Treasures

A Reading/Language Arts Program

Macmillan/McGraw-Hill

Contributors

Time Magazine, The Writers' Express, Accelerated Reader

TIME
FOR KIDS.

The Writers' Express
Immediate Impact. Lasting Transformation.   wex.org

RFB&D
learning through listening

Accelerated
Reader

Students with print disabilities may be eligible to obtain an accessible, audio version of the pupil edition of this textbook. Please call Recording for the Blind & Dyslexic at 1-800-221-4792 for complete information.

B

The McGraw-Hill Companies

 Macmillan/McGraw-Hill

Published by Macmillan/McGraw-Hill, of McGraw-Hill Education, a division of The McGraw-Hill Companies, Inc., Two Penn Plaza, New York, New York 10121.

Printed in the United States of America

3 4 5 6 7 8 9 10 WEB 15 14 13 12 11

Treasures

A Reading/Language Arts Program

Program Authors

Dr. Diane August
Senior Research Scientist, Center for
 Applied Linguistics
Washington, D.C.

Dr. Donald R. Bear
University of Nevada, Reno
Reno, Nevada

Dr. Janice A. Dole
University of Utah
Salt Lake City, Utah

Dr. Jana Echevarria
California State University, Long Beach
Long Beach, California

Dr. Douglas Fisher
San Diego State University
San Diego, California

Dr. David J. Francis
University of Houston
Houston, Texas

Dr. Vicki L. Gibson
Educational Consultant, Gibson Hasbrouck
 and Associates, Massachusetts

Dr. Jan E. Hasbrouck
Educational Consultant – J.H. Consulting
Los Angeles, California

Dr. Scott G. Paris
Center for Research and Practice,
National Institute of Education
Singapore

Dr. Timothy Shanahan
University of Illinois at Chicago
Chicago, Illinois

Dr. Josefina V. Tinajero
University of Texas at El Paso
El Paso, Texas

 Macmillan/McGraw-Hill

Program Authors

Dr. Diane August

Center for Applied Linguistics, Washington, D.C.

- Principal Investigator, Developing Literacy in Second-Language Learners: Report of the National Literacy Panel on Language-Minority Children and Youth
- Member of the New Standards Literacy Project, Grades 4–5

Dr. Donald R. Bear

University of Nevada, Reno

- Author of *Words Their Way* and *Words Their Way with English Learners*
- Director, E.L. Cord Foundation Center for Learning and Literacy

Dr. Janice A. Dole

University of Utah

- Investigator, IES Study on Reading Interventions
- National Academy of Sciences, Committee Member: Teacher Preparation Programs, 2005–2007

Dr. Jana Echevarria

California State University, Long Beach

- Author of *Making Content Comprehensible for English Learners: The SIOP Model*
- Principal Researcher, Center for Research on the Educational Achievement and Teaching of English Language Learners

Dr. Douglas Fisher

San Diego State University

- Co-Director, Center for the Advancement of Reading, California State University
- Author of *Language Arts Workshop: Purposeful Reading and Writing Instruction* and *Reading for Information in Elementary School*

Dr. David J. Francis

University of Houston

- Director of the Center for Research on Educational Achievement and Teaching of English Language Learners (CREATE)
- Director, Texas Institute for Measurement, Evaluation, and Statistics

Dr. Vicki Gibson

Educational Consultant Gibson Hasbrouck and Associates, Massachusetts

- Author of *Differentiated Instruction: Grouping for Success*

Dr. Jan E. Hasbrouck

Educational Consultant JH Consulting, Los Angeles

- Developed Oral Reading Fluency Norms for Grades 1–8
- Author of *The Reading Coach: A How-to Manual for Success*

Dr. Scott G. Paris

Center for Research and Practice, National Institute of Education, Singapore

- Principal Investigator, CIERA, 1997–2004

Dr. Timothy Shanahan

University of Illinois at Chicago

- Member, National Reading Panel
- President, International Reading Association, 2006
- Chair, National Literacy Panel and National Early Literacy Panel

Dr. Josefina V. Tinajero

University of Texas at El Paso

- Past President, NABE and TABE
- Co-Editor of *Teaching All the Children: Strategies for Developing Literacy in an Urban Setting* and *Literacy Assessment of Second Language Learners*

Consulting and Contributing Authors

Dr. Adria F. Klein
Professor Emeritus,
California State University,
San Bernardino

- President, California
Reading Association, 1995
- Co-Author of *Interactive Writing* and *Interactive Editing*

Dolores B. Malcolm
St. Louis Public Schools
St. Louis, MO

- Past President, International
Reading Association
- Member, IRA Urban
Diversity Initiatives
Commission
- Member, RIF Advisory
Board

Dr. Doris Walker-Dalhouse
Minnesota State University,
Moorhead

- Author of articles on
multicultural literature and
reading instruction in urban
schools
- Co-Chair of the Ethnicity, Race,
and Multilingualism Committee,
NRC

Dinah Zike
Educational Consultant

- Dinah-Might Activities, Inc.
San Antonio, TX

Program Consultants

Kathy R. Bumgardner
Language Arts Instructional
Specialist
Gaston County Schools, NC

Elizabeth Jimenez
CEO, GEMAS Consulting
Pomona, CA

Dr. Sharon F. O'Neal
Associate Professor
College of Education
Texas State University
San Marcos, TX

Program Reviewers

Mable Alfred
Reading/Language Arts Administrator
Chicago Public Schools, IL

Suzie Bean
Teacher, Kindergarten
Mary W. French Academy
Decatur, IL

Linda Burch
Teacher, Kindergarten
Public School 184
Brooklyn, NY

Robert J. Dandorph
Principal
John F. Kennedy Elementary School
North Bergen, NJ

Suzanne Delacruz
Principal, Washington Elementary
Evanston, IL

Carol Dockery
Teacher, Grade 3
Mulberry Elementary
Milford, OH

Karryl Ellis
Teacher, Grade 1
Durfee School, Decatur, IL

Christina Fong
Teacher, Grade 3
William Moore Elementary School
Las Vegas, NV

Lenore Furman
Teacher, Kindergarten
Abington Avenue School
Newark, NJ

Sister Miriam Kaeser
Assistant Superintendent
Archdiocese of Cincinnati
Cincinnati, OH

LaVonne Lee
Principal, Rozet Elementary School
Gillette, WY

SuEllen Mackey
Teacher, Grade 5
Washington Elementary School
Decatur, IL

Jan Mayes
Curriculum Coordinator
Kent School District
Kent, WA

Bonnie Nelson
Teacher, Grade 1
Solano School, Phoenix, AZ

Cyndi Nichols
Teacher, Grade K/1
North Ridge Elementary School
Commack, NY

Sharron Norman
Curriculum Director
Lansing School District
Lansing, MI

Renee Ottinger
Literacy Leader, Grades K–5
Coronado Hills Elementary School
Denver, CO

Michael Pragman
Principal, Woodland Elementary School
Lee's Summit, MO

Carol Rose
Teacher, Grade 2
Churchill Elementary School
Muskegon, MI

Laura R. Schmidt-Watson
Director of Academic Services
Parma City School District, OH

Dianne L. Skoy
Literacy Coordinator, Grades K–5
Minneapolis Public Schools
Minneapolis, MN

Charles Staszewski
ESL Teacher, Grades 3–5
John H. William School, No. 5
Rochester, NY

Patricia Synan
New York City Department
of Education

Stephanie Yearian
Teacher, Grade 2
W. J. Zahnow Elementary
Waterloo, IL

v

Unit 3 Essential Questions

Unit 3 The Big Question

How can words be powerful?

Enduring Understanding and Essential Questions

In this unit, students will listen, read, and write about powerful words. As they progress through the unit, they will also develop and apply key comprehension skills that good readers use as they read.

Big Idea	Enduring Understanding	Essential Questions
Theme: The Power of Words	Words spoken or written are powerful tools.	How can words be powerful?

Comprehension	Enduring Understanding	Essential Questions
Make Inferences Week 1	Good readers take details the author provides and make inferences about characters' actions and relationships.	What details help you make inferences about characters' relationships?
Draw Conclusion Week 2	Good readers connect two or more pieces of information to draw conclusions about the plot's main events.	How can drawing conclusions help you to sequence the plot's main events and explain their influence on future events?
Fact and Opinion Week 3	Good readers verify facts and distinguish them from opinions.	Why is it important to verify facts and distinguish them from opinions when you read?
Theme Week 4	Good readers can recognize and explain the message of a work of fiction as its theme.	Why is the theme of a work of fiction important?
Character, Setting, Plot Week 5	Good readers think about where the story is set, how it influences the main and future plot events, and how it affects the characters.	How does the setting affect the characters and the main and future events of the plot?

Theme: The Power of Words

Planning the Unit

Main Selections

Using the Student Book

Wrapping Up the Unit

Additional Resources

Unit Assessment

Theme: The Power of Words

Theme Opener, pp. xvi–266/267

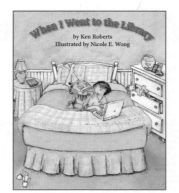

pp. 272–283

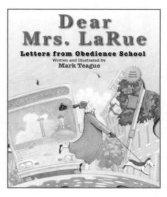

pp. 296–317

	WEEK 1	WEEK 2
ORAL LANGUAGE	**Theme** Letters **Build Background**	**Theme** The Art of Persuasion **Build Background**
• **Listening Comprehension**		
• **Speaking/Viewing**		
WORD STUDY	**Vocabulary** *weekdays, slithered, genuine, apologize, harmless, ambulance* **Word Parts:** Base Words	**Vocabulary** *neglected, appreciated, misunderstood, desperate, endured, obedience* **Word Parts:** Prefixes
• **Vocabulary**		
• **Phonics/Word Study**	**Phonics** *r*-Controlled Vowels	**Phonics** Silent Letters
• **Spelling**	**Spelling** *r*-Controlled Vowels	**Spelling** Silent Letters
READING	**Comprehension** **Strategy:** Generate Questions **Skill:** Make Inferences	**Comprehension** **Strategy:** Generate Questions **Skill:** Draw Conclusions
• **Comprehension**		
• **Fluency**	**Fluency** Repeated Reading: Phrasing and Expression	**Fluency** Repeated Reading: Expression
• **Leveled Readers**	**Approaching** *Snakes in North America* **On Level** *Snakes in North America* **Beyond** *Snakes in North America* **ELL** *North American Snakes*	**Approaching** *Melvin and the Princess* **On Level** *Fish Tricks* **Beyond** *Hopping to Victory* **ELL** *Fish Tricks*
LANGUAGE ARTS	**Writing** **Trait:** Ideas	**Writing** **Trait:** Ideas
• **Writing**		
• **Grammar**	**Grammar** Action Verbs	**Grammar** Verb Tenses

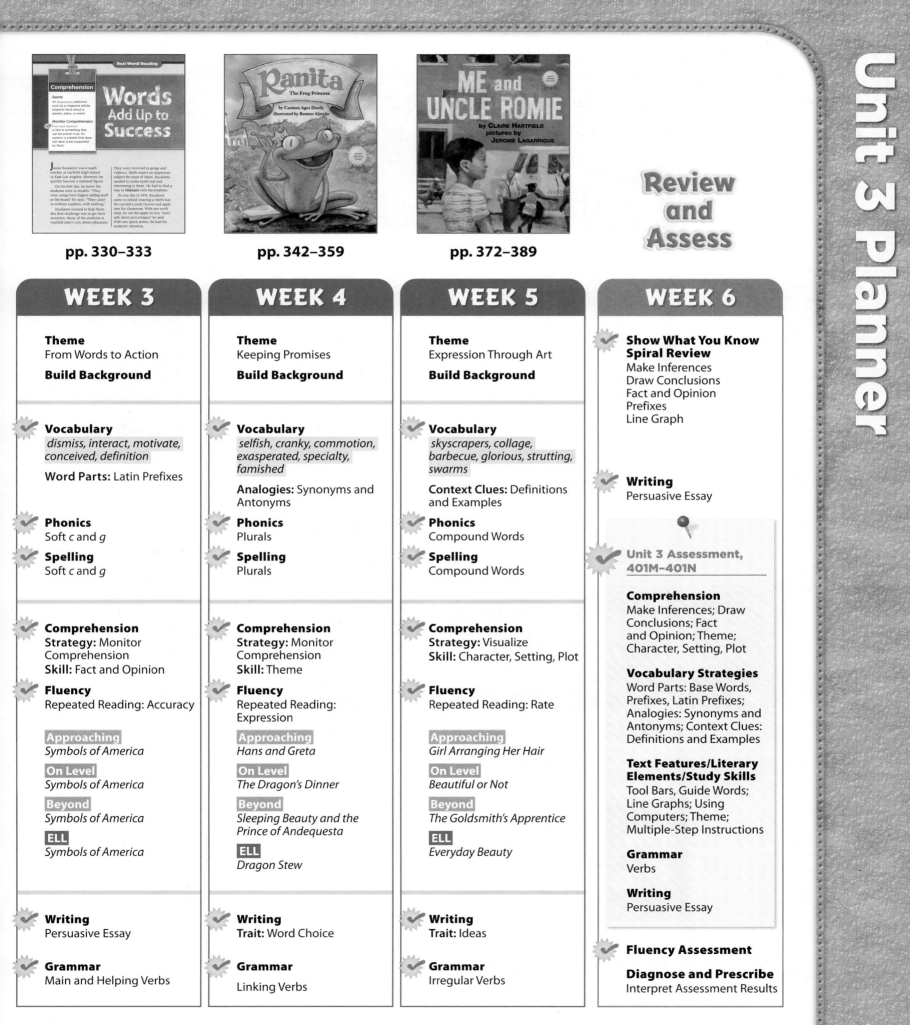

pp. 330–333   pp. 342–359   pp. 372–389

Review and Assess

WEEK 3

Theme
From Words to Action

Build Background

Vocabulary
dismiss, interact, motivate, conceived, definition
Word Parts: Latin Prefixes

Phonics
Soft *c* and *g*

Spelling
Soft *c* and *g*

Comprehension
Strategy: Monitor Comprehension
Skill: Fact and Opinion

Fluency
Repeated Reading: Accuracy

Approaching
Symbols of America
On Level
Symbols of America
Beyond
Symbols of America
ELL
Symbols of America

Writing
Persuasive Essay

Grammar
Main and Helping Verbs

WEEK 4

Theme
Keeping Promises

Build Background

Vocabulary
selfish, cranky, commotion, exasperated, specialty, famished
Analogies: Synonyms and Antonyms

Phonics
Plurals

Spelling
Plurals

Comprehension
Strategy: Monitor Comprehension
Skill: Theme

Fluency
Repeated Reading: Expression

Approaching
Hans and Greta
On Level
The Dragon's Dinner
Beyond
Sleeping Beauty and the Prince of Andequesta
ELL
Dragon Stew

Writing
Trait: Word Choice

Grammar
Linking Verbs

WEEK 5

Theme
Expression Through Art

Build Background

Vocabulary
skyscrapers, collage, barbecue, glorious, strutting, swarms
Context Clues: Definitions and Examples

Phonics
Compound Words

Spelling
Compound Words

Comprehension
Strategy: Visualize
Skill: Character, Setting, Plot

Fluency
Repeated Reading: Rate

Approaching
Girl Arranging Her Hair
On Level
Beautiful or Not
Beyond
The Goldsmith's Apprentice
ELL
Everyday Beauty

Writing
Trait: Ideas

Grammar
Irregular Verbs

WEEK 6

Show What You Know
Spiral Review
Make Inferences
Draw Conclusions
Fact and Opinion
Prefixes
Line Graph

Writing
Persuasive Essay

**Unit 3 Assessment,
401M–401N**

Comprehension
Make Inferences; Draw Conclusions; Fact and Opinion; Theme; Character, Setting, Plot

Vocabulary Strategies
Word Parts: Base Words, Prefixes, Latin Prefixes; Analogies: Synonyms and Antonyms; Context Clues: Definitions and Examples

Text Features/Literary Elements/Study Skills
Tool Bars, Guide Words; Line Graphs; Using Computers; Theme; Multiple-Step Instructions

Grammar
Verbs

Writing
Persuasive Essay

Fluency Assessment

Diagnose and Prescribe
Interpret Assessment Results

Unit 3 Resources

Literature

Student Book

StudentWorks Plus
Online and CD-ROM

Read-Aloud Anthology
Includes Plays for
Readers Theater

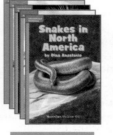

| Approaching Level | On Level | Beyond Level | ELL |

Leveled Readers

Leveled Classroom Library Books (18)

Teaching Support

Teacher's Edition

Teacher's Resource Book

cranky

slithered

Vocabulary Cards

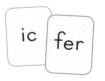

ic fer

Word-Building Cards

green

have

High-Frequency Word Cards

whale

wh_

Sound-Spelling Cards

Student Practice

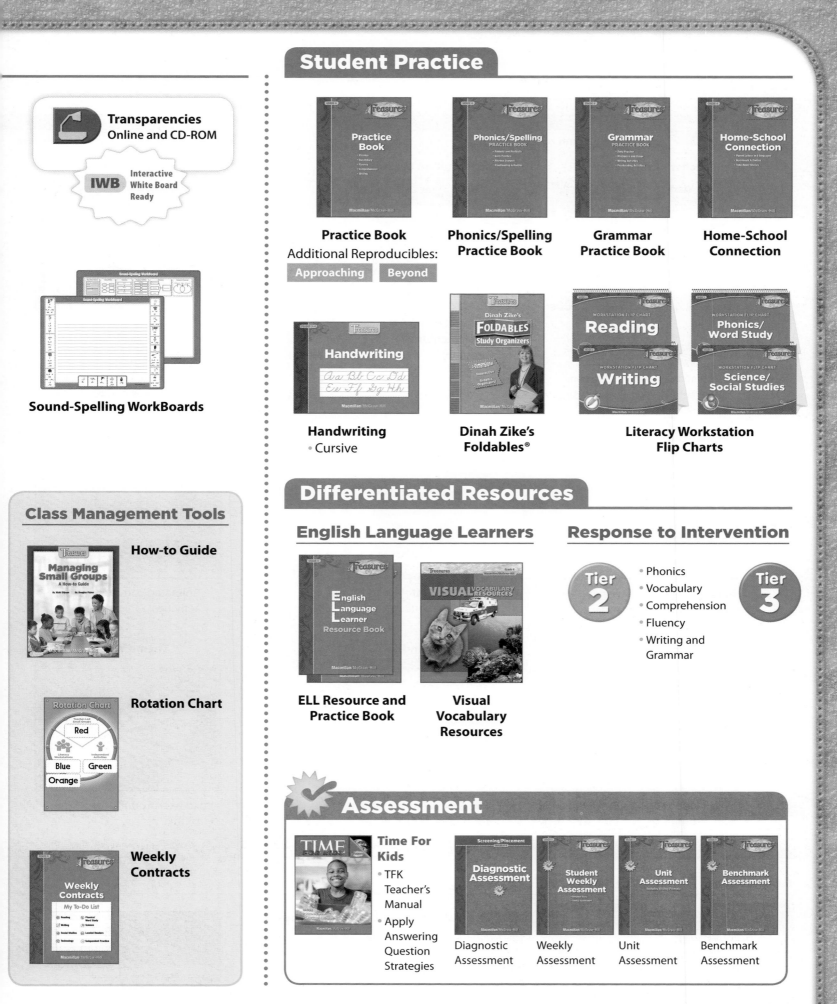

Transparencies
Online and CD-ROM

IWB Interactive White Board Ready

Sound-Spelling WorkBoards

Practice Book
Additional Reproducibles:
Approaching   Beyond

Phonics/Spelling Practice Book

Grammar Practice Book

Home-School Connection

Handwriting
• Cursive

Dinah Zike's Foldables®

Literacy Workstation Flip Charts

Class Management Tools

How-to Guide

Rotation Chart

Weekly Contracts

Differentiated Resources

English Language Learners

ELL Resource and Practice Book

Visual Vocabulary Resources

Response to Intervention

Tier 2
• Phonics
• Vocabulary
• Comprehension
• Fluency
• Writing and Grammar

Tier 3

Assessment

Time For Kids
• TFK Teacher's Manual
• Apply Answering Question Strategies

Diagnostic Assessment

Student Weekly Assessment

Unit Assessment

Benchmark Assessment

Digital Solutions

Go to **ConnectED** Online Center

http://connected.mcgraw-hill.com

☑ Prepare/Plan

ONLINE
www.macmillanmh.com

Teacher's Edition Online

TeacherWorks™ Plus
All-In-One Planner and Resource Center

Available on CD-ROM
- Interactive Teacher's Edition
- Printable Weekly Resources

Implementation Modules

- Support on how to implement the reading program

Balanced Literacy Planner

- Create customized weekly balanced literacy planners

ELL Strategies

- Teaching strategies for English Language Learners

Reading Video Library

- Video clips of instructional routines

Leadership Handbook

- Professional development for school principals

☑ Teach/Learn

ONLINE
www.macmillanmh.com

Interactive Student Book

StudentWorks™ Plus
Interactive Student Book

- Word-by-Word Reading
- Summaries in Other Languages
- Media Literacy and Research

Animated Activities

- Animated comprehension activities

Theme Videos

- Build background and concept vocabulary

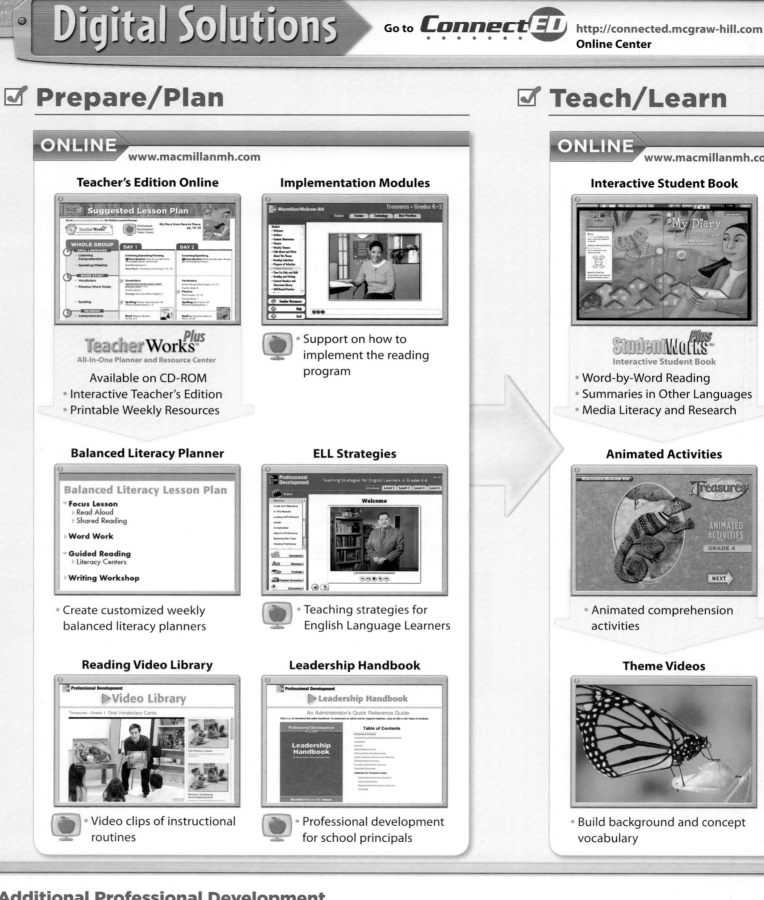

Additional Professional Development

- **Instructional Routine Handbook**
- **Writing Professional Development Guide**
- **Managing Small Groups**
- **Leadership Handbook:**
  An Administrator's Quick Reference Guide

Also available
Reading Yes!
Video Workshops
on CD-ROM

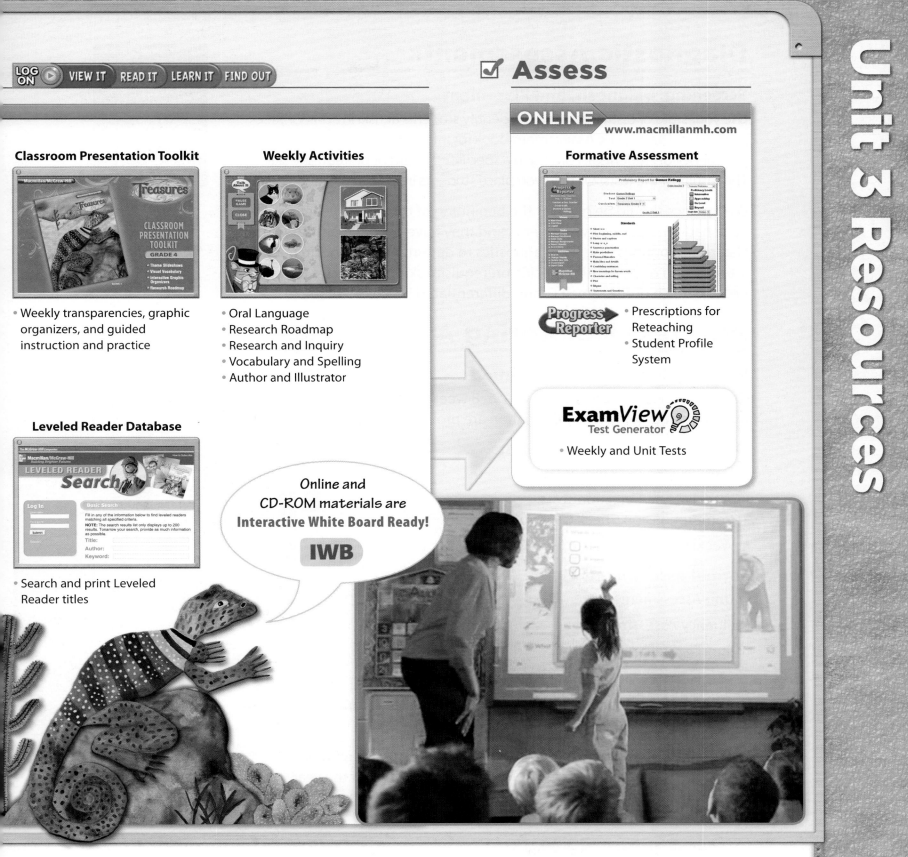

LOG ON ▶ VIEW IT READ IT LEARN IT FIND OUT

☑ **Assess**

Classroom Presentation Toolkit

- Weekly transparencies, graphic organizers, and guided instruction and practice

Weekly Activities

- Oral Language
- Research Roadmap
- Research and Inquiry
- Vocabulary and Spelling
- Author and Illustrator

ONLINE www.macmillanmh.com

Formative Assessment

Progress Reporter
- Prescriptions for Reteaching
- Student Profile System

ExamView Test Generator
- Weekly and Unit Tests

Leveled Reader Database

- Search and print Leveled Reader titles

Online and CD-ROM materials are **Interactive White Board Ready!**

IWB

Available on CD

AUDIO CD
- **Listening Library**
- **Fluency Solutions**
- **Sound Pronunciation**

CD-ROM · StudentWorks *Plus*
Interactive Student Book
- **Skill Level Up!**
- **Vocabulary PuzzleMaker**

Accelerated Reader
- Accelerated Reader Quizzes

Diagnostic Assessments

Screening, Diagnosis, and Placement

Use your state or district screener to identify students at risk. In addition, see tests in our **Diagnostic Assessment** book for information on determining the proficiency of students according to a specific standard or prerequisite skill. The results of the tests will help you place students in the program.

Diagnostics should be given at the beginning of the school year after you have had time to observe students and they have become familiar with classroom routines. Use the diagnostics to determine students in need of intervention or to identify specific prerequisite skill deficiencies that you need to teach during Small Group differentiated instruction time.

Progress Monitoring Assessments

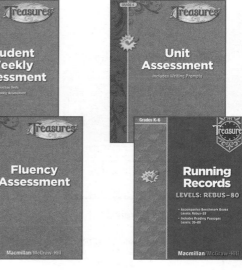

Meeting Grade-Level Expectations

Use the weekly and unit tests (every 6–8 weeks). Multiple questions and next-steps information are provided.

Ongoing Informal Assessments

- Daily Quick Check Observations
- Weekly Tests/Selection Tests; Comprehension Check Questions (Student Book)
- Weekly Fluency Practice Book Passages

Formal Assessments

- Unit Assessments
- Fluency Assessments
- Running Records

Summative Assessments

Links to the State Test

Use the State Assessment and the tests provided in the **Benchmark Assessment**. Give every trimester, midyear, or at the end of the year to determine whether students have mastered the grade-level content standards and to document long-term academic growth.

Digital Assessment

Assessment Online
- Administer the **Weekly** and **Unit Assessment** electronically
- Score all tests electronically
- Prescriptions for Reteaching
- Student Profile System

ExamView Test Generator

Test Generator
- Available on CD-ROM
- **Weekly** and **Unit Assessments**

Test Alignment

GRADE 4 UNIT 3 ASSESSED SKILLS	TerraNova/ CAT 6	SAT 10	ITBS	NAEP
COMPREHENSION STRATEGIES AND SKILLS				
• Strategies: Generate questions, monitor comprehension, visualize	◆	◆	◆	◆
• Skills: Make inferences, draw conclusions, fact and opinion, theme, character, setting, plot	◆	◆	◆	◆
VOCABULARY STRATEGIES				
• Word parts: Base words, prefixes, Latin prefixes	◆	◆	◆	◆
• Analogies: Synonyms and antonyms			◆	◆
• Context clues: Definitions and examples	◆	◆	◆	◆
PHONICS/SPELLING				
• *r*-Controlled vowels				
• Silent letters				
• Soft *c* and *g*				
• Plurals				
• Compound words				
TEXT FEATURES AND STUDY SKILLS				
• Using computers, toolbars				
• Line graphs	◆	◆	◆	◆
• Multiple-step instructions			◆	◆
GRAMMAR, MECHANICS, USAGE				
• Verbs: Action, tenses, main and helping, linking, irregular	◆	◆	◆	
• Punctuation: Dialogue, contractions	◆	◆	◆	
• Subject-verb agreement	◆	◆	◆	

KEY

TerraNova/CAT 6	TerraNova, The Second Edition
SAT 10	Stanford Early Achievement Test
ITBS	Iowa Tests of Basic Skills
NAEP	National Assessment of Educational Progress

Theme Project

Introduce the Theme Write this theme statement on the board: *Words, spoken or written, are powerful tools.* Ask: *If you could choose any written or spoken message that communicates important ideas, what would it be?*

Help students get ready for their theme projects by brainstorming famous speeches, letters, or articles they might already know about. Have them think of historical figures who were famous for their speeches and writing. Suggest that they listen to some recordings of famous speeches.

LOG ON ▶ VIEW IT

Theme Launcher Video
www.macmillanmh.com

Research and Inquiry
Self-Selected Theme Project

State the Problem and Identify Needed Information Tell students that they will be researching a famous spoken or written message and sharing with others what it says to them. Students should start by thinking of people who have made contributions to society. They will need to choose someone who has communicated his or her ideas orally or in writing. Students will choose one example of this person's writings or speeches to analyze and discuss.

Research Plan Have students make a list of all the places they can look to find information, such as library and media centers, and recordings on the Internet.

Research Strategies

Record Information
Make sure Web sites are reliable.

- Record your information in an organized way so that you can credit and cite your sources later.

- Evaluate each source. Take notes on each source. Be sure to paraphrase the information in your own words so that you do not plagiarize somebody else's ideas and words.

Gathering Sources Have students use the resources that they identified to locate famous writings or speeches of the person they have chosen. Remind students that they can consult a reference librarian or a local expert to help them with their research.

Synthesizing After students do research and take notes, have them organize the information by topic and subtopic.

See the Unit Closer on pages 401K–401L for **Step 5: Create the Presentation** and **Step 6: Review and Evaluate.**

Minilesson

Creating a Research Plan

Explain To create a research plan, first ask some open-ended questions about your topic. Then narrow the focus of your topic by picking two of the questions that interest you the most. Think about the purpose of your research. Will you write a report? Create an informational poster? Next identify what kinds of resources you will need to do your research. Will you need visual resources such as maps, charts, graphs, or time lines? **TEKS 4.24 (A) (iii)**

Discuss Ask: *What are some sources of information that would help you with your research?* (Possible sources include library and media centers, the Internet, local experts on the topic, and reference librarians.) **TEKS 4.24 (A) (ii)**

Apply As students begin creating their research plans encourage them to narrow the focus of their topic. Have them create a plan and identify the kinds of resources they will need to complete their research.

Minilesson

Creating a Works-Cited Page

Explain When you present information from a research source, you must give credit to the source on a **works-cited page.** Each source must have its own entry, and include the author's name, title of the source, publisher, place of publication, and publication year. Entries must be listed in alphabetical order. It is important to keep track of the sources you use.

Discuss Ask: *Why is it helpful to keep track of the information you will need for your works cited page as you are conducting your research?* (If you record the information as you are using the source, you will not forget any of the sources you used. You will also have all the information you need right in front of you when you are ready to create your works-cited page.)

Apply Have students create a works-cited page for the research presentation they have produced. Make sure to remind students of the correct format of a works-cited page.

LISTENING AND SPEAKING

WORKING IN GROUPS

Remind students to

- Respectfully ask questions to obtain or clarify information;

- Stay focused on the topic and ask relevant, detailed questions;

- Provide suggestions that build on the ideas of others.

See Listening and Speaking Checklists in StudentWorks Plus.

The
Big
Question

How can words
be powerful?

Theme Video
The Power of Words
www.macmillanmh.com

264

265

Introduce Theme Project

THE POWER OF WORDS

Review with students what they have learned so far about the power of words.

- Help students think of a subject they would like to communicate to others about (thoughts on: raising money for an animal shelter, energy conservation, cleaning up a park), and in what form they might like to do this (newspaper article, speech to student government, letter to mayor). Explain that these are all ways in which words can be used to influence people.

- Read and discuss the activity on page 266 of the **Student Book**. Help students begin thinking about which verbal or written message by an inspiring person they would like to explore.

Connect to Content

Gifted & Talented

Inspiring People

Abraham Lincoln, John F. Kennedy, Barbara Jordan, and Martin Luther King, Jr., are examples of people who knew the power of words and how to use them. Discuss with students an historical state figures whose words have lived on in history. What was this person trying to accomplish? Was he or she successful? Why or why not?

How can words be powerful?

Most people communicate with one another using words. Think about how often in a day you read, speak, or listen to words. Words, spoken or written, are powerful tools. We can use them to change a person's mind, to explain something, or to entertain others. Throughout history, words have helped create great changes. The words in the Declaration of Independence, the Gettysburg Address, and Martin Luther King, Jr.'s "I Have a Dream" speech have helped change the world.

Learning about the power of words can help you understand how important words and communication have been throughout history. It can help you choose your words more carefully, and it can encourage you to speak up in certain situations.

Research Activities

For this unit you will create a piece of writing that tells about a person whose words inspire you. Your writing needs to tell your audience why this person inspires you. Set your purposes for reading and research people who have made famous speeches. Write about one of them and tell how that person inspired your writing.

Keep Track of Ideas

As you read, keep track of all you are learning about the power of words. Use the **Study Book Foldable** to organize your ideas. On the front panel, write the Unit Theme: *The Power of Words*. On each of the next panels, write the facts you learn each week that will help you in your research and in your understanding of the Unit Theme.

Week 5
Week 4
Week 3
Week 2
Week 1
Unit Theme

FOLDABLES
Study Organizer

Digital Learning

LOG ON ⊙ **FIND OUT** www.macmillanmh.com

StudentWorks *Plus*
Interactive Student Book

- **Research Roadmap**
  Follow a step-by-step guide to complete your research project.

Online Resources

- Topic Finder and Other Research Tools
- Videos and Virtual Field Trips
- Photos and Drawings for Presentations
- Related Articles and Web Resources
- Web Site Links

People and Places

The Franklin Public Library
America's first public library was started in Franklin, Massachusetts, in 1781. Benjamin Franklin donated books to the town and the citizens decided that these books would be lent to the public free of charge.

KEEP TRACK OF IDEAS

Go to page 24 of the Foldables™ book for instructions on how to create the Study Book organizers for this unit. Give students time to create the organizers.

- Reread "Keep Track of Ideas" on page 267 of the **Student Book**. Model how students will be using their study organizers to keep track of ideas as they read through the stories in the unit. Explain that keeping track of ideas they read about will help them develop ideas for their own theme project.

RESEARCH TOOLS

Tell students that as they read the selections in this unit, they will learn about the different ways in which people use words. Students will be able to use the Research Tools to help them learn more about the power of words.

LOG ON ⊙

StudentWorks *Plus*
Interactive Student Book

Plan, Organize, and Synthesize Activities that assist students in research planning, organization, and presentation

Listening and Speaking Resources that will help students apply listening and speaking techniques

Week 1 ★ At a Glance

Priority Skills and Concepts

✔ Comprehension

- **Strategy:** Generate Questions
- **Skill:** Make Inferences
 - Sequence
- **Genre:** Poetry, Fiction, Expository

✔ Robust Vocabulary

- **Selection Vocabulary:** *weekdays, slithered, genuine, apologize, harmless, ambulance*
- **Strategy:** Word Parts/Base Words

✔ Fluency

- **Phrasing and Expression**

✔ Phonics/Spelling

- **Word Study:** *r*-Controlled Vowels *er, ir, ur,* Multisyllabic Words
- **Spelling Words:** *dirty, purse, birth, curl, curve, curb, person, shirt, worse, hurl, twirl, swirl, herb, turkey, turnip, purpose, blurred, sternly, serpent, pearl*
 - *slowly, quickly, beautiful*

✔ Grammar/Mechanics

- **Action Verbs**
- **Punctuation in Dialogue**

✔ Writing

- **Trait: Ideas**
- Supporting Details

Key

 ✔ Tested in program   🌀 SPIRAL REVIEW Review Skill

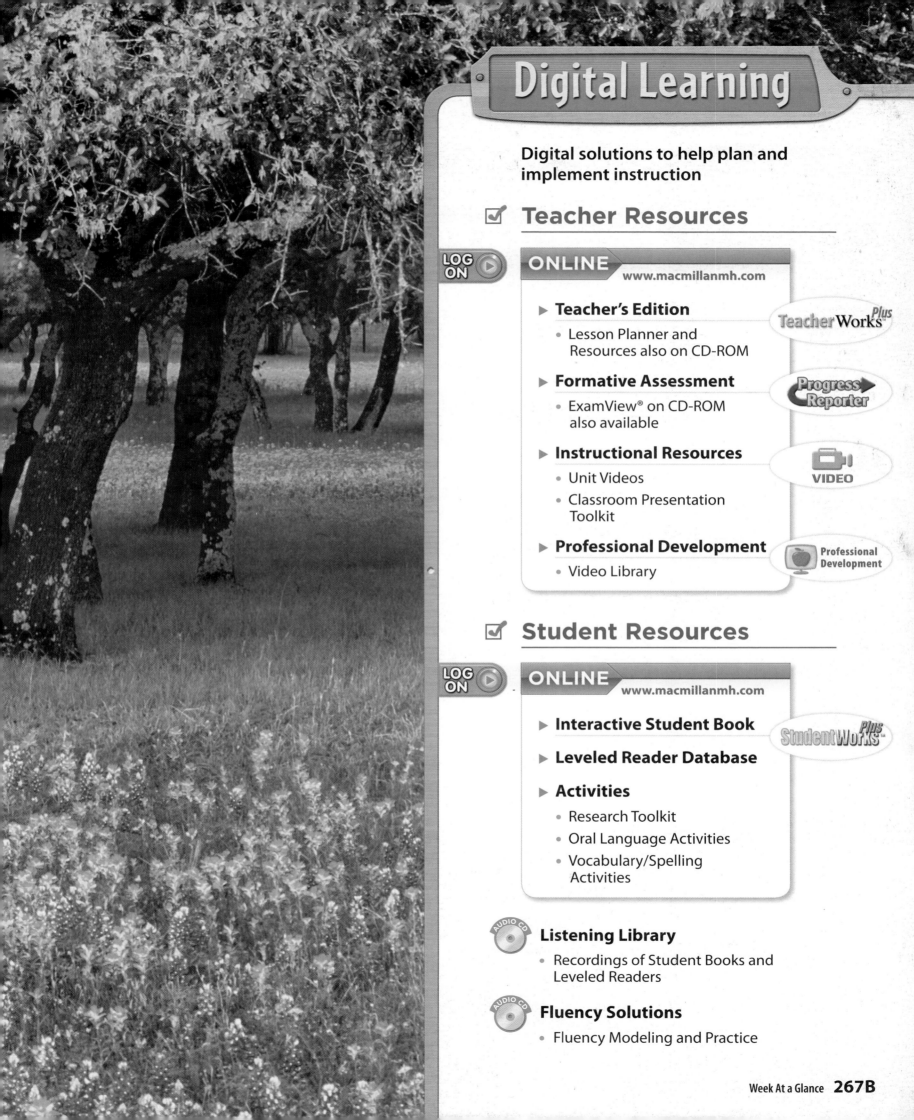

Digital Learning

Digital solutions to help plan and implement instruction

☑ Teacher Resources

LOG ON ▶

ONLINE www.macmillanmh.com

▶ **Teacher's Edition**
- Lesson Planner and Resources also on CD-ROM

TeacherWorks Plus

▶ **Formative Assessment**
- ExamView® on CD-ROM also available

Progress Reporter

▶ **Instructional Resources**
- Unit Videos
- Classroom Presentation Toolkit

VIDEO

▶ **Professional Development**
- Video Library

Professional Development

☑ Student Resources

LOG ON ▶

ONLINE www.macmillanmh.com

▶ **Interactive Student Book**

StudentWorks Plus

▶ **Leveled Reader Database**

▶ **Activities**
- Research Toolkit
- Oral Language Activities
- Vocabulary/Spelling Activities

AUDIO CD
Listening Library
- Recordings of Student Books and Leveled Readers

AUDIO CD
Fluency Solutions
- Fluency Modeling and Practice

Weekly Literature

Theme: Letters

Main Selection

Genre Humor

When I Went to the Library
by Ken Roberts
Illustrated by Nicole E. Wong

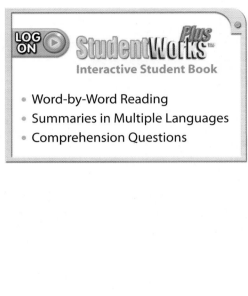

Preteach Vocabulary and Comprehension

Genre Drama

NAME THAT REPTILE
by Catherine Lutz

Paired Selection

Genre Nonfiction

Snakes

StudentWorks Plus
Interactive Student Book
- Word-by-Word Reading
- Summaries in Multiple Languages
- Comprehension Questions

Support Literature

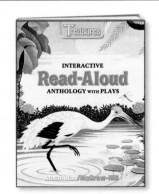

Interactive Read-Aloud Anthology
- Listening Comprehension
- Robust Vocabulary
- Readers Theater Plays for Fluency

Resources for Differentiated Instruction

Leveled Readers: Science

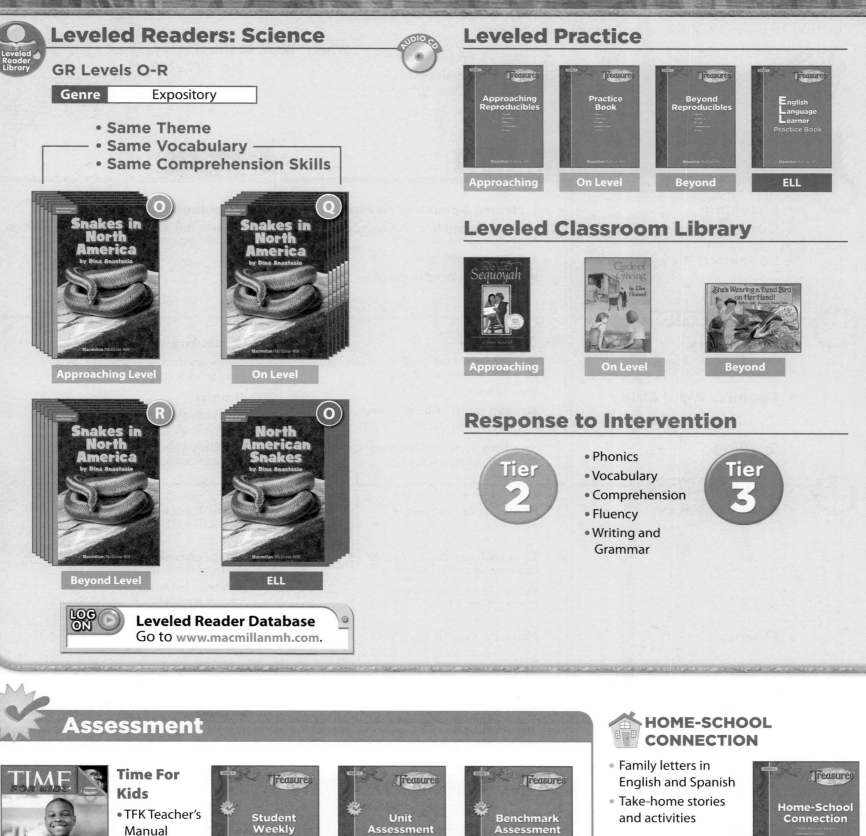

Leveled Reader Library

GR Levels O–R

Genre	Expository

- Same Theme
- Same Vocabulary
- Same Comprehension Skills

O Snakes in North America
by Dina Anastasio
Macmillan/McGraw-Hill
Approaching Level

Q Snakes in North America
by Dina Anastasio
Macmillan/McGraw-Hill
On Level

R Snakes in North America
by Dina Anastasio
Macmillan/McGraw-Hill
Beyond Level

O North American Snakes
by Dina Anastasio
Macmillan/McGraw-Hill
ELL

LOG ON ▶ **Leveled Reader Database**
Go to www.macmillanmh.com.

Leveled Practice

Treasures Approaching Reproducibles — **Approaching**

Treasures Practice Book — **On Level**

Treasures Beyond Reproducibles — **Beyond**

Treasures English Language Learner Practice Book — **ELL**

Leveled Classroom Library

Sequoyah — **Approaching**

Circle of Giving by Ellen Howard — **On Level**

She's Wearing a Dead Bird on Her Head! — **Beyond**

Response to Intervention

Tier 2

- Phonics
- Vocabulary
- Comprehension
- Fluency
- Writing and Grammar

Tier 3

Assessment

Time For Kids
- TFK Teacher's Manual
- Apply Answering Question Strategies

Treasures Student Weekly Assessment
Weekly Assessment

Treasures Unit Assessment
Unit Assessment

Treasures Benchmark Assessment
Benchmark Assessment

HOME-SCHOOL CONNECTION

- Family letters in English and Spanish
- Take-home stories and activities

Treasures Home-School Connection

LOG ON ▶ **Online Homework**
www.macmillanmh.com

Suggested Lesson Plan

Go to www.macmillanmh.com for Online Lesson Planner

TeacherWorks *Plus*
All-In-One Planner and Resource Center

Professional Development
Video Library

When I Went to the Library,
pp. 272–283

WHOLE GROUP

	DAY 1	DAY 2

ORAL LANGUAGE

- **Listening Comprehension**
- **Speaking/Viewing**

DAY 1

Listening/Speaking/Viewing

❓ Focus Question In what ways do letters help you express yourself?

Build Background, 268

Read Aloud: "A Word to the Wise," 269A–269B

DAY 2

Listening/Speaking

❓ Focus Question What do you learn when you read between the lines?

WORD STUDY

- **Vocabulary**
- **Phonics/Word Study**
- **Spelling**

DAY 1

Vocabulary

weekdays, slithered, genuine, apologize, harmless, ambulance, 271, 291C

Practice Book, 92

Strategy: Word Parts/Base Words, 270

Spelling Pretest: *r*-Controlled Vowels, 291E
Phonics/Spelling Book, 61–62

DAY 2

Vocabulary

Review Words, Base Words, 272, 291C
Practice Book, 98

Phonics

r-Controlled Vowels *er, ir, ur,* 269C–269D
Practice Book, 91

Spelling Word Sorts, 291E
Phonics/Spelling Book, 63

READING

- **Comprehension**
- **Fluency**

DAY 1

Read "Name That Reptile," 270–271

Student Book

Comprehension, 271A–271B
Strategy: Generate Questions

Skill: Make Inferences
Practice Book, 93

Fluency Model Fluency, 269B

DAY 2

Read *When I Went to the Library,* 272–283

Student Book

Comprehension, 272–283
Strategy: Generate Questions

Skill: Make Inferences
Practice Book, 94

Fluency Repeated Reading: Phrasing and Expression, 285A

LANGUAGE ARTS

- **Writing**
- **Grammar**

DAY 1

Writing

Daily Writing Name a reptile you want to see at a zoo. Write a brief explanation telling why.

Trait: Ideas
Supporting Details, 289A–289B

Grammar Daily Language Activities, 291G
Action Verbs, 291G
Grammar Practice Book, 51

DAY 2

Writing

Daily Writing Imagine a snake escaped from a cage in your house and disappeared. Make a list of adjectives describing how you would feel.

Reading/Writing Connection, 290–291

Grammar Daily Language Activities, 291G
Action Verbs, 291G
Grammar Practice Book, 52

ASSESSMENT

- **Informal/Formal**

DAY 1

Quick Check Vocabulary, 270
Comprehension, 271B

DAY 2

Quick Check Phonics, 269D
Comprehension, 283

SMALL GROUP Lesson Plan ▷ Differentiated Instruction 267G–267H

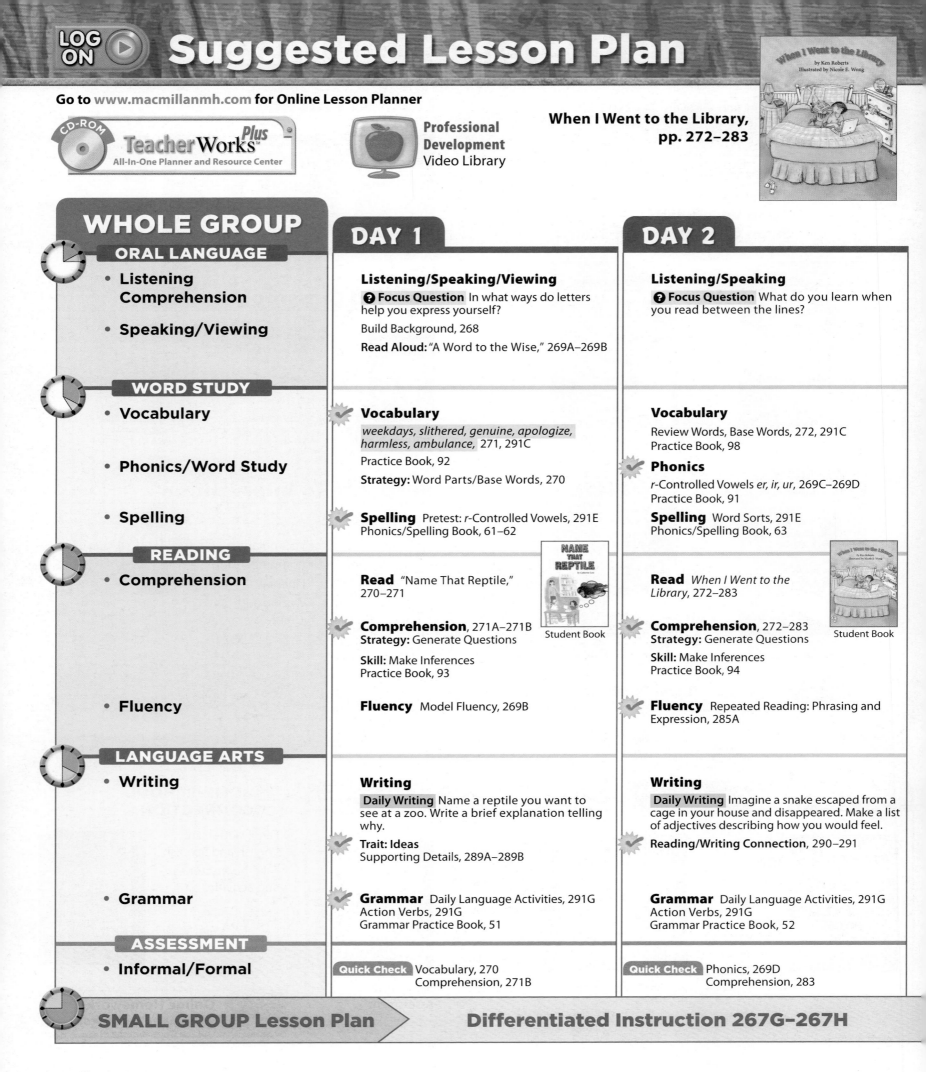

Priority Skills

Vocabulary	Comprehension	Writing	Science
Vocabulary Words	**Strategy:** Generate Questions	Trait: Ideas	Identify characteristics that allow a species to survive and reproduce.
Word Parts/Base Words	**Skill:** Make Inferences	Supporting Details	

DAY 3

Listening/Speaking

? Focus Question How do Mark's mother and Mr. Winston feel about snakes? Use details from both selections.

Summarize, 285

Vocabulary

Review Words, Related Words, 291D

Spelling Word Meanings, 291F
Phonics/Spelling Book, 64

Read *When I Went to the Library*, 272–283

Student Book

Comprehension
Comprehension Check, 285

Review Skill: Sequence, 285B
Practice Book, 96

Fluency Repeated Reading: Phrasing and Expression, 285A
Practice Book, 95

Writing

Daily Writing Write a list of safety tips on how to avoid dangerous animals in the wild.

Trait: Ideas
Supporting Details, 291A

Grammar Daily Language Activities, 291G
Mechanics and Usage, 291H
Grammar Practice Book, 53

Quick Check Fluency, 285A

DAY 4

Listening/Speaking/Viewing

? Focus Question Which of the snakes in the article you have read about would not make a good pet for Cara? Explain your answer using details from both selections.

Vocabulary

Content Vocabulary: *reptiles, camouflage, hibernate, digested,* 286
Review Words, Morphology, 291D

Spelling Proofread, 291F
Phonics/Spelling Book, 65

Read "Snakes," 286–289

Snakes
Student Book

Comprehension
Science: Electronic Encyclopedia

Text Feature: Toolbars and Guide Words, 286

Practice Book, 97

Fluency Repeated Reading: Phrasing and Expression, 285A

Time For Kids

Writing

Daily Writing Write a poem from the point of view of Cara's snake.

Trait: Ideas
Facts and Opinions, 291A

Grammar Daily Language Activities, 291G
Action Verbs, 291H
Grammar Practice Book, 54

Quick Check Vocabulary, 291D

DAY 5
Review and Assess

Listening/Speaking/Viewing

? Focus Question What makes snakes especially difficult to keep as pets? How are they different from most other animals?

Vocabulary

Assess Words, Connect to Writing, 291D

Spelling Posttest, 291F
Phonics/Spelling Book, 66

Read Self-Selected Reading, 267K
Practice Book, 99

Student Book

Comprehension
Connect and Compare, 289)

Fluency Practice, 267K

Writing

Daily Writing Imagine you have the chance to interview a caretaker in the reptile house at a zoo. List several questions you would ask.

Conferencing, 291B

Grammar Daily Language Activities, 291G
Action Verbs, 291H
Grammar Practice Book, 55

Weekly Assessment, 291II–291JJ

Differentiated Instruction

What do I do in small groups?

Teacher-Led Small Groups

Independent Activities

IF... students need additional instruction, practice, or extension based on your **Quick Check** observations for the following priority skills:

✓ **Phonics/Word Study**
r-Controlled Vowels *er, ir, ur*

✓ **Vocabulary Words**
weekdays, slithered, genuine, apologize, harmless, ambulance
Strategy: Word Parts/Base Words

✓ **Comprehension**
Strategy: Generate Questions
Skill: Make Inferences

✓ **Fluency**

THEN...

Approaching **ELL**	Preteach and Reteach Skills
On Level	Practice
Beyond	Enrich and Accelerate Learning

LOG ON ▶ **Suggested Small Group Lesson Plan**

CD-ROM **TeacherWorks** *Plus*
All-In-One Planner and Resource Center

	DAY 1	DAY 2
Approaching Level **Tier 2** • **Preteach/Reteach** **Tier 2 Instruction**	• Prepare to Read, 291I • Academic Language, 291I • Preteach Vocabulary, 291K	• Comprehension, 291M Generate Questions/Make Inferences **ELL** • Leveled Reader Lesson 1, 291N
On Level • **Practice**	• Vocabulary, 291S • Phonics, 291S *r*-Controlled Vowels *er, ir, ur* **ELL**	• Leveled Reader Lesson 1, 291U
Beyond Level • **Extend/Accelerate** **Gifted and Talented**	• Leveled Reader Lesson 1, 291Y • Analyze Information, 291Y	• Leveled Reader Lesson 2, 291Z • Synthesize Information, 291Z
ELL • **Build English Language Proficiency** • **See ELL in other levels.**	• Prepare to Read, 291AA • Academic Language, 291AA • Preteach Vocabulary, 291BB	• Vocabulary, 291BB • Preteach Main Selection, 291CC

Small Group

Focus on Leveled Readers

Leveled Reader Library

Levels O–R

Snakes in North America by Dina Anastasio (O)	Snakes in North America by Dina Anastasio (Q)	Snakes in North America by Dina Anastasio (R)	North American Snakes by Dina Anastasio (O)
Approaching	**On Level**	**Beyond**	**ELL**

Science

Teacher's Annotated Edition

Identify characteristics that allow members within a species to survive and reproduce.

Additional Leveled Readers

LOG ON

Leveled Reader Database
www.macmillanmh.com

Search by
- Comprehension Skill
- Content Area
- Genre
- Text Feature
- Guided Reading Level
- Reading Recovery Level
- Lexile Score
- Benchmark Level

Subscription also available.

Manipulatives

Sound-Spelling WorkBoards

Sound-Spelling Cards

about / today

High-Frequency Word Cards

VISUAL VOCABULARY RESOURCES

Visual Vocabulary Resources

DAY 3

- Phonics Maintenance, 291J
  r-Controlled Vowels *er, ir, ur* **ELL**
- Leveled Reader Lesson 2, 291O

- Leveled Reader Lesson 2, 291V

- Phonics, 291W
  r-Controlled Vowels *er, ir, ur* **ELL**

- Vocabulary, 291BB
- Grammar, 291EE

DAY 4

- Reteach Phonics Skill, 291J
  r-Controlled Vowels *er, ir, ur* **ELL**
- Review Vocabulary, 291L
- Leveled Reader Lesson 3, 291P

- Fluency, 291T

- Vocabulary, 291W
- Write an ABC Book, 291W
- Fluency, 291X

- Vocabulary, 291BB
- Writing/Spelling, 291FF
- Preteach Paired Selection, 291CC
- Fluency, 291DD
- Leveled Reader, 291GG

DAY 5

- High-Frequency Words, 291L
- Fluency, 291Q
- Self-Selected Independent Reading, 291R
- Book Talk, 291P

- Self-Selected Independent Reading, 291T
- Book Talk, 291V

- Self-Selected Independent Reading, 291X
- Evaluate Information, 291X
- Book Talk, 291Z

- Vocabulary, 291BB
- Leveled Reader, 291GG
- Self-Selected Independent Reading, 291DD
- Book Talk, 291HH

Managing the Class

What do I do with the rest of my class?

- Practice Book and Reproducibles
- ELL Practice Book
- Leveled Reader Activities
- Literacy Workstations
- Online Activities

Classroom Management Tools

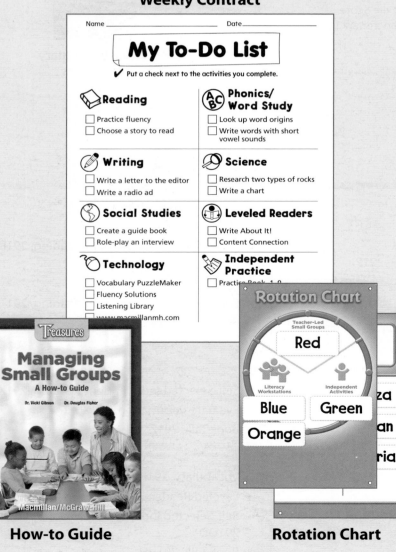

Weekly Contract

Name _____ Date _____

My To-Do List

✓ Put a check next to the activities you complete.

📖 **Reading**
- ☐ Practice fluency
- ☐ Choose a story to read

🔤 **Phonics/ Word Study**
- ☐ Look up word origins
- ☐ Write words with short vowel sounds

✏️ **Writing**
- ☐ Write a letter to the editor
- ☐ Write a radio ad

🔬 **Science**
- ☐ Research two types of rocks
- ☐ Write a chart

🌍 **Social Studies**
- ☐ Create a guide book
- ☐ Role-play an interview

📖 **Leveled Readers**
- ☐ Write About It!
- ☐ Content Connection

💻 **Technology**
- ☐ Vocabulary PuzzleMaker
- ☐ Fluency Solutions
- ☐ Listening Library
- ☐ www.macmillanmh.com

✂️ **Independent Practice**
- ☐ Practice Book 1-9

Rotation Chart

Teacher-Led Small Groups

Red

Literacy Workstations / Independent Activities

Blue   Green

Orange

How-to Guide

Treasures
Managing Small Groups
A How-to Guide
Dr. Vicki Gibson   Dr. Douglas Fisher
Macmillan/McGraw-Hill

Rotation Chart

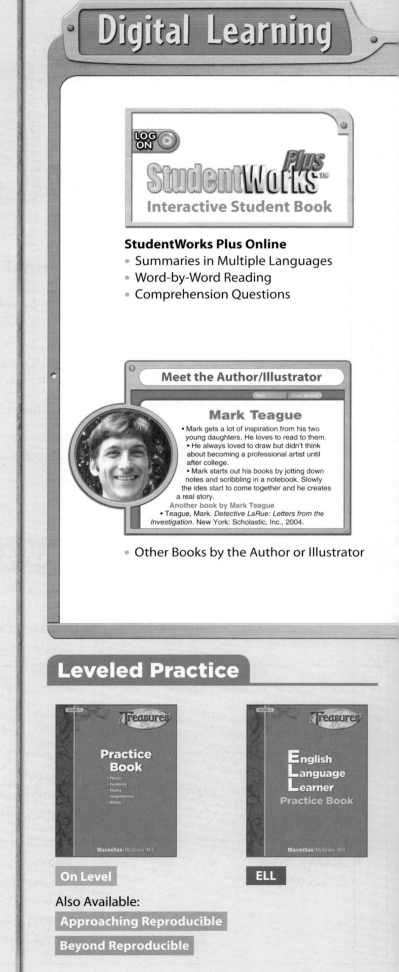

LOG ON ▶
StudentWorks Plus
Interactive Student Book

StudentWorks Plus Online
- Summaries in Multiple Languages
- Word-by-Word Reading
- Comprehension Questions

Meet the Author/Illustrator

Mark Teague
- Mark gets a lot of inspiration from his two young daughters. He loves to read to them.
- He always loved to draw but didn't think about becoming a professional artist until after college.
- Mark starts out his books by jotting down notes and scribbling in a notebook. Slowly the ides start to come together and he creates a real story.

Another book by Mark Teague
- Teague, Mark. *Detective LaRue: Letters from the Investigation.* New York: Scholastic, Inc., 2004.

- Other Books by the Author or Illustrator

Leveled Practice

Treasures
Practice Book
- Phonics
- Vocabulary
- Fluency
- Comprehension
- Writing
Macmillan/McGraw-Hill

On Level

Treasures
English Language Learner Practice Book
Macmillan/McGraw-Hill

ELL

Also Available:
Approaching Reproducible
Beyond Reproducible

Independent Activities

Oral Language Activities

- Focus on Vocabulary and Concepts
- English Language Learner Support

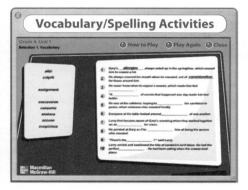

Vocabulary/Spelling Activities

- Differentiated Lists and Activities

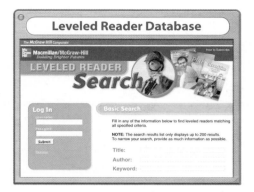

Leveled Reader Database

- Leveled Reader Database
- Search titles by level, skill, content area, and more

Research Toolkit

- Research Roadmap
- Research and Presentation Tools
- Theme Launcher Video
- Links to Science and Social Studies

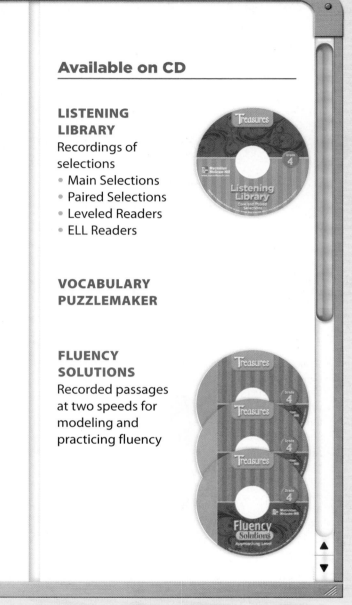

Available on CD

LISTENING LIBRARY
Recordings of selections
- Main Selections
- Paired Selections
- Leveled Readers
- ELL Readers

VOCABULARY PUZZLEMAKER

FLUENCY SOLUTIONS
Recorded passages at two speeds for modeling and practicing fluency

---

Leveled Reader Activities

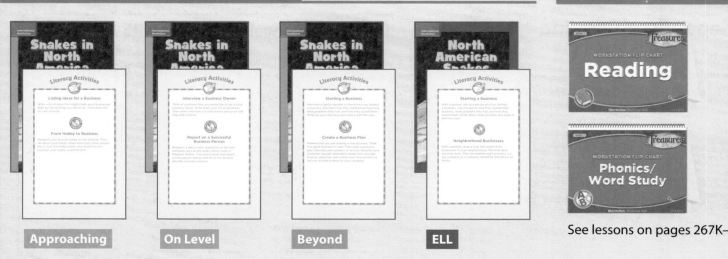

Approaching   **On Level**   **Beyond**   **ELL**

See inside cover of all Leveled Readers.

Literacy Workstations

See lessons on pages 267K–267L.

Managing the Class

Teacher-Led Small Groups
Independent Activities

What do I do with the rest of my class?

Reading

Objectives

- Develop fluency through partner-reading
- Read independently for a sustained period of time; use **Practice Book** page 99 for Reading Strategies and Reading Log

Phonics/Word Study

Objectives

- Use a dictionary to find definitions of words
- Decode and spell words with *r*-controlled vowels

Reading · **Fluency** · 20 Minutes

- Select a paragraph from the Fluency passage on page 105 of your Practice Book.
- With a partner, take turns reading the sentences aloud.
- Adjust your reading rate so that you are reading at the right speed.

Extension

- Read another paragraph from page 105 to a partner two times. The second time change your rate. Then ask your partner which way was easier to understand.
- Listen to the Audio CD.

Things you need:
- Practice Book

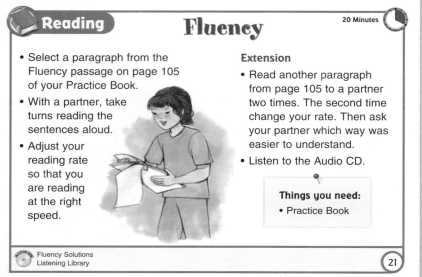

Fluency Solutions Listening Library

21

Phonics/Word Study · **Base Words** · 20 Minutes

- Write these base words on separate note cards: *harm, button, kind, play, do, fair, happy.*
- Write these prefixes and suffixes on separate cards: *-less, un-, -ness, -ful, re-, -ly.*
- Discuss the meaning of the base word with a partner.
- Tell how the meaning of the word changes when the prefix or suffix card is added to the base word card.

Extension

- Try adding different prefixes or suffixes to the base words. For example, *un-* harm *-ed.* How does the meaning change? Discuss with a partner.

harm | less

For additional vocabulary and spelling games, go to www.macmillanmh.com · Vocabulary PuzzleMaker

21

Reading · **Independent Reading** · 20 Minutes

- Look for and choose a book about animals that would make unusual pets.
- Use what you have learned about asking questions to help you understand the story.
- Discuss with a partner what kind of person might have this kind of pet.

Extension

- In your response journal, create a Character Web describing the pet owner. Write a person's name in the middle circle and their traits in the outer circles.
- Share your web with a partner.

Things you need:
- book
- pen and paper

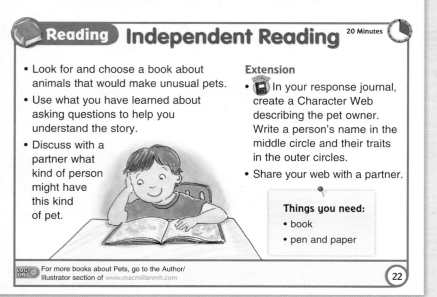

For more books about Pets, go to the Author/Illustrator section of www.macmillanmh.com

22

Phonics/Word Study · **Spelling Words with /ûr/** · 20 Minutes

- Create a Three-Pocket Foldable®.
- On the pockets, write *er, ur, ir.*
- Write these words on separate note cards: *first, hurt, third, herd, fern, burn.*
- On the back, leave blanks for the letters *er, ur,* and *ir.* Place cards in a pile with the words with blanks facing up. Draw cards with a partner. Spell the missing letters. Say the word. Sort the card in the correct pocket.

Extension

- Write new *er, ur,* and *ir* words.

FOLDABLES
- Three-Pocket Foldable®

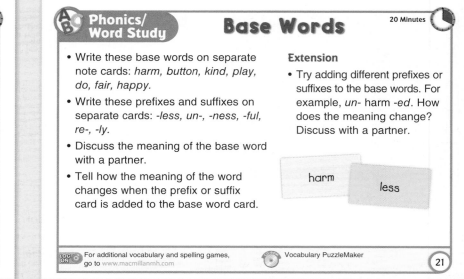

fern | er | ur | ir
fern | f__n

For additional vocabulary and spelling games, go to www.macmillanmh.com · **FOLDABLES**®

22

Literacy Workstations

Reading

Phonics/ Word Study

Writing

Science/ Social Studies

Literacy Workstation Flip Charts

Writing

Objectives

- Write a business letter to make a request
- Write a persuasive essay about the good qualities of snakes

Content Literacy

Objectives

- Use an online encyclopedia to research reptiles
- Use the Internet to research snakes

Writing — We Need More Books
20 Minutes

- Suppose you wanted to write a report about snakes, but the library had no books on the topic.
- Write a letter to the librarian. Include some ideas on how the library might be able to help its visitors.
- Be sure to use proper letter format, including date, salutation, and closing.

Extension

- Reread your letter. Is the tone polite? Are your suggestions reasonable? Find one place where you can improve your letter.
- Rewrite your letter to include your changes.

Things you need:
- pen and paper

21

Science — Reptiles
20 Minutes

- Why does a rattlesnake rattle? Use an online encyclopedia to find the answer. List the adaptations that help a rattlesnake survive in its environment.

Extension

- With a partner, list all the reptiles you can be certain live in your region.

Things you need:
- online encyclopedia
- pen and paper

Internet Research and Inquiry Activity
Students can find more facts at www.macmillanmh.com

21

Writing — Snakes Are Good
20 Minutes

- Suppose you have a friend who doesn't like snakes.
- Use an online encyclopedia to find out why snakes are good.
- Write a persuasive essay to your friend and try to change his or her opinion.

Three Good Things About Snakes

1.

2.

3.

Extension

- Create a poster that illustrates "Three Good Things About Snakes."

Things you need:
- online encyclopedia
- pen and paper
- poster board
- colored pencils or markers

22

Social Studies — Snakes
20 Minutes

- What snakes live in your state? Use the Internet to find out. Then, write a report.
- How do snakes help humans? Include the answer in your report.

Extension

- Draw and label a picture of one of the snakes from your report.

Things you need:
- online resources
- pen and paper
- colored pencils or markers

22

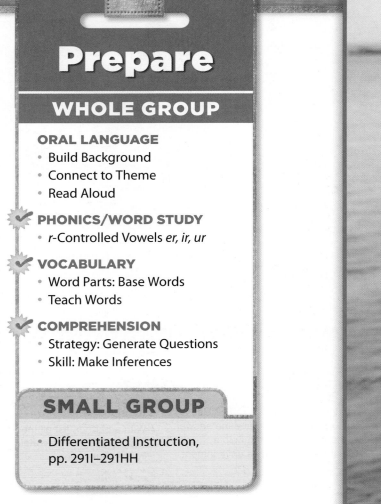

ORAL LANGUAGE
- Build Background
- Connect to Theme
- Read Aloud

✔ **PHONICS/WORD STUDY**
- *r*-Controlled Vowels *er, ir, ur*

✔ **VOCABULARY**
- Word Parts: Base Words
- Teach Words

✔ **COMPREHENSION**
- Strategy: Generate Questions
- Skill: Make Inferences

SMALL GROUP

- Differentiated Instruction, pp. 291I–291HH

Oral Language

Build Background

ACCESS PRIOR KNOWLEDGE

Share the following information: The girl in the photo is writing a letter. People write letters to tell about their experiences and to express their thoughts and emotions, or feelings. When she finishes the letter, the girl will put it in an envelope and mail it.

Write these words on the board, and briefly define each, using the **Define/Example/Ask** routine: **emotions** (feelings), **express** (put thoughts and feelings into words), **point of view** (a person's way of thinking about something).

Letters

268

FOCUS QUESTION Have a student read "Talk About It" on **Student Book** page 269. Then have students turn to a partner and describe the photo. Ask:

- How can writing a letter help you express your ideas, emotions, and point of view?

- How can reading a letter help you get to know another person better?

Talk About It

In what ways do letters help you express yourself?

 LOG ON ▶ VIEW IT

Oral Language Activities
Letters
www.macmillanmh.com

269

Use the Picture Prompt

BUILD WRITING FLUENCY

Ask students to write in their Writer's Notebooks what they know about how letters can evoke emotion and change in others. Tell them to write as much as they can. Students should write for ten minutes without stopping. Meet with individuals during Writing Conference time to provide feedback and revision assignments. Students should self-correct errors prior to the conference.

Connect to the Unit Theme

DISCUSS THE BIG IDEA

People write letters to express emotions such as regret and happiness.

Ask students to discuss what they know about how words can be used to communicate feelings.

- Why are words important in communicating emotion to others?
- When might you write a letter rather than calling or visiting someone?

USE THEME FOLDABLES

Write the **Big Idea** on the board. Ask students to copy it on their Unit Theme Foldables. Remind them to add details as they complete this week's readings.

Study Book

Objectives

- Identify the characteristics of a poem
- Develop vocabulary
- Read sentences fluently, focusing on phrasing and expression

Materials

- Read-Aloud Anthology, pp. 44-46

Read Aloud

Read "A Word to the Wise"

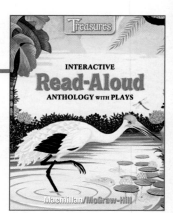

Read Aloud

GENRE: Literary Text/Poetry

Share with students the following key characteristics of a **poem**:

- A poem is arranged in lines and stanzas (similar to paragraphs in prose).

- A rhyming poem has words that rhyme. It may also have meter, or a set rhythm.

FOCUS ON VOCABULARY

Introduce the following words, using the **Define/Example/Ask** routine. Tell students that this poem is written as a riddle and that knowing these words will help them figure out more quickly what animal is speaking in the poem.

Vocabulary Routine

Use the routines below to discuss the meaning of each word.

Define: A **den** is a place where an animal sleeps or rests.
Example: The lion went back to his den and slept.
Ask: Why do some animals live in a den?

Define: To be **agile** is to move quickly and easily.
Example: Pam was not very agile with her leg in a cast.
Ask: Which living things need to be agile? Why?

Define: A **coil** is a spiral or loop.
Example: Russell made a coil by wrapping a piece of wire around his pencil.
Ask: What kinds of objects have coils in them?

LISTENING FOR A PURPOSE

Ask students to listen carefully as you read "A Word to the Wise" on **Read-Aloud Anthology** pages 44–46. Use the Think Alouds and genre study provided.

ELL **Interactive Reading** Build students' oral language by engaging them in talk about the poem's basic meaning.

- Point to the pictures of the animals on page 44. Identify the animals and have students repeat the names.

- After the second stanza, say: *Turn to your partner and discuss what you know so far about the animal who is talking. What animal do you think it might be?*

- After the fourth stanza, say: *Scales are small, flat pieces of skin that cover the bodies of fish and some other creatures. Brainstorm with your partner some animals that have scales besides fish.*

- After the last stanza, say: *Turn to your partner and discuss what you think of the snake's advice at the end of the poem.*

Think/Pair/Share Use **Copying Master 4**, "I figured out _____ because …," to help students summarize what they learned about the animal in the poem. Then have students turn to a partner and orally summarize the poem, using their responses to guide them. Finally, have a few students share their summaries with the class.

RESPOND TO THE POEM

Ask students the Think and Respond questions on page 46. Then have students work in groups to discuss other ways the author could have described the snake. Have them explain which ways they think would be most effective.

Model Fluency

Reread the poem. Tell students that this time you want them to focus on two aspects of how you read the poem—your **phrasing** and **expression**.

Point out that you read at a rate or tempo that allows you to pronounce every word correctly within a phrase, even if some words are unfamiliar to you. When you read a poem, you use expression to stress important words and phrases, such as rhyming words or phrases that repeat, and use phrasing to keep words in meaningful groups. Model an example of reading with appropriate phrasing and good expression.

Think Aloud Listen as I read the first stanza of the poem. Focus on my phrasing and expression: *I don't have to study. /I don't go to school. /I know what I know,/And I'm nobody's fool.* Did you notice how I read at a tempo that allowed me to clearly pronounce all of the words? Could you tell when I changed my expression to stress certain words? Now you try. Repeat each phrase after me, using the same phrasing and expression that I use.

Establish Fluency Focus Remind students that you will be listening for these same qualities in their reading throughout the week. You will help them improve their reading by adjusting their phrasing and using expression to emphasize key words and phrases.

Point out that good readers show their understanding of a text by reading it in these expressive ways. It shows that the reader is decoding and comprehending at the same time. That is the hallmark of a skilled, fluent reader.

Objective

- Decode multisyllabic words with *r*-controlled vowels *er, ir, ur*

Materials

- Sound-Spelling Cards
- Practice Book, p. 91
- Word-Building Cards
- Transparency 11
- Teacher's Resource Book, p. 54

ELL

Transfer Sounds Speakers of Spanish and Asian languages may have difficulties pronouncing *r*-controlled vowel sounds. Use the articulation supports on the back of the Sound-Spelling Cards to help students. Use the Approaching Level phonics lessons on page 291J for additional practice. See language transfers on pages T16–T31.

Practice Book, page 91

The /ûr/ sound can be spelled **er, ir,** and **ur.** The sound is found in words such as **serpent, bird,** and **turkey.**

A. Underline the **vowel + r combination** that represents the /ûr/ sound in each of these words.

1. b u r d e n
2. s t e r n l y
3. s e r p e n t
4. b i r t h
5. t u r n i p
6. w h i r l w i n d
7. b u r r o w
8. p u r p o s e
9. p e r s o n
10. g i r l f r i e n d

B. Now read the paragraph below. Find and circle six words that have the /ûr/ sound. Then continue the story. Circle the words with the /ûr/ sound.

One day, a raccoon climbed in the window of a house. He found a (skirt) on the floor. Holding it carefully in his mouth, he took it outside. Then he (returned) and carried away a small (purse). Finally, he (emerged) with a purple (shirt).

Responses will vary.

Approaching Reproducible, page 91
Beyond Reproducible, page 91

Phonics

✓ *r*-Controlled Vowels *er, ir, ur*

EXPLAIN/MODEL

Display the *Shirt* **Sound-Spelling Card** for *r*-controlled vowels *er, ir,* and *ur*. Tell students that when a vowel is followed by *r*, the *r* changes the vowel's sound. When the vowels *e, i,* and *u* are followed by *r*, the sound is usually /ûr/, as in *shirt*. Point to each spelling on the card and provide a sample word. Teach also the *or* spelling as in *worm*.

- **ir** as in *shirt*
- **ur** as in *burn*
- **er** as in *her*

Write the sample words on the board, underline the *r*-controlled vowel spellings, and model blending each one.

Think Aloud Look at the first word I wrote: *s-h-i-r-t*. I see the *r*-controlled vowel spelling *ir*. Listen and watch as I sound out the word: /shûrt/ *shirt*. (Run your finger under the word as you sound it out.)

PRACTICE/APPLY

Read the Words Display **Transparency 11**. The first two lines include /ûr/ words students will encounter in the upcoming selections. Have students underline the /ûr/ spelling in each word. Then have them chorally read the words.

letter	nurses	cover	flower
danger	either	yesterday	surprise
conserve	power	turn	purse
worse	gurgle	smirk	chirp
perfect	fur	perk	burn

Phonics Transparency 11

Sort the Words Ask students to sort the words by spelling pattern. Then have them write the word sort in their Writer's Notebooks.

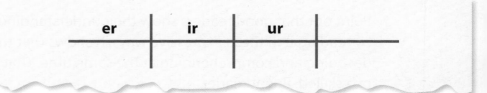

er	ir	ur	

Read Multisyllabic Words

TRANSITION TO LONGER WORDS Help students transition from reading one-syllable to multisyllabic /ûr/ words. Have students read a word in the first column, then model how to read the longer word in the second column. Point out the added syllable(s), such as a prefix or suffix, to help students gain awareness of these common word parts.

herd	shepherd	over	turnover
girl	girlfriend	world	worldwide
curd	curdle	work	workday
word	password	shirt	undershirt
birth	birthplace	whirl	whirlwind
emerge	emergency	urge	urgent

Phonics Transparency 11

BUILD WORDS Display **Word-Building Cards** *un, re, pre, birth, turn, concern, ed, ing.* Have students use the word parts to build as many *r*-controlled vowel multisyllabic words as possible. These and other words can be formed: *returned, unreturned, unconcerned, rebirth.*

CONNECT TO 6 SYLLABLE TYPES To further help students break apart longer words, explain that when a vowel is followed by the letter *r*, the vowel and the *r* must appear in the same syllable.

APPLY DECODING STRATEGY Guide students to use the Decoding Strategy to decode these words: *forever, permanent, thirsty, worthless, featherbed, merger, absurd.* Write each word. Remind students to look for common spellings in step 3 of the Decoding Strategy procedure.

Build Fluency

SPEED DRILL Distribute copies of the ***r*-Controlled Vowels Speed Drill, Teacher's Resource Book** page 54. Use the Speed Drill routine to help students become fluent reading words with /ûr/.

Quick Check

Can students read words with *r*-controlled vowels?

During **Small Group Instruction**

Tier 2

If No → | Approaching Level | Reteach the skill using the lesson on p. 291J.

If Yes → | On Level | Consolidate the learning using p. 291S.

| Beyond Level | Extend the learning using p. 291W.

DAILY **Syllable Fluency**

Use Word-Building Cards 101–110. Display one card at a time. Have students chorally read each common syllable. Repeat at varying speeds and in random order. Have students work with partners during independent time to write as many words as they can containing each syllable.

Decoding Strategy

Decoding Strategy Chart

Step 1	Look for word parts (prefixes) at the beginning of the word.
Step 2	Look for word parts (suffixes) at the end of the word.
Step 3	In the base word, look for familiar spelling patterns. Think about the six syllable-spelling patterns you have learned.
Step 4	Sound out and blend together the word parts.
Step 5	Say the word parts fast. Adjust your pronunciation as needed. Ask yourself: "Is this a word I have heard before?" Then read the word in the sentence and ask: "Does it make sense in this sentence?"

© Macmillan/McGraw-Hill

Vocabulary

STRATEGY
WORD PARTS

Base Words Remind students that adding an affix, which can be a prefix or a suffix, changes the meaning of the base word. Tell students that they can often decode the meaning of a long word that has an affix if they know the meaning of the base word.

Tell students to read "Word Parts" in the bookmark on **Student Book** page 270. Then model for students how to use a base word to determine the meaning of the word *harmless* on page 271.

Think Aloud I know that *harm* means "hurt," but I'm not sure what *harmless* means. Maybe by thinking about the base word *harm* and looking at how the word is used in context, I can figure out what *harmless* means. Because of the base word, it must have something to do with hurting. From the way it's used in the story, I think *harmless* may mean the opposite of "dangerous." So maybe it means "without hurt" or "not hurtful."

Discuss other words formed from the base word *harm,* such as *harmful* and *unharmed.* Have students apply their knowledge of the base word and affixes to determine the words' meanings.

Read "Name That Reptile"

As you read "Name That Reptile" with students, direct them to identify clues that reveal the meanings of the highlighted words. Tell students they will read these words again in *When I Went to the Library.*

Vocabulary

weekdays	genuine
slithered	harmless
apologize	ambulance

Word Parts

Base Words can help you figure out the meaning of a word.

harm = "hurt"; injure

harmless = "without hurt"

270

NAME THAT REPTILE

by Catherine Lutz

Narrator: Mark and Jean have been studying together **weekdays** after school for a big test on Friday. Jean takes a card from a cardboard box. The card has the name of a reptile on it. Now Mark will ask questions and try to name the reptile. Can you guess the answer before Mark?

Mark: Is it furry?

Jean: No. Remember, reptiles don't have fur.

Mark: That's right. Where does it live?

Jean: Mostly in the southwestern United States.

Mark: What does it eat?

Jean: It eats small birds, rabbits, mice, and squirrels.

Mark: Is it a crocodile?

Jean: No. Crocodiles live near streams, and this reptile lives where it's dry.

Mark: How big is it?

Jean: Some can be 7 feet long. Others are only 2 feet long.

Mark: It's probably not a turtle or a lizard. Is it a snake?

Jean: Yes!

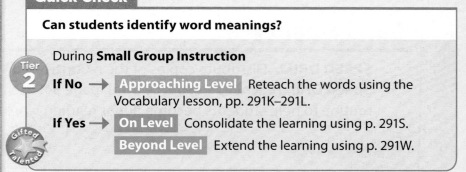

Quick Check

Can students identify word meanings?

During **Small Group Instruction**

Tier 2

If No → Approaching Level Reteach the words using the Vocabulary lesson, pp. 291K–291L.

If Yes → On Level Consolidate the learning using p. 291S.

Gifted Talented

Beyond Level Extend the learning using p. 291W.

Is it a crocodile?

Mark: Remember when my pet snake got loose? It **slithered** slowly across my mother's foot. As it slid over her foot, she screamed. Then she stood on a chair until I caught it. I had to return it to the pet store.

Jean: Did you **apologize** to your mom and say you were sorry? Was it a sincere and **genuine** apology?

Mark: Yes. I told her I was really sorry, but she didn't change her mind.

Jean: Okay, back to studying.

Mark: Does the snake crush its prey?

Jean: No.

Mark: So it's not a python. Is it **harmless**?

Jean: No. It's dangerous. Its bite can be fatal. If you get bitten, you'd need an **ambulance** to drive you to the hospital!

Mark: Yikes. Does it give a warning before it attacks?

Jean: Its tail shakes and makes noise. Each time the snake sheds, its tail gets a new segment in it.

Mark: I've got it! It's a rattlesnake!

Narrator: Did you guess the reptile before Mark did?

It's a rattlesnake!

Reread for **Comprehension**

Generate Questions

 Make Inferences When you make inferences, you use story clues to understand what is not directly stated in the story. You can also use any prior knowledge you have connected to the story. Generating questions as you read can help you make inferences about the characters and the changes they undergo. Reread the story and fill in your Inferences Web.

Clue · Clue · Inference Character · Clue · Clue

LOG ON ▶ **LEARN IT** Comprehension
www.macmillanmh.com

271

Vocabulary

✓ TEACH WORDS

Introduce each word using the **Define/Example/Ask** routine. Model reading each word using the syllable-scoop technique.

> ### Vocabulary Routine
>
> **Define:** **Weekdays** are the days of the week except Saturday and Sunday.
> **Example:** On Saturday and Sunday we have pancakes for breakfast, but on weekdays we have oatmeal.
> **Ask:** What are regular weekdays like at your house? EXPLANATION

- **Slithered** means "slid or glided like a snake." *The dog slid under the house to fetch the tennis ball and then slithered back out.* What other animals might *slither*? EXAMPLE

- If something is **genuine**, it is real or true. *A genuine person is sincere and natural.* What is an antonym for *genuine*? ANTONYM

- When you **apologize**, you tell someone that you are sorry. *Liam was sorry for breaking the vase, so he came to apologize.* Tell about a time you needed to apologize. DESCRIPTION

- Anything that is **harmless** cannot do damage or hurt you. *Pets should be harmless to protect young children from injury.* What is a synonym for *harmless*? SYNONYM

- An **ambulance** is a special vehicle that takes sick or injured people to the hospital. *After Andrew was injured, he rode in an ambulance to the hospital.* How can you tell if an ambulance is taking someone to the hospital? DESCRIPTION

ELL

Preteach Vocabulary See pages 291BB and 291K to preteach the vocabulary words to ELL and Approaching Level students. Use the **Visual Vocabulary Resources** to demonstrate and discuss each word. To further reinforce concepts, have students complete page 122 in the **ELL Resource Book**.

HOMEWORK **Practice Book,** page 92

| apologize | genuine | harmless |
| slithered | ambulance | weekdays |

A. Use the correct vocabulary word from the box to fill in the blank.

1. On our hike a snake ___slithered___ across the trail.

2. The reptile exhibit at the zoo is open ___weekdays___ from 10 A.M. to 5 P.M.

3. My encyclopedia says that the green snake we saw in my garden is ___harmless___.

4. An ___ambulance___ rushed the snakebite victim to the hospital.

5. Evan should ___apologize___ for leaving a rubber snake on his sister's pillow.

6. Danielle's snake is ___genuine___, not rubber!   **Possible responses provided.**

B. Write a sentence using one of the vocabulary words.

7. Some sharks are dangerous, but the nurse shark is *harmless*.

8. Paula has a *genuine* fear of snakes.

Approaching Reproducible, page 92
Beyond Reproducible, page 92

Objectives

- Generate questions
- Make inferences based on text evidence
- Use academic language: *generate, inferences*

Materials

- Transparencies 2, 11a, 11b
- Practice Book, p. 93

Skills Trace

Make Inferences

Introduce	9A–9B
Practice/ Apply	10–31; Practice Book, 3–4
Reteach/ Review	37M–37Z, 271A–271B, 272–285, 291M–291Z; Practice Book, 93–94
Assess	Weekly Tests; Unit 1, 3 Tests
Maintain	59B

ELL

Academic Language
Preteach the following academic language words to **ELL** and **Approaching Level** students during Small Group time: *generate questions, make inferences*. See pages 291AA and 291I.

Reread for
Comprehension

STRATEGY
GENERATE QUESTIONS

What Is It? Good readers **generate questions** as they read, such as these: *Do I understand what is taking place in this part of the story? Why has the author included this information?* These questions help them focus on the most important information and can be literal or can help them interpret or evaluate the text on a deeper level.

Why Is It Important? Tell students that generating questions will help them check their understanding and identify information that is not directly stated. Students can look for the answers as they read.

SKILL
MAKE INFERENCES

What Is It? Explain that when readers **make inferences** they use story clues and prior knowledge related to the text to make logical decisions about events and characters that are not directly stated.

Why Is It Important? Making inferences helps readers understand the interactions between characters, including their relationships and the changes they undergo.

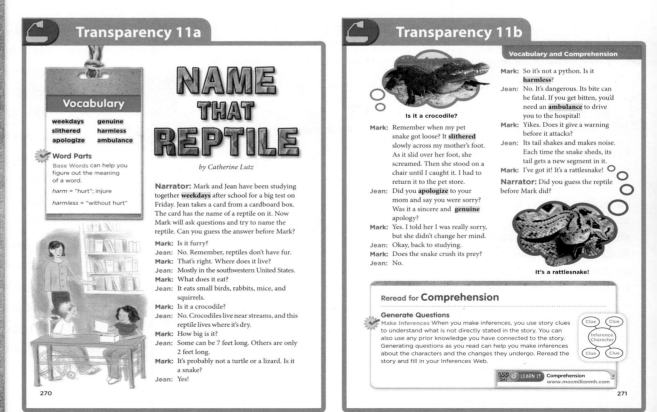

Student Book pages 270–271 available on Comprehension Transparencies 11a and 11b

- To make inferences, tell students to look for a situation in the story in which the author gives clues but does not state directly what is taking place. Students should then think about what they already know about the situation, combining story clues with their own personal experiences to make an inference, or a reasonable assumption, about what is taking place or what has happened.

- Making inferences can lead not only to conclusions about the past but also to predictions about the future. Students can look for clues in the dialogue, settings, or plot that foreshadow events to come.

MODEL

How Do I Use It? Read aloud the first page of "Name That Reptile" on **Student Book** page 270. Model making inferences.

Think Aloud I know from the introduction that Mark and Jean have been studying together. They meet weekdays after school. This is the only information that the author states directly. From these clues and my own experiences studying for a test, I can infer that Mark and Jean are probably friends, even though the author doesn't say so. Since the card Jean is holding has the name of a reptile on it, I can also assume that she and Mark are studying for a science test, not a social studies or math test.

GUIDED PRACTICE

Have students make inferences based on the text in the first column of page 271. Remind them that they should consider the dialogue between the two characters and make inferences about how Mark's mother feels about his pet snake.

APPLY

Display **Transparency 2**. Ask students to use the clues and their inferences to complete the Inferences Web. Then have students finish rereading the story. Afterward, have them identify the clues the author provided that the reptile was a rattlesnake.

Quick Check

Can students make inferences and use textual evidence to support understanding?

During Small Group Instruction

Tier 2

If No → **Approaching Level** Reteach the skill using the Comprehension lesson, pp. 291M–291P.

If Yes → **On Level** Consolidate the learning using pp. 291U–291V.

Beyond Level Extend the learning using pp. 291Y–291Z.

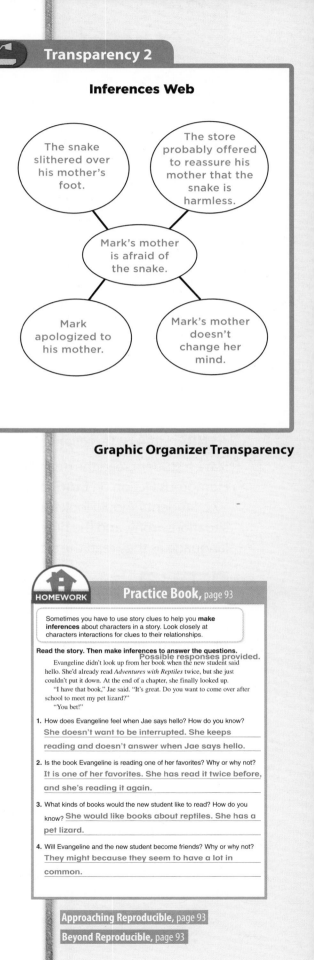

Transparency 2

Inferences Web

- The snake slithered over his mother's foot.
- The store probably offered to reassure his mother that the snake is harmless.
- Mark's mother is afraid of the snake.
- Mark apologized to his mother.
- Mark's mother doesn't change her mind.

Graphic Organizer Transparency

HOMEWORK   **Practice Book,** page 93

Sometimes you have to use story clues to help you **make inferences** about characters in a story. Look closely at characters interactions for clues to their relationships.

Read the story. Then make inferences to answer the questions.
Possible responses provided.
Evangeline didn't look up from her book when the new student said hello. She'd already read *Adventures with Reptiles* twice, but she just couldn't put it down. At the end of a chapter, she finally looked up.
"I have that book," Jae said. "It's great. Do you want to come over after school to meet my pet lizard?"
"You bet!"

1. How does Evangeline feel when Jae says hello? How do you know? She doesn't want to be interrupted. She keeps reading and doesn't answer when Jae says hello.

2. Is the book Evangeline is reading one of her favorites? Why or why not? It is one of her favorites. She has read it twice before, and she's reading it again.

3. What kinds of books would the new student like to read? How do you know? She would like books about reptiles. She has a pet lizard.

4. Will Evangeline and the new student become friends? Why or why not? They might because they seem to have a lot in common.

Approaching Reproducible, page 93

Beyond Reproducible, page 93

Read

WHOLE GROUP

MAIN SELECTION
- *When I Went to the Library*
- Skill: Make Inferences

PAIRED SELECTION
- Expository: "Snakes"
- Text Feature: Toolbars and Guide Words

SMALL GROUP

- Differentiated Instruction, pp. 291I–291HH

Main Selection

GENRE: Literary Text/Fiction

Have a student read the definition of Humorous Fiction on **Student Book** page 272. Students should look for comical situations, irony, and the humorous use of language as they read the story.

STRATEGY
GENERATE QUESTIONS

Remind students that generating questions will improve their understanding of the events in a story, and help them make inferences about the characters and the plot.

SKILL
MAKE INFERENCES

Since authors do not always tell readers directly everything that takes place in a story, readers must take what details the author does offer to make inferences about characters, their relationships, and events in the story.

Comprehension

Genre

Humor can be found in both fiction and nonfiction selections. Humorous fiction is a made-up story written to make the reader laugh.

Generate Questions

Make Inferences
As you read, fill in your Inferences Web.

Read to Find Out

What do you learn when you read between the lines?

272

Vocabulary

Vocabulary Words Review the tested vocabulary words: **apologize, genuine, ambulance, weekdays, harmless, slithered**.

Additional Selection Words Students may be unfamiliar with these words. Pronounce the words, give student-friendly explanations as needed, and help students use the previously taught vocabulary strategies: using word parts, context clues, and a dictionary.

galactic (p. 275): in the same group of stars as Earth

python (p. 278): a snake that wraps around its prey to crush it

anaconda (p. 278): another type of snake that crushes its prey

asp (p. 278): a small poisonous snake

cobra (p. 278): a poisonous snake

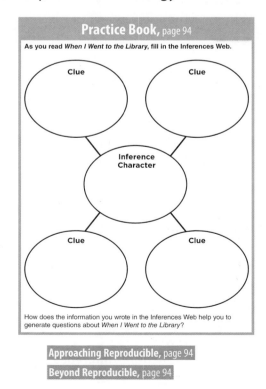

When I Went to the Library
by Ken Roberts
illustrated by Nicole E. Wong

Dear Mr. Winston,

My parents said that I have to write and **apologize**. Dad says he is going to read this letter before it's sent and that I'd better make sure my apology sounds truly **genuine**. So, I am truly, genuinely sorry for bringing that snake into the library yesterday.

My parents say that what I did was wrong, even though the cardboard box was shut, most of the time, and there was no way that snake could have escaped if you hadn't opened the box and dropped it on the floor.

273

Read the Main Selection

Preteach	Read Together	Read Independently
Have Approaching Level students and English Language Learners listen to the selection on **StudentWorks Plus**, the interactive e-Book, before reading with the class.	Use the prompts to guide comprehension and model how to complete the graphic organizer. Have students use **Think/Pair/Share** to discuss the selection.	If students can read the selection independently, have them read and complete the graphic organizer. Suggest that they use their purposes to choose their reading strategies.

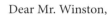

LOG ON StudentWorks Plus
Interactive Student Book

Preview and Predict

QUICK WRITE Ask students to read the title, preview the illustrations, think about the genre, and make predictions about the story. Students may also include information they already know about libraries and library etiquette.

Set Purposes

FOCUS QUESTION Discuss the "Read to Find Out" question on **Student Book** page 272. Remind students to look for the answer as they read.

Point out the Inferences Web in the Student Book and on **Practice Book** page 94. Explain that students will fill it in as they read.

Read *When I Went to the Library*

Use the questions and Think Alouds to support instruction about the comprehension strategy and skill.

Practice Book, page 94

As you read *When I Went to the Library*, fill in the Inferences Web.

- Clue
- Clue
- Inference Character
- Clue
- Clue

How does the information you wrote in the Inferences Web help you to generate questions about *When I Went to the Library*?

Approaching Reproducible, page 94
Beyond Reproducible, page 94

Develop Comprehension

1 STRATEGY
GENERATE QUESTIONS

Teacher Think Aloud Generating questions about a selection can give me a purpose for reading and help me to make inferences. For example, in the last paragraph on page 274, the girl mentions that Mr. Winston was taken away in an ambulance. Although the author does not state that he was taken to the hospital, I can infer that from this clue. So I can ask, *Did this happen because the snake escaped? Did it bite Mr. Winston?* I will keep reading to find out.

2 SKILL
MAKE INFERENCES

Does the girl think that bringing the snake inside the library was her fault? Why or why not? (No. In her letter, she explains that she brought the snake inside but says she had to do so, because Mr. Winston wouldn't let her borrow the snake book. When she uses the phrase "even for ten minutes," this is a clue that she is angry about it and blames Mr. Winston. Therefore, she does not think it is her fault.) Add this clue to your Inferences Web. When you have all four clues, fill in your inference.

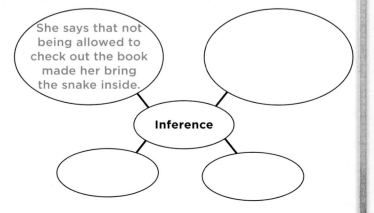

> She says that not being allowed to check out the book made her bring the snake inside.

Inference

My parents say it's my fault for having brought that snake into the library and I truly, genuinely apologize but I still don't know how I was supposed to find out what kind of snake I had inside that box without bringing the snake right into the library so I could look at snake pictures and then look at the snake and try to find a picture that matched the snake.

1   I told my parents something that I didn't get a chance to remind you about before the **ambulance** took you away. I did come into the library without the snake, first. I left the box outside, hidden under a bush and tried to borrow a thick green book with lots of snake pictures. You told me that the big green book was a reference book which meant that it had to stay inside the library and I couldn't take it

2   out, even for ten minutes.

274

Monitor Comprehension

Monitor and Clarify: *Reread to Clarify*

Explain Tell students that, as they read, they should ask themselves if they understand what is happening. If they find a passage confusing, they can read the passage again. They can also go back and reread an earlier part of the story to adjust their understanding.

Discuss Ask if any students think that Mr. Winston was bitten by the snake. Have students reread pages 274 and 275 to check if the narrator ever states that directly and to identify any clues that might clarify what happened to Mr. Winston. (Students should recognize that the narrator does not say Mr. Winston was bitten, but it is clear that the snake was somehow involved in his hospitalization.)

Apply As students read, have them self-monitor by going back and rereading to clarify any part of the story that may be confusing.

My parents say I still shouldn't have brought that snake into the library and that I have to be truly, genuinely sorry if I ever hope to watch Galactic Patrol on television again. My parents picked Galactic Patrol because it's my favorite show, although I'm not sure what not watching a television program has to do with bringing a snake into the library.

The people at the library say you hate snakes so much that you won't even touch a book with a picture of snakes on the cover and that is why you won't be back at the library for a few more weeks. If you want, you could watch Galactic Patrol. It's on at 4:00 P.M. **weekdays**, on channel 7. There are no snakes on the show because it takes place in space.

275

Develop Comprehension

3 **SKILL**
MAKE INFERENCES

According to the girl, the people at the library said Mr. Winston hates snakes. Do you think that information is correct? What can you infer about how Mr. Winston really feels from the events that have taken place in the story so far? (If Mr. Winston merely hated snakes, he would not have had to be taken away in an ambulance. The truth is that he is very afraid of snakes.)

4 **GENRE:** Literary Text/Fiction

When I Went to the Library is humorous fiction. What examples on page 275 show that this story is meant to be funny? (Even though some people really are afraid of snakes, the idea that a librarian had to be taken away in an ambulance simply because he saw one is humorous. Telling Mr. Winston to watch *Galactic Patrol* is funny because of the reason the girl gives: that there are no snakes in space.)

Phonics/Word Study

APPLY DECODING SKILLS While reading, point out words with the sound/spelling patterns, syllable types, and word parts students have recently learned. Help students blend these words. You may wish to focus on selection words with /ûr/ spelling patterns, such as *cover, flowers, danger, yesterday, perfectly,* and *ever.*

Develop Comprehension

5 STRATEGY
WORD PARTS

The girl says there are no poisonous snakes where she lives. What is the **base word** of *poisonous*? (*poison*) What other words can be made from this base word? (*poisoned, poisoning*)

6 CHARACTER'S POINT OF VIEW

From whose point of view is the story told? How does this affect your understanding of the events in the library? (The story is told from the girl's point of view. The events come to light bit by bit, because the girl talks a lot about why she is writing the letter, her parents, how she bought the snake, and so on. We have to make inferences about how the other characters think and feel based on what she says and what we already know about libraries, librarians, and parents.)

7 SEQUENCE

SPIRAL REVIEW

What main events have taken place in the story so far? Retell the events in **sequence**. (The girl is writing a letter of apology to Mr. Winston, who works at the library. She brought a snake into the library, and it scared him so much that he had to be taken to the hospital. Then she explains that she had to bring the snake inside to compare it to pictures in a book that could not be borrowed. Finally, she points out that the flowers sent to Mr. Winston are being paid for out of her allowance and that the snake is not poisonous.)

276

Vocabulary

Word Structure Clues: *Linguistic Roots*

Explain/Model Explain that words in English usually have Greek, Latin, or other linguistic roots. For example, *snake* comes from a German word meaning "to crawl" and *poison* comes from a Latin word meaning "to drink." Many English words have the Greek root *tele-*, meaning "far" or "from afar." Knowing such roots can help readers understand a long word. Point out *television* on page 275.

Think Aloud I know what a television is, but I did not realize that the word contains the root *tele-*. Since a television enables people to see events happening in far-off places, I can see the connection to the meaning of the root.

Practice/Apply Write *telescope, telephone*, and *telegram*. Discuss how the meaning of each word may relate to the Greek root *tele-*.

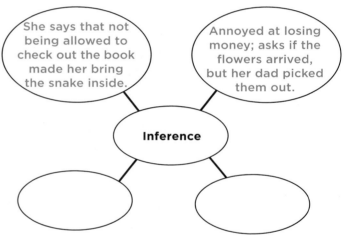

Did the flowers arrive? Dad picked them out but I have to pay for them with my allowance for the next two months. The flowers are proof that I am truly, genuinely sorry for having brought that snake into the library. I hope the people who work at the library find that snake soon! Did they look under all the chairs?

That snake isn't dangerous. It is a local snake, and there are no poisonous snakes in Manitoba. The people at the library say you know that too because that was one of the reasons you decided to move here. I bought that snake from a friend. I paid one month's allowance for it, which means that snake has cost me a total of three months' allowance and I only owned it for one hour!

Mom says I don't have to tell who sold me that snake so I won't tell you either because Dad says he is going to read this letter. Besides, I don't want you to be mad at anyone else when I am the one who brought that snake into the library yesterday. I am truly, genuinely sorry.

Make Inferences
How can you tell that the girl writing the letter is not truly sorry? Use details from the story to explain your answer.

277

Extra Support

Make Inferences

Help students make inferences about the plot by modeling the process of identifying clues. Ask: *Who told the girl to write the letter?* (her parents) *What was she told to say in the letter?* (that she is truly, genuinely sorry) *Who will read the letter before she sends it?* (her father) *Does the girl really want to write this letter?* (The girl makes a point of saying she has to write it, so she probably does not want to do so.)

Develop Comprehension

8 | **SKILL**
MAKE INFERENCES

How can you tell that the girl writing the letter is not truly sorry? Use details from the story to explain your answer. (She asks if the flowers arrived, but her dad picked them out. She is annoyed about losing her allowance money.) Add this information to your Inferences Web.

She says that not being allowed to check out the book made her bring the snake inside.

Annoyed at losing money; asks if the flowers arrived, but her dad picked them out.

Inference

9 **SELF-SELECTED STRATEGY USE**

What strategies have you used so far to help you understand the selection? Where did you use them? Why?

RETURN TO PREDICTIONS AND PURPOSES

Have students respond to the story by confirming or revising their predictions and purposes for reading. Have students revise or write additional questions to help focus their attention as they continue to read.

Stop here if you wish to read this selection over two days.

Develop Comprehension

10 STRATEGY
GENERATE QUESTIONS

Teacher Think Aloud I notice that the girl repeats certain words and expressions a lot. Does she realize that saying she is "truly, genuinely sorry" so often makes it sound as if her apology is not very genuine at all? In the first paragraph on page 278, she repeats the word *snake* five times. If she knows that Mr. Winston is afraid of snakes, why does she do that? What other questions can you ask about the girl's letter?

PARTNERS Prompt students to apply the strategy in a Think Aloud by generating questions with a partner to make inferences.

Student Think Aloud The girl has already said that Mr. Winston hates snakes. So when she is trying to tell him that the snake she brought into the library is harmless, I wonder why she mentions poisonous snakes such as cobras, as well as huge, dangerous snakes such as pythons and anacondas. Doesn't she realize that mentioning those snakes by name will upset Mr. Winston even more? It seems as though she is just explaining everything she did, but I wonder if she is trying to upset him on purpose.

I want you to know that I didn't plan to show you that snake. I didn't mean to scare you at all. I knew where the big green snake book was kept. I put the box on a table close to the book and tried to find the right picture. I looked at a picture, then at the snake, at another picture, and then the snake. I did that five times and can tell you that the snake inside the library is not a python, a rattlesnake, an anaconda, an asp, or a cobra.

Anyway, I was surprised when you wanted to see what was inside the box because I didn't ask for any help and there were plenty of people in the library who did need help.

Dad says that the fact that I said, "Nothing," instead of "A snake," is proof that I knew I was doing something wrong when I brought that snake into the library. I am truly, genuinely sorry even though my friend Jake Lambert promised me that the snake I bought from him is perfectly **harmless**.

278

Text Evidence

Make Inferences

Reread question 11. Then ask, *What did the girl do with the box when she was in the library? Point to the information in the text.* (She put the box on the table near the book about snakes (p. 278). She would look at a picture of a snake, then look in the box to see if it was a match.) *Why do you think this behavior might make Mr. Winston curious about the box?* (There was something in the box that the girl wanted to identify. The box was next to a book about snakes.) *What did the girl say that might have worried Mr. Winston?* (Mr. Winston asked the girl what was in the box, and she said, "Nothing." Obviously there was something in the box, or she would not need to look inside. The girl did not want him to know what was in the box.)

Develop Comprehension

11 | **SKILL**
MAKE INFERENCES

Do you think the girl is being honest when she says she was surprised that Mr. Winston wanted to look inside the box? Explain. (She is probably not being totally honest. The reason she gives for being surprised is not completely believable. She probably knew she was doing something wrong, as her father says. She makes it seem as though Mr. Winston should have minded his own business.) **Add this information to your Inferences Web.**

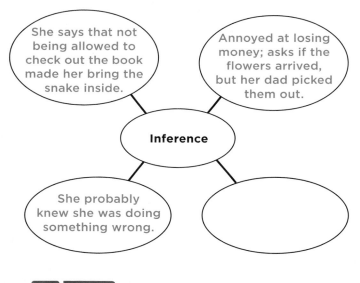

She says that not being allowed to check out the book made her bring the snake inside.

Annoyed at losing money; asks if the flowers arrived, but her dad picked them out.

Inference

She probably knew she was doing something wrong.

12 | **SKILL**
MAKE INFERENCES

Based on what you have read so far, what kind of relationship do you think the girl has with her parents? Explain. (By threatening to keep her from watching her favorite TV program, they show that they know her well. They recognize that she does not want to apologize. Her dad insists on reading the letter before she mails it, so he must know she might not be sincere.)

Develop Comprehension

13 **MONITOR AND CLARIFY: REREAD TO CLARIFY**

What self-monitoring strategies could you use to help you decide what kind of person Mr. Winston is? (Since he is only seen from the girl's point of view, I can reread to locate clues in the girl's letter. He is afraid of snakes, and he seems to be concerned about what goes on in the library. He screamed and fainted, so he may not be a strong person.)

14 **GENRE:** Literary Text/Fiction

In what ways do the girl's comments about Mr. Winston's rash add to the humor and make the mishap even funnier? (The girl acts as though she's surprised that a person can get a rash just from being upset or frightened, so we can tell that she thinks he overreacted. We can tell that the girl thinks the rash is funny, because she teases Mr. Winston about it.)

I did tell you that I didn't need any help and I did have a snake book open in front of me, so I don't know why you insisted on looking inside the box if you are so afraid of snakes and everything. I don't know why you picked up that box before opening a flap, either. If you had left the box on the table and maybe even sat down next to it, then maybe the box would have been all right when you screamed and fainted. You wouldn't have fallen so far, either, if you were sitting down.

Did you know that you broke out in a rash after you fainted? I thought a person had to touch something like poison ivy to get a rash. I didn't know it was possible to get a rash by just thinking about something but my parents say it really can happen. I think maybe you did touch something. Maybe, when you were lying on the floor, that snake **slithered** over to you and touched you! Did you know that snake skin feels dry, not wet and slimy at all?

Make Inferences
Explain how the girl is not taking responsibility for what happened to Mr. Winston.

280

281

Develop Comprehension

15 **SKILL**
MAKE INFERENCES

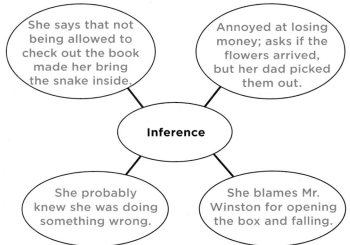

Explain how the girl is not taking responsibility for what happened to Mr. Winston. (She implies that he should have known what was in the box because of the book she was reading. She also says that he opened the box the wrong way. She even says that it is his fault he fell so far, because he should have been sitting down instead of standing up.) **Add this information to your Inferences Web.**

She says that not being allowed to check out the book made her bring the snake inside.

Annoyed at losing money; asks if the flowers arrived, but her dad picked them out.

Inference

She probably knew she was doing something wrong.

She blames Mr. Winston for opening the box and falling.

STRATEGIES FOR EXTRA SUPPORT

Question 15 MAKE INFERENCES
Clarify Discuss the meaning of the phrase "taking responsibility" and provide an example. Then ask questions to help students make inferences. Ask: *When you make a mistake or do something wrong, what do you do?* (I apologize, or say I am sorry.) Explain that apologizing is one way of taking responsibility. *Does the girl think it is her fault that Mr. Winston was injured?* (No.) *Explain your answer.* (She blames Mr. Winston for opening the box and getting injured.) *Is she telling the truth about being sorry?* (No.) *Is she taking responsibility for what happened to Mr. Winston?* (No.) *Explain your answer.* (She blames other people and does not really believe that she did anything wrong.) *Why is she apologizing?* (Her father is making her apologize.)

Develop Comprehension

16 STRATEGY
GENERATE QUESTIONS

Although she knows that Mr. Winston is afraid of snakes, the girl keeps writing about the missing snake and where it might be. What **questions** can you ask to find out why she does this?

Student Think Aloud The girl says it would be funny if the snake ended up at the hospital with Mr. Winston. Is she being mean? Is she so angry about losing the snake that she wants to make him feel worse? I think she is angry about losing the snake, and because she thinks it's silly to be afraid of snakes, she is being mean to him while sounding "genuine."

17 SKILL
MAKE INFERENCES

Based on evidence in the letter she has written, do you think Cara's apology is genuine? Explain. (No. Clearly she is only writing the letter because her parents told her to do so.) Add this information to the inference circle in your Inferences Web.

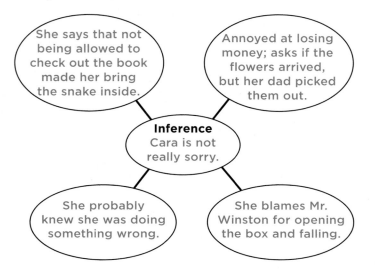

She says that not being allowed to check out the book made her bring the snake inside.

Annoyed at losing money; asks if the flowers arrived, but her dad picked them out.

Inference
Cara is not really sorry.

She probably knew she was doing something wrong.

She blames Mr. Winston for opening the box and falling.

I just thought of something. Maybe everyone's looking in the library for that snake but it's not in the library. Maybe it crawled into one of your pockets or up your sleeve and rode with you to the hospital! Wouldn't that be funny? Why don't you get one of the nurses to check? If it's not in your clothes, it might have crawled out and might be hiding inside the hospital someplace. I think people should be looking there, too.

I am sure you will be talking to the people in the library, to make sure they find that snake before you go back to work. I hope they do find it, even though my parents say that I can't keep it. If that snake is found, could you ask the people at the library to give me a call? I would be interested in knowing that it is all right. And if they do find that snake and do decide to give me a call, could you ask them if they could compare that snake with the snake pictures in that big green reference book before they call me? I would still like to know what kind of snake I owned for an hour.

I am truly, genuinely sorry.
Your friend,

Cara

282

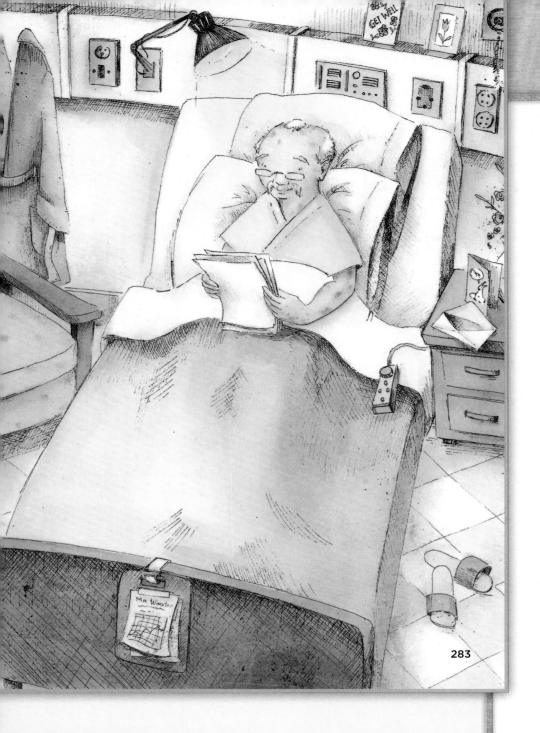

283

Develop Comprehension

RETURN TO PREDICTIONS AND PURPOSES

Review students' predictions and purposes. Were they correct? What did they learn when they read between the lines? (Cara is not truly, genuinely sorry. She is actually annoyed with Mr. Winston and blames him for the mishap.)

REVIEW READING STRATEGIES

- **Generate Questions** In what ways did generating questions about what you read help you to understand the selection?

- **Monitor and Clarify: Reread to Clarify** Do you understand the strategy of rereading to clarify when you are not sure what part of a story means? When might you use it again?

- **Decoding** What difficult words did you encounter? How did the Reading Multisyllabic Words strategy help you sound out these words?

- **Self-Selected Strategy Use** What strategies did you use to make sense of what you read? Where? How were these strategies helpful?

PERSONAL RESPONSE

Ask students to use what they have learned about writing letters to tell why someone might write a letter of apology. Encourage them to use examples from the story and to make connections to their own lives.

Quick Check

Can students use text evidence to make inferences about the characters and their relationships?

During **Small Group Instruction**

If No → **Approaching Level** Reteach the skill and have students apply it to a simpler text. Use Leveled Reader lessons, pp. 291N–291P.

If Yes → **On Level** Have students apply the skill to a new text to consolidate learning. Use Leveled Reader lessons, pp. 291U–291V.

Beyond Level Have students apply the skill to a more complex text to extend learning. Use Leveled Reader lessons, pp. 291Y–291Z.

Gifted & Talented

Author and Illustrator

IDENTIFY THE AUTHOR AND ILLUSTRATOR

Have students read the biographies of the author and the illustrator. Explain that this story is based on a real event. A fellow librarian told Ken Roberts about a time two children came up to her in the library. They showed her a snake that they wanted to identify. The librarian calmly helped the children find information about their snake.

DISCUSS

- Did it surprise you to learn that Ken Roberts is a librarian? Explain.

- What are some similarities and differences between this story and the real-life snake incident?

WRITE ABOUT IT

Author's Craft: Humor
Discuss how Mr. Winston would react to Cara's letter. Have students write a letter from Mr. Winston to Cara in response to her apology. Students should try to include humor. Remind students to include a salutation, closing, and signature.

Author's Purpose

By writing this story as a letter, the author made it more humorous. The story is written from a first-person point of view, so readers only hear Cara's side of the story. Readers must make inferences to get the full story.

Identify the
Author and Illustrator

Ken Roberts is actually a librarian. He often writes funny stories with unusual characters, like the girl in this piece. Ken has many talents. He is a storyteller, puppeteer, juggler, and magician. He was once a champion runner, too.

Nicole E. Wong has been interested in art all her life and even went to college to study it. She has been very fortunate to have turned her passion and training into her career in illustration. Nicole's artwork has appeared in several books, including Jan Wahl's *Candy Shop*, and various magazines. Nicole lives in Massachusetts with her husband, Dan, and their dog, Sable.

Another book illustrated by Nicole E. Wong

LOG ON ▶ **FIND OUT**
Author Ken Roberts
Illustrator Nicole E. Wong
www.macmillanmh.com

✔ Author's Purpose
Why did Ken Roberts write this story in the form of a letter? Identify whether he wrote the story using the first- or third-person point of view.

284

Author's Craft

Humor

- Repetition is one tool authors use to write humorous stories. Example: "I am truly, genuinely sorry." (pages 273 and 277) Cara says this line so often that readers laugh at her exaggerated sincerity. Have students discuss other repeated funny lines.

- Saying one thing but meaning something different can also make stories funny. Cara's letter to Mr. Winston may sound sincere, but when you read it carefully, you see that she is actually making him feel worse. Example: "I was surprised when you wanted to see what was inside the box because I didn't ask for any help." (page 278)

- Ask students to find other examples of contradiction and explain why they are funny.

Comprehension Check

LOG ON ▶ LEARN IT Comprehension
www.macmillanmh.com

Summarize

To summarize *When I Went to the Library* use the most important details from the selection. Information from your Inferences Web may help you.

Clue — Clue
Inference Character
Clue — Clue

Think and Compare

1. Who told Cara that she had to **apologize** to Mr. Winston? Details

2. According to Cara, what was one of the reasons Mr. Winston decided to move to Manitoba? Cause and Effect

3. Describe how Cara feels about apologizing to Mr. Winston. Explain using details from the story. Generate Questions: Make Inferences

4. Why did the author tell the story from Cara's perspective? Author's Purpose

5. Read "Name That Reptile" on pages 270–271. How do Mark's mother and Mr. Winston feel about snakes? Use details from both selections. Reading/Writing Across Texts

285

Make Connections

Text-to-Self Have students respond to the following question to make connections to their own lives. Use the Think Aloud to model a response. *If you were Cara, how would you have handled the whole situation with Mr. Winston and the snake?*

Think Aloud: I might have worried about the snake escaping if I brought it into the library. I would have taken a picture of the snake and brought that to the library instead.

Text-to-Text Have students respond to the following question to make connections to the world. Use the Think Aloud to model a response. *Will someone like Mr. Winston ever be able to see the humor in this event?*

Think Aloud: On the last page, Mr. Winston does not appear to be unhappy. Even though Cara may not realize it, her letter is funny. He probably can see that Cara is not sorry, but he may feel sympathetic toward her or find her apology humorous.

Comprehension Check

SUMMARIZE

Have partners summarize *When I Went to the Library* in their own words. Remind students to use their Inferences Web to help them maintain meaning and logical order.

THINK AND COMPARE
Text Evidence

1. **Details** <u>Answer stated in text</u> Cara's parents told her she must apologize to Mr. Winston. LOCATE

2. **Cause and Effect** <u>Answer stated in text</u> One reason Mr. Winston moved to Manitoba is that there are no poisonous snakes in the area. COMBINE

3. **Make Inferences** <u>Answer</u> Cara is not truly sorry. <u>Evidence</u> Cara points out that the snake is harmless. She tells Mr. Winston that he didn't need to look in the box. She thinks he overreacted. CONNECT

4. **Author's Purpose** <u>Answer</u> The author told the story from Cara's perspective because it made the story humorous. <u>Evidence</u> She tells her side of the story in a funny way, and it is up to the reader to figure out what really happened. ANALYZE

5. **Text-to-Text** Both Mark's mother and Mr. Winston have an extreme fear of snakes. She screamed and got up on a chair when Mark's snake crawled over her foot, and Mr. Winston ended up in the hospital after the snake incident in the library. READING/WRITING ACROSS TEXTS

Objectives

- Read fluently with appropriate phrasing and good expression
- Rate: 102–122 WCPM

Materials

- Transparency 11
- Practice Book, p. 95
- Fluency Solutions Audio CD

ELL

Develop Comprehension
Some students will need support to grasp the humor of this passage. Break the passage into chunks and use gestures and board sketches to help convey meaning. Act out the reactions of Mr. Winston as he reads this paragraph. Have students echo key phrases.

Practice Book, page 95

As I read, I will pay attention to rate and intonation.

	North America is a large area of land. It contains
10	many different climates and landscapes. Most of Mexico
18	and the southwestern United States is hot and dry. Other
28	areas, including the northeastern states and parts of Canada,
37	are cool and wet. Some areas have large mountain ranges,
47	like the Rocky Mountains in the West. Others have flat,
57	rolling plains, like the Midwest.
62	Snakes can be found in just about all of these places.
73	Snakes live in forests, canyons, and deserts. One might
82	even be living in your own backyard. Most snakes don't do
93	well in the cold. In fact, the hardy garter snake is the only
106	serpent that can survive in Alaska.
112	North America has five snake families. Two of these
121	families are poisonous, and three are not. Meet the five
131	families. As you read this book, you will get to know them
143	a lot better. 146

Comprehension Check

1. What is the main idea about snakes in this passage? **Main Idea and Details** Snakes live in all different environments in North America.
2. Why is there only one kind of snake in Alaska? **Cause and Effect** Most snakes don't do well in a cold climate.

	Words Read	–	Number of Errors	=	Words Correct Score
First Read		–		=	
Second Read		–		=	

Approaching Reproducible, page 95

Beyond Reproducible, page 95

Fluency

Repeated Reading: Phrasing and Expression

EXPLAIN/MODEL Explain that part of reading with appropriate phrasing is grouping words together in meaningful phrases. Model reading **Transparency 11** with careful phrasing, pausing at each single slash and stopping at each double slash. Have students listen for your phrasing and for how your expression changes for questions and important words or phrases that you want to emphasize.

> **Transparency 11**
>
> I just thought of something. // Maybe everyone's looking in the library for that snake but it's not in the library. // Maybe it crawled into one of your pockets or up your sleeve and rode with you to the hospital! // Wouldn't that be funny? // Why don't you get one of the nurses to check? // If it's not in your clothes, / it might have crawled out and might be hiding inside the hospital someplace. // I think people should be looking there, too. //

Fluency (from *When I Went to the Library,* p. 282)

PRACTICE/APPLY Reread the first two sentences with students. Then divide them into two groups. Have groups alternate reading sentences with appropriate phrasing and good expression. Remind students to enunciate each word and to use their voice to stress important words or phrases, such as "inside the hospital someplace."

 DAILY FLUENCY Students will practice fluency using **Practice Book** page 95 or the **Fluency Solutions Audio CD**. The passage is recorded at a slow practice speed and a faster fluent speed.

Quick Check

Can students read accurately with good phrasing and expression?

During **Small Group Instruction**

If No → **Approaching Level** Use the Fluency lesson and model, p. 291Q.

If Yes → **On Level** See Fluency, p. 291T.

Beyond Level See Fluency, p. 291X.

Comprehension

SPIRAL REVIEW

REVIEW SKILL
SEQUENCE

EXPLAIN/MODEL

- **Sequence** is the order in which events occur in a story. Sometimes an author may present events out of order, such as when a flashback to an earlier time is presented. Point out that a flashback usually explains how a past event influenced an event or a situation in the present.

- In a story, an author uses sequence, or chronological order, to develop characters and to advance the plot. Tracking the sequence of events in a story helps readers to identify the most important events and to explain how each event influences future events.

Lead a class discussion about the sequence of events in "Name That Reptile." Ask how the sequence in which the events are presented is significant to the meaning of the passage.

PRACTICE/APPLY

PARTNERS

Have students work in pairs or literature circles to evaluate the importance of identifying the sequence of events in *When I Went to the Library* in order to comprehend the story. Students should explain how each of the story's main events influences the events that follow.

- What is Cara doing at the beginning of the story? What is Mr. Winston doing at the end? (Cara is writing a letter of apology to Mr. Winston at the beginning of the story. At the end of the story, Mr. Winston is reading her letter.)

- Why did she bring the snake into the library? (She wanted to find out what kind of snake it was.)

- When did Mr. Winston pick up and open the box? (After he asked Cara what was in the box and she replied, "Nothing.")

- Why was it important that the author first describe the snake before talking about Mr. Winston's reaction to it? (The story was told from Cara's point of view, and Cara thought Mr. Winston overreacted since the snake was harmless.)

Have students work together to complete the Sequence Chart on **Teacher's Resource Book** page 265 for *When I Went to the Library*. Then have them use the chart to summarize the story, maintaining meaning and logical order.

PRACTICE BOOK See **Practice Book** page 96 for Comparing Fiction and Autobiography.

Objectives

- Sequence the main events of a story
- Explain their influence on future events

Skills Trace

Sequence

Introduce	107A–107B
Practice/ Apply	108–121; Practice Book, 39–40
Reteach/ Review	125M–125Z, 229A–229B, 230–251, 257M–257Z; Practice Book, 84–85
Assess	Weekly Tests; Units 1, 2, 5 Tests
Maintain	155B, 285B, 641A–641B, 642–659, 663M–663Z, 697B

Test Practice

TEST PREP

Answering Questions

To apply **answering questions strategies** to content-area reading, see pages 85–92 in *Time For Kids*.

Paired Selection

GENRE: Informational Text/Expository

Have students read the bookmark on **Student Book** page 286. Explain that an electronic encyclopedia

- is an expository text that provides information about various subjects;
- contains paragraphs, headings, and boldfaced words that organize the information;
- may present information graphically through photos, diagrams, or charts.

Text Features: Toolbars and Guide Words

EXPLAIN Explain that toolbars are the rows of icons, or small pictures, near the top of a computer screen. Toolbars often have pull-down menus with guide words to help focus a search.

- Toolbars make it easier to print, search for information, or return to a previous page with one or two clicks.

- The toolbars and guide words in an electronic encyclopedia provide information about the contents of a particular section of an article. Students can use these text features to get an overview of the contents of electronic text or to find information.

APPLY Have students identify how many related articles about snakes are shown on the toolbar on page 287. (4) Discuss why using an online encyclopedia can be quicker than using physical reference materials. (There are links to click on for related information, so the information is easy to access.)

Find Snakes

▼ article outline

Science

Genre

Expository selections, such as **electronic encyclopedia articles**, include facts, diagrams, and photographs on many topics.

Text Features

Toolbars and **Guide Words** help you find more information or move to a related topic in an electronic encyclopedia.

Content Vocabulary

reptiles	hibernate
camouflage	digested

Snakes

Physical Characteristics

Snakes are **reptiles**. They have flexible skeletons and no legs. Their bodies are covered with scales. Clear scales even cover their eyes. Most snakes are colored to **camouflage** them. For example, the emerald tree boa is green. This helps it hide among tree leaves. Other snakes, like coral snakes, are brightly colored to warn enemies that they are poisonous. Snakes range greatly in size. The dwarf blind snake is 10 cm (about 4 in.) long. The anaconda and reticulated python can be as long as 10 m (about 33 ft).

Timber rattlesnakes (*crotalus horridus*), northeastern United States

Behavior

Like all reptiles, snakes are cold-blooded. They cannot make their own body heat. Snakes need the sun or warm surroundings to keep them warm. In cool weather, many snakes gather underground or in other sheltered places. There they **hibernate**, meaning they stay at rest during the winter.

Printers

286

Content Vocabulary

Explain the words using the **Define/Example/Ask** routine. Definitions are provided below.

- **Reptiles** are cold-blooded animals that have backbones, lay eggs, and either slither on their belly or creep on short legs. What are the names of some reptiles?

- Animals blend in with their surroundings to **camouflage** or disguise themselves. How does camouflage help animals survive?

- When animals **hibernate**, they spend the winter in a deep sleep. What animals do you know that hibernate?

- When the body breaks down food, the food is **digested**. How do our bodies use food we have digested?

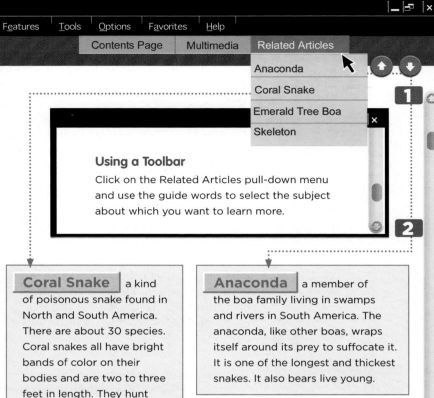

Features | Tools | Options | Favorites | Help

Contents Page | Multimedia | Related Articles

Anaconda
Coral Snake
Emerald Tree Boa
Skeleton

1

2

Using a Toolbar

Click on the Related Articles pull-down menu and use the guide words to select the subject about which you want to learn more.

Coral Snake a kind of poisonous snake found in North and South America. There are about 30 species. Coral snakes all have bright bands of color on their bodies and are two to three feet in length. They hunt lizards and other snakes.

Anaconda a member of the boa family living in swamps and rivers in South America. The anaconda, like other boas, wraps itself around its prey to suffocate it. It is one of the longest and thickest snakes. It also bears live young.

Coral snake

287

Connect to Content

CAMOUFLAGE

Have students reread the section on the physical characteristics of snakes. Tell them to visualize an emerald tree boa curled up on a tree branch, camouflaged by the leaves. Using a reference book as needed, have students list different places where snakes could live and how the snakes could camouflage themselves to blend into their surroundings. Students should then create a picture of a camouflaged snake. Have students trade pictures and try to find the hidden snakes.

Paired Selection

Read "Snakes"

Before reading, have students preview the article, think about what they would like to learn from it, and set their own purposes for reading. As students read, remind them to apply what they have learned about using toolbars and guide words to locate information. Also have students identify clues to the meanings of the highlighted words.

1 TEXT FEATURE: TOOLBAR

What section would you click on to find video clips of snakes? (Multimedia)

2 TEXT FEATURE: GUIDE WORDS

What section would you click on to find a pull-down menu about how anacondas trap their prey? (Related Articles) Which guide word would you select? (Anaconda)

Use the Interactive Question-Response Guide in the **ELL Resource Book**, pages 120–121, to help students gain access to the paired selection content.

Paired Selection

3 CONTENT VOCABULARY

Look at the word *digested* on page 288. What clues in the sentence tell you more about the meaning of the word? (the words *break down* and *eats*)

4 DRAW CONCLUSIONS

Can you make any general statements about how all snakes raise their young? (No. Some female snakes take care of their young, but others do not.)

Egg-eater snake (*Dasyreptis scabra*), savannah, South Africa

3

Cobra hatching

4

Find   Snakes

Hunting and Eating

Snakes are meat eaters but do not chew their prey. They swallow animals whole. Snakes can stretch their jaws far apart. This lets them eat animals that are bigger than their own heads.

Constrictors, such as boa constrictors, wrap themselves around their prey. These snakes suffocate their prey and then swallow it. Some snakes are venomous and kill their prey with poison. Venomous snakes, such as rattlesnakes, inject the poison through their fangs. Some poisons kill the animal. Others break down the animal's flesh so that it is partly **digested** by the time the snake eats it.

Raising Young

Most female snakes lay eggs that have soft, leathery shells. Some females stay close to guard the eggs. Others, such as pythons, coil around the eggs to keep them warm. Some snakes give birth to live babies. Garter snakes can have more than 40 baby snakes at once. Snakes do not usually take care of their young.

Printers

288

ON YOUR OWN

Practice Book, page 97

An encyclopedia is a set of books with information on a wide variety of topics. An electronic encyclopedia has the same information, but it is on a CD-ROM. You can use the **toolbar** and **guide words** to find the information you want, and gain an overview of the text.

Study the pages above to answer these questions.

1. What information is the computer user looking for? _____ information about pythons

2. Which button on the toolbar should the user click on to print out a copy of the page? _____ Print

3. If you are looking for a good map of Australia, what button on the toolbar would you click? _____ Search

4. If you are looking for more information about snakes, what button would you click? _____ Related Articles

ELL

Content Vocabulary Using the word *camouflage*, show students how to use surrounding words, such as *colored* and *hide*, to help unlock word meanings. Work with students to write the definition of *camouflage* on the board. Continue for other content vocabulary. Ask students to find surrounding word clues that unlock meanings. Elaborate on students' responses.

Approaching Reproducible, page 97

Beyond Reproducible, page 97

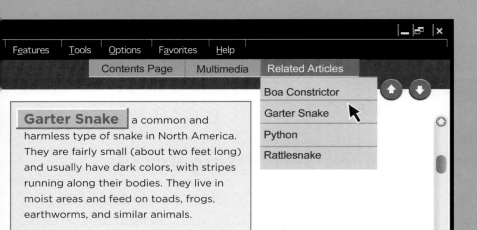

Garter Snake a common and harmless type of snake in North America. They are fairly small (about two feet long) and usually have dark colors, with stripes running along their bodies. They live in moist areas and feed on toads, frogs, earthworms, and similar animals.

✔ Connect and Compare

1. Look at the Related Articles menu on this page. Explain what guide word you would click on if you were researching venomous snakes. **Using a Toolbar and Guide Words**

2. Constrictors often hunt animals that have sharp teeth, claws, or hooves. Why would they need to kill their prey before swallowing it? **Apply**

3. Think about this article and *When I Went to the Library*. Which of the snakes discussed in this selection would not make a good pet for Cara? Explain using details from both selections. **Reading/Writing Across Texts**

Science Activity

Research a snake's life cycle and its habitat. Write a letter to a friend telling the interesting facts you learned about the snake. Don't forget to include the date on your letter.

LOG ON ▶ **FIND OUT** **Science** Snakes
www.macmillanmh.com

289

Connect to Content

RESEARCH AND INQUIRY

Harmful and Harmless Snakes

Explain that although some snakes are poisonous and even deadly, others are harmless. Have students brainstorm types of snakes as well as other types of organisms people may fear.

Review using reference materials. Have partners research a specific snake or another organism and organize their findings for a presentation.

As each pair presents their snake or other organism, remind them to tell whether it is harmful and to display a photograph or illustration of it. Have a recorder create a two-column chart to categorize each snake or other organism as harmful or harmless, and lead a class discussion about the results.

Paired Selection

Connect and Compare

1. Students would click on "Rattlesnakes" because the article mentioned how some snakes, including rattlesnakes, are venomous. USING A TOOLBAR AND GUIDE WORDS

2. They would need to kill their prey first so that the prey does not harm them. APPLY

3. **FOCUS QUESTION** Neither the coral snake nor the anaconda would make a good pet for Cara. Both snakes could be harmful to her. One squeezes its prey, and the other is poisonous. READING/WRITING ACROSS TEXTS

Science Activity

Have students read their letters to the rest of the class. While their classmates are presenting, other students can create a list of the different information presented in the letters.

WHOLE GROUP

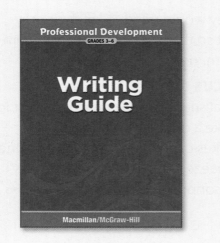

✓ **WRITING WORKSHOP**
- Developing Persuasive Writing
- Trait: Ideas
- Supporting Details

Professional Development
GRADES 3–6

Writing Guide

Macmillan/McGraw-Hill

UNIT 3

Developing Persuasive Writing

Trait: Ideas

Strong Sentences: Supporting Details

TEACH/MODEL Tell students that good writers use **supporting details** to help readers understand their ideas. **Supporting details** give more information about a subject or idea. They may explain a subject or tell why the writer believes something. They may give facts to show why something is true.

Point out that writers make their supporting sentences stronger by using precise words and descriptive phrases. This will provide readers with additional information and help readers connect to the writer's ideas. Write the sentence below on the board.

> Fruit is a good choice for an after-school snack.

Prompt students to suggest details that show why fruit is a good after-school snack. Write the details they suggest in a word web on the board.

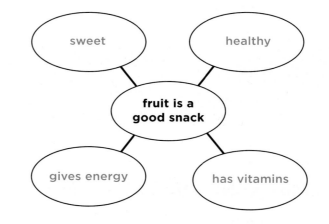

Discuss with students that these details support the idea that fruit is a good after-school snack. They explain why it is a good choice.

Teacher Write Aloud

PRACTICE/APPLY Further explore with students the use of supporting details to communicate and explain ideas by using one of the details you brainstormed to write a strong sentence.

> *Fruit provides the energy you need after school to do your homework and play sports.*

Point out that specific details like *to do your homework and play sports* support the idea that a fruit that provides energy is a good choice for an after-school snack.

Write the following sentence on the board. Then complete the Teacher Think Aloud.

> *Friday is my favorite day of the week.*

Teacher Think Aloud To explain why Friday is my favorite day of the week, I need to give supporting details. One supporting detail I might give is: *My teacher does not give homework on Fridays!* This tells readers a fact that supports the idea that Friday is my favorite day of the week.

 Draft Display the Writing Prompt on **Writing Transparency 36**. Tell students to give supporting details to explain why the day they chose is their favorite. Remind students to think of facts and descriptive details that support their choice. To prompt them, ask questions such as these:

- What do you do on the day you chose?
- What is special about this day?
- Why is this day better than others?

Circulate and provide Over-the-Shoulder Conferences as students work.

Objective

- Write supporting details that give facts, details, or explanations

Materials

- Writer's Notebooks
- Writing Transparency 36

Daily Journal Prompts

Focus on Supporting Details

Use these and other prompts for independent daily journal writing.

- Write about a book you enjoyed reading.
- Write about someone you think is a good friend.
- Write about a time you thought something was unfair.
- Write about a restaurant where you like to eat.

Transparency 36

Think about your favorite day of the week. Tell which day it is. Then give supporting details to explain why it is your favorite.

Writing Transparency

Reading and Writing Connection

✓ Trait: Ideas

SUPPORTING DETAILS

Clarify that writers support their statements with facts, details, and explanations. Using precise verbs and descriptive words and phrases can create strong, clear sentences that support the writer's main idea.

Read the Passage

Use the example from *When I Went to the Library* to show how the narrator uses supporting details to explain her decision to not tell who sold her the snake.

- Have students read the bookmark. Explain that supporting details are facts, details, and explanations that tell more about ideas, actions, or opinions.

- **Ask:** *Have you ever done something you regretted later?*

- Then have students chorally read the excerpt from *When I Went to the Library*. Direct their attention to the callout. Have students tell how Cara supports her explanation.

- **Ask:** *Do you agree with Cara's decision not to tell who sold her the snake? Do her supporting details for that decision make sense to you?*

Reading and Writing Connection

Writing

✓ Trait: Ideas

Good writers use **facts**, **details**, and **explanations** to support their ideas and opinions.

Read the passage below. Notice the details the author chose to include in the narrator's explanation.

> **An excerpt from**
> *When I Went to the Library*

The author uses supporting details to explain why Cara is not saying who sold her the snake. These details show Cara does not want anyone to get into trouble.

Mom says I don't have to tell who sold me that snake so I won't tell you either because Dad says he is going to read this letter. Besides, I don't want you to be mad at anyone else when I am the one who brought that snake into the library yesterday. I am truly, genuinely sorry.

I want you to know that I didn't plan to show you that snake. I didn't mean to scare you at all.

When I Went to the Library
by Ken Roberts
Illustrated by Nicole E. Wong

Respond to the Selection

Have students write a response to the selection.

- ☑ **Engagement** Help students deepen their connection to the text and discover their own perspective on it. *Focus on a moment when you made a mistake.*

- ☑ **Response** Help students explore more deeply their reactions to particular passages in the reading. *Focus on a moment in the story when you thought something a character did or said was funny. Use text evidence in your writing.*

- ☑ **Literary Analysis** Help students deepen their connection to the text and discover their own perspective on it. *Focus on a place in the story where you thought the author was trying to make you laugh. Use text evidence in your writing.*

Read and Find

Read Becky's writing below. What supporting details does she use to describe her dinner? Use the checklist below to help you.

Yuck!

by Becky L.

I didn't want to hurt my aunt's feelings. She had cooked my favorite recipe for pasta primavera. I took a big bite. It was awful—a mushy mass in my mouth! I drank a big gulp of milk and managed to swallow it. Luckily, Scampy, her round little dog, came waddling by. I put a forkful in my napkin and offered it to him under the table. Scampy sniffed the pasta and then waddled away.

Read about Becky's mushy mass.

Writer's Checklist

☑ What is the writer's opinion or idea?

☑ What supporting **details** does the writer give?

☐ What descriptive words show her opinion?

291

Read the Student Model

Have students chorally read the student model at the top of **Student Book** page 291. Discuss the supporting details this student writer gave to support her statement.

Journal Prompt

Draft Write the following prompt on the board. Have students write a response to the prompt.

> *Tell about a moment when you had to make a choice. Explain your choice by including supporting details.*

Tell students that you will be reading and commenting on their writing during Writing Conference time.

Model how to use the Writer's Checklist so students can write and revise their work. Then ask:

- *What is the moment you chose?*
- *What details did you provide? Will readers be able to understand why you made that choice? If not, what supporting details could you add?*

ELL ENGLISH LANGUAGE LEARNERS

Beginning	Intermediate	Advanced
Write Sentences Provide model sentences based on the Journal Prompt: *I had to choose between ___ and ___. I chose ___ because ___. It was a good choice because ___.* Help students complete the frames with supporting details.	**Explain** Ask students to write three sentences based on the Journal Prompt. Have them use the words *because* to help them show why they made that choice. Provide a frame if necessary: *I chose ___ because ___.* Read their sentences, correcting grammar and spelling as needed.	**Describe** Ask students to respond to the Journal Prompt. Have them use strong verbs and emotion words to describe their actions and feelings.

Objectives

- Write supporting details
- Write strong sentences

Materials

- Writer's Notebooks
- Teacher's Resource Book, p. 188

ELL

Connecting Words Tell students that one word they can use when writing supporting sentences is *because*. Show students that the idea they are explaining or supporting goes before the word *because*, and the detail goes after it: *It is fun to visit the library because there are lots of books to read.* Guide students to use the word *because* in some of their supporting sentences.

HOMEWORK **Teacher's Resource Book,** page 188

1. Read:
Statement 1: Exercise keeps your body healthy.
A. It is more fun than doing homework.
B. It makes your heart and lungs stronger.
My supporting detail: _____

2. Read:
Statement 2: Dogs are good pets.
A. They can protect your house.
B. Their barking can keep you awake at night.
My supporting detail: _____

3. Read:
Statement 3: It is fun to visit the library.
A. You can check out books you want to read.
B. You have to be quiet in the library.
My supporting detail: _____

Extra Practice: Write two supporting details for this statement:
    I am a good friend.
_____
_____
_____
_____

Minilessons

Minilesson 1 | Ideas/Supporting Details

TEACH/MODEL

Remind students that writers support their statements with facts, details, and explanations. A good supporting detail gives more information or explains the writer's main idea. Have students use **Teacher's Resource Book** page 188. Ask students to choose the supporting detail that best supports the statement. Then have them write an additional supporting detail.

PRACTICE/APPLY

Have students work independently. When complete, ask students to share which detail they chose for each statement and read the supporting detail they wrote. The correct details are: (1) B (2) A (3) A.

Minilesson 2 | Ideas/Facts and Opinions

TEACH/MODEL

Tell students that writers often use both facts and opinions to express their ideas. A **fact** is a piece of information that can be proved, either by personal observation or by checking a reference, such as a book. An **opinion** is a statement that tells what someone thinks or believes. It cannot be proved, but it can be supported. Writers often use facts to support their opinions. Write the following statements on the board. Have students tell whether each one is a fact or an opinion. Challenge students to tell how they would prove each fact.

> - It is better to check out books from the library than to buy them from a bookstore. (opinion)
> - It does not cost anything to check out a library book. (fact)
> - The library has made-up stories and information books. (fact)
> - The made-up stories are the best. (opinion)

PRACTICE/APPLY

Write the following topics on the board. In their Writer's Notebooks, have students choose one of the topics and write two facts and two opinions about their topic.

> - lunch in the school cafeteria
> - summer
> - a favorite book

Conferencing Routine

Dynamic Feedback System

Step 1 Read and appreciate the writing.

Step 2 Notice how the student uses the targeted skill (for example, supporting details: Ask: *What supporting details did the writer include?*).

Step 3 Write comments that show how the writing has an impact on you. Direct your comments to those places in the piece where the student has used the targeted skill.

Step 4 Meet with the student and give him or her a revision assignment.

Write Effective Comments

Ideas At least one of your comments should highlight the way the student uses **supporting details** in his or her writing. Here are some sample comments.

- These details show me just why this point is important to you.

- Can you write a detail that shows me why you think this?

- What information can you give to explain this statement?

Revision Assignments

Ideas Here are some examples of effective revision assignments for supporting details.

- ***Reread your entry.*** *This detail does not give me a lot of information. Rewrite it and include descriptive words so that your meaning is very clear.*

- **[Underline a section.]** Mark a specific section of a student's writing and then ask the student to revise it in a specific way.

- **[Underline a section.]** *Read the part that I underlined. This detail does not completely support your main idea. Rewrite it so that it gives more information about your main idea.*

Teacher-to-Teacher

Over-the-Shoulder Conferences

Use these quick, focused opportunities to comment while students are writing.

- **Step 1** Quietly move close enough to a student that you can read the journal entry he or she is writing.

- **Step 2** Read part of what you see. You don't need to start from the beginning or read the entire piece.

- **Step 3** Show the student a spot in the writing where he or she is using a particular skill or describing something that piques your interest.

- **Step 4** Whisper a sentence or two about why you noticed that spot in the writing, and ask a question that will nudge the student to add a supporting detail.

- Step 5 Move on to the next student. Select students strategically. You should see 12–15 students in a 15-minute period.

Research Proven Writing Approach

The Writers' Express
Immediate Impact. Lasting Transformation.   wex.org

Connect Language Arts

WHOLE GROUP

- ✓ **VOCABULARY**
  - Tested Words
- ✓ **SPELLING**
  - *r*-Controlled Vowels *er, ir, ur*
- ✓ **GRAMMAR**
  - Action Verbs

SMALL GROUP

- Differentiated Instruction, pp. 291I–291HH

Build Robust Vocabulary

Day 1 · Teach/Practice

CONNECT TO WORDS

- Practice this week's vocabulary words using the following prompts:

1. What do you do during the *weekdays*?
2. If an animal *slithered*, what did it do?
3. How can you tell if someone is being *genuine*?
4. What is the difference between making an *apology* and giving an explanation?
5. What kinds of habits are *harmless*?
6. How can an *ambulance* help after an accident has taken place?

ACADEMIC VOCABULARY

- Review the important academic vocabulary words for the week. These words include *dialogue, inferences, sequence, generate, humor.*

- Write each word on the board. Define each using student-friendly language, and ask students to select the word you are defining. Then point to words in random order for students to define.

Day 2 · Review

- Review the definitions of this week's vocabulary words using **Student Book** pages 270–271. Then discuss the words using these prompts:

1. Which do you enjoy more—*weekdays* or weekends? Why?
2. How might a person react if a snake *slithered* nearby?
3. When might it be good to know whether an item is *genuine*?
4. When might it be necessary to *apologize* to someone?
5. Why are *harmless* animals sometimes feared?
6. What kinds of people might work in an *ambulance*?

- Have students write their own context-rich sentences for this week's vocabulary words in their Writer's Notebooks. Direct students to the sentences in the book or model an example first.

WORD PARTS: BASE WORDS

- Remind students that knowing the meanings of base words can help them determine or clarify the meanings of unfamiliar words containing those base words.

- Display **Transparency 21**. Read the first sentence. Model how to identify and use the base word as well as the suffix to determine the meaning of the underlined word.

- Have students identify and use the base words and affixes in the remaining sentences to help them define the underlined words.

Practice Book, page 98

Prefixes and **suffixes** can be added to many words. The original word is called the **base word**. If you know what the base word is, you can figure out the meaning of the word with a prefix or suffix. You can find the meaning of prefixes and suffixes in a dictionary. Many prefixes and suffixes come from Latin, Greek, or other languages.

unhappy
The base word is **happy**. **Happy** means "feeling good."
The prefix **un-** means "the opposite of."
The word **unhappy** means "not feeling good."

Find the word with a prefix or suffix in each sentence. Circle the base word. Then tell what the word with the suffix or prefix means. **Possible responses provided.**

1. The snake's markings were (color)ful, with red and blue bands.
   Colorful means "full of colors."

2. Even small snakes can be (danger)ous sometimes.
   Dangerous means "full of danger."

3. Knowing that the snake was hidden somewhere in the room made us all un(comfort)able.
   Uncomfortable means "not able to be at ease."

4. The water moccasin swam under Khalid's boat and dis(appear)ed.
   Disappeared means "vanished or gone from sight."

5. Casey was (success)ful in finding a picture of a rattlesnake in the book.
   Successful means "having success."

Approaching Reproducible, page 98
Beyond Reproducible, page 98

Day 3 Reinforce

CONNECT TO WORDS

- Ask students to create Word Squares for each word in their Writer's Notebooks.

- In the first square, students write the word. (Example: *weekdays*)

- In the second square, students write their own definition of the word and any related words, such as synonyms. (Example: *school days, Monday through Friday*)

- In the third square, students draw a simple illustration that will help them remember the word. (Example: drawing of a calendar with weekdays circled)

- In the fourth square, students write nonexamples, including antonyms for the word. (Example: *weekends, Saturday and Sunday*)

RELATED WORDS

- Help students generate words related to *genuine*. The classification of synonyms can raise students' word consciousness and help improve students' vocabularies.

- Draw a T-chart on the board. One column is headed "Real"; the other column is headed "Fake."

- Have students list synonyms they know in each column. Direct students to use a print or online thesaurus to generate more words. Add words not included, such as (real) *authentic, valid, actual;* (fake) *counterfeit, imitation, replication, artificial.*

 **Day 4** Extend

CONNECT TO WORDS

- Review this week's vocabulary using the following sentence stems. Have students orally complete each one.

   1. During the weekdays, Matt has to _____.
   2. The snake slithered because _____.
   3. Becca was genuine about _____.
   4. Mr. Varu had to apologize for _____.
   5. The harmless insect _____.
   6. Ricardo drove the ambulance to _____.

MORPHOLOGY

- Remind students that, like other word parts, suffixes can come from Latin (such as *-able,* meaning "capable of"), Greek (such as *-logy,* meaning "the study of"), or other languages (such as *-less,* from the Old English, meaning "without").

- Then use the additional selection word *reference* as a springboard for students to learn other words.

- Write *reference.* Underline *-ence.* Explain that the suffix *-ence* comes from Latin and can mean "the act of" or "the state of" and *refer* can mean "to mention." So a *reference* relates to "the act of mentioning."

- Write *conference* and *inference* and underline *-ence* in each. Use the suffix and base to define each word. Explain *confer* can mean "to discuss." So, a *conference* involves "the act of discussing." To *infer* means "to draw a conclusion." So, an *inference* involves "the act of drawing a conclusion."

 Day 5 Assess and Reteach

POSTTEST

- Display **Transparency 22.** Have students complete the cloze sentences using one of this week's vocabulary words.

- Note how quickly and accurately students can complete this task. Work with students who make errors or require too much time to complete this task during Small Group time.

CONNECT TO WRITING

- Have students write sentences in their Writer's Notebooks using this week's vocabulary. Tell students to write sentences that provide information they learned from this week's readings.

- **ELL** Provide the Day 4 sentence stems for students needing extra support.

Go to pages T14–15 for **Differentiated Spelling Lists**.

✔ r-Controlled Vowels *er, ir, ur*

Spelling Words

dirty	shirt	turnip
purse	worse	purpose
birth	hurl	blurred
curl	twirl	sternly
curve	swirl	serpent
curb	herb	pearl
person	turkey	

Review slowly, quickly, beautiful
Challenge spurt, further

Dictation Sentences

1. My keyboard was <u>dirty</u>.
2. She bought a new leather <u>purse</u>.
3. Our cat gave <u>birth</u> to eight kittens.
4. Her hair had a little <u>curl</u>.
5. The car rounded the <u>curve</u>.
6. He fell off the <u>curb</u>.
7. A **person** ran by the window.
8. Only his <u>shirt</u> was torn.
9. The fall could have been <u>worse</u>.
10. The quarterback can <u>hurl</u> the football.
11. I <u>twirl</u> my hair around my finger.
12. <u>Swirl</u> the soapy water in the glass.
13. This <u>herb</u> will flavor the sauce.
14. We have <u>turkey</u> on Thanksgiving.
15. The <u>turnip</u> came from our garden.
16. I stated the <u>purpose</u> for my visit.
17. The writing <u>blurred</u> from the rain.
18. I lectured my dog <u>sternly</u>.
19. A <u>serpent</u> slithered past my feet.
20. There was a <u>pearl</u> in the oyster.

Review/Challenge Words

1. Can you speak more <u>slowly</u>?
2. I finished the test <u>quickly</u>.
3. That painting is <u>beautiful</u>.
4. We saw jelly <u>spurt</u> out of a sandwich.
5. Read a little <u>further</u> in your book.

Words in **bold** are from this week's selections.

Day 1 — Pretest

ASSESS PRIOR KNOWLEDGE

- Model for students how to spell the word *stir*. Segment the word sound by sound, and then attach a spelling to each sound. Point out that the *ir* spelling stands for the /ûr/ sounds.

- Use the Dictation Sentences. Say the underlined word, read the sentence, and repeat the word. Have students write the words.

- Have students self-correct their tests. Point out that the *ur* spelling is always pronounced the same way.

- Have students cut apart the **Spelling Word Cards BLM** on **Teacher's Resource Book** page 54 and figure out a way to sort them. Have them save the cards for use throughout the week.

Day 2 — Word Sorts and Review

SPIRAL REVIEW

Review suffixes such as those found in the words *slowly, quickly, beautiful,* and *lightest*. Have students find words in this week's readings with the same suffixes.

WORD SORTS

- Have students take turns sorting the spelling words and explaining how they sorted them. When students have finished the sort, discuss any words that have unexpected /ûr/ spellings (*worse*).

- Review the spelling words, pointing out the /ûr/ spellings. Use the cards on the Spelling Word Cards BLM. Write the key words *turn, stir,* and *serve* on the board. Model how to sort words by /ûr/ spellings. Place one or two cards beneath the correct key words.

ON YOUR OWN — Phonics/Spelling, pages 61–62

Fold back the paper along the dotted line. Use the blanks to write each word as it is read aloud. When you finish the test, unfold the paper. Use the list at the right to correct any spelling mistakes.

1. _____	1. dirty
2. _____	2. purse
3. _____	3. birth
4. _____	4. curl
5. _____	5. curve
6. _____	6. curb
7. _____	7. person
8. _____	8. shirt
9. _____	9. worse
10. _____	10. hurl
11. _____	11. twirl
12. _____	12. swirl
13. _____	13. herb
14. _____	14. turkey
15. _____	15. turnip
16. _____	16. purpose
17. _____	17. blurred
18. _____	18. sternly
19. _____	19. serpent
20. _____	20. pearl
Review Words 21. _____	21. slowly
22. _____	22. quickly
23. _____	23. beautiful
Challenge Words 24. _____	24. spurt
25. _____	25. further

HOMEWORK — Phonics/Spelling, page 63

birth	dirty	herb	purse	sternly
worse	hurl	curve	blurred	serpent
pearl	swirl	turnip	shirt	turkey
curl	curb	purpose	person	twirl

Write the spelling words with these spelling patterns.

words with *ir*
1. birth
2. swirl
3. dirty
4. shirt
5. twirl

words with *er*
6. person
7. sternly
8. serpent
9. herb

words with *ur*
10. hurl
11. turnip
12. purpose
13. curb
14. purse
15. curl
16. blurred
17. turkey
18. curve

Day 3 Word Meanings

CATEGORIES

Read each group of words below. Ask students to copy the words into their notebooks, completing the groups by adding a similar spelling word that matches the theme of the group.

1. pocketbook, wallet (*purse*)
2. throw, pitch (*hurl*)
3. carrot, potato (*turnip*)
4. goose, duck (*turkey*)
5. diamond, gold (*pearl*)

Challenge students to come up with other similar word groups to which they can add spelling words, review words, or challenge words.

Have partners write a sentence for each spelling word, leaving a blank space where the word should go. Direct them to exchange papers and fill in the blanks.

Day 4 Proofread

PROOFREAD AND WRITE

Write these sentences on the board. Have students circle and correct each misspelled word.

1. Her perse is the same color as her shurt. (*purse, shirt*)
2. The photo of the terkey was blirred. (*turkey, blurred*)
3. The purpos of the purl sale was to get rid of old stock. (*purpose, pearl*)
4. I only ate the turnups with the urb flavoring. (*turnips, herb*)

Error Correction Students may substitute other vowel spellings for *er, ir,* or *ur.* Since there is no simple rule to determine which spelling to use, students will need lots of reading and writing practice with these words.

Day 5 Assess and Reteach

POSTTEST

Use the Dictation Sentences on page 291E for the Posttest.

If students have difficulty with any words in the lesson, have them place the words on a list called *Spelling Words I Want to Remember* in their Writer's Notebooks. Look for students' use of these words in their writings.

If students have trouble remembering the silent letter *h* in *herb,* remind them about other words with silent letters that they already know how to spell, such as *know* and *write.* Point out that students will learn to spell more words with silent letters next week.

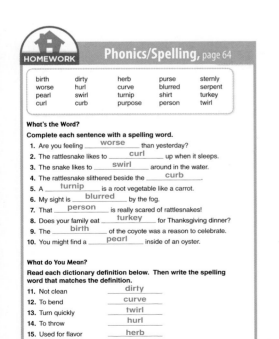

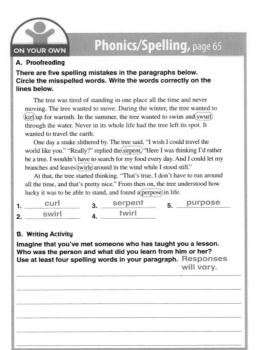

Action Verbs

Daily Language Activities

Write the sentences on the board.

DAY 1

My friend's came to my house today. We were going to the Park together.
(1: friends; 2: park)

DAY 2

I met Jans new friend today. Do you know shelley. what a nice girl she is!
(1: Jan's; 2: Shelley?; 3: What)

DAY 3

"The other team plays really well." said mr. Chen.

I asked "Can we beat them," (1: well,";
2: Mr.; 3: asked, ; 4: them?")

DAY 4

There is only one purson in our school who runs faster than George? Cindy wins more races than any of the other runner's. (1: person;
2: George.; 3: runners)

DAY 5

I asked Libby. "will you teach me to pitch better?"

"I will help you practice" said Libby".
(1: Libby, "Will; 2: practice,"; 3: Libby.)

Action Verbs Demonstrate examples of action verbs, such as *wave* or *jump* by waving or jumping. Brainstorm with students actions they do: play ball, dance, shop at the mall. Work with students to use the actions in sentences. Write the sentences on the board and ask students to underline the action verbs.

✔ Action Verbs

Day 1 · Introduce the Concept

INTRODUCE VERBS

Present the following:

- A **verb** tells what the subject **does** or **is**: Roadrunner dances. He is happy.

- A verb can include more than one word, a **main** verb and a **helping** verb: *Jenny is dancing.*

Use the **Teach/Practice/Apply** routine and the English Language Learner supports on the transparency to extend the lesson.

Day 2 · Teach the Concept

REVIEW VERBS

Review with students how verbs function in a sentence. Have students explain the difference between verbs and other parts of speech, such as nouns.

INTRODUCE ACTION VERBS

- An **action verb** tells what the subject does, did, or will do.

- A **present tense** action verb tells what is happening now: *Jen dances.*

- A **past tense** action verb tells what has already happened: *Jen danced yesterday.*

- A **future tense** action verb tells what will happen in the future: *Jen will dance tomorrow.*

See Grammar Transparency 51 for modeling and guided practice.

See Grammar Transparency 52 for modeling and guided practice.

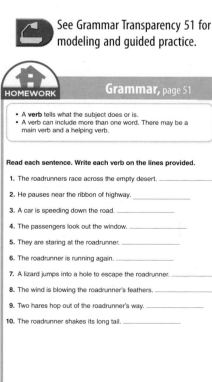

HOMEWORK — Grammar, page 51

- A **verb** tells what the subject does or is.
- A verb can include more than one word. There may be a main verb and a helping verb.

Read each sentence. Write each verb on the lines provided.

1. The roadrunners race across the empty desert. _____
2. He pauses near the ribbon of highway. _____
3. A car is speeding down the road. _____
4. The passengers look out the window. _____
5. They are staring at the roadrunner. _____
6. The roadrunner is running again. _____
7. A lizard jumps into a hole to escape the roadrunner. _____
8. The wind is blowing the roadrunner's feathers. _____
9. Two hares hop out of the roadrunner's way. _____
10. The roadrunner shakes its long tail. _____

ON YOUR OWN — Grammar, page 52

- An **action verb** tells what a subject does, did, or will do.
- Action verbs have different **tenses**. They can show action in the past, present, or future.

Read each sentence. On the lines provided, write *present*, *past*, or *future* to name the tense of each underlined verb.

1. The rattlesnake stretched out along the rocks. _____
2. His scales flash silver in the hot desert sun. _____
3. He swished his long tail. _____
4. A prairie dog scurries away when it hears the snake's rattle. _____
5. A small lizard will crawl away. _____
6. The rattlesnake reached the edge of the rock. _____
7. A bee buzzes past the snake. _____
8. The rattlesnake hurries down the rock. _____
9. He will quickly pass by a cold, shaded area. _____
10. You approached the snake with caution. _____

Day 3 Review and Practice

REVIEW ACTION VERBS

Review how to identify action verbs.

MECHANICS AND USAGE: PUNCTUATION IN DIALOGUE

- Use quotation marks before and after someone's exact words.
- Begin a quotation with a capital letter.
- Commas and periods always appear inside quotation marks.
- If the end of a quotation comes at the end of a sentence, use a period, question mark, or exclamation mark to end it.
- If the sentence continues after a quotation is given, use a comma to close the quotation.
- Use quotation marks before and after the title of a story or article.

 See Grammar Transparency 53 for modeling and guided practice.

HOMEWORK   **Grammar,** page 53

- Use quotation marks at the beginning and end of a speaker's exact words. Begin a quotation with a capital letter.
- Commas and periods always go inside quotation marks.
- Do not use quotation marks when you do not use the speaker's exact words.

Rewrite each sentence correctly by putting capital letters and quotation marks where they belong.

1. Roberto asked me, have you ever seen a rattlesnake?

2. no, I never have, I answered.

3. Roberto told me that rattlesnakes are his favorite animal.

4. Our science teacher said, rattlesnakes are related to lizards.

5. both rattlesnakes and lizards are reptiles, she explained.

6. some reptiles can even change colors, Andrea said.

7. yes, you are thinking of chameleons, Andrea, replied Ms. Giordello.

8. why do they do that? asked Hakim.

Day 4 Review and Proofread

REVIEW ACTION VERBS

Ask students to explain what a verb does in a sentence. Ask how action verbs can be identified.

PROOFREAD

Have students correct errors in the following lines of dialogue.

1. Jerry called out, "noreen, it's your ball!" ("Noreen,)

2. "I got it." yelled Sam. (it!")

3. "Where is Sam," asked Noreen. (Sam?")

4. "Right behind you, answered Sam." (1: you,"; 2: Sam.)

5. Jerry warned, "watch out, you two!" ("Watch)

 See Grammar Transparency 54 for modeling and guided practice.

ON YOUR OWN   **Grammar,** page 54

- **Action verbs** tell what the subject does, did, or will do.
- Action verbs have tenses that can show action in the present, past, or future.

Proofread the dialogue below. Look for mistakes in action verb tenses and quotations. Rewrite the dialogue, action verbs, and quotations correctly.

I am so excited! Tomorrow we arrived in Taos, New Mexico! Carla says.
Dad will reply, Yes, we should be there in about a day.
Mom points, to the mountains in the distance. She will say, stop the car so we can take some pictures.
Carla remarks, I will see a strange bird in the distance.
Dad explained, the bird was a roadrunner.
Carla watched the speedy bird. It passes close enough to see its feathers.

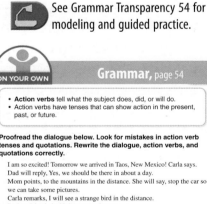

Day 5 Assess and Reteach

ASSESS

Use the Daily Language Activity and **Grammar Practice Book** page 55 for assessment.

RETEACH

Use Grammar Practice Book page 55 and selected pages from the **Grammar and Writing Handbook** for additional reteaching. Remind students that it is important to use verbs correctly as they speak and write.

Check students' writing for use of the skill and listen for it in their speaking. Assign Grammar Revision Assignments in their Writer's Notebooks as needed.

 See Grammar Transparency 55 for modeling and guided practice.

HOMEWORK   **Grammar,** page 55

A. Read each sentence. Circle the letter of the sentence that has a present-tense action verb.

1. a. The roadrunner is coming down from the mountain.
   b. He looked at the desert.
   c. The roadrunner will speed across the road.
   d. The other animals will be far away.

2. a. The rattlesnake will slide down the rocks.
   b. He saw the roadrunner.
   c. The rattlesnake was shaking his tail.
   d. The rattles make a hollow clatter.

B. Read each sentence. Fill in the blank with an action verb.

3. The roadrunner _____ across the highway.
4. The rattlesnake _____ the desert for other animals.
5. The duck _____ in the pond.
6. The mother bird _____ her babies.

Daily Planner

DAY 1	• Prepare to Read • Academic Language • Vocabulary (Preteach)
DAY 2	• Comprehension • Leveled Reader Lesson 1
DAY 3	• Phonics/Decoding • Leveled Reader Lesson 2
DAY 4	• Phonics/Decoding • Vocabulary (Review) • Leveled Reader Lesson 3
DAY 5	• High-Frequency Words • Fluency • Self-Selected Reading

LOG ON ▶ StudentWorks Plus

Interactive Student Book

If you wish to preteach the main selection, use StudentWorks Plus for:

• Vocabulary Preteaching
• Word-by-Word Highlighting
• Think Aloud Prompts

Academic Language

Academic words include those harder Tier 2 words that appear in much of students' reading materials as well as the language of instruction. The words chosen for instruction were selected from the **Living Word Vocabulary** list and Avril Coxhead's list of **High-Incidence Academic Words**.

Approaching Level

Prepare to Read

Objective Preview *When I Went to the Library*
Materials • **StudentWorks Plus** • self-stick notes

PREVIEW THE MAIN SELECTION

■ Have students preview *When I Went to the Library* using **StudentWorks Plus**, the interactive eBook. This version of the Student Book contains oral summaries in multiple languages, story recordings, word-by-word highlighting, Think Aloud prompts, and comprehension-monitoring questions.

■ Remind students that listening carefully to and following along with the word-by-word reading will help them prepare for the reading of the selection with the class. Ask students to place self-stick notes on any challenging words or places that confuse them. Discuss the confusing items with students prior to the reading of the selection with the rest of the class.

■ Ask students to write three or four sentences in their **Writer's Notebooks** telling what they learned about the girl's trip to the library.

Academic Language

Objective Teach academic language
Materials • none

PRETEACH LANGUAGE OF INSTRUCTION

Tell students that there are many important lesson words you will be using this week. You want them to become familiar with these words *before* the lessons. These words also appear in the directions of the tests they will be taking this year.

Preteach the following academic words: *generate, inferences, sequence, humor, base word, guide words,* and *toolbar.*

■ Define each word using student-friendly language. Tell students that *humor* means "something funny" or "what makes you laugh." For example, jokes are a form of humor.

■ In addition, relate each word to known words. For example, connect *sequence* to *order* or to *first, second, third,* and connect *inference* to *figuring something out* or *using clues.*

■ Highlight these words when used throughout the week and reinforce their meanings.

Approaching Level

Phonics/Decoding

Objective Decode words with *r*-controlled vowels *er, ir, ur*

Materials
- **Approaching Reproducible,** p. 91
- **Sound-Spelling WorkBoards**

PHONICS MAINTENANCE

Tier 2

- Distribute a **WorkBoard** to each student. Say a sound previously taught, including the sounds for *r*-controlled vowels, three-letter blends, and digraphs. Have students find the **Sound-Spelling Card** on the board for each sound.

- Review the spelling(s) for each sound by providing a sample word containing that spelling. Guide students to write the word on the board. Model how to segment the word and write the spelling for each sound, as needed. In addition, point out spelling hints, such as that the *er, ir,* and *ur* spellings stand for the same sound and that the sound can differ when it comes in stressed or unstressed syllables.

- Dictate the following words for students to spell: *purse, serve, street, sprint, bird, nurse,* and *verb.* Write the words on the board, and have students self-correct their work.

RETEACH SKILL

r*-Controlled Vowels *er, ir, ur Point to the /ûr/ Sound-Spelling Card on the WorkBoard, and review the spellings for this sound. State each spelling and provide a sample word.

- Write the words below on the board. Model how to decode the first word in each row, then guide students as they decode the remaining words. For the multisyllabic words, divide the words into syllables using the syllable-scoop technique to help students read one syllable at a time.

- When completed, point to the words in random order for students to chorally read. Repeat several times.

Sound-Spelling WorkBoard

clerk	perch	nerve	herd	swerve	stern
chirp	chip	first	fist	fir	twirl
burn	bun	spurt	church	blurt	lurk
percent	personal	thirteen	purchase	prefer	lurking
curl	curling	unfurl	password	birthday	return
purring	kernel	dirty	blackbird	invert	version

Approaching Reproducible, page 91

Say these words and listen for the sound of the vowel + *r*:
twirl, hurl, person. This is the /ûr/ sound.

The /ûr/ sound can have different spellings. In these three words,
/ûr/ is spelled **ir, ur,** and **er.**

Circle the vowel + *r* combination that makes the
/ûr/ sound in each of these words.

1. b u**r** n   8. f e**r** n
2. st e**r** n   9. p u**r** se
3. sh i**r** t   10. d i**r** t y
4. de s e**r** t   11. b i**r** t h
5. wh i**r** l   12. c u**r** l
6. h e**r** d   13. c u**r** v e
7. p u**r** p l e   14. p e**r** s o n

Approaching Level

Vocabulary

Objective Preteach selection vocabulary

Materials
- **Visual Vocabulary Resources**
- **Approaching Reproducible**, p. 92   • **Vocabulary Cards**

PRETEACH KEY VOCABULARY

Tier 2

Introduce the Words Use the **Visual Vocabulary Resources** to preteach the key selection words *weekdays, slithered, genuine, apologize, harmless*, and *ambulance*. Use the following routine that appears in detail on the cards.

- Define the word in English, and provide the example given.

- Define the word in Spanish, if appropriate, and indicate if the word is a cognate.

- Display the picture, and explain how it illustrates or demonstrates the word.

- Then engage students in structured partner talk about the image, using the key word.

- Ask students to chorally say the word three times.

- Point out any known sound-spellings or focus on a key aspect of phonemic awareness related to the word.

- You may wish to also distribute copies of the Vocabulary Glossary in the **ELL Resource Book**.

REVIEW PREVIOUSLY TAUGHT VOCABULARY

Display the **Vocabulary Cards** from the previous four weeks. Say the meanings of each word, one by one, and have students identify them. Then point to words in random order for students to provide definitions and related words they know.

Base Words Remind students that a base word is the simplest form of a word. Have students identify base words and affixes or inflectional endings in words from previous weeks, such as *legendary, loosened,* and *mysterious. (legend, loose, mystery)* Have students explain how the vocabulary words' meanings relate to their base words and use both the base word and the vocabulary word in the same sentence. For example: *The boy loosened the cap until it was completely loose.* Have students identify context clues in the sentence to the words' meanings.

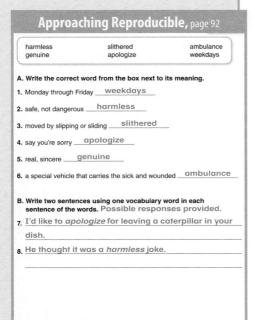

Approaching Reproducible, page 92

| harmless | slithered | ambulance |
| genuine | apologize | weekdays |

A. Write the correct word from the box next to its meaning.

1. Monday through Friday ___weekdays___

2. safe, not dangerous ___harmless___

3. moved by slipping or sliding ___slithered___

4. say you're sorry ___apologize___

5. real, sincere ___genuine___

6. a special vehicle that carries the sick and wounded ___ambulance___

B. Write two sentences using one vocabulary word in each sentence of the words. Possible responses provided.

7. I'd like to *apologize* for leaving a caterpillar in your dish.

8. He thought it was a *harmless* joke.

Approaching Level

Vocabulary

Objective Review vocabulary and high-frequency words
Materials • **Vocabulary Cards** • **High-Frequency Word Cards**

REVIEW VOCABULARY

Review the Words Display the **Vocabulary Cards** *weekdays, slithered, genuine, apologize, harmless,* and *ambulance.* Point to each word, read it aloud, and have students chorally repeat.

Have students give examples of the following:

- a *weekday*
- an animal that *slithers* and an animal that does not *slither*
- something that is *genuine*
- what you might say to *apologize* for something
- something that is *harmless* and something that is harmful
- a time when you might need an *ambulance*

HIGH-FREQUENCY WORDS

Tier 2

Top 250 Words The ability to read accurately and effortlessly the most frequently used words in written English will help students develop reading fluency. Display **High-Frequency Word Cards** 81–90. Then do the following:

- Display one card at a time, and ask students to chorally state each word.
- Have students spell each word aloud.
- Ask students to write each word in their Writer's Notebooks as they state aloud each letter. Then have them read the word again.
- When completed, quickly flip through the word card set as students chorally read the words.
- Provide opportunities for students to use the words in speaking and writing. For example, provide sentence starters, such as *I like to help* _____ for oral and written practice. Or point to a word card and ask a question such as *Which word can you use to describe what you bought at a store?* (when pointing to the *got* word card).
- Continue the routine throughout the week.

ELL

Practice Vocabulary Pair students of different proficiency. Orally model the vocabulary in sentences. For example: *Rosa apologized to Lin after she missed her birthday party.* On the board, provide sentence frames for pairs to copy and complete using the vocabulary. For example: *The snake* _____ *into the woods. (slithered)*

Word Webs

Have students create word webs in their Writer's Notebooks for each vocabulary word. Write the related words provided, and ask students to add other words, phrases, and illustrations.

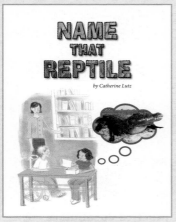

Student Book

Approaching Level

Comprehension

Objective Reteach generate questions and make inferences
Materials • **Student Book:** "Name That Reptile"

RETEACH STRATEGY: GENERATE QUESTIONS

Tier **2**

- **Define** Tell students that *generating questions* means asking yourself questions as you are reading. Generating questions helps you check and adjust your comprehension of what the author says and figure out things that the author does not directly state.

- **Relate to Real Life** Ask students to imagine that they want to visit a classmate but do not know where the classmate lives. They might ask: *Where do you live? How can I get there from my house?* They are generating questions to get information. Similarly, students can generate questions to get information when they read.

- **Set Purposes** Remind students that good readers generate questions while they read. The questions can be literal and help them figure out information, and or they can be interpretive or evaluative and help them better understand the text.

RETEACH SKILL: MAKE INFERENCES

- **Define** Write *inference* and circle the base word *infer*. Explain that *infer* means "to figure out something by using what you already know." When you make an inference, you use clues that the author gives and what you know from your own experiences (related to the text) to make logical decisions about story events and characters' actions that are not directly stated.

- **Relate to Real Life** Ask students to imagine that they are ringing the doorbell at a friend's house. They ring and ring, but no one comes to the door. Students might conclude that no one is home. When students do that, they make an inference. They see that no one is opening the door, and they know from experience that their friends' parents open the door when they are home. Thus, students infer, or figure out, that no one is home.

- **Set Purposes** Remind students that good readers generate questions to help them make inferences. Doing so will help them better understand both fiction and nonfiction writing.

- **Apply** Work with students to generate questions and make inferences about "Name That Reptile." Help them use the inferences to tell what they learned about the characters and the snakes. Students will apply this strategy and skill to a simpler text as they read *Snakes in North America*.

Approaching Level

Leveled Reader Lesson 1

Leveled Reader

Objective   Read to apply skills and strategies
Materials   • **Leveled Reader:** *Snakes in North America*

BEFORE READING

Preview and Predict Have students read the title and preview the first chapter. Ask students to make predictions about what they might learn about snakes. Have students generate a few questions about the selection before they begin reading.

 Review the Vocabulary Words Have students read the vocabulary words on the inside front cover. Briefly define each, and ask students to state related words they have learned.

Set a Purpose for Reading *Let's read to find out about snakes that live in North America.*

DURING READING

 STRATEGY
GENERATE QUESTIONS

Remind students that generating questions can help them check their comprehension as they read and can guide them in making inferences by uncovering details the author does not directly state.

SKILL
MAKE INFERENCES

Remind students to make inferences by using clues that the author gives in addition to what they already know from their own experience (related to the text). Read the Introduction and Chapter 1 with students. Have them record clues and inferences on their Inference Webs.

As you read, help students decode unknown words. In addition, ask open-ended questions to facilitate rich discussion, such as: *What does the author want you to know about snakes and their patterns?* Build on students' responses to develop a deeper understanding.

To check students' understanding, stop after every two pages, and ask students to generate questions for others to answer. If students have difficulty answering, help them reread to find the answers. Then model using the answers to make inferences.

AFTER READING

Have students compare the snakes in the book with snakes they have seen or heard about. *How are the snakes similar and different?* Ask which snakes students want to learn more about and why.

Digital Learning

Use the **Leveled Reader Audio CD** for fluency building *after* students read the book with your support during Small Group time.

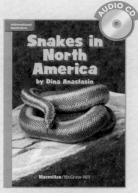

Leveled Reader

Approaching Level

Leveled Reader Lesson 2

Objective Reread to apply skills and strategies and develop fluency

Materials
• **Leveled Reader:** *Snakes in North America*
• **Approaching Reproducible,** p. 95

BEFORE READING

✔ **Review the Strategy and Skill** Review students' completed Inference Webs from the first read. Remind students that making inferences means combining clues that the author gives in the text with what they already know from their own experience. Generating questions can help them check and adjust their comprehension of what the author says, and it can enable them to make inferences about things that the author does not directly state.

✔ **Review the Vocabulary Words** Have students search the book for each vocabulary word. Ask students to read aloud the sentence containing the word and state the word's definition or provide related words. Point out examples of words whose base word offers an important clue to the word's meaning.

Set a Purpose for Reading *Let's reread to check our understanding of the information in the book and to work on our reading fluency.*

DURING READING

Reread *Snakes in North America* with students. Have them read silently, two pages at a time, or read aloud to partners. Stop and have students generate questions before they read the next two pages. Model generating questions and summarizing, as needed.

AFTER READING

Check Comprehension Have partners complete the Comprehension Check on page 20. Review students' answers. Help students find evidence for their answers in the text.

MODEL FLUENCY

Model reading the fluency passage on **Approaching Reproducible** page 95. Tell students to pay close attention to your phrasing and expression, or the way your voice rises and falls to express ideas and feelings, as you read. Read one sentence at a time and have students echo-read each sentence, copying your phrasing and expression.

During independent reading time, have students work with a partner using the fluency passage. One student reads aloud, while the other repeats each sentence back. If students need additional support, have them listen to the "practice speed" version of the passage on the **Fluency Solutions Audio CD**.

Approaching Reproducible, page 95

As I read, I will pay attention to rate and intonation.

	Snakes that live in the trees of the rain forest have a few things in
15	common. Most of these snakes are long and skinny. They also have
27	angled scales along the underside of their body. These features help the
39	snakes balance on tree branches and shrubs.
46	Snakes that live in trees have features that help them survive.
57	Some of them use camouflage. Their colors help them blend in with
69	their surroundings and hide from predators. The Amazon tree boa does
80	this by looking like a branch. But it is a genuine snake.
92	The Amazon tree boa has extra-large eyes that can spot prey. When
104	prey comes along, the snake uncoils and scoops it up. This snake stays
117	in the trees most of the time. When it spots an animal in the water, it
133	drops down and quickly swims after it. 140

Comprehension Check

1. What do snakes that live in trees in the rain forest have in common? **Main Idea and Details** Snakes that live in trees are long and skinny, have angled scales, and use camouflage.

2. What is the main idea in the third paragraph? Name three supporting details. **Main Idea and Details** The Amazon tree boa is well adapted to catch its prey; it has extra-large eyes, uses camouflage to hide in trees, and has the ability to swim after prey in the water.

	Words Read	−	Number of Errors	=	Words Correct Score
First Read		−		=	
Second Read		−		=	

Approaching Level

Leveled Reader Lesson 3

Objectives Build fluency

Materials
- **Leveled Reader:** *Snakes in North America*
- **Approaching Reproducible,** p. 95

FOCUS ON FLUENCY

Timed Reading Tell students that they will be doing a final timed reading of the fluency passage on **Approaching Reproducible** page 95 that they have been practicing. With each student, follow these directions:

- Place the passage facedown.

- When you say "Go," the student begins reading the passage aloud.

- When you say "Stop," the student stops reading the passage.

As they read, note words students mispronounce and their overall phrasing and expression. Stop after one minute. Help students record and graph the number of words they read correctly.

REREAD PREVIOUSLY READ BOOKS

- Distribute copies of the past six **Leveled Readers**. Have students select two to reread. Tell students that rereading these books will help them develop their skills. The more times they read the same words, the quicker they will learn these words. This will make the reading of other books easier.

- Circulate and listen in as students read. Stop students periodically and ask them how they are figuring out difficult words and how they are monitoring their comprehension. Note students who need additional work with specific decoding or comprehension skills.

- Encourage students to read other previously read Leveled Readers during independent reading time or for homework.

Meet Grade-Level Expectations

As an alternative to this day's lesson, guide students through a reading of the On Level Leveled Reader. See page 291U. Since both books contain the same vocabulary, phonics, and comprehension skills, the scaffolding you provided will help most students gain access to this more challenging text.

Book Talk

Bringing Groups Together Students will work with peers of various language and reading abilities to discuss this week's Leveled Readers. Refer to page 162 in the **Teacher's Resource Book** for more about how to conduct a Book Talk.

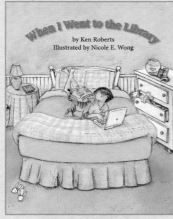

Student Book

Student Book

Approaching Level

Fluency

Objectives Reread selections to develop fluency; develop speaking skills

Materials • **Student Book:** *When I Went to the Library,* "Name That Reptile"

REREAD FOR FLUENCY

- Have students reread a portion of *When I Went to the Library.* Suggest that they focus on two to four of their favorite pages from the selection. Work with students to read the pages with the appropriate phrasing and expression.

- Provide time for students to read their sections of text to you. Comment on their phrasing and expression, and provide corrective feedback by modeling proper fluency.

DEVELOP SPEAKING/LISTENING SKILLS

- Have students practice reading the dialogue on the first half-page of "Name That Reptile."

- Work with students to read the text with appropriate phrasing and expression. Model reading a few lines of dialogue at a time. Emphasize the way that your voice goes up at the end of each question and the way that you adjust your phrasing to reflect the characters' differing ways of speaking. Have students repeat.

- Provide time for students to read aloud the dialogue with partners. Ask students to name the ways their partners used phrasing and expression to capture the character's personality.

- Challenge students to memorize and recite the dialogue with their partners for the class.

Decodable Text

Use the decodable stories in the **Teacher's Resource Book** to help students build fluency with basic decoding patterns.

Approaching Level

Self-Selected Reading

Objective Read independently to generate questions and make inferences
Materials • **Leveled Classroom Library** • other fiction books

APPLY SKILLS AND STRATEGIES TO INDEPENDENT READING

- **Read Independently** Have students choose a fiction book for sustained silent reading. (See the **Theme Bibliography** on pages T7–T8 for book suggestions.) Remind students that generating questions can help them to better understand what they are reading and that making inferences means figuring out unstated information by combining clues that the author gives with what they already know from their own experience that is connected to the text. Have students read their books and record notes about their inferences on Inference Webs.

- **Show Evidence of Reading** While reading, students may generate a reading log or journal. After reading, ask students to use their Inference Webs to write or orally state a summary of the book, maintaining meaning and logical order. Provide time for students to share their summaries and other comments through Book Talks. Ask: *What did you like best about the book? Why? Would you recommend the book to a classmate? Why or why not?*

Approaching

Leveled Classroom Library
See Leveled Classroom Library lessons on pages T2–T7.

Daily Planner

DAY 1	• Vocabulary • Phonics
DAY 2	• Leveled Reader Lesson 1
DAY 3	• Leveled Reader Lesson 2
DAY 4	• Fluency
DAY 5	• Self-Selected Reading

ELL

Practice Vocabulary Pair ELL students with native speakers. On the board, provide sentence frames for pairs to copy and complete using the vocabulary and additional words when necessary. For example: *Maria had to _____ to Serena after she broke her _____.* (*apologize; doll*)

Sound-Spelling WorkBoard

On Level

Vocabulary

Objective   Review vocabulary
Materials   • **Vocabulary Cards**

REVIEW PREVIOUSLY TAUGHT WORDS

Review the Words Display the **Vocabulary Cards** for *weekdays, slithered, genuine, apologize, harmless*, and *ambulance*. Point to each word, read it aloud, and have students chorally repeat.

Then provide the following prompts. Ask students to describe a time when they or someone they know . . .

- . . . did something special on a *weekday*.
- . . . used the word *slithered* to describe something.
- . . . found something that was valuable because it was *genuine*.
- . . . decided to *apologize* to someone.
- . . . realized that an animal or insect was *harmless*.
- . . . saw an *ambulance*.

Phonics/Word Study

Objective   Decode *r*-controlled vowels *er, ir, ur*
Materials   • **Sound-Spelling WorkBoards**

RETEACH SKILL

- *r*-**Controlled Vowels *er, ir, ur*** Point to the /ûr/ **Sound-Spelling Card** on the **WorkBoard** and review the spellings for this sound. State each spelling and provide a sample word.

- Write the words below on the board. If necessary, divide the words into syllables using the syllable-scoop technique to help students read one syllable at a time. When completed, point to the words in random order for students to chorally read.

turtle	Thursday	bluebird	turkey	person
herder	disturb	serving	unswerving	murmur
merchant	desert	shirtless	pattern	lantern

- **Spelling** Dictate the following words for students to spell on their WorkBoards: *furry, perfect, hurtful, thirsty, purple*. Guide students to use the Sound-Spelling Cards, and model how to segment words, such as spelling a word syllable by syllable.

On Level

Fluency

Objectives Reread selections to develop fluency; develop speaking skills
Materials • **Student Book:** *When I Went to the Library*, "Name That Reptile"

REREAD FOR FLUENCY

- Have students reread *When I Went to the Library*. Work with students to read with the appropriate phrasing and expression.

- Provide time for students to read a section of text to you. Comment on their phrasing and expression and provide corrective feedback.

DEVELOP SPEAKING/LISTENING SKILLS

- Have students practice reading the first page of "Name That Reptile."

- Work with students to read the text with appropriate phrasing and expression. Model reading a few lines of dialogue at a time. Emphasize the way that your voice goes up at the end of each question and the way that you adjust your phrasing to reflect the characters' differing ways of speaking. Have students repeat.

- Provide time for pairs of students to read aloud the dialogue to partners. Ask students to name the ways the readers used phrasing and expression to capture the characters' personalities.

- Challenge partners to memorize and recite the dialogue.

Self-Selected Reading

Objective Read independently to make inferences
Materials • **Leveled Classroom Library** • other fiction books

APPLY SKILLS AND STRATEGIES TO INDEPENDENT READING

- **Read Independently** Have students choose a fiction book or a **Leveled Classroom Library** book for sustained silent reading. (See the **Theme Bibliography** on pages T8 and T9 for book suggestions.) Have students read their books and record notes about their inferences on Inference Webs.

- **Show Evidence of Reading** While reading, students may generate a reading log or journal. After reading, ask students to use their Inference Webs to write a summary of the book, maintaining meaning and logical order. Provide time for students to share their summaries and comments through Book Talks. Ask: *What did you like best about the book? Why? Would you recommend the book to a classmate? Why or why not?*

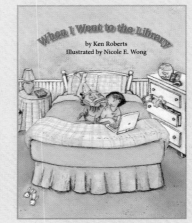

Student Book

Student Book

On Level

Leveled Classroom Library
See Leveled Classroom
Library lessons on pages T2–T7.

Leveled Reader

On Level

Leveled Reader Lesson 1

Objective   Read to apply strategies and skills

Materials   • **Leveled Reader:** *Snakes in North America*

BEFORE READING

Preview and Predict Have students read the title and preview the book by reading the chapter titles and looking at the photographs. Ask students to predict what questions about snakes the book might answer.

Review Vocabulary Words Have students read the vocabulary words on the inside front cover. Ask students to state related words they have learned. Review definitions as needed.

Set a Purpose for Reading *Let's read to find out about snakes that live in North America.*

DURING READING

> **STRATEGY**
> **GENERATE QUESTIONS**

Remind students that generating questions can help them check and adjust their comprehension as they read and can also help them uncover details that the author does not directly state.

> **SKILL**
> **MAKE INFERENCES**

Remind students that making inferences means figuring out what the author does not say directly based on clues in the text, combined with what they already know from their own experience.

Read the Introduction with students. Ask open-ended questions to facilitate rich discussion, such as *What does the author want you to know about snakes and their patterns?* Build on students' responses to help them develop a deeper understanding of the text. Have students make notes on their Inference Webs, then continue reading. Remind them to support their inferences with text evidence.

Base Words As they read, have students point out this week's vocabulary words. Discuss how each word is used. Review base words, and have students identify the base words in several words.

AFTER READING

Ask students to compare the snakes in the book with snakes they have seen or heard about. Ask: *How are the snakes similar and different?* Have students tell which snakes they want to learn more about and why.

On Level

Leveled Reader Lesson 2

Objective Reread to apply skills and strategies and develop fluency
Materials • **Leveled Reader:** *Snakes in North America*
• **Practice Book,** p. 95

Leveled Reader

BEFORE READING

Review the Strategy and Skill Review students' completed Inference Webs from the first read. Remind students that making inferences means combining clues that the author gives with what they already know from their own experiences (connected to the text) to figure out things that the author does not state directly.

Generating, or asking, questions can help students check and adjust their comprehension as they read and can enable them to make inferences about things that the author does not directly state. If students' Inference Webs are incomplete, provide a model web or use a student web and revise it as a group. Have students copy the revised Inference Web in their Writer's Notebooks.

Set a Purpose for Reading *Let's reread to check our understanding of the information in the book and to work on our reading fluency.*

DURING READING

Reread *Snakes in North America* with students. Have them read silently, two pages at a time, or read aloud to partners. Stop and have students generate questions before they read the next two pages. Model generating questions, as needed.

AFTER READING

Check Comprehension Have partners complete the Comprehension Check on page 20. Review students' answers. Help students find evidence for their answers in the text.

MODEL FLUENCY

Model reading the fluency passage on **Practice Book** page 95. Tell students to pay close attention to your phrasing and expression, especially the way your voice rises and falls, as you read. Then read one sentence at a time and have students echo-read each sentence, copying your phrasing and expression.

During independent reading time, have students work with a partner using the fluency passage. One student reads aloud while the other repeats each sentence back. If students need additional support, have them listen to the "practice speed" version of the passage on the **Fluency Solutions Audio CD**.

Book Talk

Bringing Groups Together Students will work with peers of various language and reading abilities to discuss this week's **Leveled Readers**. Refer to page 162 in the **Teacher's Resource Book** for more about how to conduct a Book Talk.

Practice Book, page 95

As I read, I will pay attention to rate and intonation.

    North America is a large area of land. It contains
10 many different climates and landscapes. Most of Mexico
18 and the southwestern United States is hot and dry. Other
28 areas, including the northeastern states and parts of Canada,
37 are cool and wet. Some areas have large mountain ranges,
47 like the Rocky Mountains in the West. Others have flat,
57 rolling plains, like the Midwest.
62   Snakes can be found in just about all of these places.
73 Snakes live in forests, canyons, and deserts. One might
82 even be living in your own backyard. Most snakes don't do
93 well in the cold. In fact, the hardy garter snake is the only
106 serpent that can survive in Alaska.
112   North America has five snake families. Two of these
121 families are poisonous, and three are not. Meet the five
131 families. As you read this book, you will get to know them
143 a lot better. 146

Comprehension Check

1. What is the main idea about snakes in this passage? **Main Idea and Details** Snakes live in all different environments in North America.
2. Why is there only one kind of snake in Alaska? **Cause and Effect** Most snakes don't do well in a cold climate.

	Words Read	–	Number of Errors	=	Words Correct Score
First Read		–		=	
Second Read		–		=	

Daily Planner

DAY 1	• Leveled Reader Lesson 1
DAY 2	• Leveled Reader Lesson 2
DAY 3	• Phonics
DAY 4	• Vocabulary • Fluency
DAY 5	• Self-Selected Reading

ELL

Self-Monitor Vocabulary
Have student pairs of different proficiency identify and define unfamiliar words from the main selection using a dictionary. Challenge students to use the new words in sentences. Monitor students as they complete the activity.

Beyond Level

Phonics/Word Study

Objective Decode multisyllabic words with *r*-controlled vowels *er, ir, ur*

Materials • none

EXTEND/ACCELERATE

- **Read Multisyllabic Words with *r*-Controlled Vowels *er, ir, ur***
  Write the words below on the board. Challenge students to read the words, using known word parts. When completed, point to the words in random order for students to chorally read.

expertly	suburban	hibernate	superbly
purchasing	birdfeeder	vertical	perspective
whirlwind	cursive	surrender	cursor
hummingbird	fertilizer	virtuous	skirmishing

- **Define the Words** Ask students to use their knowledge of word parts to figure out the meanings of the above words. Then have partners find the words in a dictionary and confirm or revise the meanings. Challenge students to use these words in this week's writing assignments.

- **Spell Words with *r*-Controlled Vowels *er, ir, ur*** Dictate the following words for students to spell: *rebirth, immerse, returning, unburdened, energetic.* Write the words for students to self-correct.

Vocabulary

Objectives Discuss ways animals move; write an ABC book

Materials • ABC books

ENRICH VOCABULARY

- **Discuss Ways Animals Move** Remind students that snakes slither. Have students demonstrate slithering. Then have students brainstorm the ways other animals move (for example: *elephants lumber, deer leap, cats crouch*). Record the words on the board.

- **Write an ABC Book** Provide some ABC books for students to look through. Then have students work with partners or in small groups to write an ABC book themselves about animals and how they move. For each letter, direct students to write a sentence that tells how an animal moves (for example: *Ants scurry in an awful hurry; Bears plod toward the berry bushes*). Tell students to be creative for difficult letters, such as *q* and *x*, and to use vivid words.

Beyond Level

Fluency

Objectives   Reread selections to develop fluency; develop speaking skills

Materials   • **Student Book:** *When I Went to the Library*, "Name That Reptile"

REREAD FOR FLUENCY

- Have students reread *When I Went to the Library*. Work with students to read the selection with the appropriate phrasing and expression.

- Provide time for students to read a section of text to you. Comment on their phrasing and expression, and provide corrective feedback.

DEVELOP SPEAKING/LISTENING SKILLS

- Have students practice reading "Name That Reptile."

- Work with students to read the text with appropriate phrasing and expression. Model reading a few lines of dialogue at a time. Emphasize the way that your voice goes up at the end of each question and the way that you adjust your phrasing to reflect the characters' differing ways of speaking. Have students repeat.

- Provide time for pairs of students to read aloud the dialogue to the class. Ask students to name ways in which the readers used phrasing and expression to capture the characters' personalities.

Self-Selected Reading

Objectives   Read independently to generate questions and make inferences

Materials   • **Leveled Classroom Library** • other fiction books

APPLY SKILLS AND STRATEGIES TO INDEPENDENT READING

- **Read Independently** Have students choose a fiction or **Leveled Classroom Library** book for sustained silent reading. (See the **Theme Bibliography** on pages T7 and T8 for suggestions.) Have students read their books and make inferences based on generated questions, and add them to an Inference Web.

- **Show Evidence of Reading** While reading, students may generate a reading log or journal. After reading, ask students to use their Inference Webs to write a summary of the book, maintaining meaning and logical order. Provide time for students to share their summaries and comments through Book Talks.

- **Evaluate** Have students imagine they are the main character of the book they read. Have them evaluate the main events of the story from the character's point of view, in the form of a letter to a friend. When they are done, students can share their letters with the class.

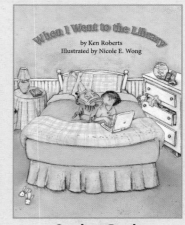

Student Book

Student Book

Beyond

Leveled Classroom Library
See Leveled Classroom
Library lessons on pages T2–T7.

Leveled Reader

Beyond Level

Leveled Reader Lesson 1

Objective	Read to apply strategies and skills
Materials	• **Leveled Reader:** *Snakes in North America*

BEFORE READING

Preview and Predict Have students preview the book by reading the title and chapter titles and looking at the photographs. Ask students to predict what questions about snakes the book might answer.

 Review the Vocabulary Words Have students read the vocabulary words on the inside front cover. Ask students to state each definition and any related words they have learned.

Set a Purpose for Reading *Let's read to find out about snakes that live in North America.*

DURING READING

 STRATEGY
GENERATE QUESTIONS

Ask students to define the term *generate questions*. Remind students that *generating questions* means asking yourself questions about what you are reading.

SKILL
MAKE INFERENCES

Ask students to define the term *make inferences*. Remind students that making inferences means figuring out what the author does not directly state by combining clues the author gives with what they already know from their own experience (connected to the text).

Read the book with students. Ask open-ended questions to facilitate rich discussion, such as *What does the author want you to know about snakes and their patterns?* Build on students' responses to help them develop a deeper understanding of the text. Have students fill in their Inference Webs independently as they read.

AFTER READING

Compare Ask students to compare the snakes in the book with snakes they have seen or heard about. Have student pairs come up with a list of questions they would like to research on the Internet during independent time.

Analyze Have students imagine they are talking to a snake expert at a job fair. Ask students to create a list of questions to ask the expert about their job, such as *What training do you need? What special classes did you take?*

Gifted & Talented

Beyond Level

Leveled Reader Lesson 2

Objective Reread to apply skills and strategies and develop fluency

Materials • **Leveled Reader:** *Snakes in North America*
• **Beyond Reproducible,** p. 95

BEFORE READING

Review the Strategy and Skill Review students' completed Inference Webs from the first read.

Remind students that generating questions can help them check and adjust their comprehension as they read and can enable them to make inferences about things that the author does not directly state. If students' Inference Webs are incomplete, provide a model web or use a student web and revise it as a group. Have students copy the revised Inferences Web in their Writer's Notebooks.

Set a Purpose for Reading *Let's reread to check our understanding of the information in the book and work on our reading fluency.*

DURING READING

Have students reread *Snakes in North America* silently or with a partner. If reading in pairs, prompt students to stop every two pages and generate questions for each other to answer.

AFTER READING

Check Comprehension Have students independently complete the Comprehension Check on page 20. Review students' answers. Help students find evidence for their answers in the text.

Synthesize Discuss with students the elements of a poem. Have students write a poem about snakes, using information from *Snakes in North America*. Students should practice reading their poems aloud and then present them to the class.

MODEL FLUENCY

Model reading the fluency passage on **Beyond Reproducible** page 95. Tell students to pay close attention to your phrasing and expression, or the way your voice rises and falls to express ideas and feelings, as you read. Then read one sentence at a time, and have students echo-read the sentences, copying your phrasing and expression.

During independent reading time, have students work with a partner using the fluency passage. One student reads aloud, while the other repeats each sentence back. Students can check their fluency by reading along with the "expert speed" version of the passage on the **Fluency Solutions Audio CD**.

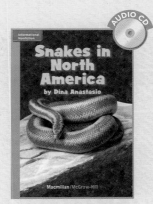

Leveled Reader

Book Talk

Bringing Groups Together Students will work with peers of various language and reading abilities to discuss this week's Leveled Readers. Refer to page 162 in the **Teacher's Resource Book** for more about how to conduct a Book Talk.

Beyond Reproducible, page 95

As I read, I will pay attention to rate and intonation.

	The puff adder is one of Africa's most common
9	venomous snakes. It can be found in dry areas like
19	woodlands, low forests, and grasslands all across Africa.
27	But it is hard to find. Its light brown, green, and black skin
40	camouflages it very well. The puff adder also blends in
50	with its habitat among rocks and fallen trees. Because the
60	puff adder is well camouflaged, people often accidentally
68	step on the snake or come too close to it.
78	The puff adder can remain motionless for long periods
87	of time. Because of this, its prey and enemies often come
98	very close to the snake without realizing it. Within
107	seconds, the puff adder can strike. It puffs up its head and
119	makes a loud hissing sound before it attacks. The puff
129	adder moves forward in a straight line instead of slithering
139	from side to side. This helps it dart even more quickly at
152	nearby prey like rodents, toads, and other snakes. 160

Comprehension Check

1. Explain why the puff adder is so dangerous. **Main Idea and Details** The puff adder is well camouflaged, can remain motionless for long periods of time, and can strike within seconds.
2. What was the author's purpose in writing this passage? **Author's Purpose** to inform readers about one of Africa's most common venomous snakes

	Words Read	–	Number of Errors	=	Words Correct Score
First Read		–		=	
Second Read		–		=	

ELL ENGLISH LANGUAGE LEARNERS

Daily Planner

DAY 1	• Build Background Knowledge • Vocabulary
DAY 2	• Vocabulary • Access to Core Content *When I Went to the Library*
DAY 3	• Vocabulary • Grammar • Access to Core Content *When I Went to the Library*
DAY 4	• Vocabulary • Writing/Spelling • Access to Core Content *"Snakes"* • Leveled Reader *North American Snakes*
DAY 5	• Vocabulary • Leveled Reader *North American Snakes* • Self-Selected Reading

LOG ON StudentWorks™ Plus
Interactive Student Book

Use StudentWorks Plus for:
• Vocabulary Preteaching
• Word-by-Word Highlighting
• Think Aloud Prompts

Cognates

Help students identify similarities and differences in pronunciation and spelling between English and Spanish cognates.

emotion	*emoción*
express	*expresar*
genuine	*genuino*
ambulance	*ambulancia*
action	*acción*
verb	*verbo*

ELL ENGLISH LANGUAGE LEARNERS

Prepare to Read

Content Objective Describe the power of words
Language Objective Use key words to describe how letters help us express feelings
Materials • **StudentWorks Plus**

BUILD BACKGROUND KNOWLEDGE

All Language Levels

■ Have students preview *When I Went to the Library* using **StudentWorks Plus**, which contains oral summaries in multiple languages, online multilingual glossaries, word-by-word highlighting, and questions that assess and build comprehension.

■ Students can build their word-reading fluency by reading along as the text is read or by listening during the first reading and, at the end of each paragraph, returning to the beginning of the paragraph and reading along.

■ Students can build their comprehension by reviewing the definitions of key words in the online glossary and by answering the comprehension questions. When appropriate, the text required to answer the question is highlighted to provide students with additional support and scaffolding.

■ Following the reading, ask students to respond in writing to a question that links the story to their experiences, such as *Have you ever had to apologize for something? How did it make you feel?*

Academic Language

Language Objective Use academic language in classroom conversations

All Language Levels

■ This week's academic words are **boldfaced** throughout the lesson. Define the word in context, and provide a clear example from the selection. Then ask students to generate an example or a word with a similar meaning.

Academic Language Used in Whole Group Instruction

Theme Words	Key Selection Words	Strategy and Skill Words
emotions **express** **point of view**	**weekdays** **slithered** **genuine** **apologize** **harmless** **ambulance**	**generate questions** **make inferences** **action verbs** **base words**

ELL ENGLISH LANGUAGE LEARNERS

Vocabulary

Language Objective Demonstrate understanding and use of key words

Materials • **Visual Vocabulary Resources**
            • **ELL Resource Book**

Visual Vocabulary Resources

PRETEACH KEY VOCABULARY

Use the **Visual Vocabulary Resources** to preteach the key selection words *weekdays, slithered, genuine, apologize, harmless,* and *ambulance*. Focus on two words per day. Use the routine below, which is detailed on the cards.

Beginning/Intermediate

- Point out any known sound-spellings, or focus on a key aspect of phonemic awareness related to the word.

All Language Levels

- Define the word in English, and provide the example given.
- Define the word in Spanish, if appropriate, and indicate if the word is a cognate.
- Display the picture, and explain how it demonstrates the word.
- Engage students in a structured activity about the image, using the key word.
- Ask students to chorally say the word three times.
- Distribute copies of the Vocabulary Glossary, **ELL Resource Book** page 122.

PRETEACH FUNCTION WORDS AND PHRASES

All Language Levels

Use the Visual Vocabulary Resources to preteach the function words and phrases *break out into, take place, pick out,* and *genuinely*. Focus on one word or phrase per day. Use the routine on the cards.

- Define the word in English and, if appropriate, in Spanish. Point out if the word is a cognate.
- Refer to the picture and engage students in talk about the word. For example, students will partner-talk using sentence frames.
- Ask students to chorally repeat the word three times.

TEACH BASIC WORDS

Beginning/Intermediate

Use the Visual Vocabulary Resources to teach the basic words *poison ivy, rash, faint, nurse, hospital,* and *first aid*. Teach these "first aid" words using the routine provided on the card.

ELL Resource Book, page 122

Use the word chart to study this week's vocabulary words.
Write a sentence using each word in your writer's notebook.

Word	Context Sentence	Illustration
weekdays	Monday through Friday are <u>weekdays</u>.	What are things you do on weekdays?
slithered	The snake <u>slithered</u> across the sand.	
genuine	My smile was <u>genuine</u>, because I really liked the gift.	
apologize	I wrote a note to my mom to <u>apologize</u> for breaking her vase.	
harmless	This spider looks scary, but it is <u>harmless</u>.	
ambulance	An <u>ambulance</u> raced down the street toward the hospital.	

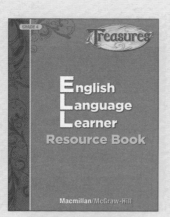

ELL Resource Book

ELL ENGLISH LANGUAGE LEARNERS

Access to Core Content

Content Objective Read grade-level text
Language Objective Discuss text, using key words and sentence frames
Materials • **ELL Resource Book,** pp. 114–121

PRETEACH MAIN SELECTION (PAGES 272–283)

All Language Levels

Use the Interactive Question-Response Guide on **ELL Resource Book** pages 114–119 to introduce students to *When I Went to the Library*. Preteach half of the selection on Day 2 and half on Day 3.

- Use the prompts provided in the guide to develop meaning and vocabulary. Use the partner-talk and whole-class responses to engage students and increase student talk.

- When completed, have partners reread the story.

PRETEACH PAIRED SELECTION (PAGES 286–289)

All Language Levels

Use the Interactive Question-Response Guide on ELL Resource Book pages 120–121 to preview the paired selection "Snakes." Preteach the selection on Day 4.

Beginning	Intermediate	Advanced
Use Visuals During the Interactive Reading, select several illustrations. Describe them and make inferences using the illustrations. Have students summarize what you said.	**Make Inferences** During the Interactive Reading, select a few lines of text. After you have read and explained it, have students make inferences based on the text.	**Make Inferences** During the Interactive Reading, select a passage of text. After you have read and explained it, have students make inferences based on the passage.

ELL ENGLISH LANGUAGE LEARNERS

Fluency

Content Objectives Reread selections to develop fluency; develop speaking skills
Language Objective Tell a partner what a selection is about
Materials • **Student Book:** *When I Went to the Library*, "Snakes"
          • **Teacher's Resource Book**

REREAD FOR FLUENCY

Beginning

■ Have students read the decodable passages on page 15 in the **Teacher's Resource Book**.

Intermediate/Advanced

■ Have students reread two to four of their favorite pages of *When I Went to the Library*, based on their levels. Help students read the pages with the appropriate pacing and intonation. For example, tell students to pay close attention to your pacing (tempo) and intonation (the way your voice rises and falls to express ideas and feelings) as you read. Then read one sentence at a time, and have students echo-read each sentence, copying your pacing and intonation.

■ Provide time for students to read their sections of text to you. Comment on their pacing and intonation, and provide corrective feedback by modeling proper fluency.

DEVELOP SPEAKING/LISTENING SKILLS

All Language Levels

■ Work with students to read their favorite section of "Snakes" to their partner, using appropriate pacing and intonation.

■ Have them tell their partner about the paragraph. Provide the sentence frame *I like this paragraph because it is about ____*.

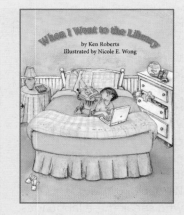

Student Book

Self-Selected Reading

Content Objective Read independently
Language Objective Orally retell information learned
Materials • **Leveled Classroom Library** • other fiction books

APPLY SKILLS AND STRATEGIES TO INDEPENDENT READING

All Language Levels

■ Have students choose a fiction book for independent reading. (See the **Theme Bibliography** on pages T8–T9.)

■ After reading, ask students to orally summarize and share their reactions to the book with classmates.

Leveled Classroom Library
See Leveled Classroom
Library lessons on pages T2–T7.

Transfer Skills

Verb Agreement There is no verb agreement in Cantonese, Haitian Creole, Hmong, Korean, and Vietnamese. Verbs do not change form to indicate the number of the subject as in English (*He apologizes, We apologize*). Students who speak these languages may have difficulty understanding the concept of adding *-s* or *-es* to a verb to indicate a singular subject. Emphasize the *-s* or *-es* verb endings as you model correct usage, and have students repeat. See language transfers on pages T16–T31.

Corrective Feedback

During Whole Group grammar lessons, follow the routine on the **Grammar Transparencies** to provide students with extra support. This routine includes completing the items with English Language Learners while other students work independently, having students reread the sentences with partners to build fluency, and providing a generative task such as writing a new sentence using the skill.

Grammar

Content Objective Identify action verbs
Language Objective Speak in complete sentences, using sentence frames.

✔ ACTION VERBS

Beginning/Intermediate

- Review action verbs. Write the following on the board: *I apologized to my best friend*. Underline the action verb (*apologized*). Tell students that this is an action verb because it tells what the subject (*I*) did. Point out that action verbs have different tenses that can show action in the present, future, and past: I <u>apologize</u> to my friend. I <u>will apologize</u> to my friend. I <u>apologized</u> to my friend.

All Language Levels

- Write sentence frames on the board, such as those provided below. Review action verbs with students. Have students provide an action verb to complete each sentence. Have them read their sentences aloud and say: *The action verb is ___.*

  Yesterday, I ___ my bike to the library.

  I ___ some books about snakes.

  Snakes ___ their skins as they grow.

  I will not ___ the box with the snake in it.

PEER DISCUSSION STARTERS

All Language Levels

- Write the following sentences on the board.

  I learned that snakes ___.   *If I had a snake, I would ___.*

- Pair students and have them complete each sentence frame. Ask them to expand on their sentences by providing as many details as they can from this week's readings. Circulate, listen in, and take note of each student's language use and proficiency.

Beginning	Intermediate	Advanced
Use Verbs Describe the illustrations in *When I Went to the Library* to students, using action verbs. Have students repeat the sentences aloud. Then ask them to point to the illustrations that the sentences describe.	**Describe** Ask students to describe the illustrations in *When I Went to the Library* using action verbs. Have them use complete sentences.	**Describe** Ask students to describe the illustrations in *When I Went to the Library* using action verbs. Have them use different tenses in their sentences.

ELL ENGLISH LANGUAGE LEARNERS

Writing/Spelling

Content Objective Spell words correctly
Language Objective Write in complete sentences, using sentence frames

All Language Levels

- Write the key vocabulary words on the board: *weekdays, slithered, genuine, apologize, harmless, ambulance*. Have students copy each word on their **WorkBoards**. Help them say each word and then write a sentence for it. Provide sentence starters, such as:

  On weekdays I go to ___.

  The snake slithered through the ___.

  They knew I was genuine when I said I was sorry because ___.

  One way to apologize for something is to ___.

  A harmless snake ___.

  An ambulance takes people ___.

Beginning/Intermediate

- Help students spell words using their growing knowledge of English sound-spelling relationships. Model how to segment the word students are trying to spell, and attach a spelling to each sound (or spellings to each syllable if a multisyllabic word). Use the **Sound-Spelling Cards** to reinforce the spellings for each English sound.

Advanced

- Dictate the following words for students to spell: *chirp, herd, burning, first, clerk, curly*. Use the Sound-Spelling Cards to guide students as they spell each word.

- When completed, review the meanings of words that can be easily demonstrated or explained. Use actions, gestures, and available pictures.

Sound-Spelling WorkBoard

Phonics/Word Study

For English Language Learners who need more practice with this week's phonics/spelling skill, see the Approaching Level lesson on page 291J. Focus on minimal contrasts, articulation, and those sounds that do not transfer from the student's first language to English. See language transfers on pages T16–T31.

Leveled Reader

ELL ENGLISH LANGUAGE LEARNERS

Leveled Reader

Content Objective Read to apply skills and strategies

Language Objective Retell information, using complete sentences

Materials • **Leveled Reader:** *North American Snakes*
• **ELL Resource Book,** p. 123
• **Visual Vocabulary Resources,** pp. 413–418

BEFORE READING

All Language Levels

- **Preview** Read the title. Ask: *What is the title? Say it again.* Repeat with the author's name. Then page through the book. Use simple language to tell about each page. Immediately follow up with questions, such as *Are all snakes poisonous? This is a coral snake. What does it look like? This snake is molting. What is happening to its skin?*

- **Review Skills** Use the inside front cover to review the comprehension skill and vocabulary words.

- **Set a Purpose** Say: *Let's read to find out about the different kinds of snakes that live in North America.*

DURING READING

All Language Levels

- Have students read each page aloud using the differentiated suggestions. Provide corrective feedback, such as modeling how to blend a decodable word or clarifying meaning by using techniques from the Interactive Question-Response Guide.

- **Retell** After every two pages, ask students to state the main ideas they have learned so far. Help them to complete the Inferences Web. Restate students' comments when they have difficulty using story-specific words. Provide differentiated sentence frames to support students' responses and engage students in partner-talk where appropriate.

Vocabulary

Preteach Vocabulary Use the routine in the **Visual Vocabulary Resources**, pages 413–418, to preteach the ELL Vocabulary listed in the inside front cover of the **Leveled Reader**.

Beginning	Intermediate	Advanced
Echo-Read Have students echo-read after you.	**Choral-Read** Have students chorally read with you.	**Choral-Read** Have students chorally read.
Check Comprehension Point to pictures and ask questions, such as *Find the rattlesnake. Do you see the rattle on the rattlesnake? Point to it.*	**Check Comprehension** Ask questions or provide prompts, such as *Describe this picture. What happens when snakes molt?*	**Check Comprehension** Ask: *What did you learn from this page about poisonous snakes? Read sentences that tell the main ideas about poisonous snakes.*

ELL ENGLISH LANGUAGE LEARNERS

AFTER READING

Use the chart below and Think and Compare questions in the **Leveled Reader** to determine students' progress.

Think and Compare	Beginning	Intermediate	Advanced
1 Look at page 7. Why do you think boas might attack people? *(Make Inferences)*	Possible responses: Nonverbal response. Step on snake.	Possible responses: People can step on snakes.	Possible responses: Boas might attack people if people step on them or bother them.
2 How did the rat snake get its name? Think of other snakes with interesting names. How do you think they got those names? *(Analyze)*	Possible responses: Nonverbal response. Eat rats. Rattlesnake has rattle.	Possible responses: Rat snakes like to eat rats. Snakes get names for being special.	Possible responses: Rat snakes got their name because they like to eat rats. Snakes are named for a special quality that makes them different.
3 Have you changed your opinion about snakes after reading this book? Why or why not? *(Evaluate)*	Possible responses: Nonverbal response. Yes. Snakes help people.	Possible responses: Yes, snakes eat rats and insects. They help people.	Possible responses: Yes, my opinion changed because I learned that snakes eat rats and insects that cause problems for people.

BOOK TALK

Develop Listening and Speaking Skills Distribute copies of **ELL Resource Book** page 123 and form small groups. Help students determine the leader to discuss the Book Talk questions. Tell students to remember the following while engaged in the activity:

- Share information in cooperative learning interactions. Remind students to work with their partners to retell the story and complete any activities. Ask: *What happened next in the story?*

- Employ self-corrective techniques and monitor their own and other students' language production. Students should ask themselves: *What parts of this passage were confusing to me? Can my classmates help me clarify a word or sentence that I don't understand?*

- Distinguish between formal and informal English and know when to use each one. Remind students to note whether the selection is written in formal or informal English. Ask: *Why do you think it is written in this way?* Remind students that they may use informal English when speaking with their classmates, but they should use formal language when they talk to teachers or write essays.

ELL Resource Book

Book Talk

Bringing Groups Together
Students will work with peers of varying language abilities to discuss the Book Talk questions. Form groups so that students who read the Beyond Level, On Level, Approaching Level, and ELL Leveled Readers are in the same group for the activity.

Progress Monitoring

Weekly Assessment

ASSESSED SKILLS

- Vocabulary: Vocabulary Words, Word Parts: Base Words
- Comprehension: Make Inferences
- Grammar: Action Verbs
- Phonics/Spelling: *r*-Controlled Vowels *er, ir, ur*

Selection Test for When I Went to the Library *Also Available*

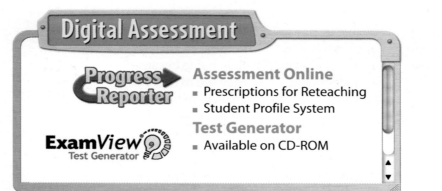

Digital Assessment

Progress Reporter

Assessment Online
- Prescriptions for Reteaching
- Student Profile System

ExamView Test Generator

Test Generator
- Available on CD-ROM

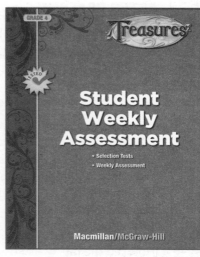

**Weekly Assessment
Unit 3 Week 1**

Fluency Assessment

Assess fluency for one group of students per week.
Use the Oral Fluency Record Sheet to track the number of words read correctly. Fluency goal for all students:
102–122 words correct per minute (WCPM).

Approaching Level	Weeks 1, 3, 5
On Level	Weeks 2, 4
Beyond Level	Week 6

Fluency Assessment

Diagnose		Prescribe
Review the assessment answers with students. Have them correct their errors. Then provide additional instruction as needed.		
	IF...	**THEN...**
VOCABULARY WORDS **VOCABULARY STRATEGY** Word Parts: Base Words	0–2 items correct …	See **Vocabulary Intervention Teacher's Edition.** **LOG ON** Online Practice: Go to www.macmillanmh.com. **CD-ROM** Vocabulary PuzzleMaker
COMPREHENSION Skill: Make Inferences	0–3 items correct …	See **Comprehension Intervention Teacher's Edition.** **SPIRAL REVIEW** See Make Inferences lesson in Unit 1 Week 2, page 59B.
GRAMMAR Action Verbs	0–1 items correct …	See **Writing and Grammar Intervention Teacher's Edition.**
PHONICS AND SPELLING *r*-Controlled Vowels *er, ir, ur*	0–1 items correct …	**LOG ON** Online Practice: Go to www.macmillanmh.com. See **Phonics Intervention Teacher's Edition.**
FLUENCY	98–101 WCPM	**AUDIO CD** Fluency Solutions Audio CD
	0–97 WCPM	See **Fluency Intervention Teacher's Edition.**

Response to Intervention

To place students in Tier 2 or Tier 3 Intervention use the *Diagnostic Assessment*.

Tier 2

- Phonics
- Vocabulary
- Comprehension
- Fluency
- Writing and Grammar

Tier 3

Week 2 ★ At a Glance

Priority Skills and Concepts

✔ Comprehension
- **Strategy:** Generate Questions
- **Skill:** Draw Conclusions
- Character
- **Genre:** Expository, Fantasy

✔ Robust Vocabulary
- **Selection Vocabulary:** *neglected, appreciated, misunderstood, desperate, endured, obedience*
- **Strategy:** Word Parts/Prefixes

✔ Fluency
- **Expression**

✔ Phonics/Spelling
- **Word Study:** Silent Letters, Multisyllabic Words
- **Spelling Words:** *hour, lambs, knew, wrench, kneel, thumbs, honest, answer, honesty, plumber, honor, known, combs, wrapper, knives, doubt, knead, wriggle, heir, wrinkle*
- *person, pearl, shirt*

✔ Grammar/Mechanics
- **Verb Tenses**
- **Subject-Verb Agreement**

✔ Writing
- **Trait: Ideas**
- Strong Reasons

Key

✔ **Tested in program**    **Review Skill**

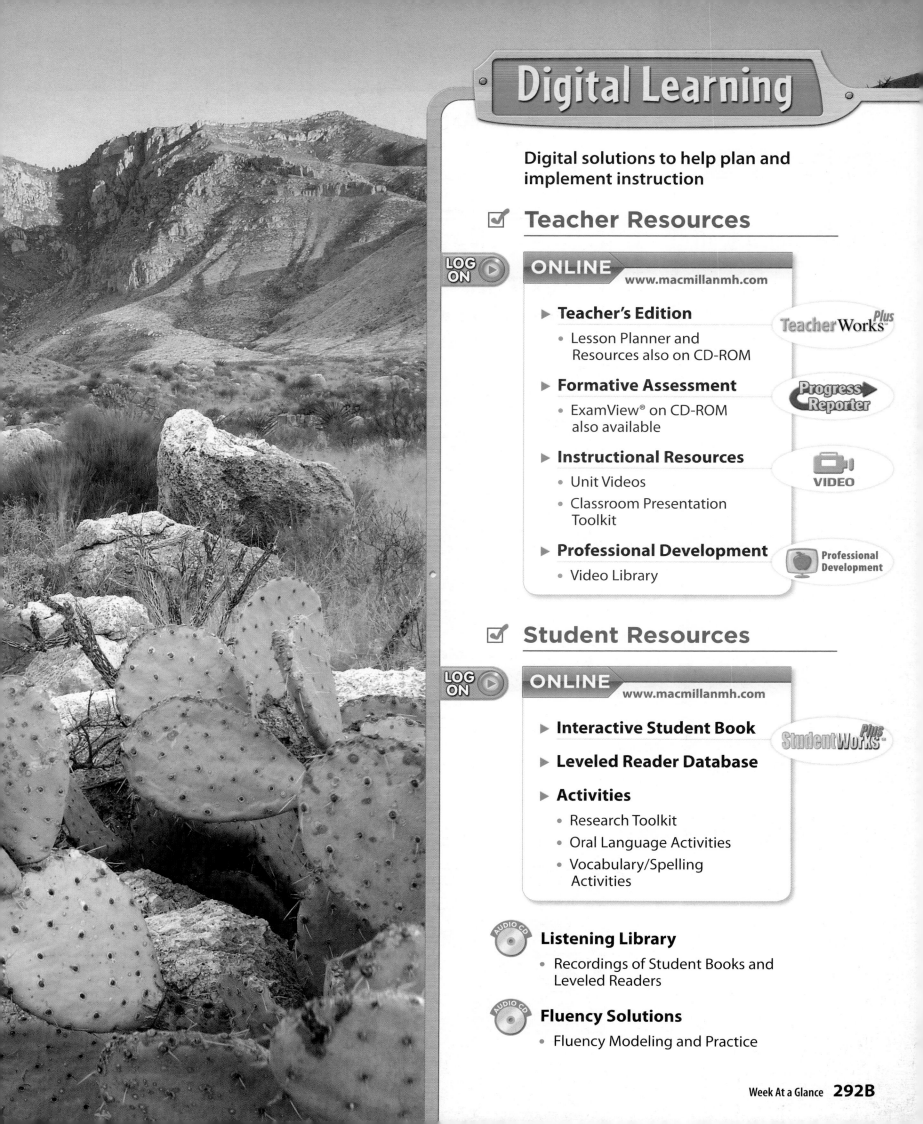

Digital Learning

Digital solutions to help plan and implement instruction

☑ Teacher Resources

LOG ON ▶

ONLINE www.macmillanmh.com

▶ **Teacher's Edition**
  • Lesson Planner and Resources also on CD-ROM

TeacherWorks Plus

▶ **Formative Assessment**
  • ExamView® on CD-ROM also available

Progress Reporter

▶ **Instructional Resources**
  • Unit Videos
  • Classroom Presentation Toolkit

VIDEO

▶ **Professional Development**
  • Video Library

Professional Development

☑ Student Resources

LOG ON ▶

ONLINE www.macmillanmh.com

▶ **Interactive Student Book**

StudentWorks Plus

▶ **Leveled Reader Database**

▶ **Activities**
  • Research Toolkit
  • Oral Language Activities
  • Vocabulary/Spelling Activities

AUDIO CD **Listening Library**
  • Recordings of Student Books and Leveled Readers

AUDIO CD **Fluency Solutions**
  • Fluency Modeling and Practice

Weekly Literature

Theme: The Art of Persuasion

LOG ON ▶ StudentWorks™ Plus
Interactive Student Book

- Word-by-Word Reading
- Summaries in Multiple Languages
- Comprehension Questions

Main Selection
Genre | Fantasy

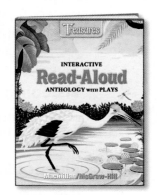

Preteach Vocabulary and Comprehension
Genre | Fiction

Paired Selection
Genre | Expository

Support Literature

Interactive Read-Aloud Anthology

- Listening Comprehension
- Robust Vocabulary
- Readers Theater Plays for Fluency

Resources for Differentiated Instruction

Leveled Readers

GR Levels O–T

AUDIO CD

Genre	Fiction

- Same Theme
- Same Vocabulary
- Same Comprehension Skills

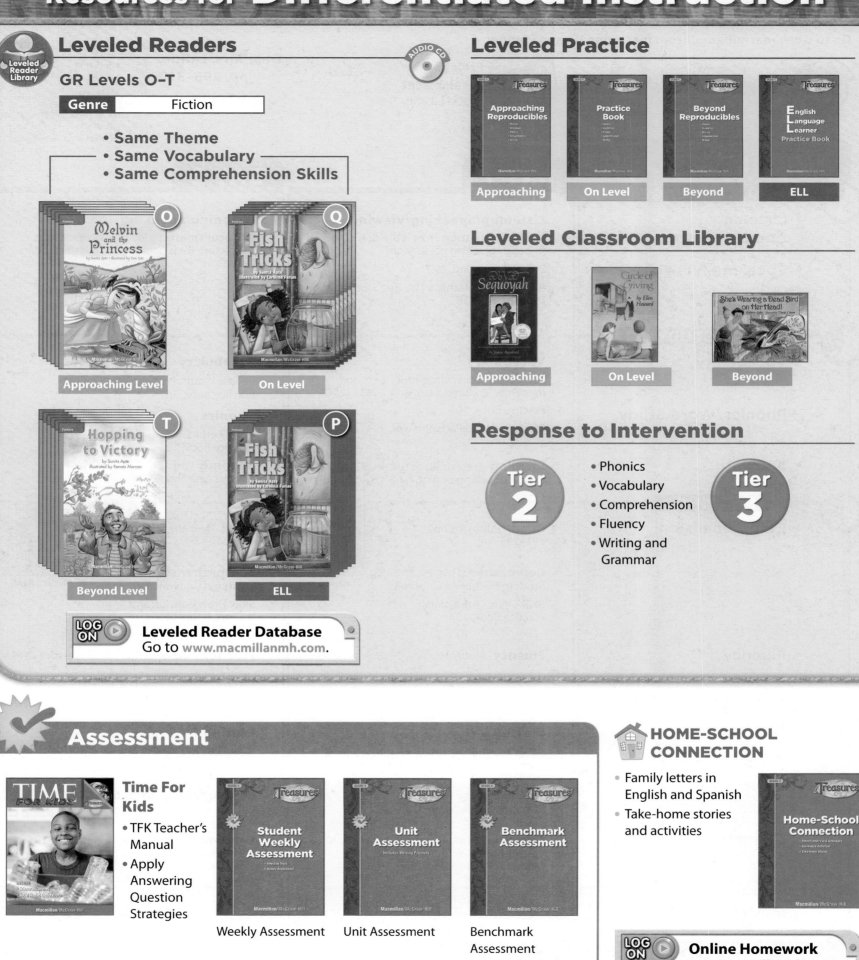

O — *Melvin and the Princess* by Sunita Apte • illustrated by Don Tate
Approaching Level

Q — *Fish Tricks* by Sunita Apte Illustrated by Carolina Farías
On Level

T — *Hopping to Victory* by Sunita Apte illustrated by Renato Alarcao
Beyond Level

P — *Fish Tricks* by Sunita Apte Illustrated by Carolina Farías
ELL

LOG ON ▶ **Leveled Reader Database**
Go to www.macmillanmh.com.

Leveled Practice

Treasures — **Approaching Reproducibles**
Approaching

Treasures — **Practice Book**
On Level

Treasures — **Beyond Reproducibles**
Beyond

Treasures — **English Language Learner Practice Book**
ELL

Leveled Classroom Library

Sequoyah
Approaching

Circle of Giving by Ellen Howard
On Level

She's Wearing a Dead Bird on Her Head!
Beyond

Response to Intervention

Tier 2

- Phonics
- Vocabulary
- Comprehension
- Fluency
- Writing and Grammar

Tier 3

Assessment

TIME FOR KIDS

Time For Kids
- TFK Teacher's Manual
- Apply Answering Question Strategies

Treasures — **Student Weekly Assessment**
Weekly Assessment

Treasures — **Unit Assessment** Includes Writing Prompts
Unit Assessment

Treasures — **Benchmark Assessment**
Benchmark Assessment

HOME-SCHOOL CONNECTION

- Family letters in English and Spanish
- Take-home stories and activities

Treasures — **Home-School Connection**

LOG ON ▶ **Online Homework**
www.macmillanmh.com

CD-ROM TeacherWorks *Plus*
All-In-One Planner and Resource Center

Professional Development
Video Library

Dear Mrs. LaRue,
pp. 296–317

Dear Mrs. LaRue
Letters from Obedience School
Written and Illustrated by
Mark Teague

WHOLE GROUP

ORAL LANGUAGE
- **Listening Comprehension**
- **Speaking/Viewing**

WORD STUDY
- **Vocabulary**
- **Phonics/Word Study**
- **Spelling**

READING
- **Comprehension**
- **Fluency**

LANGUAGE ARTS
- **Writing**
- **Grammar**

ASSESSMENT
- **Informal/Formal**

DAY 1

Listening/Speaking/Viewing
❓ Focus Question How is the dog in the photograph using persuasion?
Build Background, 292
Read Aloud: "Hachiko: The True Story of a Loyal Dog," 293A–293B

Vocabulary
neglected, appreciated, misunderstood, desperate, endured, obedience, 295, 325C
Practice Book, 101
Strategy: Word Parts/Prefixes, 294

Spelling Pretest: Silent Letters, 325E
Phonics/Spelling Book, 67–68

Read "Puppy Trouble," 294–295

Comprehension, 295A–295B
Strategy: Generate Questions
Skill: Draw Conclusions
Practice Book, 102

Puppy Trouble
Student Book

Fluency Model Fluency, 293B

Writing
Daily Writing Do you think dogs make good pets? Write a paragraph explaining why or why not.
Trait: Ideas
Strong Reasons, 323A–323B

Grammar Daily Language Activities, 325G
Verb Tenses, 325G
Grammar Practice Book, 56

Quick Check Vocabulary, 294
Comprehension, 295B

DAY 2

Listening/Speaking
❓ Focus Question How close to reality is the picture Ike is painting in his letters to Mrs. LaRue?

Vocabulary
Review Words, Prefixes, 296, 325C
Practice Book, 107
Phonics
Silent Letters, 293C–293D
Practice Book, 100
Spelling Word Sorts, 325E
Phonics/Spelling Book, 69

Read *Dear Mrs. LaRue,* 296–317

Comprehension, 296–317
Strategy: Generate Questions
Skill: Draw Conclusions
Practice Book, 103

Dear Mrs. LaRue
Student Book

Fluency Repeated Reading: Expression, 319A

Writing
Daily Writing Write a journal entry for one day from the viewpoint of a dog.

Reading/Writing Connection, 324–325

Grammar Daily Language Activities, 325G
Verb Tenses, 325G
Grammar Practice Book, 57

Quick Check Phonics, 293D
Comprehension, 317

SMALL GROUP Lesson Plan ▷ **Differentiated Instruction 292G–292H**

Priority Skills

Vocabulary	Comprehension	Writing	Science
Vocabulary Words Word Parts: Prefixes	**Strategy:** Generate Questions **Skill:** Draw Conclusions	Trait: Ideas Strong Reasons	Identify inherited traits and learned characteristics.

DAY 3

Listening/Speaking

❓ Focus Question Compare the events and characters in "Puppy Trouble" and *Dear Mrs. LaRue*. Use details from both selections in your answer.

Summarize, 319

Vocabulary

Review Words, Related Words, 325D

Spelling Word Meanings, 325F
Phonics/Spelling Book, 70

Read *Dear Mrs. LaRue*, 296–317

Student Book

Comprehension
Comprehension Check, 319

Review Skill: Character, 319B
Practice Book, 105

Fluency Repeated Reading: Expression, 319A
Practice Book, 104

Writing

Daily Writing Write a dialogue between a dog and a cat in which they argue about who makes the best pet.

Trait: Ideas
Strong Reasons, 325A

Grammar Daily Language Activities, 325G
Mechanics and Usage, 325H
Grammar Practice Book, 58

Quick Check Fluency, 319A

DAY 4

Listening/Speaking/Viewing

❓ Focus Question Think about this article and *Dear Mrs. LaRue*. What do you think Rico would say if he wrote a letter to his owner?

Vocabulary

Content Vocabulary: *intelligent, impressive, demonstrated, exposure, phrases,* 320
Review Words, Morphology, 325D

Spelling Proofread, 325F
Phonics/Spelling Book, 71

Read "Dog Amazes Scientists!" 320–323

Student Book

Comprehension
Genre: Nonfiction

Text Feature: Line Graph, 320
Practice Book, 106

Fluency Repeated Reading: Expression, 319A

Time For Kids

Writing

Daily Writing Write a poem describing a dog. You may choose a specific breed or a mutt who is the family pet.

Trait: Organization
Opinion Paragraph, 325A

Grammar Daily Language Activities, 325G
Verb Tenses, 325H
Grammar Practice Book, 59

Quick Check Vocabulary, 325D

DAY 5
Review and Assess

Listening/Speaking/Viewing

❓ Focus Question Based on your readings, what conclusions can you draw about the relationship between dogs and their owners?

Vocabulary

Assess Words, Connect to Writing, 325D

Spelling Posttest, 325F
Phonics/Spelling Book, 72

Read Self-Selected Reading, 292K
Practice Book, 108

Comprehension
Connect and Compare, 323

Student Book

Fluency Practice, 292K

Writing

Daily Writing Write a letter to Mrs. LaRue giving her advice about Ike.

Conferencing, 325B

Grammar Daily Language Activities, 325G
Verb Tenses, 325H
Grammar Practice Book, 60

Weekly Assessment, 325II–325JJ

Differentiated Instruction

What do I do in small groups?

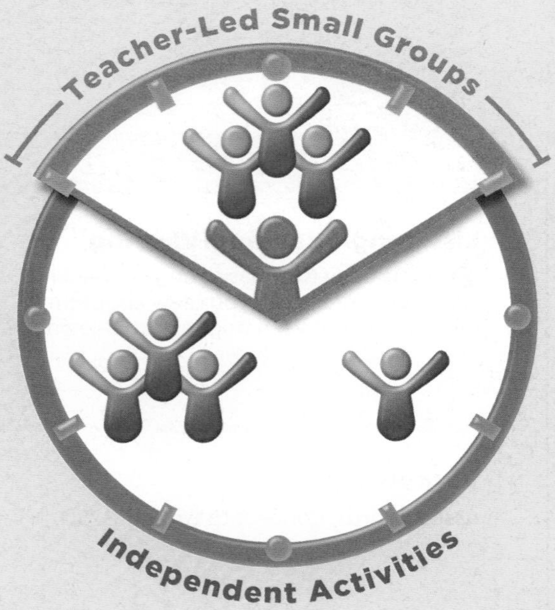

Teacher-Led Small Groups
Independent Activities

Focus on Skills

IF... students need additional instruction, practice, or extension based on your Quick Check observations for the following priority skills:

Phonics/Word Study
Silent Letters

Vocabulary Words
neglected, appreciated, misunderstood, desperate, endured, obedience
Strategy: Word Parts/Prefixes

Comprehension
Strategy: Generate Questions
Skill: Draw Conclusions

Fluency

THEN...

Approaching ELL	Preteach and Reteach Skills
On Level	Practice
Beyond	Enrich and Accelerate Learning

LOG ON Suggested Small Group Lesson Plan

CD-ROM TeacherWorks Plus All-In-One Planner and Resource Center

	DAY 1	DAY 2
Approaching Level • **Preteach/Reteach** Tier 2 **Tier 2 Instruction**	• Prepare to Read, 325I • Academic Language, 325I • Preteach Vocabulary, 325K	• Comprehension, 325M Generate Questions/Draw Conclusions ELL • Leveled Reader Lesson 1, 325N
On Level • **Practice**	• Vocabulary, 325S • Phonics, 325S Silent Letters ELL	• Leveled Reader Lesson 1, 325U
Beyond Level • **Extend/Accelerate** Gifted and Talented **Gifted and Talented**	• Leveled Reader Lesson 1, 325Y • Analyze Information, 325Y	• Leveled Reader Lesson 2, 325Z • Synthesize Information, 325Z
ELL • **Build English Language Proficiency** • **See ELL in other levels.**	• Prepare to Read, 325AA • Academic Language, 325AA • Preteach Vocabulary, 325BB	• Vocabulary, 325BB • Preteach Main Selection, 325CC

Focus on Leveled Readers

Manipulatives

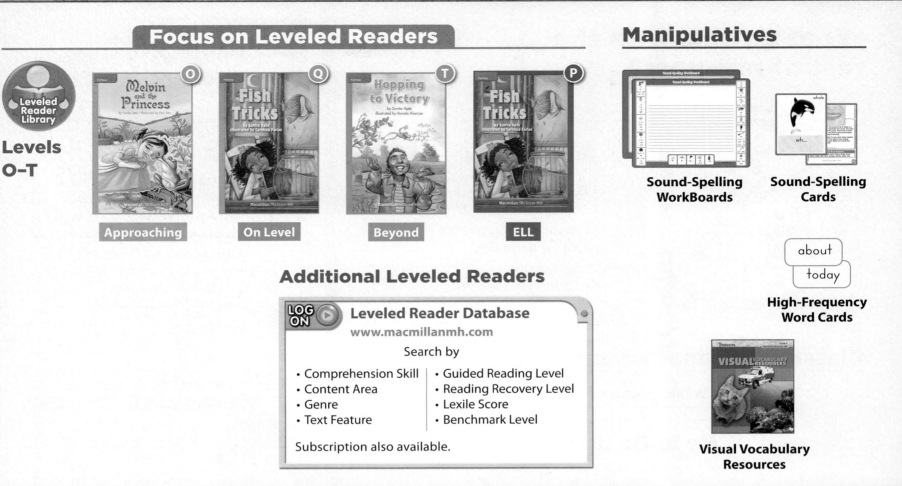

Levels O–T

Melvin and the Princess — O — Approaching

Fish Tricks — Q — On Level

Hopping to Victory — T — Beyond

Fish Tricks — P — ELL

Additional Leveled Readers

LOG ON **Leveled Reader Database**
www.macmillanmh.com

Search by
- Comprehension Skill
- Content Area
- Genre
- Text Feature
- Guided Reading Level
- Reading Recovery Level
- Lexile Score
- Benchmark Level

Subscription also available.

Sound-Spelling WorkBoards

Sound-Spelling Cards

about today

High-Frequency Word Cards

Visual Vocabulary Resources

DAY 3

- Phonics Maintenance, 325J
  Silent Letters **ELL**
- Leveled Reader Lesson 2, 325O

- Leveled Reader Lesson 2, 325V

- Phonics, 325W
  Silent Letters **ELL**

- Vocabulary, 325BB
- Grammar, 325EE

DAY 4

- Reteach Phonics Skill, 325J
  Silent Letters **ELL**
- Review Vocabulary, 325L
- Leveled Reader Lesson 3, 325P

- Fluency, 325T

- Vocabulary, 325W
- Research/Summarize News Stories, 325W
- Fluency, 325X

- Vocabulary, 325BB
- Writing/Spelling, 325FF
- Preteach Paired Selection, 325CC
- Fluency, 325DD
- Leveled Reader, 325GG

DAY 5

- High-Frequency Words, 325L
- Fluency, 325Q
- Self-Selected Independent Reading, 325R
- Book Talk, 325P

- Self-Selected Independent Reading, 325T
- Book Talk, 325V

- Self-Selected Independent Reading, 325X
- Evaluate Information, 325X
- Book Talk, 325Z

- Vocabulary, 325BB
- Leveled Reader, 325GG
- Self-Selected Independent Reading, 325DD
- Book Talk, 325HH

Managing the Class

What do I do with the rest of my class?

- Practice Book and Reproducibles
- ELL Practice Book
- Leveled Reader Activities
- Literacy Workstations
- Online Activities

Classroom Management Tools

Weekly Contract

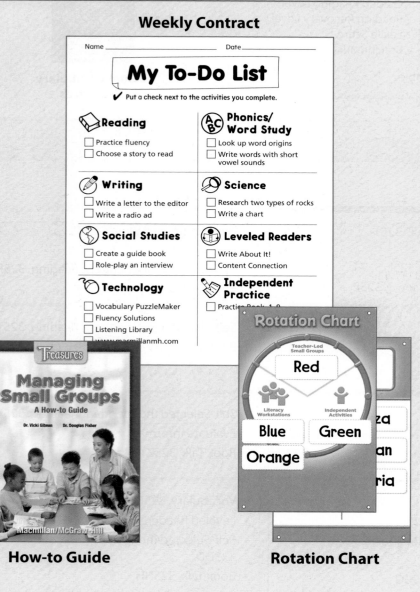

Name _____ Date _____

My To-Do List

✔ Put a check next to the activities you complete.

📖 **Reading**
- ☐ Practice fluency
- ☐ Choose a story to read

🔤 **Phonics/Word Study**
- ☐ Look up word origins
- ☐ Write words with short vowel sounds

✏️ **Writing**
- ☐ Write a letter to the editor
- ☐ Write a radio ad

🔬 **Science**
- ☐ Research two types of rocks
- ☐ Write a chart

🌎 **Social Studies**
- ☐ Create a guide book
- ☐ Role-play an interview

📖 **Leveled Readers**
- ☐ Write About It!
- ☐ Content Connection

🖱️ **Technology**
- ☐ Vocabulary PuzzleMaker
- ☐ Fluency Solutions
- ☐ Listening Library
- ☐ www.macmillanmh.com

🖌️ **Independent Practice**
- ☐ Practice Book, 1–8

Rotation Chart

Teacher-Led Small Groups

Red

Literacy Workstations Independent Activities

Blue   Green

Orange

Treasures

Managing Small Groups
A How-to Guide

Dr. Vicki Gibson   Dr. Douglas Fisher

Macmillan/McGraw-Hill

How-to Guide

Rotation Chart

Digital Learning

StudentWorks Plus
Interactive Student Book

LOG ON ▶

StudentWorks Plus Online
- Summaries in Multiple Languages
- Word-by-Word Reading
- Comprehension Questions

Meet the Author/Illustrator

Mark Teague

- Mark gets a lot of inspiration from his two young daughters. He loves to read to them.
- He always loved to draw but didn't think about becoming a professional artist until after college.
- Mark starts out his books by jotting down notes and scribbling in a notebook. Slowly the ideas start to come together and he creates a real story.

Another book by Mark Teague
- Teague, Mark. *Detective LaRue: Letters from the Investigation.* New York: Scholastic, Inc., 2004.

- Other Books by the Author or Illustrator

Leveled Practice

Treasures
Practice Book
- Phonics
- Vocabulary
- Fluency
- Comprehension
- Writing

Macmillan/McGraw-Hill

On Level

Treasures
English Language Learner Practice Book

Macmillan/McGraw-Hill

ELL

Also Available:
Approaching Reproducible

Beyond Reproducible

Independent Activities

LOG ON

ONLINE INSTRUCTION www.macmillanmh.com

Oral Language Activities

- Focus on Vocabulary and Concepts
- English Language Learner Support

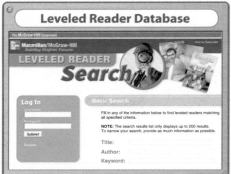

Leveled Reader Database

- Leveled Reader Database
- Search titles by level, skill, content area, and more

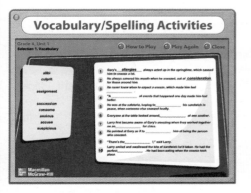

Vocabulary/Spelling Activities

- Differentiated Lists and Activities

Research Toolkit

- Research Roadmap
- Research and Presentation Tools
- Theme Launcher Video
- Links to Science and Social Studies

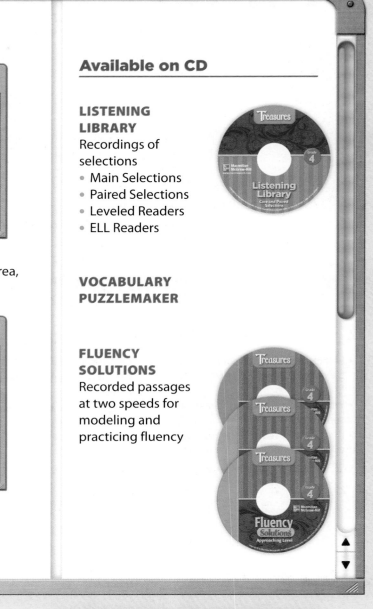

Available on CD

LISTENING LIBRARY
Recordings of selections
- Main Selections
- Paired Selections
- Leveled Readers
- ELL Readers

VOCABULARY PUZZLEMAKER

FLUENCY SOLUTIONS
Recorded passages at two speeds for modeling and practicing fluency

---

Leveled Reader Activities

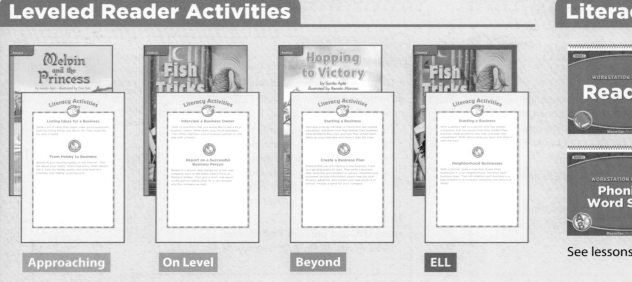

Approaching   **On Level**   **Beyond**   **ELL**

See inside cover of all Leveled Readers.

Literacy Workstations

See lessons on pages 292K–292L.

Managing the Class

What do I do with the rest of my class?

Reading

Objectives

- Practice reading with expression
- Read independently for a sustained period of time; use **Practice Book** page 108 for Reading Strategies and Reading Log

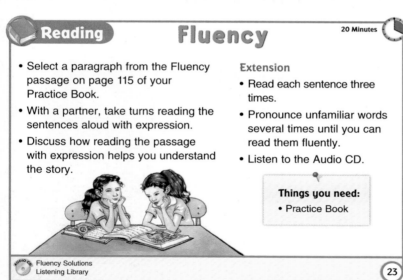

Reading — Fluency

20 Minutes

- Select a paragraph from the Fluency passage on page 115 of your Practice Book.
- With a partner, take turns reading the sentences aloud with expression.
- Discuss how reading the passage with expression helps you understand the story.

Extension

- Read each sentence three times.
- Pronounce unfamiliar words several times until you can read them fluently.
- Listen to the Audio CD.

> **Things you need:**
> - Practice Book

Fluency Solutions
Listening Library

23

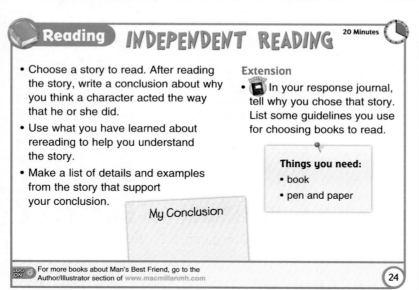

Reading — INDEPENDENT READING

20 Minutes

- Choose a story to read. After reading the story, write a conclusion about why you think a character acted the way that he or she did.
- Use what you have learned about rereading to help you understand the story.
- Make a list of details and examples from the story that support your conclusion.

My Conclusion

Extension

- In your response journal, tell why you chose that story. List some guidelines you use for choosing books to read.

> **Things you need:**
> - book
> - pen and paper

For more books about Man's Best Friend, go to the Author/Illustrator section of www.macmillanmh.com

24

Phonics/Word Study

Objectives

- Identify the silent consonants in words
- Build new words using prefixes
- Use a dictionary to find the definitions of words

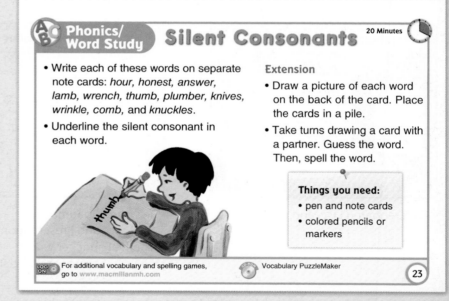

Phonics/Word Study — Silent Consonants

20 Minutes

- Write each of these words on separate note cards: *hour, honest, answer, lamb, wrench, thumb, plumber, knives, wrinkle, comb,* and *knuckles*.
- Underline the silent consonant in each word.

Extension

- Draw a picture of each word on the back of the card. Place the cards in a pile.
- Take turns drawing a card with a partner. Guess the word. Then, spell the word.

> **Things you need:**
> - pen and note cards
> - colored pencils or markers

For additional vocabulary and spelling games, go to www.macmillanmh.com

Vocabulary PuzzleMaker

23

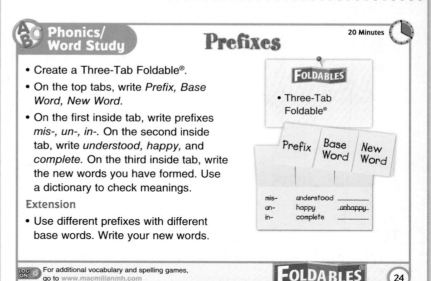

Phonics/Word Study — Prefixes

20 Minutes

- Create a Three-Tab Foldable®.
- On the top tabs, write *Prefix, Base Word, New Word.*
- On the first inside tab, write prefixes *mis-, un-, in-*. On the second inside tab, write *understood, happy,* and *complete.* On the third inside tab, write the new words you have formed. Use a dictionary to check meanings.

FOLDABLES
- Three-Tab Foldable®

Prefix	Base Word	New Word
mis-	understood	
an-	happy	unhappy
in-	complete	

Extension

- Use different prefixes with different base words. Write your new words.

For additional vocabulary and spelling games, go to www.macmillanmh.com

FOLDABLES

24

Literacy Workstations

Literacy Workstation Flip Charts

✏️ Writing

Objectives

- Write a paragraph explaining how you solved a problem
- Use topic sentences and describe events in a sequence
- Write an explanatory paragraph about training pets

🔍 Content Literacy

Objectives

- Research information about how dogs help people
- Research information about a local animal shelter
- Create a line graph

✏️ Writing — Explain It Plainly
20 Minutes

- Think of a problem that you solved. For example, did you find a way to make your dog stop barking?
- Write a paragraph about your experience. In your topic sentence, state the problem that you solved.
- Then write in order the steps you took to solve the problem.

Extension

- Share your paragraph with a classmate. Ask your classmate if your steps are clear and complete.
- Find one place where you can add more details to make your writing better.

Things you need:
- pen and paper

23

🔍 Science — How Dogs Help
20 Minutes

- Use the Internet to research guide dogs. Find out: What breeds are used and why? What qualities do guide dogs have? Write your answers on note cards.
- Use your note cards to write an article about guide dogs.

Extension

- Illustrate two ways that dogs help people.
- Write captions that give facts under each picture.

Things you need:
- online resources
- note cards
- poster board and markers
- pen and paper

LOG ON Internet Research and Inquiry Activity
Students can find more facts at www.macmillanmh.com

23

✏️ Writing — Taking Care of Pets
20 Minutes

- ⏱️ Write an explanatory paragraph about why it is important for people to train their pet dogs.
- Include a strong topic sentence and support your topic with examples and details.

Extension

- Draw a cartoon about how a badly trained dog causes problems.
- Write a humorous caption under your cartoon.

Things you need:
- pen and paper
- colored pencils or markers

24

🌎 Social Studies — Animal Shelters
20 Minutes

- Use a computer to research animal adoptions at a local animal shelter.
- Find out how many pets are placed in homes each month.

Extension

- Create a line graph based on your research. Put the name of each month at the bottom of the graph.
- On the side of the graph, list the number of pets that are adopted. Plot the numbers on the graph.

Things you need:
- online resources
- pen and paper
- ruler

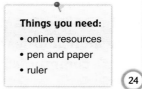

24

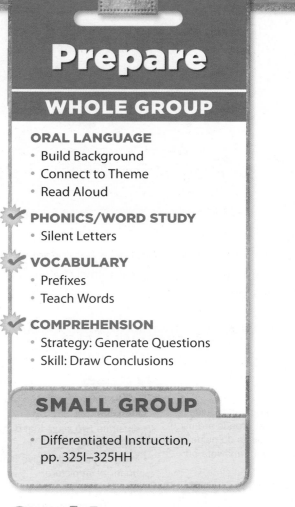

Prepare

WHOLE GROUP

ORAL LANGUAGE
- Build Background
- Connect to Theme
- Read Aloud

✓ **PHONICS/WORD STUDY**
- Silent Letters

✓ **VOCABULARY**
- Prefixes
- Teach Words

✓ **COMPREHENSION**
- Strategy: Generate Questions
- Skill: Draw Conclusions

SMALL GROUP

- Differentiated Instruction, pp. 325I–325HH

Oral Language

Build Background

ACCESS PRIOR KNOWLEDGE

Share the following information: Like many Americans, the person in this picture has a pet dog. There are about 73 million pet dogs in the United States. The most popular dogs in the United States are Labrador retrievers. Next are golden retrievers, beagles, and German shepherds. Many dog owners feel a special bond with their pets in which each is sensitive to the other's needs.

Write the following words on the board, and briefly define each one using the **Define/Example/Ask** routine: **responsibilities** (duties), **request** (ask for), **communicate** (make known or understood), **persuasion** (act of convincing).

FOCUS QUESTION Ask students to read "Talk About It" on **Student Book** page 293. Then describe the photo. Ask:

- How can a dog and its owner communicate with each other and make their feelings known?

- What acts of persuasion might a dog use to get what it wants?

The Art of Persuasion

292

Talk About It

How is this dog using persuasion?

LOG ON ▶ VIEW IT

Oral Language Activities
The Art of Persuasion
www.macmillanmh.com

293

Use the Picture Prompt

BUILD WRITING FLUENCY

Have students write in their Writer's Notebooks what they know about dogs. Have them write as much as they can for ten minutes without stopping. Provide feedback and revision assignments during Writing Conference time. Prior to meeting, students should self-correct any errors they find.

Connect to the Unit Theme

DISCUSS THE BIG IDEA

Our words can be a powerful tool to convince people to think or act in a certain way.

Discuss what students have learned about writing letters to express ideas or emotions. Discuss other ways to express ideas and emotions.

- What are creative ways in which we can express ourselves and communicate our thoughts?

- How can our words affect others?

USE THEME FOLDABLES

Write the **Big Idea** statement on the board. Ask students to copy it on their Unit Theme Foldables. Remind them to add details as they complete this week's readings.

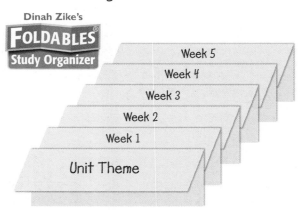

Dinah Zike's
FOLDABLES®
Study Organizer

Week 5
Week 4
Week 3
Week 2
Week 1
Unit Theme

Study Book

ELL ENGLISH LANGUAGE LEARNERS

Beginning	Intermediate	Advanced
Use Visuals Tell students about the photograph. *This dog is hungry. There is no food in the bowl. The dog wants the owner to feed him.* Then ask students to tell you what the dog in the photograph is doing. Repeat correct answers in a louder and slower voice for the class to hear.	**Describe** Ask students to describe what the dog in the photograph is doing. *What does the dog want the owner to do? What does the dog do to let the owner know?* Repeat students' responses, correcting grammar and pronunciation as needed.	**Discuss** Have students discuss having a pet. *What do pets do for owners? What do owners do for their pets?* Elaborate on their responses.

Objectives

- Identify the characteristics of narrative nonfiction
- Develop vocabulary
- Read sentences fluently, focusing on expression

Materials

- Read-Aloud Anthology, pp. 66–71

Read Aloud

Read "Hachiko: The True Story of a Loyal Dog"

Read Aloud

GENRE: Informational Text/Expository

Explain that one kind of **expository** text is narrative nonfiction. Share with students these key characteristics of narrative nonfiction:

- It tells a true story about an event.

- It is nonfiction that reads like a novel.

- A work of narrative nonfiction gives well-researched information while keeping the reader's interest with an engaging story.

FOCUS ON VOCABULARY

Introduce the following words, using the **Define/Example/Ask** routine. Tell students that knowing these words will help them understand the events in the story as you read.

Vocabulary Routine

Use the routines below to discuss the meaning of each word.

Define: **Kimonos** are loose robes tied with a sash, which are worn by some Japanese women.
Example: Kimonos are a traditional way of dress for women in Japan.
Ask: In what ways does a kimono look different from a bathrobe?

Define: **Strode** means walked confidently.
Example: The cowboys strode into the room.
Ask: What is the difference between strode and crept?

Define: **Timidly** means shyly.
Example: The boy approached the giant timidly.
Ask: What might you do timidly?

Define: A **morsel** is a very small piece of food.
Example: The mouse ate a morsel of cheese.
Ask: What is a synonym for morsel?

LISTENING FOR A PURPOSE

Ask students to listen carefully as you read "Hachiko: The True Story of a Loyal Dog" on **Read-Aloud Anthology** pages 66–71. Use the Think Alouds and Genre Study provided.

ELL **Interactive Reading** Build students' oral language by engaging them in talk about the story's meaning.

- After the first paragraph, say: *What do you think the author is going to do now?*

- After the sixth paragraph, say: *Turn to your partner, and discuss how we know the dog was happy to see the older man.*

- After the last page, say: *Why did the people build a statue of Hachiko?*

PARTNERS **Think/Pair/Share** Use **Copying Master 1,** "I wonder . . .," to help students generate questions about the story. Have students write these questions down. When completed, have them share their questions with the class.

RESPOND TO THE STORY

Ask students the Think and Respond questions on page 71. Then have students think of other ways people could have chosen to honor Hachiko.

Model Fluency

Reread the story. Tell students that this time you want them to focus on one aspect of how you read it—your **expression**.

Point out that an important part of reading aloud is being expressive with one's voice. Paying attention to punctuation and using the correct intonation will help students do this. When they see an exclamation mark, for example, they will know to add emphasis, drama, and excitement to their reading. Model an example. Students will find additional clues in the story that will help them with expression. If the text reads, "'Ouch!' he cried," they will have to yell the word *ouch*.

Think Aloud When I read the second paragraph of the story, I see that Kentaro asks his mother to take him to the train station. Then I read about his mother's reaction: *She laughed and said, "Kentaro, you have become big and brave, just like a samurai!"* The story says that Mama laughed. So I should give a little laugh when I read her line. I also notice an exclamation mark at the end of the sentence. This tells me to say the sentence with emphasis. Now you look for a line of dialogue in the story. Figure out how to read it with expression by looking at the punctuation and other clues in the story.

Establish Fluency Focus Remind students that you will be listening for these same qualities in their reading throughout the week. You will help them improve their reading by assisting them in finding clues to help them read with appropriate expression.

Readers Theater

BUILDING LISTENING AND SPEAKING SKILLS Distribute copies of "All the Money in the World," **Read-Aloud Anthology** pages 182–202. Have students practice reading the play throughout the unit. Assign parts and have the students present the play or perform it as a dramatic reading at the end of the unit.

ELL

Discuss Genre Review narrative nonfiction with students. Ask: *What kind of story does a narrative nonfiction tell? How is a narrative nonfiction similar to a fiction? How is it different? Is Hachiko a real dog? What happened to him? How is this story a narrative nonfiction?* Elicit details from the story to support students' responses.

Objective
- Decode multisyllabic words with silent letters

Materials
- Practice Book, p. 100
- Transparency 12
- Word-Building Cards
- Teacher's Resource Book, p. 131

ELL

Transfer Sounds Some English Language Learners may have difficulties with silent letters. For example, in Spanish there are only two silent letters—*h* and *u* (as in *gu* and *qu*). The letter *u* is sometimes pronounced in the *gu* spelling. Have students practice pronunciation and spelling of words with silent letters. Use the Approaching Level phonics lesson on page 325J for additional practice. See language transfers on pages T16–T31.

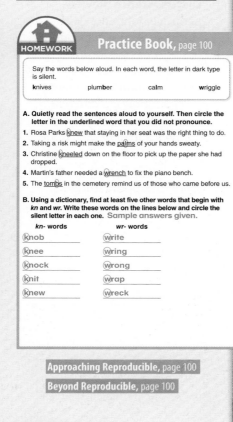

HOMEWORK **Practice Book,** page 100

Say the words below aloud. In each word, the letter in dark type is silent.

| knives | plumber | calm | wriggle |

A. Quietly read the sentences aloud to yourself. Then circle the letter in the underlined word that you did not pronounce.

1. Rosa Parks <u>knew</u> that staying in her seat was the right thing to do.
2. Taking a risk might make the <u>palms</u> of your hands sweaty.
3. Christine <u>kneeled</u> down on the floor to pick up the paper she had dropped.
4. Martin's father needed a <u>wrench</u> to fix the piano bench.
5. The <u>tombs</u> in the cemetery remind us of those who came before us.

B. Using a dictionary, find at least five other words that begin with *kn* and *wr*. Write these words on the lines below and circle the silent letter in each one. Sample answers given.

kn- words	*wr-* words
knob	write
knee	wring
knock	wrong
knit	wrap
knew	wreck

Approaching Reproducible, page 100
Beyond Reproducible, page 100

Phonics

✓ Silent Letters

EXPLAIN/MODEL

Display the *Nest* and *Rose* **Sound-Spelling Cards**. Point out the *kn* and *gn* spellings on the *Nest* card and the *wr* spelling on the *Rose* card. Explain that these spellings for /n/ and /r/ contain silent letters.

Explain that the letters *g* and *k* are often silent when they come before the letter *n*, as in *gnat* and *know*. The letter *w* is silent when it comes before the letter *r*, as in *write*. Continue by teaching the silent-letter spellings listed.

- **kn** as in *know*
- **gn** as in *gnat* or *sign*
- **wr** as in *write*
- **mb** as in *lamb*
- **bt** as in *debt*
- **gh** as in *ghost*
- **rh** as in *rhyme*
- **mn** as in *hymn*
- **l** as in *calf*

Write the words on the board, underline the silent letters, and model blending each word.

Think Aloud Look at the first word I wrote, *k-n-o-w*. I see the consonant pair *kn*. In this spelling, the letter *k* is silent, so I'll say the /n/ sound. Listen and watch as I sound out the word: /nō/, *know*. (Run your finger under the word as you sound it out.)

PRACTICE/APPLY

Read the Word List Display **Transparency 12**. Have students underline the silent letter in each word. Then have them chorally read the words.

know	sign	ghost	wrappings
rhyming	lambs	knives	ghoul
wrinkle	wrist	doubt	rhino
dumb	wrote	half	crumb
wrench	thumbs	knot	knapsack
knob	gnash	plumber	combs

Phonics Transparency 12

Sort the Words Ask students to sort the words by spelling pattern. Then have them write the word sort in their Writer's Notebooks.

wr	kn	rh	mb	gh	lf

Read Multisyllabic Words

TRANSITION TO LONGER WORDS Help students transition from reading one-syllable to multisyllabic words with silent letters. Have students read a word in the first column, then model how to read the longer word in the second column. Point out the added syllable(s), such as a prefix or suffix, to help students gain awareness of these common word parts.

knee	kneecap	knead	kneaded
know	knowledge	wrong	wrongly
wrap	unwrap	wreck	wreckage
write	rewrite	wrinkle	unwrinkled
thumb	thumbprint	doubt	doubtfully
knot	knotty	wrist	wristwatch

Phonics Transparency 12

APPLY DECODING STRATEGY Guide students in using the Decoding Strategy to decode the following words that include silent letters: *subtle, wringing, numbness, wren, debtor, wrestlers, knickknack.* Write each word on the board. Remind students to look for silent-letter spelling patterns in step 3 of the Decoding Strategy procedure.

Build Fluency

SPEED DRILL Distribute copies of **Silent Letter Speed Drill, Teacher's Resource Book** page 131. Use the Speed Drill routine to help students become fluent reading words with silent-letter spelling patterns. Remind students to apply what they learn about silent-letter patterns to their spelling.

Quick Check

Can students read words with silent letters?

During **Small Group Instruction**

Tier 2

If No → **Approaching Level** Reteach the skill using the lesson on p. 325J.

If Yes → **On Level** Consolidate the learning using p. 325S.

Beyond Level Extend the learning using p. 325W.

Use **Word-Building Cards** 110–120. Display one card at a time. Have students chorally read each common syllable. Repeat at varying speeds and in random order. Have students work with partners during independent time to write as many words as they can containing each syllable.

Decoding Strategy

Decoding Strategy Chart

Step 1	Look for word parts (prefixes) at the beginning of the word.
Step 2	Look for word parts (suffixes) at the end of the word.
Step 3	In the base word, look for familiar spelling patterns. Think about the six syllable-spelling patterns you have learned.
Step 4	Sound out and blend together the word parts.
Step 5	Say the word parts fast. Adjust your pronunciation as needed. Ask yourself: "Is this a word I have heard before?" Then read the word in the sentence and ask: "Does it make sense in this sentence?"

© Macmillan/McGraw-Hill

Vocabulary

✔ **STRATEGY**
WORD PARTS

Prefixes Review the definition of prefixes using the bookmark on **Student Book** page 294. Remind students that a prefix changes the meaning of a base word. On the board, write the word *misunderstood*. Underline *understood*.

Think Aloud Inside the word *misunderstood* I see another word—*understood*. I realize that this is the base word and that *mis-* must be a prefix. I know the meaning of *understood*. I do not know the meaning of the prefix *mis-*. I look it up in the dictionary and see that it means "badly" or "wrongly" and originally comes from an old German word meaning "go wrong." Now I know that *misunderstood* means "understood wrongly, or incorrectly."

Be sure students know that *mis-* can mean "wrongly," and have them look for other words with that prefix using a dictionary. Point out that not every word that begins with *mis-* follows the pattern of prefix + base word. Discuss nonexamples such as *mister* and *missing*.

Read "Puppy Trouble"

As you read "Puppy Trouble" with students, ask them to identify clues that reveal the meanings of the highlighted words. Tell students they will read these words again in *Dear Mrs. LaRue*.

Vocabulary

neglected	desperate
appreciated	endured
misunderstood	obedience

✔ **Word Parts**

Prefixes are added to the beginnings of words to change their meanings.
mis- = "badly" or "wrongly"
misunderstood = "wrongly understood"

Puppy Trouble

by Lana Engell

We got back from the grocery store and found the house a mess. I had **neglected** to close the bathroom door again, and because of my forgetfulness, our Saint Bernard, Bernie, had left chewed toilet paper all over the house. Bernie was happily running in circles. He had no idea that what he had done while we were away was not liked or **appreciated**.

Bernie had already chewed Mom's favorite handbag and my new shoes. He had spread garbage throughout the house and pawed the furniture. Mom didn't like that, because she's very neat. Mom was also concerned about Bernie jumping on people when I took him out for walks. She was afraid he might scare somebody.

294

Quick Check

Can students identify word meanings?

During **Small Group Instruction**

Tier 2

If No → **Approaching Level** Reteach the words using the Vocabulary lesson, pp. 325K–325L.

If Yes → **On Level** Consolidate the learning using p. 325S.

Gifted Talented

Beyond Level Extend the learning using p. 325W.

Mom said that if Bernie didn't start behaving, we couldn't keep him, and I knew Mom wasn't bluffing. I could also tell she wasn't kidding. Her message was clear, so there was no way it could be **misunderstood**. Bernie was in trouble again.

I was **desperate**. If I didn't think of something really fast, I was going to lose my dog!

Then I had a really wonderful idea. It meant I would have to give up watching some of my favorite TV shows to spend more time with Bernie. In the end, though, if I could keep him, it was worth a try.

Just then Mom finished putting the groceries away. She came into the living room and saw the mess.

"I've had it with this puppy," Mom said in a tired voice. "I'm just about out of patience, Lin."

"I know, Mom," I said. "You've **endured** Bernie's chewing and messes for three long months now. But I've never had a pet before. If I'm not training him correctly, then it's not Bernie's fault. Can we take him to **obedience** school?" I asked.

And that's just what we did.

Reread for **Comprehension**

Generate Questions

Draw Conclusions Generating questions can help you draw conclusions about what happens in the **plot** of a story. When you draw conclusions, you use information from the story as well as your own experiences connected to the story to understand the characters and events of the plot. Reread the story and use your Conclusions Chart to keep track of your conclusions.

Text Clues	Conclusion

 LOG ON **LEARN IT** Comprehension
www.macmillanmh.com

295

Preteach Vocabulary See pages 325BB and 325K to preteach the vocabulary words to ELL and Approaching Level students. Use the **Visual Vocabulary Resources** to demonstrate and discuss each word. To further reinforce concepts, have students complete page 138 in the **ELL Resource Book**.

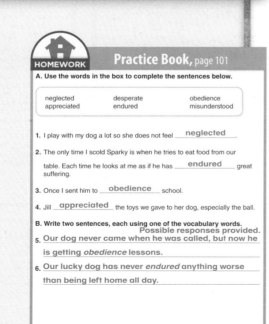

 HOMEWORK **Practice Book,** page 101

A. Use the words in the box to complete the sentences below.

neglected	desperate	obedience
appreciated	endured	misunderstood

1. I play with my dog a lot so she does not feel ___neglected___

2. The only time I scold Sparky is when he tries to eat food from our table. Each time he looks at me as if he has ___endured___ great suffering.

3. Once I sent him to ___obedience___ school.

4. Jill ___appreciated___ the toys we gave to her dog, especially the ball.

B. Write two sentences, each using one of the vocabulary words.
Possible responses provided.
5. Our dog never came when he was called, but now he is getting *obedience* lessons.

6. Our lucky dog has never *endured* anything worse than being left home all day.

Approaching Reproducible, page 101
Beyond Reproducible, page 101

Vocabulary

TEACH WORDS

Introduce each word using the **Define/Example/Ask** routine. Model reading each word using the syllable-scoop technique.

Vocabulary Routine

Define: When you **neglected** something, you forgot or failed to do it.
Example: I neglected to give Mom the phone message.
Ask: What are some reasons why homework might be neglected?
DESCRIPTION

- If you **appreciated** something, you valued it. *I appreciated the chance to attend the concert.* What have you appreciated? EXAMPLE

- If something is **misunderstood**, it is not correctly known. *I misunderstood the task, so I did extra work.* Describe a time when you misunderstood directions. DESCRIPTION

- Someone who is **desperate** will do just about anything to help or change a situation. *I was so desperate for advice, I even asked my sister.* What is the difference between being worried and being desperate? COMPARE AND CONTRAST

- Things that are **endured** are put up with. *Dad endured reading me the same bedtime story when I was little because he knew it was my favorite.* What is an antonym for *endured*? ANTONYM

- **Obedience** is doing what you are told when you are told to do it. *Obedience is expected of all students during assemblies.* When is obedience important for public safety? DESCRIPTION

Objectives
- Generate questions
- Draw conclusions about the events of a story
- Use academic language: *generate questions, draw conclusions*

Materials
- Transparencies 4, 12a, 12b
- Practice Book, p. 102

Skills Trace
Draw Conclusions

Introduce	295A–295B
Practice/Apply	296–319; Practice Book, 102–103
Reteach/Review	325M–325Z, 477A–477B, 478–497, 503M–503Z; Practice Book, 165–166
Assess	Weekly Tests; Units 3, 4, 6 Tests
Maintain	361B, 745A–745B, 746–769, 773M–773Z, 797B

Academic Language
Preteach the following academic language words to ELL and Approaching Level students during Small Group time: *generate questions, draw conclusions*. See pages 325AA and 325I.

Reread for Comprehension

STRATEGY
GENERATE QUESTIONS

What Is It? With this strategy, students ask, or **generate questions** about, a text before, during, and after reading. The questions may be literal or higher-level. Good readers learn to generate questions such as these: *Do I understand what is taking place in this part of the story? What does this word or phrase mean? How does the setting affect events?*

Why Is It Important? Generating questions will help students check their understanding of the text and focus on important ideas.

SKILL
DRAW CONCLUSIONS

What Is It? Readers **draw conclusions** when they connect two or more pieces of information in a story. Then they use this information to arrive at a new understanding of a character's actions or an event in the story.

Why Is It Important? Point out that drawing conclusions helps students get more information and ideas from their reading. It can help them summarize the plot's main events, put the events in sequential order, and explain the events' influence on future events.

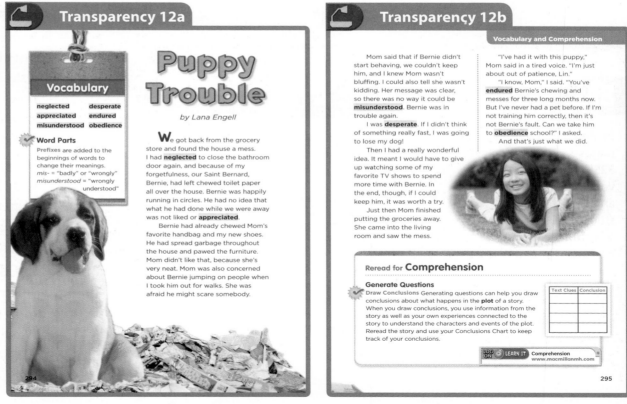

Student Book pages 294–295 available on Comprehension Transparencies 12a and 12b

- Point out that it is important to use evidence from the text to support one's conclusions. As students continue to read and get more information, they may want to revise their conclusions.

MODEL

How Do I Use It? Read aloud the first paragraph of "Puppy Trouble" from **Student Book** page 294. Model drawing a conclusion based on clues in the text.

Think Aloud The narrator says that she didn't close the bathroom door "again." I can conclude from this that she has forgotten to close it before. How many other times has Bernie made a mess with toilet paper? What other things has the puppy done in the past? I will keep reading to find out.

GUIDED PRACTICE

- Display **Transparency 4** to record text clues you identify and the conclusions you draw from them. Help students enter the first text clue and conclusion in the Conclusions Chart. (Clue: The narrator says she left the bathroom door open "again." Conclusion: The dog may have dragged the toilet paper around the house before.)

- Ask students what conclusions they can draw from the fact that Bernie "had no idea what he had done." (The narrator may not have known how to discipline Bernie properly in the past.) Have students add this conclusion to the Conclusions Chart.

APPLY

Have students reread the rest of the story and complete the Conclusions Chart. Remind them to reach their conclusions by using story clues and their own experiences related to the story. Ask them to include how things will work out for Lin and her dog, and to support their conclusions.

Quick Check

Can students draw conclusions based on evidence in the text?

During **Small Group Instruction**

Tier 2

If No → **Approaching Level** Reteach the skill using the Comprehension lesson, pp. 325M–325P.

If Yes → **On Level** Consolidate the learning using pp. 325U–325V.

Beyond Level Extend the learning using pp. 325Y–325Z.

Transparency 4

Conclusions Chart

Text Clues	Conclusion
The bathroom door was left open "again."	This has happened before.
Bernie does not know he has misbehaved.	Bernie has not been disciplined.
Lin says she has to spend more time with Bernie.	Lin will be with Bernie at obedience school.
Lin thinks she may not be training Bernie correctly.	There are correct and incorrect ways to train a dog.

Graphic Organizer Transparency

HOMEWORK   **Practice Book,** page 102

Sometimes authors don't explain how one plot event influences another, so you must **draw conclusions**. When you draw **conclusions**, you use information from the selection and your own prior experience connected to the reading selection.

Read the story. Answer the questions and draw conclusions.

Fred and Roberto lived next door to each other. Whenever Roberto looked out the window and saw that Fred's owner was taking him for a walk, Roberto would scratch at the front door and whine until Mrs. Marsh got his leash and took him out.

One day, Fred came bounding into Roberto's backyard. "I'm running away," he told Roberto. "Mr. Gomez doesn't appreciate the way I bring him his slippers when he comes home from work."

"Don't do it," Roberto advised Fred. "Give Mr. Gomez a little more time to get to know you. He will appreciate you when he gets to know you better."

"You may be right," Fred agreed. "I'll give him another chance."

1. Why did Roberto scratch on the door?
   He saw Fred going for a walk.

2. What happened after Roberto scratches on the door?
   Mrs. Marsh takes him out.

3. Why did Fred want to run away?
   His owner didn't appreciate him.

4. Why does Fred agree with Roberto?
   Fred agrees because Roberto's idea makes sense.

Approaching Reproducible, page 102
Beyond Reproducible, page 102

Read

WHOLE GROUP

✓ **MAIN SELECTION**
- *Dear Mrs. LaRue*
- Skill: Draw Conclusions

✓ **PAIRED SELECTION**
- Expository: "Dog Amazes Scientists!"
- Text Feature: Line Graph

SMALL GROUP

- Differentiated Instruction, pp. 325I–325HH

Main Selection

GENRE: Literary Text/Fiction

Point out that fantasy is a type of fiction. Read the definition of Fantasy on **Student Book** page 296. Students should look for events and situations that could not take place in real life.

STRATEGY
GENERATE QUESTIONS

Remind students that they can check their understanding of a selection by generating questions to clarify meaning. This strategy can also help them summarize the story's events and place them in the correct sequence.

SKILL
DRAW CONCLUSIONS

Remind students to look for clues in the text about the characters or events in the story when drawing conclusions. They should also consider what they know from their own experiences that relate to the reading selection.

Comprehension

Genre

A **Fantasy** is a story about characters and settings that could not exist in real life.

Generate Questions

Draw Conclusions
As you read, fill in your Conclusions Chart.

Text Clues	Conclusion

Read to Find Out

How close to reality are the events Ike is describing in his letters to Mrs. LaRue?

296

Vocabulary

Vocabulary Words Review the tested words: **neglected, appreciated, misunderstood, desperate, endured, obedience**.

Additional Selection Words Students may be unfamiliar with these words. Pronounce the words, give student-friendly explanations as needed, and help students use the previously taught vocabulary strategies: word parts, context clues, dictionary.

canine (p. 297): having to do with dogs

resident (p. 297): a person who lives in a particular place

established (p. 297): started a business meant to last a long time

melodramatic (p. 302): tending to exaggerate what is bad

visibly (p. 311): in a way that is easy to see

purchase (p. 315): to buy something

Mrs. LaRue
Letters from Obedience School
Written and Illustrated by
Mark Teague

Award Winning Selection

The Snort City Register / Gazette

September 30

LOCAL DOG ENTERS OBEDIENCE SCHOOL

"Ike LaRue"

Citing a long list of behavioral problems, Snort City resident Gertrude R. LaRue yesterday enrolled her dog, Ike, in the Igor Brotweiler Canine Academy.

Established in 1953, the Academy has a history of dealing with such issues.

"I'm at my wit's end!" said Mrs. LaRue. "I love Ike, but I'm afraid he's quite spoiled. He steals food right off the kitchen counter, chases the neighbor's cats, howls whenever I'm away, and last week while I was crossing the street he pulled me down and tore my best camel's hair coat! I just don't know what else to do!"

School officials were unavailable for comment . . .

297

Read the Main Selection

Preteach	Read Together	Read Independently
Have Approaching Level students and English Language Learners listen to the selection on **StudentWorks Plus**, the interactive e-Book, before reading with the class.	Use the prompts to guide comprehension and model how to complete the graphic organizer. Have students use **Think/Pair/Share** to discuss the selection.	If students can read the selection independently, have them read and complete the graphic organizer. Suggest that they use their purposes to choose their reading strategies.

LOG ON StudentWorks Plus
Interactive Student Book

Preview and Predict

Ask students to read the title, preview the illustrations, think about the genre, and write their predictions about what will happen. Will the story be humorous or serious? How can they tell?

Set Purposes

FOCUS QUESTION Discuss the "Read to Find Out" question on **Student Book** page 296. Remind students to look for the answer as they read and to set their own purposes for reading as well.

Point out the Conclusions Chart in the Student Book and on **Practice Book** page 103. Explain that students will fill it in as they read.

Read *Dear Mrs. LaRue*

Use the questions and Think Alouds to support instruction about the comprehension strategy and skill.

Practice Book, page 103

As you read *Dear Mrs. LaRue*, fill in the Conclusions Chart.

Text Clues	Conclusion

How does completing the Conclusions Chart help you to generate questions about *Dear Mrs. LaRue*?

Approaching Reproducible, page 103
Beyond Reproducible, page 103

Develop Comprehension

1 STRATEGY
GENERATE QUESTIONS

Teacher Think Aloud As I read, I can help myself make sure that I understand what is taking place in the story by asking **questions** and looking for the answers. I notice that the text on page 298 is made to look like a letter. The letter is signed with the name "Ike." Here are some questions I could ask: *Is Ike the dog? Who is Mrs. LaRue? Why was Ike sent there? Is the school as bad as the letter says?* I will keep reading to find out.

2 GENRE: Literary Text/Fiction

What information can you find on page 298 that lets you know that this story is a fantasy and not realistic? (The sign in front of the Academy says, "Welcome dogs!," but dogs cannot read. Ike is shown using his paws to mail a letter, but dogs cannot write or mail letters.)

Dear Mrs. LaRue,

October 1

How could you do this to me? This is a PRISON, not a school! You should see the other dogs. They are BAD DOGS, Mrs. LaRue! I do not fit in. Even the journey here was a horror. I am very unhappy and may need something to chew on when I get home. Please come right away!

Sincerely,

Ike

1

2 **3**

298

Monitor Comprehension

Monitor and Clarify: *Adjust Reading Rate*

Explain Tell students that they can adjust their reading rate if they do not understand plot events after rereading or asking themselves questions. Explain to students how to increase and decrease their reading rate to improve comprehension.

Discuss Ask students whether they should slow down or speed up their reading rates when reading dialogue and why. (Students may say that they would read more slowly so that listeners can tell when they speak as different characters.)

Apply As students read the selection, have them experiment with different reading rates for passages of dialogue and passages of narration.

IGOR
BROTWEILER
CANINE
ACADEMY

299

Develop Comprehension

3 CHARACTER

SPIRAL REVIEW What were Ike's feelings toward Mrs. LaRue? What have you learned so far about their relationship based on his letter? (There is tension between Ike and Mrs. LaRue. Ike is upset that Mrs. LaRue sent him to obedience school. Yet he likes Mrs. LaRue and wants to go home to her. Mrs. LaRue must be having a difficult time with Ike, which is why she sent him to obedience school.)

4 SKILL
DRAW CONCLUSIONS

 Look carefully at the illustrations on pages 298 and 299. What **conclusions** can you draw about Ike's description of the Academy? (The illustration on page 298 shows the Academy in a very positive light. The illustration on 299 shows it very negatively. This second illustration seems to be Ike's point of view, which is an inaccurate portrayal of what life is really like at the Academy.) How might this affect future events? (Ike may continue to report events inaccurately.)

Phonics/Word Study

APPLY DECODING SKILLS While reading, point out words with the sound/spelling patterns, syllable types, and word parts students have recently learned. Help students blend these words. You may wish to focus on selection words with silent letters, such as *know* and *honestly*.

Develop Comprehension

5 STRATEGY
WORD PARTS

On page 301, in the second paragraph, what does the word *mistreated* mean? (It means "treated badly.") Explain how knowing the meaning of the **prefix** *mis-* helps you figure out the meaning of *mistreated*. (The prefix *mis-* means "wrong," "bad," or "badly." When it is added to *treated*, the word means "treated badly.")

300

October 2

Dear Mrs. LaRue,

    Were you really upset about the chicken pie? You know, you might have discussed it with me. You could have said, "Ike, don't eat the chicken pie. I'm saving it for dinner." Would that have been so difficult? It would have prevented a lot of hard feelings.

    Needless to say, I am being horribly mistreated. You say I should be patient and accept that I'll be here through the term. Are you aware that the term lasts TWO MONTHS? Do you know how long that is in dog years?

Sincerely,

Ike

5

> ✓ **Draw Conclusions**
> What can you conclude about Ike from his letters?

6

Develop Comprehension

6 SKILL
DRAW CONCLUSIONS

✓ **What can you conclude about Ike from his letters?** (From the evidence in Ike's letter it is possible to conclude that he ate Mrs. LaRue's chicken pie. In the illustration on page 300, he is eating only one piece with a knife and fork. In reality, he probably devoured the whole pie, like a real dog would do. We also see from the newspaper article on page 297 that Ike misbehaved in additional ways. For example, he chased the neighbor's cats. Mrs. LaRue sent Ike to obedience school to teach him better behavior.) **Enter this information on your Conclusions Chart.**

Text Clues	Conclusion
Ike ate Mrs. LaRue's chicken pie. He also misbehaved in other ways, including chasing the neighbor's cats.	Mrs. LaRue sent ike to obedience school to teach him better behavior.

Develop Comprehension

7 MAKE INFERENCES

What is the most likely reason Ike tells Mrs. LaRue about the Hibbins' cats? (Ike wants to take the blame away from himself. He tells Mrs. LaRue that the cats are not the angels Mrs. Hibbins says they are and claims not to know why they were on the fire escape in January. It seems clear that Ike chased the cats onto the fire escape, and this is one of the reasons Mrs. LaRue sent him to obedience school.)

October 3

7

Dear Mrs. LaRue,

I'd like to clear up some misconceptions about the Hibbins' cats. First, they are hardly the little angels Mrs. Hibbins makes them out to be. Second, how should I know what they were doing out on the fire escape in the middle of January? They were being a bit melodramatic, don't you think, the way they cried and refused to come down? It's hard to believe they were really sick for three whole days, but you know cats.

Your dog,

Ike

8

302

Comprehension

Literary Devices: *Conflict and Resolution*

Explain A conflict, or struggle between two forces, is central to a story's plot. The conflict can be between two characters or between a character and another force, such as nature or society. When a conflict is brought to an end, there has been a *resolution*. Usually a story has one main conflict, but it may include multiple small ones.

Discuss Have students reread Ike's letter on page 302. Ask: *What conflict does Ike hint at? Which characters are involved in it?* (A conflict occurs between Ike and the cats. Ike probably led the cats onto the fire escape and then kept them from coming down.)

Apply Ike does not mention any resolution to this conflict. Do students think the conflict was resolved? If so, how? (Students may say it was partially resolved when the cats came back inside.)

Develop Comprehension

8 USE ILLUSTRATIONS

In this letter, Ike tells Mrs. LaRue what happened with the Hibbins' cats. Look at the black and white illustration. Does this show what actually happened, or what Ike wants Mrs. LaRue to believe? Why? (The illustration is drawn to show Ike imagining the scene. He is trying to be nice to the cats, offering them food, but they are being mean. One even thumbs his nose at Ike. It is probably not what actually happened.)

Develop Comprehension

9 **SKILL**
DRAW CONCLUSIONS

What **conclusions** can you draw about Ike's opinion of himself and of Mrs. LaRue from his letter of October 4? (You can tell from the letter that Ike has a very high opinion of himself. He thinks that the tasks he is supposed to be learning are ridiculous and beneath him. He implies that Mrs. LaRue is not skilled enough to cross the street on her own. He says he saved her life and she wasn't very grateful. Finally, he points out that she needs him) **Add this information to your Conclusions Chart.**

Text Clues	Conclusion
Ike ate Mrs. LaRue's chicken pie. He also misbehaved in other ways, including chasing the neighbor's cats.	Mrs. LaRue sent ike to obedience school to teach him better behavior.
Ike complains that the training is silly. He says Mrs. LaRue doesn't appreciate that he saved her from an accident.	Ike has a very high opinion of himself, and thinks Mrs. LaRue cannot get along without him.

October 4

Dear Mrs. LaRue,

You should see what goes on around here. The way my teach — I mean WARDEN, Miss Klondike, barks orders is shocking. Day after day I'm forced to perform the most meaningless tasks. Today it was "sit" and "roll over," all day long. I flatly refused to roll over. It's ridiculous. I won't do it. Of course I was SEVERELY punished.

And another thing: Who will help you cross the street while I'm away? You know you have a bad habit of not looking both ways. Think of all the times I've saved you. Well, there was that one time, anyway. I must say you weren't very grateful, complaining on and on about the tiny rip in your ratty old coat. But the point is, you need me!

Yours,

Ike

9

304

Vocabulary

Word Structure Clues: *Root Words*

Explain/Model Explain that good readers sometimes use their knowledge of root or base words to figure out the meanings of unfamiliar words in a passage.

Think Aloud: I'm not sure what the word *meaningless* means. Inside the word, though, I see the base word *meaning*. I realize that *-less must be a suffix*. I know what *meaning* means. Now I look up the definition of the suffix *-less and see that it often means* "without." Now I know that *meaningless* means "without meaning."

Practice/Apply Have students use their knowledge of root or base words to figure out the meanings of more difficult words they encounter. For example, they can take apart the word *hardship* on page 310 to figure out its meaning.

Dear Mrs. LaRue,

October 5

The GUARDS here are all caught up in this "good dog, bad dog" thing. I hear it constantly: "Good dog, Ike. Don't be a bad dog, Ike." Is it really so good to sit still like a lummox all day? Nevertheless, I refuse to be broken!

Miss Klondike has taken my typewriter. She claims it disturbs the other dogs. Does anybody care that the other dogs disturb ME?

Yours,

Ike

305

Develop Comprehension

10 STRATEGY
GENERATE QUESTIONS

Teacher Think Aloud In all the color illustrations, I see that the Brotweiler Canine Academy looks nothing like the place Ike describes in his letters to Mrs. LaRue. Since the author is also the illustrator, I can **generate questions** about the way the illustrations add to the story. How do they make the story more enjoyable? They make Ike's letters even funnier. What other questions can you ask about the effect the illustrations have on your understanding of the story?

PARTNERS Prompt students to apply the strategy in a Think Aloud by having them generate questions based on the illustrations.

Student Think Aloud How do the illustrations help me learn about Ike? I see that on page 305 Ike has a book called *Nasty Dungeons of the World* in his room. This is funny, not only because dogs can't read, but because it tells me that this is where, in the story, Ike is getting details to use in his description of the school. Next to the book there is a can of gourmet dog food, so the reality is very different. Ike obviously exaggerates and bends the truth.

Develop Comprehension

11 **SKILL**
DRAW CONCLUSIONS

Drawing conclusions can help you summarize the plot's main events and explain their influence on future events. Look at the title of the book Ike is reading on page 306. Put this fact together with other details in the text to conclude how it might influence future events in the story. (On page 306 Ike is reading a book called *50 Great Escapes*. Since Ike has been reading books like *Nasty Dungeons of the World* to help him describe the "horrible" conditions at the Academy in his letters, he may use details from *50 Great Escapes* to tell Mrs. LaRue about his escape from the Academy.)

11

Dear Mrs. LaRue,   October 6

Were the neighbors really complaining about my howling? It is hard to imagine. First, I didn't howl that much. You were away those nights, so you wouldn't know, but trust me, it was quite moderate. Second, let's recall that these are the same neighbors who are constantly waking ME up in the middle of the afternoon with their loud vacuuming. I say we all have to learn to get along.

My life here continues to be a nightmare. You wouldn't believe what goes on in the cafeteria.

Sincerely,

Ike

P.S. I don't want to alarm you, but the thought of escape has crossed my mind!

306

Text Evidence

Draw Conclusions

Reread question 12 aloud to students. Then ask, *What questions can you raise to help you draw conclusions about Ike's illness?* (Answers will include: *What are Ike's symptoms? Do they sound believable? Does Ike seem to exaggerate here as he does in his other letters? What does the doctor say about Ike's condition?*) *How might you go about finding the answers to these questions? Point to the information when you find it.* (Students would want to reread the letter on page 307, and analyze each detail. They may also want to reread previous letters, to see if the tone here is the same or different from other letters, and if Ike seems any more sincere this time.)

October 7

Dear Mrs. LaRue,

I hate to tell you this, but I am terribly ill. It started in my paw, causing me to limp all day. Later I felt queasy, so that I could barely eat dinner (except for the yummy gravy). Then I began to moan and howl. Finally, I had to be taken to the vet. Dr. Wilfrey claims that he can't find anything wrong with me, but I am certain I have an awful disease. I must come home at once.

Honestly yours,

Ike

> **Draw Conclusions**
> Is Ike's illness real? Explain using details from the story.
>
> **12**

13

307

Develop Comprehension

12 **SKILL**
DRAW CONCLUSIONS

 Is Ike's illness real? Explain using details from the story. (Ike describes his illness with strong words, but his symptoms do not seem real. He claims to have a stomachache but eats the yummy gravy. The doctor cannot find anything wrong. Ike is not really sick. He is just pretending so he can go home.) Add information to your Conclusions Chart.

Text Clues	Conclusion
Ike ate Mrs. LaRue's chicken pie. He also misbehaved in other ways, including chasing the neighbor's cats.	Mrs. LaRue sent Ike to obedience school to teach him better behavior.
Ike complains that the training is silly. He says Mrs. LaRue doesn't appreciate that he saved her from an accident.	Ike has a very high opinion of himself, and thinks Mrs. LaRue cannot get along without him.
Ike's symptoms don't seem real. His complaints seem extremely exaggerated. He is able to eat the food he likes. The doctor says nothing is wrong with him.	Ike is pretending to be sick so he will be sent home.

13 **SELF-SELECTED STRATEGY USE**

What strategies have you used to help understand the story? Where did you use them? Why? How did they help?

RETURN TO PREDICTIONS AND PURPOSES

Have students confirm or revise their predictions and purposes for reading. Encourage them to revise or write additional questions to help focus their attention as they continue to read the selection.

Stop here if you wish to read this selection over two days.

Develop Comprehension

14 **SUMMARIZE**

How would you **summarize** Ike's stay at Brotweiler Canine Academy so far? (Ike calls it a prison and insists that he does not belong there with the "bad dogs." He writes to Mrs. LaRue every day, arguing with her about her reasons for sending him to obedience school and telling her about the horrible conditions there. Though he complains about the staff and training, his life at the Academy seems quite pleasant. The worst thing that has happened is that his noisy typewriter has been taken away. Pretending to be ill is his most recent trick to try and get sent home.)

Comprehension

Evaluating Information

Explain Tell students when reading for information it is important to think about the source of the information. They can ask themselves questions as they read: *Is this source reliable? Does the author back up statements with facts? Is information missing or unclear?*

Discuss Ask students if they think Ike would be an accurate source of information about obedience schools for dogs. Why or why not? What might be a better source?

Apply Provide students with a book review or editorial from a newspaper. Read the article aloud. Have students offer opinions about the accuracy of the information in the article using evidence from the text. Discuss what other sources they could use to verify the information in the article.

October 8

Dear Mrs. LaRue,

Thank you for the lovely get well card. Still, I'm a little surprised that you didn't come get me. I know what Dr. Wilfrey says, but is it really wise to take risks with one's health? I could have a relapse, you know.

With fall here, I think about all the fine times we used to have in the park. Remember how sometimes you would bring along a tennis ball? You would throw it and I would retrieve it EVERY TIME, except for once when it landed in something nasty and I brought you back a stick instead. Ah, how I miss those days.

Yours truly,

Ike

P.S. Imagine how awful it is for me to be stuck inside my tiny cell!

P.P.S. I still feel pretty sick.

309

Develop Comprehension

15 CHARACTER

SPIRAL REVIEW Think about Ike's **character** traits and motivations. Why does Ike write the letter on page 309? Has Ike changed since he first entered the Academy? (Since Ike's other plans failed, he has come up with a new one—to talk about the "good old days," so Mrs. LaRue will miss him and send him back home. We see from this letter that Ike still has not changed. He still does not think he has done anything wrong, and he still spends all his time and energy trying to figure out ways to get sent back home.)

Develop Comprehension

16 SKILL

DRAW CONCLUSIONS

✔ How does Ike "escape" from the Academy? (Since he was never really a prisoner, he probably just leaves. The illustrations show him with a suitcase and riding in a taxi, so he probably did not have to sneak out or worry about being caught, as he suggests in his letter.)

October 9

Dear Mrs. LaRue,

By the time you read this I will be gone. I have decided to attempt a daring escape! I'm sorry it has come to this, since I am really a very good dog, but frankly you left me no choice. How sad it is not to be **appreciated**! From now on I'll wander from town to town without a home — or even any dog food, most likely. Such is the life of a **desperate** outlaw. I will try to write to you from time to time as I carry on with my life of hardship and danger.

Your lonely fugitive,

16

Ike

310

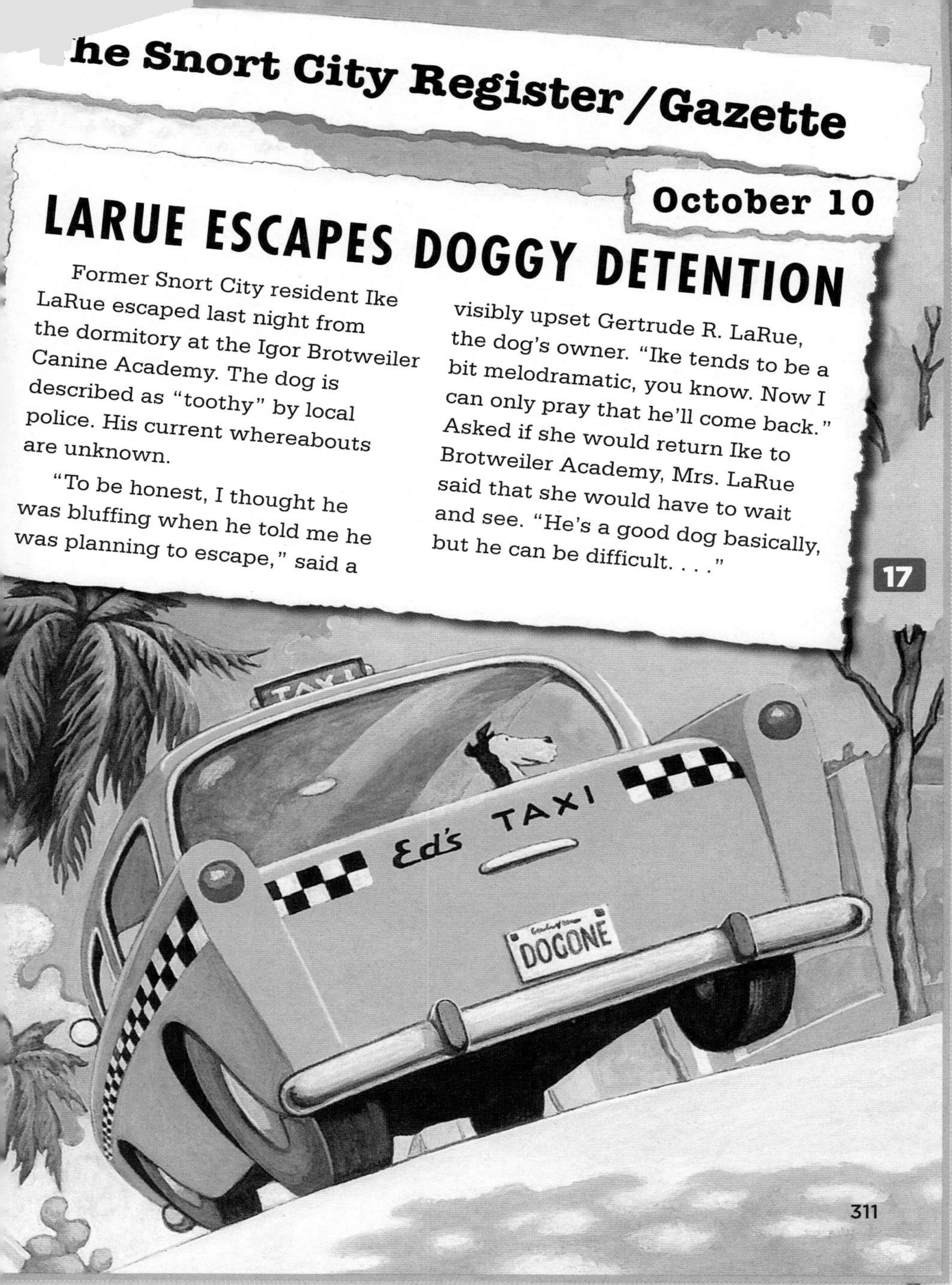

The Snort City Register/Gazette

October 10

LARUE ESCAPES DOGGY DETENTION

Former Snort City resident Ike LaRue escaped last night from the dormitory at the Igor Brotweiler Canine Academy. The dog is described as "toothy" by local police. His current whereabouts are unknown.

"To be honest, I thought he was bluffing when he told me he was planning to escape," said a visibly upset Gertrude R. LaRue, the dog's owner. "Ike tends to be a bit melodramatic, you know. Now I can only pray that he'll come back." Asked if she would return Ike to Brotweiler Academy, Mrs. LaRue said that she would have to wait and see. "He's a good dog basically, but he can be difficult. . . ."

TAXI
Ed's TAXI
DOGONE

17

311

Develop Comprehension

17 GENRE: Literary Text/Fiction

Is the newspaper story about Ike's escape realistic or a fantasy? How do you know? How does this affect what you think might happen in the story? (Fantasy. The article is written as if Ike were human, when really he is a dog. The town is called Snort City, which sounds made up, especially since dogs snort. Mrs. LaRue says that Ike can be "melodramatic," which is a term you would use to describe a person, not a dog.)

ELL ENGLISH LANGUAGE LEARNERS

STRATEGIES FOR EXTRA SUPPORT

Question 17 GENRE: Literary Text/Fiction

Practice Vocabulary Remind students of the meanings of the terms *realistic* and *fantasy*. Give familiar examples as necessary. Then direct students' attention to the name of the newspaper on page 311. Read the article aloud with them and discuss the information it contains about Ike and Mrs. LaRue. Have students say why they think the information seems realistic or like something from a fantasy. Help students express their ideas. Then restate or clarify their responses.

Develop Comprehension

18 **SKILL**
DRAW CONCLUSIONS

What **conclusions** can you draw about Ike's travels as he "escapes" the Academy? (Ike says he continues to suffer as he travels, but it has only been one day since he "escaped" from the Academy. Ike uses melodramatic language to describe his "wanderings." For example, he says that he is roaming "this barren wasteland." Yet the illustration shows that he is quite comfortable, and that he is even eating in a restaurant. Ike seems to be having a pleasurable trip.) **Add this information to your Conclusions Chart.**

Text Clues	Conclusion
Ike ate Mrs. LaRue's chicken pie. He also misbehaved in other ways, including chasing the neighbor's cats.	Mrs. LaRue sent Ike to obedience school to teach him better behavior.
Ike complains that the training is silly. He says Mrs. LaRue doesn't appreciate that he saved her from an accident.	Ike has a very high opinion of himself, and thinks Mrs. LaRue cannot get along without him.
Ike's symptoms don't seem real. His complaints seem extremely exaggerated. He is able to eat the food he likes. The doctor says nothing is wrong with him.	Ike is pretending to be sick so he will be sent home.
Ike uses more melodramatic language, which makes what he says unbelievable. The color illustrations show he is quite comfortable.	Ike is having a pleasurable trip.

October 11 — Somewhere in America

Dear Mrs. LaRue,

18 I continue to suffer horribly as I roam this barren wasteland. Who knows where my wanderings will take me now? Hopefully to someplace with yummy food! Remember the special treats you used to make for me? I miss them. I miss our nice, comfy apartment. But mostly, I miss you!

Your sad dog,

Ike

P.S. I even miss the Hibbins' cats, in a way.

312

October 12 — Still Somewhere

Dear Mrs. LaRue,

The world is a hard and cruel place for a "stray" dog. You would scarcely believe the misery I've **endured**. So I have decided to return home. You may try to lock me up again, but that is a risk I must take. And frankly, even more than myself, I worry about you. You may not know it, Mrs. LaRue, but you need a dog!

Your **misunderstood** friend,

Ike

19

313

Develop Comprehension

19 STRATEGY
GENERATE QUESTIONS

What **questions** can you ask to help you decide what causes Ike to return home?

Student Think Aloud Ike says he has suffered, but what is the real reason he wants to go home? He has only been out on his own for a couple of days. Why is he willing to risk being sent to "prison" again? Is he just lonely? Yes, he says he misses the apartment and especially Mrs. LaRue. He also realizes that being home is easier than being on his own. Will he ever admit that Mrs. LaRue was right to send him to the Academy? Probably not.

Develop Comprehension

20 SKILL
DRAW CONCLUSIONS

Based on evidence in the text so far, do you think Ike actually saved Mrs. LaRue's life, or was this another event he imagined or exaggerated, like being put in a cell at the Academy? (It seems likely that this is another exaggeration, since Ike dramatized and stretched the truth about conditions at the Academy and his "imprisonment" inside a cell.) Add this information to your Chart.

Text Clues	Conclusion
Ike ate Mrs. LaRue's chicken pie. He also misbehaved in other ways, including chasing the neighbor's cats.	Mrs. LaRue sent Ike to obedience school to teach him better behavior.
Ike complains that the training is silly. He says Mrs. LaRue doesn't appreciate that he saved her from an accident.	Ike has a very high opinion of himself, and thinks Mrs. LaRue cannot get along without him.
Ike's symptoms don't seem real. His complaints seem extremely exaggerated. He is able to eat the food he likes. The doctor says nothing is wrong with him.	Ike is pretending to be sick so he will be sent home.
Ike uses more melodramatic language, which makes what he says unbelievable. The color illustrations show he is quite comfortable.	Ike is having a pleasurable trip.
Ike ran away from the Academy. He exaggerated the conditions there, as well as the details about his escape.	It is doubtful that Ike actually saved Mrs. LaRue's life.

314

The Snort City Register/Gazette

October 13

HERO DOG SAVES OWNER! [20]

Ike LaRue, until recently a student at the Igor Brotweiler Canine Academy, returned to Snort City yesterday in dramatic fashion. In fact he arrived just in time to rescue his owner, Gertrude R. LaRue of Second Avenue, from an oncoming truck. Mrs. LaRue had made the trip downtown to purchase a new camel's hair coat. Apparently she **neglected** to look both ways before stepping out into traffic.

The daring rescue was witnessed by several onlookers, including patrolman Newton Smitzer. "He rolled right across two lanes of traffic to get at her," said Smitzer. "It was really something. I haven't seen rolling like that since I left the police academy." [21]

315

Develop Comprehension

[21] **SKILL**
DRAW CONCLUSIONS

Is this an accurate report of what happened when Ike returned home? (The newspaper report could be Ike's fantasy. It is not clear whether he really saved Mrs. LaRue or if he was just being troublesome again.)

Develop Comprehension

22 **SKILL**
DRAW CONCLUSIONS

Have Ike's experiences at obedience school and afterward changed him? Explain your answer. (He still believes he is a hero. He is responsible for tearing Mrs. LaRue's coat again. He still gets to eat chicken pie. He may have succeeded in getting Mrs. LaRue to think differently about him, but no, he has not really changed.) Use this information to complete your Conclusions Chart.

Text Clues	Conclusion
Ike ate Mrs. LaRue's chicken pie. He also misbehaved in other ways, including chasing the neighbor's cats.	Mrs. LaRue sent Ike to obedience school to teach him better behavior.
Ike complains that the training is silly. He says Mrs. LaRue doesn't appreciate that he saved her from an accident.	Ike has a very high opinion of himself, and thinks Mrs. LaRue cannot get along without him.
Ike's symptoms don't seem real. His complaints seem extremely exaggerated. He is able to eat the food he likes. The doctor says nothing is wrong with him.	Ike is pretending to be sick so he will be sent home.
Ike uses more melodramatic language, which makes what he says unbelievable. The color illustrations show he is quite comfortable.	Ike is having a pleasurable trip.
Ike ran away from the Academy. He exaggerated the conditions there, as well as the details about his escape.	It is doubtful that Ike actually saved Mrs. LaRue's life.
Ike believes he is a hero. He tears Mrs. LaRue's coat again. He eats chicken pie again.	Ike has not really changed.

Mrs. LaRue was unhurt in the incident, though her coat was badly torn. "I don't care about that," she said. "I'm just happy to have my Ike back home where he belongs!"

LaRue said she plans to throw a big party for the dog. "All the neighbors will be there, and I'm going to serve Ike's favorite dishes. . . ."

316

Listening/Speaking

Have selected students share their Personal Response letters. Remind students to establish a context that will help their listeners imagine the events as Mrs. LaRue might describe them. Listeners should ask thoughtful questions, and presenters should respond by offering further relevant details. After students listen to the final presenter, say: *Let's check our understanding. Turn to a partner and retell the events from the last letter.* Use students' retellings to check their listening comprehension.

"... I'll bet he can't wait to taste the chicken pie. . . ." **22**

WELCOME HOME

IKE

Ike

Ike

317

Develop Comprehension

RETURN TO PREDICTIONS AND PURPOSES

Review students' **predictions** and **purposes** for reading. Did they find out if the picture Ike is painting in his letters to Mrs. LaRue reflects reality?

REVIEW READING STRATEGIES

- **Generate Questions** In what ways did generating questions help you to understand the selection?

- **Monitor and Clarify: Adjust Reading Rate** Do you understand the strategy of adjusting reading rate as you read different sections of text? When might you use it again?

- **Decoding** What difficult words did you encounter? How did the Reading Multisyllabic Words strategy help you sound out these words?

- **Self-Selected Strategy Use** What strategies did you use to make sense of what you read? Where? How were these strategies helpful?

PERSONAL RESPONSE

Have students write a letter as Mrs. LaRue, retelling a particular event from the story. Then have them create a different ending using her point of view. Remind them to use details from the story in the letter.

Quick Check

Can students draw conclusions?

During **Small Group Instruction**

If No → **Approaching Level** Reteach the skill and have students apply it to a simpler text. Use Leveled Reader lessons, pp. 325N–325P.

If Yes → **On Level** Have students apply the skill to a new text to consolidate learning. Use Leveled Reader lessons, pp. 325U–325V.

Gifted Talented **Beyond Level** Have students apply the skill to a more complex text to extend learning. Use Leveled Reader lessons, pp. 325Y–325Z.

Author and Illustrator

WRITE HOME ABOUT MARK TEAGUE

Have students read the biography of the author and illustrator. Ask:

- What types of things do you think Mark Teague has seen real dogs do?

- The title of the book is taken from the letter format. What might be another appropriate title? Support your answer with details from the text.

- How do the illustrations drawn by Mark Teague make the story even funnier?

WRITE ABOUT IT

Encourage students to continue the newspaper theme in *Dear Mrs. LaRue*. Have them write a review of the book for a newspaper. They may want to discuss how the letter format shows the conflict in a humorous way.

Author's Purpose

Mark Teague used his experiences with two dogs from his childhood to write *Dear Mrs. LaRue*. He took the characteristics of each dog and rolled them into the character of Ike. Most of the story is written in first person, from Ike's point of view.

Write Home About
Mark Teague

Mark Teague says that this story is one of his favorites. He had lots of fun pretending he was Ike and writing from a dog's point of view. Mark based Ike on two dogs he and his brother had. One dog loved to eat, the other dog liked to play tricks. Now Mark has cats. He put them in this story, too. Mark gets ideas for many of his books from things he did as a boy. Then he adds a twist or two to make his stories really funny.

Other books by Mark Teague

LOG ON ▶ **FIND OUT**
Author Mark Teague
www.macmillanmh.com

★ Author's Purpose

What experiences from his real life did Mark Teague use to write *Dear Mrs. LaRue*? Explain if he wrote the story using the first-person or third-person point of view.

318

Author's Craft
Text Features

Text features are graphics that accompany stories. Sometimes they make stories more realistic.

- Have students look at the letter from Ike to Mrs. LaRue on page 298.

- Discuss how the letter format makes the letter seem more realistic than if it had been written as just part of the story.

- Have students look for and discuss the effects of the letter and how it creates humor.

Comprehension Check

Summarize

To summarize *Dear Mrs. LaRue* use the most important details from the selection. Information from your Conclusions Chart may help you.

Text Clues	Conclusion

Think and Compare

1. Who took Ike's typewriter away? Details

2. Mrs. LaRue's coat is torn twice. How is her reaction the first time it is torn different from her reaction the second time it is torn? Compare and Contrast

3. Why did Ike decide to escape from **obedience** school? Explain using details from the story. Generate Questions: Draw Conclusions

4. The author tells the story from Ike's point of view. What clues does the author give to show the reader that Ike's letters are full of exaggeration? Author's Craft

5. Compare the events and characters in "Puppy Trouble" and *Dear Mrs. LaRue*. Use details from both selections in your answer. Reading/Writing Across Texts

319

Make Connections

Text-to-Self Have students respond to the following question to make connections to their own lives. Use the Think Aloud to model a response. *If you were Mrs. LaRue, would you believe Ike?*

Think Aloud: To answer this, I would try to remember how Ike acted at home, and reread his letters. At home, according to the first newspaper article, Ike misbehaved. Yet he never admitted to doing anything wrong. Rereading Ike's letters, I see they are exaggerated. If I were Mrs. LaRue, I would not believe Ike.

Text-to-World Have students respond to the following question to make connections to the world. Use the Think Aloud to model a response. *Why do you think people exaggerate?*

Think Aloud: To answer this question, I would need to think about why Ike might have exaggerated. Ike wanted attention. He also seemed to enjoy making up an exciting story. Maybe people exaggerate for the same reasons.

Comprehension Check

TEST PREP

SUMMARIZE

Have partners summarize *Dear Mrs. LaRue* orally.

THINK AND COMPARE

Text Evidence

1. **Details** <u>Answer stated in text</u> Miss Klondike took Ike's typewriter. LOCATE

2. **Compare and Contrast** <u>Answer stated in text</u> The first time Mrs. LaRue is upset with Ike and sends him to obedience school. The second time she is just happy to have him home. COMBINE

3. **Generate Questions: Draw Conclusions** <u>Answer</u> Although obedience school was not horrible, as Ike had claimed, he wanted to be home with Mrs. LaRue. <u>Evidence</u> Ike howls when Mrs. LaRue is away. He tries to get her to bring him home, even though life at the Academy is pleasant. Ike reminisces about good times with Mrs. LaRue. It is clear that he misses her. CONNECT

4. **Author's Craft** <u>Answer</u> He uses black and white illustrations to show events that are clearly exaggerated, and he uses melodramatic language. <u>Evidence</u> Ike is shown escaping from an old-fashioned prison, wearing an old-fashioned prison uniform. He calls himself a "fugitive." ANALYZE

5. **Text-to-Text** In both stories the dogs misbehaved. In "Puppy Trouble" the dog left chewed toilet paper around the house. In *Dear Mrs. LaRue*, Ike knocked Mrs. LaRue down. Both dogs were sent to obedience school. In "Puppy Trouble" the dog learned to behave. In *Dear Mrs. LaRue* Ike did not change at all. COMPARE TEXT

Objectives

- Read fluently with expression
- Rate: 102–122 WCPM

Materials

- Transparency 12
- Practice Book, p. 104
- Fluency Solutions Audio CD

ELL

Read with Expression
Read the passage and discuss what Ike says and how he feels. Explain words such as *fit in, a horror,* and *chew.* Echo-read the passage with students, and have them mimic the expressiveness of your voice.

Practice Book, page 104

As I read, I will pay attention to expression.

	Presidents have kept a wide range of pets. These
9	animals have included cows, mice, goats, and birds. But
18	dogs have been the most popular presidential pets.
26	Dogs are loyal and loving. They make their owners
35	feel appreciated. Like other dog owners, many Presidents
43	have enjoyed the special friendship that dogs can give.
52	Many people believe that dogs help Presidents gain
60	support from Americans. Pictures of Presidents playing
67	with their dogs can make the Presidents seem likable and
77	help them win votes.
81	More than 200 dogs of various breeds have lived at the
91	White House. Some of these White House dogs served
100	as guard dogs. Others played with the Presidents' children.
109	And others clearly belonged to the Presidents and were
118	their personal four-legged friends. A few presidential
125	pooches were even as well known as their masters. Let's
135	take a look at some of the famous "First Dogs" of America. 147

Comprehension Check

1. Why might people vote for a candidate who has a dog as a pet? **Cause and Effect** People think a candidate who has a dog as a pet is probably a likable person.
2. Why did the author write this passage about presidential dogs? **Author's Purpose** The author wants you to know that presidential dogs help presidents in a number of ways.

	Words Read	–	Number of Errors	=	Words Correct Score
First Read		–		=	
Second Read		–		=	

Approaching Reproducible, page 104

Beyond Reproducible, page 104

Fluency

Repeated Reading: Expression

EXPLAIN/MODEL Explain that paying attention to punctuation will help students read with expression, to capture the meaning and emotion of the words. Read **Transparency 12** aloud. Point out that the words written in capital letters should be read with emphasis. Read one sentence at a time. Have students echo-read.

> **Transparency 12**
>
> Dear Mrs. LaRue,
>
> How could you do this to me? This is a PRISON, not a school! You should see the other dogs. They are BAD DOGS, Mrs. LaRue! I do not fit in. Even the journey here was a horror. I am very unhappy and may need something to chew on when I get home. Please come right away!
>
> Sincerely,
>
> Ike

Fluency (from *Dear Mrs. LaRue,* p. 298)

PRACTICE/APPLY Divide students into two groups. The first group reads the passage a sentence at a time. The second group echo-reads. Then groups switch roles. Remind students to read expressively, in ways that demonstrate their comprehension of what they are reading.

 DAILY FLUENCY Students will practice fluency using **Practice Book** page 104 or the **Fluency Solutions Audio CD**. The passage is recorded at a slow practice speed and a faster fluent speed.

Quick Check

Can students read fluently with expression?

During **Small Group Instruction**

If No → **Approaching Level** Use the Fluency lesson and model, p. 325Q.

If Yes → **On Level** See Fluency, p. 325T.

Beyond Level See Fluency, p. 325X.

Comprehension

REVIEW SKILL
CHARACTER

EXPLAIN/MODEL

- Authors use various methods to show what kinds of people or animals the **characters** in the story are. For example, an author may provide detailed descriptions of the characters, or the author may establish what the characters are like through their actions.

- Authors may also provide clues to a character's traits through the character's thoughts or his or her interaction with other characters.

Lead a discussion about the characters in "Puppy Trouble." Students should answer questions such as these: *What is Lin's character? What is her relationship with her mother? Does Lin's character change?*

PRACTICE/APPLY

Have partners discuss the characters in *Dear Mrs. LaRue*, using the following questions. Have them jot down important details that give textual evidence supporting their inferences and conclusions.

- How would you describe Ike's character? (Ike is melodramatic and is always exaggerating. He is also imaginative and smart. He thinks highly of himself and will not admit to doing anything wrong.)

- Based on what you read in his letters, how do you think Ike would describe his own character? (He would say he is a very well-behaved dog that helps his owner, and he is just misunderstood.)

- How would you describe the relationship between Ike and Mrs. LaRue? (They care about each other but are currently at odds. Ike is upset that Mrs. LaRue sent him to obedience school. Mrs. LaRue is fed up with Ike's behavior and wants to discipline him.)

- Did this relationship change over time? (Yes. Mrs. LaRue became worried about Ike, and was happy to have him back home, even though his behavior did not change.)

- Would you like to have a pet like Ike? Why or why not? (Students might say they would like a pet with personality, like Ike. Others might say they would not want a dog that misbehaved.)

Direct students to make connections, take a position, and share their ideas. Have them compare the dog in this story with dogs they know from other stories, films, or television shows, or dogs they know from real life.

PRACTICE BOOK See **Practice Book** page 105 for Following Directions.

Objectives

- Analyze characters and their relationships
- Describe changes that characters undergo

Skills Trace

Character, Setting, Plot

Introduce	41A–41B
Practice/ Apply	42–59; Practice Book, 12–13
Reteach/ Review	65M–65Z, 81A–81B, 82–97, 103M–103Z; Practice Book, 30–31
Assess	Weekly Tests; Units 1, 3 Tests
Maintain	121B, 319B, 371A–371B, 372–391, 395M–395Z, 429B

Test Practice

Answering Questions

To apply **answering questions strategies** to content-area reading, see pages 93–100 in *Time For Kids*.

Paired Selection

GENRE: Informational Text/Expository

Have students read the bookmark on **Student Book** page 320. Explain that a news story is one kind of expository text, and that a news story

- is factual, accurate, and up-to-date;
- answers the questions *who, what, when, where*, and *why*;
- tells about local, national, or world events;
- may tell an interesting true story, called a *human interest story*.

Text Feature: Line Graphs

EXPLAIN Point out the line graph on page 321. Have students read the title. Discuss how to read a line graph.

- **Labels** up the left-hand side and across the bottom explain what the numbers or points on the line mean.
- The **slope** of the line shows how quickly or slowly change happens. A steep slope shows change that happens quickly. A gradual slope shows a slight change over time.

PRACTICE/APPLY Have students identify how many words a child knows by the age of two. Explain that they need to look for the label "2" on the left-hand side and then follow the line across until they see the dot. Then they follow the line down to find the number of words. (300, or halfway between 200 and 400)

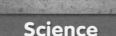

Science

Genre

Expository selections, such as **news stories**, give information about events.

✔ **Text Feature**

Line Graphs show changes over time.

Content Vocabulary

intelligent   exposure

impressive   phrases

demonstrated

DOG AMAZES SCIENTISTS!
Rico the border collie has a knack for learning words.

by Kim Christopher

GERMANY — A border collie named Rico is amazing scientists with his knowledge of human language. Rico recognizes at least 200 words and quickly learns and remembers even more.

Rico began his training when he was ten months old. His owner, Susanne Baus, put toys in different places and had Rico fetch them by name. She rewarded Rico with food or by playing with him. Rico continued to learn more and more new words. Scientists first noticed Rico when he showed off his talent on a popular German game show.

320

Content Vocabulary

Explain the words using the **Define/Example/Ask** routine. Definitions are provided for this activity.

- **Intelligent** means having or showing the ability to think, learn, and understand. What can you do to become more intelligent?

- Something that is **impressive** causes people to be amazed. What impressive events have you seen or heard about?

- When something is **demonstrated** to you, you are shown how to do it. What are some things we have demonstrated in class?

- **Exposure** is the act of making something known or understood. Can you remember your first exposure to music?

- **Phrases** are words put together to express ideas. What phrases do your friends say all the time?

Border collies are **intelligent** medium-size dogs that have a lot of energy and are easily trained. They like to stay busy, and they like to please their owners.

Even though nine-year-old Rico knows 200 words, he doesn't know as many words as even the average two-year-old person does. Human nine-year-olds know thousands and thousands of words, and they learn about ten new words a day. Still, Rico's ability to find objects by name is so **impressive** that scientists wanted to study him.

Number of Words a Child Understands

Reading a Line Graph

This line graph shows an increase in number. It shows how many words a child understands at different ages.

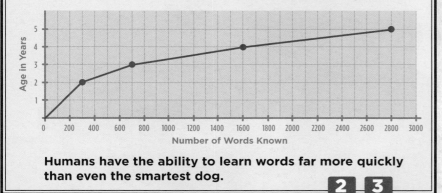

Humans have the ability to learn words far more quickly than even the smartest dog.

321

Connect to Content

INHERITED TRAITS AND LEARNED CHARACTERISTICS

Discuss how dogs, like other animals, have inherited traits and learned characteristics. An inherited trait may be the way a breed of dog looks or how smart the breed is. Learned characteristics may be behaviors or skills the dog was taught.

Ask students to think of their dream pet. What inherited traits would it have? What learned characteristics would it have? Students can refer to books or the Internet to help them find examples of different kinds of dogs.

Paired Selection

Read "Dog Amazes Scientists!"

Before students read, remind them to apply what they have learned about reading line graphs and to set their own purposes for reading. As they read, have them identify clues that help them understand the highlighted words.

1 MAIN IDEA AND DETAILS

Read the last paragraph on page 321. Use the details to figure out the main idea of the paragraph. (Details: Rico knows 200 words. The average two-year-old knows more than 200 words. The average nine-year-old knows thousands and thousands of words, and learns about ten new words a day. Main Idea: Humans learn new words much more quickly than even the smartest dog.)

2 TEXT FEATURE: LINE GRAPH

What is the purpose of this line graph? (The purpose of this line graph is to show the number of words a child understands at different ages, up to the age of five. The graph shows that each year a child grows, so does his or her vocabulary.)

3 TEXT FEATURE: LINE GRAPH

How old is a typical child who understands the same number of words as nine-year-old Rico? (about 1¼ years old)

Use the Interactive Question-Response Guide in the **ELL Resource Book**, pages 136–137, to help students gain access to the paired selection content.

Paired Selection

4 CONTENT VOCABULARY

Review the word *demonstrated* on page 322. What synonym in the next sentence helps you understand what *demonstrated* means? (The word *showed* has a similar meaning as *demonstrated*.)

5 DRAW CONCLUSIONS

How might dog owners around the world react to a finding that says that dogs can understand phrases? (The article says that most pet owners think their pets are smart, so many dog owners would want to teach their dogs phrases, too. They may start to train their dogs differently, beginning from when they are puppies—teaching them words first, and then phrases. They may give their dogs such commands as, "put the toy in the box.")

4 Scientists learned a lot about Rico as they watched him fetch familiar toys by name. Then Rico **demonstrated** something amazing. He showed scientists that he could pick out by name toys he had never seen before! Scientists put some familiar toys in a room. They added a new toy. Rico's owner asked him to fetch the new toy. Rico picked out the right toy most of the time in these tests.

Scientists think that Rico connects new words to new things. Since Rico already knows the names of old toys, he knows he should pick out a new toy when he hears a new word.

Rico can also remember the name of a new toy after just one **exposure**, or experience, with that toy. This shows scientists that even though animals are unable to talk, they can understand words. Rico's vocabulary seems to be as large as that of animals that have been trained in language. Those animals include apes, sea lions, dolphins, and parrots.

Most dog owners will tell you that their pets are very smart. But just how smart is Rico? Is he an outstanding dog in a breed known to be very intelligent? Or is Rico a "dog genius"?

322

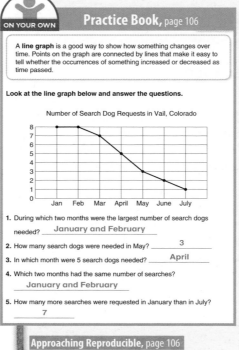

ON YOUR OWN
Practice Book, page 106

A **line graph** is a good way to show how something changes over time. Points on the graph are connected by lines that make it easy to tell whether the occurrences of something increased or decreased as time passed.

Look at the line graph below and answer the questions.

Number of Search Dog Requests in Vail, Colorado

1. During which two months were the largest number of search dogs needed? **January and February**
2. How many search dogs were needed in May? **3**
3. In which month were 5 search dogs needed? **April**
4. Which two months had the same number of searches? **January and February**
5. How many more searches were requested in January than in July? **7**

Approaching Reproducible, page 106
Beyond Reproducible, page 106

ELL

Content Vocabulary
Explain to students that a difficult word will often be defined or explained in the surrounding paragraph. Point to the word *exposure* on page 322. Have students find the definition of the word in the paragraph and read it aloud. Then have them figure out the meaning of *phrases* on page 323, based on the example given there. Provide ample time for students to respond.

Scientists are now studying Rico to learn more. They want to know if Rico can understand **phrases** such as "put the toy in the box." Rico's owner thinks that he can. The answers to questions about Rico's intelligence are still to come. The outcome of the study will be interesting to both scientists and dog owners all over the world.

5

Connect and Compare

1. Look at the line graph on page 321. How many words does a four-year-old understand? **Reading a Line Graph**

2. According to the graph, at what age does a child understand 2,800 words? **Apply**

3. Think about this article and *Dear Mrs. LaRue*. What would Rico say if he wrote a letter to his owner? Explain using details from both selections. **Reading/Writing Across Texts**

Science Activity

Research how dogs became pets. Use online sources and information from graphs to write a research report to explain how dogs have become pets over time.

 **Science** Border collies
www.macmillanmh.com

Paired Selection

Connect and Compare

1. A four-year-old child understands about 1,600 words. READING A LINE GRAPH

2. According to the graph, a child understands 2,800 words at the age of five. APPLY

3. **FOCUS QUESTION** Rico might write about his experiences being tested by the scientists. He might write about how difficult it is to remember so many words, or about how smart he is. Like Ike, Rico might tell his side of the story, which might be different from what was reported in the article. READING/WRITING ACROSS TEXTS

Science Activity

Remind students to use more than one information source and to credit those sources properly. Have volunteers present their information on how dogs became pets. Have other students ask thoughtful questions, summarize the main ideas and supporting evidence, and compare presentations.

Connect to Content

SCIENTIFIC SURVEY

Point out that scientists study the world around them by making observations, conducting experiments, and recording and interpreting their results. Have students summarize what they know about this process. Build background as needed.

Have groups perform their own study, or survey. They should think of a question to ask others in school, write down their answers, or have them fill out a questionnaire.

Finally, they should organize the information they gathered and record the results on a line graph. Have other classmates study the line graph and interpret the results.

Write

WHOLE GROUP

WRITING WORKSHOP
- Developing Persuasive Writing
- Trait: Ideas
- Strong Reasons

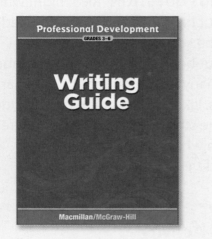

Professional Development
GRADES 3–6

Writing Guide

Macmillan/McGraw-Hill

Trait: Ideas
Strong Paragraphs: Strong Reasons

TEACH/MODEL Remind students that an opinion is a statement that tells what someone thinks or believes. It cannot be proved. To support their opinion, writers give **strong reasons**, including facts, examples, and details, that explain why they think or feel the way they do. Strong reasons can help writers establish a position and convince readers to agree with that position.

Then point out that writers build **strong paragraphs** by including reasons that connect to the main idea. Write the following sentence on the board:

> Everyone should own a pet.

Point out that this is an example of an opinion or position. To strongly establish the position, the writer must give reasons that prove it to readers. The writer must explain *why* he or she thinks this statement is true. Share the example below.

> Everyone should own a pet. Pets can keep you company and make you smile when you feel sad. Playing with a pet is also a fun way to get exercise. You might even make friends with someone else who has a pet like yours.

Point out that the writer uses different verb tenses (*make, might … make*) to give both current and possible future reasons. Discuss with students the reasons they found most effective in proving or supporting the writer's position. Then invite students to identify additional reasons. Discuss how each reason connects to the main idea.

Teacher Write Aloud

PRACTICE/APPLY Further explore with students the use of strong reasons to support a writer's position or opinion. List the position statement and reasons below on the board. Then complete the Teacher Think Aloud.

- It is important to keep our parks clean.
- Cans and broken glass can hurt children.
- Litter makes parks look messy.
- Plastic bags from snacks can make animals sick.
- Everyone likes to play at the park.

Teacher Think Aloud Remember that when you have an opinion or take a position, you need to give reasons that explain why you think or feel the way you do. In a strong paragraph, every reason supports the position. Do you see a reason listed that does not belong? The last reason does not belong because it doesn't support the opinion that it is important to keep parks clean.

Review the reasons with students. Then complete the Think Aloud by inviting students to suggest other reasons that support the opinion. Give students time to argue for their suggested reason. Try different reasons and poll students to achieve consensus.

Draft Display the Writing Prompt on **Writing Transparency 37**. Tell students to state their position and support it with strong, convincing reasons, such as facts, details, and examples. Circulate and provide Over-the-Shoulder Conferences as students work.

Objective

- Write reasons to support an opinion

Materials

- Writer's Notebooks
- Writing Transparency 37

Daily Journal Prompts

Focus on Strong Reasons

Use these and other prompts for independent daily journal writing.

- Write about something you would like to buy.

- Write about something you think people should do each day.

- Write about a person you think is a hero.

- Write about a book you would recommend to other students.

Transparency 37

Think about a field trip you think we should take. Give strong reasons that explain why you think we should take this trip.

Writing Transparency

Write

Reading and Writing Connection

Trait: Ideas

STRONG REASONS

Remind students that writers give strong reasons to explain their ideas and opinions. Every reason should support the writer's position to create a strong paragraph.

Read the Passage

Use the example from *Dear Mrs. LaRue* to show how the author uses reasons to explain why Mrs. LaRue sent Ike to school.

- Have students read the bookmark. Review that reasons explain the writer's opinion or position.

- **Ask:** *When have you felt frustrated or upset with a friend, pet, or brother or sister?*

- Then have students chorally read the excerpt from *Dear Mrs. LaRue*. Direct their attention to the callout. Have students identify the reasons Mrs. LaRue is "at her wit's end" with Ike.

- **Ask:** *How do the things Mrs. LaRue says make you feel about Ike? Why do you think the author chose these details?*

Reading and Writing Connection

Writing

✓ **Trait: Ideas**
Writers provide **good reasons** that explain their ideas or opinions.

Read the passage below. Notice how the author Mark Teague has Mrs. LaRue give her reasons for sending Ike to school.

An excerpt from *Dear Mrs. LaRue*

The author gives reasons why Mrs. LaRue is "at her wit's end." Each reason is a strong one that explains why she is feeling upset.

"I'm at my wit's end!" said Mrs. LaRue. "I love Ike, but I'm afraid he's quite spoiled. He steals food right off the kitchen counter, chases the neighbor's cats, howls whenever I'm away, and last week while I was crossing the street he pulled me down and tore my best camel's hair coat! I just don't know what else to do!"

Respond to the Selection

Have students write a response to the selection.

- ☑ **Engagement** Help students deepen their connection to the text and discover their own perspective on it. *Focus on a moment when you missed your home or family.*

- ☑ **Response** Help students explore more deeply their reactions to particular passages in the reading. *Focus on a moment in the story when you noticed that the words and the pictures didn't match. Use text evidence in your writing.*

- ☑ **Literary Analysis** Help students deepen their connection to the text and discover their own perspective on it. *Focus on a place in the story where you thought the author was trying to make you laugh. Use text evidence in your writing.*

Read and Find

Read Jaden's writing below. What reasons did she provide for her opinion? Use the checklist below to help you.

At My Grandmother's House

by Jaden S.

I think Nana's living room is the most comfortable place in the world. She has a huge tan armchair and two couches. The couches are so puffy that when you sit on them, you sink down! I also love her blue and green rug which is as soft as a fleece blanket. I can lie on it for hours. It's even better than lying on grass or sand.

> Read about how Jaden feels about Nana's living room.

Writer's Checklist

☑ What is the writer's opinion?

☑ Does the writer give **good reasons** to explain her opinion?

☑ Does each reason support her opinion?

325

Read the Student Model

Have students chorally read the student model at the top of **Student Book** page 325. Discuss the reasons this student writer gives to explain her opinion. Use the Writer's Checklist.

Journal Prompt

Draft Write the following prompt on the board. Have students write a response to the prompt.

> *What animal do you think would make the best pet? Write a paragraph giving reasons that support your choice.*

Tell students that you will be reading and commenting on their writing during Writing Conference time.

Model how to use the Writer's Checklist so students can write and revise their work. Then ask:

- *What animal did you choose?*

- *What reasons did you provide to explain why you think it would be the best? Do all of your reasons support your opinion? If not, what other reasons or supporting details could you add instead?*

Objectives
- Write strong reasons
- Write strong paragraphs

Materials
- Writer's Notebooks
- Teacher's Resource Book, p. 189

ELL

Provide Language Read each opinion statement on Teacher's Resource Book page 189 aloud to students. Then ask *Why?* Provide language as needed to help students answer the questions. Then help them turn their oral statements into written sentences.

HOMEWORK Teacher's Resource Book, page 189

Write two reasons to support each opinion.

1. Everyone should wear a bike helmet when they ride their bike.
Reason 1: _____
Reason 2: _____

2. Summer is the best season of the year.
Reason 1: _____
Reason 2: _____

3. It is important to take good care of your pets.
Reason 1: _____
Reason 2: _____

Extra Practice: Choose two of the opinions from above. Write one more reason to support each of the opinions you chose.

Minilessons

Minilesson 1 Ideas/Strong Reasons

TEACH/MODEL

Remind students that they have been working hard on giving reasons to explain their ideas and opinions. Today they will practice that again. Have students use **Teacher's Resource Book** page 189. Ask students to read the sentences silently.

PRACTICE/APPLY

Have students work independently to write two reasons for each opinion. When complete, ask students to share their work during Sharing Circle.

Minilesson 2 Organization/Opinion Paragraph

TEACH/MODEL

Tell students that writers make their work more effective and easier to understand by organizing their ideas in a clear way. Point out that in a strong paragraph one idea flows smoothly into the next. This helps readers better understand a writer's main idea or opinion. Write the following steps for organizing an opinion paragraph on the board:

> Step 1: <u>State Your Opinion:</u> State your opinion clearly and simply.
> Step 2: <u>Support Your Opinion:</u> Give at least three strong reasons to support your opinion. Remember to use specific verbs and descriptive details to make your reasons convincing and powerful. End with your strongest reason.
> Step 3: <u>Conclude:</u> End, or conclude, your paragraph by stating your opinion again and asking the reader to do something or feel a certain way.

PRACTICE/APPLY

Write the following opinion statement: *Everyone should treat his or her classmates with respect.* In their Writer's Notebooks, have students add reasons and a concluding sentence. Provide the following prompts to help students write strong reasons:

- What can happen if we aren't nice to our classmates?

- How would you feel if someone didn't share?

- Why does everyone need to listen?

- What do you want your reader to do?

Conferencing Routine

Dynamic Feedback System

Step 1 Read and appreciate the writing.

Step 2 Notice how the student uses the targeted skill (for example, strong reasons: Ask: *How did the writer support his or her ideas or opinions?*).

Step 3 Write comments that show how the writing has an impact on you. Direct your comments to those places in the piece where the student has used the targeted skill.

Step 4 Meet with and give the student a revision assignment.

Write Effective Comments

Ideas At least one of your comments should highlight the way the student supports an opinion or idea with **strong reasons**. Here are some sample comments.

- I can really understand your opinion because you explained your reasons so clearly.

- Can you add a strong verb or some more description to this reason to make it stronger?

- Your reasons convinced me to agree with your position.

Revision Assignments

Ideas Here are some examples of effective revision assignments for strong reasons.

 Reread your entry. *Choose one reason that supports your opinion. Now rewrite it, adding more detail to make it stronger and clearer.*

Revise **[Underline a section.]** Mark a specific section of a student's writing and then ask the student to revise it in a specific way.

Revise **[Underline a section.]** *Read the part that I underlined. Can you rewrite this reason to help me better understand why you think [a parrot would make the best pet]?*

Teacher-to-Teacher

Over-the-Shoulder Conferences

Use these quick, focused opportunities to comment while students are writing.

- **Step 1** Quietly move close enough to a student that you can read the journal entry he or she is writing.

- **Step 2** Read part of what you see. You don't need to start from the beginning or read the entire piece.

- **Step 3** Show the student a spot in the writing where he or she is using a particular skill or describing something that piques your interest.

- **Step 4** Whisper a sentence or two about why you noticed that spot in the writing, and ask a question that will nudge the student to add a strong reason.

- **Step 5** Move on to the next student. Select students strategically. You should see 12–15 students in a 15-minute period.

Research Proven Writing Approach

The Writers' Express
Immediate Impact. Lasting Transformation.   wex.org

5-Day Vocabulary

Connect Language Arts

WHOLE GROUP

- **VOCABULARY**
  - Tested Words
- **SPELLING**
  - Silent Letters
- **GRAMMAR**
  - Verb Tenses

SMALL GROUP

- Differentiated Instruction, pp. 325I–325HH

Practice Book, page 107

When you put the **prefix** *mis-* in front of a word, it changes the meaning of the word. *Mis-* means "badly" or "incorrectly" and derives from a German word meaning "go wrong."

Add the prefix mis- to each word. Then write a sentence with the new word.

New word

1. judge misjudge	4. read misread
2. spell misspell	5. behave misbehave
3. treat mistreat	

Sentence Possible responses provided.

1. It's easy to *misjudge* someone you don't know well.

2. Melinda tries not to *misspell* any words in her essays.

3. Owners who *mistreat* their pets should not be allowed to keep them.

4. I *misread* the directions and we went north instead of south.

5. We didn't expect them to *misbehave* in the library.

Approaching Reproducible, page 107

Beyond Reproducible, page 107

325C Unit 3 Week 2

Build Robust Vocabulary

Day 1 | Teach/Practice

CONNECT TO WORDS

- Practice this week's vocabulary words using the following prompts:

1. If you *neglected* to clean your room, what would happen?

2. What favor has someone done for you that you really *appreciated*?

3. Describe a time when you felt *misunderstood*.

4. What is the difference between needing something and being *desperate*?

5. When in history have people *endured* hardships, or difficult times?

6. How might a dog show *obedience* to its master?

ACADEMIC VOCABULARY

- Review the important academic vocabulary words for the week. These words include: *generate questions, draw conclusions, fantasy, expression, prefixes, line graph.*

- Write each word on the board. Define each using student-friendly language, and ask students to select the word you are defining. Then point to words in random order for students to define.

Day 2 | Review

CONNECT TO WORDS

- Review the definitions of this week's vocabulary words using **Student Book** pages 294–295. Then discuss each word using these prompts:

1. Have you ever *neglected* to do your homework? Why?

2. What can you give someone that will be greatly *appreciated*?

3. If you were *misunderstood* in class, what might you do?

4. When might you be *desperate* for something, and what might that something be?

5. Why might it be worth it to *endure* a difficult hike?

6. To whom should you show *obedience*?

PREFIXES

- Point out that often an unfamiliar word can be decoded by identifying and defining its prefix, or the word part that comes before the base.

- Review the prefix *mis-*, as in *misunderstood* or *mistake*, which means "wrongly" or "badly." Remind students it is rooted in an old German word meaning "go wrong."

-  Display **Transparency 23**. Read the first sentence. Model how to identify a word with *mis-* that has the same meaning as the italicized words. To which of the italicized words can *mis-* be added?

- Have students identify words with *mis-* that can replace the italicized words in the other sentences.

Day 3 **Reinforce**

CONNECT TO WORDS

- Ask students to create Word Squares for each word in their Writer's Notebooks.

- In the first square, students write the word. (Example: *appreciated*)

- In the second square, students write their own definition of the word and any related words, such as synonyms. (Example: *valued, respected, loved, grateful for, thankful for, pleased about*)

- In the third square, students draw a simple illustration that will help them remember the word. (Example: picture of a happy person saying, "Thank you!")

- In the fourth square, students write nonexamples, including antonyms for the word. (Example: *take for granted, look down upon, scorn, dislike, dismiss, be upset about*)

RELATED WORDS

- Help students generate words related to *misunderstood*.

- Write the word *misunderstood* on the board. Have students discuss its meaning.

- Draw a word web. Write *misunderstood* in the center.

- Have students fill in the word web with words or phrases with similar meanings. For help, tell them to use a print or online thesaurus. Add words or phrases not included, such as *misinterpreted, got the wrong idea*, and *did not understand correctly*.

 **Day 4** **Extend**

CONNECT TO WORDS

- Review this week's vocabulary using the following sentence stems. Have students orally complete each one.

  1. We neglected to _____, so _____.

  2. What I appreciated most about _____ was _____.

  3. You misunderstood what I meant when I said _____ .

  4. I am so desperate for _____ that I _____.

  5. I am willing to endure _____ if _____.

  6. Please show obedience to your parents by _____.

MORPHOLOGY

- Use the additional selection word *resident* as a springboard for students to learn other words.

- Write *resident*. Have students identify the base word. (*reside*) Using a dictionary, they should find the meaning of the suffix. ("one who performs a particular action")

- Explain that *reside* means "to make one's home permanently or for a time." It comes from the Latin word *residēre*, "to remain behind." Now, help students figure out the meaning of *resident*.

- Brainstorm other words with the base word *reside*, such as *residence* and *residential*. Have students look up the prefixes or suffixes (such as *-ence* and *-ial*) to figure out the meanings. Students should share their definitions and tell how the words relate to *resident*.

Day 5 **Assess and Reteach**

POSTTEST

- Display **Transparency 24**. Have students complete the cloze sentences using one of this week's vocabulary words.

- Note how quickly and accurately students can complete this task. Work with students who make errors or require too much time to complete this task during Small Group time.

CONNECT TO WRITING

- Have students write sentences in their Writer's Notebooks using this week's vocabulary. Tell students to write sentences that provide information they learned from this week's readings.

- **ELL** Provide the Day 4 sentence stems for students needing extra support.

5-Day Spelling

Go to pages T14–T15 for **Differentiated Spelling Lists**.

✓ Silent Letters

Spelling Words

hour	answer	knives
lambs	honesty	doubt
knew	plumber	knead
wrench	honor	wriggle
kneel	known	heir
thumbs	combs	wrinkle
honest	wrapper	

Review person, pearl, shirt
Challenge knuckles, wrestle

Dictation Sentences

1. The drive took an <u>hour</u>.
2. She has many <u>lambs</u> on her farm.
3. He <u>knew</u> exactly what to do.
4. The tool box had a <u>wrench</u>.
5. He had to <u>kneel</u> to see under it.
6. Many animals do not have <u>thumbs</u>.
7. It is good to be <u>honest</u>.
8. Can you <u>answer</u> that question?
9. **<u>Honesty</u>** is the best policy.
10. A <u>plumber</u> came to fix the pipe.
11. It was an <u>honor</u> to be chosen.
12. What are you **<u>known</u>** for?
13. We bought <u>combs</u> at the store.
14. Throw away the candy <u>wrapper</u>.
15. We used <u>knives</u> to cut the meat.
16. I <u>doubt</u> that I'll see her tonight.
17. The baker will <u>knead</u> the dough.
18. Don't <u>wriggle</u> in your chair.
19. The king's <u>heir</u> is his son.
20. Try not to <u>wrinkle</u> your shirt.

Review/Challenge Words

1. He is the tallest <u>person</u> in the room.
2. Erica wears a <u>pearl</u> bracelet.
3. Jake buttoned his <u>shirt</u>.
4. She scraped her <u>knuckles</u> climbing the tree.
5. I challenge you to an arm <u>wrestle</u>.

Words in **bold** are from this week's selections.

Day 1 Pretest

ASSESS PRIOR KNOWLEDGE

■ Model for students how to spell the word *wrinkle*. Segment the word syllable by syllable, then attach a spelling to each sound. Point out that *wr* makes the /r/ sound.

■ Use the Dictation Sentences. Say the underlined word, read the sentence, and repeat the word. Have students write the words.

■ Have students self-correct their tests. Point out that a *k* is silent before *n* at the beginning of a word or syllable.

■ Have students cut apart the **Spelling Word Cards BLM** on **Teacher's Resource Book** page 55 and figure out a way to sort them. Have them save the cards for use throughout the week.

Day 2 Word Sorts and Review

SPIRAL REVIEW

■ Review the /ûr/ sound in the words *person*, *pearl*, and *shirt*. Have students find words in this week's readings with the sound.

WORD SORTS

■ Have students take turns sorting the spelling words and explaining how they sorted them. When students have finished the sort, discuss any words that have unexpected vowel spellings. (*heir*)

■ Review the spelling words, pointing out the silent letter spellings. Use the cards from the Spelling Word Cards BLM. Write the key words *lambs*, *honor*, *wriggle*, and *knew* on the board. Model how to sort words by silent letters. Place one or two cards beneath the correct key words.

ON YOUR OWN — **Phonics/Spelling,** pages 67–68

Fold back the paper along the dotted line. Use the blanks to write each word as it is read aloud. When you finish the test, unfold the paper. Use the list at the right to correct any spelling mistakes.

1. _____	1. hour
2. _____	2. lambs
3. _____	3. knew
4. _____	4. wrench
5. _____	5. kneel
6. _____	6. thumbs
7. _____	7. honest
8. _____	8. answer
9. _____	9. honesty
10. _____	10. plumber
11. _____	11. honor
12. _____	12. known
13. _____	13. combs
14. _____	14. wrapper
15. _____	15. knives
16. _____	16. doubt
17. _____	17. knead
18. _____	18. wriggle
19. _____	19. heir
20. _____	20. wrinkle
Review Words 21. _____	21. person
22. _____	22. pearl
23. _____	23. shirt
Challenge Words 24. _____	24. knuckles
25. _____	25. wrestle

HOMEWORK — **Phonics/Spelling,** page 69

doubt	heir	honest	plumber	honesty
lambs	hour	wrinkle	knead	known
honor	knew	thumbs	wrapper	answer
wriggle	knives	combs	kneel	wrench

Write the spelling words with these spelling patterns.

words with silent h
1. hour
2. honesty
3. honor
4. honest
5. heir

words with silent k
11. kneel
12. knew
13. knives
14. known
15. knead

words with silent b
6. doubt
7. thumbs
8. lambs
9. combs
10. plumber

words with silent w
16. wriggle
17. wrinkle
18. wrapper
19. wrench
20. answer

Day 3 | Word Meanings

CONTEXT CLUES

Have students copy the three sentences below into their Writer's Notebooks. Say the sentences aloud, and ask students to fill in the missing blanks with a spelling word.

1. The _____ was late, so we had to go home. (*hour*)

2. The _____ is fixing our leaky faucet. (*plumber*)

3. The young _____ will soon inherit the kingdom. (*heir*)

Challenge students to come up with other sentences for spelling words, review words, or challenge words.

Have students do a word hunt for the words in weekly reading or other materials. They should identify the definition of the spelling word being used in context.

 **Day 4** | Proofread

PROOFREAD AND WRITE

Write these sentences on the board. Have students circle and correct each misspelled word. They can use print or electronic resources to help them.

1. The plummer forgot to bring his rench. (*plumber, wrench*)

2. After you nead the dough, let it rise for one our. (*knead, hour*)

3. The lams won a medal of onner for their wool. (*lambs, honor*)

4. Josh's anser showed dout in his voice. (*answer, doubt*)

5. Lucinda is nown for being onest. (*known, honest*)

Error Correction Teach students that the letter *b* is silent before *t* and after *m* unless this letter and the *b* are in separate syllables. (Example: *tumble*)

 Day 5 | Assess and Reteach

POSTTEST

Use the Dictation Sentences on page 325E for the Posttest.

If students have difficulty with any words in the lesson, have them place the words on a list called *Spelling Words I Want to Remember* in their Writer's Notebooks.

Challenge students to find words for each silent-letter spelling.

HOMEWORK — Phonics/Spelling, page 70

doubt	heir	honest	plumber	honesty
lambs	hour	wrinkle	knead	known
honor	knew	thumbs	wrapper	answer
wriggle	knives	combs	kneel	wrench

Definitions for You

Fill in the word from the spelling list that matches the definition.

1. Response to a question — answer
2. A tool for tightening or loosening — wrench
3. Young sheep — lambs
4. For untangling hair — combs
5. A measurement of time — hour
6. To place knees on ground — kneel
7. To thank or appreciate — honor
8. To squirm — wriggle
9. A paper covering — wrapper
10. One who inherits — heir
11. A line in the skin — wrinkle
12. Tools for cutting — knives
13. To be truthful — honest
14. To be unsure — doubt
15. Understood — knew
16. Not your fingers — thumbs
17. Fixes pipes — plumber
18. To press in — knead
19. Truth — honesty
20. Was or is understood — known

ON YOUR OWN — Phonics/Spelling, page 71

A. Proofreading

There are six spelling mistakes in the story below. Circle the misspelled words. Write the words correctly on the lines below.

My brother Sam could never make up his mind about what he wanted to be when he grew up. He just new that he wanted to help people.

At one time, he wanted to be a farmer. He liked sheep and lams. I think he would have liked herding them. He could have been a shepherd.

Sam also liked tools. He liked fixing his bike with a rench. He could have been a plummer. He would have liked helping people by fixing their leaky sinks.

When he decided to be a judge, I was sure that was the perfect job for him. He was always onest and fair. I had no dout that he would help a lot of people. You could just tell that he was going to make a difference, whether as a shepherd, a plumber, or a judge.

1. knew   3. wrench   5. honest
2. lambs   4. plumber   6. doubt

B. Writing Activity

Think about people like Dr. Martin Luther King and others who make a difference. Write a paragraph describing another job that involves helping people. Use at least four spelling words in your paragraph.

Responses will vary.

HOMEWORK — Phonics/Spelling, page 72

Look at the words in each set below. One word in each set is spelled correctly. Use a pencil to fill in the circle next to the correct word. Before you begin, look at the sample set of words. Sample A has been done for you. Do Sample B by yourself. When you are sure you know what to do, you may go on with the rest of the page.

Sample A:
- Ⓐ nitt
- Ⓑ niht
- Ⓒ knit ●
- Ⓓ knitt

Sample B:
- Ⓔ gnat
- Ⓕ natt
- Ⓖ nat
- Ⓗ gnatt

1.
- Ⓐ dowt
- Ⓑ dout
- Ⓒ dowbt
- Ⓓ doubt

2.
- Ⓔ lamms
- Ⓕ lams
- Ⓖ lammbs
- Ⓗ lambs

3.
- Ⓐ onor
- Ⓑ honer
- Ⓒ honor
- Ⓓ oner

4.
- Ⓔ wriggle
- Ⓕ riggle
- Ⓖ wriggel
- Ⓗ riggel

5.
- Ⓐ eir
- Ⓑ heir
- Ⓒ haire
- Ⓓ aire

6.
- Ⓔ hour
- Ⓕ ouer
- Ⓖ houer
- Ⓗ oure

7.
- Ⓐ neww
- Ⓑ knew
- Ⓒ nue
- Ⓓ knue

8.
- Ⓔ nives
- Ⓕ knifes
- Ⓖ nifes
- Ⓗ knives

9.
- Ⓐ onist
- Ⓑ honist
- Ⓒ honest
- Ⓓ onest

10.
- Ⓔ rinkle
- Ⓕ wrinkle
- Ⓖ wrenkel
- Ⓗ rinkel

11.
- Ⓐ thumms
- Ⓑ thums
- Ⓒ thumbs
- Ⓓ thummbs

12.
- Ⓔ cowms
- Ⓕ coams
- Ⓖ komes
- Ⓗ combs

13.
- Ⓐ plummer
- Ⓑ plumber
- Ⓒ plumer
- Ⓓ plummber

14.
- Ⓔ knead
- Ⓕ nead
- Ⓖ knaed
- Ⓗ neede

15.
- Ⓐ wrapper
- Ⓑ rappur
- Ⓒ wrappur
- Ⓓ rappere

16.
- Ⓔ kneel
- Ⓕ neal
- Ⓖ kneal
- Ⓗ neel

17.
- Ⓐ onestie
- Ⓑ honesty
- Ⓒ honistie
- Ⓓ onisty

18.
- Ⓔ noan
- Ⓕ known
- Ⓖ nonne
- Ⓗ knoan

19.
- Ⓐ annser
- Ⓑ ansir
- Ⓒ anserr
- Ⓓ answer

20.
- Ⓔ rench
- Ⓕ wrench
- Ⓖ wrinch
- Ⓗ rinch

5-Day Grammar

✔ Verb Tenses

Daily Language Activities

Write the sentences on the board.

DAY 1
My mother said to me you can have this. It was my grandmothers favorite necklace. (1: me, "You can have this."; 2: grandmother's)

DAY 2
I looked in the childrens' section of the library. I find a book called *Honest abe*. (1: children's; 2: found; 3: *Abe*.)

DAY 3
When I ran into Annie I helped her carry some boxes. They were full of pens, pencils and erasers. (1: Annie,; 2: boxes; 3: pencils,)

DAY 4
Annie check out a different book every week. She reads a whole book in a few ours. (1: checks; 2: hours.)

DAY 5
I new the answer to the question. I raise my hand, the teacher calling on someone else. (1: knew; 2: raised; 3: hand, but the; 4: called)

Day 1 | Introduce the Concept

INTRODUCE VERB TENSES

Present the following:

- The **tense** of a verb tells you when in time an action is happening.

- A verb has three basic tenses: past tense, present tense, and future tense.

- A **present-tense** verb shows that the action is happening now or is happening over and over: Thomas *looks* at the gray sky.

- The helping verb *be* (*is, am, are*) can be added to the *-ing* form of a verb to show present tense: The dog *is wagging* its tail.

Examples:
My teacher **checks** our homework.
The sun **rises** in the East.
Birds **are singing** in the trees.

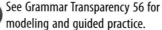 See Grammar Transparency 56 for modeling and guided practice.

HOMEWORK   **Grammar,** page 56

- A verb in the **past tense** tells about an action that already happened.
- Add *-ed* to most verbs to show past tense.
- If a verb ends with *e*, drop the *e* and add *-ed*.
- If a verb ends with a consonant and *y*, change *y* to *i* and add *-ed*.

Write the verb in parentheses in the past tense.

1. We _____ Martin Luther King, Jr.'s birthday in January. (celebrate)
2. People _____ home from school for the holiday. (stay)
3. The students in our school _____ about Dr. King before the holiday. (learn)
4. We _____ a program of events about Dr. King. (prepare)
5. Today my class _____ a play about his childhood. (perform)
6. James _____ the lead in the show. (play)
7. He _____ his lines before going onstage. (practice)
8. He _____ his Aunt Betty to come to the play. (ask)
9. Our teacher, Mrs. Clark, _____ us good luck before the play started. (wish)
10. We all _____ our best to make the show a success. (try)

Day 2 | Teach the Concept

REVIEW VERB TENSES

Review what the tense of a verb shows. Ask students what it means if a verb is in the present tense.

INTRODUCE PAST AND FUTURE TENSES

Present the following:

- A **past-tense** verb shows action that has already happened: He *ran* home.

- To form the past tense of most verbs, add *-ed*. If the verb ends in *e*, add only *d*. If it ends with a consonant and *y*, change the *y* to *i* before adding *-ed*: I *studied* all day.

- A verb in the **future tense** shows action that will happen. Form the future tense of a verb by adding a helping verb such as *will* or *shall* to the main verb: We *will scuba dive* this summer.

See Grammar Transparency 57 for modeling and guided practice.

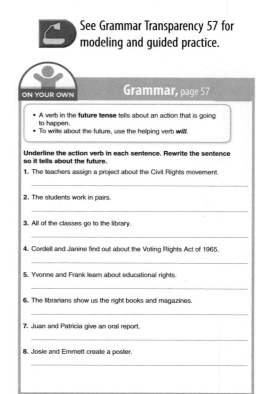

ON YOUR OWN   **Grammar,** page 57

- A verb in the **future tense** tells about an action that is going to happen.
- To write about the future, use the helping verb **will**.

Underline the action verb in each sentence. Rewrite the sentence so it tells about the future.

1. The teachers assign a project about the Civil Rights movement.
2. The students work in pairs.
3. All of the classes go to the library.
4. Cordell and Janine find out about the Voting Rights Act of 1965.
5. Yvonne and Frank learn about educational rights.
6. The librarians show us the right books and magazines.
7. Juan and Patricia give an oral report.
8. Josie and Emmett create a poster.

REVIEW VERB TENSES

Review the differences among present, past, and future tenses of verbs, and how to form each.

MECHANICS AND USAGE: SUBJECT-VERB AGREEMENT

- The form of a present-tense verb must agree with the subject of the sentence.

- With a singular third-person subject, add -s or -es to most verbs to show the present tense: Thomas *looks* at the gray sky.

- If the subject is *I* or *you*, then do not add -s or -es to a present-tense verb: I *look* at the gray sky.

- If the subject is a plural noun or pronoun, do not add -s or -es: Thomas and I *look* at the gray sky.

REVIEW VERB TENSES

Review past- and future-tense verbs. Ask students to describe the different types of subject-verb agreement in the present tense.

PROOFREAD

Have students correct errors in the following sentences.

1. I run in a race next week. (will run)

2. Yesterday, sally will fix her lunch. (Sally; fixed)

3. Tim still write his name in all capital letters. (writes)

4. Last night, I open an e-mail from my grandparents. (opened)

Day 5 **Assess and Reteach**

ASSESS

Use the Daily Language Activity and **Grammar Practice Book** page 60 for assessment.

RETEACH

Use Grammar Practice Book page 60 and selected pages from the **Grammar and Writing Handbook** for additional reteaching. Remind students that it is important to use verbs correctly as they speak and write.

Check students' writing for use of the skill and listen for it in their speaking. Assign Grammar Revision Assignments in their Writer's Notebooks as needed.

 See Grammar Transparency 58 for modeling and guided practice.

 See Grammar Transparency 59 for modeling and guided practice.

 See Grammar Transparency 60 for modeling and guided practice.

HOMEWORK **Grammar,** page 58

- The present tense must have **subject-verb agreement**. Add -s to most verbs if the subject is singular. Do not add -s if the subject is plural or *I* or *you*.
- Add -es to verbs that end in s, ch, sh, x, or z if the subject is singular. Do not add -es when the subject is plural or *I* or *you*.

Pick the correct form of the verb in each sentence below. Underline your answer.

1. Ms. Harkner's class (take, takes) a field trip today.

2. The students (visit, visits) the Martin Luther King, Jr. Historic Site.

3. The class (hurry, hurries) to the buses at 9:00 a.m.

4. The buses (reach, reaches) Atlanta at 10:00 a.m.

5. Tour guides (show, shows) us through Martin Luther King's birth home.

6. A guide (teach, teaches) us about Martin Luther King, Jr.'s childhood.

7. She (say, says) Dr. King and his family lived in Alabama.

8. Dr. Kings "I Have a Dream" speech (remain, remains) a landmark.

9. My parents and I (discuss, discusses) the speech often.

10. My sister's class (will tour, will tours) the site next week.

ON YOUR OWN **Grammar,** page 59

- A verb in the **past tense** tells about an action that already happened.
- A verb in the **future tense** tells about an action that is going to happen.

Rewrite the poem below. Change the underlined verbs to the past tense. Then circle the verb in the future tense.

Just History?

To me, it's a mystery —
Why do people think
Dr. King is just history?
He <u>stand</u> on the brink
of a change. He <u>dream</u>
of equality. He <u>speak</u>
with calm strength. His world <u>seem</u>
cold, but he <u>seek</u>
to warm it. Dr. King, we will remember
you.

HOMEWORK **Grammar,** page 60

A. Rewrite each underlined verb, using the correct past-tense form.

1. Gordon <u>help</u> Ms. Morrison decorate the classroom. _____

2. The students <u>copy</u> quotes from Dr. King onto big banners. _____

3. Gordon <u>place</u> a banner on the wall. _____

4. The corner of the banner <u>flutter</u> in the breeze. _____

5. The teacher <u>push</u> a pin into each corner of the banner. _____

B. Choose a verb from the box below to complete each sentence. Write the correct future-tense form of the verb.

fix	invite	tape	wish	worry

6. I _____ the sign to the wall.

7. The sign _____ people to our Martin Luther King, Jr. celebration.

8. Anna _____ that the sign isn't straight.

9. Ms. Morrison _____ the sign for us.

10. Our class _____ everyone welcome as they walk into the room.

Daily Planner

DAY 1	• Prepare to Read • Academic Language • Vocabulary (Preteach)
DAY 2	• Comprehension • Leveled Reader Lesson 1
DAY 3	• Phonics/Decoding • Leveled Reader Lesson 2
DAY 4	• Phonics/Decoding • Vocabulary (Review) • Leveled Reader Lesson 3
DAY 5	• High-Frequency Words • Fluency • Self-Selected Reading

LOG ON StudentWorks Plus
Interactive Student Book

If you wish to preteach the main selection, use StudentWorks Plus for:

• Vocabulary Preteaching
• Word-by-Word Highlighting
• Think Aloud Prompts

Academic Language

Academic words include those harder Tier 2 words that appear in much of students' reading materials as well as the language of instruction. The words chosen for instruction were selected from the **Living Word Vocabulary** list and Avril Coxhead's list of **High-Incidence Academic Words**.

Approaching Level

Prepare to Read

Objective Preview *Dear Mrs. LaRue*
Materials • **StudentWorks Plus** • self-stick notes

PREVIEW THE MAIN SELECTION

■ Have students preview *Dear Mrs. LaRue* using **StudentWorks Plus**. This version of the selection contains oral summaries in multiple languages, story recording, word-by-word highlighting, Think Aloud prompts, and comprehension-monitoring questions.

■ Remind students that listening carefully to and following along with the word-by-word reading will help them prepare for the reading of the selection with the class. Ask students to place self-stick notes on any challenging words or places that confuse them. Discuss the confusing items with students prior to the reading of the selection with the rest of the class.

■ Ask students to write four sentences in their Writer's Notebooks telling what they learned about the power of persuasion.

Academic Language

Objective Teach academic language
Materials • none

PRETEACH LANGUAGE OF INSTRUCTION

Tell students that there are many important lesson words you will be using this week. You want them to become familiar with these words *before* the lessons. These words also appear in the directions of the tests they will be taking this year.

Preteach the following academic words: *draw conclusions, generate questions, fantasy, prefixes*, and *expression*.

■ Define each word using student-friendly language. Tell students that *prefixes* are word parts that come *before* the base word; for example, in the word *misunderstood*, the prefix *mis-* comes before the base word *understood*. Underline the letters *pre-* in *prefix*, and tell students that *pre-* means "before."

■ Relate each word to known words; for example, connect *fantasy* to things that *cannot happen in real life*, *expression* to *feelings*, *draw conclusions* to *use clues to figure things out*, and *generate questions* to *think of questions you would like to have answered*.

■ Highlight these words when used throughout the week, and reinforce their meanings.

Approaching Level

Phonics/Decoding

Objective Decode words with silent letters

Materials • **Approaching Reproducible,** p. 100
• **Sound-Spelling WorkBoards**

Sound-Spelling WorkBoard

PHONICS MAINTENANCE

Tier 2

- Distribute a **WorkBoard** to each student. Say a sound previously taught, including the initial consonant sound /n/ represented by the letters *n, kn,* and *gn,* and the initial consonant sound /r/ represented by the letters *r* and *wr.* Have students find the **Sound-Spelling Card** on the board for each sound.

- Review the spelling(s) for each sound by providing a sample word containing that spelling. Guide students in writing the word on the board. Model how to segment the word and write the spelling for each sound, as needed. In addition, point out that some words, such as *honest,* begin with a silent *h,* while other words, such as *comb,* end with a silent *b.*

- Dictate the following words for students to spell: *now, kneel, gnaw, wreck, ride, onward, honor, comb, tumble.* Write each word on the board, and have students self-correct their work.

RETEACH SKILL

Silent Letters Point to the Sound-Spelling Cards with silent letter spellings on the WorkBoard, and review the spellings for the sounds /n/ and /r/. State each spelling and provide a sample word.

- Write the words below on the board. Model how to decode the first word in each row, then guide students as they decode the remaining words. For the multisyllabic words, divide the words into syllables using the syllable-scoop technique to help students read one syllable at a time.

- When completed, point to the words in random order for students to chorally read. Repeat several times.

knife	knives	kites	knock	kneeling	knapsack
now	know	known	gnawing	never	unknown
wrist	wrong	rotten	wrench	wrecked	wrinkle
wrote	written	writer	reader	unwrap	wrongful
honest	honor	homely	honesty	hourly	honestly
lamb	comb	climb	crumb	thumb	tumble

Approaching Reproducible, page 100

Look at these words: *kneel, climb, walk, wreck.*

In these words, one letter is silent.
• In *kneel* the silent letter is *k.*
• In *climb* the silent letter is *b.*
• In *walk* the silent letter is *l.*
• In *wreck* the silent letter is *w.*

A. Circle the silent letter in each word.
1. ⓦr i t e   5. ⓚn i t
2. ⓚn e a d   6. t a ⓛk
3. t h u m ⓑs   7. ⓦr o n g
4. ⓦr e n c h   8. l a m ⓑ

B. Now think of four other words with the same silent letters. Write the words on the blanks and circle the silent letters in each one.
Sample responses provided.
9. ___ⓚnee___
10. ___dumⓑ___
11. ___ⓦriggle___
12. ___baⓛm___

Approaching Level

Vocabulary

Objective   Preteach selection vocabulary

Materials   • **Visual Vocabulary Resources**   • **Vocabulary Cards**
               • **Approaching Reproducible,** p. 101

✓ PRETEACH KEY VOCABULARY

Tier 2

Introduce the Words Display the **Visual Vocabulary Resources** to preteach the key selection words *neglected, appreciated, misunderstood, desperate, endured*, and *obedience*. Use the following routine that appears in detail on the cards.

- Define the word in English, and provide the example given.

- Define the word in Spanish, if appropriate, and indicate if the word is a cognate.

- Display the picture, and explain how it illustrates or demonstrates the word.

- Then engage students in structured partner-talk about the image, using the key word.

- Ask students to chorally say the word three times.

- Point out any known sound-spellings or focus on a key aspect of phonemic awareness related to the word.

- You may wish to also distribute copies of the Vocabulary Glossary in the **ELL Resource Book**.

REVIEW PREVIOUSLY TAUGHT VOCABULARY

Display the **Vocabulary Cards** from the previous four weeks. Say the meanings of each word, one by one, and have students identify them. Then point to words in random order for students to provide definitions and related words they know.

Prefixes Remind students that a prefix is a word part that comes before the base word and changes its meaning. Discuss how prefixes can be added to this week's words to form words such as *disobedience* and *unappreciated*. Discuss how the new word and the vocabulary word relate in meaning. Have students write a context sentence for each pair of words. For example, *Sandra received many compliments on her work and felt very* appreciated, *but Jo did not and felt* unappreciated.

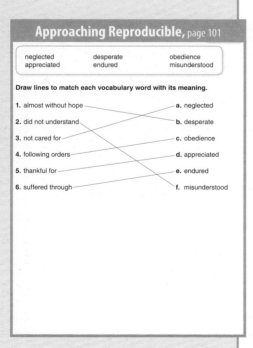

Approaching Reproducible, page 101

| neglected | desperate | obedience |
| appreciated | endured | misunderstood |

Draw lines to match each vocabulary word with its meaning.

1. almost without hope —   **a.** neglected
2. did not understand —   **b.** desperate
3. not cared for —   **c.** obedience
4. following orders —   **d.** appreciated
5. thankful for —   **e.** endured
6. suffered through —   **f.** misunderstood

Approaching Level

Vocabulary

Objective Review vocabulary and high-frequency words

Materials • **Vocabulary Cards** • **High-Frequency Word Cards**

✔ REVIEW VOCABULARY

Review Words Display the **Vocabulary Cards** for *neglected, appreciated, misunderstood, desperate, endured*, and *obedience*. Point to each word, read it aloud, and have students chorally repeat.

Have students suggest examples of the following:

- a responsibility that you *neglected* to meet

- an experience you had that you really *appreciated*

- a time when a fourth grader might feel *misunderstood*

- a situation in which a person might feel *desperate*

- a kind of experience that has to be *endured*

- how you might be rewarded for *obedience*

HIGH-FREQUENCY WORDS

Tier 2

Top 250 Words The ability to read accurately and effortlessly the most frequently used words in written English will help students develop reading fluency. Display **High-Frequency Word Cards** 91–100. Then do the following:

- Display one card at a time, and ask students to chorally state each word.

- Have students spell each word aloud.

- Ask students to write each word in their Writer's Notebooks as they state aloud each letter. Then have them read the word again.

- When completed, quickly flip through the Word Card set as students chorally read the words.

- Provide opportunities for students to use the words in speaking and writing. For example, provide sentence starters for oral and written practice, such as *I feel <u>hurt</u> when _____.* Or point to a Word Card and ask a question, such as *What word means the opposite of this word?* (when pointing to the *In* word card).

- Continue the routine throughout the week.

ELL

Practice Vocabulary Pair students of different proficiency. Orally model the vocabulary in sentences. For example: *I neglected to clean my room, so it is very messy.* On the board, provide sentence frames for pairs to copy and complete using the vocabulary. For example: *I _____ my friends for helping me with the science project.* (*appreciated*)

Word Webs

Have students create word webs in their Writer's Notebooks for each vocabulary word. Write the related words provided and ask students to add other words, phrases, and illustrations.

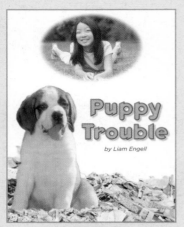

Student Book

Corrective Feedback

Read each paragraph with students. Ask: *What questions do you have about the puppy and its owners?* Write the questions on the board. If students have difficulty, model questions such as *Who is training the puppy? How could the family solve this problem?* Encourage students to look for clues to answer their questions as they read on.

Approaching Level

Comprehension

Objective	Reteach generate questions and draw conclusions
Materials	• **Student Book:** "Puppy Trouble"

Tier 2

✓ RETEACH STRATEGY: GENERATE QUESTIONS

- **Define** Tell students that when they generate questions, they ask important questions about what is happening in a story, why the characters act the way they do, and what might happen next. Then they look for clues to help them figure out the answers to their questions.

- **Relate to Real Life** Ask students to imagine that they have a friend who loves playing basketball. One day, they ask her to play basketball after school. She frowns and softly says, "No thanks. I don't feel like it." Then she walks away. Say: *What questions could you ask to help you figure out why your friend is acting this way?* Have students brainstorm a list of questions. Write them on the board.

- **Set Purposes** Remind students that good readers generate questions about a story before, during, and after reading. Then they look for story clues to help them answer those questions. Asking and answering questions helps them figure out what is happening in a story and why it is happening.

✓ RETEACH SKILL: DRAW CONCLUSIONS

- **Define** Remind students that drawing conclusions means figuring things out by finding and analyzing text clues in order to arrive at a new understanding of a character or event in a story.

- **Relate to Real Life** Refer back to the story about the friend who did not want to play basketball. Have them imagine they discovered these clues: Her brother is sick in the hospital. He is also a high school basketball star and will not be able to play this year. Ask: *What conclusions can you draw about why your friend does not want to play basketball?*

- **Set Purposes** Remind students that good readers are like detectives. They draw conclusions about story characters and events by looking for clues and thinking about what they mean. This helps them understand the reasons for the characters' actions, and analyze the relationships between characters.

- **Apply** Help students generate questions about the characters and events in "Puppy Trouble." Ask them to look for text clues to help them answer their questions and draw conclusions. Students will apply this strategy and skill to a simpler text as they read *Melvin and the Princess*.

Approaching Level

Leveled Reader Lesson 1

Objective Read to apply skills and strategies
Materials • **Leveled Reader:** *Melvin and the Princess*

Leveled Reader

BEFORE READING

Preview and Predict Have students read the title and preview the first chapter. Ask students to generate a list of questions about the book before they read.

Review Vocabulary Words Have students read the vocabulary words on the inside front cover. Briefly define each and ask students to state related words they have learned.

Set a Purpose for Reading *Let's read to find answers to our questions and draw conclusions about the characters in the story.*

DURING READING

STRATEGY
GENERATE QUESTIONS

Remind students that generating questions means asking questions about story characters and events and then looking for clues to help them answer the questions.

SKILL
DRAW CONCLUSIONS

Remind students to look for clues to help them figure things out as they read. Read Chapter 1 with students. Help students complete a Conclusions Chart. Students should use text clues and their own prior experience connected to the reading selection.

As you read, help students decode unknown words. Ask open-ended questions to facilitate rich discussion, such as *What is the author trying to tell you about the characters? What conclusions can you draw about the relationship between the girl and the frog?* Build on students' responses to help them develop a deeper understanding of the text.

Stop after every two pages, and ask students to generate questions and draw conclusions about characters and plot before reading on. If they struggle, help students reread the difficult pages or passage. Then model generating questions and drawing conclusions about the information in the chapter.

AFTER READING

Have students compare *Dear Mrs. LaRue* and *Melvin and the Princess*. Ask: *In what ways are the stories similar?*

Digital Learning

Use the **Leveled Reader Audio CD** for fluency building *after* students read the book with your support during Small Group time.

Leveled Reader

Approaching Level

Leveled Reader Library

Leveled Reader Lesson 2

Objective Reread to apply skills and strategies and develop fluency

Materials
- **Leveled Reader:** *Melvin and the Princess*
- **Approaching Reproducible,** p. 104

BEFORE READING

 Review the Strategy and Skill Review students' completed Conclusions Charts from the first read. Remind students that generating questions means asking questions and looking for clues in the text to help answer them. Drawing conclusions means figuring things out that were not stated directly in the text, based on story clues and one's own knowledge connected to the text.

Review Vocabulary Words Have students search the book for each vocabulary word. Ask students to read aloud the sentence containing the word and state the word's definition or provide related words. Point out any context clues provided, such as surrounding words.

Set a Purpose for Reading *Let's reread to try to draw more conclusions and to work on our reading fluency.*

DURING READING

Reread *Melvin and the Princess* with students. Have them read silently two pages at a time, or read aloud to a partner. Stop and have students generate questions and draw conclusions before reading the next two pages. Model your own questions and conclusions, as needed.

AFTER READING

Check Comprehension Have partners complete the Comprehension Check on page 16. Review students' answers. Help students find evidence for their answers in the text.

MODEL FLUENCY

Model reading the fluency passage on **Approaching Reproducible** page 104. Tell students to pay close attention to your expression. Then read one sentence at a time, and have students echo-read the sentences, copying your expression.

During independent reading time, have students work with a partner using the fluency passage. One student reads aloud while the other repeats each sentence back. If students need additional support, have them listen to the "practice speed" version of the passage on the **Fluency Solutions Audio CD**.

Approaching Reproducible, page 104

As I read, I will pay attention to expression.

	It takes a lot of work to be a movie dog. Mixed breeds
13	and purebreds alike must be well behaved. They must
22	know basic **obedience** commands like "sit down," "stay,"
30	and "come." They must also learn to perform difficult
39	tricks.
40	During the filming of a movie, a dog actor must follow
51	its trainer's commands quickly and properly. Sometimes
58	trainers aren't able to give a vocal command. So they
68	use simple hand signals instead. Sometimes fancy signals
76	are **misunderstood** by a dog actor.
82	Dog performers also must feel at ease on the movie set.
93	It's a place with many people, lots of noise, and bright
104	lights. Even with all these things going on, a dog actor
115	needs to stay focused on its trainer at all times. 125

Comprehension Check

1. Why do movie dogs need to know basic obedience commands? **Cause and Effect** Movie dogs need to know basic movie commands so that when they are filmed they perform in the correct way.

2. Why does the author want you to know about movie dogs? **Author's Purpose** The author wants to inform you that being a movie dog is a lot of work and that such dogs have to be well-trained.

	Words Read	–	Number of Errors	=	Words Correct Score
First Read		–		=	
Second Read		–		=	

Approaching Level

Leveled Reader Lesson 3

Objective Build fluency

Materials
- **Leveled Reader:** *Melvin and the Princess*
- **Approaching Reproducible,** p. 104

FOCUS ON FLUENCY

Timed Reading Tell students that they will be doing a final timed reading of the fluency passage on **Approaching Reproducible** page 104 that they have been practicing. With each student, follow these directions:

- Place the passage facedown.

- When you say "Go," the student begins reading the passage aloud.

- When you say "Stop," the student stops reading the passage.

As they read, note words students mispronounce and their overall expression. Stop after one minute. Help students record and graph the number of words they read correctly.

REREAD PREVIOUSLY READ BOOKS

- Distribute copies of the past six **Leveled Readers**. Have students select two to reread. Tell students that rereading these books will help them develop their skills. The more times they read the same words, the quicker they will learn these words. This will make the reading of other books easier.

- Circulate and listen in as students read. Stop students periodically and ask them how they are figuring out difficult words and how they are monitoring their comprehension. Note students who need additional work with specific decoding or comprehension skills.

- Encourage students to read other previously read Leveled Readers during independent reading time or for homework.

Meet Grade-Level Expectations

As an alternative to this day's lesson, guide students through a reading of the On Level Leveled Reader. See page 325U. Since both books contain the same vocabulary, phonics, and comprehension skills, the scaffolding you provided will help most students gain access to this more challenging text.

Book Talk

Bringing Groups Together Students will work with peers of various language and reading abilities to discuss this week's Leveled Readers. Refer to page 158 in the **Teacher's Resource Book** for more about how to conduct a Book Talk.

Student Book

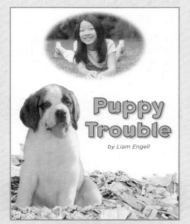

Student Book

Approaching Level

Fluency

Objectives Reread selections to develop fluency; develop speaking skills

Materials • **Student Book:** *Dear Mrs. LaRue*, "Puppy Trouble"

✓ REREAD FOR FLUENCY

- Have students reread a portion of *Dear Mrs. LaRue*. Suggest that they focus on two to four of their favorite pages from the selection. Work with students on reading the pages with the appropriate expression.

- Provide time for students to read their sections of text to you. Comment on their expression, and provide corrective feedback by modeling proper fluency.

DEVELOP SPEAKING/LISTENING SKILLS

- Have pairs of students reread the selection "Puppy Trouble."

- Ask students to tell their partner about an experience they have had involving a pet or other animal that misbehaved and caused problems for people. Have them explain why the experience was funny or unforgettable.

- Provide time for students to practice telling their narrative to partners. Ask students to name ways in which their partner used words and vocal expression to help the listener imagine the circumstances of the experience.

- Challenge students to deliver their narrative presentations to the class. Remind them to speak loudly, clearly, and smoothly and to use appropriate gestures to amplify their meaning. Encourage listeners to ask relevant questions and make pertinent comments related to the narrative.

Approaching Level

Self-Selected Reading

Objective Read independently to generate questions and draw conclusions

Materials • **Leveled Classroom Library** • other fiction books

APPLY SKILLS AND STRATEGIES TO INDEPENDENT READING

- **Read Independently** Have students choose a fiction book for sustained silent reading. (See the **Theme Bibliography** on pages T8–T9 for book suggestions.) Remind them to generate questions and look for clues in the text to answer their questions. This process can help them draw conclusions about the story. Have students read their books and record text clues and conclusions on a Conclusions Chart.

- **Show Evidence of Reading** While reading, suggest that students generate a reading log or journal. After reading, ask students to use their Conclusions Chart and logs to paraphrase the content of the book, maintaining meaning and logical order. They may write or orally state a summary of the book. Ask students to share their summaries and reactions to the book while participating in Book Talks. Ask: *Could you figure out why the characters in this book acted the way they did? Why or why not?*

Approaching

Leveled Classroom Library
See Leveled Classroom
Library lessons on pages T2–T7.

Daily Planner

DAY 1	• Vocabulary • Phonics
DAY 2	• Leveled Reader Lesson 1
DAY 3	• Leveled Reader Lesson 2
DAY 4	• Fluency
DAY 5	• Self-Selected Reading

ELL

Practice Vocabulary Pair ELL students with native speakers. On the board, provide sentence frames for pairs to copy and complete using the vocabulary and additional words when necessary. For example: *I _____ to clean my room so now it is very _____.* (*neglected; messy*)

Sound-Spelling WorkBoard

On Level

Vocabulary

Objective Review vocabulary

Materials • **Vocabulary Cards**

REVIEW PREVIOUSLY TAUGHT WORDS

Review the Words Display the **Vocabulary Cards** for *neglected, appreciated, misunderstood, desperate, endured,* and *obedience.* Point to each word, read it aloud, and have students chorally repeat.

Then ask students to answer each question below, justifying their answer. Allow other students to respond. Use the discussions to determine each student's depth of word knowledge.

■ What would happen if you *neglected* to help around the house?

■ What did someone once tell you that you really *appreciated*?

■ When you feel *misunderstood,* do you feel happy or sad? Why?

■ What kinds of situations might make someone feel *desperate*?

■ When you have *endured* something boring, have you enjoyed it?

Phonics/Word Study

Objective Decode multisyllabic words with silent letters

Materials • **Sound-Spelling WorkBoards**

RETEACH SKILL

■ **Words with Silent Letters** Point to the **Sound-Spelling Cards** for the sounds /n/ and /r/ on the **WorkBoard**, and review the silent letter spellings for each sound. Review words that begin with a silent *h* and those ending with a silent *b*. State each spelling, and provide a sample word for each sound-spelling combination.

■ Write the words below on the board. If necessary, divide the words into syllables using the syllable-scoop technique to help students read one syllable at a time. When completed, point to the words in random order for students to chorally read.

knives	gnawing	unknown	nowhere	knickknack
wreath	wretched	wristband	wrongful	dumbfound
honesty	hourly	climbing	thumbtack	dishonestly

■ **Spelling** Dictate the following words for students to spell on their WorkBoards: *kneecap, knighthood, wristwatch, honorable, plumber.* Guide students in using the Sound-Spelling Cards, and model how to segment words, such as spelling a word syllable by syllable.

On Level

Fluency

Objectives   Reread selections to develop fluency; develop speaking skills

Materials   • **Student Book:** *Dear Mrs. LaRue*, "Puppy Trouble," "Dog Amazes Scientists!"

REREAD FOR FLUENCY

- Have students reread *Dear Mrs. LaRue*. Work with students to read with appropriate expression. Model as needed.

- Provide time for students to read a section of text to you. Comment on their expression and provide corrective feedback as needed.

DEVELOP SPEAKING/LISTENING SKILLS

- Have pairs of students reread the selections "Puppy Trouble" and "Dog Amazes Scientists!"

- Have students tell their partners about an experience they had involving an animal that misbehaved or showed how smart it was. Have them explain why the experience was funny or memorable.

- Provide time for students to practice telling their narrative to partners. Ask students to name ways in which their partner used words and vocal expression to help the listener imagine the circumstances of the experience.

- Challenge students to deliver their narrative presentations.

Self-Selected Reading

Objective   Read independently to generate questions and draw conclusions

Materials   • **Leveled Classroom Library**   • other fiction books

APPLY SKILLS AND STRATEGIES TO INDEPENDENT READING

- **Read Independently** Have students choose a fiction book for sustained silent reading. (See the **Theme Bibliography** on pages T8–T9 for book suggestions.) Have students read their books and record text clues and conclusions on a Conclusions Chart.

- **Show Evidence of Reading** While reading, students may generate a reading log or journal. After reading, ask students to use their Conclusions Charts and logs to paraphrase the content of the book, maintaining meaning and logical order. They may write or orally state a summary of the book. Provide time for students to share their summaries and reactions to the book while participating in Book Talks. Ask: *Could you draw conclusions about the characters in this book and why they acted the way they did? Explain your answer.*

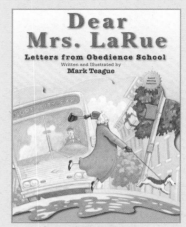

Student Book

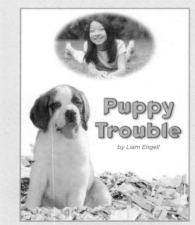

Student Book

On Level

Leveled Classroom Library
See Leveled Classroom
Library lessons on pages T2–T7.

Leveled Reader

On Level

Leveled Reader Lesson 1

Objective Read to apply strategies and skills
Materials • **Leveled Reader:** *Fish Tricks*

BEFORE READING

Preview and Predict Have students read the title and preview the book by reading the chapter titles and looking at the illustrations. Ask students to predict what this book is about and to generate a list of questions they would like to answer as they read.

 Review Vocabulary Words Have students read the vocabulary words on the inside front cover. Ask students to state related words they have learned. Review definitions, as needed.

Set a Purpose for Reading *Let's read to find out what conclusions we can draw about Maddie and her fish.*

DURING READING

 STRATEGY
GENERATE QUESTIONS

Remind students to generate questions about the characters in the book and then look for clues to answer their questions.

SKILL
DRAW CONCLUSIONS

Remind students to look for clues to help them answer their questions and draw conclusions as they read.

Read Chapter 1 with students. Ask open-ended questions to facilitate rich discussion, such as *What did the author want you to know about Maddie's problem? What conclusions can you draw about Maddie's relationship with her aunt?* Build on students' responses to help them develop a deeper understanding of the text. Have students fill in the first section of the Conclusions Chart before they continue reading.

Prefixes As they read, have students point out this week's new vocabulary words and look for words with prefixes. Students should identify any context clues the author provides for these words, such as nearby words with similar meanings or definitions or examples.

AFTER READING

Ask students what they would do if they had a pet like Minnie. Have them give an explanation based on details in the text. Ask: *What conclusions can you draw about Maddie's relationship with Minnie?*

On Level

Leveled Reader Lesson 2

Objective Reread to apply skills and strategies and develop fluency

Materials • **Leveled Reader:** *Fish Tricks* • **Practice Book,** p. 104

BEFORE READING

Review the Strategy and Skill Review students' completed Conclusions Charts from the first read. Remind students that they can draw conclusions by looking for clues in the text to answer their questions about the book.

If students' conclusions are incomplete, choose important details from the book, write them on a Conclusions Chart on the board, and model drawing conclusions from the details. Have students copy the revised Conclusions Chart in their Writer's Notebooks.

Set a Purpose for Reading *Let's reread to draw more conclusions and to work on our reading fluency*.

DURING READING

Reread *Fish Tricks* with students. Have them read silently two pages at a time, or read aloud to a partner. Stop and have students summarize before reading the next two pages. Model oral summaries, as needed.

AFTER READING

Check Comprehension Have partners complete the Comprehension Check on page 20. Review students' answers. Help students find evidence for their answers in the text.

MODEL FLUENCY

Model reading the fluency passage on **Practice Book** page 104. Tell students to pay close attention to your expression as you read. Then read one sentence at a time, and have students echo-read the sentences, copying your expression.

During independent reading time, have students work with a partner using the fluency passage. One student reads aloud while the other repeats each sentence back. If students need additional support, have them listen to the "practice speed" version of the passage on the **Fluency Solutions Audio CD**.

Leveled Reader

Book Talk

Bringing Groups Together Students will work with peers of various language and reading abilities to discuss this week's **Leveled Readers**. Refer to page 158 in the **Teacher's Resource Book** for more about how to conduct a Book Talk.

Practice Book, page 104

As I read, I will pay attention to expression.

	Presidents have kept a wide range of pets. These
9	animals have included cows, mice, goats, and birds. But
18	dogs have been the most popular presidential pets.
26	Dogs are loyal and loving. They make their owners
35	feel appreciated. Like other dog owners, many Presidents
43	have enjoyed the special friendship that dogs can give.
52	Many people believe that dogs help Presidents gain
60	support from Americans. Pictures of Presidents playing
67	with their dogs can make the Presidents seem likable and
77	help them win votes.
81	More than 200 dogs of various breeds have lived at the
91	White House. Some of these White House dogs served
100	as guard dogs. Others played with the Presidents' children.
109	And others clearly belonged to the Presidents and were
118	their personal four-legged friends. A few presidential
125	pooches were even as well known as their masters. Let's
135	take a look at some of the famous "First Dogs" of America. 147

Comprehension Check

1. Why might people vote for a candidate who has a dog as a pet? **Cause and Effect** People think a candidate who has a dog as a pet is probably a likable person.
2. Why did the author write this passage about presidential dogs? **Author's Purpose** The author wants you to know that presidential dogs help presidents in a number of ways.

	Words Read	−	Number of Errors	=	Words Correct Score
First Read		−		=	
Second Read		−		=	

Daily Planner

DAY 1	• Leveled Reader Lesson 1
DAY 2	• Leveled Reader Lesson 2
DAY 3	• Phonics
DAY 4	• Vocabulary • Fluency
DAY 5	• Self-Selected Reading

ELL

Self-Monitor Vocabulary
Have student pairs of
different proficiency identify
and define unfamiliar
words from the main
selection using a dictionary.
Challenge students to use
the new words in sentences.
Monitor students as they
complete the activity.

Beyond Level

Phonics/Word Study

Objective Decode multisyllabic words with silent letters

Materials • none

EXTEND/ACCELERATE

■ **Read Multisyllabic Words with Silent Letters** Write the words
below on the board. Challenge students to read the words, using
known word parts such as roots and bases. When completed,
point to the words in random order for students to chorally read.

knapsack	knickknack	gnawingly	noticeable
wristband	wristwatch	wraparound	handwritten
honorably	dishonesty	dishonorable	hitchhiker
plumbing	climber	combing	thumbnail

■ **Define Words** Ask students to use their knowledge of word
parts to figure out the meanings of the above words. Then have
partners check the meanings in a dictionary. Challenge students
to use these words in this week's writing assignments.

■ **Spell Words with Silent Letters** Dictate these words for students
to spell: *thumbtack, wrestling, knitwear, gnashing, hourglass*. Write
the words for students to self-correct.

Vocabulary

Objectives Review news stories; research and summarize news stories

Materials • Internet search engine

ENRICH VOCABULARY

■ **Review News Stories** Remind students that *Dear Mrs. LaRue*
included fantasy news stories, while the selection "Dog Amazes
Scientists!" was a real news story, which included interesting
facts about the accomplishments of a real dog. It answered the
questions *who, what, when, where*, and *why* about real events.

■ **Research and Summarize News Stories** Have students
search newspapers and news Web sites for news stories about
amazing pets. Have them write brief summaries of two articles to
share with the class. Each summary should answer the questions
who, what, when, where, and *why* about the pet and its owners.
Direct students to analyze how different authors treat similar
concepts, themes, or events involving amazing pets. Students
should collect interesting vocabulary words from their reading.

Gifted & Talented

Beyond Level

Fluency

Objectives Reread selections to develop fluency; develop speaking skills

Materials • **Student Book:** *Dear Mrs. LaRue*, "Puppy Trouble," "Dog Amazes Scientists!"

REREAD FOR FLUENCY

- Have students reread *Dear Mrs. LaRue*. Work with students to read the book with appropriate expression.

- Provide time for students to read a section of text to you. Comment on their expression and provide corrective feedback.

DEVELOP SPEAKING/LISTENING SKILLS

- Review "Puppy Trouble" and "Dog Amazes Scientists!"

- Have students prepare a presentation about an experience they had with an animal that either misbehaved or showed how smart it was. Ask them to include details to help listeners imagine the experience and understand why it was memorable.

- Have students make their presentations to a partner. Ask partners to name ways in which the speaker used words and vocal expression to help the listener imagine the experience.

- Challenge students to deliver their presentations to the class.

Self-Selected Reading

Objective Read independently to generate questions and draw conclusions

Materials • **Leveled Classroom Library** • other fiction books

APPLY SKILLS AND STRATEGIES TO INDEPENDENT READING

- **Read Independently** Have students choose a fiction book for sustained silent reading. (See the **Theme Bibliography** on pages T8–T9 for book suggestions.) Have students read their books and record text clues and conclusions on a Conclusions Chart.

- **Show Evidence of Reading** While reading, students may generate a reading log or journal. After reading, have students use their Conclusions Charts and logs to paraphrase the content of the book, maintaining meaning and logical order. They may write or orally state a summary of the book. Ask students to share their summaries and reactions to the book while participating in Book Talks. Ask: *What conclusions could you draw about the characters in this book? What evidence did you use?*

- **Evaluate** Have students use text evidence to explain which character in the book they would most like to have as a friend.

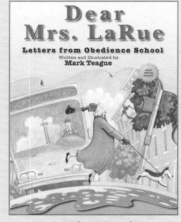

Student Book

Student Book

Beyond

Leveled Classroom Library
See Leveled Classroom Library lessons on pages T2–T7.

Leveled Reader

Beyond Level

Leveled Reader Lesson 1

Objective	Read to apply strategies and skills
Materials	• **Leveled Reader:** *Hopping to Victory*

BEFORE READING

Preview and Predict Have students preview the book by reading the title and chapter titles and looking at the illustrations. Ask students to generate questions they would like to answer as they read the book.

Review Vocabulary Words Have students read the vocabulary words on the inside front cover. Ask students to state each definition and any related words they have learned.

Set a Purpose for Reading *Let's read to answer our questions and draw conclusions about* Hopping to Victory.

DURING READING

STRATEGY
GENERATE QUESTIONS

Ask students to define the term *generate questions*. Remind students to ask questions about the characters or events in the book and then to look for clues in the text to help them answer the questions. Their questions can be both literal and higher level.

SKILL
DRAW CONCLUSIONS

Ask students to define the term *draw conclusions*. Remind students that they can use clues in the text, plus their own experiences connected to the text, to help them figure things out as they read.

Read the book with students. Ask open-ended questions to facilitate rich discussion, such as: *What does the author want to tell us about friendships? What conclusions can you draw about Ted and Eduardo's relationship?* Build on students' responses to help them develop a deeper understanding of the text. Have students fill in their Conclusions Charts independently as they read.

AFTER READING

Compare Ask students to compare Eduardo in *Hopping to Victory* to Ike in *Dear Mrs. LaRue* and Bernie in "Puppy Trouble."

Analyze Ask students to think about why a pet can make a good companion. Have them consider what they learned in their readings and any personal experiences they may have had with pets.

Week 3 ★ At a Glance

Priority Skills and Concepts

 Comprehension
- **Strategy:** Monitor Comprehension
- **Skill:** Fact and Opinion
- Cause and Effect
- **Genre:** Autobiography, Expository

 **Robust Vocabulary**
- **Selection Vocabulary:** *dismiss, interact, motivate, conceived, definition*
- **Strategy:** Latin Prefixes

 Fluency
- Accuracy

 **Phonics/Spelling**
- **Word Study:** Soft *c* and *g*, Multisyllabic Words
- **Spelling Words:** *center, once, scene, germs, spice, bridge, badge, circus, cement, glance, strange, police, certain, orange, ounce, ginger, wedge, arrange, sponge, village*
- *combs, kneel, wrench*

 **Grammar/Mechanics**
- **Main and Helping Verbs**
- **Punctuation in Contractions**

 Writing
- **Persuasive Essay**

Key

✔ Tested in program   Review Skill

Diagnose	IF...	Prescribe / THEN...
VOCABULARY WORDS **VOCABULARY STRATEGY** Prefixes	0–2 items correct …	See **Vocabulary Intervention Teacher's Edition.** **LOG ON** ▶ Online Practice: Go to **www.macmillanmh.com**. **CD-ROM** Vocabulary PuzzleMaker
COMPREHENSION Skill: Draw Conclusions	0–3 items correct …	See **Comprehension Intervention Teacher's Edition.** **SPIRAL REVIEW** See Draw Conclusions lesson in Unit 3 Week 4, page 361B.
GRAMMAR Verb Tenses	0–1 items correct …	See **Writing and Grammar Intervention Teacher's Edition.**
PHONICS AND SPELLING Silent Letters	0–1 items correct …	**LOG ON** ▶ Online Practice: Go to **www.macmillanmh.com**. See **Phonics Intervention Teacher's Edition.**
FLUENCY	98–101 WCPM	**AUDIO CD** Fluency Solutions Audio CD
	0–97 WCPM	See **Fluency Intervention Teacher's Edition.**

Review the assessment answers with students. Have them correct their errors. Then provide additional instruction as needed.

Response to Intervention

To place students in Tier 2 or Tier 3 Intervention use the *Diagnostic Assessment*.

- Phonics
- Vocabulary
- Comprehension
- Fluency
- Writing and Grammar

Progress Monitoring
Weekly Assessment

ASSESSED SKILLS

- Vocabulary: Vocabulary Words, Prefixes
- Comprehension: Draw Conclusions
- Grammar: Verb Tenses
- Phonics/Spelling: Silent Letters

Selection Test for* Dear Mrs. LaRue *Also Available

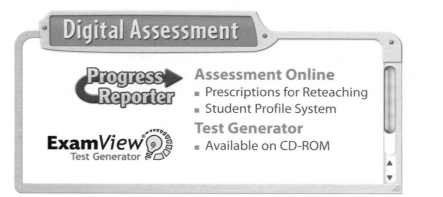

Digital Assessment

Progress Reporter

Assessment Online
- Prescriptions for Reteaching
- Student Profile System

ExamView Test Generator

Test Generator
- Available on CD-ROM

Weekly Assessment
Unit 3 Week 2

Fluency Assessment

Assess fluency for one group of students per week. Use the Oral Fluency Record Sheet to track the number of words read correctly. Fluency goal for all students: **102–122 words correct per minute (WCPM).**

Approaching Level	Weeks 1, 3, 5
On Level	Weeks 2, 4
Beyond Level	Week 6

Fluency Assessment

AFTER READING

Use the chart below and Think and Compare questions in the **Leveled Reader** to determine students' progress.

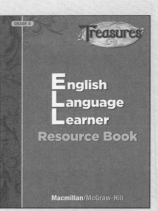

ELL Resource Book

Think and Compare	Beginning	Intermediate	Advanced
1 What conclusions can you draw about how Minnie changed Maddie's life? *(Draw Conclusions)*	Possible responses: Nonverbal response. Help Maddie. Get friends.	Possible responses: Minnie helped Maddie make friends.	Possible responses: Maddie was shy, so Minnie helped Maddie become more comfortable meeting new people.
2 Would you like to have Minnie as a pet? Explain *(Evaluate)*	Possible responses: Nonverbal response. Yes. Fun. Teach tricks.	Possible responses: Yes, I want to have Minnie as a pet. I can teach her tricks.	Possible responses: Yes, I would like to have Minnie as a pet because it would be fun to talk to her and teach new tricks to her.
3 How can pets change people's lives? *(Apply)*	Possible responses: Nonverbal response. Help. Make better.	Possible responses: Pets can help people and make lives better. Pets make people feel good.	Possible responses: Pets can make people's lives better because pets can make people feel good and they can do fun things with people.

BOOK TALK

Develop Listening and Speaking Skills Distribute copies of **ELL Resource Book** page 139 and form small groups. Help students determine the leader to discuss the Book Talk questions. Tell students to remember the following while engaged in the activity:

- Narrate, describe, and explain with specificity and detail. Ask: *Where did the story take place? Can you describe the setting? What else did you notice?*

- Express opinions, ideas, and feelings on a variety of social and academic topics. Ask: *What do you think about the characters in the story?*

- Use high-frequency English words to describe people, places, and objects.

- Share information in cooperative learning interactions. Remind students to work with their partners to retell the story and complete any activities. Ask: *What happened next in the story?*

Book Talk

Bringing Groups Together
Students will work with peers of varying language abilities to discuss the Book Talk questions. Form groups so that students who read the Beyond Level, On Level, Approaching Level, and ELL Leveled Readers are in the same group for the activity.

Leveled Reader

ELL ENGLISH LANGUAGE LEARNERS

Leveled Reader

Content Objective Read to apply skills and strategies

Language Objective Retell information, using complete sentences

Materials
- **Leveled Reader:** *Fish Tricks*
- **ELL Resource Book,** p. 139
- **Visual Vocabulary Resources,** pp. 419–424

BEFORE READING

> **All Language Levels**

- **Preview** Read the title *Fish Tricks*. Ask: *What's the title? Say it again*. Repeat with the author's name. Then page through the book. Use simple language to tell about each page. Immediately follow up with questions, such as *Can fish do tricks? What tricks would they do? What would you like to see a fish do?*

- **Review Skills** Use the inside front cover to review the comprehension skill and vocabulary words.

- **Set a Purpose** Say: *Let's read to find out about what tricks the fish can do.*

DURING READING

> **All Language Levels**

- Have students read each page aloud using the differentiated suggestions. Provide corrective feedback, such as modeling how to blend a decodable word or clarifying meaning by using techniques from the Interactive Question-Response Guide.

- **Retell** After every two pages, ask students to state the main ideas they have learned so far. Help them to complete the Conclusions Chart. Restate students' comments when they have difficulty using story-specific words. Provide differentiated sentence frames to support students' responses and engage students in partner-talk where appropriate.

Vocabulary

Preteach Vocabulary Use the routine in the **Visual Vocabulary Resources**, pages 419–424, to preteach the ELL Vocabulary listed in the inside front cover of the **Leveled Reader**.

Beginning	Intermediate	Advanced
Echo-Read Have students echo-read after you.	**Choral-Read** Have students chorally read with you.	**Choral-Read** Have students chorally read.
Check Comprehension Point to pictures and ask questions, such as *Where does the fish live? What tricks can Minnie do?*	**Check Comprehension** Ask questions/prompts, such as *Does Maddie think that fish make a good pet? Why? Who is Minnie? What can she do?*	**Check Comprehension** Ask: *What kind of pet does Maddie want to have? Why does Minnie want to show her tricks to Aunt Irene? How does Minnie help Maddie?*

Writing/Spelling

Content Objective Spell words correctly
Language Objective Write in complete sentences, using sentence frames

All Language Levels

■ Write the key vocabulary words on the board: *neglected, appreciated, misunderstood, desperate, endured,* and *obedience.* Have students copy each word on their **WorkBoards**. Help them say each word and then write a sentence for it. Provide sentence starters such as:

> *Sometimes I feel neglected when ____.*
>
> *Being appreciated feels good because ____.*
>
> *I misunderstood my mom when she told me to ____.*
>
> *People feel desperate when ____.*
>
> *The longest day I ever endured was when ____.*
>
> *We show obedience when the teacher says ____.*

Beginning/Intermediate

■ Help students spell words using their growing knowledge of English sound-spelling relationships. Model how to segment the word students are trying to spell, and attach a spelling to each sound (or spellings to each syllable if a multisyllabic word). Use the **Sound-Spelling Cards** to reinforce the spellings for each English sound.

Advanced

■ Dictate the following words for students to spell: *know, comb, sign, write, honor, climb, knife, gnaw, honest.* Use the Sound-Spelling Cards to guide students as they spell each word.

■ When completed, review the meanings of words that can be easily demonstrated or explained. Use actions, gestures, and available pictures.

Sound-Spelling WorkBoard

Phonics/Word Study

For English Language Learners who need more practice with this week's phonics/spelling skill, see the Approaching Level lesson on page 325J. Focus on minimal contrasts, articulation, and those sounds that do not transfer from the student's first language to English. See language transfers on pages T16–T31.

Transfer Skills

Verbs Tenses There is no agreement of present-tense verbs in Cantonese, Haitian Creole, Hmong, Korean, and Vietnamese. Verbs do not change form to indicate the number of the subject. (*Hector tells, Hector and Ana tells*) Also, verbs in Hmong and Khmer do not change form to express tense. Model correct usage, and have students repeat for additional practice. See language transfers on pages T16–T31.

Corrective Feedback

During Whole Group grammar lessons, follow the routine on the **Grammar Transparencies** to provide students with extra support. This routine includes completing the items with English Language Learners while other students work independently, having students reread the sentences with partners to build fluency, and providing a generative task such as writing a new sentence using the skill.

Grammar

Content Objective Identify present-, past-, and future-tense verbs
Language Objective Speak in complete sentences, using sentence frames

✓ VERB TENSES

Beginning/Intermediate

■ Write these sentences on the board. Underline the verbs: *The dog wags its tail. The dog is wagging its tail. The dog wagged its tail. The dog will wag its tail.* Review that the tense of a verb tells when an action happens: a present-tense verb shows actions that happen now; a form of *be* can be added to the *-ing* form of a verb to show present tense; a past-tense verb shows action that has already happened, and a future-tense verb shows action that will happen. Remind students to add *-ed* to most verbs to form the past tense, and *will* to the main verb to form the future tense.

All Language Levels

■ Review verb tenses. Write the sentences below on the board. Have students underline the verb in each sentence. Have them say: ____ is a ____-tense verb.

 My dog Pete finished obedience school last summer.

 However, yesterday Pete barked at the neighbor.

 Pete tries to behave. He is wagging his tail right now!

 I think we will send him back to school soon.

PEER DISCUSSION STARTERS

All Language Levels

■ Write these sentences on the board:
 Dogs have to learn to ____. I learned that some dogs ____.

■ Have partners complete each sentence frame. Ask them to expand on their sentences by providing details from this week's readings. Circulate, listen in, and note students' language use.

Beginning	Intermediate	Advanced
Use Visuals Describe the illustrations in *Dear Mrs. LaRue* to students. Ask: *What do you see?* Help students point and name verbs. Work with them to form sentences based on the illustrations, using verb tenses.	**Describe** Ask students to describe the illustrations in *Dear Mrs. LaRue*. Have them use complete sentences with different verb tenses. Model sentences as needed.	**Discuss** Ask students to discuss the illustrations in *Dear Mrs. LaRue*. Have them describe in complete sentences, using different verb tenses. Have them use each verb tense at least once.

ELL ENGLISH LANGUAGE LEARNERS

Fluency

Content Objectives Reread selections to develop fluency; develop speaking skills
Language Objective Tell a partner what a selection is about
Materials • **Student Book:** *Dear Mrs. LaRue*, "Dog Amazes Scientists!"
• **Teacher's Resource Book**

REREAD FOR FLUENCY

Beginning

- Have students read the decodable passages on page 16 in the **Teacher's Resource Book**.

Intermediate/Advanced

- Have students reread two to four of their favorite pages of *Dear Mrs. LaRue*, based on their levels. Help students read the pages with the appropriate expression. For example, read each sentence of the first page and have students echo. Then have students chorally read additional pages. Remind them to use vocal expression to help listeners imagine Ike's experience.

- Provide time for students to read their sections of text to you. Comment on their expression, and provide corrective feedback by modeling proper fluency.

DEVELOP SPEAKING/LISTENING SKILLS

All Language Levels

- Have students practice reading "Dog Amazes Scientists!" Work with them to read with the appropriate expression.

- Provide time for students to read aloud the article to a partner. Ask students to summarize the article. Provide the sentence frame *This article is about ____*.

Self-Selected Reading

Content Objective Read independently
Language Objective Orally retell information learned
Materials • **Leveled Classroom Library** • other fiction books

APPLY SKILLS AND STRATEGIES TO INDEPENDENT READING

All Language Levels

- Have students choose a fiction book for independent reading. (See the **Theme Bibliography** on pages T8–T9.)

- After reading, ask students to orally summarize and share their reactions to the book with classmates. Ask: *Would you recommend this book to a classmate? Why or why not?*

Student Book

Leveled Classroom Library
See Leveled Classroom
Library lessons on pages T2–T7.

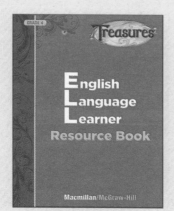

ELL Resource Book

ELL ENGLISH LANGUAGE LEARNERS

Access to Core Content

Content Objective Read grade-level text

Language Objective Discuss text using key words and sentence frames

Materials • **ELL Resource Book,** pp. 124–137

PRETEACH MAIN SELECTION (PAGES 296–317)

All Language Levels

Use the Interactive Question-Response Guide on **ELL Resource Book** pages 124–135 to introduce students to *Dear Mrs. LaRue.* Preteach half of the selection on Day 2 and half on Day 3.

- Use the prompts provided in the guide to develop meaning and vocabulary. Use the partner-talk and whole-class responses to engage students and increase student talk.

- When completed, have partners reread the story.

PRETEACH PAIRED SELECTION (PAGES 320–323)

All Language Levels

Use the Interactive Question-Response Guide on ELL Resource Book pages 136–137 to preview the paired selection, "Dog Amazes Scientists!" Preteach the selection on Day 4.

Beginning	Intermediate	Advanced
Use Visuals During the Interactive Reading, select several illustrations. Describe them to students. Then work with students to draw conclusions based on the illustrations.	**Draw Conclusions** During the Interactive Reading, select a few lines of text. After you have read and explained it, have students draw conclusions based on the text.	**Draw Conclusions** During the Interactive Reading, select a passage of text. After you read and explain it, have students draw conclusions based on the passage.

Vocabulary

Visual Vocabulary Resources

Language Objective Demonstrate understanding and use of key words by discussing persuasion

Materials • **Visual Vocabulary Resources**
• **ELL Resource Book**

PRETEACH KEY VOCABULARY

Use the **Visual Vocabulary Resources** to preteach the key selection words *neglected, appreciated, misunderstood, desperate, endured,* and *obedience.* Focus on two words per day. Use the following routine, which appears in detail on the cards.

Beginning/Intermediate

■ Point out any known sound-spellings, or focus on a key aspect of phonemic awareness related to the word.

All Language Levels

■ Define the word in English, and provide the example given.

■ Define the word in Spanish, if appropriate, and indicate if the word is a cognate.

■ Display the picture and explain how it illustrates the word. Engage students in structured activity, using the key word.

■ Ask students to chorally say the word three times.

■ Distribute copies of the Vocabulary Glossary on **ELL Resource Book** page 138.

PRETEACH FUNCTION WORDS AND PHRASES

All Language Levels

Use the Visual Vocabulary Resources to preteach the phrases *to be a horror, to clear up* [something], *wait and see,* and *feel queasy.* Focus on one phrase per day. Use the detailed routine on the cards.

■ Define the word in English and, if appropriate, in Spanish. Point out if the word is a cognate.

■ Refer to the picture and engage students in talk about the word. For example, students will partner-talk using sentence frames.

■ Ask students to chorally repeat the word three times.

TEACH BASIC WORDS

Beginning/Intermediate

Use the Visual Vocabulary Resources to teach the basic words *get-well card, letter, typewriter, mail, envelope,* and *stamp.* Teach these "letter-writing" words using the routine provided on the card.

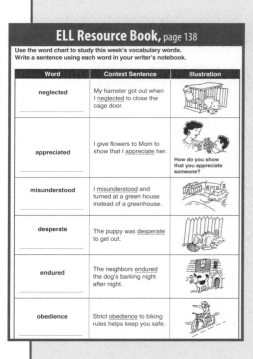

ELL Resource Book, page 138

Use the word chart to study this week's vocabulary words.
Write a sentence using each word in your writer's notebook.

Word	Context Sentence	Illustration
neglected	My hamster got out when I neglected to close the cage door.	
appreciated	I give flowers to Mom to show that I appreciate her.	How do you show that you appreciate someone?
misunderstood	I misunderstood and turned at a green house instead of a greenhouse.	
desperate	The puppy was desperate to get out.	
endured	The neighbors endured the dog's barking night after night.	
obedience	Strict obedience to biking rules helps keep you safe.	

ELL ENGLISH LANGUAGE LEARNERS

Daily Planner

DAY 1	• Build Background Knowledge • Vocabulary
DAY 2	• Vocabulary • Access to Core Content *Dear Mrs. LaRue*
DAY 3	• Vocabulary • Grammar • Access to Core Content *Dear Mrs. LaRue*
DAY 4	• Vocabulary • Writing/Spelling • Access to Core Content "Dog Amazes Scientists!" • Leveled Reader *Fish Tricks*
DAY 5	• Vocabulary • Leveled Reader *Fish Tricks* • Self-Selected Reading

LOG ON StudentWorks Plus
Interactive Student Book

Use StudentWorks Plus for:
- Vocabulary Preteaching
- Word-by-Word Highlighting
- Think Aloud Prompts

Cognates

Help students identify similarities and differences in pronunciation and spelling between English and Spanish cognates.

responsibilities	*responsabilidades*
communicate	*comunicar*
persuasion	*persuación*
obedience	*obediencia*
prefix	*prefijo*

ELL ENGLISH LANGUAGE LEARNERS

Prepare to Read

Content Objective Explore the power of words
Language Objective Use key words to discuss persuasion through written letters
Materials • StudentWorks Plus

BUILD BACKGROUND KNOWLEDGE

All Language Levels

- Have students preview *Dear Mrs. LaRue* using **StudentWorks Plus**, which contains oral summaries in multiple languages, online multilingual glossaries, word-by-word highlighting, and questions that assess and build comprehension.

- Students can build their word-reading fluency by reading along as the text is read or by listening during the first reading and, at the end of each paragraph, returning to the beginning of the paragraph and reading along.

- Students can build their comprehension by reviewing the definitions of key words in the online glossary and by answering the comprehension questions. When appropriate, the text required to answer the question is highlighted to provide students with additional support and scaffolding.

- After reading, ask students to write a response to a question that links the story to their personal experiences, such as *Do you have a dog or know someone who has one? How does that dog behave?*

Academic Language

Language Objective Use academic language in classroom conversations

All Language Levels

- This week's academic words are **boldfaced** throughout the lesson. Define the word in context, and provide a clear example from the selection. Then ask students to generate an example or a word with a similar meaning.

Academic Language Used in Whole Group Instruction

Theme Words	Key Selection Words	Strategy and Skill Words
responsibilities **request** **communicate** **persuasion**	**neglected** **appreciated** **misunderstood** **desperate** **endured** **obedience**	**draw conclusions** **generate questions** **prefixes** **verb tenses**

Beyond Level

Leveled Reader Lesson 2

Objective Reread to apply skills and strategies and develop fluency

Materials
- **Leveled Reader:** *Hopping to Victory*
- **Beyond Reproducible,** p. 104

BEFORE READING

Review the Strategy and Skill Review students' completed Conclusions Charts from the first read. Remind students that they can draw conclusions by looking for clues in the text to answer their questions about the book.

If students' conclusions are incomplete, draw a Conclusions Chart on the board. Generate questions about the book, and find text evidence to answer them. Model drawing conclusions from the clues, and write them in the chart. Have students copy the revised chart in their Writer's Notebooks.

Set a Purpose for Reading *Let's reread to draw more conclusions about our story and to work on our reading fluency.*

DURING READING

Have students reread *Hopping to Victory* silently or with a partner. If reading in pairs, prompt students to stop every two pages and draw conclusions or ask their partner probing questions.

AFTER READING

Check Comprehension Have students independently complete the Comprehension Check on page 20. Review students' answers. Help students find evidence for their answers in the text.

Synthesize Have students decide whether or not having a pet is a good idea. Then have them write a short essay trying to convince their classmates of their opinion. Ask students to make strong arguments based on facts, and to use supporting details.

MODEL FLUENCY

Model reading the fluency passage on **Beyond Reproducible** page 104. Tell students to pay close attention to your expression as you read. Then read one sentence at a time and have students echo-read the sentences, copying your expression.

During independent reading time, have students work with a partner using the fluency passage. One student reads aloud while the other repeats each sentence back. Students can check their fluency by reading along with the "expert speed" version of the passage on the **Fluency Solutions Audio CD.**

Leveled Reader

Book Talk

Bringing Groups Together Students will work with peers of various language and reading abilities to discuss this week's **Leveled Readers.** Refer to page 158 in the **Teacher's Resource Book** for more about how to conduct a Book Talk.

Beyond Reproducible, page 104

As I read, I will pay attention to expression.

	Dogs and people go together. For thousands of years, they have
11	lived in each other's company.
16	Dogs helped hunters search for game and shepherds tend their
26	flocks. Dogs protected their human masters from danger and
35	unwelcome intruders.
37	Dogs are social animals too. They offer love and companionship
47	to the people around them.
52	Today most dogs live as pets. But some have jobs that require
64	special training. These dogs serve as helpers and companions to
74	people in need. They are well trained for the work they do.
86	Some helping dogs work in partnership with visually challenged
95	people. Others work with the hearing or physically challenged.
104	These dogs enable their human partners to live more independent lives.
115	Helping dogs also work in group facilities like nursing homes or
126	hospitals. These dogs provide welcome company for the many
135	residents or patients staying there.
140	Each type of helping work that a dog does demands certain skills.
152	It's often hard work for a dog to learn them. But for those dogs that
167	succeed, their benefit to humans is tremendous. Amazingly, all that
177	these dogs ask for in return is praise and loving care. 188

Comprehension Check

1. Why are dogs so easy to train? **Cause and Effect** Dogs are social animals and love praise.
2. Why did the author write this passage? **Author's Purpose** To inform the reader about helping dogs.

	Words Read	−	Number of Errors	=	Words Correct Score
First Read		−		=	
Second Read		−		=	

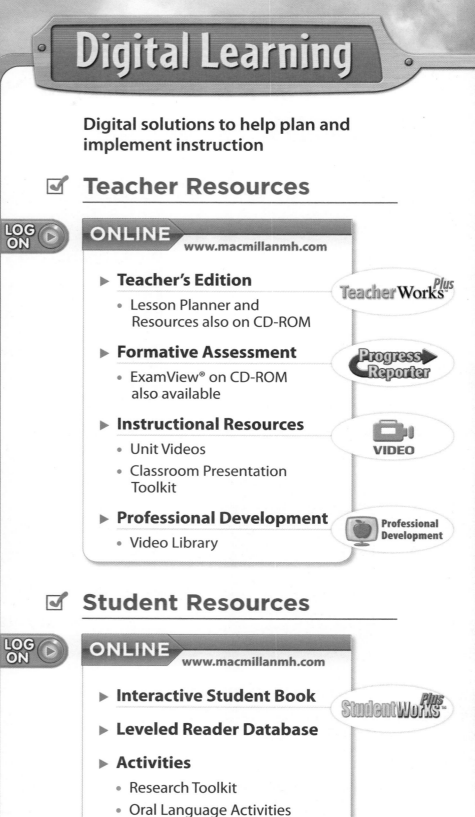

Digital Learning

Digital solutions to help plan and implement instruction

☑ Teacher Resources

LOG ON ▶

ONLINE www.macmillanmh.com

▶ **Teacher's Edition**
- Lesson Planner and Resources also on CD-ROM

TeacherWorks Plus

▶ **Formative Assessment**
- ExamView® on CD-ROM also available

Progress Reporter

▶ **Instructional Resources**
- Unit Videos
- Classroom Presentation Toolkit

VIDEO

▶ **Professional Development**
- Video Library

Professional Development

☑ Student Resources

LOG ON ▶

ONLINE www.macmillanmh.com

▶ **Interactive Student Book**

StudentWorks Plus

▶ **Leveled Reader Database**

▶ **Activities**
- Research Toolkit
- Oral Language Activities
- Vocabulary/Spelling Activities

 Listening Library
- Recordings of Student Books and Leveled Readers

Fluency Solutions
- Fluency Modeling and Practice

Weekly Literature

Theme: From Words to Action

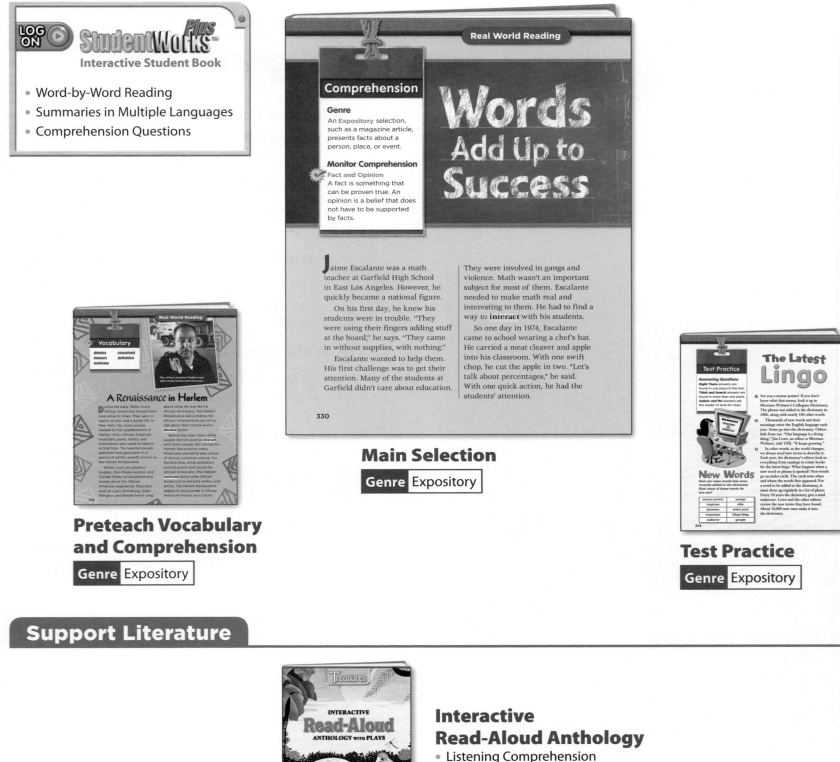

LOG ON StudentWorks™ Plus
Interactive Student Book

- Word-by-Word Reading
- Summaries in Multiple Languages
- Comprehension Questions

Real World Reading

Comprehension

Genre
An Expository selection, such as a magazine article, presents facts about a person, place, or event.

Monitor Comprehension
✓ Fact and Opinion
A fact is something that can be proven true. An opinion is a belief that does not have to be supported by facts.

Words Add Up to Success

Jaime Escalante was a math teacher at Garfield High School in East Los Angeles. However, he quickly became a national figure.

On his first day, he knew his students were in trouble. "They were using their fingers adding stuff at the board," he says. "They came in without supplies, with nothing."

Escalante wanted to help them. His first challenge was to get their attention. Many of the students at Garfield didn't care about education.

They were involved in gangs and violence. Math wasn't an important subject for most of them. Escalante needed to make math real and interesting to them. He had to find a way to **interact** with his students.

So one day in 1974, Escalante came to school wearing a chef's hat. He carried a meat cleaver and apple into his classroom. With one swift chop, he cut the apple in two. "Let's talk about percentages," he said. With one quick action, he had the students' attention.

330

Main Selection
Genre Expository

Real World Reading

Vocabulary

dismiss   conceived
interact   definition
motivate

The writer Langston Hughes was part of the Harlem Renaissance.

A Renaissance in Harlem

Preteach Vocabulary and Comprehension
Genre Expository

Test Practice

Test Practice

Answering Questions
Right There answers are found in one place in the text. **Think and Search** answers are found in more than one place. **Author and Me** answers ask the reader to look for clues.

New Words

The Latest Lingo

1. Are you a mouse potato? If you don't know what that means, look it up in Merriam-Webster's Collegiate Dictionary. The phrase was added to the dictionary in 2006, along with nearly 100 other words.

2. Thousands of new words and their meanings enter the English language each year. Some go into the dictionary. Others fade from use. "Our language is a living thing," Jim Lowe, an editor at Merriam-Webster, told TFK. "It keeps growing."

3. In other words, as the world changes, we always need new terms to describe it. Each year, the dictionary's editors look in everything from catalogs to comic books for the latest lingo. What happens when a new word or phrase is spotted? New words go on index cards. The cards note when and where the words first appeared. For a word to be added to the dictionary, it must show up regularly in a lot of places. Every 10 years the dictionary gets a total makeover. Lowe and the other editors review the new terms they have found. About 10,000 new ones make it into the dictionary.

mouse potato	manga
ringtone	ollie
spyware	warm pool
supersize	bling-bling
unibrow	google

324

Test Practice
Genre Expository

Treasures
INTERACTIVE Read-Aloud ANTHOLOGY WITH PLAYS
Macmillan McGraw-Hill

Interactive Read-Aloud Anthology
- Listening Comprehension
- Robust Vocabulary
- Readers Theater Plays for Fluency

Resources for Differentiated Instruction

Leveled Readers: Social Studies

AUDIO CD

GR Levels O–S

Genre	Expository

- Same Theme
- Same Vocabulary
- Same Comprehension Skills

O — Approaching Level

Q — On Level

S — Beyond Level

O — ELL

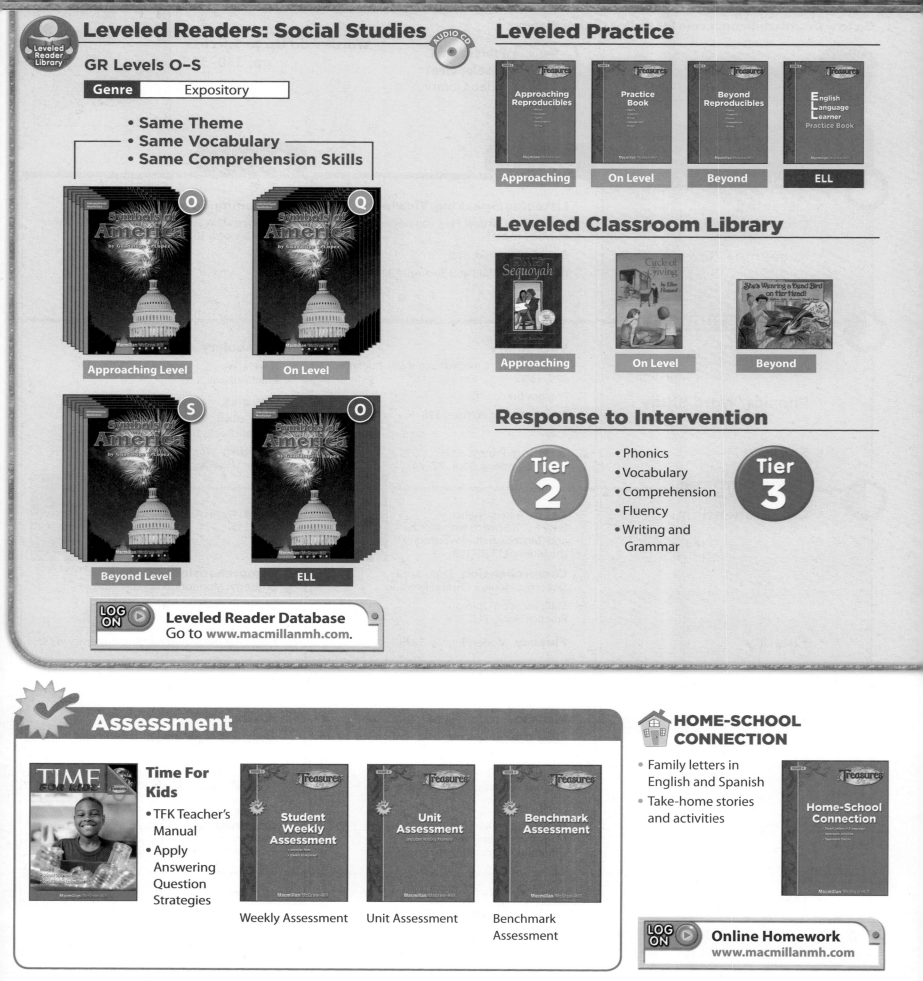

Leveled Reader Library

LOG ON ▶ **Leveled Reader Database**
Go to www.macmillanmh.com.

Leveled Practice

Approaching Reproducibles — **Approaching**

Practice Book — **On Level**

Beyond Reproducibles — **Beyond**

English Language Learner Practice Book — **ELL**

Leveled Classroom Library

Sequoyah — **Approaching**

Circle of Giving by Ellen Howard — **On Level**

She's Wearing a Dead Bird on Her Head! — **Beyond**

Response to Intervention

Tier 2

- Phonics
- Vocabulary
- Comprehension
- Fluency
- Writing and Grammar

Tier 3

Assessment

TIME FOR KIDS

Time For Kids

- TFK Teacher's Manual
- Apply Answering Question Strategies

Student Weekly Assessment — Weekly Assessment

Unit Assessment — Unit Assessment

Benchmark Assessment — Benchmark Assessment

HOME-SCHOOL CONNECTION

- Family letters in English and Spanish
- Take-home stories and activities

Home-School Connection

LOG ON ▶ **Online Homework**
www.macmillanmh.com

Suggested Lesson Plan

Go to www.macmillanmh.com for Online Lesson Planner

CD-ROM TeacherWorks™ Plus
All-In-One Planner and Resource Center

Professional Development Video Library

Words Add Up to Success, pp. 330–333

WHOLE GROUP

ORAL LANGUAGE

- Listening Comprehension
- Speaking/Viewing

WORD STUDY

- Vocabulary
- Phonics/Word Study
- Spelling

READING

- Comprehension
- Fluency

LANGUAGE ARTS

- Writing
- Grammar

ASSESSMENT

- Informal/Formal

DAY 1

Listening/Speaking/Viewing

❓ Focus Question How can powerful words move us to act?

Build Background, 326

Read Aloud: "Wild and Swampy," 327A–327B

Vocabulary

dismiss, interact, motivate, conceived, definition, 329, 337G

Practice Book, 110

Strategy: Latin Prefixes, 328

Spelling Pretest, 337I
Phonics/Spelling Book, 73–74

Read "A Renaissance in Harlem," "A Speech with Reach," and "Most-Searched Words on the Internet," 328–329

Comprehension, 329A–329B
Strategy: Monitor Comprehension

Skill: Fact and Opinion
Practice Book, 111

Fluency Model Fluency, 327B

Writing

Daily Writing Describe a time when you heard someone use words powerfully.

Persuasive Essay, Plan/Prewrite, 337A

Grammar Daily Language Activities, 337K
Main and Helping Verbs, 337K
Grammar Practice Book, 61

Quick Check Vocabulary, 329
Comprehension, 329B

DAY 2

Listening/Speaking

❓ Focus Question How did Jaime Escalante use his words to make a difference?

Vocabulary

Review Words, Latin Prefixes, 330, 337G
Practice Book, 116

Phonics

Soft *c* and *g*, 327C–327D
Practice Book, 109

Spelling Word Sorts, 337I
Phonics/Spelling Book, 75

Read *Words Add Up to Success,* 330–333

Comprehension, 330–333
Strategy: Monitor Comprehension

Skill: Fact and Opinion
Practice Book, 112

Fluency Repeated Reading: Accuracy, 333A

Writing

Daily Writing Write a journal entry for one day from the viewpoint of a teacher.

Persuasive Essay, Draft, 337B

Grammar Daily Language Activities, 337K
Main and Helping Verbs, 337K
Grammar Practice Book, 62

Quick Check Phonics, 327D
Comprehension, 333

Student Book

SMALL GROUP Lesson Plan ▶ Differentiated Instruction 326G–326H

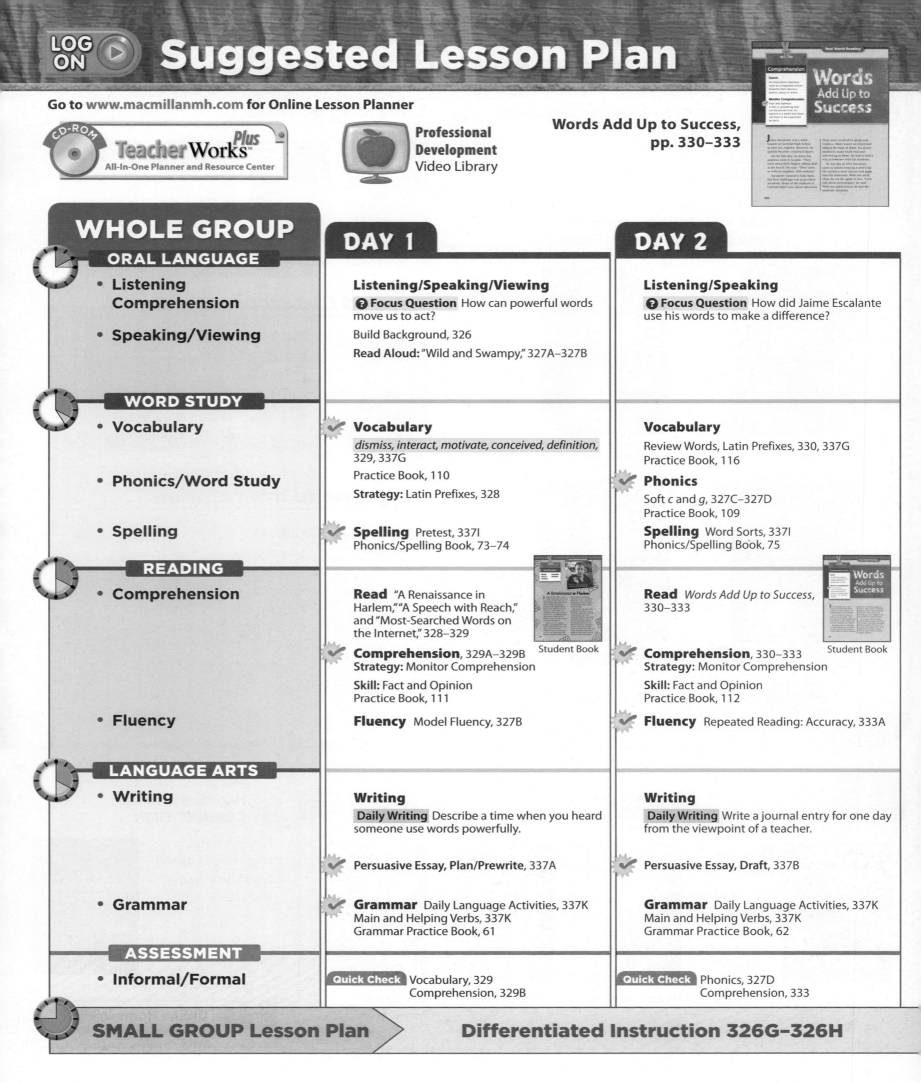

Priority Skills

Vocabulary	Comprehension	Writing	Social Studies
Vocabulary Words Latin Prefixes	**Strategy:** Monitor Comprehension **Skill:** Fact and Opinion	Persuasive Essay	Explain the meaning of patriotic symbols and landmarks.

DAY 3

Listening/Speaking

? Focus Question What do the speechmakers in "A Speech with Reach" have in common with Jaime Escalante?

Summarize, 333

Vocabulary
Review Words, Related Words, 337H

Spelling Word Meanings, 337J
Phonics/Spelling Book, 76

Read *Words Add Up to Success*, 330–333

Student Book

Comprehension
Comprehension Check, 333BS

Review Skill: Cause and Effect, 333B
Practice Book, 114

Fluency Repeated Reading: Accuracy, 333A
Practice Book, 113

Writing

Daily Writing Write a paragraph about a memorable class.

Persuasive Essay, Revise and Conferencing, 337C–337E

Grammar Daily Language Activities, 337K
Mechanics and Usage, 337L
Grammar Practice Book, 63

Quick Check Fluency, 333A

DAY 4

Listening/Speaking/Viewing

? Focus Question Why do you think the dictionary gets a total makeover every ten years?

Vocabulary
Review Words, Morphology, 337H

Spelling Proofread, 337J
Phonics/Spelling Book, 77

Read "The Latest Lingo," 334–335

Test Practice
Answering Questions

Research and Study Skills
Using a Computer, 333C–333D
Practice Book, 115

Student Book

Fluency Repeated Reading: Accuracy, 333A

Time For Kids

Writing

Daily Writing Write five questions that you would like to ask the editor of a dictionary.

Writing Prompt, 336–337

Persuasive Essay, Conferencing, Proofread/ Edit, 337E–337F

Grammar Daily Language Activities, 337K
Main and Helping Verbs, 337L
Grammar Practice Book, 64

Quick Check Vocabulary, 337H

DAY 5
Review and Assess

Listening/Speaking/Viewing

? Focus Question What are one fact and opinion you learned about the power of words this week?

Vocabulary
Assess Words, Connect to Writing, 337H

Spelling Posttest, 337J
Phonics/Spelling Book, 78

Read Self-Selected Reading, 326K
Practice Book, 117

Student Book

Comprehension
Strategy: Monitor Comprehension

Skill: Fact and Opinion

Fluency Practice, 326K

Writing

Daily Writing Write an advice column for younger students about why they should learn to use words precisely.

Persuasive Essay, Publish and Share, 337F

Grammar Daily Language Activities, 337K
Main and Helping Verbs, 337L
Grammar Practice Book, 65

Weekly Assessment, 337MM–337NN

Differentiated Instruction

What do I do in small groups?

Teacher-Led Small Groups

Independent Activities

LOG ON ▶

Focus on Skills

IF... students need additional instruction, practice, or extension based on your **Quick Check** observations for the following priority skills:

- ✔ **Phonics/Word Study**
  Soft *c* and *g*

- ✔ **Vocabulary Words**
  dismiss, interact, motivate, conceived, definition
  Strategy: Latin Prefixes

- ✔ **Comprehension**
  Strategy: Monitor Comprehension
  Skill: Fact and Opinion

- ✔ **Fluency**

THEN...

Approaching **ELL**	Preteach and Reteach Skills
On Level	Practice
Beyond	Enrich and Accelerate Learning

Suggested Small Group Lesson Plan

CD-ROM **TeacherWorks** *Plus*
All-In-One Planner and Resource Center

	DAY 1	DAY 2
Approaching Level • **Preteach/Reteach** **Tier 2 Instruction**	• Prepare to Read, 337M • Academic Language, 337M • Preteach Vocabulary, 337O	• Comprehension, 337Q Monitor Comprehension/Fact and Opinion **ELL** • Leveled Reader Lesson 1, 337R
On Level • **Practice**	• Vocabulary, 337W • Phonics, 337W Soft *c* and *g* **ELL**	• Leveled Reader Lesson 1, 337Y
Beyond Level • **Extend/Accelerate** **Gifted and Talented**	• Leveled Reader Lesson 1, 337CC • Analyze Information, 337CC	• Leveled Reader Lesson 2, 337DD • Synthesize Information, 337DD
ELL • **Build English Language Proficiency** • See **ELL** in other levels.	• Prepare to Read, 337EE • Academic Language, 337EE • Preteach Vocabulary, 337FF	• Vocabulary, 337FF • Preteach Main Selection, 337GG

Focus on Leveled Readers

Levels O–S

Approaching — O

On Level — Q

Beyond — S

ELL — O

Social Studies

Teacher's Annotated Edition

Explain the meaning of selected patriotic symbols and landmarks.

Additional Leveled Readers

LOG ON

Leveled Reader Database
www.macmillanmh.com

Search by

- Comprehension Skill
- Content Area
- Genre
- Text Feature
- Guided Reading Level
- Reading Recovery Level
- Lexile Score
- Benchmark Level

Subscription also available.

Manipulatives

Sound-Spelling WorkBoards

Sound-Spelling Cards

High-Frequency Word Cards

Visual Vocabulary Resources

DAY 3

- Phonics Maintenance, 337N
  Soft *c* and *g* **ELL**
- Leveled Reader Lesson 2, 337S

- Leveled Reader Lesson 2, 337Z

- Phonics, 337AA
  Soft *c* and *g* **ELL**

- Vocabulary, 337FF
- Grammar, 337II

DAY 4

- Reteach Phonics Skill, 337N
  Soft *c* and *g* **ELL**
- Review Vocabulary, 337P
- Leveled Reader Lesson 3, 337T

- Fluency, 337X

- Vocabulary, 337AA
- Discuss Inspiring People, 337AA
- Fluency, 337BB

- Vocabulary, 337FF
- Writing/Spelling, 337JJ
- Fluency, 337HH
- Leveled Reader, 337KK

DAY 5

- High-Frequency Words, 337P
- Fluency, 337U
- Self-Selected Independent Reading, 337V
- Book Talk, 337T

- Self-Selected Independent Reading, 337X
- Book Talk, 337Z

- Self-Selected Independent Reading, 337BB
- Evaluate Information, 337BB
- Book Talk, 337DD

- Vocabulary, 337FF
- Leveled Reader, 337KK
- Self-Selected Independent Reading, 337HH
- Book Talk, 337LL

Managing the Class

What do I do with the rest of my class?

- Practice Book and Reproducibles
- ELL Practice Book
- Leveled Reader Activities
- Literacy Workstations
- Online Activities

Classroom Management Tools

Weekly Contract

Name _____ Date _____

My To-Do List

✔ Put a check next to the activities you complete.

📖 **Reading**
- ☐ Practice fluency
- ☐ Choose a story to read

🔤 **Phonics/Word Study**
- ☐ Look up word origins
- ☐ Write words with short vowel sounds

✏️ **Writing**
- ☐ Write a letter to the editor
- ☐ Write a radio ad

🔬 **Science**
- ☐ Research two types of rocks
- ☐ Write a chart

🌎 **Social Studies**
- ☐ Create a guide book
- ☐ Role-play an interview

📖 **Leveled Readers**
- ☐ Write About It!
- ☐ Content Connection

🖱 **Technology**
- ☐ Vocabulary PuzzleMaker
- ☐ Fluency Solutions
- ☐ Listening Library
- ☐ www.macmillanmh.com

🖌 **Independent Practice**
- ☐ Practice Book, 1–9

Rotation Chart

Teacher-Led Small Groups

Red

Literacy Workstations | Independent Activities

Blue | **Green**

Orange

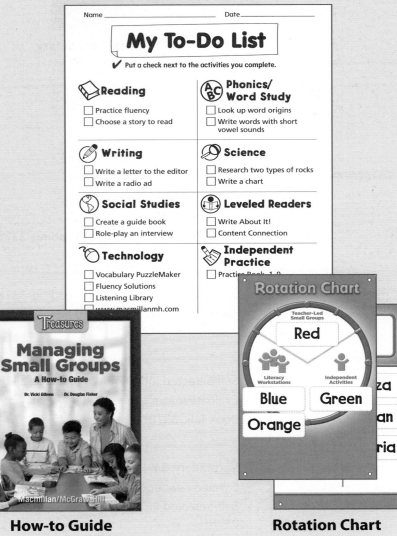

How-to Guide

Rotation Chart

Digital Learning

StudentWorks *Plus*
Interactive Student Book

StudentWorks Plus Online
- Summaries in Multiple Languages
- Word-by-Word Reading
- Comprehension Questions

Meet the Author/Illustrator

Mark Teague

- Mark gets a lot of inspiration from his two young daughters. He loves to read to them.
- He always loved to draw but didn't think about becoming a professional artist until after college.
- Mark starts out his books by jotting down notes and scribbling in a notebook. Slowly the ides start to come together and he creates a real story.

Another book by Mark Teague
- Teague, Mark. *Detective LaRue: Letters from the Investigation.* New York: Scholastic, Inc., 2004.

- Other Books by the Author or Illustrator

Leveled Practice

Practice Book
- Phonics
- Vocabulary
- Fluency
- Comprehension
- Writing

Macmillan/McGraw-Hill

On Level

English Language Learner Practice Book

Macmillan/McGraw-Hill

ELL

Also Available:
Approaching Reproducible
Beyond Reproducible

Independent Activities

 LOG ON

ONLINE INSTRUCTION www.macmillanmh.com

Oral Language Activities

- Focus on Vocabulary and Concepts
- English Language Learner Support

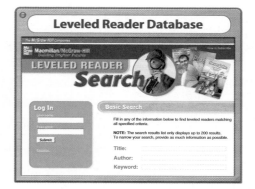

Leveled Reader Database

- Leveled Reader Database
- Search titles by level, skill, content area, and more

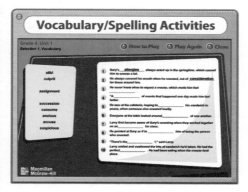

Vocabulary/Spelling Activities

- Differentiated Lists and Activities

Research Toolkit

- Research Roadmap
- Research and Presentation Tools
- Theme Launcher Video
- Links to Science and Social Studies

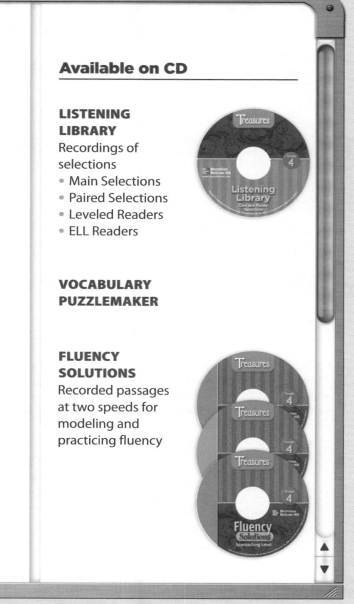

Available on CD

LISTENING LIBRARY
Recordings of selections
- Main Selections
- Paired Selections
- Leveled Readers
- ELL Readers

VOCABULARY PUZZLEMAKER

FLUENCY SOLUTIONS
Recorded passages at two speeds for modeling and practicing fluency

Leveled Reader Activities

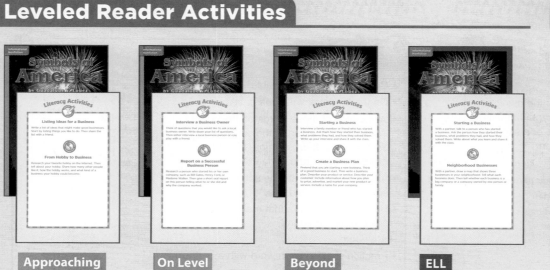

Approaching   **On Level**   **Beyond**   **ELL**

See inside cover of all Leveled Readers.

Literacy Workstations

Reading · Writing · Phonics/Word Study · Science/Social Studies

See lessons on pages 326K–326L.

Managing the Class

What do I do with the rest of my class?

📖 Reading

Objectives

- Practice reading with accuracy
- Read independently for a sustained period of time; use **Practice Book** page 117 for Reading Strategies and Reading Log

---

Reading — **Fluency** — 20 Minutes

- Select a paragraph from the Fluency passage on page 125 of your Practice Book.
- With a partner, take turns reading the sentences with accuracy.
- Vary your reading rate as you read each sentence.

Extension

- With your partner, read a paragraph out loud together. Practice until you can read it smoothly.
- Listen to the Audio CD.

> **Things you need:**
> - Practice Book

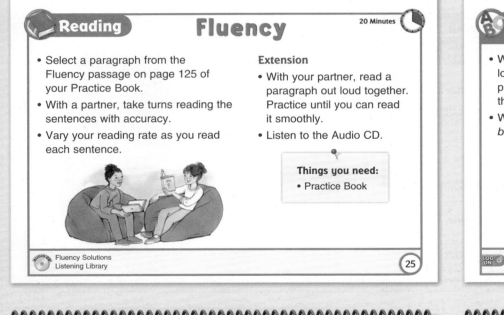

Fluency Solutions
Listening Library

(25)

Reading — **Independent Reading** — 20 Minutes

- Read a magazine article.
- 📱 Write down the statements that you think are facts and the ones you feel are opinions in your response journal.

Extension

- Choose one of the opinions. Write a paragraph that tells why you agree or disagree with this opinion.

> **Things you need:**
> - magazines
> - pen and paper

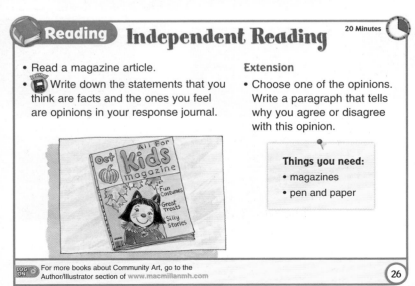

For more books about Community Art, go to the Author/Illustrator section of www.macmillanmh.com

(26)

🔤 Phonics/Word Study

Objectives

- Identify and use words with Latin prefixes
- Identify and sort words with soft *c* and *g* sounds

Phonics/Word Study — **Latin Prefixes** — 20 Minutes

- Work with a partner. Using a dictionary look up words that begin with the prefix *bi-*. The prefix *bi-* comes from the Latin word meaning "two."
- Write down three words that begin with *bi-* and the definition of each word.

Extension

- Write sentences using each word.
- Read your sentences aloud to your partner.

> **Things you need:**
> - pen and paper
> - dictionary

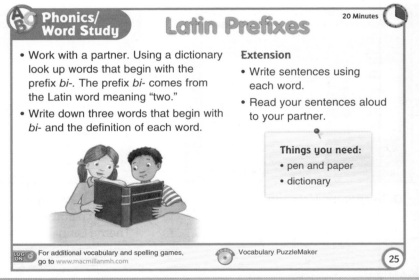

For additional vocabulary and spelling games, go to www.macmillanmh.com   Vocabulary PuzzleMaker

(25)

Phonics/Word Study — **Soft *c* and *g* Sounds** — 20 Minutes

- Create a Two-Tab Foldable®.
- On the top tabs, write *soft c, soft g*.
- Write each of these words on the correct inside tab according to the soft sounds: *center, once, germs, spice, circus, badge, bridge,* and *dance*.
- Add more words with the soft *c* and *g* sounds to your Foldable.
- Underline the letters that make the soft *c* or soft *g* sound.

Extension

- Practice spelling each word with a partner.

FOLDABLES
- Two-Tab Foldable®

soft c | soft g

circus | bridge

For additional vocabulary and spelling games, go to www.macmillanmh.com   **FOLDABLES®**

(26)

Literacy Workstations

Reading | **Phonics/ Word Study** | **Writing** | **Science/ Social Studies**

Literacy Workstation Flip Charts

Writing

Objectives

- Write an essay about an important personal experience
- List facts about an event in the news
- Write a paragraph that expresses an opinion

Content Literacy

Objectives

- Research information about an inspiring scientist
- Write a thank-you letter
- Write clues about a famous historical person, place, or event

---

Writing — A Personal Essay
20 Minutes

- Write a personal essay about how you overcame an obstacle.
- In your essay, clearly express your opinions about the experience. How did it make you feel? What did you think at the time? What do you think now?

Extension

- At the end of your essay, write a few sentences summarizing why the experience you described is important to you.

Things you need:
- pen and paper

25

Science — Inspiring Scientist
20 Minutes

- What famous scientist has inspired you and why? Use an encyclopedia or the Internet to research the scientist and list his or her accomplishments.

Lives of the GREAT SCIENTISTS

Extension

- Write a thank-you letter to the scientist, telling how he or she inspired you. Be sure to use date, salutation, and closing.

Things you need:
- encyclopedia or online resources
- pen and paper

25

Writing — Current Events
20 Minutes

- Read a newspaper or magazine article about something interesting that recently happened in the world.
- Write three important facts you learned about the event.

Extension

- Using your facts, write an essay that expresses your opinions about the event. Your opinions can be about any detail mentioned in the article or the author's point of view.
- Exchange your paragraph with a partner.

Things you need:
- newspaper or magazine article
- pen and paper

26

Social Studies — History Mystery Game
20 Minutes

- Think of a famous historical person, place, or event.
- Write down as many clues as you can.

Extension

- Using your clues, play a guessing game. Give a partner one statement after another about your history mystery until he or she guesses the answer.
- Switch roles with your partner.

Things you need:
- pen and paper

26

Prepare

WHOLE GROUP

ORAL LANGUAGE
- Build Background
- Connect to Theme
- Read Aloud

✓ **PHONICS/WORD STUDY**
- Soft *c* and *g*

✓ **VOCABULARY**
- Latin Prefixes
- Teach Words

✓ **COMPREHENSION**
- Strategy: Monitor Comprehension
- Skill: Fact and Opinion

SMALL GROUP

- Differentiated Instruction, pp. 337M–337LL

Oral Language

Build Background

ACCESS PRIOR KNOWLEDGE

Share this information: The student in the photo is reading a book. We read by understanding words. Words give this student the power to speak, read, write, and express himself. Words can lead directly to actions.

Write the following words on the board, and briefly define each one using the **Define/Example/Ask** routine: **inspire** (make one want to do something), **engrossed in** (taking all of one's attention), **powerful** (strong), **imagination** (creative thoughts).

FOCUS QUESTION Ask students to read "Talk About It" on **Student Book** page 326. Then have students turn to a partner and describe the photo. Ask:

- Is the student engrossed in, or giving all his attention to, the book? Explain.

- How do powerful words in books inspire you, or make you want to do something? How do they affect your imagination, or creative thoughts?

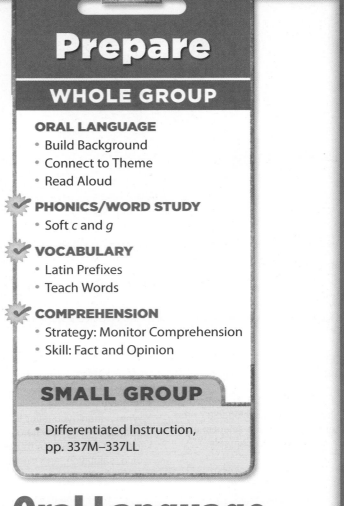

Talk About It

How can powerful words move us to act?

LOG ON ▶ VIEW IT

Oral Language Activities
From Words to Action
www.macmillanmh.com

From Words to ACTION

326

Use the Picture Prompt

BUILD WRITING FLUENCY

Ask students to write in their Writer's Notebooks about how words lead to action. Tell students to write as much as they can for ten minutes. Meet with individuals during Writing Conference time to provide feedback and revision assignments. Students should self-correct errors prior to the conference.

Connect to the Unit Theme

DISCUSS THE BIG IDEA

Words can influence people in many ways, making them feel happy, sad, inspired, or fearful.

Ask students what they have learned so far in this unit about the power of words.

- What are some ways in which people use words to express their thoughts?

- Which are more powerful—spoken words or written words? Why do you think so?

USE THEME FOLDABLES

Write the **Big Idea** statement on the board. Ask students to copy it on their Unit Theme Foldables. Remind them to add details as they complete this week's readings.

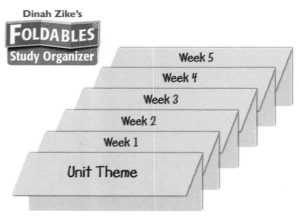

Study Book

Beginning	Intermediate	Advanced
Use Visuals Tell students about the photograph. *The boy is reading the words in the book. We use words to speak, read, and write. Words can inspire, or make us do things.* Ask students to tell you what the boy is doing. Repeat correct responses in a louder and slower voice for the class to hear.	**Describe** Ask students to tell what the boy in the photograph is doing. *What is the boy doing? How do words affect people?* Repeat students' responses, correcting grammar and pronunciation as needed.	**Discuss** Ask students to discuss how using words can lead to action. Elicit examples to support their responses.

Objectives

- Identify the characteristics of an autobiography
- Develop vocabulary
- Read sentences fluently, focusing on accuracy

Materials

- Read Aloud Anthology, pp. 24–27

Read Aloud

Read "Wild and Swampy"

Read Aloud

GENRE: Literary Nonfiction/Autobiography

Share with students the following key characteristics of an **autobiography**:

- An autobiography is the true story of a person's life, written by that person.

- In an autobiography, the author reflects upon, or looks back on, parts of his or her life and shares personal thoughts and feelings about them.

- Authors often use adjectives, or describing words, to tell about real experiences. The adjectives help readers visualize the experiences and the author's feelings about them.

FOCUS ON VOCABULARY

Introduce the following words, using the **Define/Example/Ask** routine. Tell students that knowing these words will help them visualize what the author describes.

Vocabulary Routine

Use the routine below to discuss the meaning of each word.

Define: **Leaching** is the removal of material by way of separation through water.
Example: The minerals are leaching out of the soil.
Ask: If something is leaching out of the soil, is it going into the soil or leaving the soil?

Define: **Planks** are wooden boards.
Example: We used planks to make a bridge across the stream.
Ask: What are some other items that can be made out of planks?

Define: To have **scurried** is to have moved quickly.
Example: A mouse suddenly scurried across the kitchen floor.
Ask: What is a synonym for *scurried*? What is an antonym for it?

LISTENING FOR A PURPOSE

Ask students to listen carefully as you read "Wild and Swampy" on **Read-Aloud Anthology** pages 24–27. Use the Think Alouds and Genre Study prompts provided.

ELL **Interactive Reading** Build students' oral language by engaging them in discussion about the passage's basic meaning.

- Point to the picture of the raccoon and the alligator. Name each and have students repeat. Discuss the animals and their surroundings.

- After the first four paragraphs, say: *Turn to your partner and describe the brown water snake.*

- After the first paragraph on the second page, say: *Tell your partner what the raccoon and the alligator were doing.*

- At the end of the passage, say: *Explain why you think the author stays in a mangrove swamp until the last light of day.*

Think/Pair/Share Use **Copying Master 3**, "I was able to picture in my mind . . . ," to help students visualize the images described. Then have students turn to a partner and orally summarize the passage, using their responses to guide them. Finally, have a few students share their summaries with the class.

RESPOND TO THE AUTOBIOGRAPHY

Ask students the Think and Respond questions on page 27. Then have students describe the water, plants, and animals in a swamp. Have them share and solve riddles about something that they would see in a swamp.

Model Fluency

Reread the passage. Tell students that this time you want them to focus on your **accuracy**, or how carefully you read.

Explain that reading with accuracy means saying every word and pronouncing every word correctly. Reading with accuracy enables the speaker and the listener to understand and enjoy the content being read. Model reading with accuracy.

Think Aloud Listen as I read the sentence about mammals in the swamp. There are many animal names in the sentence. Listen to how I read accurately to enhance my understanding and yours, too: *Raccoons, opossums, otters, bobcats, black bear, and deer all thrive in swampland.* Did you hear me say every word? Did you notice how I pronounced each mammal's name carefully and correctly? Now you try. Repeat the sentence after me, using the good accuracy that I am using.

Establish Fluency Focus Remind students that you will be listening for this same quality in their reading throughout the week. You will help them improve their reading by increasing their accuracy.

Readers Theater

BUILDING LISTENING AND SPEAKING SKILLS Distribute copies of "All the Money in the World," **Read-Aloud Anthology** pages 182–202. Have students practice reading the play throughout the unit. Assign parts and have the students present the play or perform it as a dramatic reading at the end of the unit.

ELL

Discuss Genre Review autobiography with students. Ask: *What kind of story is an autobiography? Who is the author of an autobiography? What does Jim Arnosky write about in "Wild and Swampy"? How did he feel?* Provide ample time for students to respond. Elicit details and specific information to support students' responses.

Objective
- Decode multisyllabic words with soft *c* and *g*

Materials
- Sound-Spelling Cards
- Practice Book, p. 109
- Word-Building Cards
- Transparency 13
- Teacher's Resource Book, p. 132

ELL

Transfer Sounds Speakers of Spanish, Vietnamese, Hmong, Cantonese, and Korean may have difficulties pronouncing and perceiving the /j/ sound. Use the Approaching Level phonics lesson on page 337N for additional practice. Also use the articulation supports on the Sound-Spelling Cards. See language transfers on pages T16–T31.

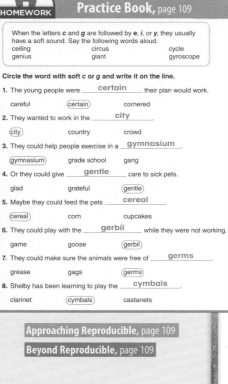

HOMEWORK

Practice Book, page 109

When the letters *c* and *g* are followed by *e*, *i*, or *y*, they usually have a soft sound. Say the following words aloud.
ceiling   circus   cycle
genius   giant   gyroscope

Circle the word with soft *c* or *g* and write it on the line.

1. The young people were ___certain___ their plan would work.
   careful   (certain)   cornered
2. They wanted to work in the ___city___.
   (city)   country   crowd
3. They could help people exercise in a ___gymnasium___
   (gymnasium)   grade school   gang
4. Or they could give ___gentle___ care to sick pets.
   glad   grateful   (gentle)
5. Maybe they could feed the pets ___cereal___
   (cereal)   corn   cupcakes
6. They could play with the ___gerbil___ while they were not working.
   game   goose   (gerbil)
7. They could make sure the animals were free of ___germs___
   grease   gags   (germs)
8. Shelby has been learning to play the ___cymbals___
   clarinet   (cymbals)   castanets

Approaching Reproducible, page 109
Beyond Reproducible, page 109

Phonics

Soft *c* and *g*

EXPLAIN/MODEL

Display the *Jump* and *Sun* **Sound-Spelling Cards**. Tell students that the letters *c* and *g* can have either a hard or soft sound. The letter *c* has a hard /k/ sound in *cold* and a soft /s/ sound in *cement*. The letter *g* has a hard /g/ sound in *good* and a soft /j/ sound in *germ*. When *c* comes before the letters *i* or *e*, it usually has an /s/ sound. When *g* comes before the letters *i* or *e*, it usually has a /j/ sound. The soft *g* sound can also be spelled *dge* at the ends of words.

- rec̲eive
- g̲em (or g̲eese)
- fu̲dge
- c̲inammon
- g̲iant (or g̲iggle)

Write the sample words on the board, underline the soft *c* and *g* spellings, and model each one.

Think Aloud Look at the first word I wrote: *receive*. I see the *c* before the letter *e*, so the sound should be soft. Listen and watch as I sound out the word /ri sēv/, *receive*. (Run your finger under the word as you sound it out.)

PRACTICE/APPLY

Read the Word List Display **Transparency 13**. The first two lines include soft *c* and *g* words students will encounter in the upcoming selections. Have students underline the soft *c* and *g* spelling in each word. Then have them chorally read the words.

princess	certain	viceroy	innocently
Germany	gentle	village	gem
ledge	bridge	ginger	gifted
strange	cinder	celery	sponge
gender	gentleman	gear	budget
recent	danger	gorge	central

Phonics Transparency 13

Sort the Words Ask students to sort the words by sound pattern. Then have them write the word sort in their Writer's Notebooks.

ce	ge	ci	gi	__dge

Read Multisyllabic Words

TRANSITION TO LONGER WORDS Help students transition from reading one-syllable to multisyllabic soft *c* and *g* words. Have students read a word in the first column, then model how to read the longer word in the second column. Point out the added syllable(s), such as a prefix or suffix, to help students gain awareness of these common word parts.

cent	central	edge	edgy
cell	cellular	cyst	cystic
gym	gymnasium	charge	recharge
germ	germinal	change	changeable
gem	gemstone	prince	princely
voice	invoice	juice	juicer

Phonics Transparency 13

BUILD WORDS Use **Word-Building Cards** *gen, der, tle, er, al, ate, ous, cen, sus, ter, tral, tury*. Display the cards. Have students use the word parts on the cards to build as many multisyllabic soft *c* and *g* words as possible. These and other words can be formed: *gender, gentle, general, generous, generate, census, center, central, century*.

APPLY DECODING STRATEGY Guide students to use the Decoding Strategy to decode the following words: *enlargement, exchange, centuries, deceitful, gentlemanly, incident, recession*. Write each word on the board. Remind students to look for vowel-team syllables and final *e* spellings in step 3 of the Decoding Strategy procedure.

Build Fluency

SPEED DRILL Distribute copies of the **Soft *c* and *g* Speed Drill** on **Teacher's Resource Book** page 132. Use the Speed Drill routine to help students become fluent reading words with soft *c* and *g* spelling patterns.

Quick Check

Can students read words with soft *c* and *g*?

During **Small Group Instruction**

Tier 2

If No → Approaching Level Reteach the skill using the lesson on p. 337N.

If Yes → On Level Consolidate the learning using p. 337W.

Beyond Level Extend the learning using p. 337AA.

DAILY **Syllable Fluency**

Use Word-Building Cards 121–130. Display one card at a time. Have students chorally read each common syllable. Repeat at varying speeds and in random order. Have students work with partners during independent time to write as many words as they can containing each syllable.

Decoding Strategy

Decoding Strategy Chart

Step 1	Look for word parts (prefixes) at the beginning of the word.
Step 2	Look for word parts (suffixes) at the end of the word.
Step 3	In the base word, look for familiar spelling patterns. Think about the six syllable-spelling patterns you have learned.
Step 4	Sound out and blend together the word parts.
Step 5	Say the word parts fast. Adjust your pronunciation as needed. Ask yourself: "Is this a word I have heard before?" Then read the word in the sentence and ask: "Does it make sense in this sentence?"

© Macmillan/McGraw-Hill

Vocabulary

STRATEGY
WORD PARTS

Latin Prefixes Explain that a prefix is a word part that can be added to the beginning of a word. Adding a prefix changes the word's meaning. Point out that, like other word parts, prefixes often come from Greek, Latin, or other languages. Many prefixes, such as *dis-*, *non-*, and *inter-*, are derived from Latin, the language of ancient Rome.

Ask students to read the vocabulary words on the bookmark on **Student Book** page 328. Then model for students how to find the meaning of the word *interact*.

Think Aloud When I look at the word *interact*, I notice that it is made up of a base word, *act*, and a prefix, *inter-*. I know that *inter* is a Latin prefix that means "between," so *interact* means "act between." *Interact* describes the way two people communicate or work together.

Have students follow a similar procedure with the words *interleague* and *interstate*. Also discuss examples of words with the prefixes *dis-* (meaning "from") and *non-* (meaning "not"), such as *displace* and *nonfiction*.

Read "A Renaissance in Harlem"

As you read "A Renaissance in Harlem," "A Speech with Reach," and "The Top 5 Most-Searched Words on the Internet" with students, have them identify clues to the meanings of the highlighted words. Tell students they will read these words again in *Words Add Up to Success*.

Real World Reading

Vocabulary

dismiss	conceived
interact	definition
motivate	

The writer Langston Hughes was part of the Harlem Renaissance.

A Renaissance in Harlem

During the early 1920s, many African Americans moved from rural areas to cities. They were in search of jobs and a better life. In New York City, many people headed to the neighborhood of Harlem. Many African American musicians, poets, artists, and entertainers also came to Harlem at that time. The talented people gathered here gave birth to a period of artistic growth, known as the Harlem Renaissance.

Writers such as Langston Hughes, Zora Neale Hurston, and Claude McKay wrote poems and stories about the African American experience. Musicians such as Louis Armstrong, Duke Ellington, and Bessie Smith sang about what life was like for African Americans. The Harlem Renaissance was a chance for African Americans to use art to talk about their culture and to **dismiss** racism.

Before this time, many white people did not want to **interact** with black people. But during the Harlem Renaissance, many Americans started to take notice of African American culture. For the first time, white publishers printed poems and stories by African Americans. This helped **motivate** many other African Americans to become writers and artists. The Harlem Renaissance helped to boost pride in African American history and culture.

328

ELL

Preteach Vocabulary See pages 337FF and 337O to preteach the vocabulary words to **ELL** and **Approaching Level** students. Use the **Visual Vocabulary Resources** to demonstrate and discuss each word. To further reinforce concepts, have students complete page 142 in the **ELL Resource Book**.

HOMEWORK — Practice Book, page 110

dismiss	interact	motivate
conceived	definition	

A. From each pair of words below, circle the word that best completes the sentence. Then write the correct word on the line provided.

1. What is the (**definition**/interact) of the word *genius*? ___definition___

2. Hearing the music of Louis Armstrong might (dismiss/**motivate**) you to play the trumpet. ___motivate___

3. When he played, Armstrong liked to (**interact**/motivate) with the people who watched him. ___interact___

4. My sister and I (**conceived**/definition) of a way of playing like Louis Armstrong. ___conceived___

5. Mom will probably (**dismiss**/interact) our idea of starting a family band. ___dismiss___

B. Write new sentences for three of the vocabulary words used above. Underline the vocabulary word in each sentence. Possible responses provided.

6. I <u>conceived</u> of a new game.

7. The <u>definition</u> of *hilarious* is "very funny."

8. My dog does not <u>interact</u> much with my cat.

Approaching Reproducible, page 110
Beyond Reproducible, page 110

A Speech with Reach

TIME FOR KIDS

Great speeches use powerful words to move people. Throughout history, speeches have caused people to think and to act. Here are some famous lines from well-known speeches.

"General Secretary Gorbachev, if you seek peace, if you seek prosperity..., if you seek liberalization: Come here to this gate! Mr. Gorbachev, open this gate! Mr. Gorbachev, tear down this wall!"

— President Ronald Reagan, delivered in West Berlin on June 12, 1987

"Fourscore and seven years ago our fathers brought forth on this continent a new nation, **conceived** in liberty, and dedicated to the proposition that all men are created equal."

— President Abraham Lincoln, Gettysburg Address, 1863

The Top 5 Most-Searched Words on the Internet

When you don't know the **definition** of a word, do you look it up? Over the past 10 years, people have most often looked up on an online dictionary the following words:

1. effect (i-fekt) noun: an event, condition, or state of affairs that is produced by a cause

2. affect (a-fekt) verb: to produce a significant influence upon or change in

3. love (luhv) noun: a quality or feeling of strong or constant affection for and dedication to another being or thing

4. blog (blawg) noun: [short for "weblog"] a Web site that contains an online personal journal often with hyperlinks provided by the writer

5. integrity (in-te-gruh-tee) noun: the condition of being free from damage or defect

Source: merriam-webster.com

329

Quick Check

Can students identify word meanings?

During **Small Group Instruction**

Tier 2

If No → **Approaching Level** Reteach the words using the Vocabulary lesson, pp. 337O–337P.

If Yes → **On Level** Consolidate the learning using p. 337W.

Beyond Level Extend the learning using p. 337AA.

Gifted Talented

Vocabulary

TEACH WORDS

Introduce each word using the **Define/Example/Ask** routine. Model reading each word using the syllable-scoop technique.

Vocabulary Routine

Define: When you **dismiss** something, you forget about it or put it aside.
Example: We can dismiss that idea because it will not work.
Ask: Why might you dismiss an idea that someone presented to you? EXPLANATION

- If you **interact** with another person, you speak to that person or do something together. *I interact with the students at school.* Who are some of the people with whom you interact? EXAMPLE

- When you **motivate** someone, you make that person want to take action. *Seeing the movie helped motivate me to read the book.* What is a synonym for *motivate*? SYNONYM

- If people **conceived** of a way to do something, they thought of an idea or a plan. *Mom conceived of the perfect way to get me to do my chores—paying me.* When is the last time you conceived of a good idea? What was that idea? DESCRIPTION

- A **definition** explains what a word means. *The word* mollify *was new to me, so I looked up its definition in an online dictionary.* Why is it important to understand the definition of a word? EXPLANATION

Objectives

- Monitor comprehension of a text
- Distinguish facts from opinions
- Explain how to verify facts
- Use academic language: *monitor comprehension, fact, opinion*

Materials

- Transparency 13
- Practice Book, p. 111

Skills Trace

Fact and Opinion

Introduce	329A–329B
Practice/ Apply	330–333; Practice Book, 111–112
Reteach/ Review	337Q–337DD, 733A–733B, 734–737, 741Q–741DD; Practice Book, 246–247
Assess	Weekly Tests; Units 3, 6 Tests
Maintain	455B, 527B, 769B

ELL

Academic Language
Preteach the following academic language words to **ELL** and **Approaching Level** students during Small Group time: *fact, opinion.*
See pages 337EE and 337M.

Reread for
Comprehension

STRATEGY
MONITOR COMPREHENSION

What Is It? Remind students that when they monitor their comprehension of a text, they check their understanding through self-correction techniques such as rereading aloud or paraphrasing.

Why Is It Important? By monitoring their comprehension, students can figure out independently whether their understanding of a text is accurate. They can adjust their understanding as necessary.

SKILL
FACT AND OPINION

What Is It? Point out that a **fact** is something that can be verified or proven true. An **opinion** is what someone believes or thinks. Words such as *I think, I feel*, and *the best* can signal opinions.

Why Is It Important? To understand informational text, readers need to be able to distinguish between facts and opinions. Then they can **verify the facts** by looking them up in books or other sources.

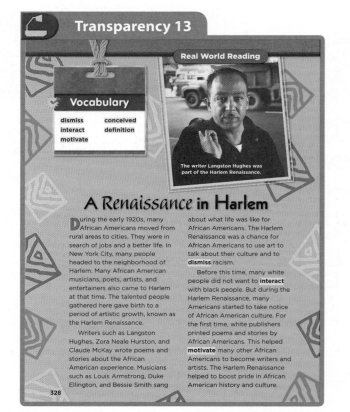

Student Book page 328 available on Comprehension Transparency 13

- To distinguish between fact and opinion, students should read the text and ask themselves, *Can this statement be checked and proven correct?* If so, then it is a fact. If it is a statement that cannot be proven correct and tells what someone thinks or believes, then it is an opinion.

- Distinguishing fact from opinion will enable students to form their own opinions on topics and seek out facts to substantiate them.

MODEL

How Do I Use It? Read aloud the first paragraph of "A Renaissance in Harlem" on **Student Book** page 328.

Think Aloud The first sentence is a fact. It tells that many African Americans moved to cities in the 1920s. I can look that up to prove that it is true. The paragraph states other facts: People looked for jobs. They moved to Harlem. Some were musicians, poets, artists, and entertainers. The last sentence gives an opinion, though. The author says that talented people gathered in Harlem. It's the author's opinion that the people were talented.

GUIDED PRACTICE

Help students determine that most of the sentences in the article are facts because they can be proven to be true. Discuss sources readers can use to verify the facts, such as an encyclopedia or a history book. Then have students examine the article's final sentence and explain whether it expresses a fact or an opinion. Ask students to state their own opinion on the influence of the Harlem Renaissance.

APPLY

After students distinguish between fact and opinion in "A Renaissance in Harlem" on Student Book page 328, have them apply the same technique to "A Speech with Reach" and "The Top 5 Most-Searched Words on the Internet" on Student Book page 329. Have them explain how they would verify the facts.

Quick Check

Can students distinguish facts from opinions in a text?

During **Small Group Instruction**

Tier 2

If No → **Approaching Level** Reteach the skill using the Comprehension lesson, pp. 337Q–337T.

If Yes → **On Level** Consolidate the learning using pp. 337Y–337Z.

Beyond Level Extend the learning using pp. 337CC–337DD.

HOMEWORK

Practice Book, page 111

A **fact** is a statement that can be proven true.
An **opinion** is a statement that tells someone's feelings or ideas. It cannot be proven true.
Facts and opinions can appear together.

A. Read the following sentences. After each sentence write *fact* or *opinion*.

1. Our class went on a field trip to the art museum last week. _fact_
2. We saw one painting that was almost 500 years old. _fact_
3. It is harder to be a painter than to be a writer. _opinion_
4. The best painters are from the United States. _opinion_
5. Some painters study art in college. _fact_
6. Going to the art museum is a great way to spend an afternoon. _opinion_

B. Write one fact about art. Then write one opinion about art. Possible responses provided.

7. Fact: We have two art museums in our city.
8. Opinion: Making things with clay is fun.

Approaching Reproducible, page 111
Beyond Reproducible, page 111

Read

WHOLE GROUP

✓ **MAIN SELECTION**
- *Words Add Up to Success*
- Skill: Fact and Opinion

✓ **TEST PRACTICE**
- "The Latest Lingo"
- Answering Questions

SMALL GROUP

- Differentiated Instruction, pp. 337M–337LL

Main Selection

GENRE: Informational Text/Expository

Have a student read the definition of an Expository selection on **Student Book** page 330. Remind students to look for factual information in the photographs and captions as well as in the text itself.

✓ **STRATEGY**
MONITOR COMPREHENSION

Tell students to pause at regular intervals in their reading to monitor and adjust their understanding of the facts and opinions presented in the text.

✓ **SKILL**
FACT AND OPINION

Explain to students that a fact can be proven to be true, whereas an opinion is what someone thinks or believes. To fully understand a text, readers need to be able to distinguish facts from opinions. They also need to understand how to verify facts.

Comprehension

Genre
An **Expository** selection, such as a magazine article, presents facts about a person, place, or event.

Monitor Comprehension
Fact and Opinion
A fact is something that can be proven true. An opinion is a belief that does not have to be supported by facts.

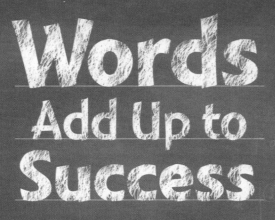

Words Add Up to Success

Jaime Escalante was a math teacher at Garfield High School in East Los Angeles. However, he quickly became a national figure.

On his first day, he knew his students were in trouble. "They were using their fingers adding stuff at the board," he says. "They came in without supplies, with nothing."

Escalante wanted to help them. His first challenge was to get their attention. Many of the students at Garfield didn't care about education.

They were involved in gangs and violence. Math wasn't an important subject for most of them. Escalante needed to make math real and interesting to them. He had to find a way to **interact** with his students.

So one day in 1974, Escalante came to school wearing a chef's hat. He carried a meat cleaver and apple into his classroom. With one swift chop, he cut the apple in two. "Let's talk about percentages," he said. With one quick action, he had the students' attention.

330

Vocabulary

Vocabulary Words Review the tested words while reading: **dismiss, interact, motivate, conceived, definition**.

Additional Selection Words Students may be unfamiliar with these words. Pronounce the words, give student-friendly explanations as needed, and help students use the previously taught vocabulary strategies: context clues, dictionary, word origins.

encouragement (p. 331): support that makes you want to do well

impact (p. 332): powerful effect or influence

determination (p. 332): strong desire to get something done

attitudes (p. 332): ways you think or feel

influence (p. 333): power to cause change or to make a difference

Working Wonders

From that day forward, Escalante used his imagination to reach students. He **conceived** of different ways to keep them interested in the lessons. He wanted the students to understand that school and math were important to their lives.

Escalante believed that his job was to **motivate** as well as teach students. He used jokes and real-life examples to keep their interest. He also made sure his students took class seriously. **1**

If someone wasn't paying attention, Escalante would nudge him or her with a little red pillow. If students were late, they had to sit in a chair built for a kindergartener. The students felt embarrassed. As a result, they got to class on time and focused on their work.

Escalante sometimes used tough words to shake up his class. However, he also gave his students plenty of encouragement. He often told them, "You are the best, you are our hope for the future. Remember that." Those words inspired his students to try harder and do better.

331

Read the Main Selection

Preteach	Read Together	Read Independently
Have Approaching Level students and English Language Learners listen to the selection on **StudentWorks Plus** and use the **ELL Resource Book**, pages 140–141, before reading with the class.	Use the prompts to guide comprehension and model how to complete the graphic organizer. Have students use **Think/Pair/Share** to discuss the selection.	If students can read the selection independently, have them read and complete the graphic organizer. Suggest that they use their purposes to choose their reading strategies.

LOG ON **StudentWorks** *Plus*
Interactive Student Book

Preview and Predict

QUICK WRITE Ask students to read the title, preview the illustrations, think about the genre, and make predictions. Students may include what they know about classroom interaction.

Set Purposes

FOCUS QUESTION Discuss with students the title of the article on **Student Book** page 330. Ask: *How can words add up to success?*

Point out the Fact and Opinion Chart on **Practice Book** page 112. Explain that students will use it to distinguish facts from opinions in this article.

Read *Words Add Up to Success*

Use the questions and Think Alouds to support instruction about the comprehension strategy and skill.

1 **STRATEGY**
MONITOR COMPREHENSION

Teacher Think Aloud To check my understanding, I am going to reread the second paragraph on page 331. The author says Escalante *believed* his job was to motivate and teach. I understand that this statement is Escalante's opinion, because it tells what he believed about his job. What facts are presented in this paragraph?

Prompt students to apply the strategy in a Think Aloud.

Student Think Aloud When I reread the paragraph, I understand that Escalante interested his students in school through jokes and real-life examples. This is a fact I can verify by reading other articles about him.

Develop Comprehension

2 **CAUSE AND EFFECT**

SPIRAL REVIEW

Why did the students' opinions of themselves change after the test? (They felt better about themselves because their hard work had produced success. They knew they were capable of doing well.) Use this information to form your own opinion about Escalante. Explain why you formed this opinion. (Most students will express approval of Escalante because many of his students did well on the test.)

3 SKILL
FACT AND OPINION

What did the people in charge of the test think at first? How do you know that this was their **opinion**? (They thought that the students had cheated because they did not believe students from a poor school could do that well. The words *thought* and *believe* signal an opinion.) Use this information as you complete your Fact and Opinion Chart.

Fact	Opinion
Escalante used jokes and examples to motivate students.	School and math are important.
The students did well on the advanced math test.	Escalante believed that his job was to motivate.
	The people in charge of the test believed that the students had cheated.

Jaime Escalante speaks to audiences, such as this one at Lyon College, about his experiences.

Making an Impact

Escalante's words and determination made his students want to do well—and they did. Many of his students studied hard and passed an advanced math test. The test was so difficult, only two percent of all high school seniors passed it each year. About 80 percent of Escalante's students passed the test. The students' attitudes changed when they got good grades. They knew the **definition** of hard work and now, success. They felt better about **2** themselves, and they wanted to do well in school.

3 The people in charge of the test thought the students from Garfield had cheated. They didn't believe students from an urban school, like Garfield, could do so well. Escalante's students took the test again and did just as well the second time. Through their scores the students were able to **dismiss** any doubt, and the testers had to admit they were wrong! A movie director heard this story and decided to make a movie about Escalante and his students. He knew other people would also be inspired by them.

332

Quick Check

Can students distinguish facts from opinions in a text?

During **Small Group Instruction**

If No → **Approaching Level** Reteach the skill and have students apply it to a simpler text. Use Leveled Reader lessons, pp. 337R–337T.

If Yes → **On Level** Have students apply the skill to a new text to consolidate learning. Use Leveled Reader lessons, pp. 337Y–337Z.

Gifted Talented

Beyond Level Have students apply the skill to a more complex text to consolidate learning. Use Leveled Reader lessons, pp. 337CC–337DD.

From the Classroom to the Big Screen

The film *Stand and Deliver* was a box office hit in 1988, and it made Escalante famous. The movie also brought attention to Garfield High School. Companies gave hundreds of thousands of dollars to improve the school's many programs. Students and teachers were helped by the movie's success.

Escalante no longer teaches at Garfield, but his words and actions live on. Maria Torres is one example of his influence. She was a student of Escalante's at Garfield. When she graduated from high school, she entered college at UCLA. "Many teachers merely instruct you," reports Torres. "Mr. Escalante's secret is he really cares. He made us feel powerful, that we could do anything."

Actor Edward James Olmos played Escalante in *Stand and Deliver*.

Think and Compare

1. What percentage of Escalante's students passed the advanced math test?

2. Identify an opinion in the article and explain why it is an opinion.

3. What is this article mainly about? Use details from the text to support your answer.

4. What do the speech makers in "A Speech with Reach" have in common with Jaime Escalante?

333

Reproducible, page 174

Cause/Effect Writing Frame

Summarize "Words Add Up to Success."
Use the Cause/Effect Writing Frame below.

Jaime Escalante's students were in trouble. They were in trouble **because** _____

This **caused** Jaime Escalante to _____

He **also** _____

In addition, he _____

As a result of Jaime Escalante's efforts, _____

Rewrite the completed summary on another sheet of paper. Keep it as a model for writing a summary of an article or selection using this text structure.

Develop Comprehension

Comprehension Check

SUMMARIZE

Have students summarize the selection using the Nonfiction Text Structure Writing Frame Reproducible on **Teacher's Resource Book** page 174. Remind them to use their Fact and Opinion Charts as they complete their summaries.

THINK AND COMPARE
Text Evidence

1. **Details** <u>Answer stated in text</u> About 80% of his students passed the test. LOCATE

2. **Fact and Opinion** <u>Answer</u> Students should point out an opinion and be able to cite its page number. <u>Evidence</u> They should recognize that the opinion they chose cannot be verified. They should identify any relevant opinion words such as *believe* or *think*. COMBINE

3. **Main Idea and Details** <u>Answer</u> Jaime Escalante was a math teacher who used his imagination to inspire students to learn. <u>Evidence</u> He taught percentages by cutting an apple and used jokes and tough words. His methods worked so well that 80% of his students did well on a difficult test. CONNECT

4. **Text-to-Text** The speech makers and Escalante both used words to influence, motivate, and persuade. COMPARE TEXT

Objectives
- Read fluently with accuracy
- 102–122 WCPM

Materials
- Transparency 13
- Practice Book, p. 113
- Fluency Solutions Audio CD

ELL

Develop Comprehension
Make sure students understand the passage. Help students identify the problem—few supplies, little interest in math, an overall lack of attention. Point out that reading with accuracy means not skipping over the details. Then have students describe the main idea of the passage in phrases or complete sentences.

Practice Book, page 113

As I read, I will pay attention to accuracy.

	Thousands of years ago in China, people made an
9	important discovery. They found out that caterpillars of
17	one kind of moth spin cocoons of silk. And better yet, they
29	found out that the cocoons could be unwound and the silk
40	thread could be woven into fabric.
46	Silk fabric is shiny. It is soft and smooth to the touch.
58	It is very light in weight. And it can be dyed in many
71	colors.
72	For thousands of years, the Chinese were the only
81	people who knew how to produce silk cloth. People in
91	other countries wanted to trade for the precious silk
100	fabric. Traders traveled to and from China on one
109	main road. They traded goods such as spices, glass,
118	and gold for silk. Sometimes they even traded horses
127	for silk. Over time, this route became known as the Silk
138	Road. 139

Comprehension Check

1. Are the statements in the second paragraph facts or opinions? **Main Idea and Details** facts

2. What is the main idea of the third paragraph? **Main Idea and Details**
   Traders traveled to China to trade goods for silk.

	Words Read	–	Number of Errors	=	Words Correct Score
First Read		–		=	
Second Read		–		=	

Approaching Reproducible, page 113
Beyond Reproducible, page 113

Fluency
Repeated Reading: Accuracy

EXPLAIN/MODEL Tell students that they will be doing an echo-reading. Remind them that an important part of fluent reading is accuracy—that is, saying every word and pronouncing it correctly. Model reading **Transparency 13** for them with accuracy.

Transparency 13

Jaime Escalante was a math teacher at Garfield High School in East Los Angeles. However, he quickly became a national figure.

On his first day, he knew his students were in trouble. "They were using their fingers adding stuff at the board," he says. "They came in without supplies, with nothing."

Escalante wanted to help them. His first challenge was to get their attention. Many of the students at Garfield High School didn't care about education. They were involved in gangs and violence. Math wasn't an important subject for most of them. Escalante needed to make math real and interesting to them. He had to find a way to interact with his students.

Fluency (from *Words Add Up to Success*, p. 330)

PRACTICE Have cooperative-learning partners echo-read each sentence. First, one partner reads each sentence and the other echoes. Then they switch roles. Tell students to help their partners by reminding them to read accurately and giving them feedback.

DAILY FLUENCY Students will practice fluency using **Practice Book** page 113 or the **Fluency Solutions Audio CD**. The passage is recorded at a slow practice speed and a faster fluent speed.

Quick Check

Can students read fluently?

During **Small Group Instruction**

If No ➞ **Approaching Level** Use the Fluency lesson and model, p. 337U.

If Yes ➞ **On Level** See Fluency, p. 337X.

Beyond Level See Fluency, p. 337BB.

Comprehension

REVIEW SKILL
CAUSE AND EFFECT

EXPLAIN/MODEL

Remind students that a **cause** is what makes something happen. An **effect** is what happens as the result of a cause. Note that some expository texts are organized by cause and effect.

- Point out that recognizing relationships between causes and effects will enable students to better understand why the events in a selection happen, and why people behave as they do.

- Explain that cause-and-effect relationships are sometimes explicitly stated. Words such as *because* or *since* may signal cause and effect. Sometimes cause-and-effect relationships are implicit. Then readers need to look carefully for clues in the text.

Discuss how to identify cause-and-effect relationships in "A Renaissance in Harlem." Model asking questions such as "Why did many African Americans move to cities in the early 1920s?"

PRACTICE/APPLY

Discuss whether the cause-and-effect text structure in *Words Add Up to Success* is explicit or implicit. Have partners skim the selection and identify any cause-and-effect clue words, such as "as a result" on page 331. Help students conclude that the causes and effects are mainly implied. Ask partners to use the following questions to identify and describe implicit causes and effects in *Words Add Up to Success*.

- Why weren't many of Escalante's students interested at first in education? (Math did not seem relevant to them. Many were involved in gangs and violence.)

- What effect did Escalante's efforts have on his students? (He captured their attention, motivated them to work hard, and helped them realize they could be successful in school.)

- Why did a film director decide to make a movie about Escalante and his students? Explain. (The film director heard how Escalante's students retook the advanced math test and proved the test administrators wrong. The director thought this story was inspiring.)

Remind partners to support their answers with evidence from the text. Have pairs share their answers with the class.

PRACTICE BOOK See **Practice Book** page 114 for Verifying Facts.

Objective

- Identify and describe explicit and implicit cause-and-effect relationships

Skills Trace

Cause and Effect	
Introduce	203A–203B
Practice/ Apply	204–219; Practice Book, 75–76
Reteach/ Review	225M–225Z, 707A–B, 708–723, 729M–729Z; Practice Book, 237–238
Assess	Weekly Tests; Units 2, 6 Tests
Maintain	251B, 333B, 737B

Test Practice

Answering Questions

To apply **answering questions strategies** to content-area reading, see pages 101–108 in *Time For Kids*.

Research
Study Skills

Objectives

- Use a computer
- Locate and explore relevant sources of research

Materials

- Transparency 3
- Practice Book, p. 115

Using a Computer

EXPLAIN

Tell students that to locate and explore information about a specific topic, they can use a computer in the school's media center. Review how to use a computer to find information. Have students think of a topic they would like to learn more about and develop a research plan for gathering information from different types of sources, including performing online searches. Detail the following resources:

- Use a computer to e-mail someone you know personally to ask a question or to request information about your topic.

- Depending on your topic and the expertise of the person you e-mail, you can conduct an online interview, request the names of other individuals to contact, or ask for advice on relevant sources.

- The Internet is a collection of millions of computer networks that share information. Search engines review these collections to match the key words you submit.

- To begin a search, select a search engine, go to the search engine's home page, type in your key words, and click on "Search." Choose specific key words. For example, a general search for windmills would result in thousands of choices.

- The listings that the search engine finds will have a title, a phrase with your key word, and the URL, or address, of the Web page. Click on a title to go to that site.

- If you already have the title and address of a Web page suggested by a teacher, librarian, or another expert, you can start your search by going to that site first.

- Select sources you can trust. Sites sponsored by the government (*.gov*) or a university (*.edu*) are generally very reliable. Sites sponsored by nonprofit organizations (*.org*) are often more trustworthy than sites sponsored by commercial companies (*.com*).

- Record and save the information you collect. Save it in a computer file if you have permission to do so, print it out, or write important facts on note cards. It is important to keep track of your sources.

MODEL

Display **Transparency 3**.

Transparency 3

Using a Computer

Follow this process to use the computer for research. Obey the school's acceptable-use policy as you complete the steps below.

1. Choose a topic.
2. Narrow the topic so that you get only the material you need.
3. If you know someone with information about your topic, e-mail that person. Ask for an online interview or for suggestions of good online sources.
4. Select a search engine. Type your topic into the search area and click on "Search."
5. Look at the Web sites. Choose ones that seem reliable.
6. Go to the sites. Be sure to record and save useful information.

Study Skill Transparency

Think Aloud I want to learn more about windmill farms in Texas. I will start by using the computer to e-mail a friend who knows a lot about windmill farms. I will ask for her recommendations for my research. Then, while I wait for her answer, I will select a search engine, type in the key words *windmill farms Texas*, and click on "Search." The screen shows me many Web sites. The first one says *state.tx.us* in the address. That sounds like a state-sponsored Web site, so I'll try that one first.

PRACTICE/APPLY

Have students use the computer to search for Web sites about windmill farms in Texas. Have them print out the first page of the search results. Discuss with students which Web sites seem most reliable and why.

Have students consult two Web sites about windmill farms. Explore with them any differences they notice in the facts they find on the sites. Discuss the next steps students might take to gather information for a research project about Texas windmill farms.

Practice Book, page 115

The **Internet** is a collection of computer networks. A **search engine** reviews that collection to help you find information.

To use a search engine:
• Type a key word or a phrase in the Search box.
• The search engine will come back with a list of Web pages that contain the key words.
• When choosing a Web page, select trustworthy sources.

Use the Web page to answer the questions.

1. What words have been entered in the search box? __solar power__
2. If you clicked on the first Web page listed, what information would you find? __I would find an article about solar power.__
3. If you wanted to find information about solar power in California, what words would you put in the search box? __solar power, California__
4. If you entered the word "California" in the search box, what information would you find? __information about California__

Approaching Reproducible, page 115
Beyond Reproducible, page 115

Test Practice

Answering Questions

EXPLAIN

Good test takers know how to answer the question that's asked.

- **Read the selection**.

- **Read** the **question** and all the **answers**.

- **Paraphrase** the question. Put it into your own words to make sure you understand what the question is asking.

- **Reread** or **scan** the selection to determine the best answer.

- Some answers are **stated**. An answer stated in one place is **right there**. When an answer is in two places, **think and search** to locate and combine the information.

- Sometimes the answer is **not stated**. **Connect** clues and evidence from the selection or **analyze** the text evidence to determine the answer.

MODEL

Remind students to record their answers on a separate sheet of paper.

Question 1 Read the question and all of the answer choices.

Think Aloud This question is asking what new phrase was added to the dictionary in 2006. I can **combine** information from different parts of the selection to determine the answer. The first sentence of the article asks about a "mouse potato." The last sentence of the paragraph explains that this phrase was added

---

Test Practice

Answering Questions

Right There answers are found in one place in the text. **Think and Search** answers are found in more than one place. **Author and Me** answers ask the reader to look for clues.

The Latest Lingo

❶ Are you a mouse potato? If you don't know what that means, look it up in Merriam-Webster's Collegiate Dictionary. The phrase was added to the dictionary in 2006, along with nearly 100 other words.

❷ Thousands of new words and their meanings enter the English language each year. Some go into the dictionary. Others fade from use. "Our language is a living thing," Jim Lowe, an editor at Merriam-Webster, told TFK. "It keeps growing."

❸ In other words, as the world changes, we always need new terms to describe it. Each year, the dictionary's editors look in everything from catalogs to comic books for the latest lingo. What happens when a new word or phrase is spotted? New words go on index cards. The cards note when and where the words first appeared. For a word to be added to the dictionary, it must show up regularly in a lot of places. Every 10 years the dictionary gets a total makeover. Lowe and the other editors review the new terms they have found. About 10,000 new ones make it into the dictionary.

New Words

Here are some words that were recently added to the dictionary. How many of these words do you use?

mouse potato	manga
ringtone	ollie
spyware	wave pool
supersize	bling-bling
unibrow	google

334

Answering Questions

QAR Strategies

A good reader thinks about **question-answer relationships** and different ways to reread a text to answer questions.

Right There: The answer is stated in the text. You can locate the answer in one place.

Think and Search: The reader combines information stated in different parts of the text to find the answer.

Author and Me: The answer is not directly stated. The reader must infer the answer by finding clues in the text.

Use "The Latest Lingo" to answer questions 1–4.

1 What new phrase was added to the dictionary in 2006?

A   latest lingo
B   mouse potato
C   bling-bling
D   wave pool

2 Paragraph 2 is mostly about —

F   new words on index cards
G   Jim Lowe's job
H   the idea that language is a living thing
J   a dictionary makeover

3 For a new word to be added to the dictionary it must —

A   show up in a lot of places
B   appear on a Web site
C   be in a catalog and comic book
D   be in the dictionary already

4 Which is the best summary of this article?

F   Jim Lowe has a great job. He is an editor of Merriam-Webster's Collegiate Dictionary. He thinks that language is a living thing. He likes to look for new words in catalogs and comic books.

G   Every 10 years, all the editors at Merriam-Webster decide to look for new words. They write new words and phrases like "mouse potato" and "spyware" on index cards.

H   Every year, new words enter the English language. The editors of Merriam-Webster's Collegiate Dictionary keep track of these new words. If a word is used regularly in enough places, it will eventually make it into the dictionary.

J   The words "supersize" and "manga" were added to Merriam-Webster's Collegiate Dictionary. The dictionary is revised every 10 years. Lowe and his editors review about 10,000 new words.

335

Monitor Comprehension

Self-Monitoring for Reading Comprehension

Ask yourself:

• Am I determining my answer by using personal experience instead of real proof from the selection?
• Am I adding information that is not connected to the selection to determine my answer?
• Can I prove my answer with text evidence?
• Is there a logical connection between my answer and the text evidence I am using to prove my answer?

in 2006. When I combine this information, the **stated answer** is that the phrase "mouse potato" was added to the dictionary in 2006. The best answer is B.   **THINK AND SEARCH**

GUIDED PRACTICE

Question 2 Read Question 2. Ask: *How can you restate this incomplete sentence as a question?* (What is paragraph 2 mostly about?) *What details and text evidence can you find in paragraph 2 to answer the question?* (New words enter the English language every year. An editor said that language is a living thing that keeps growing.) *How can you **connect** these details to the main idea?* (The English language changes and grows each year, like a living thing.) *What is the best answer?* (The best answer is H.)   **AUTHOR AND ME**

APPLY

Question 3 Read Question 3. Ask: *How can you turn this incomplete sentence into a question?* (Why would a new word be added to the dictionary?) Have students reread or scan the selection to **locate** information about how and why new words are added. Ask: *What answer can you locate in the selection?* (The **stated answer** is that a new word must show up regularly in many places. So, the best answer is A.)
RIGHT THERE

Have students answer question 4.

Question 4 After students have selected a summary, say: *What are the most important ideas in this selection that should be included in a summary?* (The summary should include the ideas that new words enter the English language each year and that editors add new words if they are used often. Answer H is the best summary.)   **AUTHOR AND ME**

Writing Prompt

EXPLAIN

Tell students that they may be asked to write to a prompt when taking a test. Explain that a prompt is a writing assignment. It tells you the **topic** to write about on the test.

Point out that prompts sometimes tell you the **purpose** of your composition or writing. Sometimes they also tell you what **genre** to use. Sometimes prompts do not give this information. Then you need to decide on your purpose and choose the most appropriate genre.

- You can write to entertain. (imaginative or personal narrative)

- You can write to influence. (persuasive)

- You can write to explain or inform. (expository)

MODEL

Determine the Topic and Purpose
Read the prompt on **Student Book** page 336. Ask: *What is this composition supposed to be about?* (It is about starting a new project.) Ask: *For what purpose would you write about starting a new project?* (Students should recognize that the purpose of the composition could be expository, persuasive, or entertaining.) Point out the suggestions in the boxes beneath the prompt.

Determine the Genre or Writing Mode Note that this student has decided to write a persuasive composition in response to the prompt. The composition expresses the writer's opinion and attempts to influence others to agree.

✏ Write to a Prompt

> Write a composition about starting a new project.

> Think about how to clearly express your ideas and opinions.

> As you write, think about what makes an effective sentence.

Below, see how one student begins a response to the prompt above.

> The writer included an opinion to express a point of view.

Sometimes, it is hard for kids in our class to relate to what they read. That is why I have started a magazine only for kids. I call it Kids Today. The magazine will be written and run by kids. It will talk about topics that are important and interesting to us.

First, I am looking for kids my age who want to write for the magazine. I have decided to arrange the writing by subject: school, news, sports, music, and movies. Second, I need kids to edit the articles.

This magazine is such a great way to reach our classmates and to talk about what interests us and is important to us. Come join Kids Today and help make it a success!

Writing Prompt

Respond in writing to the prompt below. Review the hints below before and after you write.

> Write a composition about how you could help your classmates.

Writing Hints

- ☑ Remember to write about helping your classmates. Think about the genre.
- ☑ Form an opinion about a topic.
- ☑ Plan your writing by organizing your ideas.
- ☑ Include important details.
- ☑ Use correct spelling and grammar.
- ☑ Review and edit your writing.

337

PRACTICE

Topic Have students read the prompt on page 337 and restate the topic.

Purpose The student is being asked to suppose that he or she could help classmates. The student must think about what he or she would do to help them and then try to convince readers that these actions would be useful.

Genre or Writing Mode Point out the prompt asks students to try to influence others. It is a persuasive prompt.

APPLY

Writing Prompt Students can practice writing from the prompt, simulating a test-taking situation. Distribute paper for students' responses.

Tell students: *You may use scrap paper to organize your thoughts before you begin to draft your essay. Use the Writing Hints to make sure you have followed all the necessary steps for responding to the prompt.*

For a guided writing process lesson, see pages 337A–337F.

4-POINT SCORING RUBRIC			
4 Excellent	**3** Good	**2** Fair	**1** Unsatisfactory
Focus and Coherence Sustained focus shows sense of completeness and how ideas are related.	**Focus and Coherence** Focus generally shows sense of completeness and clear relationship between ideas.	**Focus and Coherence** Somewhat focused paragraphs and/or composition has some sense of completeness but may shift quickly from idea to idea.	**Focus and Coherence** Weak connection to prompt and abrupt shifts from idea to idea show lack of focus and little or no sense of completeness.
Organization Logical progression of thought, with meaningful transitions and effective presentation of ideas.	**Organization** Generally logical progression of thought, with mostly meaningful transitions and generally effective organizational strategy.	**Organization** Progression of thought may not be completely logical and requires more meaningful transitions; organizational strategy is not effective.	**Organization** Progression of thought is not logical, and transitions are minimal or lacking; no evidence of organizational strategy.
Development of Ideas Thorough, insightful, and specific development of ideas shows interesting connections and willingness to take compositional risks.	**Development of Ideas** Development of ideas may be thoughtful but shows little evidence of willingness to take compositional risks.	**Development of Ideas** Development of ideas, using lists or brief explanations, is superficial, inconsistent, or contrived.	**Development of Ideas** Development of ideas is general or vague.
Voice Authentic and original writing expresses unique perspective.	**Voice** Mostly authentic and original writing generally expresses unique perspective.	**Voice** Shows some authenticity or originality but has difficulty expressing unique perspective.	**Voice** Shows little or no sense of individual voice.
Conventions Demonstrates consistent command of spelling, capitalization, punctuation, grammar, usage, and sentence structure.	**Conventions** Generally demonstrates good command of spelling, capitalization, punctuation, grammar, usage, and sentence structure.	**Conventions** Demonstrates limited command of spelling, capitalization, punctuation, grammar, usage, and sentence structure.	**Conventions** Demonstrates little or no command of spelling, capitalization, punctuation, grammar, usage, and sentence structure.

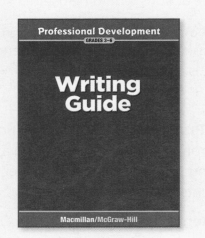

Persuasive Essay

Plan/Prewrite

TEACH/MODEL

Define the Genre Tell students that a persuasive essay is an essay in which the writer argues a position or gives an opinion about a topic and explains why the opinion makes sense. The writer's purpose is to get the reader to agree and possibly take action. Discuss the features of a persuasive essay.

Transparency 38

Features of a Persuasive Essay:

• It is a nonfiction work.

• It states the writer's opinion or position.

• It tries to get others to agree with the writer's thinking.

• It supports the opinion or position with convincing arguments.

• It organizes reasons in logical order, includes helpful transition words, and has a strong conclusion.

• It includes opinion words, such as *should, must, best*, and other persuasive language.

Writing Transparency

Set the Purpose Explain to students that they are going to choose a Writer's Notebook entry and turn it into a persuasive essay. Remind students that they have been working on many different pieces of writing that have explained and supported their ideas and opinions. In a few moments they are going to look at an example of a persuasive essay. The author started out with a journal entry and added reasons and details to support his opinion.

Consider the Audience In a persuasive essay, the writer's purpose is to convince a reader to think, believe, or do something. Writers choose details that they think will persuade or convince their intended audience. As students look at this persuasive essay, prompt them to think about how the author used strong reasons to support his opinion or position.

DISCUSS THE STUDENT SAMPLE

Student Sample Display **Writing Transparencies 39** and **40**. Read the pages aloud. On chart paper or the board, write students' ideas about what makes this example a strong persuasive essay.

Ask the following:

- *What opinion is the writer trying to support?* (Even kids can help in the community.)

- *Who is the writer's audience? How can you tell?* (His audience is someone his age. He chooses activities and reasons that would appeal to this audience.)

- *What are some reasons the writer gives for helping out?* (meet people, make the community better, feel good about yourself)

- *What does the writer want his audience to do?* (volunteer in the community)

Select a Journal Entry Students can select one or two entries from their Writer's Notebooks. See Selecting Journal Entries for guidance on how to help students identify appropriate journal entries that they will take through the writing process.

Brainstorm Ideas Students can also select a new topic to write about. Have students work in pairs to discuss opinions they would like to share. Remind students to review the features of a persuasive essay as they choose their topic.

Organize Your Ideas Once students have chosen their topics, they can complete an Organizing Web. Tell students to write their opinion statement in the center oval and reasons and supporting details in the outer ovals. See page 257 in the **Teacher's Resource Book**.

✓ Draft

Have students begin their drafts. Students can work on their selected journal entries by adding strong reasons and details that support their opinions and convince their audience. Prompt them to think about how the writer of the sample used strong reasons that appealed to his audience to convince them to take action.

Students who choose to write about a new event should review their Organizing Webs. Before they start to write, tell students to think about the reasons and details on their webs as support for the opinion. Each reason should convince the audience to think, believe, or do something. Remind students to state their position at the beginning of the essay and give support in the paragraphs that follow.

Objectives

- Define genre of persuasive essay
- Plan/prewrite a draft
- Develop a draft

Materials

- Writer's Notebooks
- Writing Transparencies 39–40
- Teacher's Resource Book, page 257

Selecting Journal Entries

This quick classroom routine encourages students to reread their work with a purpose and make some judgments about their own writing.

1. Read each student's Writer's Notebook, select two of the strongest entries from recent student writing, and flag them with self-stick notes.

2. Explain that you have posted a self-stick note on two pieces that you thought were strong. The student's job is to reread them and choose one of the pieces for you to give an individual Revision Assignment. Give the student a basis for choosing the entry, and post the criteria. For example:

- ☑ Choose a piece in which you've expressed an opinion that you want to share with others.
- ☑ Choose a piece that you think will convince your audience to think or believe as you do.
- ☑ After deciding on a piece, write a big check mark (√) on the self-stick note attached to the entry that you want me to read.

Objectives
- Use persuasive language
- Revise draft

Materials
- Writer's Notebooks
- Writing Transparencies 38, 41–42

ELL

Words of Degree Help students understand that words have degrees of meaning. For example, *must* is a stronger word than *should*. Help students choose between words such as *good* and *best* to properly emphasize their reasons and details.

Teacher-to-Teacher

In order to save time when reading Writer's Notebooks, it's important to just focus on the goal you have for that reading. For example, for today you just need to underline a place where students could add persuasive language. Don't worry about making lots of comments or reading carefully for other revision assignments. This way, you'll be able to get through the journals in much less time.

Persuasive Essay

Minilesson 1: Word Choice/Persuasive Language

TEACH/MODEL

Set the Purpose Tell students that one way to convince readers to think, believe, or act is to include positive persuasive words, such as *best* or *proud*, or words that call to action, such as *should* or *must*.

Use Persuasive Language Remind students that the purpose of yesterday's sample persuasive essay was to persuade young people to help in their community. Display **Writing Transparency 41**.

> ### Transparency 41
>
> **Example 1:** Finally, helping others makes you *feel good about yourself* and *shows your pride* in your community.
> **Example 2:** Everyone *must* do their share.

Writing Transparency

Read Example 1. Ask: *How does the writer want you to feel?* (good; proud) Read Example 2. Ask: *What does the writer want you to do?* (help in the community) Point out that *must* is a stronger word than *should*, and shows how important the writer thinks it is to help.

✓ Revise

PRACTICE/APPLY

Review the persuasive essay traits on **Writing Transparency 38**. Tell students they will now add persuasive language to their essays. Ask them to:

> ### Transparency 42
>
> 1. Reread your Writer's Notebook entry.
> 2. Circle a sentence that shows how you want the reader to feel. Rewrite it. Add positive words, such as *best* or *proud*.
> 3. Underline a sentence that shows what you want the reader to do. Rewrite it. Add a word that calls to action, such as *can, should,* or *must*.

Writing Transparency

Have students share their revisions. Point out good examples.

Summarize Learning Discuss the following: *Did you add persuasive words? Writing is more convincing when it appeals to readers' feelings.*

Persuasive Essay

Minilesson 2: Organization/Logical Order

TEACH/MODEL

Set the Purpose Tell students that writing is more persuasive and easier to follow when it is organized in a logical way. Organizing reasons in a persuasive essay from weakest to strongest builds the writer's argument and ends the essay in a powerful way. Write the following on the board and complete the Teacher Think Aloud:

> Everyone should recycle. You can save our planet by not filling up our landfills and using natural resources to make new products. You can earn extra money by bringing in your cans. Cans, bottles, and boxes are good for art projects. Start recycling today.

Teacher Think Aloud Which reason is the strongest reason for recycling? They are all good reasons. I think the strongest reason is that it saves our planet. This should be the last reason before the concluding sentence to end the essay in a powerful way.

Guide students to rewrite the paragraph, rearranging the reasons. Read the revised paragraph aloud when you are done. Discuss how the order of the reasons made a stronger argument.

 **Revise**

PRACTICE/APPLY

Tell students that now they will look at their essay to find places where they need to reorder their reasons. Remind them that the strongest reasons are those that will most convince their audience.

Transparency 44

1. Reread your journal entry.
2. Underline the reasons you gave to support your opinion.
3. Number the reasons in order from weakest to strongest. Start with number 1 for your weakest reason.
4. Rewrite your entry so that the reasons that support your opinion are arranged from weakest to strongest.

Writing Transparency

Summarize Learning Discuss the following: *Were you able to rearrange your reasons? Is your essay more persuasive? Organizing your reasons from weakest to strongest builds your argument and leaves readers with a strong impression of why they should agree with you.*

Objective

- Organize reasons in a logical way

Materials

- Writer's Notebooks
- Writing Transparency 43, 44
- Teacher's Resource Book, p. 190

CREATING RUBRICS

Teacher Developed Rubric As a follow-up, display **Writing Transparency 43.** Have students refer to **Teacher's Resource Book** page 190. Work with students to fill in the rubric for this week's writing. Tell students that you will use this rubric to evaluate their completed pieces. They should refer to the rubric as they write, revise, and proofread.

ON YOUR OWN **Teacher's Resource Book,** page 190

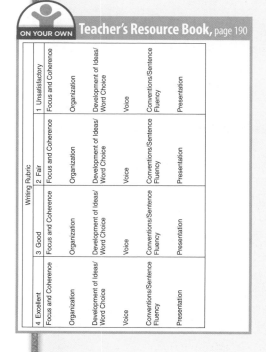

Peer Review

Think, Pair, Share Ask students to read their revised drafts aloud to partners. Listeners should be able to state what the writer wants them to think, believe, or do. Ask them to point out which reasons were persuasive and which ones were not. Encourage writers to use their partners' input when revising their drafts.

Flexible Pairing Option Consider pairing students who do not know each other well or do not regularly work together.

Research Proven Writing Approach

The Writers' Express
Immediate Impact. Lasting Transformation.   wex.org

Conferencing Routine

Dynamic Feedback System

Step 1 Read and appreciate the writing.

Step 2 Notice how the student uses the targeted skill (for example, word choice: Ask: *How did the writer use persuasive language to make the argument convincing?*).

Step 3 Write comments that show how the writing has an impact on you. Direct your comments to those places in the piece where the student has used the targeted skill.

Step 4 Meet with the student and give him or her a revision assignment.

Write Effective Comments

Persuasive Essay At least one of your comments should highlight the way the student uses the skills related to the genre. Here are some sample comments. Use these comments to get you started. Once you're comfortable, you can craft your own comments to be more specific to a particular entry.

- This first sentence lets me know right away what you think.

- I'm really able to see your point from your reasons.

- What are some other reasons I should agree with you?

- This last sentence tells me what you want me to do.

Revision Assignments

Persuasive Essay Below are examples of effective revision assignments. Use them to get started.

 I underlined a sentence where I think you could add persuasive language to make the reason stronger. Rewrite it and add words that will convince your reader to agree with you.

 I underlined your last sentence because it does not clearly state what you want the reader to do. Rewrite it so that the reader knows what you want him or her to do, think, or feel after reading your essay.

Persuasive Essay

✔ Edit/Proofread: Conventions

During the editing process, students should proofread their own work for spelling, grammar, and punctuation. Remind students to

- check for complete sentences;
- make sure their subjects and verbs agree;
- begin new sentences with capital letters;
- end sentences with proper punctuation;
- check for correct use and punctuation of contractions;
- read their writing aloud and check for errors in syntax.

Use the Grammar, Mechanics, and Spelling lessons on pages 337I–337L for minilessons on conventions in which students may have difficulty.

Publish and Share

Ask students to type or write, in cursive script or manuscript printing, a final copy of their persuasive essays. Remind them to use their best handwriting to correctly form letters. Model for them how to create documents with appropriate spacing between words, sentences, paragraphs, and correct margins.

It is important to post students' work. Post examples of strong reasons and clearly stated opinions.

Have students publish their essays in the editorial section of a class newspaper. They can draw pictures to illustrate their essays.

Presentations Ask students to present their persuasive essays to the class. Remind them to make eye contact with the audience and use gestures and appropriate volume to emphasize important points.

Objectives

- Edit drafts for grammar, mechanics, and spelling
- Publish a written work for a specific purpose

WRITING RUBRIC

Evaluate Students' Writing Use the rubric on page 401G. Review your evaluation with each student. Refer to the rubric you created with students to clearly identify strengths in their writing and areas on which they should focus.

Connect
Language Arts

WHOLE GROUP

VOCABULARY
- Tested Words

SPELLING
- Soft *c* and *g*

GRAMMAR
- Main and Helping Verbs

SMALL GROUP

- Differentiated Instruction, pp. 337M–337LL

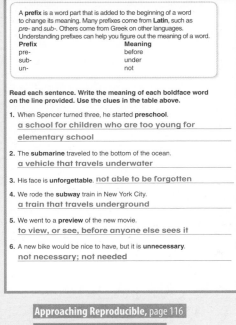

Practice Book, page 116

A **prefix** is a word part that is added to the beginning of a word to change its meaning. Many prefixes come from **Latin**, such as *pre-* and *sub-*. Others come from Greek or other languages. Understanding prefixes can help you figure out the meaning of a word.

Prefix	Meaning
pre-	before
sub-	under
un-	not

Read each sentence. Write the meaning of each boldface word on the line provided. Use the clues in the table above.

1. When Spencer turned three, he started **preschool**.
   a school for children who are too young for elementary school

2. The **submarine** traveled to the bottom of the ocean.
   a vehicle that travels underwater

3. His face is **unforgettable**. not able to be forgotten

4. We rode the **subway** train in New York City.
   a train that travels underground

5. We went to a **preview** of the new movie.
   to view, or see, before anyone else sees it

6. A new bike would be nice to have, but it is **unnecessary**.
   not necessary; not needed

Approaching Reproducible, page 116

Beyond Reproducible, page 116

Build Robust Vocabulary

Day 1 Teach/Practice

CONNECT TO WORDS

- Practice this week's vocabulary words using the following prompts:

  1. How does your teacher *dismiss* you from class?

  2. Which adults do you *interact* with at school?

  3. What would *motivate* you to help with a household chore, such as setting the table for dinner?

  4. How do you think an idea for writing a book is *conceived*?

  5. What is a *definition* for the word *school*?

ACADEMIC VOCABULARY

- Review the important academic vocabulary words for the week. These words include: *autobiography, prefix, expository, fact, opinion, cause, effect.*

- Write each word on the board. Define each using student-friendly language, and ask students to select the word you are defining. Then point to words in random order for students to define.

Day 2 Review

CONNECT TO WORDS

- Review the definitions of this week's vocabulary words using **Student Book** pages 328–329. Then discuss each word using the following prompts:

  1. If you *dismiss* an idea, is the idea important? Explain.

  2. When you *interact* with your friends, are you alone? Explain.

  3. How would you *motivate* a dog to learn to sit or to stay?

  4. If you *conceived* of a new way to study spelling words, what would you have done?

  5. What is a synonym for *definition*?

LATIN PREFIXES

- Review that a prefix is a word part that can be added to the beginning of a word to change the word's meaning. Remind students that recognizing common Latin prefixes can help readers determine the meanings of some unfamiliar words.

-  Display **Transparency 25.** Discuss the prefixes on the chart and their meanings. Then have students read the first sentence. Ask them to find the word with the prefix and to use the word parts to determine its meaning.

- Have students follow a similar procedure for the remaining sentences. Ask students to say another word with each prefix. Allow the use of a dictionary, if needed.

Day 3 Reinforce

CONNECT TO WORDS

- Ask students to create Word Squares for each word in their Writer's Notebooks.

- In the first square, students write the word. (Example: *dismiss*)

- In the second square, students write their own definition of the word and related words, such as synonyms. (Example: *reject, get rid of*)

- In the third square, students draw a simple illustration that will help them remember the word. (Example: drawing of a person waving his hand to dismiss another person who is talking)

- In the fourth square, students write nonexamples, including antonyms for the word. (Example: *accept, invite*)

RELATED WORDS

- Help students generate words related to *motivate*. The classification of synonyms can help improve students' vocabularies.

- Draw a word web on the board. Write *motivate* in the middle.

- Have students brainstorm words they associate with *motivate*. They can use a thesaurus or dictionary to help them. Record their responses, which may include *inspire, move,* and *encourage*.

- Direct students to use each of the related words in a sentence that shows its meaning. They may also use the words in analogies.

Day 4 Extend

CONNECT TO WORDS

- Review this week's vocabulary using the following sentence stems. Have students orally complete each one.

1. When you dismiss someone or something, you ____.

2. I like to interact with ____.

3. My teacher can motivate me by ____.

4. When I thought of ____, I conceived of a great idea.

5. It is important to know the definition of a word because ____.

MORPHOLOGY

- Learning about suffixes and roots can help raise students' word consciousness. Use the additional selection word *encouragement* as a springboard for students to learn other words.

- Write *encouragement* on the board. Underline *-ment*. Explain that *encourage* is rooted in the Latin word *cor*, meaning "heart," and *-ment* is a suffix that comes from the Latin *mentum*. The suffix *-ment* means "the act of." So, *encouragement* means "the act of encouraging."

- Write *statement, enjoyment, argument,* and *entertainment* on the board. Have students underline the suffix in each word and discuss the meaning of the base word. Help students use the word parts to define each word by completing this phrase: *the act of ____.* (*stating, enjoying, arguing, entertaining*)

Day 5 Assess and Reteach

POSTTEST

- Display **Transparency 26**. Have students complete the cloze sentences using one of this week's vocabulary words.

- Note how quickly and accurately students can complete this task. Work with students who make errors or require too much time to complete this task during Small Group time.

CONNECT TO WRITING

- Have students write sentences in their Writer's Notebooks using this week's vocabulary. Tell students to write sentences that provide information they learned from this week's readings.

- **ELL** Provide the Day 4 sentence stems for students needing extra support.

5-Day Spelling

Go to pages T14–T15 for **Differentiated Spelling Lists**.

✔ Soft *c* and *g*

Spelling Words

center	circus	ounce
once	cement	ginger
scene	glance	wedge
germs	strange	arrange
spice	police	sponge
bridge	certain	village
badge	orange	

Review combs, kneel, wrench
Challenge general, ceremony

Dictation Sentences

1. What's in the center of the candy?
2. We practice once a week.
3. I loved the last scene of the play.
4. Wash the germs off your hands.
5. Add a little spice to your food.
6. Let's cross the bridge.
7. I earned a badge at the scout meeting.
8. I like the lions in the circus.
9. Watch out for that wet cement!
10. Glance at the mirror.
11. That is really strange.
12. You can trust the police.
13. Are you certain you saw a bear?
14. Peel the orange.
15. Add one ounce of sugar.
16. Do you like the taste of ginger?
17. I asked, "May I have a wedge of cheese?"
18. Please arrange the books neatly.
19. Use a sponge to wash the table.
20. In which village do you live?

Review/Challenge Words

1. He combs his hair every morning.
2. You have to kneel to get that low.
3. Use a wrench to fix that.
4. The general store has everything.
5. That was a lovely ceremony.

Day 1 Pretest

ASSESS PRIOR KNOWLEDGE

- Model for students how to spell the word *village*. Segment the word syllable by syllable, then attach a spelling to each sound. Point out the soft *g* spelling pattern -*age*.

- Use the Dictation Sentences. Say the underlined word, read the sentence, and repeat the word. Have students write the words.

- Have students self-correct their tests. Point out that the soft *c* and *g* sounds are more common at the ends of words.

- Have students cut apart the **Spelling Word Cards BLM** on **Teacher's Resource Book** page 56 and figure out a way to sort them. Have them save the cards for use throughout the week.

Day 2 Word Sorts and Review

SPIRAL REVIEW

- Review the silent letters in *honesty*, *combs*, *kneel*, and *wrench*. Have students find words in this week's readings with the same silent letters.

WORD SORTS

- Have students take turns sorting the spelling words and explaining how they sorted them. Discuss any problems.

- Review the words, pointing out the soft *c* and *g* formations. Use the cards from the Spelling Word Cards BLM. Write the key words *germs*, *badge*, and *glance* on the board. Model how to sort words with the soft *c* or /s/ sound, spelled *c* before *e* or *i*. Model how to sort words with the soft *g* or /j/ sound, spelled *g* before *e* or *i*, and spelled -*dge* at the end of a word. Place one or two cards beneath each key word.

ON YOUR OWN **Phonics/Spelling,** pages 73–74

Fold back the paper along the dotted line. Use the blanks to write each word as it is read aloud. When you finish the test, unfold the paper. Use the list at the right to correct any spelling mistakes.

1. _____		1. center
2. _____		2. once
3. _____		3. scene
4. _____		4. germs
5. _____		5. spice
6. _____		6. bridge
7. _____		7. badge
8. _____		8. circus
9. _____		9. cement
10. _____		10. glance
11. _____		11. strange
12. _____		12. police
13. _____		13. certain
14. _____		14. orange
15. _____		15. ounce
16. _____		16. ginger
17. _____		17. wedge
18. _____		18. arrange
19. _____		19. sponge
20. _____		20. village
Review Words 21. _____		21. combs
22. _____		22. kneel
23. _____		23. wrench
Challenge Words 24. _____		24. general
25. _____		25. ceremony

HOMEWORK **Phonics/Spelling,** page 75

arrange	glance	wedge	bridge	once
badge	cement	strange	orange	spice
circus	center	germs	ounce	sponge
certain	scene	ginger	police	village

Pattern Power
Write the spelling words with these spelling patterns.

words with *soft c*
1. cement
2. police
3. center
4. once
5. circus
6. scene
7. spice
8. certain
9. glance
10. ounce

words with *soft g*
11. arrange
12. germs
13. badge
14. ginger
15. bridge
16. wedge
17. orange
18. sponge
19. strange
20. village

Day 3 **Word Meanings**

CATEGORIES

Write these groups of words on the board. Have students copy them into their Writer's Notebooks and complete each group by adding a spelling word.

1. apple, banana, _____ (*orange*)
2. town, city, _____ (*village*)
3. middle, inside, _____ (*center*)
4. ton, pound, _____ (*ounce*)
5. mop, towel, _____ (*sponge*)

Challenge students to come up with other word groups using spelling words, review words, or challenge words.

Have students do a word hunt for the words in the weekly reading or other materials. They should define the spelling word being used in context and point out any clues to its meaning.

 **Day 4** **Proofread**

PROOFREAD AND WRITE

Write these sentences on the board. Have students circle and correct each misspelled word.

1. The clowns did a sceen at the cercus. (*scene, circus*)
2. Did the polis officer show you her bage? (*police, badge*)
3. At the senter of our villij, we have a park. (*center, village*)
4. Does it seem strang that the bridje was closed? (*strange, bridge*)
5. My favorite spise is jinjer. (*spice, ginger*)

Error Correction Some students may continue to use the more common spellings for /s/ and /j/. Provide these students with additional reading and writing practice with common soft *c* and *g* spelling patterns (e.g., *-ace, -age*).

Day 5 **Assess and Reteach**

POSTTEST

Use the Dictation Sentences on page 337I for the Posttest.

If students have difficulty with any words in the lesson, have them place the words on a list called *Spelling Words I Want to Remember* in their Writer's Notebooks. Look for students' use of these words in their writings.

Challenge students to find words with letters that spell soft *c* and *g* and add them to their Writer's Notebooks.

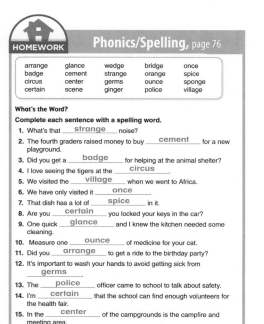

HOMEWORK Phonics/Spelling, page 76

arrange	glance	wedge	bridge	once
badge	cement	strange	orange	spice
circus	center	germs	ounce	sponge
certain	scene	ginger	police	village

What's the Word?
Complete each sentence with a spelling word.
1. What's that ___strange___ noise?
2. The fourth graders raised money to buy ___cement___ for a new playground.
3. Did you get a ___badge___ for helping at the animal shelter?
4. I love seeing the tigers at the ___circus___.
5. We visited the ___village___ when we went to Africa.
6. We have only visited it ___once___.
7. That dish has a lot of ___spice___ in it.
8. Are you ___certain___ you locked your keys in the car?
9. One quick ___glance___ and I knew the kitchen needed some cleaning.
10. Measure one ___ounce___ of medicine for your cat.
11. Did you ___arrange___ to get a ride to the birthday party?
12. It's important to wash your hands to avoid getting sick from ___germs___.
13. The ___police___ officer came to school to talk about safety.
14. I'm ___certain___ that the school can find enough volunteers for the health fair.
15. In the ___center___ of the campgrounds is the campfire and meeting area.
16. I need a damp ___sponge___ to clean up these dirty counters.

ON YOUR OWN Phonics/Spelling, page 77

A. Proofreading
There are six spelling mistakes in the story below. Circle the misspelled words. Write the words correctly on the lines below.

Ana read an article in the newspaper about a fire at a house in a nearby *vilage.* No one was hurt, but the family lost all of their belongings. Many people were helping them out, but the children didn't have clothes and books for school.

She thought about how *strang* it would be to lose her own stuff. She was *certain* she could find a way to help out. Ana decided to *arranje* a way for them to get the things they needed.

She started asking people to help. She started with her parents. They gave her a few dollars. Then she asked her grandparents. They gave a little, too. Then she asked her teacher, and next her neighbors. Pretty soon, she had the courage to ask everyone—the *polise* and even the clowns at the local *sircus.* When she collected enough money, her dad drove her to the store. She bought new clothes, books, and school supplies. She even bought some new toys. Then she loaded her purchases in a big box and got ready to drop them off to their new owners.

1. ___village___ 3. ___certain___ 5. ___police___
2. ___strange___ 4. ___arrange___ 6. ___circus___

B. Writing Activity
Imagine that you read about a family who needs help in your town. What might it be? How could you follow Ana's example and do something to fix it? Use at least three spelling words in your paragraph. **Answers will vary.**

HOMEWORK Phonics/Spelling, page 78
Look at the words in each set below. One word in each set is spelled correctly. Use a pencil to fill in the circle next to the correct word. Before you begin, look at the sample set of words. Sample A has been done for you. Do Sample B by yourself. When you are sure you know what to do, you may go on with the rest of the page.

Sample A:
Ⓐ city
Ⓑ sitty
Ⓒ sitie
Ⓓ citie

Sample B:
Ⓔ jiant
Ⓕ giant
Ⓖ gient
Ⓗ jyent

1. Ⓐ arrange Ⓑ arranje Ⓒ arange Ⓓ aranje
2. Ⓔ badge Ⓕ bajj Ⓖ badje Ⓗ bage
3. Ⓐ cerkis Ⓑ sirkus Ⓒ circus Ⓓ sircus
4. Ⓔ serten Ⓕ certain Ⓖ certin Ⓗ sirtain
5. Ⓐ glantz Ⓑ glance Ⓒ glanse Ⓓ glansce

6. Ⓔ siment Ⓕ sement Ⓖ cement Ⓗ cemint
7. Ⓐ senter Ⓑ scenter Ⓒ sinter Ⓓ center
8. Ⓔ scene Ⓕ sceen Ⓖ secne Ⓗ csene
9. Ⓐ wedje Ⓑ wej Ⓒ weg Ⓓ wedge
10. Ⓔ stranje Ⓕ strange Ⓖ straynje Ⓗ straine

11. Ⓐ jerms Ⓑ girms Ⓒ jirms Ⓓ germs
12. Ⓔ jinjer Ⓕ jinger Ⓖ ginger Ⓗ ginjer
13. Ⓐ brijj Ⓑ bridje Ⓒ brige Ⓓ bridge
14. Ⓔ orange Ⓕ ornje Ⓖ oranje Ⓗ ornge
15. Ⓐ ownse Ⓑ ounce Ⓒ ounse Ⓓ ownce

16. Ⓔ poleese Ⓕ polease Ⓖ police Ⓗ poleece
17. Ⓐ wonce Ⓑ wunse Ⓒ onse Ⓓ once
18. Ⓔ spise Ⓕ spyce Ⓖ spyse Ⓗ spice
19. Ⓐ sponge Ⓑ spunje Ⓒ spunge Ⓓ sponje
20. Ⓔ villaje Ⓕ vilage Ⓖ vilidge Ⓗ village

5-Day Grammar

Main and Helping Verbs

Daily Language Activities
Write the sentences on the board.

DAY 1
We was at the park yesterday Then it, started to rain. We left and goed to the mall? (1: were; 2: yesterday.; 3: it started; 4: and went to; 5: mall.)

DAY 2
I wants a dog? I am gonna feed it in the morning. I will happy all the time. (1: want; 2: dog.; 3: am going to feed; 4: will be happy)

DAY 3
I am been here before. By the end of last summer, I have ridden on all the rides. And I has seen all the shows already? (1: have been; 2: I had ridden; 3: I had seen; 4: already.)

DAY 4
You arent going yet. First, lets' clean up the mess we maked. Then we will going to your hous. (1: aren't; 2: let's; 3: we made.; 4: will go; 5: house.)

DAY 5
I do asked for a chocolate shake. Didnt' they fix it yet? I have hungry. (1: did ask; 2: Didn't; 3: am hungry.)

Day 1 — Introduce the Concept

INTRODUCE MAIN AND HELPING VERBS

Present the following:

- The **main verb** in a sentence tells what the subject does or is: *They* work *for me.*

- A **helping verb** tells more about when an action takes place. The helping verb comes before the main verb in statements: *They* are *working for me.* (present)

- The verbs *have, has, had, is, am, are, was, were,* and *will* are used as helping verbs.

- Forms of the helping verb *have* are used in the **present perfect** tense. The present perfect shows an action that began in the past and was only just completed or is still going on. I *have met* her. He *has worked* hard.

See Grammar Transparency 61 for modeling and guided practice.

Day 2 — Teach the Concept

REVIEW MAIN AND HELPING VERBS

Review with students how to identify the main verb and the helping verb.

INTRODUCE HELPING VERBS AND TENSES

Present the following:

- The helping verbs *am, is,* and *are* are used to show present tense: *I* am *eating.* The helping verbs *was* and *were* are used to show past tense: *I* was *eating.* The helping verb *will* is used to show future tense: *I* will *eat tomorrow.*

- The helping verbs *have, has,* and *had* can be used with the past-tense form of a verb to show an action that has already happened: *I* had *eaten, I* have *eaten.*

See Grammar Transparency 62 for modeling and guided practice.

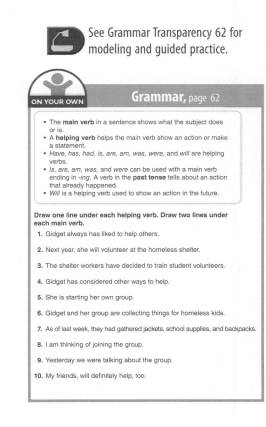

HOMEWORK — **Grammar,** page 61

- The **main verb** in a sentence shows what the subject does or is.
- A **helping verb** helps the main verb show an action or make a statement.
- *Have, has,* and *had* can be helping verbs.
- *Is, are, am, was, were,* and *will* can be helping verbs.

Write a main verb or helping verb to complete each sentence.

1. Charlie _____ searched for a place to volunteer.

2. He has _____ lists of groups.

3. Charlie _____ worrying about choosing the right place to help.

4. He _____ visit different groups.

5. The people in the soup kitchen are _____ vegetables.

6. Many people _____ donated clothes to this group.

7. This afternoon Charlie is _____ for people who couldn't leave their homes.

8. He has _____ floors at the animal shelter.

9. Charlie _____ pitch in wherever he can.

10. The leaders of the groups are _____ him and telling him he's done a great job.

ON YOUR OWN — **Grammar,** page 62

- The **main verb** in a sentence shows what the subject does or is.
- A **helping verb** helps the main verb show an action or make a statement.
- *Have, has, had, is, are, am, was, were,* and *will* are helping verbs.
- *Is, are, am, was,* and *were* can be used with a main verb ending in *-ing*. A verb in the **past tense** tells about an action that already happened.
- *Will* is a helping verb used to show an action in the future.

Draw one line under each helping verb. Draw two lines under each main verb.

1. Gidget always has liked to help others.

2. Next year, she will volunteer at the homeless shelter.

3. The shelter workers have decided to train student volunteers.

4. Gidget has considered other ways to help.

5. She is starting her own group.

6. Gidget and her group are collecting things for homeless kids.

7. As of last week, they had gathered jackets, school supplies, and backpacks.

8. I am thinking of joining the group.

9. Yesterday we were talking about the group.

10. My friends, will definitely help, too.

 Day 3 Review and Practice

REVIEW MAIN VERBS AND HELPING VERBS

Review how to form verb phrases using the helping verbs *be* and *have*.

MECHANICS AND USAGE: PUNCTUATION IN CONTRACTIONS

- A **contraction** is a word that combines two words and leaves out some of the letters from one or both of the words.

- Use an **apostrophe** for the letters that have been left out. The word *don't* is a contraction for the words *do* and *not*. The letter *o* has been left out of the word *not*.

- Ask students to identify contractions that can be made using the verbs *be* and *have*.

 Day 4 Review and Proofread

REVIEW CONTRACTIONS WITH HELPING VERBS

Have students explain how to use helping verbs. Ask them what punctuation is used to make a contraction and where that punctuation should be placed.

PROOFREAD

Have students correct errors in the following sentences.

1. Im' going to the mall. (I'm or I am)
2. There willn't be time left to go to the store. (won't or will not)
3. I do'nt like the circus. (don't or do not)
4. She wasnt nice. (wasn't or was not)
5. I amn't going to come with you. (am not or I'm not)

Day 5 Assess and Reteach

ASSESS

Use the Daily Language Activity and **Grammar Practice Book** page 65 for assessment.

RETEACH

Use Grammar Practice Book page 65 and selected pages from the **Grammar and Writing Handbook** for additional reteaching. Remind students that it is important to use verbs and contractions correctly as they speak and write.

Check students' writing for use of the skill and listen for it in their speaking. Assign Grammar Revision Assignments in their Writer's Notebooks as needed.

 See Grammar Transparency 63 for modeling and guided practice.

 See Grammar Transparency 64 for modeling and guided practice.

See Grammar Transparency 65 for modeling and guided practice.

Daily Planner

DAY 1	• Prepare to Read • Academic Language • Vocabulary (Preteach)
DAY 2	• Comprehension • Leveled Reader Lesson 1
DAY 3	• Phonics/Decoding • Leveled Reader Lesson 2
DAY 4	• Phonics/Decoding • Vocabulary (Review) • Leveled Reader Lesson 3
DAY 5	• High-Frequency Words • Fluency • Self-Selected Reading

Interactive Student Book

If you wish to preteach the main selection, use StudentWorks Plus for:

• Vocabulary Preteaching
• Word-by-Word Highlighting
• Think Aloud Prompts

Academic Language

Academic words include those harder Tier 2 words that appear in much of students' reading materials as well as the language of instruction. The words chosen for instruction were selected from the **Living Word Vocabulary** list and Avril Coxhead's list of **High-Incidence Academic Words**.

Approaching Level

Prepare to Read

Objective   Preview *Words Add Up to Success*
Materials   • **StudentWorks Plus**   • self-stick notes

PREVIEW THE MAIN SELECTION

- Have students preview *Words Add Up to Success* using **StudentWorks Plus**. This version of the selection contains oral summaries in multiple languages, story recording, word-by-word highlighting, Think Aloud prompts, and comprehension-monitoring questions.

- Remind students that listening carefully to and following along with the word-by-word reading will help them prepare for the reading of the selection with the class. Ask students to place self-stick notes on any challenging words or places that confuse them. Discuss these with students prior to the reading of the selection with the rest of the class.

- Ask students to write three or four sentences in their Writer's Notebooks telling what they learned about how Jaime Escalante's words helped young people become successful.

Academic Language

Objective   Teach academic language
Materials   • none

PRETEACH LANGUAGE OF INSTRUCTION

Tell students that there are many important lesson words you will be using this week. You want them to become familiar with these words *before* the lessons. These words also appear in the directions of the tests they will be taking this year.

Preteach the following academic words: *expository, fact, opinion, prefix*.

- Define each word using student-friendly language. Relate the word *expository* to the word *expose*, or "to make known." Explain that when authors write expository text, they are giving information about a topic.

- In addition, relate each word to known words. For example, connect *fact* to *proven* and *opinion* to *believed*.

- Highlight these words when used throughout the week and reinforce their meanings.

Approaching Level

Phonics/Decoding

Objective   Decode words with soft *c* and *g*

Materials
- **Approaching Reproducible,** p. 109
- **Sound-Spelling WorkBoards**

PHONICS MAINTENANCE

Tier 2

- Distribute a **WorkBoard** to each student. Say a sound previously taught, including *r*-controlled vowels and hard and soft *c* and *g*. Have students find the **Sound-Spelling Card** on the board for each sound.

- Review the spelling(s) for each sound by providing a sample word containing that spelling. Guide students to write the word on the board. Model how to segment the word and write the spelling for each sound, as needed. In addition, point out spelling hints, such as the letter *e* after the letter *c* usually makes the *c* have a soft sound as in *ceiling*.

- Dictate the following words for students to spell: *serve, turn, like, are, central, place, change*, and *gentle*. Write each word on the board, and have students self-correct their work.

RETEACH SKILL

Soft *c* and *g*   Point to the soft *c* and *g* Sound-Spelling Cards on the WorkBoard, and review the spellings for these sounds. State each spelling and provide a sample word.

- Write the words below on the board. Model how to decode the first word in each row, and then guide students as they decode the remaining words. For the multisyllabic words, divide the words into syllables using the syllable-scoop technique to help students read one syllable at a time.

- When completed, point to the words in random order for students to chorally read. Repeat several times.

cold	cent	gem	good	cone	circus
dance	prance	ring	chance	glance	ginger
rage	range	twinge	strange	badge	budget
hinge	cringe	wince	price	center	cement
since	prince	germ	age	stage	city
ice	spice	certain	cell	cellar	stranger

Sound-Spelling WorkBoard

ELL

Minimal Contrasts Focus on articulation. Make the soft *c* and *g* sounds: /s/ and /j/. Have students repeat. Use hand mirrors, if available, to have students watch their mouths when shaping sounds. Repeat for both sounds. Then have students make the hard *c* and *g* sounds: /k/ and /g/. Note any differences in their mouth positions. Continue by having students read minimal contrast words such as *hug/huge, can't/cent, place/placard, rag/rage.*

Approaching Reproducible, page 109

When *c* and *g* are followed by *e*, *i*, or *y*, their sounds are soft.
- The soft *c* is pronounced like the letter **s**:
  Examples: *certain, center*
- The soft *g* is pronounced like the letter *j*:
  Examples: *village, ginger*

Circle each soft c or g in the following words.
1. citizen
2. fragile
3. cage
4. gymnasium
5. license
6. cycle

7. Explain the pronunciation of the *c* and *g* in *cage*.
   The *c* is followed by *a* — hard; the *g* is followed by *e* — soft.

8. Explain the pronunciation of the 2 *cs* in *cycle*.
   The first *c* is followed by *y* — soft; the second *c* is followed by a consonant — hard.

Approaching Level

Vocabulary

Objective   Preteach selection vocabulary

Materials   • **Visual Vocabulary Resources**   • **Approaching Reproducible,** p. 110
                • **Vocabulary Cards**

PRETEACH KEY VOCABULARY

Tier 2

Introduce the Words   Use the **Visual Vocabulary Resources** to preteach the key selection words *dismiss, interact, motivate, conceived*, and *definition*. Use the following routine that appears in detail on the cards.

- Define the word in English, and provide the example given.

- Define the word in Spanish, if appropriate, and indicate if the word is a cognate.

- Display the picture, and explain how it illustrates or demonstrates the words.

- Then engage students in structured partner-talk about the image, using the key word.

- Ask students to chorally say the word three times.

- Point out any known sound-spellings or focus on a key aspect of phonemic awareness related to the word.

- You may wish to also distribute copies of the Vocabulary Glossary in the **ELL Resource Book**.

REVIEW PREVIOUSLY TAUGHT VOCABULARY

Display the **Vocabulary Cards** from the previous four weeks. Say the meanings of the words, one by one, and have students identify them. Then point to words in random order for students to provide definitions and related words they know.

Latin Prefixes   Remind students that prefixes are word parts added to the beginning of a word, and that many prefixes come from Latin. Review the meanings of the prefixes *non-, dis-,* and *inter-*. Ask: What is the meaning of the word *nonviolence*? Which part of the word is the prefix? How does the prefix change the meaning of the original word?

Corrective Feedback

Throughout the lessons, provide feedback based on students' responses. If the answer is correct, ask another question. If the answer is tentative, restate key information to assist the student. If the answer is wrong, provide corrective feedback such as hints or clues, refer to a visual such as a Sound-Spelling Card or story illustration, or probe with questions to help the student clarify any misunderstanding.

Approaching Reproducible, page 110

| motivate | dismiss | conceived |
| interact | definition | |

A. Match each word in column 1 with the correct clue in column 2. Write the letter of the clue next to the correct vocabulary word.

Column 1	Column 2
1. interact _d_	a. make someone want to take action
2. definition _e_	b. thought of or planned
3. conceived _b_	c. put something aside
4. motivate _a_	d. speak to or do something with a person
5. dismiss _c_	e. the meaning of a word

B. Complete the sentence with the correct word in parentheses.

6. Watching the talent show on TV might (motivate/interact) ___motivate___ me to take singing lessons.

7. The (definition/dismiss) ___definition___ of the word *instruct* is "to teach."

8. Tess and Tia (dismiss/interact) ___interact___ every day in art class.

Approaching Level

Vocabulary

Objective Review vocabulary and high-frequency words
Materials • **Vocabulary Cards** • **High-Frequency Word Cards**

REVIEW VOCABULARY

Review Words Display the **Vocabulary Cards** for *dismiss, interact, motivate, conceived,* and *definition*. Point to each word, read it aloud, and have students chorally repeat.

Then provide the following word sets. Have students tell which word or phrase has almost the same meaning as the first word in each group:

- **dismiss**, remove, protect
- **interact**, communicate, hide
- **motivate**, design, encourage
- **conceived**, thought up, ignored
- **definition**, feeling, meaning

HIGH-FREQUENCY WORDS

Tier 2

Top 250 Words The ability to read accurately and effortlessly the most frequently used words in written English will help students develop reading fluency. Display **High-Frequency Word Cards** 101–110. Then do the following:

- Display one card at a time, and ask students to chorally state each word.
- Have students spell each word aloud.
- Ask students to write each word in their Writer's Notebooks as they state aloud each letter. Then have them read the word again.
- When completed, quickly flip through the Word Card set as students chorally read the words.
- Provide opportunities for students to use the words in speaking and writing. For example, provide sentence starters, such as *That _____ made me laugh*, for oral and written practice. Or point to a Word Card and ask a question, such as *What word is a synonym for jump?* (*leap*)
- Continue the routine throughout the week.

ELL

Practice Vocabulary Pair students of different proficiency. Orally model the vocabulary in sentences. For example: *I use a dictionary to find the definition of a word*. On the board, provide sentence frames for pairs to copy and complete using the vocabulary. For example: *After the school bell rings, the teacher will _____ the class.* (*dismiss*)

Word Webs

Have students create word webs in their Writer's Notebooks for each vocabulary word. Write the related words provided, and ask students to add other words, phrases, and illustrations.

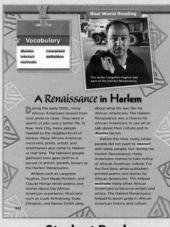

Student Book

Corrective Feedback

Remind students that a fact can be proven to be true, while an opinion is someone's belief. Give a pair of statements such as: *There was a Renaissance in Harlem. The best musicians in the world performed in Harlem.* Have students identify the first statement as a fact and the second as an opinion. Then ask students to state facts and opinions for the class to identify.

Approaching Level

Comprehension

Objective Reteach monitor comprehension and identify fact and opinion

Materials • **Student Book:** "A Renaissance in Harlem"

RETEACH STRATEGY: MONITOR COMPREHENSION

Tier 2

- **Define** Tell students that good readers monitor their comprehension to be sure they understand what they read. To fully understand expository text, they are careful to distinguish between facts and opinions.

- **Relate to Real Life** Have students imagine that they are shopping for a new pair of sneakers. Do they want the black ones with red stripes or the plain blue ones? The blue sneakers fit better, but they like the black ones more. Once they understand and can distinguish between facts and their own preference or opinion, students can make an informed choice about which sneakers they want to buy and why.

- **Set Purposes** Remind students that good readers identify and distinguish between facts and opinions in an expository selection.

RETEACH SKILL: FACT AND OPINION

- **Define** Tell students that a fact can be proven to be true. An opinion tells what someone thinks or believes. Words like *I think* or *the best* can signal opinions.

- **Relate to Real Life** Ask students to tell about a movie that they have seen. Prompt them with questions such as: *Who was the main character? Did you like the movie? Who was the best actor?* Point out that when they name characters and events from the movie, they are giving facts. They can prove that those characters and events were in the movie. When they tell how they feel about the movie, they are giving opinions. They are saying what they think about the movie. Other people might have different opinions.

- **Set Purposes** Point out that good readers distinguish between facts and opinions as they read. Doing so helps them better understand the text and enables them to decide whether the facts support the opinions. Have students explain how they can verify facts using reference books or other sources.

- **Apply** Work with students to distinguish between facts and opinions in "A Renaissance in Harlem." Then use the facts and opinions to model how readers can monitor their comprehension of the article. Students will apply this strategy and skill to a simpler text as they read *Symbols of America*.

Approaching Level

Leveled Reader Lesson 1

Leveled Reader

Objective   Read to apply skills and strategies

Materials   • **Leveled Reader:** *Symbols of America*

BEFORE READING

Preview and Predict Have students read the title and preview the book by reading the chapter titles and looking at the photographs. Ask them to make predictions about the facts and opinions that they may find in this book. Students should note any questions they have before they read.

Review Vocabulary Words Have students read the vocabulary words on the inside front cover. Briefly define each and ask students to state related words they have learned.

Set a Purpose for Reading *Let's read to find out about symbols of America—what they are and what they mean.*

DURING READING

STRATEGY
MONITOR COMPREHENSION

Remind students that when they monitor comprehension, they check and adjust their understanding of what they are reading.

SKILL
FACT AND OPINION

Remind students to distinguish between facts and opinions as they read *Symbols of America*. Help students complete their Fact and Opinion Charts.

As you read, help students decode unknown words. In addition, ask open-ended questions to facilitate rich discussion, such as *What facts about American symbols does the author give? What opinions does the author share?* Build on students' responses to help them develop a deeper understanding of the text.

Stop after every two pages and ask students to summarize the information they read to check their understanding. Help struggling students reread difficult pages or passages. Then model identifying facts and opinions.

AFTER READING

Ask students to comment on and share opinions about what they have learned. *What fact about an American symbol most interested you? Why? What are some of the author's opinions about these symbols? What are some of your opinions about them?*

Leveled Reader

Approaching Level

 Leveled Reader Library

Leveled Reader Lesson 2

Objective Reread to apply skills and strategies and develop fluency
Materials
- **Leveled Reader:** *Symbols of America*
- **Approaching Reproducible,** p. 113

BEFORE READING

Review the Strategy and Skill Review students' completed Fact and Opinion Charts from the first read. Remind students that a fact is a statement that can be proven, whereas an opinion is a statement of feeling or belief. Understanding the difference between facts and opinions enables students to better understand what they are reading.

Review Vocabulary Words Have students search the book for each vocabulary word. Ask students to read aloud the sentence containing the word and state the word's definition or provide related words. Remind students that knowing Latin prefixes can help them understand some word meanings. Have students use Latin prefixes to help them define unfamiliar words, as applicable.

Set a Purpose for Reading *Let's reread to check our understanding of the information in the book and to work on our reading fluency.*

DURING READING

Reread *Symbols of America* with students. Have students read silently, two pages at a time, or read aloud to a partner. Stop and have students monitor their comprehension of the text before they read on. Model techniques for checking understanding, as needed.

AFTER READING

Check Comprehension Have partners complete the Comprehension Check on page 20. Review students' answers. Help students find evidence for their answers in the text.

MODEL FLUENCY

Model reading the fluency passage on **Approaching Reproducible** page 113. Tell students to pay close attention to your accuracy as you read. Then read one sentence at a time, and have students copy your accuracy as they echo-read.

During independent reading time, have students work with a partner using the fluency passage. One student reads aloud, while the other repeats each sentence back. If students need additional support, have them listen to the "practice speed" version of the passage on the **Fluency Solutions Audio CD**.

Approaching Reproducible, page 113

As I read, I will pay attention to accuracy.

	Giant pandas spend their days eating bamboo. Pandas
8	cannot digest the plant easily. So it is hard for their bodies
20	to use bamboo's nutrients. Pandas need to eat a lot of
31	bamboo in order to stay healthy.
37	Pandas have to peel off the hard outside part of the
48	bamboo to get at the softer part under it. Their wrists have
60	a long bone that they can use like a thumb. Having this
72	bone lets them grab and tear the bamboo. Then the pandas
83	crush the bamboo stems and leaves in their mouths. Panda
93	jaws are strong and their teeth are flat.
101	Pandas have to spend up to 14 hours a day eating. It
112	takes a long time to chew on the 20 to 40 pounds
122	(9 to 18 kg) of bamboo they need each day. 130

Comprehension Check

1. Why do pandas need to eat a lot of bamboo? Explain. **Main Idea and Details** It is physically difficult for them to get the nutrients they need from bamboo. Because of this, pandas must eat large quantities of bamboo.

2. What is the main idea of the second paragraph? **Main Idea and Details** Pandas' wrists, jaws, and teeth are made to help them eat large amounts of bamboo.

	Words Read	−	Number of Errors	=	Words Correct Score
First Read		−		=	
Second Read		−		=	

Approaching Level

Leveled Reader Lesson 3

Objective Build fluency

Materials
- **Leveled Reader:** *Symbols of America*
- **Approaching Reproducible,** p. 113

FOCUS ON FLUENCY

Timed Reading Tell students that they will be doing a final timed reading of the fluency passage on **Approaching Reproducible** page 113, which they have been practicing. With each student, follow these directions:

- Place the passage facedown.
- When you say "Go," the student begins reading the passage aloud.
- When you say "Stop," the student stops reading the passage.

As they read, note words students mispronounce and their overall intonation. Stop after one minute. Help students record and graph the number of words they read correctly.

REREAD PREVIOUSLY READ BOOKS

- Distribute copies of the past six **Leveled Readers**. Have students select two to reread. Tell students that rereading these books will help them develop their skills. The more times they read the same words, the quicker they will learn these words. This will make the reading of other books easier.

- Circulate and listen in as students read. Stop students periodically and ask them how they are figuring out difficult words and how they are monitoring their comprehension. Note students who need additional work with specific decoding or comprehension skills.

- Encourage students to read other previously read Leveled Readers during independent reading time or for homework.

Meet Grade-Level Expectations

As an alternative to this day's lesson, guide students through a reading of the On Level Leveled Reader. See page 337Y. Since both books contain the same vocabulary, phonics, and comprehension skills, the scaffolding you provided will help most students gain access to this more challenging text.

Book Talk

Bringing Groups Together Students will work with peers of various language and reading abilities to discuss this week's Leveled Readers. Refer to page 162 in the **Teacher's Resource Book** for more about how to conduct a Book Talk.

Student Book

Student Book

Decodable Text

Use decodable stories in the **Teacher's Resource Book** to help students build fluency with basic decoding patterns.

Approaching Level

Fluency

Objectives Reread selections to develop fluency; develop speaking skills

Materials • **Student Book:** *Words Add Up to Success*, "A Speech with Reach"

REREAD FOR FLUENCY

- Have students reread a portion of *Words Add Up to Success*. Suggest that they focus on their favorite passage from the selection. Work with students to read the passage with accuracy.

- Provide time for students to read their passages to you. Comment on their accuracy, and provide corrective feedback by modeling proper fluency.

DEVELOP SPEAKING/LISTENING SKILLS

- Have students practice reading two of the quotations in "A Speech with Reach."

- Work with students to read with accuracy. Model reading each quotation. Emphasize the way in which reading with accuracy— saying every word and pronouncing every word correctly—makes information clear. Have students repeat.

- Provide time for students to read aloud the quotations to partners. Ask students to discuss how their partner's accuracy made the meaning of each quotation clear.

- Challenge students to memorize and recite one or both of the quotations to the class.

Approaching Level

Self-Selected Reading

Objective   Read independently to identify facts and opinions
Materials   • **Leveled Classroom Library**   • other nonfiction books

APPLY SKILLS AND STRATEGIES TO INDEPENDENT READING

- **Read Independently** Have students choose an informational book for sustained silent reading. (See the **Theme Bibliography** on pages T8–T9 for book suggestions.) Remind them that a fact can be proven to be true, whereas an opinion tells what someone thinks or believes. Have students read their books and record the facts and opinions on a Fact and Opinion Chart. Discuss how they can verify facts.

- **Show Evidence of Reading** While reading, students may generate a reading log or journal. After reading, ask students to use their Fact and Opinion Charts to paraphrase the content of the book, maintaining meaning and logical order. They may write or orally state a summary of the book. Provide time for students to share their summaries and their reactions to the book while participating in Book Talks. Ask: *What facts did you learn from this book? What is your opinion of the book—for example, would you recommend it to a friend? Why or why not?*

Approaching

Leveled Classroom Library
See Leveled Classroom
Library lessons on pages T2–T7.

On Level

Daily Planner

DAY 1	• Vocabulary • Phonics
DAY 2	• Leveled Reader Lesson 1
DAY 3	• Leveled Reader Lesson 2
DAY 4	• Fluency
DAY 5	• Self-Selected Reading

ELL

Practice Vocabulary Pair ELL students with native speakers. On the board, provide sentence frames for pairs to copy and complete using the vocabulary and additional words when necessary. For example: *The coach decided to _____ the _____ early, so we could watch the championship game on TV.* (*dismiss; practice*)

Sound-Spelling WorkBoard

Vocabulary

Objective Review vocabulary

Materials • **Vocabulary Cards**

REVIEW PREVIOUSLY TAUGHT WORDS

Review the Words Display **Vocabulary Cards** for *dismiss, interact, motivate, conceived,* and *definition*. Point to each word, read it aloud, and have students chorally repeat. Then have students answer these questions. Allow time for students to discuss their answers. Use the discussions to determine each student's depth of word knowledge.

- If you had been planning a bike ride and then decided not to go, did you *interact* the idea or *dismiss* the idea?

- When you tell a friend what a word means, do you give a *definition* or *interact* a word?

- When your mom says that you can have dessert when you finish your homework, is she trying to *dismiss* you or *motivate* you?

- If you just thought of a great idea for your school project, did you *conceive* of the idea or *motivate* the idea?

- When you do a school project with a group of your classmates, do you *interact* with the group or *conceive* of a *definition*?

Phonics/Word Study

Objective Decode multisyllabic words with soft *c* and *g*

RETEACH SKILL

- **Words with Soft *c* and *g*** Point to the /s/ and /j/ **Sound-Spelling Cards** on the **WorkBoard**, and review the soft *c* and *g* spellings for these sounds. State each spelling and provide a sample word.

- Write the words below on the board. If necessary, divide the words into syllables using the syllable-scoop technique to help students read one syllable at a time. When completed, point to the words in random order for students to chorally read.

notice	receive	princess	recess	spicy
giant	gentle	village	garage	gadget
circle	central	certain	unhinge	oblige

- **Spelling** Dictate the following words for students to spell on their WorkBoards: *ranger, dancing, ginger, cereal, icy*. Guide students to use the Sound-Spelling Cards, and model how to segment words, such as spelling a word syllable by syllable.

On Level

Fluency

Objectives Reread selections to develop fluency; develop speaking skills
Materials • **Student Book:** *Words Add Up to Success*, "A Speech with Reach"

✔ REREAD FOR FLUENCY

- Have students reread *Words Add Up to Success.* Work with students to read with accuracy.

- Provide time for students to read a section of text to you. Comment on their accuracy, and provide corrective feedback.

DEVELOP SPEAKING/LISTENING SKILLS

- Have students practice reading the quotations in "A Speech with Reach."

- Work with students to read with accuracy. Model reading each quotation. Emphasize the way in which reading with accuracy— saying every word, and pronouncing every word correctly—makes information clear. Have students repeat.

- Provide time for students to read aloud the quotations to the class. Ask students to discuss how the reader's accuracy made the meaning of each quotation clear.

- Challenge students to memorize and recite the quotations to the class.

Student Book

Student Book

Self-Selected Reading

Objective Read independently to identify facts and opinions
Materials • **Leveled Classroom Library** • other informational books

APPLY SKILLS AND STRATEGIES TO INDEPENDENT READING

- **Read Independently** Have students choose an informational book for sustained silent reading, such as a **Leveled Classroom Library** book. (See the **Theme Bibliography** on pages T8–T9 for book suggestions.) Have students read their books and record the facts and opinions on a Fact and Opinion Chart.

- **Show Evidence of Reading** While reading, students may generate a reading log or journal. After reading, ask students to use their Fact and Opinion Charts to paraphrase what the reading was about, maintaining meaning and logical order. Allow students to share their summaries and reactions to the book while participating in Book Talks. Ask: *What facts did you learn from this book? How can you check them? What is your opinion of the book— for example, would you recommend it to a friend? Why or why not?*

On Level

Leveled Classroom Library
See Leveled Classroom Library lessons on pages T2–T7.

Leveled Reader

On Level

Leveled Reader Lesson 1

Objective	Read to apply strategies and skills
Materials	• **Leveled Reader:** *Symbols of America*

BEFORE READING

Preview and Predict Have students read the title and preview the book by reading the chapter titles and looking at the photographs. Ask them to make predictions about the facts and opinions that they may find in this book.

 Review Vocabulary Words Have students read the vocabulary words on the inside front cover. Ask students to state related words they have learned. Review definitions, as needed.

Set a Purpose for Reading *Let's read to find out about American symbols—what they are and what they mean.*

DURING READING

 STRATEGY
MONITOR COMPREHENSION

Remind students that monitoring their comprehension means pausing to check and adjust their understanding as they read.

SKILL
FACT AND OPINION

Remind students that a fact can be proven to be true, whereas an opinion tells what someone believes. As they read, students should distinguish between facts and opinions.

Read Chapter 1 with students. Ask open-ended questions to facilitate rich discussion, such as *What facts does the author give about things that symbolize America? What opinions does the author share?* Build on students' responses to help them develop a deeper understanding of the text. Have students fill in the first section of the Fact and Opinion Chart before they continue reading.

Latin Prefixes As they read, have students point out this week's new vocabulary words and words with Latin prefixes, as applicable.

AFTER READING

Ask students to comment on and share opinions about what they have learned. Ask: *What fact about a particular symbol interested you most? What are some of the author's opinions? Which of these opinions do you agree with?* Have students generate questions that they would like to ask the author about some of these symbols.

On Level

Leveled Reader Lesson 2

Objective   Reread to apply skills and strategies and develop fluency
Materials   • **Leveled Reader:** *Symbols of America*
                  • **Practice Book,** p. 113

BEFORE READING

Leveled Reader

Review the Strategy and Skill Review students' completed Fact and Opinion Charts from the first read. Remind students that monitoring their comprehension means checking to make sure they understand what they are reading.

Review with students that a fact is a statement that can be proven whereas an opinion is a statement of feeling or belief. If students' Fact and Opinion Charts are incomplete, provide a model chart or use a student chart and revise it as a group. Have students copy the revised chart into their Writer's Notebooks.

Set a Purpose for Reading *Let's reread to check our understanding of the information in the book and to work on our reading fluency.*

DURING READING

Reread *Symbols of America* with students. Have students read silently, two pages at a time, or read aloud to a partner. Stop and have students monitor their comprehension of the text before they read on. Model techniques for checking understanding, as needed.

AFTER READING

Check Comprehension Have partners complete the Comprehension Check on page 20. Review students' answers. Help them find evidence for their answers in the text.

MODEL FLUENCY

Model reading the fluency passage on **Practice Book** page 113. Tell students to pay close attention to your accuracy as you read. Then read one sentence at a time, and have students copy your accuracy as they echo-read.

During independent reading time, have students work with a partner using the fluency passage. One student reads aloud, and the other repeats each sentence. If students need additional support, have them listen to the "practice speed" version of the passage on the **Fluency Solutions Audio CD**.

Book Talk

Bringing Groups Together Students will work with peers of various language and reading abilities to discuss this week's **Leveled Readers**. Refer to page 162 in the **Teacher's Resource Book** for more about how to conduct a Book Talk.

Practice Book, page 113

As I read, I will pay attention to accuracy.

	Thousands of years ago in China, people made an
9	important discovery. They found out that caterpillars of
17	one kind of moth spin cocoons of silk. And better yet, they
29	found out that the cocoons could be unwound and the silk
40	thread could be woven into fabric.
46	Silk fabric is shiny. It is soft and smooth to the touch.
58	It is very light in weight. And it can be dyed in many
71	colors.
72	For thousands of years, the Chinese were the only
81	people who knew how to produce silk cloth. People in
91	other countries wanted to trade for the precious silk
100	fabric. Traders traveled to and from China on one
109	main road. They traded goods such as spices, glass,
118	and gold for silk. Sometimes they even traded horses
127	for silk. Over time, this route became known as the Silk
138	Road. 139

Comprehension Check

1. Are the statements in the second paragraph facts or opinions? **Main Idea and Details** facts

2. What is the main idea of the third paragraph? **Main Idea and Details**
   Traders traveled to China to trade goods for silk.

	Words Read	–	Number of Errors	=	Words Correct Score
First Read		–		=	
Second Read		–		=	

Daily Planner

DAY 1	• Leveled Reader Lesson 1
DAY 2	• Leveled Reader Lesson 2
DAY 3	• Phonics
DAY 4	• Vocabulary • Fluency
DAY 5	• Self-Selected Reading

ELL

Self-Monitor Vocabulary
Have student pairs of different proficiency identify and define unfamiliar words from the main selection using a dictionary. Challenge students to use the new words in sentences. Monitor students as they complete the activity.

Beyond Level

Phonics/Word Study

Objective Decode multisyllabic words with soft *c* and *g*
Materials • **none**

EXTEND/ACCELERATE

- **Read Multisyllabic Words with Soft *c* and *g*** Write the words below on the board. Challenge students to read the words, using known word parts. When completed, point to the words in random order for students to chorally read.

excellently	experiencing	noticeable	principle
tragedy	discouragement	rearrangement	advantage
ceremonial	circumference	centrifugal	concentration
gentleman	gigantic	vacancy	efficiency

- **Define Words** Ask students to use their knowledge of word parts to figure out the meanings of the above words. Then have partners find the words in a dictionary and confirm or revise the meanings. Challenge students to use these words in this week's writing assignments.

- **Spell Words with Soft *c* and *g*** Dictate these words for students to spell: *circular, intelligence, cancellation, generally, policy*. Write the words for students to self-correct.

Vocabulary

Objectives Review fact and opinion; compare works on a theme

ENRICH VOCABULARY

- **Review Fact and Opinion** Remind students that a fact is a statement that can be verified, whereas an opinion is an expression of preference or belief. Have students discuss reasons why they do or do not admire Jaime Escalante, using the vocabulary words from the selection to express their opinions. For example, they might note that they admire Escalante because he motivated students or interacted with them in imaginative ways.

- **Discuss Inspiring People** Have the class discuss inspiring individuals who have helped change their lives or ideas in some way. Direct students to use cause-and-effect signal words to describe the impact this person had on them. For example, they might say that they study harder because of a great teacher.

Gifted & Talented

Beyond Level

Fluency

Objectives   Reread selections to develop fluency; develop speaking skills
Materials   • **Student Book:** *Words Add Up to Success*, "A Speech with Reach"

REREAD FOR FLUENCY

- Have students reread *Words Add Up to Success*. Work with students to read with accuracy.

- Provide time for students to read a section of text to you. Comment on their accuracy and provide corrective feedback.

DEVELOP SPEAKING/LISTENING SKILLS

- Have students practice reading the quotations in "A Speech with Reach."

- Work with students to read with accuracy. Model reading each quotation. Emphasize the way in which reading with accuracy makes information clear. Have students repeat.

- Provide time for students to read aloud the quotations to the class. Ask students to discuss how the reader's accuracy made the meaning of each quotation clear.

- Challenge students to memorize and recite the quotations to the class.

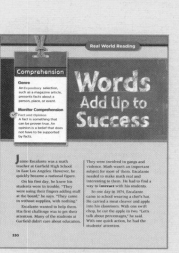

Student Book

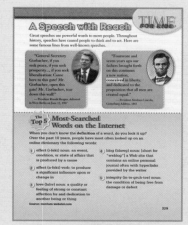

Student Book

Self-Selected Reading

Objective   Read independently to distinguish facts and opinions
Materials   • **Leveled Classroom Library**   • other informational books

APPLY SKILLS AND STRATEGIES TO INDEPENDENT READING

- **Read Independently** Have students choose an informational book for sustained silent reading. (See the **Theme Bibliography** on pages T8–T9 for book suggestions.) Have students read their books and record facts and opinions on a Fact and Opinion Chart.

- **Show Evidence of Reading** While reading, students may generate a reading log or journal. After reading, ask students to use their Fact and Opinion Charts to paraphrase what the reading was about, maintaining meaning and logical order. Provide time for students to share their summaries and comment on their reactions to the book while participating in Book Talks. Ask: *What facts did you learn from this book? What is your opinion of the book?*

- **Evaluate** Have students evaluate whether the facts in the book support the opinions. Ask: *How would you verify the facts?* Have students brainstorm resources to check the information.

Beyond

Leveled Classroom Library
See Leveled Classroom
Library lessons on pages T2–T7.

Leveled Reader

Beyond Level

Leveled Reader Lesson 1

Objective Read to apply strategies and skills
Materials • **Leveled Reader:** *Symbols of America*

BEFORE READING

Preview and Predict Have students preview the book by reading the title and chapter titles and looking at the photographs. Ask them to make predictions about the facts and opinions that they may find in this book.

Review Vocabulary Words Have students read the vocabulary words on the inside front cover. Ask students to state each definition and any related words they have learned.

Set a Purpose for Reading *Let's read to find out about symbols of America—what they are and what they mean.*

DURING READING

STRATEGY
MONITOR COMPREHENSION

Ask students to define the word *comprehension*. Remind them that monitoring their comprehension means pausing to check their understanding and using self-correction techniques as needed.

SKILL
FACT AND OPINION

Ask students to define the terms *fact* and *opinion*. Remind them that a fact can be verified. An opinion tells what someone believes.

Read the book with students. Ask open-ended questions to facilitate rich discussion, such as *What facts does the author give about things that symbolize America? What opinions does the author share?* Build on students' responses to help them develop a deeper understanding of the text. Have students fill in the Fact and Opinion Chart independently as they read.

AFTER READING

Author's Purpose Remind students that authors write to entertain, inform, or persuade. Ask: *Why did the author write this book? How would the book be different if the author had a different purpose for writing about this topic?*

Analyze Have partners choose a symbol and analyze why it has come to represent something important to Americans.

Gifted & Talented

Beyond Level

Leveled Reader Lesson 2

Objective   Reread to apply skills and strategies and develop fluency
Materials   • **Leveled Reader:** *Symbols of America*
• **Beyond Reproducible,** p. 113

Leveled Reader

BEFORE READING

Review the Strategy and Skill   Review students' completed Fact and Opinion Charts from the first read. Remind students to pause and monitor their comprehension as they read.

Review with students that a fact is a statement that can be proven whereas an opinion is a statement of feeling or belief. If students' Fact and Opinion Charts are incomplete, provide a model chart or use a student chart and revise it as a group. Have students copy the revised chart into their Writer's Notebooks.

Set a Purpose for Reading   *Let's reread to check our understanding of the information in the book and to work on our reading fluency.*

DURING READING

Have students reread *Symbols of America* silently or with a partner. If reading in pairs, prompt students to stop every two pages and evaluate the text or ask their partner probing questions.

AFTER READING

Check Comprehension   Have students independently complete the Comprehension Check on page 20. Review students' answers. Help students find evidence for their answers in the text.

Synthesize   Ask students to compare one of the symbols in the book with a symbol that means something to them personally, such as a school mascot or family heirloom. Have students create a Venn diagram showing how their personal symbol and the symbol from the book are alike and different.

Gifted & Talented

MODEL FLUENCY

Model reading the fluency passage on **Beyond Reproducible** page 113. Tell students to pay close attention to your accuracy as you read. Then read one sentence at a time, and have students copy your accuracy as they echo-read.

During independent reading time, have students work with a partner using the fluency passage. One student reads aloud, while the other repeats each sentence back. Students can check their fluency by reading along with the "expert speed" version of the passage on the **Fluency Solutions Audio CD.**

Book Talk

Bringing Groups Together   Students will work with peers of various language and reading abilities to discuss this week's **Leveled Readers.** Refer to page 162 in the **Teacher's Resource Book** for more about how to conduct a Book Talk.

Beyond Reproducible, page 113

As I read, I will pay attention to accuracy.

	You have just arrived by boat at a city on a great river.
13	The town is built on a cliff high above the riverbank. You
25	walk up 300 steps from the dock to reach the city gate.
36	The gate is built into the city's old stone wall. A nearby
48	market sells everything from pears to high-heeled shoes.
56	Near the city gate is a terrace. There are tables and
67	chairs where you can sit and look out over the mighty river
79	below. In the distance is the entrance to a magnificent gorge.
90	The cliffs of the river canyon rise steeply into the sky.
101	Boats look small from where you sit.
108	This is the town of Fengjie (FUNG-jee), China. It is
117	on the banks of the Yangtze (YANK-see) River, the longest
126	river in all of Asia. But Fengjie won't be here much longer.
138	By the year 2009, the entire town will be under water. 148

Comprehension Check

1. When the author states that the town is built on a cliff, is that a fact or an opinion? **Main Idea and Details** The author is stating a fact.

2. Name three details from the first paragraph that support the idea that Fengjie is an old city that has not seen many modern changes. **Main Idea and Details** Fengjie is reached from the river by a stone stairway of 300 steps. It is surrounded by an old stone wall. Visitors must enter the city through a main gate.

	Words Read	−	Number of Errors	=	Words Correct Score
First Read		−		=	
Second Read		−		=	

ELL ENGLISH LANGUAGE LEARNERS

Daily Planner

DAY 1	• Build Background Knowledge • Vocabulary
DAY 2	• Vocabulary • Access to Core Content *Words Add Up to Success*
DAY 3	• Vocabulary • Grammar • Access to Core Content *Words Add Up to Success*
DAY 4	• Vocabulary • Writing/Spelling • Access to Core Content *Words Add Up to Success* • Leveled Reader *Symbols of America*
DAY 5	• Vocabulary • Leveled Reader *Symbols of America* • Self-Selected Reading

LOG ON ▶ StudentWorks™ Plus
Interactive Student Book

Use StudentWorks Plus for:
• Vocabulary Preteaching
• Word-by-Word Highlighting
• Think Aloud Prompts

Cognates

Help students identify similarities and differences in pronunciation and spelling between English and Spanish cognates.

inspire	*inspirar*
imagination	*imaginación*
interact	*interactuar*
motivate	*motivar*
conceive	*concebir*
definition	*definición*
comprehension	*comprensión*
opinion	*opinión*
prefix	*prefijo*
verb	*verbo*

ELL ENGLISH LANGUAGE LEARNERS

Prepare to Read

Content Objective Explore the expression of community values through words
Language Objective Use key words to discuss community values
Materials • **StudentWorks Plus**

BUILD BACKGROUND KNOWLEDGE

All Language Levels

■ Have students preview *Words Add Up to Success* using **StudentWorks Plus**, which contains oral summaries in multiple languages, online multilingual glossaries, word-by-word highlighting, and questions that assess and build comprehension.

■ Students can build their word-reading fluency by reading along as the text is read or by listening during the first reading and, at the end of each paragraph, returning to the beginning of the paragraph and reading along.

■ Students can build their comprehension by reviewing the definitions of key words in the online glossary and by answering the comprehension questions. When appropriate, the text required to answer the question is highlighted to provide students with additional support and scaffolding.

■ After reading, ask students to respond in writing to a question that links the story to their personal experiences, such as *Who has motivated you to do well? How have they motivated you?*

Academic Language

Language Objective Use academic language in classroom conversations

All Language Levels

■ This week's academic words are **boldfaced** throughout the lesson. Define the word in context, and provide a clear example from the selection. Then ask students to generate an example or a word with a similar meaning.

Academic Language Used in Whole Group Instruction

Theme Words	Key Selection Words	Strategy and Skill Words
inspire	dismiss	monitor comprehension
engrossed in	interact	fact and opinion
powerful	motivate	Latin prefixes
imagination	conceived	main verbs
	definition	helping verbs

ELL ENGLISH LANGUAGE LEARNERS

Vocabulary

Language Objective Demonstrate understanding and use of key words by talking about motivation

Materials • **Visual Vocabulary Resources**
• **ELL Resource Book**

✓ PRETEACH KEY VOCABULARY

Use the **Visual Vocabulary Resources** to preteach the key selection words *dismiss, interact, motivate, conceived*, and *definition*. Focus on two words per day. The below routine is detailed on the cards.

Beginning/Intermediate

■ Point out any known sound-spellings, or focus on a key aspect of phonemic awareness related to the word.

All Language Levels

■ Define the word in English, and provide the example given.

■ Define the word in Spanish, if appropriate, and indicate if the word is a cognate.

■ Display the picture, and explain how it illustrates the word. Engage students in a structured activity using the key word.

■ Ask students to chorally say the word three times.

■ Distribute copies of the Vocabulary Glossary on **ELL Resource Book** page 142.

PRETEACH FUNCTION WORDS AND PHRASES

All Language Levels

Use the Visual Vocabulary Resources to preteach the function words and phrases *to bring attention to, to be the best, hope for the future*, and *from that day forward*. Focus on one word or phrase per day. Use the detailed routine on the cards.

■ Define the word in English and, if appropriate, in Spanish. Point out if the word is a cognate.

■ Refer to the picture and engage students in talk about the word. For example, students will partner-talk using sentence frames.

■ Ask students to chorally repeat the word three times.

TEACH BASIC WORDS

Beginning/Intermediate

Use the Visual Vocabulary Resources to teach the basic words *high school, board, supplies, example, attention*, and *success*. Teach these "school" words using the routine provided on the card.

Visual Vocabulary Resources

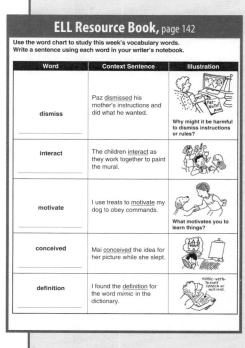

ELL Resource Book, page 142

Use the word chart to study this week's vocabulary words. Write a sentence using each word in your writer's notebook.

Word	Context Sentence	Illustration
dismiss	Paz dismissed his mother's instructions and did what he wanted.	Why might it be harmful to dismiss instructions or rules?
interact	The children interact as they work together to paint the mural.	
motivate	I use treats to motivate my dog to obey commands.	What motivates you to learn things?
conceived	Mai conceived the idea for her picture while she slept.	
definition	I found the definition for the word mimic in the dictionary.	

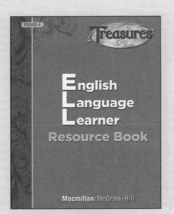

ELL Resource Book

Access to Core Content

Content Objective Read grade-level text

Language Objective Discuss text, using key words and sentence frames

Materials • **ELL Resource Book,** pp. 140–141

PRETEACH MAIN SELECTION (PAGES 330–333)

All Language Levels

Use the Interactive Question-Response Guide on **ELL Resource Book** pages 140–141 to introduce students to *Words Add Up to Success*. Preteach half of the selection on Day 2 and half on Day 3.

■ Use the prompts provided in the guide to develop meaning and vocabulary. Use the partner-talk and whole-class responses to engage students and increase student talk.

■ When completed, have partners reread the story.

Beginning	Intermediate	Advanced
Use Visuals During the Interactive Reading, select several photographs. Describe a fact and an opinion about the photographs. Then have students retell the fact and opinion.	**Describe** During the Interactive Reading, select a few lines of text. After you have read and explained it, have students identify one fact and then tell one opinion based on the text.	**Explain** During the Interactive Reading, select a passage of text. After you have read and explained it, have students describe facts and tell their opinions based on the text.

ELL ENGLISH LANGUAGE LEARNERS

Fluency

Content Objectives Reread selections to develop fluency; develop speaking skills

Language Objective Tell a partner what a selection is about

Materials • **Student Book:** *Words Add Up to Success*, "The Latest Lingo"
• **Teacher's Resource Book**

REREAD FOR FLUENCY

Beginning

■ Have students read the decodable passages on page 17 in the **Teacher's Resource Book**.

Intermediate/Advanced

■ Have students reread two to four of their favorite pages from *Words Add Up to Success*, based on their levels. Help students to read the pages with accuracy. For example, read each sentence of the first paragraph and have students echo. Then have students chorally reread additional paragraphs.

■ Have students read their sections of text to you. Comment on their accuracy, and provide corrective feedback by modeling proper fluency.

DEVELOP SPEAKING/LISTENING SKILLS

All Language Levels

■ Have students practice reading "The Latest Lingo." Work with students to read with accuracy.

■ Provide time for students to read aloud the article to a partner. Have students tell their partner one interesting fact they learned from the article. Provide the sentence frame *I learned that _____*.

Self-Selected Reading

Content Objective Read independently

Language Objective Orally retell information learned

Materials • **Leveled Classroom Library** • other nonfiction books

APPLY SKILLS AND STRATEGIES TO INDEPENDENT READING

All Language Levels

■ Have students choose a nonfiction book for independent reading. (See the **Theme Bibliography** on pages T8–T9.)

■ After reading, ask students to orally summarize and share their reactions to the book with classmates. Ask: *Would you recommend this book to a classmate? Why or why not?*

Student Book

Leveled Classroom Library
See Leveled Classroom
Library lessons on pages T2–T7.

Transfer Skills

Verbs *Have* and *Be* In Spanish, the verbs *have* and *be* are used differently. For example, the verb *have* is used to express states of being such as age or hunger (*She has ten years; I have hunger*). Provide additional practice using the verbs *have* and *be* for Spanish-speaking students. Give immediate corrective feedback, and have students repeat. See language transfers on pages T16–T31.

Corrective Feedback

During Whole Group grammar lessons, follow the routine on the **Grammar Transparencies** to provide students with extra support. This routine includes completing the items with English Language Learners while other students work independently, having students reread the sentences with partners to build fluency, and providing a generative task such as writing a new sentence using the skill.

ELL ENGLISH LANGUAGE LEARNERS

Grammar

Content Objective Identify main and helping verbs
Language Objective Speak in complete sentences, using sentence frames

MAIN AND HELPING VERBS

Beginning/Intermediate

- Review main and helping verbs with students. Explain that the main verb tells what the subject does or is, and a helping verb tells when the action takes place. Write on the board: *I am teaching this class.* Underline *am teaching.* Point out the main and helping verbs. Explain that the helping verb comes before the main verb.

All Language Levels

- Review main and helping verbs. Write on the board: *We are reading a book. We have read a book. We will read a book.* Explain that we use *am, is*, and *are* to show present tense; *have, has*, and *had* to show past tense; and *will* to show future tense. Write the sentences below on the board. Have students identify main and helping verbs. Have them say: *The helping verb is ____. The main verb is ____.*

  Mom has promised us a puppy.   *We have finished our work.*

  We are scrubbing the tires now.   *We will eat ice cream.*

PEER DISCUSSION STARTERS

All Language Levels

- Write the following sentence on the board.

  It's important to keep promises because ____.

- Have pairs complete the sentence frame. Ask them to expand on their sentence by providing details from this week's readings. Circulate, listen in, and take note of each student's language use and proficiency.

Beginning	**Intermediate**	**Advanced**
Use Visuals Describe the photographs in *Words Add Up to Success* to students. Ask: *What do you see?* Help them point and form sentences using main and helping verbs.	**Describe** Ask students to describe the photographs in *Words Add Up to Success*. Have them use main and helping verbs in complete sentences. Encourage them to use more than one verb tense.	**Discuss** Ask students to describe the photographs in *Words Add Up to Success*. Have them use sentences with main and helping verbs in different tenses.

ELL ENGLISH LANGUAGE LEARNERS

Writing/Spelling

Content Objective Spell words correctly

Language Objective Write in complete sentences, using sentence frames

All Language Levels

- Write the key vocabulary words on the board: *dismiss, interact, motivate, conceived, definition*. Have students copy each word on their **WorkBoards**. Help them say each word and then write a sentence for it. Provide sentence starters, such as:

  Some people dismiss kids' ideas because ____.

  I like to interact with other kids because ____.

  It is possible to motivate dogs to do tricks by ____.

  I wish I had conceived of ____.

  Knowing the definition of a word can ____.

Beginning/Intermediate

- Help students spell words using their growing knowledge of English sound-spelling relationships. Model how to segment the word students are trying to spell, and attach a spelling to each sound (or spellings to each syllable if a multisyllabic word). Use the **Sound-Spelling Cards** to reinforce the spellings for each English sound.

Advanced

- Dictate the following words for students to spell: *city, face, force, change, large, stingy*. Use the Sound-Spelling Cards to guide students as they spell each word.

- When completed, review the meanings of words that can be easily demonstrated or explained. Use actions, gestures, and available pictures.

Sound-Spelling WorkBoard

Phonics/Word Study

For English Language Learners who need more practice with this week's phonics/spelling skill, see the Approaching Level lesson on page 337N. Focus on minimal contrasts, articulation, and those sounds that do not transfer from the student's first language to English. See language transfers on pages T16–T31.

Leveled Reader

ELL ENGLISH LANGUAGE LEARNERS

Leveled Reader

Content Objective Read to apply skills and strategies

Language Objective Retell information, using complete sentences

Materials
- **Leveled Reader:** *Symbols of America*
- **ELL Resource Book,** p. 143
- **Visual Vocabulary Resources,** pp. 425–430

BEFORE READING

All Language Levels

- **Preview** Read the title *Symbols of America*. Ask: *What is the title? Say it again*. Repeat with the author's name. Then page through the book. Use simple language to tell about each page. Immediately follow up with questions, such as *What kinds of things or places do you see? Do they represent our country?*

- **Review Skills** Use the inside front cover to review the comprehension skill and vocabulary words.

- **Set a Purpose** Say: *Let's read to find out about the different symbols that represent America.*

DURING READING

All Language Levels

- Have students read each page aloud using the differentiated suggestions. Provide corrective feedback, such as modeling how to blend a decodable word or clarifying meaning by using techniques from the Interactive Question-Response Guide.

- **Retell** After every two pages, ask students to state the main ideas they have learned so far. Help them to complete the Fact and Opinion Chart. Restate students' comments when they have difficulty using story-specific words. Provide differentiated sentence frames to support students' responses and engage students in partner-talk where appropriate.

Vocabulary

Preteach Vocabulary Use the routine in the **Visual Vocabulary Resources**, pages 425–430, to preteach the ELL Vocabulary listed in the inside front cover of the Leveled Reader.

Beginning	Intermediate	Advanced
Echo-Read Have students echo-read after you.	**Choral-Read** Have students chorally read with you.	**Choral-Read** Have students chorally read.
Check Comprehension Point to pictures and ask questions, such as *What do you see on this page? Is this a symbol of America?*	**Check Comprehension** Ask questions or provide prompts, such as *Describe the American flag. What do the stars and stripes represent?*	**Check Comprehension** Ask: *How has the American flag changed from the original design? Why is the Statue of Liberty an important symbol?*

AFTER READING

Use the chart below and Think and Compare questions in the **Leveled Reader** to determine students' progress.

Think and Compare	Beginning	Intermediate	Advanced
1 These statements are from page 4: "The flag is one of the most important symbols of America. The flag has 50 stars." Which is an opinion? How do you know? *(Fact and Opinion)*	Possible responses: Nonverbal response. First sentence. Author feeling.	Possible responses: The first sentence is an opinion. The author feels that the flag is an important symbol.	Possible responses: The first sentence is an opinion because it shows how the author feels about the flag.
2 You read about several landmarks. Which one would you like to visit? Why? *(Apply)*	Possible responses: Nonverbal response. The White House. President lives there.	Possible responses: I want to visit the White House. The President lives and works there.	Possible responses: I would like to visit the White House because the President lives and works there.
3 Tourists often visit landmarks. Why are these places important to them? What do they learn by visiting them? *(Evaluate)*	Possible responses: Nonverbal response. See places. Learn history.	Possible responses: Tourists can see famous places. They can learn about our history.	Possible responses: Landmarks are important because tourists can see and learn about famous events. They learn about our country's history.

ELL Resource Book

BOOK TALK

Develop Listening and Speaking Skills Distribute copies of **ELL Resource Book** page 143 and form small groups. Help students determine the leader to discuss the Book Talk questions. Tell students to remember the following while engaged in the activity:

- Employ self-corrective techniques and monitor their own and other students' language production. Students should ask themselves: *What parts of this passage were confusing to me? Can my classmates help me clarify a word or sentence that I don't understand?*

- Distinguish between formal and informal English and know when to use each one. Remind students to note whether the selection is written in formal or informal English. Ask: *Why do you think it is written in this way?* Remind students that they may use informal English when speaking with their classmates, but they should use formal language when they talk to teachers or write essays.

Book Talk

Bringing Groups Together Students will work with peers of varying language abilities to discuss the Book Talk questions. Form groups so that students who read the Beyond Level, On Level, Approaching Level, and ELL Leveled Readers are in the same group for the activity.

Progress Monitoring

Weekly Assessment

ASSESSED SKILLS

- Vocabulary: Vocabulary Words, Word Parts/Latin Prefixes
- Comprehension: Fact and Opinion
- Grammar: Main and Helping Verbs
- Phonics/Spelling: Soft *c* and *g*

Selection Test for Words Add Up to Success *Also Available*

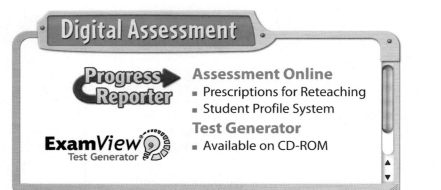

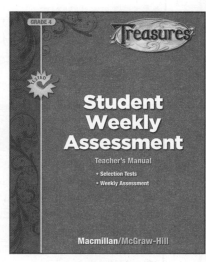

**Weekly Assessment
Unit 3 Week 3**

Fluency Assessment

Assess fluency for one group of students per week.
Use the Oral Fluency Record Sheet to track the number of
words read correctly. Fluency goal for all students:
102–122 words correct per minute (WCPM).

Approaching Level	Weeks 1, 3, 5
On Level	Weeks 2, 4
Beyond Level	Week 6

Fluency Assessment

Diagnose		Prescribe

Review the assessment answers with students. Have them correct their errors. Then provide additional instruction as needed.

	IF...	THEN...
VOCABULARY WORDS **VOCABULARY STRATEGY** Latin Prefixes	0–2 items correct . . .	See **Vocabulary Intervention Teacher's Edition.** **LOG ON** Online Practice: Go to **www.macmillanmh.com.** **CD-ROM** Vocabulary PuzzleMaker
COMPREHENSION Skill: Fact and Opinion	0–3 items correct . . .	See **Comprehension Intervention Teacher's Edition.** **SPIRAL REVIEW** See Fact and Opinion lesson in Unit 4 Week 2, page 455B.
GRAMMAR Main and Helping Verbs	0–1 items correct . . .	See **Writing and Grammar Intervention Teacher's Edition.**
PHONICS AND SPELLING Soft *c* and *g*	0–1 items correct . . .	**LOG ON** Online Practice: Go to **www.macmillanmh.com.** See **Phonics Intervention Teacher's Edition.**
FLUENCY	98–101 WCPM	**AUDIO CD** Fluency Solutions Audio CD
	0–97 WCPM	See **Fluency Intervention Teacher's Edition.**

Response to Intervention

To place students in Tier 2 or Tier 3 Intervention use the *Diagnostic Assessment*.

Tier 2

- Phonics
- Vocabulary
- Comprehension
- Fluency
- Writing and Grammar

Tier 3

Week 4 ★ At a Glance

Priority Skills and Concepts

✔ Comprehension
- **Strategy:** Monitor Comprehension
- **Skill:** Theme
-  Draw Conclusions
- **Genre:** Poetry, Drama, Expository

✔ Robust Vocabulary
- **Selection Vocabulary:** *selfish, cranky, commotion, exasperated, specialty, famished*
- **Strategy:** Analogies/Synonyms and Antonyms

✔ Fluency
- **Expression**

✔ Phonics/Spelling
- **Word Study:** Plurals, Multisyllabic Words
- **Spelling Words:** *clams, mints, props, arches, dresses, parents, caves, glasses, hobbies, engines, couches, arrows, enemies, babies, ranches, patches, mistakes, supplies, mosses, armies*
- *circus, germs, spice*

✔ Grammar/Mechanics
- **Linking Verbs**
- **Agreement of Subject and Linking Verb**

✔ Writing
- **Trait: Word Choice**
- Use Descriptive Language

Key

✔ **Tested in program**   🌀 **Review Skill**

Digital Learning

Digital solutions to help plan and implement instruction

☑ Teacher Resources

LOG ON ▶

ONLINE www.macmillanmh.com

▶ **Teacher's Edition**
- Lesson Planner and Resources also on CD-ROM

TeacherWorks Plus

▶ **Formative Assessment**
- ExamView® on CD-ROM also available

Progress Reporter

▶ **Instructional Resources**
- Unit Videos
- Classroom Presentation Toolkit

VIDEO

▶ **Professional Development**
- Video Library

Professional Development

☑ Student Resources

LOG ON ▶

ONLINE www.macmillanmh.com

▶ **Interactive Student Book**

StudentWorks Plus

▶ **Leveled Reader Database**

▶ **Activities**
- Research Toolkit
- Oral Language Activities
- Vocabulary/Spelling Activities

AUDIO CD
Listening Library
- Recordings of Student Books and Leveled Readers

AUDIO CD
Fluency Solutions
- Fluency Modeling and Practice

Weekly Literature

Theme: Keeping Promises

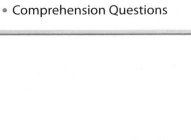

StudentWorks *Plus*

Interactive Student Book

- Word-by-Word Reading
- Summaries in Multiple Languages
- Comprehension Questions

Ranita

The Frog Princess

by Carmen Agra Deedy
illustrated by Renato Alarcão

Award Winning Author

Main Selection

Genre | Drama

The Frog Prince

by Marcia Stevens

**Preteach Vocabulary
and Comprehension**

Genre | Drama

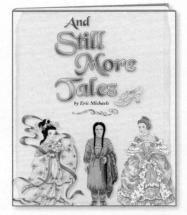

And Still More Tales

by Eric Michaels

Paired Selection

Genre | Expository

Support Literature

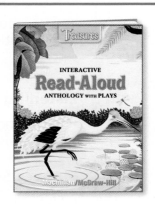

Treasures

INTERACTIVE Read-Aloud

ANTHOLOGY WITH PLAYS

Macmillan/McGraw-Hill

**Interactive
Read-Aloud Anthology**

- Listening Comprehension
- Robust Vocabulary
- Readers Theater Plays for Fluency

Resources for Differentiated Instruction

Leveled Readers

GR Levels O–U

Genre	Drama

- Same Theme
- Same Vocabulary
- Same Comprehension Skills

O
Play
Hans and Greta
by Rebecca Motil
illustrated by Liz Callen
Macmillan/McGraw-Hill

Approaching Level

R
Play
The Dragon's Dinner
by Rebecca Motil
illustrated by Liz Callen
Macmillan/McGraw-Hill

On Level

U
Play
Sleeping Beauty and the Prince of Andequesta
by Rebecca Motil
illustrated by Adam Gustavson
Macmillan/McGraw-Hill

Beyond Level

P
Play
Dragon Stew
by Rebecca Motil
illustrated by Liz Callen
Macmillan/McGraw-Hill

ELL

LOG ON ▶ **Leveled Reader Database**
Go to www.macmillanmh.com.

Leveled Practice

AUDIO CD

Approaching	On Level	Beyond	ELL
Treasures — Approaching Reproducibles	Treasures — Practice Book	Treasures — Beyond Reproducibles	Treasures — English Language Learner Practice Book

Leveled Classroom Library

Approaching	On Level	Beyond
Sequoyah	Circle of Giving by Ellen Howard	She's Wearing a Dead Bird on Her Head!

Response to Intervention

Tier 2

- Phonics
- Vocabulary
- Comprehension
- Fluency
- Writing and Grammar

Tier 3

Assessment

TIME FOR KIDS
Macmillan/McGraw-Hill

Time For Kids
- TFK Teacher's Manual
- Apply Answering Question Strategies

Weekly Assessment	Unit Assessment	Benchmark Assessment
Treasures — Student Weekly Assessment	Treasures — Unit Assessment (Includes Writing Prompts)	Treasures — Benchmark Assessment
Macmillan/McGraw-Hill	Macmillan/McGraw-Hill	Macmillan/McGraw-Hill

HOME-SCHOOL CONNECTION

- Family letters in English and Spanish
- Take-home stories and activities

Treasures — **Home-School Connection**
Macmillan/McGraw-Hill

LOG ON ▶ **Online Homework**
www.macmillanmh.com

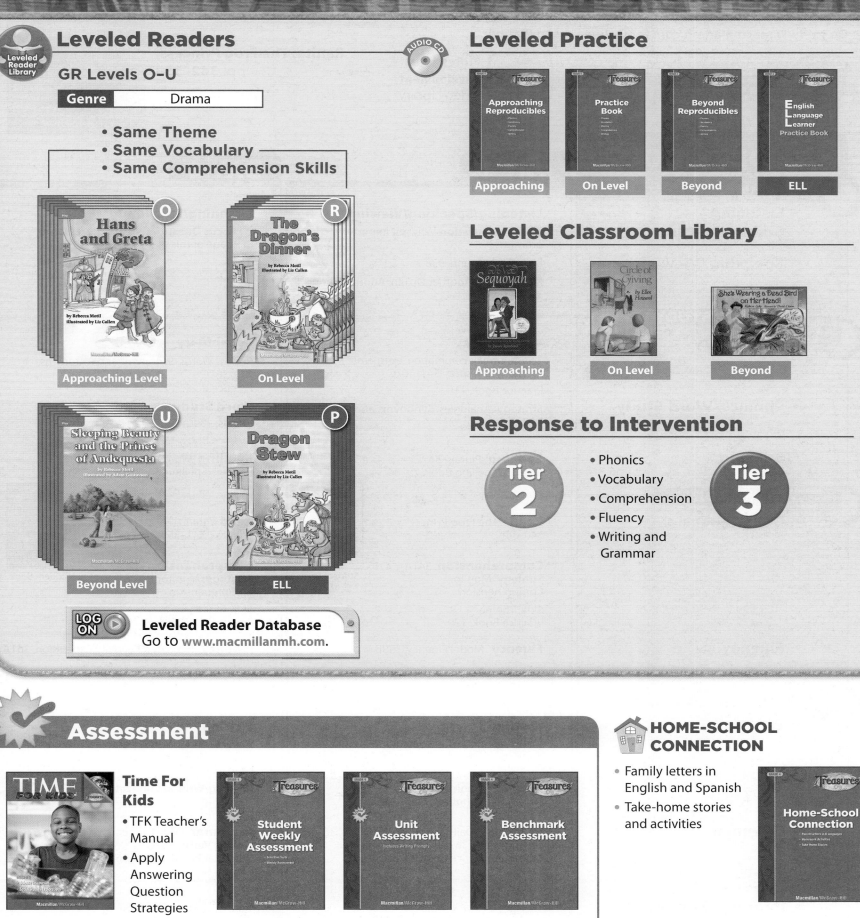

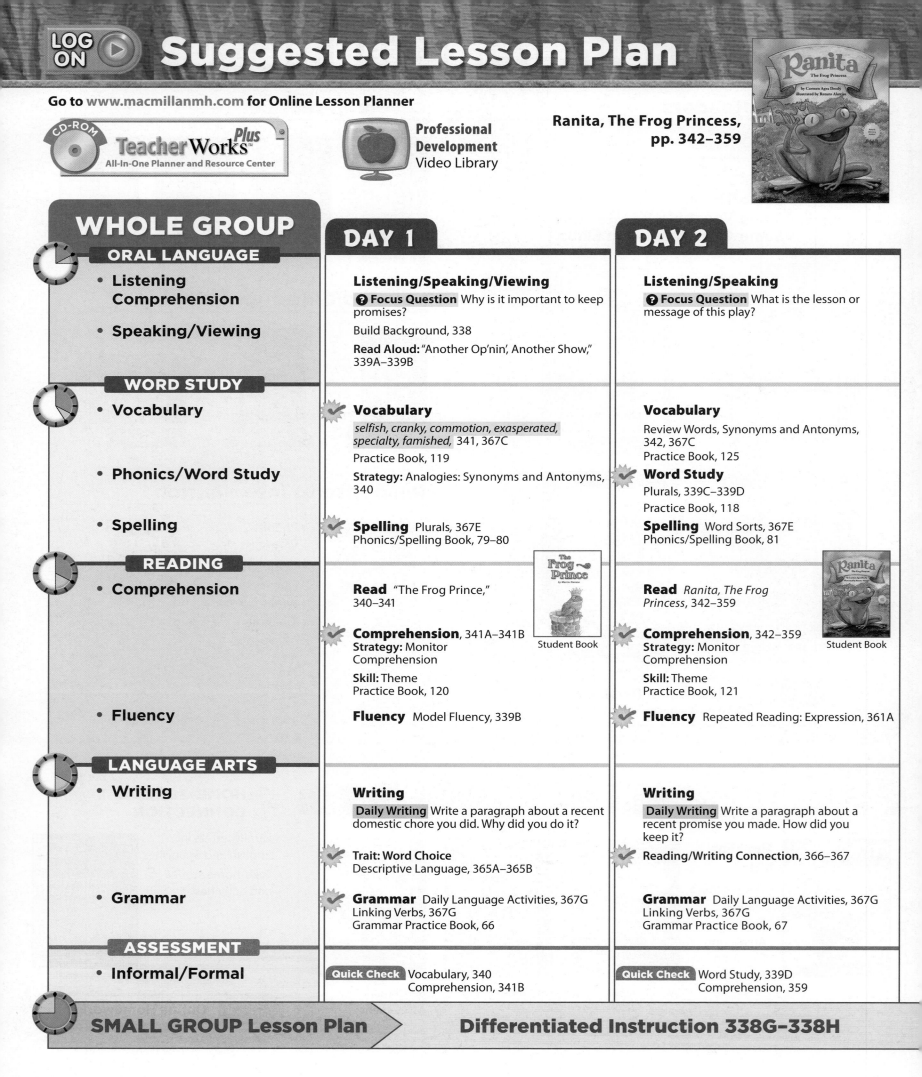

CD-ROM **TeacherWorks** *Plus*
All-In-One Planner and Resource Center

Professional Development Video Library

Ranita, The Frog Princess, pp. 342–359

WHOLE GROUP

ORAL LANGUAGE

- Listening Comprehension
- Speaking/Viewing

WORD STUDY

- Vocabulary
- Phonics/Word Study
- Spelling

READING

- Comprehension
- Fluency

LANGUAGE ARTS

- Writing
- Grammar

ASSESSMENT

- Informal/Formal

DAY 1

Listening/Speaking/Viewing

❓**Focus Question** Why is it important to keep promises?

Build Background, 338

Read Aloud: "Another Op'nin', Another Show," 339A–339B

Vocabulary
selfish, cranky, commotion, exasperated, specialty, famished, 341, 367C
Practice Book, 119
Strategy: Analogies: Synonyms and Antonyms, 340

Spelling Plurals, 367E
Phonics/Spelling Book, 79–80

Read "The Frog Prince," 340–341

The Frog Prince
Student Book

Comprehension, 341A–341B
Strategy: Monitor Comprehension
Skill: Theme
Practice Book, 120

Fluency Model Fluency, 339B

Writing
Daily Writing Write a paragraph about a recent domestic chore you did. Why did you do it?

Trait: Word Choice
Descriptive Language, 365A–365B

Grammar Daily Language Activities, 367G
Linking Verbs, 367G
Grammar Practice Book, 66

Quick Check Vocabulary, 340
Comprehension, 341B

DAY 2

Listening/Speaking

❓**Focus Question** What is the lesson or message of this play?

Vocabulary
Review Words, Synonyms and Antonyms, 342, 367C
Practice Book, 125
Word Study
Plurals, 339C–339D
Practice Book, 118
Spelling Word Sorts, 367E
Phonics/Spelling Book, 81

Read *Ranita, The Frog Princess,* 342–359

Ranita
Student Book

Comprehension, 342–359
Strategy: Monitor Comprehension
Skill: Theme
Practice Book, 121

Fluency Repeated Reading: Expression, 361A

Writing
Daily Writing Write a paragraph about a recent promise you made. How did you keep it?

Reading/Writing Connection, 366–367

Grammar Daily Language Activities, 367G
Linking Verbs, 367G
Grammar Practice Book, 67

Quick Check Word Study, 339D
Comprehension, 359

SMALL GROUP Lesson Plan ▶ **Differentiated Instruction 338G–338H**

Priority Skills

Vocabulary	Comprehension	Writing
Vocabulary Words Analogies: Synonyms and Antonyms	**Strategy:** Monitor Comprehension **Skill:** Theme	Trait: Word Choice Descriptive Language

DAY 3

Listening/Speaking

❓ Focus Question How are the characters and events in "The Frog Prince" and *Ranita, The Frog Princess* similar?

Summarize, 349

Vocabulary

Review Words, Related Words, 367D

Spelling Word Meanings, 367F
Phonics/Spelling Book, 82

Read *Ranita, The Frog Princess*, 342–359

Comprehension
Comprehension Check, 361

Review Skill: Draw Conclusions, 361B
Practice Book, 123

Fluency Repeated Reading: Expression, 361A
Practice Book, 122

Student Book

Writing

Daily Writing Write an invitation to a family member inviting him or her to your school play.

Trait: Word Choice
Descriptive Language, 367A

Grammar Daily Language Activities, 367G
Mechanics and Usage, 367H
Grammar Practice Book, 68

Quick Check Fluency, 361A

DAY 4

Listening/Speaking/Viewing

❓ Focus Question Think about the characters described in this article and those in *Ranita, The Frog Princess*. How are the characters alike? How are they different?

Vocabulary

Review Words, Morphology, 367D

Spelling Proofread, 367F
Phonics/Spelling Book, 83

Read "And Still More Tales" 362–365

Comprehension
Genre: Expository

Literary Elements: Theme, 362
Practice Book, 124

Fluency Repeated Reading:
Expression, 361A

Student Book

Time For Kids

Writing

Daily Writing Write a dialogue between two frog characters. In the dialogue, have them discuss their daily routines.

Trait: Sentence Fluency
Sentence Variety, 367A

Grammar Daily Language Activities, 367G
Linking Verbs, 367H
Grammar Practice Book, 69

Quick Check Vocabulary, 367D

DAY 5
Review and Assess

Listening/Speaking/Viewing

❓ Focus Question How would you treat a friend who did not honor a promise? Would you be willing to forgive him or her? Explain why or why not.

Vocabulary

Assess Words, Connect to Writing, 367D

Spelling Posttest, 367F
Phonics/Spelling Book, 84

Read Self-Selected Reading, 338K
Practice Book, 126

Comprehension
Connect and Compare, 365

Student Book

Fluency Practice, 338K

Writing

Daily Writing Suppose you have the chance to act in the school play, make the scenery, or design the costumes. Which would you choose and why?

Conferencing, 367B

Grammar Daily Language Activities, 367G
Linking Verbs, 367H
Grammar Practice Book, 70

Weekly Assessment, 367II–367JJ

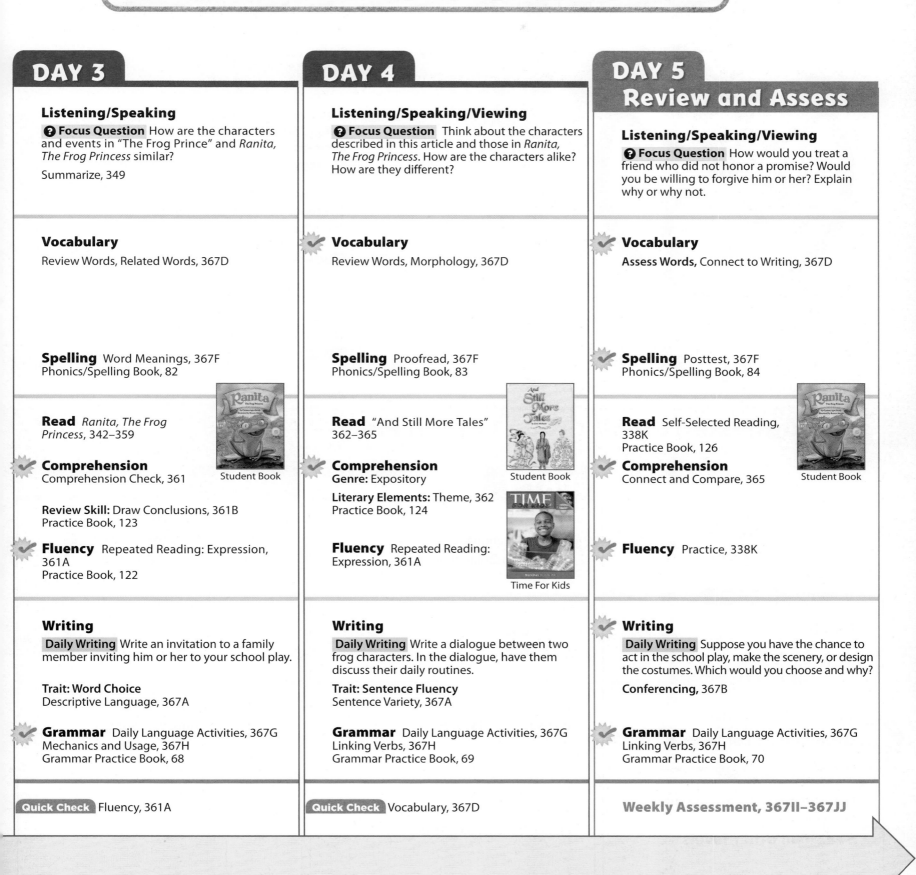

Differentiated Instruction

What do I do in small groups?

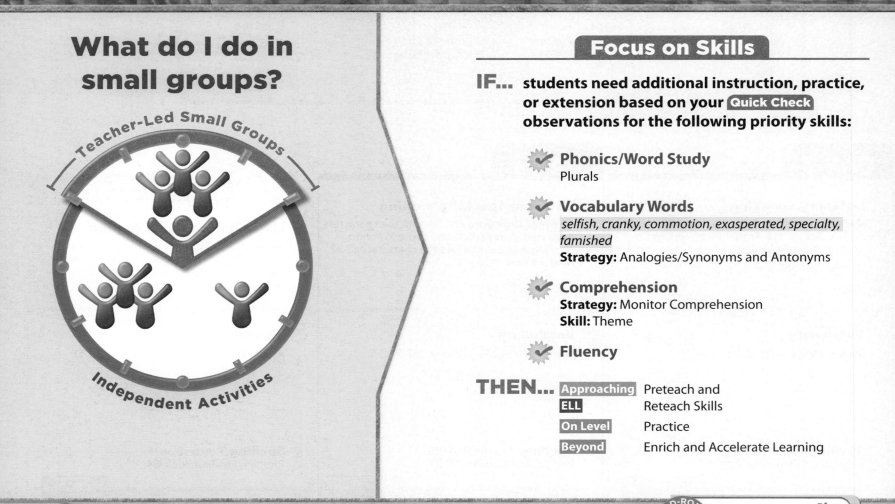

Teacher-Led Small Groups

Independent Activities

Focus on Skills

IF... students need additional instruction, practice, or extension based on your **Quick Check** observations for the following priority skills:

✔ **Phonics/Word Study**
Plurals

✔ **Vocabulary Words**
selfish, cranky, commotion, exasperated, specialty, famished
Strategy: Analogies/Synonyms and Antonyms

✔ **Comprehension**
Strategy: Monitor Comprehension
Skill: Theme

✔ **Fluency**

THEN... **Approaching ELL** Preteach and Reteach Skills
On Level Practice
Beyond Enrich and Accelerate Learning

LOG ON ▶ ## Suggested Small Group Lesson Plan

CD-ROM TeacherWorks *Plus*
All-In-One Planner and Resource Center

	DAY 1	DAY 2
Approaching Level **Tier 2** • **Preteach/Reteach** **Tier 2 Instruction**	• Prepare to Read, 367I • Academic Language, 367I • Preteach Vocabulary, 367K	• Comprehension, 367M Monitor Comprehension/Theme **ELL** • Leveled Reader Lesson 1, 367N
On Level • **Practice**	• Vocabulary, 367S • Phonics, 367S Plurals **ELL**	• Leveled Reader Lesson 1, 367U
Beyond Level **Gifted Talented** • **Extend/Accelerate** **Gifted and Talented**	• Leveled Reader Lesson 1, 367Y • Compare Fairy Tales, 367Y	• Leveled Reader Lesson 2, 367Z • Synthesize Information, 367Z
ELL • **Build English Language Proficiency** • See **ELL** in other levels.	• Prepare to Read, 367AA • Academic Language, 367AA • Preteach Vocabulary, 367BB	• Vocabulary, 367BB • Preteach Main Selection, 367CC

Focus on Leveled Readers

Leveled Reader Library

Levels O–U

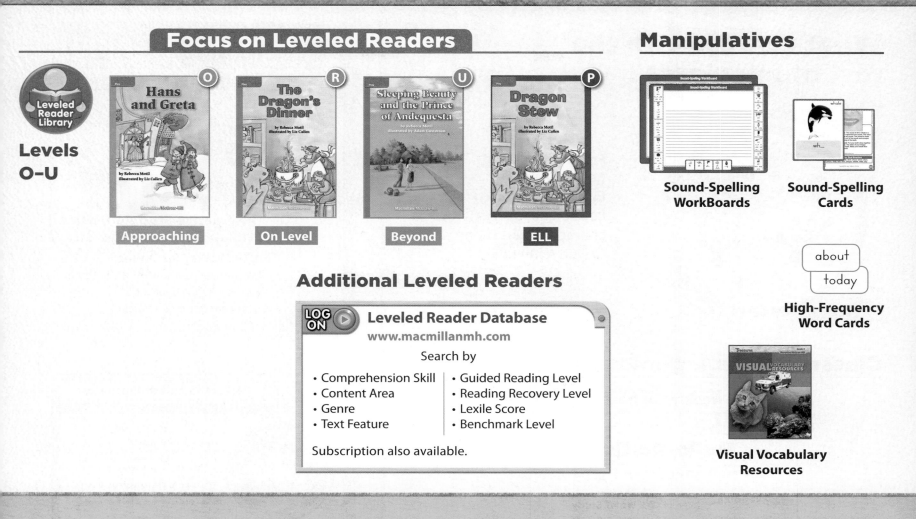

Ⓞ Hans and Greta
by Rebecca Motil
illustrated by Liz Callen
Approaching

Ⓡ The Dragon's Dinner
by Rebecca Motil
illustrated by Liz Callen
On Level

Ⓤ Sleeping Beauty and the Prince of Andequesta
by Rebecca Motil
illustrated by Adam Gustavson
Beyond

Ⓟ Dragon Stew
by Rebecca Motil
illustrated by Liz Callen
ELL

Manipulatives

Sound-Spelling WorkBoards

Sound-Spelling Cards

about today

High-Frequency Word Cards

Visual Vocabulary Resources

Additional Leveled Readers

LOG ON ▶ **Leveled Reader Database**
www.macmillanmh.com

Search by

- Comprehension Skill
- Content Area
- Genre
- Text Feature

- Guided Reading Level
- Reading Recovery Level
- Lexile Score
- Benchmark Level

Subscription also available.

DAY 3	DAY 4	DAY 5
• Phonics Maintenance, 367J Plurals **ELL** • Leveled Reader Lesson 2, 367O	• Reteach Phonics Skill, 367J Plurals **ELL** • Review Vocabulary, 367L • Leveled Reader Lesson 3, 367P	• High-Frequency Words, 367L • Fluency, 367Q • Self-Selected Independent Reading, 367R • Book Talk, 367P
• Leveled Reader Lesson 2, 367V	• Fluency, 367T	• Self-Selected Independent Reading, 367T • Book Talk, 367V
• Phonics, 367W Plurals **ELL**	• Vocabulary, 367W • Write a Description, 367W • Fluency, 367X	• Self-Selected Independent Reading, 367X • Evaluate Information, 367X • Book Talk, 367Z
• Vocabulary, 367BB • Grammar, 367EE	• Vocabulary, 367BB • Writing/Spelling, 367FF • Preteach Paired Selection, 367CC • Fluency, 367DD • Leveled Reader, 367GG	• Vocabulary, 367BB • Leveled Reader, 367GG • Self-Selected Independent Reading, 367DD • Book Talk, 367HH

Managing the Class

What do I do with the rest of my class?

- Practice Book and Reproducibles
- ELL Practice Book
- Leveled Reader Activities
- Literacy Workstations
- Online Activities

Classroom Management Tools

Weekly Contract

Name _____ Date _____

My To-Do List

✔ Put a check next to the activities you complete.

Reading
- ☐ Practice fluency
- ☐ Choose a story to read

Phonics/Word Study
- ☐ Look up word origins
- ☐ Write words with short vowel sounds

Writing
- ☐ Write a letter to the editor
- ☐ Write a radio ad

Science
- ☐ Research two types of rocks
- ☐ Write a chart

Social Studies
- ☐ Create a guide book
- ☐ Role-play an interview

Leveled Readers
- ☐ Write About It!
- ☐ Content Connection

Technology
- ☐ Vocabulary PuzzleMaker
- ☐ Fluency Solutions
- ☐ Listening Library
- ☐ www.macmillanmh.com

Independent Practice
- ☐ Practice Book, 1–9

Rotation Chart

Teacher-Led Small Groups
Red

Literacy Workstations

Independent Activities

Blue   Green
Orange

Treasures
Managing Small Groups
A How-to Guide
Dr. Vicki Gibson Dr. Douglas Fisher
Macmillan/McGraw-Hill

How-to Guide

Rotation Chart

Digital Learning

LOG ON ▶
StudentWorks *Plus*
Interactive Student Book

StudentWorks Plus Online
- Summaries in Multiple Languages
- Word-by-Word Reading
- Comprehension Questions

Meet the Author/Illustrator

Print   Close Window

Mark Teague
- Mark gets a lot of inspiration from his two young daughters. He loves to read to them.
- He always loved to draw but didn't think about becoming a professional artist until after college.
- Mark starts out his books by jotting down notes and scribbling in a notebook. Slowly the ides start to come together and he creates a real story.

Another book by Mark Teague
- Teague, Mark. *Detective LaRue: Letters from the Investigation*. New York: Scholastic, Inc., 2004.

- Other Books by the Author or Illustrator

Leveled Practice

GRADE 4
Treasures
Practice Book
- Phonics
- Vocabulary
- Fluency
- Comprehension
- Writing
Macmillan/McGraw-Hill

On Level

GRADE 4
Treasures
English Language Learner Practice Book
Macmillan/McGraw-Hill

ELL

Also Available:
Approaching Reproducible
Beyond Reproducible

Independent Activities

 LOG ON ▶ **ONLINE INSTRUCTION** www.macmillanmh.com

Oral Language Activities

- Focus on Vocabulary and Concepts
- English Language Learner Support

Vocabulary/Spelling Activities

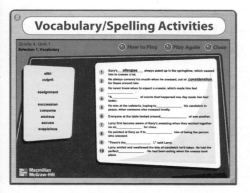

- Differentiated Lists and Activities

Leveled Reader Database

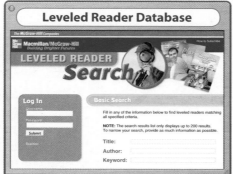

- Leveled Reader Database
- Search titles by level, skill, content area, and more

Research Toolkit

- Research Roadmap
- Research and Presentation Tools
- Theme Launcher Video
- Links to Science and Social Studies

Available on CD

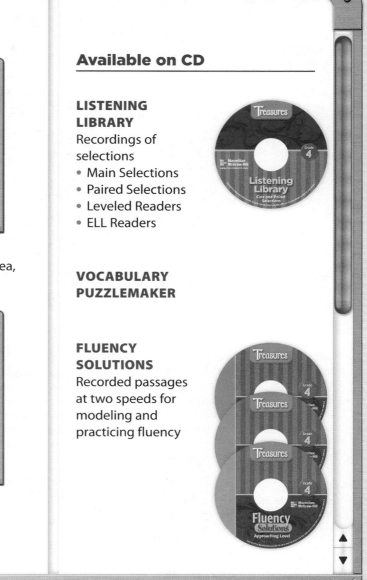

LISTENING LIBRARY
Recordings of selections
- Main Selections
- Paired Selections
- Leveled Readers
- ELL Readers

VOCABULARY PUZZLEMAKER

FLUENCY SOLUTIONS
Recorded passages at two speeds for modeling and practicing fluency

Leveled Reader Activities

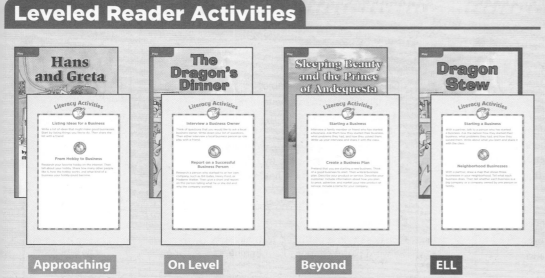

Approaching — Hans and Greta

On Level — The Dragon's Dinner

Beyond — Sleeping Beauty and the Prince of Andequesta

ELL — Dragon Stew

See inside cover of all Leveled Readers.

Literacy Workstations

WORKSTATION FLIP CHART — **Reading**

WORKSTATION FLIP CHART — **Writing**

WORKSTATION FLIP CHART — **Phonics/Word Study**

WORKSTATION FLIP CHART — **Science/Social Studies**

See lessons on pages 338K–338L.

Managing the Class

Teacher-Led Small Groups · Independent Activities

What do I do with the rest of my class?

Reading

Objectives

- Develop fluency through partner-reading
- Read independently for a sustained period of time; use **Practice Book** page 126 for Reading Strategies and Reading Log

Reading — Fluency
20 Minutes

- Read sentences with dialogue from the Fluency passage on page 135 of your Practice Book.
- With a partner, take parts and read the dialogue aloud. Read the dialogue again with accuracy. Pay attention to the stage directions.
- What was different about reading the dialogue with accuracy? Discuss with a partner.

Extension

- Try reading the dialogue without pausing between sentences. Discuss how the dialogue changes when you ignore end punctuation marks.
- Listen to the Audio CD.

Things you need:
- Practice Book

Fluency Solutions Listening Library

(27)

Reading — Independent Reading
20 Minutes

- Read a play. As you read, think about the main character. Do you agree with what he or she is saying and doing? What message or lesson is the author trying to share through this character?
- Make and fill in a Theme Map about the story, filling in the first two squares only.

| What the character says: | + | What the character does: | = | Theme: |

Extension

- Share your graphic organizer with a partner. Have your partner use the information to fill in the last square with a message or lesson the author may be trying to share with the reader.

Things you need:
- books of plays
- pen and paper

For more books about Putting on a Play, go to the Author/Illustrator section of www.macmillanmh.com

(28)

Phonics/Word Study

Objectives

- Create analogies using synonyms and antonyms
- Use plural rules to spell words

Phonics/Word Study — Analogies
20 Minutes

- Analogies compare two pairs of words, usually using synonyms or antonyms. *Cranky* is to *mad* as *thin* is to *slim* is an analogy using synonyms. *Short* is to *tall* as *up* is to *down* is an analogy using antonyms.
- Try writing your own analogies using synonyms and antonyms. Use a thesaurus if you need help.

Extension

- Pick one analogy, and draw a picture. Then, share it with a partner.

Things you need:
- pen and paper
- thesaurus
- colored pencils or markers

For additional vocabulary and spelling games, go to www.macmillanmh.com — Vocabulary PuzzleMaker

(27)

Phonics/Word Study — Plural Words
20 Minutes

- Create a Two-Tab Foldable®.
- On the first inside tab, write *mint, arch, dress, couch, hobby, berry, compass, parent.*
- On the second inside tab, write the plural form of each word by adding -*s*, -*es*, or changing the final consonant -*y* to -*i* and adding *es*.
- Write a funny story using your words.

Extension

- Discuss with a partner how making a word plural changes its meaning.

FOLDABLES
- Two-Tab Foldable®

For additional vocabulary and spelling games, go to www.macmillanmh.com

FOLDABLES®

(28)

Literacy Workstations

Reading

Phonics/ Word Study

Writing

Science/ Social Studies

Literacy Workstation Flip Charts

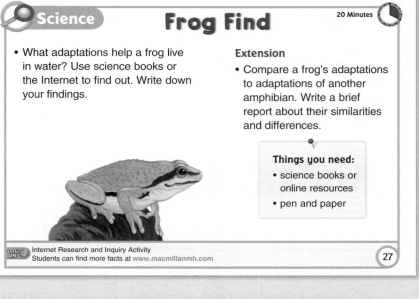

Writing

Objectives

- Create a poster to advertise a play
- Practice using strong, vivid adjectives
- Write a short dialogue

Content Literacy

Objectives

- Use the Internet to research frogs
- Practice taking notes from reference materials
- Write questions to ask your favorite actor

Writing — It's a Great Play
20 Minutes

- Imagine that your class is putting on a school play.
- Create a poster to advertise the play.
- Use strong, vivid adjectives to describe the play. Your goal is to persuade others to come see the play.

Extension

- Illustrate your poster. In your drawing, show something that is connected to an action from the play, such as a scene or character.

Things you need:
- poster board
- colored pencils or markers

Internet Research and Inquiry Activity
Students can find more facts at www.macmillanmh.com

27

Science — Frog Find
20 Minutes

- What adaptations help a frog live in water? Use science books or the Internet to find out. Write down your findings.

Extension

- Compare a frog's adaptations to adaptations of another amphibian. Write a brief report about their similarities and differences.

Things you need:
- science books or online resources
- pen and paper

Internet Research and Inquiry Activity
Students can find more facts at www.macmillanmh.com

27

Writing — Write Dialogue
20 Minutes

- Create two characters for a play. Write a short dialogue that the two characters might have with each other.
- Give your play a name.

Extension

- Write stage directions telling the actors where they should stand and what actions they are to perform. For example, you can tell how the characters should say their lines, or where the characters should move on the stage.

Things you need:
- pen and paper

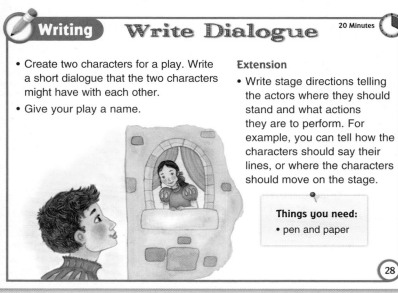

28

Social Studies — An Actor's Life
20 Minutes

- What does an actor need to be in a play? Make a list.
- Imagine that you could interview your favorite actor. What questions would you ask him or her?
- Write a list of five questions.

Extension

- Role-play the interview with a partner. One person should ask the questions, while the other answers them.

Things you need:
- pen and paper

1) Where did you grow up?
2) What's your favorite color?
3) What's your favorite movie?

28

338

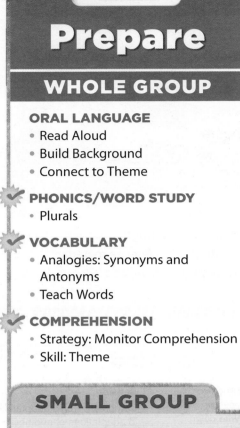

Prepare

WHOLE GROUP

ORAL LANGUAGE
- Read Aloud
- Build Background
- Connect to Theme

✓ **PHONICS/WORD STUDY**
- Plurals

✓ **VOCABULARY**
- Analogies: Synonyms and Antonyms
- Teach Words

✓ **COMPREHENSION**
- Strategy: Monitor Comprehension
- Skill: Theme

SMALL GROUP

- Differentiated Instruction, pp. 367I–367HH

Oral Language

Build Background

ACCESS PRIOR KNOWLEDGE

Share the following: Look at the girl helping to wash dishes so that they are clean. Washing dishes is a common chore, or task, for young people to help with. The girl is wearing rubber gloves to protect her hands from soap suds, or bubbles. The adult is not wearing gloves. The girl is placing the dishes in the dish rack.

Write the following words on the board, and briefly define each using the **Define/Example/Ask** routine: **promise** (a statement made by a person that something will be done), **domestic** (relating to the home), **assist** (help).

FOCUS QUESTION Ask a volunteer to read "Talk About It" on **Student Book** page 339 and describe the photo. Ask:

- Have you ever you made a promise to help with domestic chores—chores around the house? With what chores did you promise to help? Did you keep your promise?

- Why is it important to be careful about making promises?

Talk About It

Why is it important to keep promises?

LOG ON ▶ VIEW IT

Oral Language Activities
Keeping Promises
www.macmillanmh.com

Keeping Promises

339

Use the Picture Prompt

BUILD WRITING FLUENCY

Ask students to write in their Writer's Notebooks about keeping promises. Tell students to write as much as they can for ten minutes without stopping. Meet with individuals during Writing Conference time to provide feedback and revision assignments. Students should correct errors prior to meeting.

Connect to the Unit Theme

DISCUSS THE BIG IDEA

Our words are taken seriously by listeners, and we must be truthful and stick by what we say.

Ask students what they have learned about keeping promises in this unit.

- Think about how the main characters in the first two selections used words. How could you tell when they were using words truthfully or falsely?

- What other powerful ways to use words do you know about?

USE THEME FOLDABLES

Write the **Big Idea** statement on the board. Ask students to copy it on their Unit Theme Foldables. Remind them to add details as they complete this week's readings.

Dinah Zike's
FOLDABLES®
Study Organizer

Week 5
Week 4
Week 3
Week 2
Week 1
Unit Theme

Study Book

Objectives

- Identify the characteristics of poetry
- Develop vocabulary
- Read sentences fluently, focusing on expression

Materials

- Read-Aloud Anthology, pp. 90–92

Read Aloud

Read "Another Op'nin', Another Show"

Read Aloud

GENRE: Poetry

Point out that **song lyrics,** or the words to a song, are often considered a form of **poetry** and are meant to be sung. Song lyrics

- are written in lines, like a poem
- usually rhyme and usually include a refrain, or set of repeated lines
- often contain figurative language and other imagery

FOCUS ON VOCABULARY

Introduce the following words, using the **Define/Example/Ask** routine. Tell students that knowing these words will help them evaluate why Cole Porter, the composer of this song, decided to use certain lyrics.

Vocabulary Routine

Use the routine below to discuss the meaning of each word.

Define: An **op'nin'** is a short form of *opening*; refers to the first night of a new show.
Example: The man said, "The op'nin' went well even though the hound dogs got loose."
Ask: What op'nin' night would you like to participate in? Why?

Define: An **ulcer** is a sore often caused by stress.
Example: The ulcer was cured by antibiotics.
Ask: What stressful events might cause an ulcer?

Define: An **overture** is the music that is played before a show begins.
Example: The overture made us feel excited about the show.
Ask: Why might a musician write an overture?

LISTENING FOR A PURPOSE

Ask students to listen carefully as you read "Another Op'nin', Another Show" in the **Read-Aloud Anthology** pages 90–92. Use the Think Alouds and Genre Study provided.

ELL Interactive Reading Build students' oral language by engaging them in discussion about the song's basic meaning.

- Point to the masks denoting comedy and tragedy at the top of **Read-Aloud Anthology** page 90. As you point to the corresponding masks, say: *Comedy is funny, and tragedy is sad.* Have students repeat.

- After the twelfth line, say: *These people's jobs are as singers in a show. How long do they rehearse before an opening?*

- After the nineteenth line ("In Philly, Boston, or Baltimo'"), ask: *What do you think is the refrain or chorus?*

- After the last line, ask: *What does "It's curtain time and away we go" mean?*

PARTNERS

Think/Pair/Share Use **Copying Master 2**, "I made a connection when …," to help students summarize and evaluate what they learned about an actor's life on the road. When completed, ask students to turn to a partner and orally summarize the lyrics.

RESPOND TO THE LYRICS

Ask students the Think and Respond questions on page 92. Then have students generate a list of tips for people who might want to be stage actors. Encourage students to share their lists.

Model Fluency

Reread the song lyrics. Tell students that this time you want them to focus on one aspect of how you read—your **expression**.

Point out that when you see end punctuation such as a question mark or an exclamation point, you need to be expressive with your voice. You should often read a question by inflecting your voice up at the end of a sentence. Excitement should ring in your voice when you read an exclamatory sentence. Model an example.

Think Aloud Listen as I read the part beginning with, "One week, will it ever be right?/ Then out o' the hat, it's that first big night!" Notice how I ask a definite question and then express excitement. Expression is particularly important if you are reading or singing lyrics. Your expression helps give meaning to the lyrics. Now you try. Repeat each line after me, using the same expression as I do.

Establish Fluency Focus Remind students that you will be listening for them to use these same qualities in their reading throughout the week. You will help them improve their reading by using the appropriate expression.

Readers Theater

BUILDING LISTENING AND SPEAKING SKILLS Distribute copies of "All the Money in the World," **Read-Aloud Anthology** pages 182–202. Have students practice reading the play throughout the unit. Assign parts and have the students present the play or perform it as a dramatic reading at the end of the unit.

ELL

Discuss Genre Review song lyrics with students. Ask: *How are song lyrics written? Do song lyrics rhyme? How are song lyrics similar to poetry? What are some details that are in the song lyrics in "Another Op'nin', Another Show"?* Correct the meaning of students' responses as needed.

Objective

- Decode plural words

Materials

- Practice Book, p. 118
- Word-Building Cards
- Transparency 14
- Teacher's Resource Book, p. 133

ELL

Transfer Sounds In most Asian languages, there are no plural forms for nouns. For example, students may say, "I have many toy," rather than, "I have many toys." Model a sentence using plural nouns. Then work with students to form new sentences using plural nouns. Use the Approaching Level phonics lesson on page 367J for additional practice. See language transfers on pages T16–T31.

HOMEWORK

Practice Book, page 118

Plurals are formed in the following ways:
- Most plural nouns end in **-s**.
- When a word ends in **-s, -ss, -sh, -ch,** or **-x, -es** is added.
- When a word ends in a **vowel** + **y, -s** is added.
- When a word ends in a **consonant** + **y,** the **y** is dropped and **-ies** is added.

Write the correct plural form of the underlined word on the line.

1. Many talented <u>artist</u> _____ **artists** _____ have lived and worked in California.
2. Many of them study in <u>city</u> _____ **cities** _____ such as Los Angeles and San Francisco.
3. The artist Ansel Adams took many <u>photo</u> _____ **photos** _____ of the state.
4. His work showed high mountains and lush <u>valley</u> _____ **valleys** _____
5. The state is home to many famous <u>writer</u> _____ **writers** _____, too.
6. The writer Gary Soto writes about his childhood hopes and <u>wish</u> _____ **wishes** _____
7. He writes <u>story</u> _____ **stories** _____ about his family.
8. Soto turns his <u>memory</u> _____ **memories** _____ into art.

Approaching Reproducible, page 118
Beyond Reproducible, page 118

Word Study

✔ Plurals

EXPLAIN/MODEL

Write *swamp.* Explain that *swamp* is a singular noun and that it means "one swamp." Point out that when *-s* is added, a plural noun is formed and that *swamps* means "more than one swamp." Discuss these rules for many plural endings:

- Add *-s* to most singular nouns to make them plural.
- Add *-es* to singular nouns that end in *-s, -ss, -sh, -ch,* or *-x.*
- Change the *y* to *i* and add *-es* to most singular nouns that end in a consonant followed by *-y.*
- Add *-s* to nouns that end in a vowel followed by *-y.*

Write *dictionaries* on the board, and underline *-ies.*

Think Aloud I see that *dictionaries* ends in *-ies.* I know that if a word ends in a consonant and *-y,* I should change the *y* to *i* before I add *-es.* This word follows that pattern, so I know that *dictionaries* is the plural form of *dictionary.* It means "more than one dictionary."

PRACTICE/APPLY

Read the Word List Display **Transparency 14.** The first two lines include plurals of nouns that students will encounter in the upcoming selections. Have students underline the plural ending in each word. Then have them chorally read the words.

cities	jobs	stories	words
lines	years	facts	gangs
classes	ways	jokes	scores
grades	books	keys	peaches
foxes	flies	dishes	toys
babies	cards	losses	watches

Phonics Transparency 14

Sort the Words Ask students to sort the words by plural ending. (Remind students that the addition of *-s* covers two spelling rules.)

-s	-es	-ies

Read Multisyllabic Words

TRANSITION TO LONGER WORDS Help students transition to reading longer plural words. Have students chorally read each singular noun in the first column. Direct them to look at the ending of the plural form in the second column. Then model how to read each plural word, and have students chorally repeat. Finally, point to each plural word in random order, at varying speeds, and have students read the word aloud.

writer	writers	speech	speeches
artist	artists	mailbox	mailboxes
workbench	workbenches	tax	taxes
paintbrush	paintbrushes	princess	princesses
sandwich	sandwiches	teacher	teachers
supply	supplies	valley	valleys

Phonics Transparency 14

APPLY DECODING STRATEGY Guide students to use the Decoding Strategy to decode the following words: *alleys, ponies, toothbrushes, successes, poets, places, toolboxes, pennies, hundreds, butterflies.* Write each word on the board. Remind students to sound out and blend the word parts in step 4 of the Decoding Strategy.

Build Fluency

SPEED DRILL Distribute copies of the **Plurals Speed Drill** on **Teacher's Resource Book** page 133. Use the Speed Drill routine to help students become fluent reading plural words.

Quick Check

Can students read plural words?

During **Small Group Instruction**

Tier 2

If No → **Approaching Level** Reteach the skill using the lesson on p. 367J.

If Yes → **On Level** Consolidate the learning using p. 367S.

Beyond Level Extend the learning using p. 367W.

DAILY Syllable Fluency

Use **Word-Building Cards** 131–140. Display one card at a time. Have students chorally read each common syllable. Repeat at varying speeds and in random order. Have students work with partners during independent time to write as many words as they can containing each syllable.

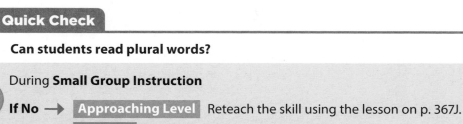

Decoding Strategy

Decoding Strategy Chart

Step 1	Look for word parts (prefixes) at the beginning of the word.
Step 2	Look for word parts (suffixes) at the end of the word.
Step 3	In the base word, look for familiar spelling patterns. Think about the six syllable-spelling patterns you have learned.
Step 4	Sound out and blend together the word parts.
Step 5	Say the word parts fast. Adjust your pronunciation as needed. Ask yourself: "Is this a word I have heard before?" Then read the word in the sentence and ask: "Does it make sense in this sentence?"

© Macmillan/McGraw-Hill

Vocabulary

✓ STRATEGY
ANALOGIES

Analogies compare two pairs of words usually using **synonyms** and **antonyms**. Remind students that synonyms are words that have similar meanings and antonyms are words that have opposite meanings.

Have students read "Analogies" on the bookmark on **Student Book** page 340. Model for students how to complete the analogy *cranky* is to *mad* as *thin* is to _____.

Think Aloud I know a cranky person is someone who is unhappy or in a bad mood. Someone who is mad is also unhappy or in a bad mood. So, *cranky* and *mad* are synonyms. To complete the analogy, I will think of a word that has a similar meaning to *thin*. Using a thesaurus, I see that some synonyms for *thin* are *slim, skinny,* and *slender*. These words can help me complete the analogy.

Have students create their own analogies using known synonyms and antonyms. Have partners exchange their analogies. Remind students that they can use a thesaurus to help them.

Read "The Frog Prince"

As you read "The Frog Prince" with students, ask them to identify clues that reveal the meanings of the highlighted words. Tell students they will read these words again in *Ranita, The Frog Princess*.

Vocabulary

selfish	exasperated
cranky	specialty
commotion	famished

✓ Analogies

Analogies compare two pairs of words usually using Synonyms or Antonyms. *Cranky* is to *mad* as *thin* is to *slim*.

The Frog Prince
by Maryn Stevens

Narrator: There once was a beautiful princess whose favorite object was a golden ball. One day the princess tossed the ball too high, and it landed in the well. As the princess cried over her lost treasure, she heard someone ask a question.

Frog: Why are you crying, princess?

Narrator: The princess looked around and saw only a frog.

Princess: I am crying because my favorite golden ball fell into the well.

Frog: I can retrieve it for you, but first you must agree to one condition. You must promise to take me home and be my friend.

Narrator: The princess had no intention of being friends with a frog, but she promised anyway. When the frog brought her the ball, the princess snatched it from him and scampered home.

Frog: What a **selfish** princess. She only cares about herself. I'm certain she has forgotten her promise. I'll just hop over to the castle to remind her.

Narrator: The frog hopped through the meadow and knocked on the heavy door of the castle.

Princess: What are you doing here, you bumbling frog?

340

Quick Check

Can students identify word meanings?

During **Small Group Instruction**

Tier 2

If No → **Approaching Level** Reteach the words using the Vocabulary lesson, pp. 367K–367L.

If Yes → **On Level** Consolidate the learning using p. 367S.

Gifted Talented **Beyond Level** Extend the learning using p. 367W.

Frog: My, aren't we grouchy and **cranky**? Bumbling? I wasn't the one who dropped the ball into the well. I am here to remind you of the promise you made.

Narrator: The princess slammed the door in the frog's face with a big BANG.

King: I heard a door slam. What's all the **commotion**? If you made a promise, you must honor it.

Narrator: A frustrated and **exasperated** princess obeyed her father. The king, the princess, and the frog ate dinner together. It was beef stew, the cook's favorite recipe, his famous **specialty**.

Frog: I was **famished**, but now I'm full. Thank you for dinner. Kindly show me to my bed now.

Narrator: The princess did as she was asked, but the frog looked sad.

Frog: You have welcomed me into your home, but I can tell that you don't want to be my friend.

Narrator: The princess blushed, for what the frog said was true. She bent down to kiss the frog, but ended up kissing a prince.

Frog: I am a prince who was turned into a frog, and your kiss turned me back. Thank you, dear friend!

Narrator: The prince and princess were wonderful friends from that day on and lived happily ever after.

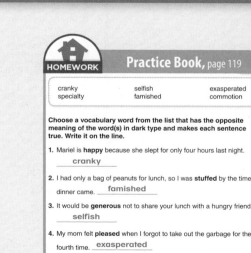

Reread for **Comprehension**

Monitor Comprehension

Theme The theme of a selection is the lesson or message about life an author wants to communicate to readers in a story. One way to identify the theme is to pay attention to the characters' words, actions, and what happens as a result of their actions.

Use the Theme Chart to help you monitor your comprehension and identify clues in the text about the theme of "The Frog Prince."

Detail
Detail
Detail
Theme

LOG ON ▶ **LEARN IT** Comprehension
www.macmillanmh.com

341

Vocabulary

TEACH WORDS

Introduce each word using the **Define/Example/Ask** routine. Model reading each word using the syllable-scoop technique.

> ## Vocabulary Routine
>
> **Define:** People who are **selfish** are concerned mainly with themselves.
> **Example:** The boy was too selfish to share his snack with the birds.
> **Ask:** What are some things people do that seem selfish? DESCRIPTION

- If you are **cranky**, you are irritated easily. *The baby was cranky because she needed a nap.* What is an antonym for *cranky*? ANTONYM

- A **commotion** occurs when there is great noise and activity. *When the batter hit a home run in the ninth inning, there was a commotion in the stands.* Where and when have you heard a commotion? EXAMPLE

- When you are **exasperated**, you have no patience and are annoyed. *He was so exasperated at the way the show ended, he turned off the television.* What is a reason that someone would get exasperated? DESCRIPTION

- A **specialty** is something that you do or know very well. *The specialty of our favorite restaurant was lasagna.* What is a specialty of yours? EXAMPLE

- To be **famished** is to feel extreme hunger. *After our hard work cleaning the beach, we were famished.* How are the adjectives *famished* and *hungry* alike and different? COMPARE AND CONTRAST

HOMEWORK **Practice Book,** page 119

cranky	selfish	exasperated
specialty	famished	commotion

Choose a vocabulary word from the list that has the opposite meaning of the word(s) in dark type and makes each sentence true. Write it on the line.

1. Mariel is **happy** because she slept for only four hours last night. ___cranky___

2. I had only a bag of peanuts for lunch, so I was **stuffed** by the time dinner came. ___famished___

3. It would be **generous** not to share your lunch with a hungry friend. ___selfish___

4. My mom felt **pleased** when I forgot to take out the garbage for the fourth time. ___exasperated___

5. Tyler's dog caused a **peaceful pause** when it escaped and ran through a grocery store. ___commotion___

Use one of the vocabulary words in a sentence of your own.

6. Possible response: We all felt *cranky* after riding in the car for hours.

Approaching Reproducible, page 119
Beyond Reproducible, page 119

Objectives

- Monitor comprehension
- Summarize and explain the theme of a story
- Use academic language: *monitor comprehension, theme*

Materials

- Transparencies 10, 14a, 14b
- Practice Book, p. 120

Skills Trace

Theme	
Introduce	341A–341B
Practice/ Apply	342–361; Practice Book, 120–121
Reteach/ Review	367M–367Z, 409A–409B, 410–429, 435M–435Z; Practice Book, 138–139
Assess	Weekly Tests; Units 3, 4 Tests
Maintain	391B, 497B, 591B

ELL

Academic Language

Preteach the following academic language words to **ELL** and **Approaching Level** students during Small Group time: *monitor comprehension, theme*. See pages 367I and 367AA.

Reread for
Comprehension

STRATEGY
MONITOR COMPREHENSION

What Is It? Remind students that when they **monitor** their **comprehension**, they check to be sure they understand what they are reading. They can adjust their comprehension using self-correction techniques such as rereading a passage or generating questions to help them understand what is taking place in a story.

Why Is It Important? By monitoring their comprehension, students can determine whether they understand what is taking place in a story. Understanding why events happen and what changes the characters undergo can help readers identify a story's theme.

SKILL
THEME

What Is It? The **theme** is the overall message or lesson about life that an author wants readers to understand when they read a story. A theme may be stated directly, or it may be implied.

Why Is It Important? By summarizing and explaining the theme of a story, readers will better understand the relationships between characters and events, as well as what the author feels is meaningful.

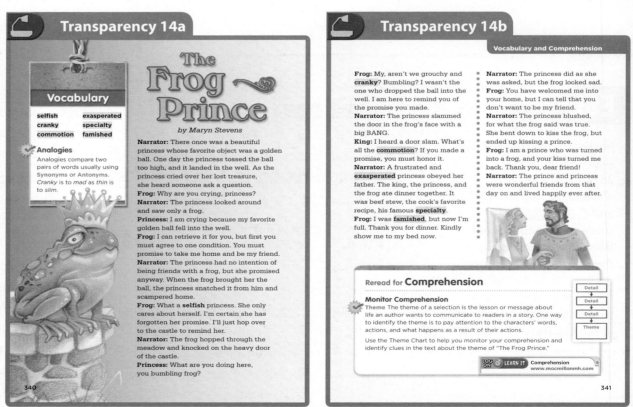

Student Book pages 340–341 available on Comprehension Transparencies 14a and 14b

Themes often express universal truths and represent morals or lessons about life. A reader can identify and analyze a theme by examining the characters, actions, and images in a story.

Have students use the following steps to identify and explain the theme of a selection as they read:

■ Think about what the characters say and do, what happens as a result of the characters' actions, the problem they face and its outcome, and where and when the story takes place.

■ Ask, "What message does the author want to get across?"

MODEL

How Do I Use It? Read aloud Frog's second speech in "The Frog Prince" on Student Book page 340. Use Transparency 10 to record clues to the play's theme on the Theme Chart.

Think Aloud As I read, I will look for clues to the play's theme in the words and actions of the characters. In this passage, Frog tells the princess he will retrieve her golden ball if she will promise to be his friend. I wonder if the princess will keep her promise to the Frog. I will read on to see if making promises has something to do with the theme of this story.

GUIDED PRACTICE

Help students begin filling in the Theme Chart by identifying the first clue. (Frog asks the princess to promise to be his friend.)

Ask students to read the remaining dialogue on page 340. Remind students to examine the characters' words, actions, and what happens as a result of their actions.

APPLY

Have students read the remainder of "The Frog Prince" and complete the Theme Chart. Ask students to describe how the characters in the play changed. Also have students discuss what the author wanted to express in this play. Then have them use the clues or details they recorded to summarize the play's theme. Ask students to explain how they identified the theme and relate it to their own lives.

Quick Check

Can students summarize and explain the theme of the play?

During **Small Group Instruction**

Tier 2

If No → **Approaching Level** Reteach the skill using the Comprehension lesson, pp. 367M–367P.

If Yes → **On Level** Consolidate the learning using pp. 367U–367V.

Beyond Level Extend the learning using pp. 367Y–367Z.

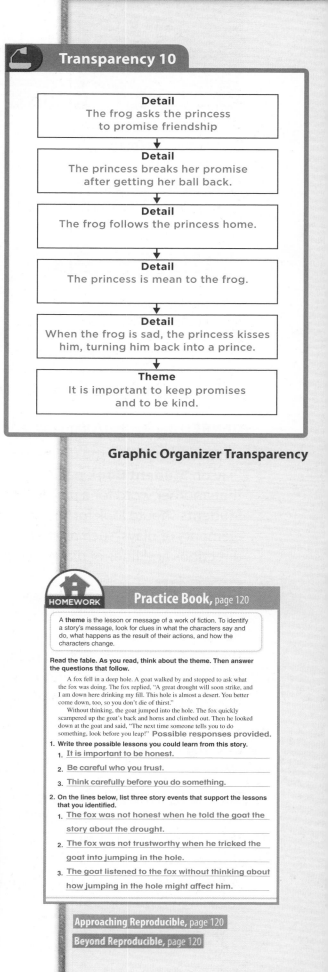

Transparency 10

| Detail |
| The frog asks the princess to promise friendship |

| Detail |
| The princess breaks her promise after getting her ball back. |

| Detail |
| The frog follows the princess home. |

| Detail |
| The princess is mean to the frog. |

| Detail |
| When the frog is sad, the princess kisses him, turning him back into a prince. |

| Theme |
| It is important to keep promises and to be kind. |

Graphic Organizer Transparency

HOMEWORK **Practice Book,** page 120

A **theme** is the lesson or message of a work of fiction. To identify a story's message, look for clues in what the characters say and do, what happens as the result of their actions, and how the characters change.

Read the fable. As you read, think about the theme. Then answer the questions that follow.

A fox fell in a deep hole. A goat walked by and stopped to ask what the fox was doing. The fox replied, "A great drought will soon strike, and I am down here drinking my fill. This hole is almost a desert. You better come down, too, so you don't die of thirst."

Without thinking, the goat jumped into the hole. The fox quickly scampered up the goat's back and horns and climbed out. Then he looked down at the goat and said, "The next time someone tells you to do something, look before you leap!" Possible responses provided.

1. Write three possible lessons you could learn from this story.
   1. It is important to be honest.
   2. Be careful who you trust.
   3. Think carefully before you do something.

2. On the lines below, list three story events that support the lessons that you identified.
   1. The fox was not honest when he told the goat the story about the drought.
   2. The fox was not trustworthy when he tricked the goat into jumping in the hole.
   3. The goat listened to the fox without thinking about how jumping in the hole might affect him.

Approaching Reproducible, page 120
Beyond Reproducible, page 120

Read

WHOLE GROUP

 MAIN SELECTION
- *Ranita, The Frog Princess*
- Skill: Theme

 PAIRED SELECTION
- Expository: "And Still More Tales"
- Literary Element: Theme

SMALL GROUP

- Differentiated Instruction, pp. 367I–367HH

Main Selection

GENRE: Literary Text/Drama

Have students read the definition of a Play on **Student Book** page 342. Note that another word for a *play* is a *drama*. Students should look for the structural elements of plays, such as stage directions and lines of dialogue.

STRATEGY
MONITOR COMPREHENSION

Remind students to monitor, or check, their comprehension as they read. Students should stop often to ask themselves if they understand what they are reading.

SKILL
THEME

Remind students that theme is the overall idea, or message about life, that the author wants to convey to readers. By discovering the theme of a story, readers will understand what an author thinks is meaningful and important.

Comprehension

Genre

A **Play** is a story that is intended to be performed and has features such as dialogue, stage directions, and scene descriptions.

Monitor Comprehension

Theme

As you read, use your Theme Chart.

Detail
↓
Detail
↓
Detail
↓
Theme

Read to Find Out

What is the lesson or message of this play?

342

Vocabulary

Vocabulary Words Review the tested words while reading: **selfish**, **cranky**, **commotion**, **exasperated**, **specialty**, and **famished**.

Additional Selection Words Students may be unfamiliar with these words. Pronounce the words, give student-friendly explanations as needed, and help students use the previously taught vocabulary strategies: word parts, dictionary, context clues.

viceroy (p. 344): a nobleman

banquet (p. 350): a large, fancy feast

oath (p. 354): a promise

tadpole (p. 359): a newly hatched baby frog

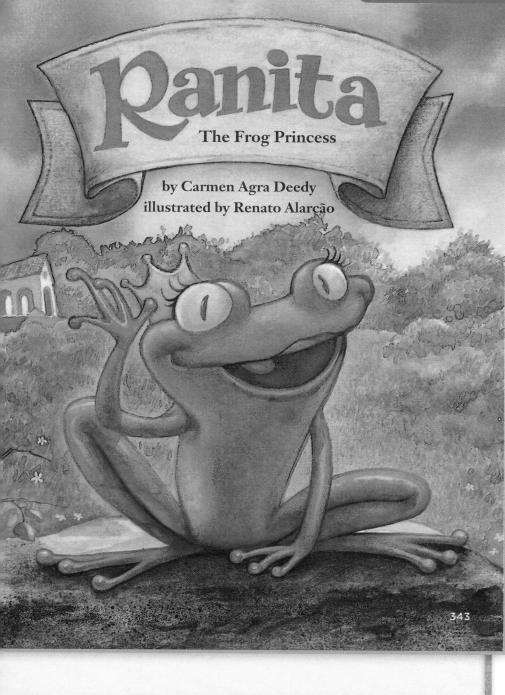

Ranita

The Frog Princess

by Carmen Agra Deedy
illustrated by Renato Alarção

343

Read the Main Selection

Preteach	Read Together	Read Independently
Have Approaching Level students and English Language Learners listen to the selection on **StudentWorks Plus**, the interactive e-Book, before reading with the class.	Use the prompts to guide comprehension and model how to complete the graphic organizer. Have students use **Think/Pair/Share** to discuss the selection.	If students can read the selection independently, have them read and complete the graphic organizer. Suggest that they use their purposes to choose their reading strategies.

LOG ON ▶ **StudentWorks** Plus
Interactive Student Book

Preview and Predict

QUICK WRITE Ask students to read the title, preview the illustrations, think about the genre, and make predictions. Students may also include their own experiences reading or watching plays.

Set Purposes

FOCUS QUESTION Discuss the "Read to Find Out" question on **Student Book** page 342. Remind students to look for the answer as they read and have them also set their own purposes for reading.

Point out the Theme Chart in the **Student Book** and on **Practice Book** page 121. Explain that students will fill in the chart as they read.

Read *Ranita, The Frog Princess*

Use the questions and Think Alouds to support instruction about the comprehension strategy and skill.

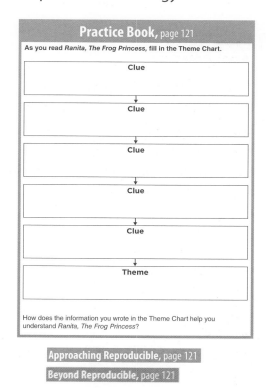

Practice Book, page 121

As you read *Ranita, The Frog Princess*, fill in the Theme Chart.

Clue
↓
Clue
↓
Clue
↓
Clue
↓
Clue
↓
Theme

How does the information you wrote in the Theme Chart help you understand *Ranita, The Frog Princess*?

Approaching Reproducible, page 121
Beyond Reproducible, page 121

Develop Comprehension

1 GENRE: Literary Text/Drama

What structural features of a play can you find on this page? (A list of the cast of characters, and the location where the play is set.) Based on the descriptions of the first five characters that the playwright provides, what predictions can you make about the conflicts and problems that might develop between these characters? (Felipe is described as "rotten," so he may be mean or spoiled. Pepe is called mistreated, so he may be angry about being treated badly. This could create a problem between Felipe and Pepe. Ranita's past is described as mysterious, so she may have a secret. Vieja Sabia is described as cranky, so she may not be very patient, which could cause problems.)

2 STRATEGY
ANALOGIES

Think about the word *mysterious* here. What are two synonyms for this word? (unknown, strange) What are two antonyms? (known, obvious) Let's complete an analogy using these words: *mysterious* is to *obvious* as *unknown* is to _____. (known)

SETTING

Long ago in Mexico. The Viceroy's hunting lodge in Chapultapec forest.

1 PLAYERS

FELIPE, the Viceroy's rotten son

2 PEPE, Felipe's mistreated servant

RANITA, a little frog with a mysterious past

VIEJA SABIA, a wise but **cranky** old woman

VICEROY, the representative of the Spanish throne

VICEROY'S WIFE

COOK

MAN ONE

MAN TWO

SERVANT ONE

SERVANT TWO

MAN THREE

EXTRAS: Members of hunting party, servants attending dinner, noblemen and ladies

344

Monitor Comprehension

Monitor and Clarify: *Self-Correct*

Explain Tell students that they can self-correct misunderstandings while they are reading. Stopping and asking open-ended questions such as *Why? What if?* and *How?* can help them make sense of challenging material.

Discuss Tell students that stage directions in a play are provided in parentheses. They give information about what is happening on stage, which actors are entering or exiting, and how a character feels. If they are confused at any time, they should try rereading the stage directions to make sure they understand what is taking place.

Apply Make sure students stop if they become confused. Have them ask open-ended questions and review the stage directions.

Scene 1

In a forest clearing, men are frantically searching the ground. From a nearby stone well, Ranita watches but remains unnoticed.

Man One: *(Frustrated)* Keep looking! If we don't find that golden arrow—

Man Two: —we'll be on *tortillas* and water for the next month!

(Men, grumbling, all agree.)

(Enter Felipe.)

Felipe: *(Loud and demanding)* Well? Have you found my golden arrow yet?

Man Three: Not yet, Señor!

Felipe: *(Sweetly, hand over heart)* It was a gift from my dear mother. *(Turning suddenly and hissing)* Find it or I will feed you to the jaguars—starting with my bumbling servant, Pepe. It's his fault I missed my mark. Now, out of my sight, all of you!

(Men exit hurriedly.)

3
4

345

Develop Comprehension

3 **STRATEGY**
MONITOR COMPREHENSION

Teacher Think Aloud As I read this play, I need to monitor my comprehension to make sure I understand what is happening. I notice that the setting of Scene 1 is described as a forest clearing. The text also tells me that men are frantically searching the ground. The stage directions in parentheses tell me what the characters are feeling and doing. I notice that at the bottom of the page, the three men exit, so the scene or the setting may change on the next page.

4 **SKILL**
THEME

Based on what he says and does on page 345, what word best describes Felipe? (Felipe yells at the men and insults Pepe. A good word to describe him would be "nasty.") How might his actions relate to the play's theme? (The theme might have something to do with the way people treat one another.)

Phonics/Word Study

APPLY DECODING SKILLS While reading, point out words with the sound-spelling patterns, syllable types, and word parts students have recently learned. Help students blend these words. You may wish to focus on selection words that are plurals: *servants, members, ladies, canes.*

Develop Comprehension

5 **MONITOR AND CLARIFY: SELF-CORRECT**

What was the final stage direction on page 345? (Men exit hurriedly.) Why is it important to read this stage direction if you want to understand what is taking place in the play at this point? (If you did not know that the men who were looking for the arrow had exited the stage, you might think they could overhear the conversation between Felipe and Ranita.)

6 **GENRE:** Literary Text/Drama

What details tell you that this selection is a fairy tale written as a play? (Ranita is a talking frog, which is the kind of character that readers would expect to find in a fairy tale. She says she is under a spell, which is also a plot device that is used in fairy tales.)

346

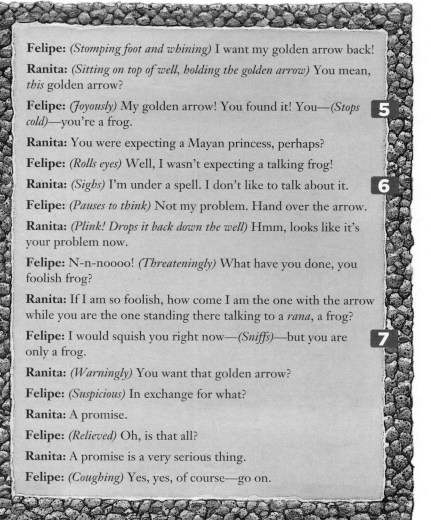

Felipe: (*Stomping foot and whining*) I want my golden arrow back!

Ranita: (*Sitting on top of well, holding the golden arrow*) You mean, *this* golden arrow?

Felipe: (*Joyously*) My golden arrow! You found it! You—(*Stops cold*)—you're a frog. **5**

Ranita: You were expecting a Mayan princess, perhaps?

Felipe: (*Rolls eyes*) Well, I wasn't expecting a talking frog!

Ranita: (*Sighs*) I'm under a spell. I don't like to talk about it. **6**

Felipe: (*Pauses to think*) Not my problem. Hand over the arrow.

Ranita: (*Plink! Drops it back down the well*) Hmm, looks like it's your problem now.

Felipe: N-n-noooo! (*Threateningly*) What have you done, you foolish frog?

Ranita: If I am so foolish, how come I am the one with the arrow while you are the one standing there talking to a *rana*, a frog?

Felipe: I would squish you right now—(*Sniffs*)—but you are only a frog. **7**

Ranita: (*Warningly*) You want that golden arrow?

Felipe: (*Suspicious*) In exchange for what?

Ranita: A promise.

Felipe: (*Relieved*) Oh, is that all?

Ranita: A promise is a very serious thing.

Felipe: (*Coughing*) Yes, yes, of course—go on.

> ✔ **Theme**
> Think about Felipe's character.
> Does he take promises seriously?

8

347

Develop Comprehension

7 MAKE PREDICTIONS

Ranita has found Felipe's arrow, which is an important event in the plot. How might the fact that the arrow was found by a talking frog under a spell affect future events in the story? (The promise Ranita wants Felipe to make will probably involve assisting her to break the spell that has been placed on her.)

8 SKILL
THEME

✔ Think about Felipe's character. Does he take promises seriously? (When Ranita asks for a promise, Felipe is relieved. He says, "Oh, is that all?" Felipe does not act like someone who can be trusted.) **What does Ranita's answer tell you about her character?** (Her answer suggests that she is honorable.) **Enter her response on your Theme Chart.**

Detail
Ranita tells Felipe a promise is a very serious thing.

Develop Comprehension

9 **SKILL**
THEME

Remember that Ranita takes promises very seriously. Why does she want Felipe to promise her all these things in exchange for the arrow? (Ranita says she is under a spell. Eating from Felipe's plate, sleeping in his bed, and being kissed by him sound like things that could break the spell. She is probably hoping that giving Felipe what he wants will help her get what she needs. She very much needs him to keep his promise.)

9 **Ranita:** IF I rescue your golden arrow, you must promise to let me eat from your *plato*, sleep in your *cama*, and give me a *beso* when the sun comes up.

Felipe: *(Just stares)* Eat from my plate? Sleep in my bed? KISS you? *That* is disgusting!

Ranita: No promise, no golden arrow.

Felipe: *(Crossing his fingers behind his back)* I promise.

(Ranita fetches the arrow. Felipe bows and runs off.)

Ranita: *Espera*! Wait! I can't hop that fast! *(Hangs her head and begins to cry)* He's gone. Now I'll never break this evil spell.

348

(*Enter wise woman, leaning on two canes.*)

10

Vieja Sabia: It doesn't feel very good, does it?

Ranita: (*Blows nose*) Please, no lectures today, old woman.

Vieja Sabia: My name is Vieja *Sabia*.

Ranita: Sorry, *Wise* Old Woman. (*Sadly*) You've already turned me into a frog. Isn't that enough?

Vieja Sabia: You wouldn't be a frog if you hadn't refused to give me a drink from this well, so long ago.

Ranita: I was a **selfish** child then. I have paid for that, haven't I? I have learned what it is like to be alone and forgotten.

11

Vieja Sabia: Perhaps you have . . .

Ranita: (*Brightening*) Then, you will turn me into a girl again?

Vieja Sabia: No. But I will take you as far as the Viceroy's hunting lodge. You must make the leap from there.

(*Exit Vieja Sabia and Ranita.*)

349

Develop Comprehension

10 **STRATEGY**
ANALOGIES

Look at the word *wise* in the stage directions at the top of page 349. What words or phrases are **antonyms** for *wise*? (*foolish, ignorant, unwise, dim-witted, naive*) Create an analogy comparing two pairs of words. Use the word *wise* with one of its antonyms, and the word *selfish* with one of its antonyms. For example, the analogy would be *wise* is to *foolish* as *selfish* is to _____.

11 **SKILL**
THEME

Why did Vieja Sabia turn Ranita into a frog? What clues can you find to the story's theme in the characters' actions? (Ranita was a selfish child. She refused to give Vieja Sabia a drink. Ranita says she has learned from this what it is like to be alone and forgotten.) Add the reason for Vieja Sabia's action as a clue to your Theme Chart.

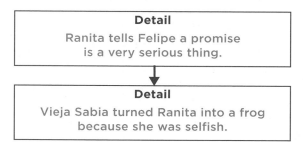

Detail
Ranita tells Felipe a promise is a very serious thing.

↓

Detail
Vieja Sabia turned Ranita into a frog because she was selfish.

Develop Comprehension

12 DRAW CONCLUSIONS

What were Felipe's mother's feelings toward Felipe? How is this relationship different from the one Felipe has with his servants? (His mother thinks Felipe is sweet and kind. She calls him "dear boy." He must behave differently around her. He is rude to the servants. They think he is spoiled and rotten.)

Scene 2

Hunting lodge with Viceroy, his wife, noblemen and women, all seated at long banquet table. Servants scurry in and out with bowls of food.

Servant One: *(Placing bowl of soup before Viceroy)* Sopa, Señor?

Viceroy: (**Exasperated**) Sí, sí. Where is Felipe?

Viceroy's Wife: *(Wistfully)* Dear boy. He is probably feeding the birds.

Servant Two: *(Aside)* To the cat.

12 **Servant One:** *(Muffles laugh)*

(Enter Felipe.)

Felipe: I am **famished**. What a day I've had today. First, I lost my golden arrow—

(Shouting from the kitchen can be heard.)

350

Comprehension

Comparing Tales Across Cultures

Explain Certain types of characters and plots are common in traditional literature from different time periods and different cultures around the world.

Discuss Ask students what stories they have read that feature a character like Vieja Sabia. Have students write a paragraph explaining the similarities and differences between Vieja Sabia and a similar character from another story they have read.

Apply Provide time for students to share their paragraphs when completed. Ask: *How is the character of the old woman similar in tales across cultures? How is it different? Why might authors across cultures have this character in their stories?*

Felipe: (Louder)—then I met this ridiculous, demanding—
(Enter Ranita, running from the kitchen chased by cook and servants.)

Felipe: (Slack-jawed)—frog.

Cook: You hop back here! (To servant) Stop her, right now!

Servant One: (Tries to catch frog) Aaaaayyyy! She's a slippery one!

Servant Two: Oooooeeeeee! She bit me!

Cook: Get her, Pepe. (Pepe catches Ranita under the table, smiles, and lets her go. A **commotion** follows as the cook and servants chase Ranita.)

13

✓ Theme
How does Felipe feel about his promise to Ranita?

Develop Comprehension

13 SKILL
THEME

 How does Felipe feel about his promise to Ranita? (Felipe calls Ranita "ridiculous" and "demanding." He is disdainful of her because she is just a frog. He thinks she is not someone worth paying attention to, and he certainly does not take the promise he made to a lowly frog seriously.)

Vocabulary

Word Structure Clues: *Suffixes*

Explain/Model Explain that suffixes are word parts added to the end of a base word. Suffixes change a word's meaning and may change its part of speech. Identifying a suffix in a word can help the reader figure out its meaning. The suffix -*ful* comes from Old English and means "full of," or "likely to." Write *hopeful* on the board.

Think Aloud I see the base word *hope* with the suffix -*ful* added. I know that -*ful* can mean "full of." When I put the meaning of the suffix and the base word together, I get "full of hope."

Practice/Apply Display the words *tasteful* and *successful*. Have students identify the suffix and tell what the words mean. Then have them find words on pages 350–351 with other suffixes. Discuss them together. (*probably, louder, slippery*)

Develop Comprehension

14 STRATEGY
MONITOR COMPREHENSION

Teacher Think Aloud I want to make sure I understand what is happening. Felipe tells his father, the Viceroy, that he does not remember making a promise to Ranita. Do you think Felipe really does not remember making a promise? Why or why not?

PARTNERS Prompt students to apply this strategy in a Think Aloud by asking them to draw a conclusion based on story clues.

Student Think Aloud Felipe makes light of promises when he speaks with Ranita. Then he runs off and does not keep his promise to her. When he is back at the lodge, he says he met a demanding frog. I think Felipe remembers making the promise to Ranita but does not want to get in trouble with his father for breaking the promise.

15 SUMMARIZE

Summarize the main events of the play so far. (Felipe is the spoiled, mean son of the Viceroy. Ranita, a frog who can speak because she is under a spell, finds Felipe's lost golden arrow. She says she will return it to him if he promises to let her eat from his plate, sleep in his bed, and get a kiss from him. Felipe agrees but does not think he will have to keep his promise. Vieja Sabia, the woman who put the spell on Ranita, takes Ranita to the Viceroy's house, and Ranita tells him about the promise. The Viceroy says that Felipe must do as he promised.)

352

Text Evidence

Theme

Reread the Teacher Think Aloud in Question 14. Ask, *Where would you look to find out whether Felipe made a promise to Ranita?* (To the part of the play where Felipe meets Ranita, in Scene 1.) *On what page number can this information be found? Point to the information when you find it.* (Felipe meets Ranita on page 347, after he loses his golden arrow.) *What do Felipe's actions in this encounter reveal about his character?* (He is tricky and a liar. He sees the opportunity to get his arrow back without keeping his promise to Ranita.) *Why is this important to remember when determining the theme of this story?* (Before readers can determine the theme of a story, they have to think about what the characters do and say and what happens in the story as a result of the characters' actions.)

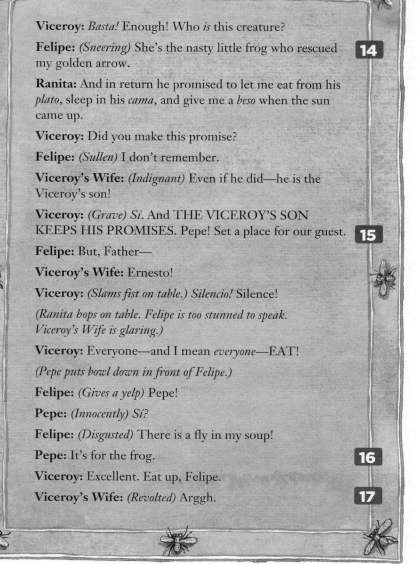

Viceroy: *Basta!* Enough! Who *is* this creature?

Felipe: (*Sneering*) She's the nasty little frog who rescued my golden arrow.

Ranita: And in return he promised to let me eat from his *plato*, sleep in his *cama*, and give me a *beso* when the sun came up.

Viceroy: Did you make this promise?

Felipe: (*Sullen*) I don't remember.

Viceroy's Wife: (*Indignant*) Even if he did—he is the Viceroy's son!

Viceroy: (*Grave*) *Sí.* And THE VICEROY'S SON KEEPS HIS PROMISES. Pepe! Set a place for our guest. **15**

Felipe: But, Father—

Viceroy's Wife: Ernesto!

Viceroy: (*Slams fist on table.*) *Silencio!* Silence!

(*Ranita hops on table. Felipe is too stunned to speak. Viceroy's Wife is glaring.*)

Viceroy: Everyone—and I mean *everyone*—EAT!

(*Pepe puts bowl down in front of Felipe.*)

Felipe: (*Gives a yelp*) Pepe!

Pepe: (*Innocently*) *Sí?*

Felipe: (*Disgusted*) There is a fly in my soup!

Pepe: It's for the frog. **16**

Viceroy: Excellent. Eat up, Felipe.

Viceroy's Wife: (*Revolted*) Arggh. **17**

353

Develop Comprehension

16 **SKILL**
THEME

In what way are the Viceroy and his son different? (Keeping a promise is important to the Viceroy. He is angry that Felipe did not keep his promise.) How might this difference be important to the theme? (The Viceroy says that his son keeps his promises. These words are in all caps, so it's an important point the author wants to emphasize.) Add this information to your Theme Chart.

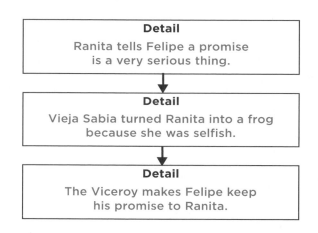

Detail
Ranita tells Felipe a promise is a very serious thing.

↓

Detail
Vieja Sabia turned Ranita into a frog because she was selfish.

↓

Detail
The Viceroy makes Felipe keep his promise to Ranita.

17 **SELF-SELECTED STRATEGY USE**

What strategies have you used to help you understand the selection? Where did you use them? How did they help?

 RETURN TO PREDICTIONS AND PURPOSES

Have students respond to the play by confirming or revising their predictions and purposes. Direct them to revise or write questions to help focus their attention as they continue to read.

Stop here if you wish to read this selection over two days.

Develop Comprehension

18 AUTHOR'S CRAFT: WORD CHOICE

Why do you think the playwright uses the adjective *snappish* rather than *angry* to describe the way Felipe says his second line on page 354? (The word *snappish* is more precise. It suggests that Felipe is snapping as he speaks, almost as if he is using words to bite Pepe.)

Scene 3

(Felipe's bedroom)

Felipe: *(On bed)* I refuse to sleep next to a FROG. Pepe!!!!!!!!

Pepe: *(Enters immediately)* Sí, Señor?

Felipe: *(Snappish)* What took you so long? Hurry—tell my father I can't do this. *(Desperate)* Tell him I'll get warts.

(Enter Viceroy.)

Viceroy: *(Annoyed)* With any luck, you will get one on your oath-breaking tongue, boy.

Felipe: *(Whining)* Father—

Viceroy: You made a promise, Felipe. *(To Pepe)* Help him keep his word, eh, Pepe?

(Exit Viceroy.)

354

Social Studies

Connect to Content

STATE GOVERNMENT

The Viceroy in *Ranita, The Frog Princess* is a royal official, representing the Spanish king in the Mexican government. Discuss with students the structure of the United States government. What are the different arms of the government?

Have students think about the structure of their state government. Working in small groups, have students research the history of their state government.

Students can write a brief report summarizing their research. Encourage them to create a time line showing the most important dates.

Felipe: *(Throws pillow at Pepe. Falls on bed and begins to wail.)* AAAAAAAYYYYYYYY!

Pepe: *(Blows out candle and sits in chair.)* Hasta mañana . . . until tomorrow. Sweet dreams, Felipe.

Felipe: *(Growls)* I will dream of roasted frog legs.

Ranita: I'm telling.

Felipe: Bug breath!

Ranita: Big baby!

Pepe: *(Sighs)* It's going to be a long night.

(Next morning)

Ranita: *(Cheerful) Despierta,* wake up! It's "beso time!"

[Felipe rubs eyes, sees Ranita, and shrieks.]

Felipe: *(Whimpers, clutching his blanket)* It wasn't a bad dream, after all. Forget it, frog! I am not kissing you!

Ranita: *(Stubbornly)* You promised.

Felipe: Well, *(Smiles slowly)* I've just had a better idea. *(Kicks chair to wake his servant)* Pepe!

Pepe: *(Groggy) Señor!*

Felipe: You are sworn to obey me in all things, *sí*?

Pepe: *(Confused) Sí,* Señor.

355

Develop Comprehension

19 DRAW CONCLUSIONS

SPIRAL REVIEW What did Pepe do to make sure Felipe kept his promise to Ranita? Use clues from the play to draw a conclusion. (The Viceroy tells Pepe he must help Felipe keep his word. The next morning, Felipe kicks a chair in his room to wake Pepe. So Pepe must have spent the night in Felipe's room, sleeping in a chair, to make sure he kept his promise to Ranita.)

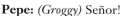

Vocabulary

Semantic/Meaning Cues

Explain Tell students that good readers use context clues and background knowledge to help them understand what they read.

Discuss Discuss the word *groggy* near the bottom of page 355. Say, *I am not familiar with the word* groggy. *It is used in a stage direction so it tells the actor playing Pepe how to say the line. The stage direction that comes before it tells Felipe to kick Pepe's chair to wake him up. I know that when someone wakes me up, I am still sleepy. I think* groggy *means "sleepy."*

Apply Tell students to use context clues and their background knowledge to help them with other difficult words such as *wail* and *whimpers* on this page.

Develop Comprehension

20 **STRATEGY**
MONITOR COMPREHENSION

How does Felipe change? In what ways does he stay the same? How does his relationship with Ranita change?

Student Think Aloud To monitor my comprehension of the play, I will reread the beginning of the story. Felipe treats Ranita badly at the beginning of the play. Now, when Ranita turns into a Mayan princess, Felipe is dazzled and bows to her. After Ranita explains that she is lucky because she does not have to marry a spoiled brat, Felipe has a screaming tantrum. He acts as he did at the beginning of the play. His relationship with her has changed, though, because she no longer needs his help.

Felipe: *(Smug)* KISS . . . THE . . . FROG.

[Pepe shrugs and kisses Ranita's cheek.]

(No longer a frog, Ranita is now a beautiful Mayan Princess.)

Felipe: *(Dazzled)* I—but who? *(Bowing)* Allow me to introduce myself, I am—

Ranita: —the Spanish Viceroy's Rotten Son. And I am . . . the Mayan Emperor's Lucky Daughter.

(Felipe and Pepe fall on their knees.)

Ranita: I have been enchanted for 200 years.

Felipe: *(Looks up)* You've been a frog for 200 years? What's so LUCKY about that?

20 **Ranita:** I'll tell you. As a princess, I could have ended up the wife of a spoiled brat like you. Instead, I found myself a prince . . . *(Takes Pepe's hand)* a prince of a husband, that is.

21 *(Pepe kisses the Princess's hand, while Felipe has a screaming tantrum.)*

356

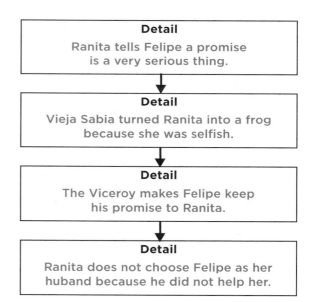

Develop Comprehension

21 SKILL
THEME

What clues can you find in the characters' actions that might be a clue to the play's theme? (Felipe does not keep his promise to Ranita. He makes Pepe kiss Ranita. Pepe is rewarded when Ranita turns into a princess and takes him as her husband. Felipe throws a tantrum because Ranita does not choose him. Ranita does not choose Felipe because he only kept his promises when he was forced to do so. I think the fact that he did not keep his final promise is a clue to the play's theme.) **Add this information to your Theme Chart.**

Detail
Ranita tells Felipe a promise is a very serious thing.

↓

Detail
Vieja Sabia turned Ranita into a frog because she was selfish.

↓

Detail
The Viceroy makes Felipe keep his promise to Ranita.

↓

Detail
Ranita does not choose Felipe as her huband because he did not help her.

Develop Comprehension

22 SKILL
THEME

Think about the message the author wants to communicate to readers. What is the theme of *Ranita, The Frog Princess?* (Felipe is punished because he did not keep his promise to Ranita. Pepe is rewarded when Ranita turns into a princess and takes him as her husband. These are clues that the play's theme is about the importance of keeping promises and treating others kindly.) Add this information to complete your Theme Chart.

Detail
Ranita tells Felipe a promise is a very serious thing.

↓

Detail
Vieja Sabia turned Ranita into a frog because she was selfish.

↓

Detail
The Viceroy makes Felipe keep his promise to Ranita.

↓

Detail
Ranita does not choose Felipe as her huband because he did not help her.

↓

Detail
Felipe is rude to Vieja Sabia. She turns him into a frog.

↓

Theme
Keep promises and be kind to others.

358

Listening/Speaking

Have selected students share the plays they create in the Personal Response activities. Assign roles to small groups of students. Remind the readers to speak loudly and clearly, employing eye contact, speaking rate, and the conventions of language to communicate their ideas effectively.

Suggest that the writer both introduce the scene, explaining the setting, and present a conclusion at the end. Discuss whether any language usage in the play reflects the region and/or culture in which the play is set. How would the characters, plot, and dialogue be different if the play took place in your community today?

Epilogue

The same clearing in the forest as in Scene 1

Felipe: *(Kicks a stone)* If they think I'm going to their ridiculous wedding . . . ha! May they have a dozen ugly tadpole children!

(Enter Vieja Sabia.)

Vieja Sabia: *Agua!* Water from the well, my son, before I die of thirst.

Felipe: *(Snarling)* I'm no water boy. I'm the Viceroy's son! Get your own water, you old *cucaracha!*

Vieja Sabia: *(With gentle concern)* Cockroach? It's very rude to speak to your elders that way. Has no one taught you manners?

Felipe: *(Puzzled)* No.

Vieja Sabia: *(Smiling wickedly)* Well *(pointing finger at Felipe)*, that is my **specialty**.

*(**POOF** Felipe the Frog hops onto the top of the well.)*

22

23

Vieja Sabia: *(to audience)* And now you know how the Frog Prince ended up in that well.

359

Develop Comprehension

23 COMPARE AND CONTRAST

Compare what happens to Felipe with what had happened to Ranita. (As with Ranita, Vieja Sabia turns Felipe into a frog because he refuses to get water for her. It is different because he should have learned from Ranita's experience.)

RETURN TO PREDICTIONS AND PURPOSES

Review students' predictions and purposes. Did students predict what the happy ending would be? (Ranita is turned back into a princess and finds a "prince of a husband.")

REVIEW READING STRATEGIES

- **Monitor Comprehension** How did understanding the characters help you identify the play's theme?

- **Monitor and Clarify: Self-Correct** When was using a self-correction technique helpful? Explain.

- **Decoding** What difficult words did you encounter? How did the Reading Multisyllabic Words strategy help you sound out these words?

- **Self-Selected Strategy Use** What strategies did you use to make sense of what you read? When? How were these strategies helpful?

PERSONAL RESPONSE

Have students write a short play or a fairy tale that teaches a lesson. The dialogue should be appropriate to the characters. Invite students to share or perform their writings.

Quick Check

Can students summarize and explain the theme of a story?

During **Small Group Instruction**

If No → **Approaching Level** Reteach the skill and have students apply it to a simpler text. Use Leveled Reader lessons, pp. 367N–367P.

If Yes → **On Level** Have students apply the skill to a new text to consolidate learning. Use Leveled Reader lessons, pp. 367U–367V.

Gifted Talented

Beyond Level Have students apply the skill to a more complex text to extend learning. Use Leveled Reader lessons, pp. 367Y–367Z.

Author and Illustrator

ONCE UPON A TIME ...

Have students read the biographies of the author and the illustrator. Ask:

- Why did Carmen Agra Deedy set her fairy tale in Latin America?

- How would the tale be different if it were set in Norway or Africa?

- How might Renato Alarcão's illustrations look as murals on buildings?

WRITE ABOUT IT

Author's Craft: Structural Elements of a Play Have students reexamine the play elements found on page 359. Then have them write a short scene between two of the play's characters, such as Ranita and Pepe. Remind them to use parentheses when including stage directions.

Author's Purpose

Have students check the play for clues to Carmen Agra Deedy's purpose for writing *Ranita, The Frog Princess* as a play. Most students will conclude that Carmen Agra Deedy wrote to entertain and that the lively scenes are meant to be performed and seen.

Once Upon a Time . . .

Carmen Agra Deedy came to the United States from Cuba in 1960, after a revolution made it dangerous for her family to live there. Hoping for a more peaceful life, Carmen and her family settled in Georgia. Carmen has not forgotten her Cuban heritage. She combines it with the heritage of the southern United States when writing her stories.

Other books by Carmen Agra Deedy

Renato Alarcão was born, raised, and currently lives in Rio de Janeiro, Brazil. Among his many art projects was the creation of 13 murals around Paterson and Passaic, New Jersey, all done with a team of artists and local teens.

✓ Author's Purpose

Why did the author write *Ranita, The Frog Princess* as a play?

LOG ON ▶ **FIND OUT**

Author Carmen Agra Deedy
Illustrator Renato Alarcão
www.macmillanmh.com

360

✎ Author's Craft
Structural Elements of a Play

- A play has features such as characters' names followed by a colon and stage directions in parentheses that tell actors how to act, where to move, and how to say the lines. Bold type sets off the play's title, scenes, characters' names, and acts.

- Example: "**Felipe:** (*Loud and demanding*) Well? Have you found my golden arrow yet?" (page 345) The name tells us that Felipe is speaking; the words in parentheses tell us how to say the line.

- Ask how stage directions help readers "hear and see" the story. For example, "**Pepe:** (*Groggy*) Señor!" (page 355) as well as text that sets the scene: "*Hunting lodge with Viceroy, his wife, noblemen and women, all seated at long banquet table.*" (page 350)

Comprehension Check

Summarize

To summarize *Ranita, The Frog Princess* use the most important details from the play. Information from your Theme Chart may help you.

Detail
↓
Detail
↓
Detail
↓
Theme

Think and Compare

1. Why did Vieja Sabia turn Ranita into a frog? Details

2. Reread the epilogue of the play. What is Vieja Sabia's **specialty**? Make Inferences

3. Why does the Viceroy believe that Felipe should keep the promise he made to Ranita? Monitor Comprehension: Theme

4. What other structural elements of a play besides dialogue does the author use to help tell the story of Ranita? Author's Craft

5. How are the characters and events in "The Frog Prince" and *Ranita, The Frog Princess* similar? Use details from both texts to explain your answer. Reading/Writing Across Texts

361

Make Connections

Text-to-Self Have students respond to the following question to make connections to their own lives. Use the Think Aloud to model a response. *How would you respond to Ranita's offer to Felipe?*

Think Aloud: Let me think how I would feel if Ranita made the same offer to me as Felipe. I think I would respond to her offer by accepting it. I would keep my promise to her because I would feel sorry for her and would want to help.

Text-to-World Have students respond to the following question to make connections to the world. Use the Think Aloud to model a response. *Did Felipe deserve the punishment he received for being selfish?*

Think Aloud: Did Felipe deserve his punishment? I think he did. He only thought about his own wishes and needed to be taught a lesson. It's important for people to be kind to others.

Comprehension Check

SUMMARIZE

Have partners summarize *Ranita, The Frog Princess* in their own words. Remind students to include only the most important events and to use their Theme Charts to help them organize their summaries.

THINK AND COMPARE
Text Evidence

1. **Details** Answer stated in text Ranita was turned into a frog because she refused to give Vieja Sabia a drink. LOCATE

2. **Make Inferences** Answer stated in text Vieja Sabia's specialty is teaching good manners. COMBINE

3. **Monitor Comprehension: Theme** Answer The Viceroy believes it is important to be trustworthy. Evidence He emphasizes that his son should keep promises, even though the Viceroy's wife thinks their son should not have to do so. CONNECT

4. **Author's Craft** Answer The author includes elements such as scenes and stage directions. Evidence Each scene is numbered and has a different setting. The stage directions are in parentheses. ANALYZE

5. **Text-to-Text** The stories have similar characters and are like fairy tales. In "The Frog Prince," the princess and prince become friends. In *Ranita*, Felipe never changes into a nice person. COMPARE TEXTS

Objectives

- Read fluently with appropriate expression
- Rate: 102–122 WCPM

Materials

- Transparency 14
- Practice Book, p. 122
- Fluency Solutions Audio CD

ELL

Develop Comprehension
Discuss what is happening in the scene. Echo-read each character's lines with students, and discuss the character's feelings. Echo-read the lines with students a second time, mimicking your expressions and gestures. Then ask students to describe the main idea of the passage.

Practice Book, page 122

As I read, I will pay attention to expression.

	[*Dean Dragon's kitchen. Matthew is struggling to light a*
9	*fire with a match under a cauldron of stew. Dean Dragon*
20	*steps up and lights it with his dragon breath. Priscilla uses*
31	*a large wooden spoon to stir the stew, while Matthew*
41	*starts chopping carrots.*]
44	**Princess Priscilla:** [*inhaling a spoonful of stew with a*
53	*look of pleasure*] Mmm. That smells good already.
61	**Matthew:** Wait until it's finished. It's delicious.
68	**Dean Dragon:** [*smiling*] My vegetable stew is good, if
77	I do say so myself. It's famous among dragons.
86	**Princess Priscilla:** I can see why. [*She smiles at Dean,*
96	*then goes back to stirring the stew.*] I'd just like to get my
109	hands on that Knight Never-Do-Well. He woke me up in
121	the middle of the night and told me that my family was in
134	danger. So of course I came. Then when we got here, he tied
147	me to the tree, told me not to worry, and said he'd be back to
162	rescue me soon. I'd like to take a can opener to that shiny
175	armor of his. 178

Comprehension Check

1. Do you think Knight Never-Do-Well is a reliable person? **Plot Development** No, because it sounds like he tricked Princess Priscilla.
2. Do these characters enjoy working together? Why? **Plot Development** Yes, the passage describes them working together while talking and smiling.

	Words Read	–	Number of Errors	=	Words Correct Score
First Read		–		=	
Second Read		–		=	

Approaching Reproducible, page 122

Beyond Reproducible, page 122

Fluency

Repeated Reading: Expression

EXPLAIN/MODEL Model reading **Transparency 14** with the proper expression in a way that captures the characters' meaning and emotions. Explain that the words in capital letters mean that what the character is saying is very important and should be read in a strong voice with lots of expression.

> ### Transparency 14
>
> **Viceroy:** *Basta!* Enough! Who *is* this creature?
> **Felipe:** (*Sneering*) She's the nasty little frog who rescued my golden arrow.
> **Ranita:** And in return he promised to let me eat from his *plato*, sleep in his *cama*, and give me a *beso* when the sun came up.
> **Viceroy:** Did you make this promise?
> **Felipe:** (*Sullen*) I don't remember.
> **Viceroy's Wife:** (*Indignant*) Even if he did—he is the Viceroy's son!
> **Viceroy:** (*Grave*) *Sí.* And THE VICEROY'S SON KEEPS HIS PROMISES. Pepe! Set a place for our guest.
> **Felipe:** But, Father—
> **Viceroy's Wife:** Ernesto!
> **Viceroy:** (*Slams fist on table.*) Silencio! Silence!
> (*Ranita hops on table. Felipe is too stunned to speak. Viceroy's wife is glaring.*)
> **Viceroy:** Everyone—and I mean *everyone*—EAT!

Fluency (from *Ranita, The Frog Princess*, page 353)

PRACTICE Have students work in small groups. Assign each member a character's role, and have one student read the sentences in parentheses. Have groups practice reading their dialogue at least three times. Give each group a chance to read the script to the class.

DAILY FLUENCY Students will practice fluency using **Practice Book** page 122 or the **Fluency Solutions Audio CD**. The passage is recorded at a slow practice speed and a faster fluent speed.

Quick Check

Can students read fluently with expression?

During **Small Group Instruction**

If No → **Approaching Level** Use the Fluency lesson and model, p. 367Q.

If Yes → **On Level** See Fluency, p. 367T.

Beyond Level See Fluency, p. 367X.

Comprehension

SPIRAL REVIEW

REVIEW SKILL
DRAW CONCLUSIONS

EXPLAIN/MODEL

▪ Remind students that when they **draw conclusions** about story characters, they use logical reasoning to arrive at a new understanding of the characters' traits, their similarities and differences, and relationships. Students also should examine how the characters interact and change in the course of the story.

▪ To draw conclusions, students should use details from the story along with relevant information from their own experience.

Have students discuss the dialogue in "The Frog Prince." Read aloud the Frog's last speech on page 341. Say: *I understand that the kiss changed the Frog. How did the kiss show that the Princess had changed? Why did they become wonderful friends?* Help students draw the conclusion that the interaction between the Frog and the Princess changed them both for the better.

PARTNERS

PRACTICE/APPLY

Have students work with partners or in cooperative groups to draw conclusions about the characters and their actions in *Ranita, The Frog Princess*. One student should record each pair's or group's responses to these questions.

▪ What conclusions can you draw about Felipe and Pepe from how they treat the frog? (Felipe is nasty to the frog and is not a very nice person. Pepe is kind to the frog and is a nice person.)

▪ What conclusions can you draw about Ranita and Felipe from how they treat Vieja Sabia? (Ranita begins to treat Vieja Sabia with respect. Ranita is someone who learns from her experiences. Felipe remains rude. He does not seem able to learn a lesson.)

▪ Which character in the play do you admire the most? Which character do you admire the least? Why? (Students should support their ideas with evidence from the text and based on their own experiences related to the text.)

Students can also draw conclusions about other characters in "The Frog Prince" and in *Ranita, The Frog Princess*. Have them analyze, for example, the King, the Viceroy, and the Viceroy's wife.

PRACTICE BOOK See **Practice Book** page 123 for Elements of a Play.

Objective

- Draw conclusions about story characters and plot events

Skills Trace

Draw Conclusions	
Introduce	295A–295B
Practice/ Apply	296–319; Practice Book, 102–103
Reteach/ Review	325M–325Z, 477A–477B, 478–497, 503M–503Z; Practice Book, 165–166
Assess	Weekly Tests; Units 3, 4, 6 Tests
Maintain	361B, 745A–745B, 746–769, 773M–773Z, 797B

TEST PREP

Test Practice

Answering Questions

To apply **answering questions strategies** to content-area reading, see pages 109–116 in *Time For Kids*.

Paired Selection

GENRE: Informational Text/Expository

Have students read the bookmark on **Student Book** page 362. Remind them that an expository article or essay

- presents information and facts about a topic
- may include graphic aids such as photos and captions, maps, or charts
- usually begins with an introductory paragraph that explains the main idea of the article or essay

✔ Literary Element: Theme

EXPLAIN Remind students that the theme of a literary text is the lesson or message communicated to readers. Often, the same theme can be found in different texts throughout the world. Details and settings might be different, but the message is the same. The theme of a small but clever character triumphing over someone bigger and stronger occurs in stories all over the world. Similarly, stories from many different times and cultures incorporate the theme that kindness to strangers or to the elderly brings unexpected rewards.

APPLY Ask students to name other common literary themes and to compare how the same theme is treated in different stories. How are the main characters alike and different? To help them get started, students can look back at the table of contents in the **Student Book**. Tell students they will learn more about themes as they read "And Still More Tales."

Language Arts

Genre

Expository texts such as magazine articles give facts and information about a topic. They often include graphic aids, such as maps.

✔ Literary Element

Theme is the main message of a story. Sometimes, the same theme can be found in different texts throughout the world.

And Still More Tales

by Eric Michaels

You are reading a fairy tale or folktale for the first time. Suddenly you think: *This character is familiar! And so is the story!* Don't be surprised. Many tales have different versions. The settings may change, but the characters and the events can be very similar. For example, the fairy tale Cinderella is enjoyed by many different people around the world. Each culture tells the tale in its own way. However, the tales all share the same theme.

362

Comprehension

Literature from Around the World

Explain Tell students that each country and culture has its own tales and legends. Have students brainstorm some legends that are familiar to them.

Discuss Divide students into groups and allow them to choose a legend to research such as the legend of King Arthur or Robin Hood. Remind students that legends can be found all over the world. Legends from England, Australia, Hawaii, and Indonesia are just four examples of research ideas. Have groups research the legend, its origin and cultural aspects, and its message or theme.

Apply After each group's research is complete, have them present their findings to the class. Ask students to identify any recurring themes among the legends that are presented.

Cinderella
A Fairy Tale by the Brothers Grimm

Jacob and Wilhelm Grimm were two storyteller brothers from Germany. Their version of the Cinderella story is familiar to many people. In this tale, Cinderella lives with her wicked stepmother and stepsisters. They make her work very hard and give her nothing but ragged clothes to wear. When the king decides to have a ball, Cinderella cannot go because she does not have a gown.

A bird throws a beautiful dress and a pair of slippers to Cinderella from a special tree. The clothes must be returned by midnight. Cinderella goes to the ball looking like a princess. Of course, the king's son falls in love with her. In her rush to get home, Cinderella loses one of the slippers. The prince finds the slipper and searches for its owner. He tries the slipper on every girl in the kingdom. Finally, he tries it on Cinderella, and the slipper fits! Cinderella and the prince live happily ever after.

EUROPE

Germany

1

ASIA

China

Yeh-Shen
A Cinderella Story from China

Yeh-Shen is often called the Chinese Cinderella and is considered by some to be the earliest version of the story. Yeh-Shen also lives with a mean stepmother who mistreats her. Like Cinderella, Yeh-Shen loses a slipper at a spring festival. This time the king is the one who realizes that Yeh-Shen is the slipper's owner. Yeh-Shen and the king marry and live happily ever after.

2

363

ELL ENGLISH LANGUAGE LEARNERS

Develop Vocabulary Help students understand difficult words by using the illustrations and by asking guided questions. For example, to explain the meaning of *trickster*, use the illustrations on page 364. Point to the rabbit and say: *This rabbit is up to something. Look at his body and face. What do they tell us?* Say: *He looks smart. He also looks like he is going to trick someone. A trickster is someone smart who tricks others.* Then have students tell you what a trickster is. Elicit examples to support students' responses.

Paired Selection

Read "And Still More Tales"

As they read, remind students to apply what they have learned about reading expository articles and about themes. Also have students set their own purposes for reading.

1 LITERARY ELEMENT: THEME

From what country is the most familiar version of Cinderella? (Germany) How does retelling the familiar tale set the stage for less familiar versions? (By restating the familiar Cinderella, the author gives the reader something to recall. Then the reader can compare and contrast the familiar story with the less familiar versions.)

2 DRAW CONCLUSIONS

SPIRAL REVIEW

What conclusions can you draw about Cinderella and Yeh-Shen's personalities? (They are both patient and sad.) How can you tell? (They both live with mean families and have no way out. They put up with abuse so they must be patient, and since their lives are difficult, they are probably sad.)

Use the Interactive Question-Response Guide in the **ELL Resource Book**, pages 154–155, to help students gain access to the paired selection content.

Paired Selection

3 LITERARY ELEMENT: THEME

How is "The Rough-Face Girl" similar to the other Cinderella tales? ("The Rough-Face Girl" has similarities to Cinderella tales in that a gentle girl is mistreated by her sisters, but her goodness is rewarded when she is rescued by and marries a powerful male figure.)

4 DRAW CONCLUSIONS

Tricksters are smart and quick, but they are not usually the kindest of characters. What conclusions can you draw about why they remain among the most popular throughout the world? (Trickster characters tend to be very clever and thus can outwit much bigger creatures. They may be popular because people like underdogs who are not expected to prevail.)

5 TEXT FEATURES: MAPS

Look at the map on page 365. What do the animals represent? (The animals represent popular trickster characters from the specific regions on the map to which they are connected. For example, the rabbit is a trickster common in the folklore of the American South.)

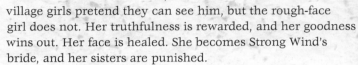

The Rough-Face Girl
A Native American Tale from Canada

The Native American culture also has a Cinderella tale. In this Algonquin tale, a beautiful, gentle girl is mistreated by her sisters. They are jealous of her and scar her face to make it rough. A warrior named Strong Wind, who has the power to make himself invisible, says he will marry the first girl who can see him. Of course, this is a test. The village girls pretend they can see him, but the rough-face girl does not. Her truthfulness is rewarded, and her goodness wins out. Her face is healed. She becomes Strong Wind's **3** bride, and her sisters are punished.

Trickster Tales

Like "Cinderella," versions of trickster tales are told around the world. In a trickster tale, the main character is a clever animal. Each culture has a favorite trickster.

All tricksters share common traits. They are smart and quick. They can outwit everyone, even those who are bigger, stronger, and more powerful. Once you read a few trickster tales, you'll understand why these clever characters are favorites around the world.

Brer Rabbit appears in many folktales from the American South. He is smart and always gets the best of others.

Coyote appears in tales from Mexico and the American Southwest. You can count on Coyote to be cunning and smart.

In parts of Africa, many people say that all stories belong to Anansi, the spider. Anansi uses his wits to capture the other animals, so that he can own all of the stories. How does Anansi accomplish this? He is a trickster!

364

ON YOUR OWN | **Practice Book,** page 124

A **theme** is the lesson or message of a work of fiction. To identify the theme, look for clues in what the characters say and do, what happens because of their actions, and how the characters change.

Read the passage. As you read, think about the theme. Then answer the questions.

Once upon a time there was a man who had three daughters. The older daughters were very vain and selfish. The youngest, Cinderella, was a kind girl who loved animals. The father was going on a trip and said to his daughters, "What would you like me to bring you when I return?" The oldest demanded a fancy dress, the other, a fine hat. Cinderella said, "A little bird, please." Her sisters thought it was a silly request, but her father did as she asked and brought her a bird.

Later, the family was invited to a ball at the king's court. "Cinderella!" her oldest sister said. "If you had asked for a dress, you could have come to the ball with us. You are so foolish!" When everyone had left, Cinderella's bird helped to make her beautiful. He gave her a flowing green dress, and so many diamonds that it blinded you to look at her. She went to the ball, and as soon as she entered the castle the king asked her to dance. They danced all night long, until the ball was almost over. "I need to get back home before my family notices I'm gone!" Cinderella cried. In her hurry to get home, one of her slippers fell off outside the castle.

When she got home, Cinderella asked the bird to make her ugly again, but he would not obey. Just then there was a knock on the door. It was the king, and he was holding Cinderella's slipper. "It is you!" he cried. Cinderella's family came home just in time to see the king place the slipper on Cinderella's foot. Their mouths fell open in surprise, and they opened even wider when the king asked Cinderella to be his wife.

1. What is a possible theme for this story? good things can happen to good people

2. On the lines below, list two story events that support that theme. Cinderella was kind; the king asked her to marry him.

Approaching Reproducible, page 124
Beyond Reproducible, page 124

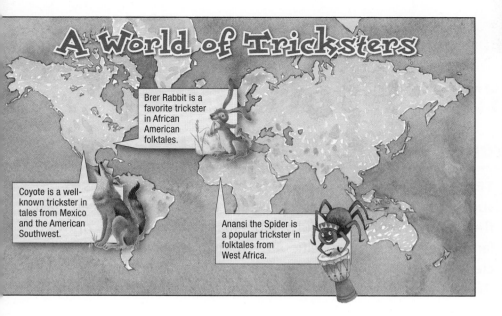

A World of Tricksters

Brer Rabbit is a favorite trickster in African American folktales.

Coyote is a well-known trickster in tales from Mexico and the American Southwest.

Anansi the Spider is a popular trickster in folktales from West Africa.

Connect and Compare

1. What theme do all three Cinderella tales share? **Theme**

2. Use the map to identify the cultures that have trickster tales. Use details from the article to explain what common traits characters in trickster tales share. **Apply**

3. Think about the Cinderella tales in this article and *Ranita, The Frog Princess*. How are they alike? How are they different? **Reading/Writing Across Texts**

4. Read two trickster tales such as an Anansi tale and a Coyote tale. Use a Venn diagram to compare the adventures of the characters in the two tales. **Apply**

365

Connect to Content

MEXICAN-AMERICAN CULTURE

Remind students that Coyote appears in tales from Mexico and those from the American Southwest, including Texas. Many people came to what is today Texas from Mexico and settled there and elsewhere in the Southwest. In doing so, they changed the region's culture.

Have student groups research where those early settlements were located and when they flourished. Make sure students consult maps and time lines.

Have students present their information in oral reports with visuals such as maps and time lines. They should focus on how Mexican culture influenced American culture over time.

Paired Selection

Connect and Compare

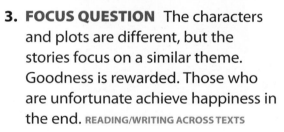

1. They share the theme that goodness and selflessness will be rewarded. **THEME**

2. Trickster tales exist in the cultures of Mexico, the American South and Southwest, and West Africa. Tricksters are usually small, weak, and smart. Anansi the Spider and Brer Rabbit are two good examples because they seem so small and powerless, yet they end up prevailing over more powerful creatures. **APPLY**

3. **FOCUS QUESTION** The characters and plots are different, but the stories focus on a similar theme. Goodness is rewarded. Those who are unfortunate achieve happiness in the end. **READING/WRITING ACROSS TEXTS**

4. Direct students to create a Venn Diagram with two circles that overlap in the center. Tell students to write the ways the characters' adventures are similar in the center of the Venn Diagram. **APPLY**

Write

WHOLE GROUP

✦ **WRITING WORKSHOP**
- Developing Persuasive Writing
- Trait: Word Choice
- Descriptive Language

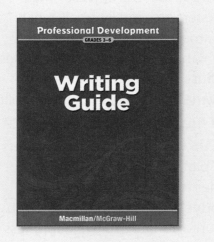

Trait: Word Choice

Strong Sentences: Descriptive Language

TEACH/MODEL Remind students that writers give reasons to support their opinions or positions. Tell them that writers can make their reasons more powerful and persuasive by using descriptive language and strong, specific verbs to make their ideas and feelings clear. This language helps readers picture the ideas and experience the writer's feelings. Explain that readers that engage this way are more likely to agree with the writer's opinion.

Point out that choosing precise, vivid language can help writers build **strong sentences** that explain their ideas and feelings. Write the sentence in the box below on the board.

> The Rock-Your-Socks-Off roller coaster is a fun ride.

Ask students if this sentence helps them picture the roller coaster and why it is fun. Then write the sentence below on the board.

> The Rock-Your-Socks-Off roller coaster is a breathtaking thrill ride with steep drops and sharp turns.

Discuss with students how the addition of strong descriptive words and phrases such as *breathtaking thrill ride, steep drops*, and *sharp turns* helps readers better imagine why the writer thinks the ride is fun.

Teacher Write Aloud

PRACTICE/APPLY Further explore with students the use of descriptive language to support opinions. Write the sentences below on the board. Then complete the Teacher Think Aloud.

- Lisa is a good student.
- The muffin was good.
- The movie was bad.

Teacher Think Aloud These sentences are not very descriptive. I don't know what makes Lisa a good student. I don't know why the muffin was good or why the movie was bad. To make these ideas clear, we need to add descriptive words and phrases. Let's think about what makes someone a good student: they do their homework carefully, they work hard, and they often get good grades. Now let's use one of these details to change the word *good* to a more descriptive word: *Lisa is a careful student.*

Work with students to add descriptive language to the remaining sentences. Invite suggestions for descriptions of a good muffin. Discuss ways people behave when a movie is bad. Remind students to think of vivid words and phrases that will create pictures in readers' minds. Add appropriate words one at a time to the sentence. Stop after each sentence to emphasize the added detail.

> The muffin was warm, soft, and sweet.
> The movie was so boring that the audience fell asleep.

Draft Display the Writing Prompt on **Writing Transparency 45**. Tell students to include descriptive words and phrases that will help readers picture their ideas and understand their feelings. Circulate and provide Over-the-Shoulder Conferences as students work.

Objective
- Write strong sentences with descriptive language

Materials
- Writer's Notebooks
- Writing Transparency 45

Daily Journal Prompts

Focus on Descriptive Language

Use these and other prompts for independent daily journal writing.

- Write about a person you think is a good friend.
- Write about a food you think everyone should try.
- Write about an activity you like to do.
- Write about your favorite place to spend time with your friends.

Transparency 45

Think about a place you have visited that you would recommend others to visit. Explain why you recommend that place, using descriptive language to make your position clear.

Writing Transparency

Reading and Writing Connections

✓ Trait: Word Choice

DESCRIPTIVE LANGUAGE

Remind students that using descriptive language is one way to make their ideas and feelings clear to readers. Description helps readers picture the writer's ideas and understand the writer's feelings. Choosing strong verbs and precise adjectives can help writers build strong sentences that express their ideas in a powerful way.

Read the Passage

Use the example from *Ranita, The Frog Princess* to show the author's skilled use of descriptive language.

- Have students read the bookmark. Explain that descriptive language includes words and phrases that help readers clearly picture the writer's ideas.

- **Ask:** *When have you lost something important to you?*

- Then have students chorally read the excerpt from *Ranita, The Frog Princess*. Direct their attention to the callout. Have students identify details the writer uses to show Ranita's feelings when Felipe breaks his promise and runs off.

- **Ask:** *How would you feel if someone broke a promise to you?*

Writing

✓ **Trait: Word Choice**
Good writers use **descriptive language** to make their ideas clear for readers.

Reading and Writing Connection

Read the passage below. Notice how the author Carmen Agra Deedy uses stage directions to add descriptive detail.

> *An excerpt from*
> *Ranita, The Frog Princess*

A play is told through dialogue, the lines characters say to each other. In a play the author adds descriptive detail using stage directions. The stage directions give details about how the characters act and feel.

Ranita: No promise, no golden arrow.

Felipe: (*Crossing his fingers behind his back*) I promise.

(*Ranita fetches the arrow. Felipe bows and runs off.*)

Ranita: *Espera*! Wait! I can't hop that fast! (*Hangs her head and begins to cry*) He's gone. Now I'll never break this evil spell.

366

Respond to the Selection

Have students write a response to the selection.

☑ **Engagement** Help students deepen their connection to the text and discover their own perspective on it. *Focus on a moment when you made a promise to someone.*

☑ **Response** Help students explore more deeply their reactions to particular passages in the reading. *Focus on one part of the story where you understood how Felipe feels. Use text evidence in your writing.*

☑ **Literary Analysis** Help students deepen their connection to the text and discover their own perspective on it. *Focus on a place in the play when the author uses details to describe Ranita and Felipe that helped you imagine them. Use text evidence in your writing.*

Read and Find

Read John's writing below. What descriptive details does he include to make his opinion clear for readers? Use the checklist below to help you.

Lunch Disaster

by John P.

Dropping a lunch tray in front of everyone is really embarrassing! My lunch tray hit the tile floor with a loud clatter. Everyone started clapping, as I stood in a puddle of warm spaghetti sauce and noodles. My sneakers felt damp from the splatters of oily red sauce on them.

Read about John's lunch disaster.

Writer's Checklist

☑ What is the writer's feeling or opinion?

☑ What **descriptive details** does he use?

☑ What words appeal to a sense of touch?

367

Read the Student Model

Have students chorally read the student model at the top of **Student Book** page 367. Discuss this student writer's use of descriptive language to make his opinion clear to readers. Use the Writer's Checklist.

Journal Prompt

Draft Write the following prompt on the board. Have students write a response to the prompt.

> Tell about a moment when you asked someone to help you find something important that you had lost.

Tell students that you will be reading and commenting on their writing during Writing Conference time.

Model how to use the Writer's Checklist so students can write and revise their work. Then ask:

- *What is the moment you chose?*
- *Will readers be able to clearly picture that moment? Will they be able to understand how you felt? If not, what descriptive details could you add?*

ELL ENGLISH LANGUAGE LEARNERS

Beginning	Intermediate	Advanced
Write Sentences Provide model sentences based on the Journal Prompt: *When I lost ____ I felt ____. I asked ____ to help me find it. I said ____.* Circle words that are not strong and guide students to replace them with more descriptive ones.	**Describe** Ask students to write three sentences based on the Journal Prompt. Tell students to try to picture in their heads the object they lost. Then have them use words and phrases to describe it. Provide a model if necessary.	**Narrate** Ask students to respond to the Journal Prompt. Have them use descriptive language to tell how they felt in that moment.

Write

Objectives

- Write using descriptive language
- Write strong sentences

Materials

- Writer's Notebooks
- Teacher's Resource Book, p. 191

Minilessons

Minilesson 1 Word Choice/Descriptive Language

TEACH/MODEL

Remind students that they have been working hard on using descriptive language to explain their ideas and feelings. Today they will use descriptive details as support for their opinions. Write the examples below on the board and model.

> The park is fun. There is a lot to do there.
>
> The park is fun. You can swing really, really high on the swing sets.

Point out that both examples state an opinion, but the second example has a stronger reason than the first because it describes an activity that people do at the park. Then have students use **Teacher's Resource Book** page 191. Ask them to read the sentences silently.

PRACTICE/APPLY

Have students work independently to add descriptive details. When complete, ask students to share their work during Sharing Circle.

Minilesson 2 Sentence Fluency/Sentence Variety

TEACH/MODEL

Tell students that writers use different sentence lengths and types to make their writing more interesting and to communicate their ideas. Writers use questions to engage readers, exclamations to emphasize information, commands to tell readers what to do, and statements to give information. Write the example below on the board.

> You might like soccer. It is fun to kick and run. It is fun to play on a team with your friends. You can sign up to join my team if you want to. The sign-up ends tomorrow, so you should hurry.

Read it aloud. Then rewrite the first two sentences: *Do you like to kick and run? Soccer might be the sport for you!* Read them aloud. Discuss how varying sentence type made the writing more interesting.

PRACTICE/APPLY

In their Writer's Notebooks, have students rewrite the rest of the paragraph, varying sentence length and type. Remind students that they can combine simple sentences to make ideas flow smoothly, or use simple sentences to give emphasis.

Conferencing Routine

Dynamic Feedback System

Step 1 Read and appreciate the writing.

Step 2 Notice how the student uses the targeted skill (for example, descriptive language: Ask: *How did the writer show his or her ideas and feelings?*).

Step 3 Write comments that show how the writing has an impact on you. Direct your comments to those places in the piece where the student has used the targeted skill.

Step 4 Meet with each student and give him or her a revision assignment.

Write Effective Comments

Word Choice At least one of your comments should highlight the student's use of **descriptive language**. Here are some sample comments.

- This detail helps me understand why you feel that way.

- This sounds like a good reason, but can you tell me more about it?

- The word "good" tells me you like this, but can you choose a stronger, more specific word?

Revision Assignments

Word Choice Here are some examples of effective revision assignments for descriptive language.

- **Revise** — **Reread your entry.** *Choose one detail in your writing. Now add rewrite the detail adding descriptive words and phrases.*

- **Revise** — **[Underline a section.]** Mark a specific section of a student's writing and then ask the student to revise it in a specific way.

- **Revise** — **[Underline a section.]** *Read the part that I underlined. Now add two or three sentences with descriptive language that makes your feelings clear.*

Teacher-to-Teacher

Over-the-Shoulder Conferences

Use these quick, focused opportunities to comment while students are writing.

- **Step 1** Quietly move close enough to a student that you can read the journal entry he or she is writing.

- **Step 2** Read part of what you see. You don't need to start from the beginning or read the entire piece.

- **Step 3** Show the student a spot in the writing where he or she is using a particular skill or describing something that piques your interest.

- **Step 4** Whisper a sentence or two about why you noticed that spot in the writing, and ask a question that will nudge the student to add descriptive language.

- **Step 5** Move on to the next student. Select students strategically. You should see 12–15 students in a 15-minute period.

Research Proven Writing Approach

The Writers' Express
Immediate Impact. Lasting Transformation.   wex.org

Connect
Language Arts

✦ **VOCABULARY**
- Tested Words

✦ **SPELLING**
- Plurals

✦ **GRAMMAR**
- Linking Verbs

SMALL GROUP

- Differentiated Instruction, pp. 367I–367HH

Practice Book, page 125

Analogies compare two pairs of words usually using **Synonyms** or **Antonyms**. For example, cranky is to mad as thin is to slim is an analogy using synonyms. Big is to little as short is to tall is an analogy using antonyms.

Read each analogy. Fill in the blank using a synonym or antonym.

1. *Truth* is to _____lie_____ as *hot* is to *cold*.
2. *Good* is to *bad* as *morning* is to _____night_____.
3. *Careful* is to _____careless_____ as *up* is to *down*.
4. *Load* is to *fill* as *hit* is to _____strike_____.
5. _____Lost_____ is to *found* as *happy* is to *sad*.
6. *Skip* is to *jump* as *speak* is to _____talk_____.

Approaching Reproducible, page 125
Beyond Reproducible, page 125

Build Robust Vocabulary

Day 1 — Teach/Practice

CONNECT TO WORDS

- Practice this week's vocabulary words using the following prompts:

  1. Would you be more inclined to help someone who was *selfish* or *generous*? Why?

  2. When might you feel *cranky*?

  3. What actions might cause a *commotion*?

  4. Which situation would leave you *exasperated*—waiting on line for hours or watching a movie at home? Why?

  5. Which item is NOT a chef's *specialty*—stoves, desserts, or vegetables? Why?

  6. How is being *famished* different from being hungry?

ACADEMIC VOCABULARY

- Review the important academic vocabulary words for the week. These words include: *monitor comprehension, theme, analogies, synonyms, antonyms.*

- Write each word on the board. Define each using student-friendly language, and ask students to select the word you are defining. Then point to words in random order for students to define.

Day 2 — Review

CONNECT TO WORDS

- Review the definitions of this week's vocabulary words using **Student Book** pages 340–341. Then discuss each word using the following prompts:

  1. What is *selfish* about someone talking about himself all the time?

  2. Would a *cranky* person be fun to travel with?

  3. Would a *commotion* in the classroom be good? Why?

  4. Did you ever feel *exasperated* while studying? When?

  5. Why might we like *specialty* items better than ones that are sold or served everywhere?

  6. Would you more likely be *famished* after taking a long hike or after watching TV?

ANALOGIES

- Remind students that an antonym is a word that means the opposite of another word. For example, *heavy* and *light* are antonyms. Synonyms, such as *heavy* and *weighty,* are words with the same meaning.

- Point out that analogies compare two pairs of words. Analogies often include antonyms or synonyms.

-  Display **Transparency 27**. Read the first analogy. Model how to use a thesaurus to complete it.

- Have students complete the remaining analogies by filling in the blank word in each pair with a synonym or antonym as needed.

Day 3 **Reinforce**

CONNECT TO WORDS

- Ask students to create Word Squares for each word in their Writer's Notebooks.

- In the first square, students write the word. (Example: *selfish*)

- In the second square, students write their own definition of the word and any related words, such as synonyms. (Example: *greedy, self-involved, uncaring about others*)

- In the third square, students draw a simple illustration that will help them remember the word. (Example: a drawing of a person not sharing food while others look hungry)

- In the fourth square, students write nonexamples, including antonyms for the word. (Example: *selfless, giving, generous*)

RELATED WORDS

- Help students generate words related to *famished*.

- Explain that *famished* comes from the Latin *fames*, meaning "hunger." The word *famine* comes from the same root and means "extreme hunger throughout a region."

- Draw a T-chart with columns for synonyms and antonyms. Ask students to use a print or digital thesaurus to find synonyms and antonyms for *famished*. (*ravenous, starving, empty; sated, full, gorged*)

- Help students use the synonyms and antonyms in analogies.

 **Day 4** **Extend**

CONNECT TO WORDS

- Review this week's vocabulary using the following sentence stems. Have students orally complete each one.

1. The selfish boy never gave _____ to _____.

2. The _____ was always cranky because _____.

3. They caused a huge commotion when _____.

4. You would feel exasperated if you had to wait for _____.

5. The chef's specialty was _____, not _____.

6. We felt famished after _____.

MORPHOLOGY

- Tell students that learning about Latin roots can help raise their word consciousness. Use the additional selection vocabulary word *cultures* as a springboard for students to learn other words.

- Write *cultures* on the board. Explain that the word comes from the Latin *cultura*, meaning "the tilling of the land." Over time, *culture* came to mean the tilling of the mind through education and the arts.

- Write the words *cultivate, cultural,* and *culture* on the board. Explain that these words all come from the Latin *cultura*. They are related to tilling, or growing, as in *cultivate* crops, a *cultural* experience, and a throat *culture*.

Day 5 **Assess and Reteach**

POSTTEST

- Display **Transparency 28**. Have students complete the cloze sentences using one of this week's vocabulary words.

- Note how quickly and accurately students can complete this task. Work with students who make errors or require too much time to complete this task during Small Group time.

CONNECT TO WRITING

- Have students write sentences in their Writer's Notebooks using this week's vocabulary. Tell students to write sentences that provide information they learned from this week's readings.

- **ELL** Provide the Day 4 sentence stems for students needing extra support.

5-Day Spelling

Go to pages T14–T15 for **Differentiated Spelling Lists**.

✓ Plurals

Spelling Words

clams	glasses	ranches
mints	hobbies	patches
props	engines	mistakes
arches	couches	supplies
dresses	arrows	mosses
parents	enemies	armies
caves	babies	

Review circus, germs, spice
Challenge batteries, compasses

Dictation Sentences

1. <u>Clams</u> live in the mud.
2. <u>Mints</u> have a refreshing taste!
3. Jenna made <u>props</u> for the play.
4. She painted the stone <u>arches</u>.
5. The actresses wore <u>dresses</u>.
6. Your <u>parents</u> will love the play!
7. Spelunkers explore <u>caves</u>.
8. Have you seen my <u>glasses</u>?
9. One of her <u>hobbies</u> is knitting.
10. The drivers started their <u>engines</u>.
11. Sit on one of the <u>couches</u>.
12. Green <u>arrows</u> pointed us home.
13. We were friends, not <u>enemies</u>.
14. There were six <u>babies</u> in the nursery.
15. Zack visited two <u>ranches</u>.
16. Kate sewed <u>patches</u> on her jeans.
17. Julio made no <u>mistakes</u> on his test.
18. We bought <u>supplies</u> for our trip.
19. Some <u>mosses</u> look like tiny trees.
20. Where did the <u>armies</u> fight?

Review/Challenge Words

1. Clowns are my favorite <u>circus</u> act.
2. Which <u>germs</u> cause measles?
3. Cinnamon is a popular <u>spice</u>.
4. My flashlight needs new <u>batteries</u>.
5. The hikers brought <u>compasses</u>.

Day 1 Pretest

ASSESS PRIOR KNOWLEDGE

- Model for students how to spell the plural form of the word *baby*. Segment the word syllable-by-syllable, then determine that the *y* is preceded by a consonant and therefore must be changed to *i*. Then, *es* must be added to form the word *babies*.

- Use the Dictation Sentences. Say the underlined word, read the sentence, and repeat the word. Have students write the words.

- Have students self-correct their tests. Point out that words ending in *y* will take the plural ending *-ies*.

- Have students cut apart the **Spelling Word Cards BLM** on **Teacher's Resource Book** page 57 and figure out a way to sort them. Have them save the cards for use throughout the week.

Day 2 Word Sorts

SPIRAL REVIEW

Review soft *c* and soft *g* sounds in the words *circus, mice, cycle, spice, charge, germs, sage,* and *digit*. Have students find words in this week's readings with the same sounds.

WORD SORTS

- Have students take turns sorting spelling word cards and explaining how they sorted them. When students have finished the sort, discuss any words that students found challenging to pluralize.

- Review the spelling words, pointing out the plural endings. Use the cards on the Spelling Word Cards BLM. Write the key words *props, arches,* and *hobbies.* on the board. Model how to sort the words by plural ending. Place one card beneath the correct key words.

ON YOUR OWN — Phonics/Spelling, pages 79–80

Fold back the paper along the dotted line. Use the blanks to write each word as it is read aloud. When you finish the test, unfold the paper. Use the list at the right to correct any spelling mistakes.

1.	1. clams
2.	2. mints
3.	3. props
4.	4. arches
5.	5. dresses
6.	6. parents
7.	7. caves
8.	8. glasses
9.	9. hobbies
10.	10. engines
11.	11. couches
12.	12. arrows
13.	13. enemies
14.	14. babies
15.	15. ranches
16.	16. patches
17.	17. mistakes
18.	18. supplies
19.	19. mosses
20.	20. armies
Review Words 21.	21. circus
22.	22. germs
23.	23. spice
Challenge Words 24.	24. batteries
25.	25. compasses

HOMEWORK — Phonics/Spelling, page 81

mosses	supplies	dresses	hobbies	parents
arches	caves	engines	enemies	patches
babies	clams	glasses	mistakes	mints
armies	arrows	couches	props	ranches

Pattern Power
Write the spelling words with these spelling patterns.

words with -s
1. caves
2. clams
3. arrows
4. engines
5. mistakes
6. props
7. parents
8. mints

words with -es
9. mosses
10. arches
11. dresses
12. glasses
13. couches
14. patches
15. ranches

words with -ies
16. babies
17. armies
18. supplies
19. hobbies
20. enemies

ANALOGIES

Remind students that analogies show relationships between two pairs of words. Read the analogies below. Ask students to complete each analogy with a spelling word. Point out the analogies use synonyms, antonyms, and examples

1. Infants are to _____ as grown-ups are to adults. (*babies*)

2. Friends are to _____ as high is to low. (*enemies*)

3. Candy is to _____ as fruit is to apples. (*mints*)

4. Errors are to _____ as pants are to trousers. (*mistakes*)

Have partners write sentences for each spelling word, leaving blank spaces where the words should go. They can exchange papers and fill in the blanks.

PROOFREAD AND WRITE

Write these sentences on the board. Have students circle and correct each misspelled word.

1. She sewed colorful patchs on the dreses. (*patches, dresses*)

2. The parentes of the twin babys looked very tired. (*parents, babies*)

3. We found ten new types of moss's in the cavees. (*mosses, caves*)

4. Without my glases, I make many mistakies. (*glasses, mistakes*)

Error Correction Reinforce that the first step in forming a plural word is to look at the last letter of its singular spelling. Then the rules for forming a plural word can be applied.

POSTTEST

Use the Dictation Sentences on page 367E for the Posttest.

If students have difficulty with any words in the lesson, have them place the words on a list called *Spelling Words I Want to Remember* in their Writer's Notebooks. Look for students' use of these words in their writings. Challenge students to find words for each plural ending and add them to their Writer's Notebooks.

EXTEND

Point out that plurals for words that end in *f* or *fe* are often irregular. Contrast these word pairs: *chief/chiefs* and *thief/thieves; safe/safes* and *wife/wives; waif/waifs* and *leaf/leaves*. Also review other irregular plural nouns, such as *men, feet,* and *children*. Encourage students to memorize the spelling of plurals they find difficult.

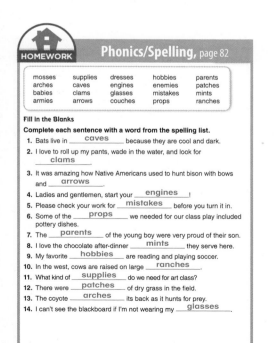

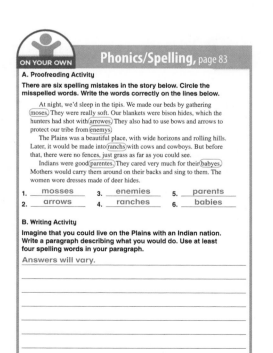

Look at the words in each set below. One word in each set is spelled correctly. Use a pencil to fill in the circle next to the correct word. Before you begin, look at the sample set of words. Sample A has been done for you. Do Sample B by yourself. When you are sure you know what to do, you may go on with the rest of the page.

Sample A:
- Ⓐ yeers
- Ⓑ yeres
- Ⓒ yeares
- Ⓓ years ●

Sample B:
- Ⓔ sitties
- Ⓕ cities
- Ⓖ citys
- Ⓗ sitys

1. Ⓐ mossus Ⓑ mossis Ⓒ mosses Ⓓ mosss
2. Ⓔ archis Ⓕ arches Ⓖ archs Ⓗ arshes
3. Ⓐ babies Ⓑ babyes Ⓒ babys Ⓓ baibies
4. Ⓔ armies Ⓕ armees Ⓖ armys Ⓗ armeez
5. Ⓐ supplies Ⓑ supplyes Ⓒ supplys Ⓓ supplis
6. Ⓔ cavees Ⓕ cavvies Ⓖ kaves Ⓗ caves
7. Ⓐ clames Ⓑ klams Ⓒ clams Ⓓ klames
8. Ⓔ airoes Ⓕ arrows Ⓖ arrowes Ⓗ airos
9. Ⓐ dresss Ⓑ dresses Ⓒ dressus Ⓓ dressis
10. Ⓔ injins Ⓕ engines Ⓖ enjins Ⓗ ingines
11. Ⓐ glassus Ⓑ glasss Ⓒ glassis Ⓓ glasses
12. Ⓔ couchs Ⓕ kowches Ⓖ cowches Ⓗ couches
13. Ⓐ hobbys Ⓑ hobbyes Ⓒ hobbies Ⓓ hobbis
14. Ⓔ enemees Ⓕ enemies Ⓖ inemies Ⓗ enemys
15. Ⓐ mistakees Ⓑ mistakes Ⓒ mistackes Ⓓ misstakes
16. Ⓔ props Ⓕ propse Ⓖ propes Ⓗ propps
17. Ⓐ parents Ⓑ pairents Ⓒ parentes Ⓓ parinse
18. Ⓔ patchs Ⓕ paches Ⓖ pachs Ⓗ patches
19. Ⓐ mintz Ⓑ mintes Ⓒ mints Ⓓ ments
20. Ⓔ ranchs Ⓕ ranches Ⓖ ranshs Ⓗ ranches

Linking Verbs

Daily Language Activities

Write the sentences on the board.

DAY 1
I am reading a book called "My New School." It tell about a students experiences at a new school. (1: My New School; 2: tells; 3: student's)

DAY 2
We went to the Pawnee Indian Village museum. It is in kansas. We likes museums. (1: Museum; 2: Kansas; 3: like)

DAY 3
This book are interesting. The details seems true. I finish it later tonight. (1: book is; 2: seem; 3: will finish)

DAY 4
It becamed late, so we waited on the curb for the bus. What time are our parentes picking us up? Marsha asked. (1: became; 2: "What; 3: parents; 4: up?")

DAY 5
My favorite mintes are green. They selled candy in the gift shop. What did you by. (1: mints; 2: sold; 3: buy?)

Day 1 Introduce the Concept

INTRODUCE LINKING VERBS

- A **linking verb** links, or connects, the subject of a sentence to a noun, a pronoun, or an adjective that describes the subject: *The chief is wise.*

- A linking verb does not show action.

- Linking verbs are most often forms of *be (is, am, are, was, were).*

- Other linking verbs include such words as *look, seem, appear, become, feel, grow, smell,* and *taste: The horse looked* strong.

Use the **Teach/Model/Apply** routine and the English Language Learner supports on the transparency to provide additional instruction and guided practice.

Day 2 Teach the Concept

REVIEW LINKING VERBS

Review linking verbs with students by using yesterday's **Grammar Book** page, page 66. Have them describe how linking verbs differ from action verbs or helping verbs.

INTRODUCE TENSE AND AGREEMENT OF LINKING VERBS

- The form of a present-tense linking verb changes to agree with the subject of the sentence or clause.

- The form of *be* changes to agree with the subject of the sentence or clause both in the present tense and the past tense. Forms of *be* include *am, is, are, was,* and *were*: I *am* amazed. You *are* honest. They *were* cold.

See Grammar Transparency 66 for modeling and guided practice.

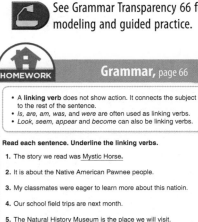

HOMEWORK   **Grammar,** page 66

- A **linking verb** does not show action. It connects the subject to the rest of the sentence.
- *Is, are, am, was,* and *were* are often used as linking verbs.
- *Look, seem, appear* and *become* can also be linking verbs.

Read each sentence. Underline the linking verbs.

1. The story we read was Mystic Horse.

2. It is about the Native American Pawnee people.

3. My classmates were eager to learn more about this natioin.

4. Our school field trips are next month.

5. The Natural History Museum is the place we will visit.

6. The museum's exhibit on the Plains Native Americans is wonderful.

7. I am Native American on my mother's side of the family.

8. The stories are unusual, but exciting.

See Grammar Transparency 67 for modeling and guided practice.

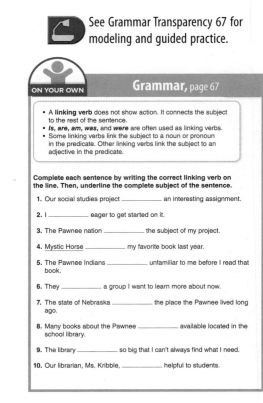

ON YOUR OWN   **Grammar,** page 67

- A **linking verb** does not show action. It connects the subject to the rest of the sentence.
- *Is, are, am, was,* and *were* are often used as linking verbs.
- Some linking verbs link the subject to a noun or pronoun in the predicate. Other linking verbs link the subject to an adjective in the predicate.

Complete each sentence by writing the correct linking verb on the line. Then, underline the complete subject of the sentence.

1. Our social studies project _____ an interesting assignment.

2. I _____ eager to get started on it.

3. The Pawnee nation _____ the subject of my project.

4. Mystic Horse _____ my favorite book last year.

5. The Pawnee Indians _____ unfamiliar to me before I read that book.

6. They _____ a group I want to learn more about now.

7. The state of Nebraska _____ the place the Pawnee lived long ago.

8. Many books about the Pawnee _____ available located in the school library.

9. The library _____ so big that I can't always find what I need.

10. Our librarian, Ms. Kribble, _____ helpful to students.

Day 3 | **Review and Practice**

REVIEW TENSE AND AGREEMENT OF LINKING VERBS

Review how to identify linking verbs and their verb tenses.

MECHANICS AND USAGE: AGREEMENT OF SUBJECT AND LINKING VERB

- The present forms of *be* are *am, is,* and *are:* I *am* in the fourth grade.

- The past-tense forms of *be* are *was* and *were:* Last year, I *was* in the third grade.

- The future tense of *be* is *will be:* Next year, I *will be* in the fifth grade.

- Use *am, was,* or *will be* with *I.*

- Use *is, was,* or *will be* with *he, she, it,* or singular subjects.

- Use *are, were,* or *will be* with *you, we, they,* or plural subjects.

 Day 4 | **Review and Proofread**

REVIEW LINKING VERBS

Review what a linking verb does. Have students explain how the verb *be* changes to show past and future tense and how it agrees with its subject.

PROOFREAD

Have students correct the errors in the following sentences.

1. The clock hands was on the one and nine when she called. (hands were)

2. The cake look like it is vanilla under the frosting. (cake looks)

3. Everyone feel the winter weather when they walked outside. (Everyone felt)

4. You is coming to the theater in our car. (You are)

Day 5 | **Assess and Reteach**

ASSESS

Use the Daily Language Activity and **Grammar Practice Book** page 70 for assessment.

RETEACH

Use Grammar Practice Book page 70 and selected pages from the **Grammar and Writing Handbook** for additional reteaching. Remind students that it is important to use verbs correctly as they speak and write.

Check students' writing for use of the skill and listen for it in their speaking. Assign Grammar Revision Assignments in their Writer's Notebooks, as needed.

 See Grammar Transparency 68 for modeling and guided practice.

See Grammar Transparency 69 for modeling and guided practice.

See Grammar Transparency 70 for modeling and guided practice.

HOMEWORK | **Grammar,** page 68

- Use *am* or *was* with *I.* Use *am* in the present tense. Use *was* in the past tense.
- Use *is* or *was* with **singular subjects** or with *he, she,* or *it.* Use *is* in the present tense. Use *was* in the past tense.
- Use *are* or *were* with **plural subjects** or with *you, we,* or *they.* Use *are* in the present tense. Use *were* in the past tense.
- Use *will be* for all subjects in the future tense.

A. Write *am, is,* or *are* to complete each sentence.

1. Mr. Hernandez _____ a teacher at our school.

2. I _____ in his history class.

3. I think he _____ a great teacher.

4. His words _____ a great inspiration to me.

5. They _____ words to listen to and learn from.

B. Write *was, were,* or *will be* to complete each sentence.

6. Yesterday, our lesson _____ about Abraham Lincoln.

7. He _____ the sixteenth president of the United States.

8. The Gettysburg Address _____ one speech that he gave.

9. The words he spoke _____ simple, but very meaningful.

10. In the future, I _____ ready to spread his message of hope and equality.

ON YOUR OWN | **Grammar,** page 69

- A **linking verb** does not show action. It connects the subject to the rest of the sentence.
- *Is, are, am, was,* and *were* are often used as linking verbs.
- Some linking verbs link the subject to a noun in the predicate.
- Some linking verbs link the subject to an adjective in the predicate.

Rewrite the lines of this play. Correct any linking verbs that are used incorrectly. Be sure to use proper punctuation for a play.

T.J.: I need an idea for my social studies project. I can't think of anything. (*T.J. paces the room nervously.*)
CARA (*confidently*): My project are about Pawnee folktales.
T.J.: "That's a good idea, Cara." *CARA opens the book and points to a picture.*
CARA: The Plains nation is very interesting to read about.
T.J. (*excitedly*): This were a great idea.

HOMEWORK | **Grammar,** page 70

A. Find the linking verb in each sentence. Write it on the line.

1. The college my sister Sharon attends is in Nebraska. _____

2. Sharon and her friends were hard workers in high school.
_____

3. Even as a girl, she was interested in the Pawnee.
_____

4. Pawnee folktales are part of what she studies in college.
_____

B. Find the noun or adjective in the predicate that is linked to the subject by a linking verb. Write the noun or adjective on the line.

5. Pedro's favorite book is Mystic Horse. _____

6. The lives of the Plains Indians were different from ours.
_____

7. Dr. Gonzalez and Dr. Lasser are experts on the Pawnee nation.
_____

8. Pedro's report on the Plains Indians was very detailed.
_____

Daily Planner

DAY 1	• Prepare to Read • Academic Language • Vocabulary (Preteach)
DAY 2	• Comprehension • Leveled Reader Lesson 1
DAY 3	• Phonics/Decoding • Leveled Reader Lesson 2
DAY 4	• Phonics/Decoding • Vocabulary (Review) • Leveled Reader Lesson 3
DAY 5	• High-Frequency Words • Fluency • Self-Selected Reading

Interactive Student Book

If you wish to preteach the main selection, use StudentWorks Plus for:

• Vocabulary Preteaching
• Word-by-Word Highlighting
• Think Aloud Prompts

Academic Language

Academic words include those harder Tier 2 words that appear in much of students' reading materials as well as the language of instruction. The words chosen for instruction were selected from the **Living Word Vocabulary** list and Avril Coxhead's list of **High-Incidence Academic Words**.

Approaching Level

Prepare to Read

Objective Preview *Ranita, The Frog Princess*
Materials • **StudentWorks Plus** • self-stick notes

PREVIEW TEXT

- Have students preview *Ranita, The Frog Princess* using **StudentWorks Plus**, the interactive eBook. This version of the Student Book contains oral summaries in multiple languages, online multilingual glossaries, word-by-word highlighting, and questions that assess and build comprehension.

- Remind students that listening carefully to and following along with the word-by-word reading will help them prepare for the reading of the selection with the class. Ask students to place self-stick notes on any challenging words or places that confuse them. Discuss these with students prior to the reading of the selection with the rest of the class.

- Ask students to write three or four sentences in their **Writer's Notebooks** telling what they learned about the results of being selfish, dishonest, and rude.

Academic Language

Objective Teach academic language
Materials • none

PRETEACH LANGUAGE OF INSTRUCTION

Tell students that there are many important lesson words they will be using this week. You want them to become familiar with these words *before* the lessons. These words also appear in the directions of the tests they will be taking this year.

Preteach the following academic words: *monitor comprehension, draw conclusions, theme, antonyms, synonyms, analogies*, and *drama*.

- Define each word using student-friendly language. Tell students that *to comprehend something* means *to understand it.* When you comprehend what someone is saying to you, you clearly understand the meaning of that person's statement.)

- In addition, relate each word to known words. For example, connect *draw conclusions* to *decisions based on what you know*, and *antonyms* to *words with opposite meanings.*

- Highlight these words when used throughout the week, and reinforce their meanings.

Approaching Level

Phonics/Decoding

Objective   Decode plural words

Materials
- **Approaching Reproducible**, p. 118
- **Sound-Spelling WorkBoards**

Sound-Spelling WorkBoard

PHONICS MAINTENANCE

Tier 2

- Distribute a **WorkBoard** to each student. Say sounds previously taught, including the sounds for soft *c*, soft *g*, three-letter blends, and *r*-controlled vowels. Have students find the **Sound-Spelling Card** on the board for each sound.

- Review the spelling(s) for each sound and for silent letters and plurals by providing a sample word with that sound or ending. Guide students to write the word. Model how to segment it and write the spelling for each sound or word part. In addition, point out spelling hints, such as that the ending -*es* is added to singular nouns that end in -*s*, -*ss*, -*sh*, -*ch*, or -*x*.

- Dictate the following words for students to spell: *large, bird, porch, porches, lights, lambs, circles, boxes*. Write the words on the board, and have students self-correct their work.

RETEACH SKILL

Plural Words   Write *ladies, kisses,* and *viceroys*. Review that you can add -*s* or -*es* to many singular nouns to make them plural. Add -*es* to singular nouns that end in -*s*, -*ss*, -*sh*, -*ch*, or -*x*. If a singular noun ends in a consonant followed by -*y*, change the *y* to *i* and add -*es*. If a singular noun ends in a vowel followed by -*y*, however, just add -*s*.

- Write the words below on the board. Model how to decode the first word in each row, then guide students as they decode the remaining words. Divide multisyllabic words into syllables using the syllable-scoop technique to help students read the words.

- When completed, point to the words in random order for students to chorally read. Repeat several times.

cube	cubes	bridge	bridges	store	stores
marches	goats	gangs	horses	stories	inches
nurses	jobs	herds	arches	brushes	sharks
perches	babies	churches	dresses	boxes	mornings
races	places	benches	torches	beaches	pledges
wages	marshes	pages	pennies	storms	turkeys

ELL

Minimal Contrasts   Focus on articulation of the ending sounds in most plurals. Make the /s/ sound, and point out your mouth position. Have students repeat. (Use hand mirrors, if available.) Repeat for /z/. Then have students say each sound together, noticing the slight difference in mouth position. Continue by having students read minimal contrast word pairs, such as *walk/walks*, *dog/dogs, bus/buses*.

Approaching Reproducible, page 118

A **plural** is a form of a noun that names more than one thing. You can form plurals in the following ways:
- To change most nouns to a plural, add -**s**.
- If a word ends in -**s**, -**ss**, -**sh**, -**ch**, or -**x**, add -**es**.
- If a word ends in a **vowel** + **y**, add -**s**.
- If a word ends in a **consonant** + **y**, change the *y* to *i* and add -**es**.

Complete the word equations to write the plural form of each word.

1. kiss + es = _____ kisses
2. family − y + ies = _____ families
3. pinch + es = _____ pinches
4. valley + s = _____ valleys
5. fox + es = _____ foxes
6. journey + s = _____ journeys
7. table + s = _____ tables
8. turkey + s = _____ turkeys
9. city − y + ies = _____ cities
10. bus + es = _____ buses

Approaching Level

Vocabulary

Objective   Preteach selection vocabulary
Materials   • **Visual Vocabulary Resources**   • **Vocabulary Cards**
    • **Approaching Reproducible**, p. 119

✓ PRETEACH KEY VOCABULARY

Tier 2

Introduce the Words Use the **Visual Vocabulary Resources** to preteach the key selection words *selfish, cranky, commotion, exasperated, specialty*, and *famished*. Use the following routine that appears in detail on the cards.

- Define the word in English, and provide the example given.

- Define the word in Spanish, if appropriate, and indicate if the word is a cognate.

- Display the picture, and explain how it illustrates or demonstrates the words.

- Then engage students in structured partner-talk about the image, using the key word.

- Ask students to chorally say the word three times.

- Point out any known sound-spellings or focus on a key aspect of phonemic awareness related to the word.

- You may wish to also distribute copies of the Vocabulary Glossary in the **ELL Resource Book**.

REVIEW PREVIOUSLY TAUGHT VOCABULARY

Display the **Vocabulary Cards** from the previous four weeks. Say the meanings of each word, one by one, and have students identify them. Then point to words in random order for students to provide definitions and related words they know.

Analogies Remind students that analogies compare two pairs of words, often using synonyms and antonyms. Write this example on the board: *Neglected* is to *appreciated* as *desperate* is to _____. Guide students in completing the example. Direct them to create or complete analogies using other vocabulary words from this week and the previous four weeks. Have students share their analogies.

Corrective Feedback

Review that analogies are comparisons that may use synonyms and antonyms. Ask: *What do analogies do?* Remind students that analogies compare two pairs of words. On the board write, *I was exasperated by her behavior.* Then write, *exasperated* is to *annoyed* as *beautiful* is to _____. Model using a thesaurus to find an appropriate synonym for *beautiful*.

Approaching Reproducible, page 119

| cranky | selfish | exasperated |
| specialty | famished | commotion |

A. Write the vocabulary word that best fits each clue.

1. concerned with your own interests and needs ___selfish___

2. annoyed and frustrated ___exasperated___

3. lots of noise and activity ___commotion___

4. an uncommon ability or product ___specialty___

5. very hungry ___famished___

6. easily irritated ___cranky___

B. Write the vocabulary word that best fits the blank in each sentence.

7. Siri was so busy that she skipped lunch, and by 5 o'clock she was ___famished___

8. There was such a ___commotion___ in the dining hall that I couldn't hear myself think.

9. That was so ___selfish___! There were only five slices of pizza left, and Dave and Dana took four of them.

10. It's not something that many people still do nowadays, but baking bread is my ___specialty___.

Approaching Level

Vocabulary

Objective Review vocabulary and high-frequency words

Materials • **Vocabulary Cards** • **High-Frequency Word Cards**

✔ REVIEW VOCABULARY

Review the Words Display the **Vocabulary Cards** for *selfish, cranky, commotion, exasperated, specialty*, and *famished*. Point to each word, read it aloud, and have students chorally repeat.

Then provide the following Yes/No questions. Have students answer *yes* or *no* to each:

- Will a *selfish* person usually share?
- Does a *cranky* person smile often?
- Is a *commotion* noisy?
- When you feel *exasperated,* are you calm?
- Is a *specialty* something that someone does very well?
- Will you be *famished* after eating a big meal?

HIGH-FREQUENCY WORDS

Top 250 Words The ability to read accurately and effortlessly the most frequently used words in written English will help students develop reading fluency. Display **High-Frequency Word Cards 111–120**. Then do the following:

- Display one card at a time, and have students chorally state each word.
- Have students spell each word aloud.
- Tell students to write each word in their Writer's Notebooks as they state aloud each letter. Then have them read the word again.
- When completed, quickly flip through the Word Card set as students chorally read the words.
- Provide opportunities for students to use the words in speaking and writing. For example, provide sentence starters, such as *In my room, I have _____,* for oral and written practice. Or point to a word card and ask a question, such as *What word means the opposite of this word?* (when pointing to the *many* Word Card).
- Continue the routine throughout the week.

Student Book

Corrective Feedback

To help students monitor their comprehension of "The Frog Prince," read each section of dialogue with them and then pause. Ask: *Do you understand what the character is saying here? Do you need to reread any parts out loud?*

Approaching Level

Comprehension

Tier 2

Objective	Reteach monitor comprehension and theme
Materials	• **Student Book:** "The Frog Prince"

RETEACH STRATEGY: MONITOR COMPREHENSION

- **Define** Explain that one definition of *monitor* is to *observe*, and that *comprehension* means *understanding*. Tell students that when they monitor their comprehension of a text, they pause at regular intervals to observe whether they understand what they are reading. If they are confused by something, they can use self-correction techniques to adjust their understanding.

  Remind students that one way to better understand what they are reading is to ask themselves questions such as why the author chose to include certain settings, characters, and events.

- **Relate to Real Life** Tell students to think of an advertisement they have seen in a magazine. To understand the ad's effectiveness, they should ask themselves why particular words and images are included and be able to answer in a way that makes sense.

- **Set Purposes** Point out to students that good readers stop and ask themselves questions as they read. If the reader can figure out such things as why the characters act as they do, he or she reads on. If not, the reader must ask more questions or choose another self-correction strategy such as rereading text aloud.

RETEACH SKILL: THEME

- **Define** Remind students that the theme of a literary text is the message about life that the author wants readers to understand.

- **Relate to Real Life** Ask students if they can remember watching a movie or television show and learning something about life from the interaction of the characters on screen. Ask: *How did the characters change by the end of the show? What message was the screenwriter trying to communicate through these characters?*

- **Set Purposes** Note that good readers look for clues to the theme of a literary text by examining the characters' words, actions, and what happens as a result of their actions.

- **Apply** Have students describe the interaction of the characters in "The Frog Prince." Then ask students to summarize and explain the play's theme. Discuss with students how understanding the characters' words and actions enabled them to understand the theme. Students will apply this strategy and skill to a simpler text as they read *Hans and Greta*.

Approaching Level

Leveled Reader Lesson 1

Objective   Read to apply skills and strategies

Materials   • **Leveled Reader:** *Hans and Greta*

Leveled Reader

BEFORE READING

Preview and Predict   Have students read the title and preview the first scene. Ask students to make predictions about what will happen to the characters in the play. Students should note any questions they have before reading. Review the elements of a play as needed.

Review the Vocabulary Words   Have students read the vocabulary words on the inside front cover. Briefly define each and ask students to state related words they have learned.

Set a Purpose for Reading   *Let's read to find out what Hans and Greta are like and what happens as a result of their actions.*

DURING READING

STRATEGY

MONITOR COMPREHENSION

Remind students that when they monitor comprehension, they ask themselves questions about what they are reading, and they think the answers over carefully. They look closely at characters' actions to be sure they understand them.

SKILL

THEME

Remind students to look for clues to the theme of the play in the characters' dialogue and behavior. Read the play with students. Help students complete a Theme Chart.

As you read, help students decode unknown words. In addition, ask open-ended questions to facilitate rich discussion, such as *What is the author telling us about the characters? Compare and contrast the behavior of Hans and Greta with the behavior of the Cat.* Build on students' responses to help them develop a deeper understanding.

Stop after each scene, and ask students to check their understanding of the characters and events before reading on. If they struggle, help students reread the difficult scene or passage.

AFTER READING

Discuss how the characters interact in this play. *What did you think of the characters and their actions? Was the author trying to teach a lesson?* Have students identify text details that support their answers.

Digital Learning

Use the **Leveled Reader Audio CD** for fluency building *after* students read the book with your support during Small Group time.

Leveled Reader

Approaching Level

 Leveled Reader Lesson 2

Objectives Reread to apply skills and strategies and develop fluency

Materials
- **Leveled Reader:** *Hans and Greta*
- **Approaching Reproducible**, p. 122

BEFORE READING

 Review the Strategy and Skill Review students' completed Theme Charts from the first read. Remind students that understanding what the characters say and do and the effects of the characters' actions is essential to understanding the theme of a story. Point out that summarizing and explaining the theme includes identifying whether ideas or actions in a text—for example, what the characters do—are good or bad.

Review the Vocabulary Words Have students search the book for each vocabulary word. Ask students to read aloud the sentence containing the word and state the word's definition or provide related words. Direct students to look up synonyms and antonyms of vocabulary words using a thesaurus.

Set a Purpose for Reading *Let's reread to check our understanding of the play and to work on our reading fluency.*

DURING READING

Reread *Hans and Greta* with students. Have them read silently, a few lines at a time, or read aloud to a partner. Stop and have students check their understanding of the characters and their actions before reading the next scene. Model monitoring comprehension.

AFTER READING

Check Comprehension Have partners complete the Comprehension Check on page 16. Review students' answers. Help students find evidence for their answers in the text.

MODEL FLUENCY

Model reading the passage on **Approaching Reproducible** page 122. Tell students to pay close attention to your expression—the way you read the dialogue so that it expresses each character's feelings. Then read one sentence at a time and have students echo-read.

During independent reading time, have students work with a partner using the fluency passage. One student reads aloud while the other repeats each sentence back. If students need additional support, have them listen to the "practice speed" version of the passage on the **Fluency Solutions Audio CD**.

Approaching Reproducible, page 122

As I read, I will pay attention to expression.

	[Hans and Greta are walking through the woods. They are going
11	*to Grandma Maggie's house. As they walk they eat sandwiches,*
21	*leaving a trail of crumbs. Their stepmother and father stand*
31	*together, waving good-bye.]*
34	**Stepmother:** Good-bye! Be sure to go straight to Grandma
43	Maggie's. Don't get lost.
47	**Father:** *[smiling and shaking his head]* If they get lost, they
58	can always follow the trail of crumbs back to our house.
69	**Stepmother:** *[nods her head, then shakes a finger at Hans and*
80	*Greta]* And don't play any of your tricks on Grandma.
90	**Hans and Greta:** We won't, Stepmother. Good-bye, Father!
98	*[Hans and Greta walk a little farther, then look at each other*
110	*and laugh.]*
112	**Greta:** I won't play tricks on Grandma Maggie. I'll play them
123	on the cat. 126

Comprehension Check

1. What do you know about Hans and Greta? **Plot Development** They can go to their grandmother's house by themselves. They like to play tricks and are not always obedient.

2. What problem might the children face and how does the father suggest they solve it? **Problem and Solution** Hans and Greta may get lost. Their father suggests that they can follow the trail of bread crumbs back to the house.

	Words Read	−	Number of Errors	=	Words Correct Score
First Read		−		=	
Second Read		−		=	

Approaching Level

Leveled Reader Lesson 3

Objective Build fluency

Materials
- **Leveled Reader:** *Hans and Greta*
- **Approaching Reproducible,** p. 122

FOCUS ON FLUENCY

Timed Reading Tell students that they will be doing a final timed reading of the fluency passage on **Approaching Reproducible** page 122 that they have been practicing. With each student, follow these directions:

- Place the passage facedown.

- When you say "Go," the student begins reading the passage aloud.

- When you say "Stop," the student stops reading the passage.

As they read, note words students mispronounce and their overall expression. Stop after one minute. Help students record and graph the number of words they read correctly.

REREAD PREVIOUSLY READ BOOKS

- Distribute copies of the past six **Leveled Readers**. Have students select two to reread. Tell students that rereading these books will help them develop their skills. The more times they read the same words, the quicker they will learn these words. This will make the reading of other books easier.

- Circulate and listen in as students read. Stop students periodically and ask them how they are figuring out difficult words and how they are monitoring their comprehension. Note students who need additional work with specific decoding or comprehension skills.

- Encourage students to read other previously read Leveled Readers during independent reading time or for homework.

Meet Grade-Level Expectations

As an alternative to this day's lesson, guide students through a reading of the On Level Leveled Reader. See page 367U. Since both books contain the same vocabulary, phonics, and comprehension skills, the scaffolding you provided will help most students gain access to this more challenging text.

Book Talk

Bringing Groups Together Students will work with peers of various language and reading abilities to discuss this week's Leveled Readers. Refer to page 159 in the **Teacher's Resource Book** for more about how to conduct a Book Talk.

Student Book

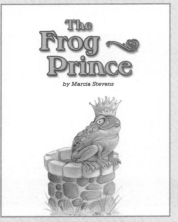

Student Book

Decodable Text

Use the decodable stories in the **Teacher's Resource Book** to help students build fluency with basic decoding patterns.

Approaching Level

Fluency

Objectives Reread play to develop fluency; develop speaking skills
Materials • **Student Book:** *Ranita, The Frog Princess*, "The Frog Prince"

✔ REREAD FOR FLUENCY

- Have students reread a portion of *Ranita, The Frog Princess*. Suggest that they focus on two to four of their favorite pages from the play. Work with students to read the dialogue with the appropriate expression.

- Provide time for students to read their passages of dialogue to you. Comment on their expression, and provide corrective feedback by modeling proper fluency.

DEVELOP SPEAKING/LISTENING SKILLS

- Have students practice reading a half page of the play "The Frog Prince."

- Work with students to read with appropriate expression. Model reading a few lines of dialogue at a time. Emphasize the way you use your voice to show that different characters are speaking and to express the emotion of each character. Have students repeat.

- Provide time for students to read aloud the dialogue to partners. Have students name ways in which their partner expressed emotion or interest with his or her voice.

- Challenge partners to select a passage of dialogue by two characters, practice, and then present a dramatic reading of that passage to the class. Remind students to read at an appropriate rate and with appropriate expression and phrasing, in ways that show their comprehension of what they are reading.

Approaching Level

Self-Selected Reading

Objective Read independently to monitor comprehension and identify theme

Materials • **Leveled Classroom Library** • other plays and fairy tales

APPLY SKILLS AND STRATEGIES TO INDEPENDENT READING

- **Read Independently** Have students choose another play or fairy tale or a **Leveled Classroom Library** book for sustained silent reading. (See the **Theme Bibliography** on pages T8–T9 for suggestions.) Remind them to monitor their comprehension as they read. Point out that summarizing and explaining the author's theme helps readers better understand the message the author wants to communicate. Have students read their books and record clues to the theme or message of their reading on a Theme Chart.

- **Show Evidence of Reading** While reading, students may generate a reading log or journal. After reading, ask students to use their Theme Chart to paraphrase what the reading was about, maintaining meaning and logical order. They may write or orally state a summary of the book. Provide time for students to share their summaries and reactions to the book while participating in Book Talks. Ask: *Why is the theme of this book an important one for readers to understand?*

Approaching

Leveled Classroom Library
See Leveled Classroom
Library lessons on pages T2–T7.

Daily Planner

DAY 1	• Vocabulary • Phonics
DAY 2	• Leveled Reader Lesson 1
DAY 3	• Leveled Reader Lesson 2
DAY 4	• Fluency
DAY 5	• Self-Selected Reading

ELL

Practice Vocabulary Pair ELL students with native speakers. On the board, provide sentence frames for pairs to copy and complete using the vocabulary and additional words when necessary. For example: *I always feel _____ when I don't get enough _____.* (cranky; sleep)

On Level

Vocabulary

Objective   Review vocabulary

Materials   • **Vocabulary Cards**

REVIEW PREVIOUSLY TAUGHT WORDS

Review the Words Display the **Vocabulary Cards** for *selfish, cranky, commotion, exasperated, specialty*, and *famished*. Point to each word, read it aloud, and have students chorally repeat.

Then provide the following discussion questions. Allow several students to respond to each. Use the discussions to determine each student's depth of word knowledge.

- In what situations might you end up feeling *cranky*?
- What are some ways that people can be *selfish*?
- Have you ever caused a *commotion*? When? Where?
- For what jobs might someone have a *specialty*?
- Would you feel *exasperated* if your pet never obeyed you? Why?
- How do you feel and act when you are *famished*?

Phonics/Word Study

Objective   Decode multisyllabic plural words

Materials   • none

RETEACH SKILL

- **Plural Words** Write: *bluebirds, circles, ponies, Mondays*. Circle each *-s, -es,* or *-ies* ending. Remind students that these endings make nouns (in these examples, *bluebird, circle, pony,* and *Monday*) plural. State each spelling and provide a sample word.

- Write the words below on the board. If necessary, divide the words into syllables using the syllable-scoop technique to help students read one syllable at a time. When completed, point to the words in random order for students to chorally read.

birches	thousands	worries	sandboxes	birthdays
bridges	donkeys	choruses	pencils	horseflies
circuses	toothbrushes	artists	valleys	workbenches

- **Spelling** Dictate these words for students to spell: *berries, birdbaths, workdays, witnesses, goldfinches*. Model how to segment words, such as spelling a word syllable by syllable.

On Level

Fluency

Objectives Reread selections to develop fluency; develop speaking skills
Materials • **Student Book:** *Ranita, The Frog Princess*, "The Frog Prince"

REREAD FOR FLUENCY

- Have students reread *Ranita, The Frog Princess*. Work with students to read with the appropriate expression. Model as needed.

- Provide time for students to read a passage of dialogue to you. Comment on their expression and provide corrective feedback.

DEVELOP SPEAKING/LISTENING SKILLS

- Have students practice reading a page from "The Frog Prince."

- Work with students to read with appropriate expression. Model reading a few lines of dialogue at a time. Emphasize the way you use your voice to show that different characters are speaking and to express the emotion of each character. Have students repeat.

- Provide time for partners to read aloud the dialogue. Have students tell how their partner expressed emotion or interest.

- Challenge students to select a passage of dialogue, choose parts, practice, and then present a dramatic reading of that passage for the class, including appropriate gestures.

Self-Selected Reading

Objective Read independently to monitor comprehension and identify theme
Materials • **Leveled Classroom Library** • other plays and fairy tales

APPLY SKILLS AND STRATEGIES TO INDEPENDENT READING

- **Read Independently** Have students choose another play or fairy tale or a **Leveled Classroom Library** book for sustained silent reading. (See the **Theme Bibliography** on pages T8–T9 for suggestions.) Remind them to monitor their comprehension as they read. Point out that explaining the author's theme helps readers understand his or her message. Have students read the books and record clues to the theme on a Theme Chart.

- **Show Evidence of Reading** While reading, students may generate a reading log or journal. After reading, ask students to use their Theme Chart to paraphrase what the reading was about, maintaining meaning and logical order. Allow students to share their summaries, and comment on their reactions to the book while participating in Book Talks. Ask: *Would you recommend this book to a classmate? Why or why not?*

Student Book

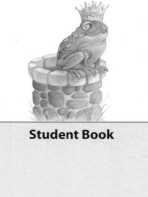

Student Book

On Level

Leveled Classroom Library
See Leveled Classroom
Library lessons on pages T2–T7.

Leveled Reader

On Level

 Leveled Reader Library

Leveled Reader Lesson 1

Objective   Read to apply strategies and skills

Materials   • **Leveled Reader:** *The Dragon's Dinner*

BEFORE READING

Preview and Predict Have students read the title and preview the play by looking at the illustrations. Ask students to predict what this play might be about and what its characters might be like. Review the elements of a play as needed.

 Review the Vocabulary Words Have students read the vocabulary words on the inside front cover. Ask students to state related words they have learned. Review definitions, as needed.

Set a Purpose for Reading *Let's read to find out what the dragon eats for dinner and what happens as a result.*

DURING READING

 STRATEGY
MONITOR COMPREHENSION

Remind students that when they monitor comprehension, they ask themselves questions about what they are reading and think the answers over carefully. They use self-correction strategies as needed, such as rereading a portion, paraphrasing, or reading more slowly.

SKILL
THEME

Remind students to look for clues to the theme of the play in the characters' dialogue and behavior. Read the play aloud with students. Have students complete a Theme Chart.

Read *The Dragon's Dinner* with students. Ask open-ended questions to facilitate rich discussion, such as *What does the dragon do? What do the results of that action tell you about the dragon?* Build on their responses to help them deepen their understanding. Have students fill in a Theme Chart as they read.

Analogies: Synonyms and Antonyms As they read, have students point out this week's new vocabulary words. Encourage them to use a thesaurus to find synonyms and antonyms for vocabulary words.

AFTER READING

Discuss the theme. *What did you think of the characters and their actions? Does this story have a message?* Have students identify text details that support their conclusions about the way in which the characters handled their problem.

On Level

Leveled Reader Lesson 2

Leveled Reader

Objectives Reread to apply skills and strategies and develop fluency
Materials • **Leveled Reader:** *The Dragon's Dinner* • **Practice Book**, p. 122

BEFORE READING

✔ **Review the Strategy and Skill** Review students' completed Theme Charts from the first read. Remind students that understanding what the characters say and do and the effects of the characters' actions is essential to understanding the theme of a story. Point out that summarizing and explaining the theme includes making judgments about whether ideas or actions in a text are good or bad. For example, students should decide which characters' actions are mainly good and which characters' actions are mainly bad.

If students' Theme Charts are incomplete, provide a model chart or use a student chart and revise it as a group. Have students copy the revised chart in their Writer's Notebooks.

Set a Purpose for Reading *Let's reread to check our understanding of the play's characters and to work on our reading fluency.*

DURING READING

Reread *The Dragon's Dinner* with students. Have them read silently, two pages at a time, or read aloud to a partner. Stop and have students monitor their comprehension before reading the next two pages. Model summarizing and explaining the theme, as needed.

AFTER READING

Check Comprehension Have partners complete the Comprehension Check on page 20. Review students' answers. Help students find evidence for their answers in the text.

MODEL FLUENCY

Model reading the fluency passage on **Practice Book** page 122. Tell students to pay close attention to your expression—that is, the way that you read the dialogue so that you express each character's feelings. Then read one sentence at a time, and have students echo-read the sentences, copying your expression.

During independent reading time, have students work with a partner using the fluency passage. One student reads aloud while the other repeats each sentence back. If students need additional support, have them listen to the "practice speed" version of the passage on the **Fluency Solutions Audio CD**.

Book Talk

Bringing Groups Together Students will work with peers of various language and reading abilities to discuss this week's **Leveled Readers**. Refer to page 159 in the **Teacher's Resource Book** for more about how to conduct a Book Talk.

Practice Book, page 122

As I read, I will pay attention to expression.

	[*Dean Dragon's kitchen. Matthew is struggling to light a*
9	*fire with a match under a cauldron of stew. Dean Dragon*
20	*steps up and lights it with his dragon breath. Priscilla uses*
31	*a large wooden spoon to stir the stew, while Matthew*
41	*starts chopping carrots.*]
44	**Princess Priscilla:** [*inhaling a spoonful of stew with a*
53	*look of pleasure*] Mmm. That smells good already.
61	**Matthew:** Wait until it's finished. It's delicious.
68	**Dean Dragon:** [*smiling*] My vegetable stew is good, if
77	I do say so myself. It's famous among dragons.
86	**Princess Priscilla:** I can see why. [*She smiles at Dean,*
96	*then goes back to stirring the stew.*] I'd just like to get my
109	hands on that Knight Never-Do-Well. He woke me up in
121	the middle of the night and told me that my family was in
134	danger. So of course I came. Then when we got here, he tied
147	me to the tree, told me not to worry, and said he'd be back to
162	rescue me soon. I'd like to take a can opener to that shiny
175	armor of his. 178

Comprehension Check

1. Do you think Knight Never-Do-Well is a reliable person? **Plot Development**
No, because it sounds like he tricked Princess Priscilla.
2. Do these characters enjoy working together? Why? **Plot Development**
Yes, the passage describes them working together while talking and smiling.

	Words Read	–	Number of Errors	=	Words Correct Score
First Read		–		=	
Second Read		–		=	

Daily Planner

DAY 1	• Leveled Reader Lesson 1
DAY 2	• Leveled Reader Lesson 2
DAY 3	• Phonics
DAY 4	• Vocabulary • Fluency
DAY 5	• Self-Selected Reading

ELL

Self-Monitor Vocabulary
Have student pairs of different proficiency identify and define unfamiliar words from the main selection using a dictionary. Challenge students to use the new words in sentences. Monitor students as they complete the activity.

Beyond Level

Phonics/Word Study

Objective   Decode multisyllabic plural words
Materials   • none

EXTEND/ACCELERATE

- **Read Multisyllabic Plural Words**   Write the words below on the board. Challenge students to read the words, using known word parts. When completed, point to the words in random order for students to chorally read.

companies	explorers	memories	marshmallows
editors	purchases	walruses	escalators
catalogs	armchairs	wristwatches	rhinoceroses
ostriches	archduchesses	butterflies	factories

- **Define the Words**   Have students use their knowledge of word parts to figure out the meanings of the words. Then have partners confirm or revise the meanings using a dictionary. Challenge students to use the words in this week's writing assignments.

- **Spell Plural Words**   Dictate the following words for students to spell on their **WorkBoards**: *curtsies, princesses, eyelashes, stingrays, cockroaches, wives.* Write the words for students to self-correct.

Vocabulary

Objectives   Review analogies with synonyms and antonyms; write descriptions
Materials   • thesauruses

ENRICH VOCABULARY

- **Analogies: Synonyms and Antonyms**   Explain that analogies are comparisons between two pairs of words that have a similar relationship. Have students define *synonym* and *antonym* and point out a thesaurus often includes both. Remind students that, in *Ranita, The Frog Princess,* Felipe threatens to feed his *bumbling* servant to the jaguars. Model how to find an antonym for *bumbling* and then how to create an analogy using the word.

- **Write a Description**   Instruct students to write a paragraph that describes Felipe. Tell students to underline each adjective and use a thesaurus to find an antonym for it. Then they should rewrite the paragraph, replacing each adjective describing Felipe with an antonym. Have them invent a new name for Felipe's opposite and tell which character they would rather meet and why.

Beyond Level

Fluency

Objectives Reread selections to develop fluency; develop speaking skills
Materials • **Student Book:** *Ranita, The Frog Princess*, "The Frog Prince"

REREAD FOR FLUENCY

- Have students reread *Ranita, The Frog Princess*. Work with students to read the dialogue with appropriate expression.

- Provide time for students to read a passage of dialogue to you. Comment on their expression and provide corrective feedback.

DEVELOP SPEAKING/LISTENING SKILLS

- Have students practice reading "The Frog Prince."

- Work with students to read with appropriate expression. Model reading a few lines of dialogue at a time. Emphasize the way you use your voice to show that different characters are speaking and to express the emotion of each character. Have students repeat.

- Provide time for students to read the dialogue to partners. Have students tell how their partner expressed emotion or interest.

- Challenge partners to select a passage of dialogue, choose parts, memorize their lines, practice, and then present a dramatic reading of that passage for the class, including gestures and body language, as well as clear diction, tempo, volume, and phrasing.

Student Book

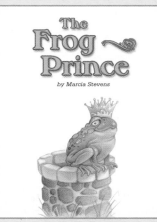

Student Book

Self-Selected Reading

Objective Read independently to identify the theme of a selection
Materials • **Leveled Classroom Library** • other plays and fairy tales

APPLY SKILLS AND STRATEGIES TO INDEPENDENT READING

- **Read Independently** Have students choose another play or a fairy tale for sustained silent reading. (See the **Theme Bibliography** on pages T8–T9 for suggestions.) Have students create a Theme Chart as they read.

- **Show Evidence of Reading** While reading, students may generate a reading log or journal. After reading, ask students to use their Theme Chart to paraphrase the story, maintaining meaning and logical order. Allow students to share their summaries and comment on their reactions while participating in Book Talks. Ask: *What was the message of this story? Do you agree or disagree? Explain.*

- **Evaluate** Have students evaluate how effectively the author conveyed the theme of the story. Ask: *How could the author have made the message of the story clearer?*

Beyond

Classroom Library
See Leveled Classroom Library lessons on pages T2–T7.

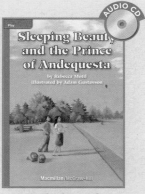

Leveled Reader

Beyond Level

Leveled Reader Lesson 1

Objective   Read to apply strategies and skills
Materials   • **Leveled Reader:** *Sleeping Beauty and the Prince of Andequesta*

BEFORE READING

Preview and Predict Have students preview the book by reading the title and looking at the illustrations. Ask students to predict what this play might be about and what its characters might be like.

 Review the Vocabulary Words Have students read the vocabulary words on the inside front cover. Ask students to state each definition and any related words they have learned.

Set a Purpose for Reading *Let's read to find out who Sleeping Beauty and the Prince of Andequesta are and what they are like.*

DURING READING

 STRATEGY
MONITOR COMPREHENSION

Remind students that when they monitor comprehension, they ask themselves questions about what they are reading and use self-correction strategies as needed to adjust their understanding. They analyze the characters' actions to be sure they understand them.

SKILL
THEME

Remind students to look for clues to the theme of the play in the characters' dialogue and behavior. Read the play aloud together with students. Have students complete a Theme Chart.

Ask open-ended questions to facilitate rich discussion, such as *How do the characters' actions affect the plot? Which character do you admire the most, or the least, and why?* Build on students' responses to help them develop a deeper understanding of the text. Have students fill in the Theme Chart independently as they read.

AFTER READING

Analyze Discuss the theme of this play. *Do you feel the results of the characters' actions were appropriate? Did the characters' behaviors lead to results that you expected? Explain.* Have students identify text details that support their view.

Compare Fairy Tales Prompt students to find out about fairy tales from other cultures that have a similar theme or similar characters. Suggest they use the Internet to research during independent time.

Beyond Level

Leveled Reader Lesson 2

Objective   Reread to apply skills and strategies and develop fluency
Materials   • **Leveled Reader:** *Sleeping Beauty and the Prince of Andequesta*
   • **Beyond Reproducible**, p. 122

Leveled Reader

BEFORE READING

Review the Strategy and Skill   Review students' completed Theme Charts from the first read.

Suggest that one way to think about the theme of a story is to decide what lesson can be learned from the events or from a character's actions. If students' Theme Charts are incomplete, provide a model chart or use a student chart and revise it as a group. Have students copy the revised chart in their Writer's Notebooks.

Set a Purpose for Reading   *Let's reread to check our ideas about the theme and work on our reading fluency.*

DURING READING

Have students reread *Sleeping Beauty and the Prince of Andequesta* silently or with a partner. If reading in pairs, prompt students to stop after every two pages to evaluate the text or ask each other probing questions.

AFTER READING

Check Comprehension   Have students independently complete the Comprehension Check on page 20. Review students' answers. Help students find evidence for their answers in the text.

Synthesize   Discuss how this play differs from familiar versions of *Sleeping Beauty*. Have students brainstorm how to create funny versions of other fairy tales. For example, how could they retell the story of *Snow White* or *Little Red Riding Hood* in a humorous way?

Gifted & Talented

MODEL FLUENCY

Model reading the fluency passage on **Beyond Reproducible** page 122. Tell students to pay close attention to your expression—that is, the way that you read the dialogue so that it expresses each character's feelings. Then read one sentence at a time, and have students echo-read the sentences, copying your expression.

During independent reading time, have students work with a partner using the fluency passage. One student reads aloud while the other repeats each sentence back. Students can check their fluency by reading along with the "expert speed" version of the passage on the **Fluency Solutions Audio CD**.

Book Talk

Bringing Groups Together Students will work with peers of various language and reading abilities to discuss this week's Leveled Readers. Refer to page 159 in the **Teacher's Resource Book** for more about how to conduct a Book Talk.

Beyond Reproducible, page 122

As I read, I will pay attention to expression.

	[Enter Rafael and Pauline from opposite sides of the stage. Rafael is
12	*carrying a soccer ball under his arm and a math test in his hand.*
26	*Pauline is carrying an armful of books.]*
33	*Rafael:* [*smiling and waving a math test*] Hey, Pauline! I got an "A" on
47	my math test. Thanks for your help!
54	*Pauline:* [*peers over the top of the books she's holding*] Good job! And
67	guess what? I got an "A" on the French test.
77	*Rafael:* [*takes some of her books*] That's great! Why don't we
88	celebrate? We could go to the park and kick a soccer ball around.
101	*Pauline:* No, thanks. I have rehearsal for *Sleeping Beauty* tonight, and I
113	need to finish my homework. Why don't we just study?
123	*Rafael:* [*exasperated*] You know what? You still haven't learned how to
134	have any fun.
137	*Pauline:* Yeah? Well, you're just a silly boy. [*Rafael and Pauline glare*
149	*at one another. Enter a man in a suit holding a cell phone.]*
162	*Man in Suit:* [*to Rafael*] Excuse me, your highness. The king wishes to
175	speak to you.
178	*Rafael:* [*taking the cell phone and speaking into it*] Dad? 188

Comprehension Check

1. Why did Pauline choose homework over relaxing? **Plot Development** Pauline's character trait is to be responsible.

2. What facts suggest that if Rafael and Pauline can stop arguing, they might make a good team? **Main Idea and Details** Pauline helped Rafael with his math test. Rafael helped Pauline with her French test. Both received good scores.

	Words Read	−	Number of Errors	=	Words Correct Score
First Read		−		=	
Second Read		−		=	

Daily Planner

DAY 1	• Build Background Knowledge • Vocabulary
DAY 2	• Vocabulary • Access to Core Content *Ranita, The Frog Princess*
DAY 3	• Vocabulary • Grammar • Access to Core Content *Ranita, The Frog Princess*
DAY 4	• Vocabulary • Writing/Spelling • Access to Core Content "And Still More Tales" • Leveled Reader *Dragon Stew*
DAY 5	• Vocabulary • Leveled Reader *Dragon Stew* • Self-Selected Reading

Interactive Student Book

Use StudentWorks Plus for:

• Vocabulary Preteaching
• Word-by-Word Highlighting
• Think Aloud Prompts

Cognates

Help students identify similarities and differences in pronunciation and spelling between English and Spanish cognates.

promise	*prometer*
domestic	*doméstico*
assist	*asistir*
commotion	*conmoción*
exasperated	*exasperado*
specialty	*especialidad*
analogy	*analogía*
theme	*tema*
synonym	*sinónimo*
antonym	*antónimo*

Prepare to Read

Content Objective Discuss the importance of keeping promises
Language Objective Use key words to discuss keeping promises
Materials • **StudentWorks Plus**

BUILD BACKGROUND KNOWLEDGE

All Language Levels

■ Have students preview *Ranita, The Frog Princess* using **StudentWorks Plus**, the interactive eBook. This version of the Student Book contains oral summaries in multiple languages, online multilingual glossaries, word-by-word highlighting, and questions that assess and build comprehension.

■ Students can build their word-reading fluency by reading along as the text is read or by listening during the first reading and, at the end of each paragraph, returning to the beginning of the paragraph and reading along.

■ Students can build their comprehension by reviewing the definitions of key words in the online glossary and by answering the comprehension questions. When appropriate, the text required to answer the question is highlighted to provide students with additional support and scaffolding.

■ After reading, ask students to respond to this question: *How would you feel if someone broke a promise to you?*

Academic Language

Language Objective Use academic language in classroom conversations

All Language Levels

■ This week's academic words are **boldfaced** throughout the lesson. Define the word in context, and provide a clear example from the selection. Then ask students to generate an example or a word with a similar meaning.

Academic Language Used in Whole Group Instruction

Theme Words	Key Selection Words	Strategy and Skill Words
promise **domestic** **assist**	**selfish** **cranky** **commotion** **exasperated** **specialty** **famished**	**monitor comprehension** **theme** **analogies** **synonyms** **antonyms** **linking verbs**

ELL ENGLISH LANGUAGE LEARNERS

Vocabulary

Language Objective Demonstrate understanding and use of key words by discussing promises

Materials • **Visual Vocabulary Resources**
      • **ELL Resource Book**

PRETEACH KEY VOCABULARY

Use the **Visual Vocabulary Resources** to preteach the key selection words *selfish, cranky, commotion, exasperated, specialty,* and *famished*. Focus on two words per day. Use the following routine, which appears in detail on the cards.

Beginning/Intermediate

- Point out any known sound-spellings, or focus on a key aspect of phonemic awareness related to the word.

All Language Levels

- Define the word in English, and provide the example given.
- Define the word in Spanish, if appropriate, and indicate if the word is a cognate.
- Show the picture and explain how it illustrates the word. Engage students in a structured partner activity using the key word.
- Ask students to chorally say the word three times.
- Distribute copies of the Vocabulary Glossary in the **ELL Resource Book** on page 156.

PRETEACH FUNCTION WORDS AND PHRASES

All Language Levels

Use the Visual Vocabulary Resources to preteach the function words and phrases *hand over heart, end up, roll eyes,* and *muffle a laugh*. Focus on one word or phrase per day. Use the detailed routine on the cards.

- Define the word in English and, if appropriate, in Spanish. Point out if the word is a cognate.
- Refer to the picture and engage students in talk about the word. For example, students will partner-talk using sentence frames.
- Ask students to chorally repeat the word three times.

TEACH BASIC WORDS

Beginning/Intermediate

Use the Visual Vocabulary Resources to teach the basic words *sneer, growl, muffle, whimper, hiss,* and *brighten*. Teach these "stage direction" words using the routine provided on the card.

Visual Vocabulary Resources

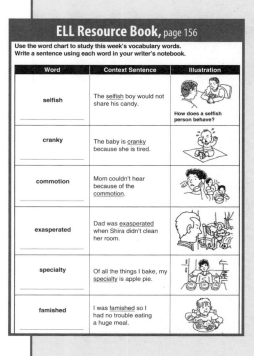

ELL Resource Book, page 156

Use the word chart to study this week's vocabulary words.
Write a sentence using each word in your writer's notebook.

Word	Context Sentence	Illustration
selfish	The selfish boy would not share his candy.	How does a selfish person behave?
cranky	The baby is cranky because she is tired.	
commotion	Mom couldn't hear because of the commotion.	
exasperated	Dad was exasperated when Shira didn't clean her room.	
specialty	Of all the things I bake, my specialty is apple pie.	
famished	I was famished so I had no trouble eating a huge meal.	

ELL Resource Book

ELL ENGLISH LANGUAGE LEARNERS

Access to Core Content

Content Objective Read grade-level text

Language Objective Discuss text, using key words and sentence frames

Materials • **ELL Resource Book**, pp. 144–155

PRETEACH MAIN SELECTION (PAGES 342–359)

All Language Levels

Use the Interactive Question-Response Guide on **ELL Resource Book** pages 144–153 to introduce students to *Ranita, The Frog Princess*. Preteach half of the selection on Day 2 and half on Day 3.

- Use the prompts provided in the guide to develop meaning and vocabulary. Use the partner-talk and whole-class responses to engage students and increase student talk.

- When completed, have partners reread the story.

PRETEACH PAIRED SELECTION (PAGES 362–365)

All Language Levels

Use the Interactive Question-Response Guide on English Learner Resource Book pages 154–155 to preview the paired selection "And Still More Tales." Preteach the selection on Day 4.

Beginning	Intermediate	Advanced
Use Visuals During the Interactive Reading, select several illustrations. Describe the illustrations and explain the theme. Have students summarize what you said.	**Describe** During the Interactive Reading, select a few lines of text. After you have read and explained it, have students describe the theme based on the text.	**Discuss** During the Interactive Reading, select a passage of text. After you have read and explain it, have students discuss the theme based on the passage.

ELL ENGLISH LANGUAGE LEARNERS

Fluency

Content Objectives Reread selections to develop fluency; develop speaking skills

Language Objective Tell a partner what a selection is about

Materials • **Student Book:** *Ranita, The Frog Princess,* "And Still More Tales"
• **Teacher's Resource Book**

REREAD FOR FLUENCY

Beginning

■ Have students read the decodable passages in the **Teacher's Resource Book**, page 18.

Intermediate/Advanced

■ Have students reread two to four of their favorite pages of *Ranita, The Frog Princess*, based on their levels. Help students read the pages with the appropriate expression. For example, read the first page and have students echo. Then have students chorally read additional pages. Remind them to use their voices to show and express the emotion of each character.

■ Provide time for students to read their sections of text to you. Comment on their expression, and provide corrective feedback by modeling proper fluency.

Student Book

DEVELOP SPEAKING/LISTENING SKILLS

All Language Levels

■ Have students practice reading "And Still More Tales." Work with them to read with the appropriate expression.

■ Provide time for students to read aloud the article to a partner. Ask students to tell their partner about the article. Provide the sentence frame: *This article is mostly about ____.*

Self-Selected Reading

Content Objective Read independently

Language Objective Orally retell information learned

Materials • **Leveled Classroom Library** • other plays

APPLY SKILLS AND STRATEGIES TO INDEPENDENT READING

All Language Levels

■ Have students choose a play for independent reading. (See the **Theme Bibliography** on pages T8–T9 for book suggestions.)

■ After reading, ask students to orally summarize and share their reactions to the book with classmates. Ask: *Would you recommend this book to a classmate? Why or why not?*

Leveled Classroom Library
See Leveled Classroom
Library lessons on pages T2–T7.

Transfer Skills

The Verb to *Be* In Hmong, the verb to *be* is not used for adjectives or places (Math test hard. This our class.) and may be omitted with prepositional phrases (The test at 3:00.). Provide students additional practice for using the verb to *be*. Write several sentences with different forms of the verb to *be*. Have students circle the verb. Then read the sentences aloud. Have students repeat after you. See language transfers on pages T16–T31.

Corrective Feedback

During Whole Group grammar lessons, follow the routine on the **Grammar Transparencies** to provide students with extra support. This routine includes completing the items with English Language Learners while other students work independently, having students reread the sentences with partners to build fluency, and providing a generative task, such as writing a new sentence using the skill.

Grammar

Content Objective Identify linking verbs
Language Objective Speak in complete sentences, using sentence frames

LINKING VERBS

Beginning/Intermediate

■ Review linking verbs. Write the following on the board: *Jaime Escalante was a math teacher.* Underline the linking verb *was*. Tell students that the subject—*Jaime Escalante*—names one person. Repeat with the sentence *His students were in trouble,* to review matching the linking verb with a plural subject.

All Language Levels

■ Write linking verbs on the board and identify them. Write sentences on the board, such as those provided below. Have students choose the verb form that correctly completes each sentence. Then have them say: *The subject is ___. The linking verb is ___.*

> *Some students ___ late. (was, were)*
> *The math test ___ very difficult. (was, were)*
> *Escalante said, "You ___ all the best." (is, are)*
> *I ___ glad I didn't have to take it! (am, is)*

PEER DISCUSSION STARTERS

All Language Levels

■ Write the following sentence on the board:

> *Tough words can ___.   Words have power because ___.*

■ Pair students and have them complete the sentence frame. Have them expand on their sentence by providing as many details as they can from this week's readings. Circulate, listen in, and take note of each student's language use and proficiency.

Beginning	Intermediate	Advanced
Develop Vocabulary Describe the illustrations in *Ranita, The Frog Princess* to students. Ask: *What do you see?* Help them point and name things in the illustrations. Help them form sentences using linking verbs.	**Use Linking Verbs** Ask students to describe illustrations in *Ranita, The Frog Princess*. Have them use linking verbs in complete sentences. Model sentences if necessary.	**Use Linking Verbs** Ask students to describe the illustrations in *Ranita, The Frog Princess* using linking verbs.

ELL ENGLISH LANGUAGE LEARNERS

Writing/Spelling

Content Objective Spell words correctly

Language Objective Write in complete sentences, using sentence frames

All Language Levels

- Write the key vocabulary words on the board: *selfish, cranky, commotion, exasperated, specialty, famished*. Have students copy each word on their **WorkBoards**. Help them say each word and then write a sentence for it. Provide sentence starters, such as:

  When you have plenty to share, it is selfish to ____.

  I always feel cranky when ____.

  There was a commotion outside so I couldn't ____.

  I get exasperated when ____.

  The specialty at my favorite bakery is ____.

  You will be famished later if you ____.

Beginning/Intermediate

- Help students spell words using their growing knowledge of English sound-spelling relationships. Model how to segment the word students are trying to spell, and attach a spelling to each sound (or spellings to each syllable if a multisyllabic word). Use the **Sound-Spelling Cards** to reinforce the spellings for each English sound.

Advanced

- Dictate the following words for students to spell: *storms, benches, stories, gangs, beaches, cities*. Use the Sound-Spelling Cards to guide students as they spell each word.

- When completed, review the meanings of words that can be easily demonstrated or explained. Use actions, gestures, and available pictures.

Sound-Spelling WorkBoard

Phonics/Word Study

For English Language Learners who need more practice with this week's phonics/spelling skill, see the Approaching Level lesson on page 367J. Focus on minimal contrasts, articulation, and those sounds that do not transfer from the student's first language to English. See language transfers on pages T16–T31.

Leveled Reader

Vocabulary

Preteach Vocabulary Use the routine in the **Visual Vocabulary Resources**, pages 431–434, to preteach the ELL Vocabulary listed in the inside front cover of the **Leveled Reader**.

ELL ENGLISH LANGUAGE LEARNERS

Leveled Reader

Content Objective Read to apply skills and strategies

Language Objective Retell information, using complete sentences

Materials • **Leveled Reader:** *Dragon Stew*
• **ELL Resource Book,** p. 157
• **Visual Vocabulary Resources,** pp. 431–434

BEFORE READING

All Language Levels

- **Preview** Read the title *Dragon Stew*. Ask: *What's the title? Say it again.* Repeat with the author's name. Then page through the book. Use simple language to tell about each page. Immediately follow up with questions, such as *Is this a dragon or a dinosaur? What is cooking in this pot? Would like to eat this stew?*

- **Review Skills** Use the inside front cover to review the comprehension skill and vocabulary words.

- **Set a Purpose** Say: *Let's read to find out about a dragon who does not eat meat.*

DURING READING

All Language Levels

- Have students read each page aloud using the differentiated suggestions. Provide corrective feedback, such as modeling how to blend a decodable word or clarifying meaning by using techniques from the Interactive Question-Response Guide.

- **Retell** After every two pages, ask students to state the main ideas they have learned so far. Help them to complete the Theme Chart. Restate students' comments when they have difficulty using story-specific words. Provide differentiated sentence frames to support students' responses and engage students in partner-talk where appropriate.

Beginning	Intermediate	Advanced
Echo-Read Have students echo-read after you.	**Choral-Read** Have students chorally read with you.	**Choral-Read** Have students chorally read.
Check Comprehension Point to pictures and ask questions, such as *Do you see the princess on this page? Point to her.*	**Check Comprehension** Ask questions/prompts, such as *Why did the dragon not want to eat Knight Never-Do-Well.*	**Check Comprehension** Ask: *What was funny about this play? Read sentences where the author includes humor.*

AFTER READING

Use the chart below and **Think and Compare** questions in the Leveled Reader to determine students' progress.

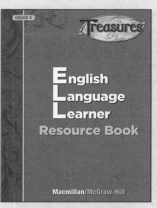

ELL Resource Book

Think and Compare	Beginning	Intermediate	Advanced
1 Think about the play. What lesson does the knight learn about his behavior? *(Theme)*	Possible responses: Nonverbal response. Be nice.	Possible responses: The knight learned that he should be nice to people.	Possible responses: The knight learned that he can't succeed by being mean to other people.
2 The Queen gets cranky when she is hungry. What makes you cranky? What do you do to feel better? *(Synthesize)*	Possible responses: Nonverbal response. Sick. Sleep.	Possible responses: I get cranky when I am sick. I rest to feel better.	Possible responses: I get cranky when I am sick, so I sleep and get a lot of rest so I can get better and feel well.
3 Why does the Queen cause commotion when she looks for her daughter? Do people act like this when they are upset? *(Analyze)*	Possible responses: Nonverbal response. Worried. Sometimes.	Possible responses: The queen is worried about the princess. Sometimes people get upset and act out.	Possible responses: The queen causes commotion because she is worried about her daughter. Sometimes people cause commotion because they are very upset at the situation.

BOOK TALK

Develop Listening and Speaking Skills Distribute copies of **ELL Resource Book**, page 157, and form small groups. Help students determine the leader to discuss the Book Talk questions. Tell students to remember the following while engaged in the activity:

- Ask and give information using abstract and content-based vocabulary. Remind students to ask thoughtful questions and respond questions with appropriate elaboration.

- Distinguish between formal and informal English and know when to use each one. Remind students to note whether the selection is written in formal or informal English. Ask: *Why do you think it is written in this way?* Remind students that they may use informal English when speaking with their classmates, but they should use formal language when they talk to teachers or write essays.

- Express opinions, ideas, and feelings on a variety of social and academic topics. Ask: *What do you think about the characters in the story?*

Book Talk

Bringing Groups Together
Students will work with peers of varying language abilities to discuss the questions for the Book Talk activity. Form groups so that students who read Beyond Level, On Level, Approaching Level, and ELL Leveled Readers are in the same group for the activity.

Progress Monitoring

Weekly Assessment

ASSESSED SKILLS

- Vocabulary: Vocabulary Words, Analogies: Synonyms and Antonyms
- Comprehension: Theme
- Grammar: Linking Verbs
- Phonics/Spelling: Plurals

Selection Test for* Ranita, The Frog Princess *Also Available

**Weekly Assessment
Unit 3 Week 4**

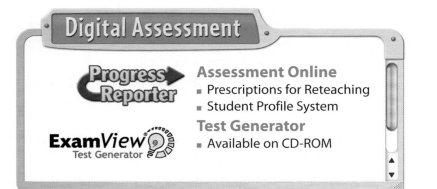

Digital Assessment

Progress Reporter

Assessment Online
- Prescriptions for Reteaching
- Student Profile System

ExamView Test Generator

Test Generator
- Available on CD-ROM

Fluency Assessment

Assess fluency for one group of students per week.
Use the Oral Fluency Record Sheet to track the number of words read correctly. Fluency goal for all students:
102–122 words correct per minute (WCPM).

Approaching Level	Weeks 1, 3, 5
On Level	Weeks 2, 4
Beyond Level	Week 6

Fluency Assessment

Diagnose		Prescribe
Review the assessment answers with students. Have them correct their errors. Then provide additional instruction as needed.		
	IF...	**THEN...**
VOCABULARY WORDS VOCABULARY STRATEGY Analogies: Synonyms and Antonyms	0–2 items correct ...	See **Vocabulary Intervention Teacher's Edition.** **LOG ON** ▶ Online Practice: Go to **www.macmillanmh.com.** **CD-ROM** Vocabulary PuzzleMaker
COMPREHENSION Skill: Theme	0–3 items correct ...	See **Comprehension Intervention Teacher's Edition.** **SPIRAL REVIEW** See Theme lesson in Unit 3 Week 5, page 391B.
GRAMMAR Linking Verbs	0–1 items correct ...	See **Writing and Grammar Intervention Teacher's Edition.**
PHONICS AND SPELLING Plurals	0–1 items correct ...	**LOG ON** ▶ Online Practice: Go to **www.macmillanmh.com.** See **Phonics Intervention Teacher's Edition.**
FLUENCY	98–101 WCPM	**AUDIO CD** Fluency Solutions Audio CD
	0–97 WCPM	See **Fluency Intervention Teacher's Edition.**

Response to Intervention

To place students in Tier 2 or Tier 3 Intervention use the *Diagnostic Assessment*.

- Phonics
- Vocabulary
- Comprehension
- Fluency
- Writing and Grammar

Week 5 ★ At a Glance

Priority Skills and Concepts

✔ Comprehension

- **Strategy:** Visualize
- **Skill:** Character, Setting, Plot
- **SPIRAL REVIEW** Theme
- **Genre:** Expository, Fiction

✔ Robust Vocabulary

- **Selection Vocabulary:** *skyscrapers, collage, barbecue, glorious, strutting, swarms*
- **Strategy:** Context Clues/Definitions and Examples

✔ Fluency

- Rate

✔ Phonics/Spelling

- **Word Study:** Compound Words, Multisyllabic Words
- **Spelling Words:** *fishbowl, lookout, backyard, desktop, campfire, overhead, waterproof, grandparent, railroad, snowstorm, loudspeaker, bookcase, bedroom, blindfold, newborn, bedspread, yourself, overdo, clothesline, undertake*
- **SPIRAL REVIEW** *dresses, arrows, babies*

✔ Grammar/Mechanics

- Irregular Verbs
- Correct Verb Usage

✔ Writing

- **Trait:** Ideas
- Strengthen an Argument

Key

✔ Tested in program   SPIRAL REVIEW Review Skill

Digital Learning

Digital solutions to help plan and implement instruction

☑ Teacher Resources

LOG ON ▶

ONLINE
www.macmillanmh.com

▶ **Teacher's Edition**
- Lesson Planner and Resources also on CD-ROM

TeacherWorks Plus

▶ **Formative Assessment**
- ExamView® on CD-ROM also available

Progress Reporter

▶ **Instructional Resources**
- Unit Videos
- Classroom Presentation Toolkit

VIDEO

▶ **Professional Development**
- Video Library

Professional Development

☑ Student Resources

LOG ON ▶

ONLINE
www.macmillanmh.com

▶ **Interactive Student Book**

StudentWorks Plus

▶ **Leveled Reader Database**

▶ **Activities**
- Research Toolkit
- Oral Language Activities
- Vocabulary/Spelling Activities

Listening Library
- Recordings of Student Books and Leveled Readers

Fluency Solutions
- Fluency Modeling and Practice

Weekly Literature

Theme: Expression Through Art

Student Book

StudentWorks Plus
Interactive Student Book

- Word-by-Word Reading
- Summaries in Multiple Languages
- Comprehension Questions

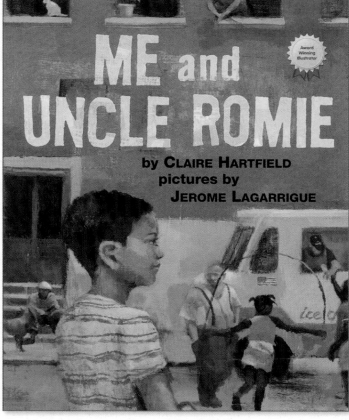

ME and UNCLE ROMIE
by Claire Hartfield
pictures by Jerome Lagarrigue

Main Selection
Genre Historical Fiction

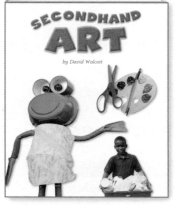

Preteach Vocabulary and Comprehension
Genre Fiction

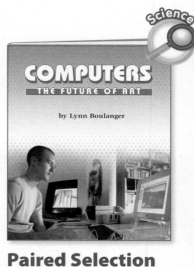

COMPUTERS: THE FUTURE OF ART
by Lynn Boulanger

Paired Selection
Genre Expository

Support Literature

Interactive Read-Aloud Anthology

- Listening Comprehension
- Robust Vocabulary
- Readers Theater Plays for Fluency

Resources for Differentiated Instruction

Leveled Readers

Leveled Reader Library

GR Levels O–U

| Genre | Fiction |

- Same Theme
- Same Vocabulary
- Same Comprehension Skills

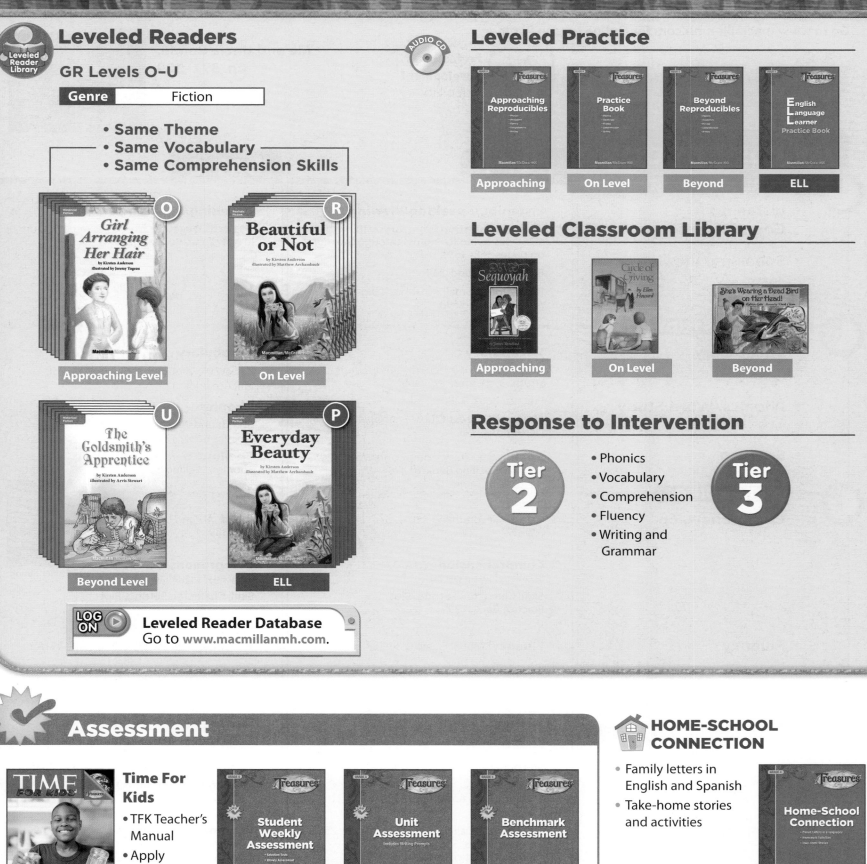

O — Girl Arranging Her Hair by Kirsten Anderson, illustrated by Jeremy Tugeau
Approaching Level

R — Beautiful or Not by Kirsten Anderson, illustrated by Matthew Archambault
On Level

U — The Goldsmith's Apprentice by Kirsten Anderson, illustrated by Arvis Stewart
Beyond Level

P — Everyday Beauty by Kirsten Anderson, illustrated by Matthew Archambault
ELL

LOG ON ▶ **Leveled Reader Database**
Go to www.macmillanmh.com.

Leveled Practice

Approaching Reproducibles — Approaching
Practice Book — On Level
Beyond Reproducibles — Beyond
English Language Learner Practice Book — ELL

Leveled Classroom Library

Sequoyah — Approaching
Circle of Giving by Ellen Howard — On Level
She's Wearing a Dead Bird on Her Head! — Beyond

Response to Intervention

Tier 2

- Phonics
- Vocabulary
- Comprehension
- Fluency
- Writing and Grammar

Tier 3

Assessment

TIME FOR KIDS

Time For Kids
- TFK Teacher's Manual
- Apply Answering Question Strategies

Student Weekly Assessment — Weekly Assessment

Unit Assessment — Unit Assessment

Benchmark Assessment — Benchmark Assessment

HOME-SCHOOL CONNECTION

- Family letters in English and Spanish
- Take-home stories and activities

Home-School Connection

LOG ON ▶ **Online Homework**
www.macmillanmh.com

Suggested Lesson Plan

Go to www.macmillanmh.com for Online Lesson Planner

TeacherWorks Plus
All-In-One Planner and Resource Center

Professional Development
Video Library

Me and Uncle Romie,
pp. 372–389

WHOLE GROUP

ORAL LANGUAGE

- **Listening Comprehension**
- **Speaking/Viewing**

WORD STUDY

- **Vocabulary**
- **Phonics/Word Study**
- **Spelling**

READING

- **Comprehension**
- **Fluency**

LANGUAGE ARTS

- **Writing**
- **Grammar**

ASSESSMENT

- **Informal/Formal**

DAY 1

Listening/Speaking/Viewing
❓ **Focus Question** What do you think the artist was trying to express through the mural on pages 368–369?
Build Background, 368
Read Aloud: "Small Artist Has a Big Appeal," 369A–369B

Vocabulary
skyscrapers, collage, barbecue, glorious, strutting, swarms, 371, 395C
Practice Book, 128
Strategy: Context Clues/Examples and Definitions, 370

Spelling Pretest: Compound Words, 395E
Phonics/Spelling Book, 85–86

Read "Secondhand Art," 370–371

Comprehension, 371A–371B
Strategy: Visualize
Skill: Character, Setting, Plot
Practice Book, 129

Student Book

Fluency Model Fluency, 369B

Writing
Daily Writing Whom do you admire? Write a short paragraph that explains why you admire him or her.
Trait: Ideas
Strengthen an Argument, 393A–393B

Grammar Daily Language Activities, 395G
Irregular Verbs, 395G
Grammar Practice Book, 71

Quick Check Vocabulary, 370
Comprehension, 371B

DAY 2

Listening/Speaking
❓ **Focus Question** How does James's summer in New York City change him?

Vocabulary
Review Words, Context Clues, 372, 395C
Practice Book, 134
Phonics
Compound Words, 369C–369D
Practice Book, 127
Spelling Word Sorts, 395E
Phonics/Spelling Book, 87

Read *Me and Uncle Romie,* 372–389

Comprehension, 372–389
Strategy: Visualize
Skill: Character, Setting, Plot
Practice Book, 130

Student Book

Fluency Repeated Reading: Rate, 391A

Writing
Daily Writing Write a paragraph about someone you are proud of. Tell why.

Reading/Writing Connection, 394–395

Grammar Daily Language Activities, 395G
Irregular Verbs, 395G
Grammar Practice Book, 72

Quick Check Phonics, 369D
Comprehension, 389

SMALL GROUP Lesson Plan ▶ Differentiated Instruction 368G–368H

Priority Skills

Vocabulary	Comprehension	Writing	Science
Vocabulary Words Context Clues/Examples and Definitions	**Strategy:** Visualize **Skill:** Character, Setting, Plot	Trait: Ideas Strengthen an Argument	Evaluate the impact of research on society.

DAY 3

Listening/Speaking

❓ Focus Question Compare the artwork in "Secondhand Art" with the artwork in *Me and Uncle Romie*. How is it alike? How is it different?

Summarize, 391

Vocabulary

Review Words, Related Words, 395D

Spelling Word Meanings, 395F
Phonics/Spelling Book, 88

Read *Me and Uncle Romie*, 372–389

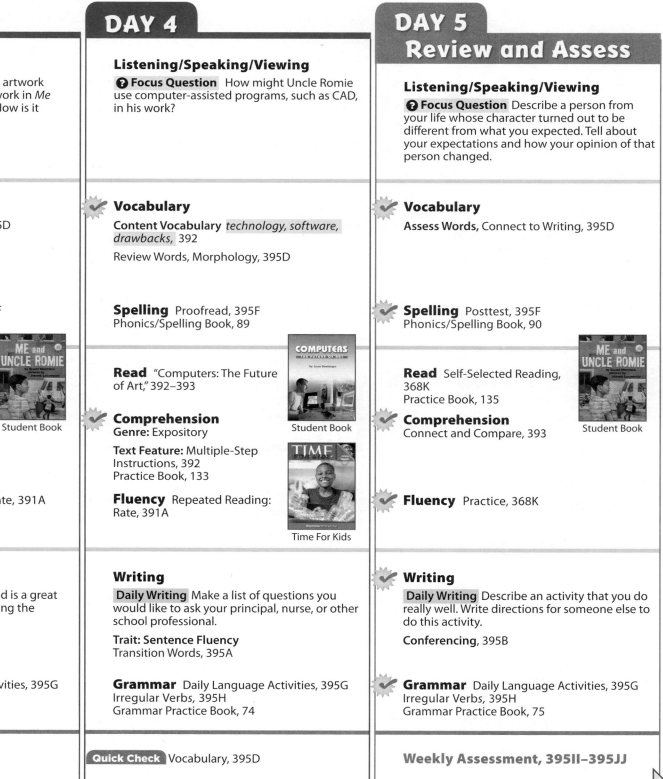

Comprehension
Comprehension Check, 391

Student Book

Review Skill: Theme, 391B
Practice Book, 132

Fluency Repeated Reading: Rate, 391A
Practice Book, 131

Writing

Daily Writing Suppose your friend is a great artist. Write a short paragraph listing the reasons why he or she is so great.

Trait: Ideas
Strengthen an Argument, 395A

Grammar Daily Language Activities, 395G
Mechanics and Usage, 395H
Grammar Practice Book, 73

Quick Check Fluency, 391A

DAY 4

Listening/Speaking/Viewing

❓ Focus Question How might Uncle Romie use computer-assisted programs, such as CAD, in his work?

Vocabulary

Content Vocabulary *technology, software, drawbacks,* 392

Review Words, Morphology, 395D

Spelling Proofread, 395F
Phonics/Spelling Book, 89

Read "Computers: The Future of Art," 392–393

Student Book

Comprehension
Genre: Expository

Text Feature: Multiple-Step Instructions, 392
Practice Book, 133

Fluency Repeated Reading: Rate, 391A

Time For Kids

Writing

Daily Writing Make a list of questions you would like to ask your principal, nurse, or other school professional.

Trait: Sentence Fluency
Transition Words, 395A

Grammar Daily Language Activities, 395G
Irregular Verbs, 395H
Grammar Practice Book, 74

Quick Check Vocabulary, 395D

DAY 5
Review and Assess

Listening/Speaking/Viewing

❓ Focus Question Describe a person from your life whose character turned out to be different from what you expected. Tell about your expectations and how your opinion of that person changed.

Vocabulary

Assess Words, Connect to Writing, 395D

Spelling Posttest, 395F
Phonics/Spelling Book, 90

Read Self-Selected Reading, 368K
Practice Book, 135

Comprehension
Connect and Compare, 393

Student Book

Fluency Practice, 368K

Writing

Daily Writing Describe an activity that you do really well. Write directions for someone else to do this activity.

Conferencing, 395B

Grammar Daily Language Activities, 395G
Irregular Verbs, 395H
Grammar Practice Book, 75

Weekly Assessment, 395II–395JJ

Differentiated Instruction

What do I do in small groups?

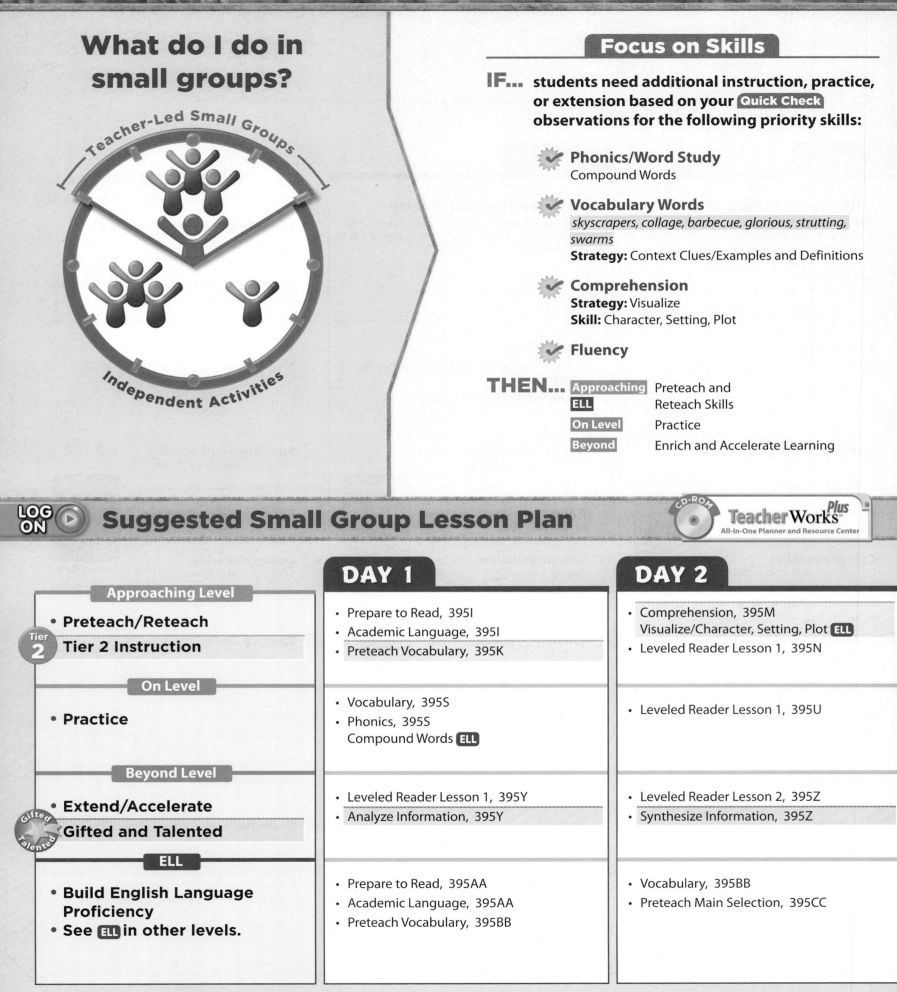

Teacher-Led Small Groups

Independent Activities

IF... students need additional instruction, practice, or extension based on your **Quick Check** observations for the following priority skills:

✓ **Phonics/Word Study**
Compound Words

✓ **Vocabulary Words**
skyscrapers, collage, barbecue, glorious, strutting, swarms
Strategy: Context Clues/Examples and Definitions

✓ **Comprehension**
Strategy: Visualize
Skill: Character, Setting, Plot

✓ **Fluency**

THEN... **Approaching** Preteach and
ELL Reteach Skills
On Level Practice
Beyond Enrich and Accelerate Learning

LOG ON ▶ **Suggested Small Group Lesson Plan**

CD-ROM TeacherWorks *Plus*
All-In-One Planner and Resource Center

	DAY 1	**DAY 2**
Approaching Level **Tier 2** • **Preteach/Reteach** **Tier 2 Instruction**	• Prepare to Read, 395I • Academic Language, 395I • Preteach Vocabulary, 395K	• Comprehension, 395M Visualize/Character, Setting, Plot **ELL** • Leveled Reader Lesson 1, 395N
On Level • **Practice**	• Vocabulary, 395S • Phonics, 395S Compound Words **ELL**	• Leveled Reader Lesson 1, 395U
Beyond Level • **Extend/Accelerate** **Gifted and Talented**	• Leveled Reader Lesson 1, 395Y • Analyze Information, 395Y	• Leveled Reader Lesson 2, 395Z • Synthesize Information, 395Z
ELL • **Build English Language Proficiency** • See **ELL** in other levels.	• Prepare to Read, 395AA • Academic Language, 395AA • Preteach Vocabulary, 395BB	• Vocabulary, 395BB • Preteach Main Selection, 395CC

Focus on Leveled Readers

Levels O–U

Girl Arranging Her Hair
by Kirsten Anderson
illustrated by Jeremy Tugeau
Macmillan/McGraw-Hill
O

Approaching

Beautiful or Not
by Kirsten Anderson
illustrated by Matthew Archambault
Macmillan/McGraw-Hill
R

On Level

The Goldsmith's Apprentice
by Kirsten Anderson
illustrated by Arvis Stewart
Macmillan/McGraw-Hill
U

Beyond

Everyday Beauty
by Kirsten Anderson
illustrated by Matthew Archambault
Macmillan/McGraw-Hill
P

ELL

Additional Leveled Readers

LOG ON ▶

Leveled Reader Database
www.macmillanmh.com

Search by

- Comprehension Skill
- Content Area
- Genre
- Text Feature

- Guided Reading Level
- Reading Recovery Level
- Lexile Score
- Benchmark Level

Subscription also available.

Manipulatives

Sound-Spelling WorkBoards

Sound-Spelling Cards

about
today

High-Frequency Word Cards

Visual Vocabulary Resources

DAY 3	DAY 4	DAY 5
• Phonics Maintenance, 395J Compound Words **ELL** • Leveled Reader Lesson 2, 395O	• Reteach Phonics Skill, 395J Compound Words **ELL** • Review Vocabulary, 395L • Leveled Reader Lesson 3, 395P	• High-Frequency Words, 395L • Fluency, 395Q • Self-Selected Independent Reading, 395R • Book Talk, 395P
• Leveled Reader Lesson 2, 395V	• Fluency, 395T	• Self-Selected Independent Reading, 395T • Book Talk, 395V
• Phonics, 395W Compound Words **ELL**	• Vocabulary, 395W • Write a Personal Narrative, 395W • Fluency, 395X	• Self-Selected Independent Reading, 395X • Evaluate Information, 395X • Book Talk, 395Z
• Vocabulary, 395BB • Grammar, 395EE	• Vocabulary, 395BB • Writing/Spelling, 395FF • Preteach Paired Selection, 395CC • Fluency, 395DD • Leveled Reader, 395GG	• Vocabulary, 395BB • Leveled Reader, 395GG • Self-Selected Independent Reading, 395DD • Book Talk, 395HH

Managing the Class

What do I do with the rest of my class?

- Practice Book and Reproducibles
- ELL Practice Book
- Leveled Reader Activities
- Literacy Workstations
- Online Activities

Classroom Management Tools

Weekly Contract

Name _____ Date _____

My To-Do List

✔ Put a check next to the activities you complete.

📖 Reading
- ☐ Practice fluency
- ☐ Choose a story to read

🔤 Phonics/Word Study
- ☐ Look up word origins
- ☐ Write words with short vowel sounds

✏️ Writing
- ☐ Write a letter to the editor
- ☐ Write a radio ad

🔬 Science
- ☐ Research two types of rocks
- ☐ Write a chart

🌎 Social Studies
- ☐ Create a guide book
- ☐ Role-play an interview

📖 Leveled Readers
- ☐ Write About It!
- ☐ Content Connection

💻 Technology
- ☐ Vocabulary PuzzleMaker
- ☐ Fluency Solutions
- ☐ Listening Library
- ☐ www.macmillanmh.com

🖌 Independent Practice
- ☐ Practice Book 1-9

Rotation Chart

Teacher-Led Small Groups

Red

Literacy Workstations   **Independent Activities**

Blue   **Green**

Orange

Treasures

Managing Small Groups
A How-to Guide

Dr. Vicki Gibson   Dr. Douglas Fisher

Macmillan/McGraw-Hill

How-to Guide   **Rotation Chart**

Digital Learning

LOG ON ▶

StudentWorks Plus

Interactive Student Book

StudentWorks Plus Online
- Summaries in Multiple Languages
- Word-by-Word Reading
- Comprehension Questions

Meet the Author/Illustrator

Mark Teague
- Mark gets a lot of inspiration from his two young daughters. He loves to read to them.
- He always loved to draw but didn't think about becoming a professional artist until after college.
- Mark starts out his books by jotting down notes and scribbling in a notebook. Slowly the ideas start to come together and he creates a real story.

Another book by Mark Teague
- Teague, Mark. *Detective LaRue: Letters from the Investigation.* New York: Scholastic, Inc., 2004.

- Other Books by the Author or Illustrator

Leveled Practice

Treasures
Practice Book
- Phonics
- Vocabulary
- Fluency
- Comprehension
- Writing

Macmillan/McGraw-Hill

On Level

Treasures
English Language Learner Practice Book

Macmillan/McGraw-Hill

ELL

Also Available:
Approaching Reproducible
Beyond Reproducible

Independent Activities

Oral Language Activities

- Focus on Vocabulary and Concepts
- English Language Learner Support

Leveled Reader Database

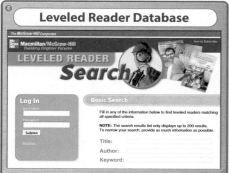

- Leveled Reader Database
- Search titles by level, skill, content area, and more

Vocabulary/Spelling Activities

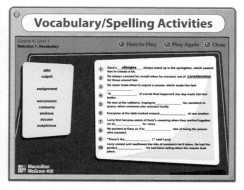

- Differentiated Lists and Activities

Research Toolkit

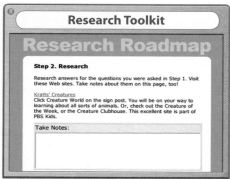

Research Roadmap

Step 2. Research

Research answers for the questions you were asked in Step 1. Visit these Web sites. Take notes about them on this page, too!

Kratts' Creatures
Click Creature World on the sign post. You will be on your way to learning about all sorts of animals. Or, check out the Creature of the Week, or the Creature Clubhouse. This excellent site is part of PBS Kids.

Take Notes:

- Research Roadmap
- Research and Presentation Tools
- Theme Launcher Video
- Links to Science and Social Studies

Available on CD

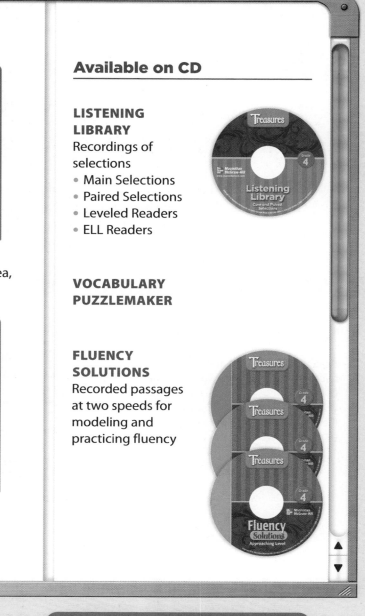

LISTENING LIBRARY
Recordings of selections
- Main Selections
- Paired Selections
- Leveled Readers
- ELL Readers

VOCABULARY PUZZLEMAKER

FLUENCY SOLUTIONS
Recorded passages at two speeds for modeling and practicing fluency

Leveled Reader Activities

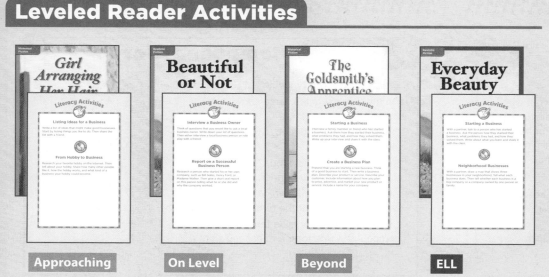

Girl Arranging Her Hair	Beautiful or Not	The Goldsmith's Apprentice	Everyday Beauty
Approaching	**On Level**	**Beyond**	**ELL**

See inside cover of all Leveled Readers.

Literacy Workstations

Reading — **Writing**

Phonics/Word Study — **Science/Social Studies**

See lessons on pages 368K–368L.

Managing the Class

What do I do with the rest of my class?

Reading

Objectives

- Develop fluency through partner-reading
- Read independently for a sustained period of time; use **Practice Book** page 135 for Reading Strategies and Reading Log

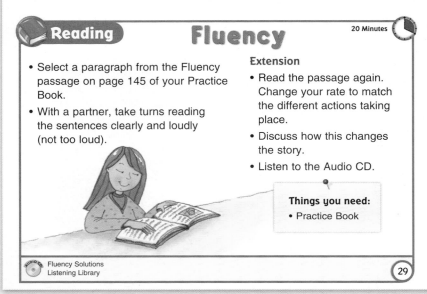

Reading — Fluency
20 Minutes

- Select a paragraph from the Fluency passage on page 145 of your Practice Book.
- With a partner, take turns reading the sentences clearly and loudly (not too loud).

Extension

- Read the passage again. Change your rate to match the different actions taking place.
- Discuss how this changes the story.
- Listen to the Audio CD.

Things you need:
- Practice Book

Fluency Solutions Listening Library

29

Reading — Independent Reading
20 Minutes

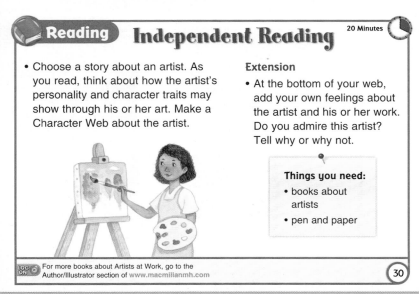

- Choose a story about an artist. As you read, think about how the artist's personality and character traits may show through his or her art. Make a Character Web about the artist.

Extension

- At the bottom of your web, add your own feelings about the artist and his or her work. Do you admire this artist? Tell why or why not.

Things you need:
- books about artists
- pen and paper

For more books about Artists at Work, go to the Author/Illustrator section of www.macmillanmh.com

30

Phonics/Word Study

Objectives

- Use a dictionary to find the definitions of words
- Write sentences using context clues
- Write sentences with compound words

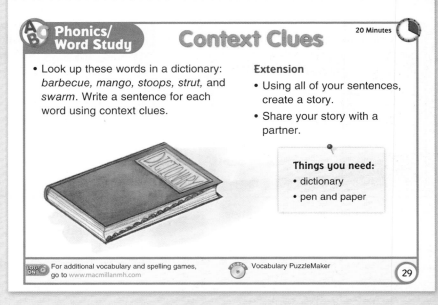

Phonics/Word Study — Context Clues
20 Minutes

- Look up these words in a dictionary: *barbecue, mango, stoops, strut,* and *swarm.* Write a sentence for each word using context clues.

Extension

- Using all of your sentences, create a story.
- Share your story with a partner.

Things you need:
- dictionary
- pen and paper

For additional vocabulary and spelling games, go to www.macmillanmh.com — Vocabulary PuzzleMaker

29

Phonics/Word Study — Compound Words
20 Minutes

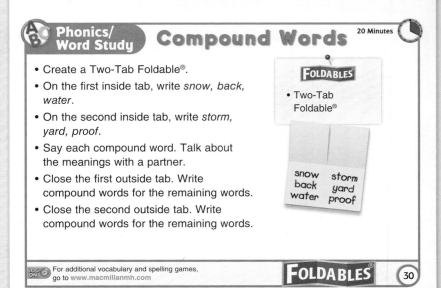

- Create a Two-Tab Foldable®.
- On the first inside tab, write *snow, back, water.*
- On the second inside tab, write *storm, yard, proof.*
- Say each compound word. Talk about the meanings with a partner.
- Close the first outside tab. Write compound words for the remaining words.
- Close the second outside tab. Write compound words for the remaining words.

FOLDABLES
- Two-Tab Foldable®

For additional vocabulary and spelling games, go to www.macmillanmh.com

FOLDABLES

30

Literacy Workstations

Literacy Workstation Flip Charts

Writing

Objectives

- Write a paragraph introducing a famous actor
- Practice writing and expressing opinions
- Write a description of a painting you like

Content Literacy

Objectives

- Research information about making a color wheel
- Make a color wheel with primary and secondary colors
- Research a statue or monument and its purpose

Writing · An Introduction
20 Minutes

- Imagine that a famous actor will speak at your school. You have been asked to introduce this person. What would you want to include in your introduction to persuade people to come to the event? Write your introduction.

Extension

- Share your introduction with a classmate. Ask him or her to give you more ideas to include. Try to come up with five more things.

Things you need:
- pen and paper

29

Science · Crayons and Color
20 Minutes

- Did you ever wonder how crayons are made? Use the Internet to find out.
- How does the state of matter change during the crayon-making process? Write an explanation.

Extension

- Write directions that explain how to mix two primary colors together to make the colors orange, green, and purple.
- Illustrate each step of your directions.

Things you need:
- online resources
- pen and paper
- colored pencils or markers

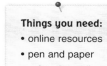

29

Writing · My Favorite Painting
20 Minutes

- Look through an art book and choose a painting you like. Write a description of the painting including what colors and textures the artist used. Describe the feeling that the painting expresses.

Extension

- Discuss your personal opinion of the painting with a partner. Would you persuade people to purchase the painting? Why or why not?

Things you need:
- art books
- pen and paper

Internet Research and Inquiry Activity
Students can find more facts at www.macmillanmh.com

30

Social Studies · Monuments
20 Minutes

- Design a monument that celebrates an important person in your state. Draw your design.
- Write the information for the plaque that will go with the monument. Be sure to include a description of the person, and tell why he or she is important.

Extension

- Role-play a dedication ceremony with a partner. One person can be the presenter. The other can be the person being honored.

Things you need:
- history books or encyclopedia
- pen and paper
- poster board
- markers

30

368

Oral Language

Build Background

ACCESS PRIOR KNOWLEDGE

Share the following information: Art can help people express their feelings about people and events. This photo depicts a mural, or large painting, of Martin Luther King, Jr. He was the civil rights leader in the 1960s whom you learned about in *My Brother Martin*.

Write these words on the board and briefly define each using the **Define/Example/Ask** routine: **expression** (showing feelings through words or other media), **memorial** (something that serves as a reminder of a person or group of people who have died, such as a statue or ceremony), **mural** (large painting on a wall).

FOCUS QUESTION Read "Talk About It" on **Student Book** page 369. Then have partners describe the photo. Ask:

- Think about Martin Luther King, Jr. Why has the artist created this memorial, or work to preserve King's memory? Explain.

- Why do you think the artist chose a mural, or large painting, to express himself or herself?

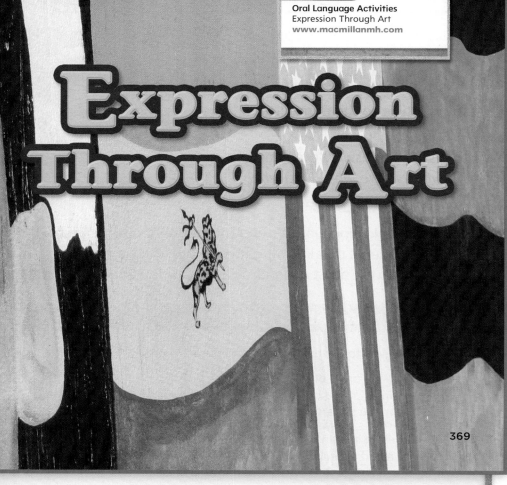

Talk About It

What do you think the artist was trying to express through this mural?

LOG ON ▶ VIEW IT

Oral Language Activities
Expression Through Art
www.macmillanmh.com

Expression Through Art

369

Use the Picture Prompt

BUILD WRITING FLUENCY

Have students write in their Writer's Notebooks about their memories of a person or an event. Tell students to write as much as they can for 10 minutes without stopping. Meet with individuals during Writing Conference time to provide feedback and revision assignments. Students should self-correct any errors they notice prior to the conference.

Connect to the Unit Theme

DISCUSS THE BIG IDEA

People use words, artwork, and other creative media to express themselves.

Ask what students have learned so far in this unit about creative expression.

- What ways of expressing ourselves have we read about so far?

- Why is expressing yourself important to communicating well with others?

USE THEME FOLDABLES

Write the **Big Idea** statement on the board. Ask students to copy it on their Unit Theme Foldables. Remind them to add details as they complete this week's readings.

Dinah Zike's
FOLDABLES®
Study Organizer

Study Book

Read Aloud

Read "Small Artist Has a Big Appeal"

Read Aloud

GENRE: Informational Text/Expository

Share with students the following key characteristics of an **expository** news article:

- A news article contains important, newsworthy facts.

- A news article answers the questions *who, what, where, when,* and *why.*

FOCUS ON VOCABULARY

Introduce the following words, using the **Define/Example/Ask** routine. Tell students that knowing these words will help them understand who the artist Alejandro Fernández is and how he works.

Vocabulary Routine

Use the routine below to discuss the meaning of each word.

Define: A **canvas** is a piece of cloth on which an artist paints.
Example: The painter pulled out a large canvas and began to work.
Ask: Where might you see artists' canvases?

Define: A **muse** is an imaginary person or thing that provides inspiration.
Example: Pedro relied upon his muse to guide his writing.
Ask: Why might an author find the idea of having a muse useful?

Define: A **trance** is a sleeplike state occurring during intense concentration.
Example: Nellie was in a trance as soon as she saw the giant boulder.
Ask: When might you be in a trance?

LISTENING FOR A PURPOSE

Ask students to listen carefully as you read "Small Artist Has a Big Appeal" in the **Read-Aloud Anthology**, pages 97–100. Use the Think Alouds and Genre Study provided.

ELL **Interactive Reading** Build students' oral language by engaging them in talk about the passage's basic meaning.

- Point to the picture of the boy with the paintbrush. Name the materials he has with him, and have students repeat. Explain that the tubes contain the paint Alejandro uses to create his work.

- After the first six paragraphs, say: *Turn to your partner and discuss why Alejandro might have left the painting for three or four days.*

- After the last paragraph on page 98, say: *Explain the pressures Alejandro's parents might be concerned about.*

- After the last paragraph, say: *Tell your partner why Alejandro's mother is important to his work.*

Think/Pair/Share Use **Copying Master 1**, "I wonder …," to help students check their understanding of Alejandro and his artwork. Then have students turn to a partner and orally summarize the article, using their responses to guide them. Finally, have a few students share their summaries with the class.

RESPOND TO THE EXPOSITORY NEWS ARTICLE

Ask students the Think and Respond questions on page 100. Then have students think about why painting might be so important to Alejandro. Have them discuss their thoughts with a partner.

Model Fluency

Reread the article. Tell students that this time you want them to focus on one aspect of how you read the article—your **rate**.

Point out that you read at a steady rate, or tempo, emphasizing particularly important words as you go. Model an example.

Think Aloud Listen as I read the part where the author describes Alejandro's journey to the United States. Listen to my rate as I read the passage.

"He left Cuba just a year ago after he and his mother won the U.S. visa lottery and were able to join his dad, who left the island for Mexico and crossed the border into the United States hoping to later reunite his family."

Did you notice how I read at a steady rate, emphasizing key points in each sentence? Now you try. Repeat each sentence after me, using the same rate and emphasis that I use.

Establish Fluency Focus Remind students that you will be listening for this same quality in their reading throughout the week. You will help them improve their reading by adjusting their rate to express meaning.

Readers Theater

BUILDING LISTENING AND SPEAKING SKILLS
Distribute copies of "All the Money in the World," **Read-Aloud Anthology** pages 182–202. Have students practice reading the play throughout the unit. Assign parts and have the students present the play or perform it as a dramatic reading at the end of the unit.

ELL

Discuss Genre Review expository news articles with students. Say: *What kind of information can you find in a news article? Who is Alejandro Fernández? What does he do? What other information did you learn from the article?* Elaborate on students' responses. Then ask students to describe the main idea of the article in phrases or sentences, based on their levels.

Objective

- Decode compound words

Materials

- Practice Book, p. 127
- Word-Building Cards
- Transparency 15
- Teacher's Resource Book, p. 134

ELL

Word Recognition Some students may find it challenging to identify short words within a longer word, particularly if their vocabulary is limited. Have students cover the compound word with their hand and reveal one letter at a time, continuing until they recognize a short word within the longer, compound word. Begin with easily identifiable words, such as *weekday, hallway,* and *backpack.* See language transfers on pages T16–T31.

HOMEWORK **Practice Book,** page 127

A **compound word** is made up of two short words. The two words together make a new word with a new meaning.

When I was at camp this summer, we built a campfire to keep warm at night.

camp + fire = campfire
camp: an outdoor place with tents or cabins
fire: the flame, heat, and light given off when wood burns
campfire: an outdoor fire for cooking or keeping warm in a camp

Draw a line dividing the two words that make up the compound word in each sentence. Then write the letter that matches the meaning of each word.

1. We had a bad snowstorm.	e and g	a. long, thin rope
2. Bentley loved snowflakes.	e and c	b. coming into being
3. Hail is made from raindrops.	h and j	c. small, thin, flat pieces
4. The child took the towels off the clothesline when the hail came.	f and a	d. plants with many long, thin leaves
5. The child's birthday was in January.	b and i	e. white crystals of ice
6. The grasshopper hid during the storm.	d and k	f. what people wear
		g. windy, unsettled weather
		h. water from clouds
		i. twenty-four hours
		j. small balls of something
		k. someone or something that jumps

Approaching Reproducible, page 127

Beyond Reproducible, page 127

Word Study

✔ Compound Words

EXPLAIN/MODEL

Explain to students that some words are made up of smaller words such as *classroom,* which is made up of the words *class* and *room,* and *birdhouse,* which is made up of the words *bird* and *house.* These words are called **compound words**.

Write the compound words below on the board. Explain that some compound words are written with two or more words joined together, some are written with a hyphen, and others are written as two separate words.

- bathtub
- passer-by
- high school

Think Aloud Let's look at each word I wrote. They are all compound words, but there is something different about how each one is written. The word *bathtub* is a regular compound word. It is made up of the words *bath* and *tub.* These two words are joined together to form one word.

However, the next two compound words are different. The compound word *passer-by* is made up of two words, but the words are written with a hyphen to separate them. In the compound word *high school,* the two words are not joined when we write them.

Explain to students that they can use the two or more words that make up a compound word to figure out its meaning.

Think Aloud Let's look again at each compound word I wrote. I can often use the smaller words in a compound word to figure out its meaning. For example, a *bathtub* is a tub in which people take a bath, a *passer-by* is a person who passes by someone or something, and a *high school* is a school of the highest level that public school students must attend.

Read Multisyllabic Words

TRANSITION TO LONGER WORDS Display **Transparency 15**. Have students underline the words that make up each compound word, and check to see if they can decode each word. Then have them chorally read the compound words. Revisit the words to determine their meanings. Have students use the smaller words to figure out a meaning. Then have them consult a dictionary to check.

afternoon	blueberry	fire escape	newspaper
airmail	collarbone	give-and-take	pillowcase
anybody	countdown	handshake	playground
bandleader	diving board	high-rise	rainbow
basketball	downtown	homesick	scrapbook
bedspread	father-in-law	masterpiece	windshield

Phonics Transparency 15

BUILD WORDS Display **Word-Building Cards** *night, back, light, hand, sun, gown, bone, door, field, ground, yard, house, candle, made, book, stand, burn, rise, shine*. Have students use them to build as many compound words as possible. These and other words can be formed: *nightgown, backbone, backfield, handmade, handstand, sunburn*.

APPLY DECODING STRATEGY Guide students to use the Decoding Strategy to decode the following words: *anteater, doubleheader, candlestick, firefighter, grasshopper, homegrown, saucepan, shoreline, supermarket, toothache, underground, wristwatch*. Write each word on the board. Remind students to look for smaller words and common spelling patterns in step 3 of the Decoding Strategy procedure.

Build Fluency

SPEED DRILL Distribute copies of the **Compound Words Speed Drill** on **Teacher's Resource Book** page 134. Use the Speed Drill routine to help students become fluent reading compound words.

Quick Check

Can students read compound words?

During **Small Group Instruction**

Tier 2

If No → **Approaching Level** Reteach the skill using the lesson on p. 395J.

If Yes → **On Level** Consolidate the learning using p. 395S.

Beyond Level Extend the learning using p. 395W.

Syllable Fluency

DAILY

Use **Word-Building Cards 141–150**. Display one card at a time. Have students chorally read each short word. Have students work with partners during independent time to write as many compound words as they can that contain at least one word from the card.

Decoding Strategy

Decoding Strategy Chart

Step 1	Look for word parts (prefixes) at the beginning of the word.
Step 2	Look for word parts (suffixes) at the end of the word.
Step 3	In the base word, look for familiar spelling patterns. Think about the six syllable-spelling patterns you have learned.
Step 4	Sound out and blend together the word parts.
Step 5	Say the word parts fast. Adjust your pronunciation as needed. Ask yourself: "Is this a word I have heard before?" Then read the word in the sentence and ask: "Does it make sense in this sentence?"

© Macmillan/McGraw-Hill

Vocabulary

Examples and Definitions Remind students that, if they find an unfamiliar word, they should look for context clues, or words or phrases in nearby sentences that can help them figure out the meaning of the word. Point out that those clues may take different forms, such as synonyms, antonyms, examples, or grammar/syntax clues. Explain that examples and definitions in the paragraph may also help them understand the unfamiliar word.

Ask students to read "Context Clues" in the bookmark on **Student Book** page 370. Then model how to use context clues to determine the meaning of the word *skyscrapers*.

Think Aloud Emma's first suggestion is to make models of "skyscrapers." I'm not sure what *skyscrapers* means, but there seem to be good context clues nearby. The words "really tall buildings" seem like a definition of *skyscrapers,* and the next sentence uses the Empire State Building as an example. So, *skyscrapers* must mean "very tall buildings," or buildings that seem to touch or scrape the sky.

Have students identify and use context clues for *barbecue* on page 371.

Read "Secondhand Art"

As you read "Secondhand Art" with students, ask them to identify clues that reveal the meanings of the highlighted words. Tell students they will read these words again in *Me and Uncle Romie.*

SECONDHAND ART

by Amir Ferry

Vocabulary

skyscrapers	glorious
collage	strutting
barbecue	swarms

✓ **Context Clues**

Examples and **Definitions** can help you figure out the meaning of unfamiliar words. Use the example in the story to figure out the meaning of *skyscrapers*.

Danny and Emma are working together on their project for the school art contest. They still have not decided what to make.

"Danny, maybe we should make models of those really tall buildings called **skyscrapers**. The Empire State Building is a skyscraper. I know how much you love tall buildings. Isn't it your dream to design the world's tallest building?" Emma asked.

"Yes, it is. That's a great idea, Emma, but it might be too hard for us," said Danny. "We could make a **collage**."

"We could," said Emma, "but lots of kids will make collages. Let's try to be different!"

370

Quick Check

Can students identify word meanings?

During **Small Group Instruction**

Tier 2

If No → **Approaching Level** Reteach the words using the Vocabulary lesson, pp. 395K–395L.

If Yes → **On Level** Consolidate the learning using p. 395S.

Gifted Talented

Beyond Level Extend the learning using p. 395W.

Danny's mom came into the kitchen to remind Danny to put the recycling bin in her car. Danny's eyes lit up.

"I've got it!" he said. "Emma, we can use the recycling. Let's make a papier-mâché city out of that stuff!"

"Great idea," agreed Emma.

They got right to work. There were tons of cans from last week's outdoor grilled chicken **barbecue**.

They cut strips of newspaper and made a paste from flour and water. Then they used the strips of paper and paste to cover the cans and make papier-mâché buildings. At last Danny and Emma were ready to paint.

"Let's use bright yellow," Emma suggested. "It's such a **glorious** color, isn't it?"

Danny giggled. "You're so dramatic, Emma."

He started **strutting** around like a rooster. "Yellow is such a *glorious* color," he teased. Emma flicked her paintbrush at him.

The next day Danny and Emma presented their art project. Everyone loved their "recycled city." Danny and Emma won first prize. **Swarms** of people came up to congratulate them.

"I always told you recycling could be a lot of fun!" Emma exclaimed.

"You were right, Emma. And the best part was that I didn't have to haul everything into Mom's car," said Danny.

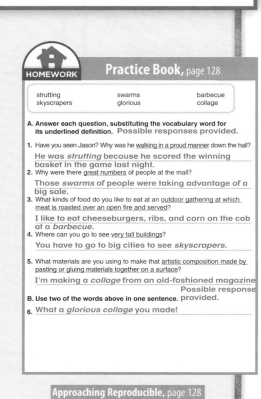

Reread for **Comprehension**

Visualize

Character, Setting, Plot Identifying and visualizing the setting of a story can help readers think about how the setting affects both the characters and the main events of the plot. For example, a change in setting is a main event that can influence future events in the story. A Story Flowchart can help you keep track of the setting, plot events, and a character's reactions in a story. Reread "Secondhand Art" and fill in the Story Flowchart.

Setting

Event	→	Character's Reaction

Event	→	Character's Reaction

Event	→	Character's Reaction

LOG ON ▶ LEARN IT Comprehension
www.macmillanmh.com

371

Vocabulary

TEACH WORDS

Introduce each word using the **Define/Example/Ask** routine. Model reading each word using the syllable-scoop technique.

Vocabulary Routine

Define: **Skyscrapers** are very tall buildings.
Example: The first skyscrapers were built in New York City and Chicago.
Ask: Are there any skyscrapers in your community? PRIOR KNOWLEDGE

- A **collage** is made from many small pieces put together to form a picture. *We cut pictures from old greeting cards to make a holiday collage.* Tell about a time you put together a collage. DESCRIPTION

- If you eat a meal that has been prepared on a grill, you are eating **barbecue**. *We ate chicken and shrimp barbecue.* What other ways can you use the word *barbecue*? MULTIPLE-MEANINGS

- Something that is **glorious** is full of beauty and wonder. *The maple leaves are glorious in the fall.* What is an antonym for the word *glorious*? ANTONYM

- Someone who is **strutting** is walking proudly, often in an exaggerated manner. *The rooster has been strutting around the chicken coop.* When have you seen people or animals strutting? PRIOR KNOWLEDGE

- When there are **swarms** of something, there are many together in a group. *We ran from the swarms of bees that we had accidentally stirred up.* How are swarms similar to and different from herds? COMPARE AND CONTRAST

ELL

Preteach Vocabulary See pages 395BB and 395K to preteach the vocabulary words to ELL and Approaching Level students. Use the **Visual Vocabulary Resources** to demonstrate and discuss each word. To further reinforce concepts, have students complete page 170 in the **ELL Resource Book**.

HOMEWORK **Practice Book,** page 128

| strutting | swarms | barbecue |
| skyscrapers | glorious | collage |

A. Answer each question, substituting the vocabulary word for its underlined definition. Possible responses provided.

1. Have you seen Jason? Why was he walking in a proud manner down the hall?
   He was *strutting* because he scored the winning basket in the game last night.
2. Why were there great numbers of people at the mall?
   Those *swarms* of people were taking advantage of a big sale.
3. What kinds of food do you like to eat at an outdoor gathering at which meat is roasted over an open fire and served?
   I like to eat cheeseburgers, ribs, and corn on the cob at a *barbecue*.
4. Where can you go to see very tall buildings?
   You have to go to big cities to see *skyscrapers*.
5. What materials are you using to make that artistic composition made by pasting or gluing materials together on a surface?
   I'm making a *collage* from an old-fashioned magazine
   Possible response
B. Use two of the words above in one sentence. provided.
6. What a *glorious collage* you made!

Approaching Reproducible, page 128

Beyond Reproducible, page 128

Me and Uncle Romie **371**

Objectives

- Visualize
- Analyze character, setting, and plot
- Use academic language: *character traits, setting, plot, visualize*

Materials

- Transparencies 7, 15a, 15b
- Practice Book, p. 129

Skills Trace

Character, Setting, Plot	
Introduce	41A–41B
Practice/ Apply	42–59; Practice Book, 12–13
Reteach/ Review	65M–65Z, 81A–81B, 82–97, 103M–103Z; Practice Book, 30–31
Assess	Weekly Tests; Units 1, 3 Tests
Maintain	121B, 319B, 371A–371B, 372–391, 395M–395Z, 429B

ELL

Academic Language
Preteach the following academic language words to **ELL** and **Approaching Level** students during Small Group time: *visualize, setting, plot, character.* See pages 395AA and 395I.

Reread for Comprehension

STRATEGY
VISUALIZE

What Is It? Explain that when you **visualize**, you use the descriptive details a writer provides to create pictures in your mind that help you understand what you are reading.

Why Is It Important? Point out that in order to visualize, readers must pay close attention to the details in the text and use logical reasoning to create a picture in their mind. Visualizing also helps readers recognize how an author's metaphors and similes create these images.

SKILL
CHARACTER, SETTING, PLOT

What Is It? Explain that the **setting** is when and where a story takes place. The **plot** is the series of events that takes place in the story. The **characters** are the people in the story.

Why Is It Important? Readers need to be able to identify the characters, setting, and plot in order to understand the main events of the story.

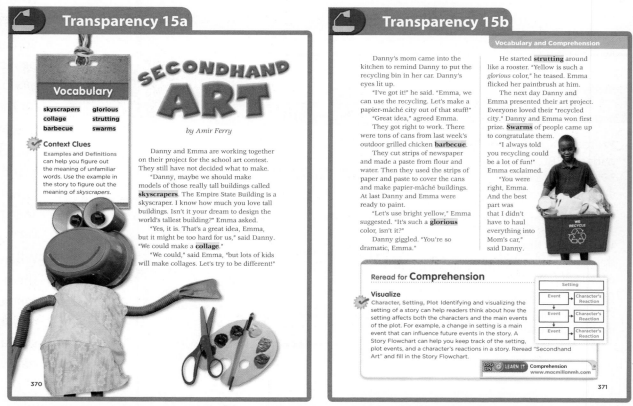

Transparency 15a

Vocabulary

skyscrapers	glorious
collage	strutting
barbecue	swarms

Context Clues
Examples and Definitions can help you figure out the meaning of unfamiliar words. Use the example in the story to figure out the meaning of *skyscrapers*.

SECONDHAND ART

by Amir Ferry

Danny and Emma are working together on their project for the school art contest. They still have not decided what to make.

"Danny, maybe we should make models of those really tall buildings called **skyscrapers**. The Empire State Building is a skyscraper. I know how much you love tall buildings. Isn't it your dream to design the world's tallest building?" Emma asked.

"Yes, it is. That's a great idea, but it might be too hard for us," said Danny. "We could make a **collage**."

"We could," said Emma, "but lots of kids will make collages. Let's try to be different!"

Transparency 15b

Vocabulary and Comprehension

Danny's mom came into the kitchen to remind Danny to put the recycling bin in her car. Danny's eyes lit up.

"I've got it!" he said. "Emma, we can use the recycling. Let's make a papier-mâché city out of that stuff!"

"Great idea," agreed Emma.

They got right to work. There were tons of cans from last week's outdoor grilled chicken **barbecue**.

They cut strips of newspaper and made a paste from flour and water. Then they used the strips of paper and paste to cover the cans and make papier-mâché buildings. At last Danny and Emma were ready to paint.

"Let's use bright yellow," Emma suggested. "It's such a **glorious** color, isn't it?"

Danny giggled. "You're so dramatic, Emma."

He started **strutting** around like a rooster. "Yellow is such a *glorious* color," he teased. Emma flicked her paintbrush at him.

The next day Danny and Emma presented their art project. Everyone loved their "recycled city." Danny and Emma won first prize. **Swarms** of people came up to congratulate them.

"I always told you recycling could be a lot of fun!" Emma exclaimed.

"You were right, Emma. And the best part was that I didn't have to haul everything into Mom's car," said Danny.

Reread for Comprehension

Visualize
Character, Setting, Plot Identifying and visualizing the setting of a story can help readers think about how the setting affects both the characters and the main events of the plot. For example, a change in setting is a main event that can influence future events in the story. A Story Flowchart can help you keep track of the setting, plot events, and a character's reactions in a story. Reread "Secondhand Art" and fill in the Story Flowchart.

LOG ON LEARN IT Comprehension www.macmillanmh.com

Setting

Event	→	Character's Reaction
↓		
Event	→	Character's Reaction
↓		
Event	→	Character's Reaction

Student Book pages 370–371 available on Comprehension Transparencies 15a and 15b

■ Sometimes, the setting of a story has a big impact on the plot. The conditions, time period, and environment in which the story is taking place may affect how the characters behave and influence certain plot events.

■ To identify the plot, readers must find the problem the main character faces, as well as the steps taken to solve the problem. They they locate the turning point—the point at which the main character begins to find a solution to the problem—and identify the events that lead to the solution. Sequencing and summarizing the plot's main events can help readers explain their influence on future events and help readers predict a resolution to the problem.

MODEL

How Do I Use It? Read aloud the first page of "Secondhand Art" on **Student Book** page 370. Display **Transparency 7** and explain that you will use a Story Flowchart to record details about setting, character, and plot, focusing on the way characters react to events.

Think Aloud I notice that Danny and Emma seem to be good friends who like to joke, but they are also serious about their art project. They are trying to be both realistic and original, so they won't settle for the first idea that comes to mind. I have a feeling they will come up with a really good idea for a project.

GUIDED PRACTICE

Help students begin filling in the Story Flowchart. Continue by helping students identify details about character, setting, and plot in the first column on page 371. Direct students to look for the ways in which the characters react to events.

APPLY

Have students analyze the characters, setting, and plot for the second column on page 371. Have them complete the Story Flowchart. Then help them use the chart to summarize the selection.

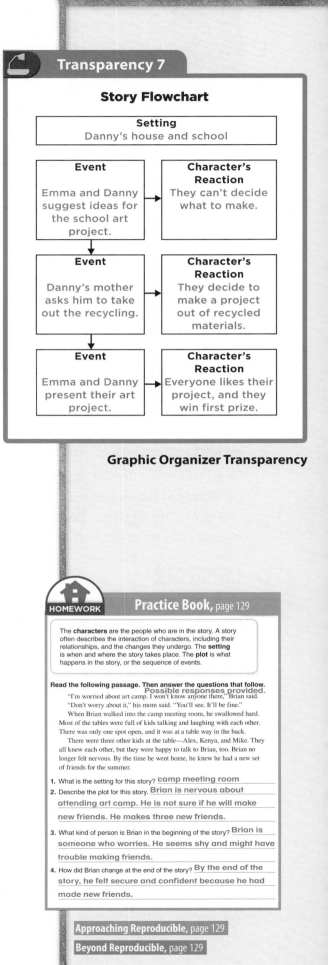

Transparency 7

Story Flowchart

Setting
Danny's house and school

Event	Character's Reaction
Emma and Danny suggest ideas for the school art project.	They can't decide what to make.
Danny's mother asks him to take out the recycling.	They decide to make a project out of recycled materials.
Emma and Danny present their art project.	Everyone likes their project, and they win first prize.

Graphic Organizer Transparency

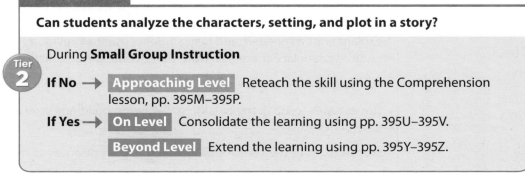

HOMEWORK **Practice Book,** page 129

The **characters** are the people who are in the story. A story often describes the interaction of characters, including their relationships, and the changes they undergo. The **setting** is when and where the story takes place. The **plot** is what happens in the story, or the sequence of events.

Read the following passage. Then answer the questions that follow.
Possible responses provided.
"I'm worried about art camp. I won't know anyone there," Brian said.
"Don't worry about it," his mom said. "You'll see. It'll be fine."
When Brian walked into the camp meeting room, he swallowed hard. Most of the tables were full of kids talking and laughing with each other. There was only one spot open, and it was at a table way in the back.
There were three other kids at the table—Alex, Kenya, and Mike. They all knew each other, but they were happy to talk to Brian, too. Brian no longer felt nervous. By the time he went home, he knew he had a new set of friends for the summer.

1. What is the setting for this story? camp meeting room
2. Describe the plot for this story. Brian is nervous about attending art camp. He is not sure if he will make new friends. He makes three new friends.
3. What kind of person is Brian in the beginning of the story? Brian is someone who worries. He seems shy and might have trouble making friends.
4. How did Brian change at the end of the story? By the end of the story, he felt secure and confident because he had made new friends.

Approaching Reproducible, page 129
Beyond Reproducible, page 129

WHOLE GROUP

✔ **MAIN SELECTION**
- *Me and Uncle Romie*
- Skill: Character, Setting, Plot

✔ **PAIRED SELECTION**
- "Computers: The Future of Art"
- Text Feature: Multiple-Step Instructions

SMALL GROUP

- Differentiated Instruction, pp. 395I–395HH

Main Selection

GENRE: Historical Fiction

Read the definition of Historical Fiction on **Student Book** page 372. Point out the character of Uncle Romie is based on the collage artist Romare Bearden.

STRATEGY
VISUALIZE

Remind students that visualizing means forming mental images based on clues, including metaphors and similes, that the author provides in the text.

SKILL
CHARACTER, SETTING, PLOT

Remind students that the setting is where and when a story takes place. The plot is the series of events that happen in a story. The characters are who the story is about. Describing the interaction of characters, including changes they undergo, can help students summarize the plot's main events.

Comprehension

Genre

Historical Fiction has real and fictional characters taking part in actual historical events.

Visualize

Character, Setting, Plot As you read, fill in your Story Flowchart.

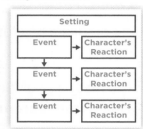

Setting
Event → Character's Reaction
Event → Character's Reaction
Event → Character's Reaction

Read to Find Out

How does James's summer in New York change him?

372

Vocabulary

Vocabulary Words Review the tested words while reading: **strutting, swarms, collage, barbecue, glorious**, and **skyscrapers.**

Additional Selection Words Students may be unfamiliar with these words. Pronounce the words, give student-friendly explanations as needed, and help students use the previously taught vocabulary strategies: word parts, context clues, dictionary.

studio (p. 379): the place where an artist works

fire escapes (p. 381): the outside stairways on buildings used as emergency exits

stoops (p. 381): the sets of steps leading to the entrances of houses

saxophone (p. 382): a musical instrument used by jazz musicians

mango (p. 382): a sweet tropical fruit

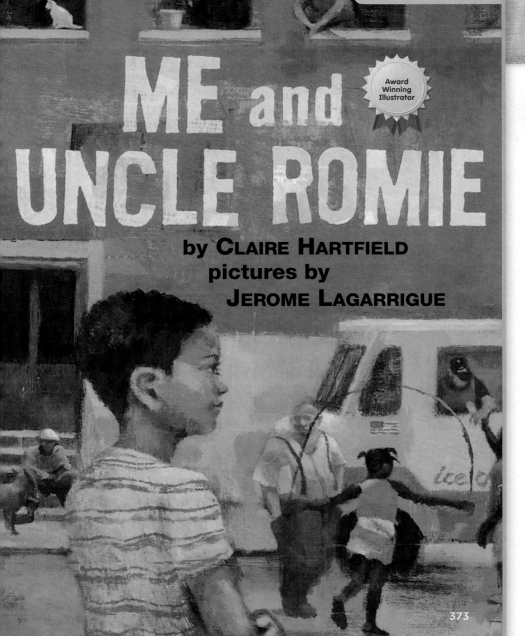

ME and UNCLE ROMIE

Award Winning Illustrator

by CLAIRE HARTFIELD
pictures by
JEROME LAGARRIGUE

373

Read the Main Selection

Preteach	Read Together	Read Independently
Have Approaching Level students and English Language Learners listen to the selection on **StudentWorks Plus**, the interactive e-Book, before reading with the class.	Use the prompts to guide comprehension and model how to complete the graphic organizer. Have students use **Think/Pair/Share** to discuss the selection.	If students can read the selection independently, have them read and complete the graphic organizer. Suggest that they use their purposes to choose their reading strategies.

LOG ON StudentWorks Plus
Interactive Student Book

Preview and Predict

QUICK WRITE Have students read the title, preview the illustrations, consider the genre, and make predictions about the story. Students may include their knowledge of being away from home.

Set Purposes

FOCUS QUESTION Discuss the "Read to Find Out" question on **Student Book** page 372. Tell students to look for the answer as they read and to set their own reading purposes as well.

Point out the Story Flowchart in the Student Book and on **Practice Book** page 130. Explain that students will fill it in as they read.

Read *Me and Uncle Romie*

Use the questions and Think Alouds to support instruction about the comprehension strategy and skill.

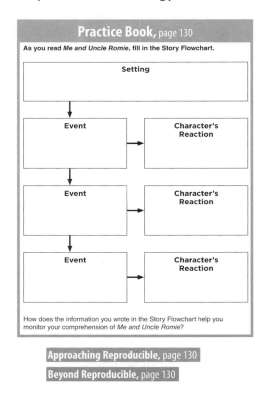

Practice Book, page 130

As you read *Me and Uncle Romie*, fill in the Story Flowchart.

Setting

Event → Character's Reaction

Event → Character's Reaction

Event → Character's Reaction

How does the information you wrote in the Story Flowchart help you monitor your comprehension of *Me and Uncle Romie*?

Approaching Reproducible, page 130
Beyond Reproducible, page 130

Develop Comprehension

1 SKILL
CHARACTER, SETTING, PLOT

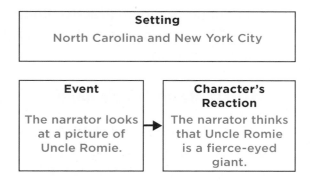

Uncle Romie's name is in the title of the story, so we know he will be a major **character**. What is the narrator's first impression of Uncle Romie based on his picture? (Based on a picture of Uncle Romie, the narrator thinks he is "a bald-headed, fierce-eyed giant.") Add this information to your Story Flowchart.

Setting
North Carolina and New York City

Event		Character's Reaction
The narrator looks at a picture of Uncle Romie.	→	The narrator thinks that Uncle Romie is a fierce-eyed giant.

It was the summer Mama had the twins that I first met my uncle Romie. The doctor had told Mama she had to stay off her feet till the babies got born. Daddy thought it was a good time for me to visit Uncle Romie and his wife, Aunt Nanette, up north in New York City. But I wasn't so sure. Mama had told me that Uncle Romie was some kind of artist, and he didn't have any kids. I'd seen his picture too. He looked scary—a bald-headed, fierce-eyed giant. No, I wasn't sure about this visit at all.

1
2

The day before I left home was a regular North Carolina summer day. "A good train-watching day," my friend B.J. said.

We waited quietly in the grass beside the tracks. B.J. heard it first. "It's a'coming," he said. Then I heard it too—a low rumbling, building to a roar. *WHOOO—OOO!*

"The *Piedmont*!" we shouted as the train blasted past.

374

Monitor Comprehension

Monitor and Clarify: *Adjust Reading Rate*

Explain Tell students that they can adjust their reading rates if they do not understand plot events after rereading or asking themselves questions. Model for students how to increase and decrease their reading rates to improve comprehension.

Discuss Ask whether students should slow down or speed up their reading rates when reading dialogue, and have them explain their response. (They would slow down to follow speaker changes.)

Apply As students read the selection, have them experiment with different reading rates for narrative passages and passages with dialogue.

"I'm the greatest train-watcher ever," B.J. boasted.

"Yeah," I answered, "but tomorrow I'll be *riding* a train. I'm the lucky one."

Lucky, I thought as we headed home. *Maybe.*

That evening I packed my suitcase. Voices drifted up from the porch below.

"Romie's got that big art show coming up," Mama said quietly. "I hope he's not too busy for James, especially on his birthday."

"Romie's a good man," Daddy replied. "And Nanette'll be there too."

> ✓ **Character, Setting, Plot**
> How does James feel about visiting Uncle Romie in New York City?

375

Read
Main Selection

Develop Comprehension

2 **STRATEGY**
VISUALIZE

✓ **Teacher Think Aloud** The details on page 374 help me to visualize how Uncle Romie looks. The narrator, James, says he looked like a "bald-headed, fierce-eyed giant." This description helps me to picture someone who is very tall and whose eyes look cruel and threatening. From his description, I can tell that James has never met Uncle Romie. I can understand why he is nervous about leaving North Carolina and traveling to New York.

3 **SKILL**
CHARACTER, SETTING, PLOT

✓ How does James feel about visiting Uncle Romie in New York City? (He is nervous. Based on the picture of Uncle Romie, James thinks he is a scary man.)

Phonics/Word Study

APPLY DECODING SKILLS While reading, point out words with the sound/spelling patterns, syllable types, and word parts students have recently learned. Help students blend these words. You may wish to focus on selection words that are compound words, such as in *suitcase, birthday, outside, everything,* and *rooftop.*

ELL — ENGLISH LANGUAGE LEARNERS

Beginning

Access Content Preteach story content build language, and develop meaning using the Interactive Question-Response Guide in the **ELL Resource Book**, pages 158–167. Give ample time for students to respond. They may point or use words or short phrases to respond.

Intermediate

Describe Preteach story content, build language, and develop meaning using the Interactive Question-Response Guide in the ELL Resource Book, pages 158–167. Have students respond in complete sentences. Repeat their responses, correcting pronunciation or grammar as needed.

Advanced

Explain Complete the Intermediate task with students. Elaborate on their responses.

Develop Comprehension

4 MONITOR AND CLARIFY: ADJUST READING RATE

This page describes an emotional good-bye. How would you adjust your reading rate to understand how James feels as he talks to his mom, and later boards the train to New York? (Students should read the text more slowly to understand how James feels. He will not only miss his mother, but the fact that he holds tight to a jar of jelly his mother had given him for Uncle Romie reveals that he is still nervous about this trip, and whether Uncle Romie will like him.)

The light faded. Mama called me into her bedroom. "Where's my good-night kiss?" she said.

I curled up next to her. "I'll miss the way you make my birthday special, Mama. Your lemon cake and the baseball game."

4

"Well," Mama sighed, "it won't be those things. But Uncle Romie and Aunt Nanette are family, and they love you too. It'll still be a good birthday, honey."

Mama pulled me close. Her voice sang soft and low. Later, in my own bed, I listened as crickets began their song and continued into the night.

The next morning I hugged Mama good-bye, and Daddy and I headed for the train. He got me seated, then stood waving at me from the outside. I held tight to the jar of pepper jelly Mama had given me for Uncle Romie.

376

Comprehension

Mood

Explain The mood, or atmosphere, of a story is the feeling it gives the reader. Authors create mood by using sensory words to describe the setting and characters. Events in the plot are also carefully developed to bring about a particular emotional response.

Discuss Ask students to look for descriptive details on page 376 that help establish the mood of this part of the story. (*light faded; curled up next to her; pulled me close; sang soft and low; crickets began their song; held tight to the jar*) What mood is the author creating? (The mood is quiet and tense.)

Apply Have students continue to scan the text for descriptive details that signal mood. Ask them to keep a list of the major plot events in the story and to identify the associated mood for each.

"ALL A-BOARD!" The conductor's voice crackled over the loudspeaker.

The train pulled away. *Chug-a-chug-a-chug-a-chug.* I watched my town move past my window—bright-colored houses, chickens **strutting** across the yards, flowers everywhere.

After a while I felt hungry. Daddy had packed me a lunch and a dinner to eat one at a time. I ate almost everything at once. Then my belly felt tight and I was kind of sleepy. I closed my eyes and dreamed about Mama and Daddy getting ready for those babies. Would they even miss me?

Later, when I woke up, I ate the last bit of my dinner and thought about my birthday. Would they make my lemon cake and take me to a baseball game in New York?

The sky turned from dark blue to black. I was getting sleepy all over again.

"We're almost there, son," the man next to me said.

Then I saw it . . . New York City. Buildings stretching up to the sky. So close together. Not like North Carolina at all. **5** **6**

377

5 NARRATIVE POINT OF VIEW

Think about the **point of view** the author uses in this story. How does the author make the first-person narrator sound like a child instead of an adult? (The author shows us how the boy experiences the train ride. The narrator notes all the sights and sounds, as would a child who has not traveled like this before. In the sentence "My belly felt tight and I was kind of sleepy," the author uses simple words that a child might use.) Why is this important to James's role as narrator? (The author wants us to experience the trip through James's eyes, and to feel what it is like for a child to travel for the first time to an unfamiliar place.)

6 **SKILL**
CHARACTER, SETTING, PLOT

How would you describe James's **character** now that you have learned more about him? (James seems shy and fearful about leaving his family, but he is also brave because he rode the train from North Carolina to New York City by himself.)

Develop Comprehension

7 FIGURATIVE LANGUAGE

Reread the last sentence on page 378. Does it have a literal or a **figurative** meaning? Explain. (This is a figure of speech—a metaphor. It means that Aunt Nanette's smile is so big and warm that James feels as if it can reach out and hug him. A smile cannot actually reach out, so it has a figurative meaning.)

"Penn Station! Watch your step," the conductor said, helping me down to the platform. I did like Daddy said and found a spot for myself close to the train. **Swarms** of people rushed by. Soon I heard a silvery voice call my name. This had to be Aunt Nanette. I turned and saw her big smile reaching out to welcome me.

7

378

Vocabulary

Word Structure Clues: *Suffixes*

Explain/Model Explain that good readers sometimes use context clues, word structure, and grammar to help them understand an unfamiliar word.

Think Aloud I see the word *silvery* on this page. I am not sure what it means. I see the base word *silver* and the suffix *-y*. Other words I have seen that have the suffix *-y* are adjectives, such as *dirty* or *lucky*. In this context, *silvery* describes the sound of Aunt Nanette's voice, so *silvery* must be an adjective describing her music as "sparkly," like the sound of a silver bell.

Practice/Apply Have students use structural clues to help them determine the meanings of other difficult words. For example, what other suffixes show that a word is an adjective?

She took my hand and guided me through the rushing crowds onto an underground train called the subway. "This will take us right home," she explained.

Home was like nothing I'd ever seen before. No regular houses anywhere. Just big buildings and stores of all kinds—in the windows I saw paints, fabrics, radios, and TVs.

We turned into the corner building and climbed the stairs to the apartment—five whole flights up. *Whew!* I tried to catch my breath while Aunt Nanette flicked on the lights. **8**

"Uncle Romie's out talking to some people about his big art show that's coming up. He'll be home soon," Aunt Nanette said. She set some milk and a plate of cookies for me on the table. "Your uncle's working very hard, so we won't see much of him for a while. His workroom—we call it his studio—is in the front of our apartment. That's where he keeps all the things he needs to make his art."

379

Develop Comprehension

8 **SKILL**
CHARACTER, SETTING, PLOT

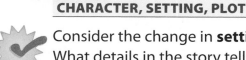

Consider the change in **setting**. What details in the story tell you how North Carolina is different from New York City? (On the train ride out of his hometown, James talks about seeing grass, chickens in the yards, and flowers all over. Upon arriving in New York City, he describes tall buildings and store windows, and walking up five flights of stairs to his aunt's apartment.)

Develop Comprehension

9 **SKILL**
CHARACTER, SETTING, PLOT

What new information does Aunt Nanette offer James about Uncle Romie? (She says that Uncle Romie is preparing for an art show and is working very hard.) How might this information influence future events in the plot? (As Uncle Romie is so busy preparing for a show, Aunt Nanette will probably have to show James around the neighborhood.)

"Doesn't he just paint?" I asked.

"Uncle Romie is a **collage** artist," Aunt Nanette explained. "He uses paints, yes. But also photographs, newspapers, cloth. He cuts and pastes them onto a board to make his paintings."

"That sounds kinda easy," I said.

Aunt Nanette laughed.

"Well, there's a little more to it than that, James. When you see the paintings, you'll understand. Come, let's get you to bed."

Lying in the dark, I heard heavy footsteps in the hall. A giant stared at me from the doorway. "Hello there, James." Uncle Romie's voice was deep and loud, like thunder. "Thanks for the pepper jelly," he boomed. "You have a good sleep, now." Then he disappeared down the hall.

9

380

Text Evidence

Character, Setting, Plot

Reread question 9. Then ask, *Why has Uncle Romie been so busy? Point to the information when you find it.* (He has been preparing for a big art show.) *Why does James think that Uncle Romie's art is easy to do?* (Because James thinks he is just gluing pictures onto a board.) *Does Aunt Nanette agree with this?* (No. She points out that Uncle Romie's art is more complicated than it sounds, and that he has been working very hard to get ready for his art show.) *What other information does the author provide to tell the reader that Uncle Romie is hardworking? (*Aunt Nanette says that James will not see Uncle Romie a lot [page 379]. He does not get home until late at night when James is already in bed.)

The next morning the door to Uncle Romie's studio was closed. But Aunt Nanette had plans for both of us. "Today we're going to a neighborhood called Harlem," she said. "It's where Uncle Romie lived as a boy."

Harlem was full of people walking, working, shopping, eating. Some were watching the goings-on from fire escapes. Others were sitting out on stoops greeting folks who passed by—just like the people back home calling out hellos from their front porches. Most everybody seemed to know Aunt Nanette. A lot of them asked after Uncle Romie too. **10**

We bought peaches at the market, then stopped to visit awhile. I watched some kids playing stickball. "Go on, get in that game," Aunt Nanette said, gently pushing me over to join them. When I was all hot and sweaty, we cooled off with double chocolate scoops from the ice cream man. Later we shared some **barbecue** on a rooftop way up high. I felt like I was on top of the world. **11**

381

Develop Comprehension

10 SKILL
CHARACTER, SETTING, PLOT

Notice the new details about the **setting**. How does Harlem in New York compare to James's hometown in North Carolina? (Harlem is busier and has more people than James's hometown. There are tall apartment buildings with concrete walkways instead of small homes with grass and trees. But people in Harlem call out "Hello!" from their buildings, just as people do in James's North Carolina neighborhood. The places are more alike than James first thought.)

11 SKILL
CHARACTER, SETTING, PLOT

When James says, "I felt like I was on top of the world," what do we learn about him? (Although James is actually sitting on a rooftop, the fun he is having in this new place makes him feel as if there is no better place to be in the world.)

ENGLISH LANGUAGE LEARNERS

STRATEGIES FOR EXTRA SUPPORT

Question 11 CHARACTER, SETTING, PLOT
Figurative Language Explain the expression *I felt like I was on top of the world*. Convey its literal meaning using a sketch of the world or globe, and then explain its figurative meaning. Ask students to retell what James did that day. You may need to explain words such as *fire escapes, stoops, front porches, stickball,* and *rooftop*. Ask students why they think James felt so happy. *Would you feel on top of the world if you had the same kind of day? Why or why not? What would make you feel on top of the world?* Repeat students' responses, correcting grammar and pronunciation as needed.

Develop Comprehension

12 STRATEGY
VISUALIZE

Teacher Think Aloud Reading the descriptive words and phrases the author uses on this page can help me visualize James's experiences in New York, and also how he felt about them. What verbs and adjectives does the author use to help you picture James's tour of New York City, and his experiences in Harlem?

Prompt partners to apply the strategy in a Think Aloud by sharing ideas.

Student Think Aloud Through James's descriptions, I imagine that his days with Aunt Nanette are packed with adventures. He uses words like *zoom* and *gobble*, which make me think of speed. I can picture him riding a fast elevator to the top of a very tall skyscraper, and then quickly eating a hot dog while walking through a big park.

As the days went by, Aunt Nanette took me all over the city—we rode a ferry boat to the Statue of Liberty . . . zoomed 102 floors up at the Empire State Building . . . window-shopped the fancy stores on Fifth Avenue . . . gobbled hot dogs in Central Park.

But it was Harlem that I liked best. I played stickball with the kids again . . . and on a really hot day a whole bunch of us ran through the icy cold water that sprayed out hard from the fire hydrant. In the evenings Aunt Nanette and I sat outside listening to the street musicians playing their saxophone songs.

On rainy days I wrote postcards and helped out around the apartment. I told Aunt Nanette about the things I liked to do back home—about baseball games, train-watching, my birthday. She told me about the special Caribbean lemon and mango cake **12** she was going to make.

382

My uncle Romie stayed hidden away in his studio. But I wasn't worried anymore. Aunt Nanette would make my birthday special.

4...3...2...1... My birthday was almost here! And then Aunt Nanette got a phone call.

"An old aunt has died, James. I have to go away for her funeral. But don't you worry. Uncle Romie will spend your birthday with you. It'll be just fine."

That night Aunt Nanette kissed me good-bye. I knew it would not be fine at all. Uncle Romie didn't know about cakes or baseball games or anything except his dumb old paintings. My birthday was ruined.

When the sky turned black, I tucked myself into bed. I missed Mama and Daddy so much. I listened to the birds on the rooftop—their songs continued into the night.

13 **14**

Develop Comprehension

13 THEME

SPIRAL REVIEW Think about James's character. How is he handling his new life in New York City? What does this suggest about one theme of this story? (James enjoys touring the city with his aunt and sees people doing the same things they do in North Carolina. He has learned to enjoy New York City, even though he was nervous about going there because it was so far from home. This suggests that one theme of the story is the importance of being open to new places and new experiences, however different they might seem at first.)

14 SELF-SELECTED STRATEGY USE

What strategies have you used so far to help you understand the story? Where did you use them? How did they help?

 RETURN TO PREDICTIONS AND PURPOSES

Have students respond to the story by revising their predictions for reading. Direct them to write additional questions as they continue reading.

Extra Support

Character, Setting, Plot

Help students check their understanding of the characters by modeling self-monitoring questions such as the following: *What is James like?* (He is a somewhat fearful boy, but he has overcome most of his fears.) *How do I know?* (He got to New York by himself and is enjoying his tour of the city.) *What are his Aunt Nanette, mother, and father like?* (They are very loving toward James.) *How do James and Aunt Nanette get along?* (They get along very well, right from the start.) *What do I know about Uncle Romie?* (He is an artist and works all day.) *What do I think he is like, based on what I know?* (He seems a bit frightening, but he did thank James for the pepper jelly, so he may not be too fierce. Also, a nice woman like Aunt Nanette is married to him.)

Stop here if you wish to read this selection over two days.

Me and Uncle Romie **383**

Develop Comprehension

15 **SKILL**
CHARACTER

What do the paintings that James discovers in Uncle Romie's studio reveal about his character? (James finds paintings with all sorts of pieces pasted together. He sees saxophones, birds, fire escapes, and brown faces. He realizes that Uncle Romie sees Harlem the same way that he does, and he can feel Harlem's beat and bounce in his uncle's paintings. Suddenly, Uncle Romie does not seem like a fierce giant, but like someone who appreciates the same things James does.)

15 The next morning everything was quiet. I crept out of bed and into the hall. For the first time the door to Uncle Romie's studio stood wide open. What a **glorious** mess! There were paints and scraps all over the floor, and around the edges were huge paintings with all sorts of pieces pasted together.

I saw saxophones, birds, fire escapes, and brown faces. *It's Harlem*, I thought. *The people, the music, the rooftops, and the stoops.* Looking at Uncle Romie's paintings, I could *feel* Harlem—its beat and bounce.

Then there was one that was different. Smaller houses, flowers, and trains. "That's home!" I shouted.

"Yep," Uncle Romie said, smiling, from the doorway. "That's the Carolina I remember."

"Mama says you visited your grandparents there most every summer when you were a kid," I said.

384

"I sure did, James. *Mmm.* Now that's the place for pepper jelly. Smeared thick on biscuits. And when Grandma wasn't looking . . . I'd sneak some on a spoon."

"Daddy and I do that too!" I told him.

We laughed together, then walked to the kitchen for a breakfast feast—eggs, bacon, grits, and biscuits.

"James, you've got me remembering the pepper jelly lady. People used to line up down the block to buy her preserves."

"Could you put someone like that in one of your paintings?" I asked.

"I guess I could." Uncle Romie nodded. "Yes, that's a memory just right for sharing. What a good idea, James. Now let's get this birthday going!"

385

Develop Comprehension

16 **PROBLEM AND SOLUTION**

James was worried about being alone with Uncle Romie. How is the **problem** being solved? (James realizes that Uncle Romie's collages are all about life in Harlem and in North Carolina. They begin to talk about what things Uncle Romie puts into his paintings, and James suggests an idea that his uncle likes very much. It seems as though the two have found a way to relate to each other.)

Develop Comprehension

17 **SKILL**
CHARACTER, SETTING, PLOT

What new **character** traits does James see in Uncle Romie when he talks to him about his childhood? (James sees that Uncle Romie is very kind and friendly. He finds that he and Uncle Romie have many things to talk about because they have a lot in common.) **Add this information to your Story Flowchart.**

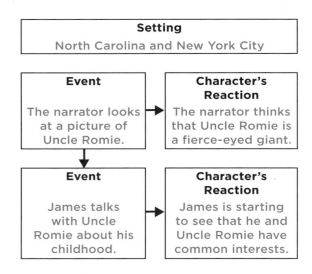

Setting
North Carolina and New York City

Event		Character's Reaction
The narrator looks at a picture of Uncle Romie.	→	The narrator thinks that Uncle Romie is a fierce-eyed giant.

Event		Character's Reaction
James talks with Uncle Romie about his childhood.	→	James is starting to see that he and Uncle Romie have common interests.

18 **COMPARE AND CONTRAST**

How is James's birthday different from what he expected it to be like? **Compare and contrast** his expectations with the actual event. (James didn't think his uncle knew about cakes or baseball, so he was sure his birthday would be ruined. But it turns out that Uncle Romie knows all about baseball and takes James to a game. They also get to know each other and find that they have a lot in common. It is a fun birthday after all.)

He brought out two presents from home. I tore into the packages while he got down the pepper jelly and two huge spoons. Mama and Daddy had picked out just what I wanted—a special case for my baseball cards, and a model train for me to build.

"Pretty cool," said Uncle Romie. "I used to watch the trains down in North Carolina, you know."

How funny to picture big Uncle Romie lying on his belly!

"B.J. and me, we have contests to see who can hear the trains first."

"Hey, I did that too. You know, it's a funny thing, James. People live in all sorts of different places and families. But the things we care about are pretty much the same. Like favorite foods, special songs, games, stories . . . and like birthdays." Uncle Romie held up two tickets to a baseball game!

It turns out Uncle Romie knows all about baseball—he was even a star pitcher in college. We got our mitts and set off for the game.

386

Social Studies

Connect to Content

IMMIGRATION: SETTLING IN A NEW COUNTRY

Explain that every day, people travel to new places just as James does in *Me and Uncle Romie*. Some people like the places they visit so much that they choose to settle there.

Point out that those who move to other countries go through a process called *immigration*. They make their home in a new place. The United States saw a surge in immigration in the late 1800s and early 1900s. Many of those immigrants arrived in the United States to make better lives for their families.

Using textbooks or the Internet, have students identify the areas where large groups of people have immigrated to their state. Ask *Why do you think people chose these areas?*

Discuss: How might immigrants have felt upon arriving in the United States? What concerns do you think they had? How might their feelings have been similar to James's feelings?

Way up in the bleachers, we shared a bag of peanuts, cracking the shells with our teeth and keeping our mitts ready in case a home run ball came our way. That didn't happen—but we sure had fun.

Aunt Nanette came home that night. She lit the candles and we all shared my Caribbean birthday cake. **18**

After that, Uncle Romie had to work a lot again. But at the end of each day he let me sit with him in his studio and talk. Daddy was right. Uncle Romie is a good man. **19**

The day of the big art show finally came. I watched the people laughing and talking, walking slowly around the room from painting to painting. I walked around myself, listening to their conversations.

"Remember our first train ride from Chicago to New York?" one lady asked her husband.

"That guitar-playing man reminds me of my uncle Joe," said another.

All these strangers talking to each other about their families and friends and special times, and all because of how my uncle Romie's paintings reminded them of these things. **20**

387

Develop Comprehension

19 GENRE: Historical Fiction

What information on page 387 might not have actually happened the way the author says it did? (The author probably does not know what people actually said at the art exhibit, so the dialogue that James overhears at the opening of the show was probably made up by the author.)

20 SKILL
CHARACTER, SETTING, PLOT

Based on the paintings in his art exhibit, what other character trait of Uncle Romie's can you identify? (Uncle Romie is very committed to his community. He tries to bring people together through his art.)

STRATEGIES FOR EXTRA SUPPORT

Question 20 CHARACTER, SETTING, PLOT
To help students identify a character trait of Uncle Romie, have students think about what motivates him to create his art. Ask: *What were people talking about as they looked at Uncle Romie's collages?* (trips they took together, and people they knew) Then have students reread the conversation Uncle Romie and James had on page 386. Ask: *What did they talk about?* (friends and fun times) *How does Uncle Romie want people to feel when they look at his art? What does this tell us about him?* Correct the meaning of students' responses as needed.

Develop Comprehension

21 **STRATEGY**
VISUALIZE

What descriptive details help you visualize the setting on page 389?

Student Think Aloud The author describes James lying in the soft grass, watching birds that "streak across the sky." Tiger lilies bend in the wind. These descriptive words create images that contrast with the "beat and bounce of Harlem."

22 **SKILL**
CHARACTER, SETTING, PLOT

Explain how James's feelings about Uncle Romie change during the story. (At first, James thinks his uncle will be scary. When he gets to New York, he doesn't get to spend time with him until his birthday, when he realizes that his uncle is kind and friendly.) Complete the Story Flowchart.

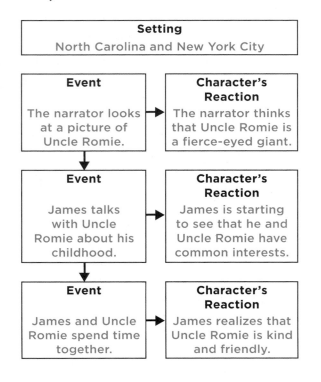

Setting
North Carolina and New York City

Event	Character's Reaction
The narrator looks at a picture of Uncle Romie.	The narrator thinks that Uncle Romie is a fierce-eyed giant.

Event	Character's Reaction
James talks with Uncle Romie about his childhood.	James is starting to see that he and Uncle Romie have common interests.

Event	Character's Reaction
James and Uncle Romie spend time together.	James realizes that Uncle Romie is kind and friendly.

Later that night Daddy called. I had a brand-new brother and sister. Daddy said they were both bald and made a lot of noise. But he sounded happy and said how they all missed me.

This time Aunt Nanette and Uncle Romie took me to the train station.

"Here's a late birthday present for you, James," Uncle Romie said, holding out a package. "Open it on the train, why don't you. It'll help pass the time on the long ride home."

I waved out the window to Uncle Romie and Aunt Nanette until I couldn't see them anymore. Then I ripped off the wrappings!

And there was my summer in New York. Bright sky in one corner, city lights at night in another. Tall buildings. Baseball ticket stubs. The label from the pepper jelly jar. And trains. One going toward the **skyscrapers**. Another going away.

21

22

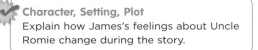
Character, Setting, Plot
Explain how James's feelings about Uncle Romie change during the story.

388

Back home, I lay in the soft North Carolina grass. It was the first of September, almost Uncle Romie's birthday. I watched the birds streak across the sky.

Rooftop birds, I thought. *Back home from their summer in New York, just like me.* Watching them, I could still feel the city's beat inside my head.

A feather drifted down from the sky. In the garden tiger lilies bent in the wind. *Uncle Romie's favorite flowers.* I yanked off a few blossoms. And then I was off on a treasure hunt, collecting things that reminded me of Uncle Romie.

I painted and pasted them together on a big piece of cardboard. Right in the middle I put the train schedule. And at the top I wrote:

389

Quick Check

Can students analyze character, setting, and plot?

During **Small Group Instruction**

If No → **Approaching Level** Reteach the skill and have students apply it to a simpler text. Use Leveled Reader lessons, pp. 395N–395P.

If Yes → **On Level** Have students apply the skill to a new text to consolidate learning. Use Leveled Reader lessons, pp. 395U–395V.

Beyond Level Have students apply the skill to a more complex text to extend learning. Use Leveled Reader lessons, pp. 395Y–395Z.

Develop Comprehension

RETURN TO PREDICTIONS AND PURPOSES

Review students' predictions and purposes for reading. Did they discover why it is important not to judge people right away? (It is important because people may not act the way you expect; it is possible not to like someone and then to like them more and more once you get to know them, just like James and Uncle Romie.)

REVIEW READING STRATEGIES

- **Visualize** In what ways did visualizing help you to understand the selection?

- **Monitor and Clarify: Adjust Reading Rate** Do you understand the strategy of adjusting your reading rate? When might you use it again?

- **Decoding** What difficult words did you encounter? How did the Reading Multisyllabic Words strategy help you sound out these words?

- **Self-Selected Strategy Use** What strategies did you use to make sense of what you read? Where? How were these strategies helpful?

PERSONAL RESPONSE

Ask students to use what they have learned about making friends to write about the process by which James and Uncle Romie became friends. Prompt them to use examples from the text to support their writing.

Author and Illustrator

VISIT THE STUDIOS OF CLAIRE AND JEROME

Have students read the biographies of the author and the illustrator. Ask:

- Why did Claire Hartfield choose to write about an artist?
- How do the details in Jerome Lagarrigue's illustrations help give the story a sense of place?

✏️ **WRITE ABOUT IT**

Author's Craft: Word Choice

Discuss with students different paintings or photographs they have seen. Have them write about what they notice and enjoy in their favorite types of artwork. Then ask students to share their observations with the class and explain their word choice.

Author's Purpose

Remind students that an author's personal life can often play a part in that author's writing. Have students look in the author's biography and in the story for clues to Claire Hartfield's purpose for writing. For example, students should notice that Claire Hatfield enjoys making works of art, just like Uncle Romie.

Visit the Studios of Claire and Jerome

Claire Hartfield based this story on African American artist Romare Bearden. She likes his collages because they seem to tell stories. Claire wrote her story to show how we can use art to share ideas. She's been expressing herself through art since she was young. Claire was a shy child, and she found that dance and art helped her share her feelings.

Jerome Lagarrigue comes from a family of artists. He grew up in France, but came to the United States to study art. Jerome illustrates books and magazines. He also teaches art.

Other books by Jerome Lagarrigue

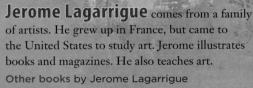

LOG ON ▶ FIND OUT

Author Claire Hartfield
Illustrator Jerome Lagarrigue
www.macmillanmh.com

✓ **Author's Purpose**

Why did Claire Hartfield write this story? How did the author's own love of art affect her purpose for writing? Explain using details from the story.

390

✏️ # Author's Craft

Word Choice

Authors carefully choose the words they write to show readers what they mean and to set the mood, or atmosphere, of the story.

- Word choice can make a difference in what readers see and hear in the story. For example, in the phrase "the train blasted past" (page 374), the word *blasted* tells readers that the train was going fast and making a lot of noise.

- Ask students which descriptive word choices helped create the mood. Have students find and discuss examples, such as "Swarms of people rushed by" (page 378). The words create an image of a swarm of bees, making the crowd seem frightening, as it might to a young boy who has just come to the big city.

Comprehension Check

Summarize

To summarize *Me and Uncle Romie* use the most important details from the selection. Information from your Story Flowchart may help you.

Setting
Event → Character's Reaction
Event → Character's Reaction
Event → Character's Reaction

Think and Compare

1. What kind of artist is Uncle Romie? Details

2. How does James's **glorious** birthday experience change his relationship with Uncle Romie? Cause and Effect

3. What can you tell about James from the birthday card he makes for Uncle Romie? Explain using details from the story. Visualize: Character, Setting, Plot

4. What point of view is the story told from? Explain why the author chose this point of view. Author's Purpose

5. Read "Secondhand Art" on pages 370–371. Compare the artwork with the artwork in *Me and Uncle Romie*. How is it alike? How is it different? Use details from both selections to explain. Reading/Writing Across Texts

Make Connections

Text-to-Self Have students respond to the following question to make connections to their own lives. Use the Think Aloud to model a response. *When have you discovered that you misjudged something, or someone, based on appearance?*

Think Aloud: Once I had a new classmate who did not talk or smile very much. Because of this, I thought that she was unfriendly when we first met. I later realized she was just shy, and we eventually became good friends.

Text-to-World Have students respond to the following question to make connections to the world. Use the Think Aloud to model a response. *Why is art a good way to express feelings and ideas?*

Think Aloud: Art can tell a story about who you are or what you are thinking. It can also remind you about something from the past. Other people can see a piece of art and understand what the artist was feeling or thinking when it was created.

Comprehension Check

SUMMARIZE

Have partners summarize *Me and Uncle Romie* in their own words. Remind students to use their Story Flowchart to help them.

THINK AND COMPARE
Text Evidence

1. **Details** Answer stated in text Uncle Romie is a collage artist. He uses paints, pictures, and other objects to create works of art. LOCATE

2. **Cause and Effect** Answer stated in text James was worried about spending his birthday with Uncle Romie. But after his birthday, James learned that Uncle Romie is kind, and they become close friends. COMBINE

3. **Character, Setting, Plot** Answer The card shows that James is creative and thoughtful. It also shows how his relationship with Uncle Romie has changed. Evidence The card proves that although he is back home, James is still thinking of the good times he had with his uncle after they got to know each other. CONNECT

4. **Author's Purpose** Answer This story is told from a first-person point of view. Evidence James narrates the story using words such as *I* and *me*. The author did this so that the reader could understand what James is thinking and feeling. ANALYZE

5. **Text-to-Text** Uncle Romie, Danny, and Emma are all artists who work with materials other than paint. Uncle Romie makes collages in *Me and Uncle Romie*. "Secondhand Art" focuses on making art from recycled materials. COMPARE TEXT

Objectives

- Read with the appropriate rate
- Rate: 102–122 WCPM

Materials

- Transparency 15
- Practice Book, p. 131
- Fluency Solutions Audio CD

ELL

Develop Comprehension
Discuss what James sees and does in the passage and how he feels. Read the passage expressively as you act it out ("I turned … I heard … took my hand … big buildings … climbed the stairs") to help convey meaning. Then echo-read the passage with students. Encourage them to mimic your expressiveness. Provide ample time for students to read after you.

Practice Book, page 131

As I read, I will pay attention to my reading rate in order to match the action in the story.

	Carly held her breath as the broad-tailed hummingbird
8	fluttered near the cluster of wildflowers. She stared into
17	her camera, waiting. A fly landed on Carly's arm. She
27	flicked it away with a finger. The bird flew near a flower.
39	The flower wasn't red enough, though. Carly waited.
47	The bird flew to another flower. This one was too small.
58	Finally, the bird hesitated over the largest, reddest flower.
67	Carly began to snap pictures. She was certain that these
77	would be some of the best pictures she had ever taken.
88	Carly raced home and uploaded the pictures onto her
97	computer. She couldn't wait to see the results.
105	But when the pictures came up on the screen, she was
116	disappointed. Carly studied them, then opened her photo
124	journal. She wrote: "Hummingbird pictures: The bird's
131	wings are a blur, not enough detail on flower, bird isn't
142	close enough to the flower in any shot. Why aren't these
153	the way I thought they would be?" 160

Comprehension Check

1. What do you learn about Carly in this passage? **Plot Development** Carly is patient. She thinks and writes about what she is doing so she can do it better next time.
2. How might the journal help Carly take better pictures in the future? **Plot Development** The photo journal might help Carly take better pictures because she can learn from her mistakes and not make them again.

	Words Read	−	Number of Errors	=	Words Correct Score
First Read		−		=	
Second Read		−		=	

Approaching Reproducible, page 131

Beyond Reproducible, page 131

Fluency

Repeated Reading: Rate

EXPLAIN/MODEL Remind students that they may need to adjust their rate, or how fast they read, to comprehend the meaning of a passage. As you model the passage on **Transparency 15**, increase the speed the second and third times you read through the sentences. Have students echo-read the entire passage after you again, increasing your rate to underscore the brisk pace and bustle of people in the city.

> ### Transparency 15
>
> Swarms of people rushed by. Soon I heard a silvery voice call my name. This had to be Aunt Nanette. I turned and saw her big smile reaching out to welcome me.
>
> She took my hand and guided me through the rushing crowd onto an underground train called the subway. "This will take us right home," she explained.
>
> Home was like nothing I'd ever seen before. No regular houses anywhere. Just big buildings and stores of all kinds— in the windows I saw paints, fabrics, radios, and TVs.
>
> We turned into the corner building and climbed the stairs to the apartment—five whole flights up.

Fluency (from *Me and Uncle Romie*, pp. 378–379)

PRACTICE Divide students into two groups. Have the first group read the passage a sentence at a time at a slow rate. Next, ask the second group to echo-read. The groups can then switch roles. Have students repeat twice more while increasing their rate.

DAILY FLUENCY Students will practice fluency using **Practice Book** page 131 or the **Fluency Solutions Audio CD**. The passage is recorded at a slow practice speed and a faster fluent speed.

Quick Check

Can students read fluently?

During **Small Group Instruction**

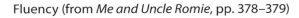

If No → **Approaching Level** Use the Fluency lesson and model, p. 395Q.

If Yes → **On Level** See Fluency, p. 395T.

Beyond Level See Fluency, p. 395X.

Comprehension

SPIRAL REVIEW

REVIEW SKILL
THEME

EXPLAIN/MODEL

- Remind students that the **theme** is the overall message or lesson in a story. Readers should look for clues in the story to find the message the author wants them to see.

- A theme may be stated directly in the text, or it may be implied.

  Briefly discuss what clues you can find in the text about the theme of "Secondhand Art." Model identifying clues to the theme for students by talking about the characters and how they find new life for items other people would throw away. Then summarize the theme of the story.

PRACTICE/APPLY

PARTNERS

Ask partners to determine the theme in *Me and Uncle Romie* by using the following questions.

- Why is James worried about spending his birthday with Uncle Romie? (He has not had time to get to know his uncle, and he is afraid he will not have a good time.)

- How did their relationship change over the course of the story? (James and Uncle Romie found out that they had a lot in common. James learned that his uncle was a good man.)

- Aunt Nanette has to leave for a funeral right before James's birthday. If this unexpected situation had not arisen, how might the story have been different? (James might have spent his birthday with Aunt Nanette. Perhaps he never would have had the same opportunity to get to know Uncle Romie.)

- What is the theme of this story? (Do not make decisions about someone before you have a chance to get to know them.) **Explain why this message is important.** (If you rely on only first impressions, you will often misjudge people. It takes time to get to know someone.)

Have partners take turns summarizing their themes. When they have finished, have pairs discuss the clues they found in the text that led them to the theme.

PRACTICE BOOK See **Practice Book** page 132 for Reading and Writing Letters.

Objective

- Summarize and explain the theme of a story

Skills Trace

Theme	
Introduce	341A–341B
Practice/ Apply	342-361; Practice Book, 120–121
Reteach/ Review	367M–367Z, 409A–409B, 410–429, 435M–435Z; Practice Book, 138–139
Assess	Weekly Tests; Units 3, 4 Tests
Maintain	391B, 497B, 591B

Test Practice

Answering Questions

To apply **answering questions strategies** to content-area reading, see pages 117–124 in *Time For Kids*.

Paired Selection

GENRE: Informational Text/Expository

Have students read the bookmark on **Student Book** page 392. Explain that an expository article

- provides carefully researched facts about a topic;

- often includes headings that give readers an overview and charts, sidebars, and/or other text features that present additional information.

Text Feature: Multiple-Step Instructions

EXPLAIN Point out that multiple-step instructions, or directions, give the steps required to do or make something.

- Instructions are often numbered. This helps the reader see what to do first, second, third, and so forth.

- Instructions can also be written in paragraph form. Look for sequence words, such as *first, next, then*, and *last*, to indicate order.

- Some instructions may include a materials list that tells the reader what supplies are needed to complete the task.

APPLY Have students brainstorm times when they might write instructions. Discuss why including a clear sequence, or order, is important. (Students might write instructions for reaching their home or school or for assembling a product; if the sequence is unclear, the person following the instructions might get confused or products could be damaged or ruined.)

Science

Genre

Expository selections, such as **articles**, explain a topic by presenting facts. They can also include photos.

Text Feature

Multiple-Step Instructions are the steps you follow in order to do or make something.

Content Vocabulary

technology   **drawbacks**

software

COMPUTERS
THE FUTURE OF ART

by Lynn Boulanger

What do you think of when you hear the word *artist*? Most people picture someone painting or drawing on a canvas. Others see a person using a hammer to create a sculpture. Today, **technology** allows artists to express themselves using new and exciting tools.

1

Reading Multiple-Step Instructions
The following instructions tell how to install a software program like CAD:

Instructions:
1. Check that your computer meets the requirements of the software.
2. Close other programs.
3. Follow the exact instructions in the manual.
4. Install other necessary programs if prompted to do so.

392

Content Vocabulary

Explain the words using the **Define/Example/Ask** routine. Definitions are provided for this activity.

- **Technology** is the methods and devices used to make things faster and easier. What types of technology do you use on a daily basis?

- **Software** is the program a computer uses to perform tasks. What computer software are you most familiar with?

- **Drawbacks** are disadvantages, or things making a plan difficult or unpleasant. What are drawbacks of writing a report by hand?

Art and Technology

Computers are the latest tool artists are using to create new art. Computer-assisted design (CAD) is a **software** program sculptors can use to plan their art. At one time, artists sketched plans for a new piece on paper. Now many of them bring their ideas to life by using computer programs such as these. With CAD, artists can play around with the size of their creations. CAD can even produce images of three-dimensional shapes. These images can help artists plan or change their work before they actually create it.

Even though this new technology has many benefits, it also has some **drawbacks**. Computer-assisted programs are expensive. An artist has to buy the program in order to use it. Also, some of these programs can be hard for artists to understand. Other programs require artists to take a class, so that they can learn the programs' special features. In spite of the drawbacks, computers are changing the way artists create art!

Connect and Compare

1. Look at the Reading Multiple-Step Instructions box on page 392. What should you do after you close all other programs on your computer? **Reading Multiple-Step Instructions**

2. How does the author feel about artists using technology to create art? Explain using details from the article. **Apply**

3. Think about this article and *Me and Uncle Romie*. How might computer-assisted programs, such as CAD, help Uncle Romie in his work? Explain using details from both selections. **Reading/Writing Across Texts**

Science Activity

On your own, research another form of technology artists are using today. Give an oral report and restate the steps that are needed to use this technology.

LOG ON ► FIND OUT **Science** Computers www.macmillanmh.com

393

---

1 TEXT FEATURE: MULTIPLE-STEP INSTRUCTIONS

 What is the last step you should take when installing a software program like CAD? (Install other necessary programs if prompted to do so.)

2 CONTENT VOCABULARY

What clues help the reader figure out the meaning of *software*? (The words *computer* and *program* can help the reader figure out that software is the program that directs a computer.)

Use the Interactive Question-Response Guide in the **ELL Resource Book**, pages 168–169, to help students gain access to the paired selection content.

Connect and Compare

 1. He or she should follow the exact instructions in the manual. READING MULTIPLE-STEP INSTRUCTIONS

2. The author thinks that technology can help artists. It can produce images that help an artist plan their work in advance. However, the programs can be expensive and hard to understand. APPLY

3. FOCUS QUESTION Computer-assisted programs could help Uncle Romie by making it faster for him to plan and finish his art. READING/WRITING ACROSS TEXTS

 ## Science Activity

Have students present their summaries about the technology that artists use. Remind them to emphasize points in ways that help listeners follow key ideas and concepts.

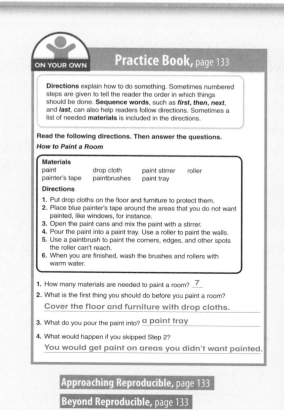

ON YOUR OWN **Practice Book,** page 133

Directions explain how to do something. Sometimes numbered steps are given to tell the reader the order in which things should be done. **Sequence words,** such as *first, then, next,* and *last,* can also help readers follow directions. Sometimes a list of needed **materials** is included in the directions.

Read the following directions. Then answer the questions.
How to Paint a Room

Materials
paint   drop cloth   paint stirrer   roller
painter's tape paintbrushes   paint tray

Directions
1. Put drop cloths on the floor and furniture to protect them.
2. Place blue painter's tape around the areas that you do not want painted, like windows, for instance.
3. Open the paint cans and mix the paint with a stirrer.
4. Pour the paint into a paint tray. Use a roller to paint the walls.
5. Use a paintbrush to paint the corners, edges, and other spots the roller can't reach.
6. When you are finished, wash the brushes and rollers with warm water.

1. How many materials are needed to paint a room? __7__
2. What is the first thing you should do before you paint a room?
   Cover the floor and furniture with drop cloths.
3. What do you pour the paint into? a paint tray
4. What would happen if you skipped Step 2?
   You would get paint on areas you didn't want painted.

Approaching Reproducible, page 133
Beyond Reproducible, page 133

Write

WHOLE GROUP

✓ **WRITING WORKSHOP**
- Developing Persuasive Writing
- Trait: Ideas
- Strengthen an Argument

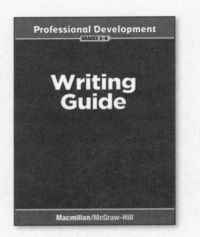

Professional Development
GRADES 3–6

Writing Guide

Macmillan/McGraw-Hill

UNIT 3
Developing Persuasive Writing

WEEK 1	**Strong Sentences/Trait: Ideas** Supporting Details
WEEK 2	**Strong Paragraphs/Trait: Ideas** Strong Arguments
WEEK 3	**Persuasive Essay**
WEEK 4	**Strong Sentences/Trait: Word Choice** Descriptive Language
WEEK 5	**Strong Paragraphs/Ideas** Strengthen an Argument, 393A–393B • Reading/Writing Connection, 394–395 • Minilessons, 395A Ideas: Strengthen an Argument Sentence Fluency: Transition Words • Conferencing Routine, 395B
WEEK 6	**Persuasive Essay**

Trait: Ideas

Strong Paragraphs: Strengthen an Argument

TEACH/MODEL Review with students that the purpose of a persuasive essay is to get readers to agree with an opinion or argument. To do this, writers support and strengthen their arguments with facts, details, and reasons that explain their position. They consider their audience and choose reasons that they think will convince that group.

Explain that a **strong persuasive paragraph** includes a clearly stated opinion or position and is followed by descriptive sentences that further explain with facts, examples, and details. It concludes, or ends, by stating the opinion again and asking the reader to do something or feel a certain way. Write the paragraph in the box on the board.

> I believe that my bedtime should be 30 minutes later. Having more time in the evening would make me feel less rushed as I do my homework. I would also have time to relax and read a good book before bed. Going to bed relaxed will help me fall asleep faster, so I'll still get the same amount of sleep. If I find that I'm too tired, I can always go to bed a little earlier. Please consider letting me have an extra half-hour before bed so that I can relax, read, and get a good night's sleep.

Have students identify the audience for this piece of writing (parent/caregiver). Then work with them to list details the writer gives to make the argument strong and convincing. Point out that the writer gives details that are particularly appealing to the audience, such as *less rushed during homework, extra time to read*, and *falling asleep faster*. Invite students to give examples of other details they might include to make the argument stronger.

- more time to spend with the family
- more time to help with chores, such as washing dishes or walking the dog

Teacher Write Aloud

PRACTICE/APPLY Further explore with students the use of reasons and details to strengthen a persuasive argument. Write the sentences below on the board. Then complete the Teacher Think Aloud.

> Everyone should have a library card. You can check out books for free.

Teacher Think Aloud The first sentence states the argument or position. The second sentence gives a reason. I think the audience is someone who likes books. To make this reason stronger, I can add a detail that gives more information and appeals to the audience. For example, I might say: *Imagine how many more books you could read if you did not have to pay for them.*

Then complete the Teacher Think Aloud by adding the sentence to those posted. Point out how you appealed to the audience by adding the detail, *many more books.* Then add the following details.

> The library has an enormous selection of books to choose from. Each book is numbered and organized, so it is easy to find what you are looking for.

Read the new paragraph aloud. Discuss how the details you added strengthen the argument. Work with students to add more reasons.

 Draft Display the Writing Prompt on **Writing Transparency 46**. Remind students to provide reasons and details to support their argument. Circulate and provide Over-the-Shoulder Conferences as students work.

Objective
- Write details that strengthen an argument

Materials
- Writer's Notebooks
- Writing Transparency 46

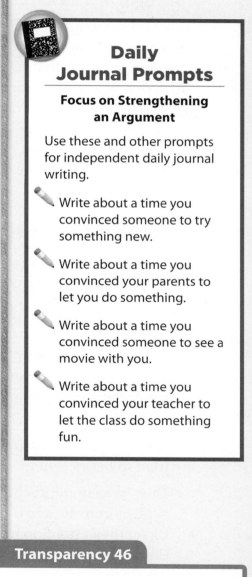

Daily Journal Prompts

Focus on Strengthening an Argument

Use these and other prompts for independent daily journal writing.

- Write about a time you convinced someone to try something new.

- Write about a time you convinced your parents to let you do something.

- Write about a time you convinced someone to see a movie with you.

- Write about a time you convinced your teacher to let the class do something fun.

Transparency 46

Think about a job you would like to have. Explain why you would be perfect for this job.

Writing Transparency

Reading and Writing Connection

✓ Trait: Ideas

STRENGTHEN AN ARGUMENT

Remind students that one way to strengthen an argument is to add reasons or details that support your idea or opinion. In a strong persuasive paragraph, the opinion or argument is clearly stated. The other sentences give details and reasons that help convince the reader that what the writer thinks or believes is true.

Read the Passage

Use the example from *Me and Uncle Romie* to show how the author uses reasons and details to show why James likes Harlem.

- Have students read the bookmark. Explain that reasons and details strengthen an argument or opinion and make it more convincing.

- **Ask:** *Can you think of a time when you went somewhere fun?*

- Then have students chorally read the excerpt from *Me and Uncle Romie*. Direct their attention to the callout. Have them identify the reasons and details the author gives to support the character's opinion.

- **Ask:** *What details does the writer give are things you like to do?*

Writing

✓ Trait: Ideas
Good writers use **strong reasons and details** to convince readers.

Reading and Writing Connection

Read the passage below. Notice how Claire Hartfield uses strong reasons and details in her story.

An excerpt from
Me and Uncle Romie

> But it was Harlem that I liked best. I played stickball with the kids again . . . and on a really hot day a whole bunch of us ran through the icy cold water that sprayed out hard from the fire hydrant. In the evenings Aunt Nanette and I sat outside listening to the street musicians playing their saxophone songs.

The author gives three reasons why James likes Harlem. Each reason is made stronger by the rich details that she uses to describe what James did, saw, felt, and heard.

Respond to the Selection

Have students write a response to the selection.

☑ **Engagement** Help students deepen their connection to the text and discover their own perspective on it. *Focus on a moment when you spent time with a relative.*

☑ **Response** Help students explore more deeply their reactions to particular passages in the reading. *Focus on a moment in the story when you felt relieved for James. Use text evidence in your writing.*

☑ **Literary Analysis** Help students deepen their connection to the text and discover their own perspective on it. *Focus on a place in the story where the author did a good job of using reasons and details to support an idea or opinion. Use text evidence in your writing.*

Read and Find

Read Krysta's writing below. What reasons and details does she give for feeling great? Use the checklist below to help you.

Go Kyle!
by Krysta D.

Read about a big game.

Even though I was sitting on a hard wooden bench and the cold December air was biting my cheeks, I felt great. My brother's football team was playing under the bright lights at the high school and was about to win! I could smell mud and crushed grass as they lined up near the end zone. "Go Kyle! Go! Woo hoo!" I shouted to my brother.

Writer's Checklist

✓ Does the writer state her opinion or feelings?

✓ Does she support her statement with **convincing reasons**?

☑ What words does Krysta use to convince the reader to agree with her opinion or argument?

395

Write

Read the Student Model

Have students chorally read the student model at the top of **Student Book** page 395. Discuss the reasons the student writer gave to explain why she felt great, even in an uncomfortable place. Use the Writer's Checklist.

Journal Prompt

Draft Write the following prompt on the board. Have students write a response to the prompt.

> *Think of a place or relative that you would like to visit. Write a paragraph to convince your parents or caregiver to let you do so.*

Tell students that you will be reading and commenting on their writing during Writing Conference time.

Model how to use the Writer's Checklist so students can write and revise their work. Then ask:

- *Where did you choose to visit?*
- *What reasons and details did you give to convince your audience? Will your reasons be convincing? If not, what details could you add to make them stronger?*

Objectives

- Write reasons and details to strengthen an argument
- Write strong paragraphs

Materials

- Writer's Notebooks
- Teacher's Resource Book, p. 192

ELL

Strong Words People often write to persuade others to think the way they do about something. One way to do this is to use words that seem to say that some thing or idea is good or bad. Make a two-column chart on the board. Help students list positive words, such as *best, important*, and *proud*, and negative words, such as *worst, disaster*, and *terrible*. Guide students to use strong powerful words to make their arguments stronger.

HOMEWORK **Teacher's Resource Book,** page 192

Read the following statements. Tell the audience. Then write two sentences including reasons and details to strengthen the argument.

Example: Our park needs to be restored.

Audience: The community

The playground equipment is broken and is a danger to the children.

We will take pride in our community if we have a beautiful park.

1. We deserve a longer recess.

Audience: _____

_____

2. We should start a baseball league!

Audience: _____

_____

Minilesson 1 | Ideas/Strengthen An Argument

TEACH/MODEL

Remind students that they have been working hard to strengthen their arguments by giving strong reasons and details. Today they will practice that again. Have students use **Teacher's Resource Book** page 192. Ask students to read the sentences silently.

PRACTICE/APPLY

Have students work independently to add reasons and details to the argument. When complete, ask students to share their work during Sharing Circle. Discuss which reasons and details were particularly strong and convincing and why.

Minilesson 2 | Sentence Fluency/Transition Words

TEACH/MODEL

Tell students that one way writers make their paragraphs more readable is to be sure that the ideas are connected and flow smoothly from one to the next. Write this chart of common transitions on the board. Point out that transitions that continue an argument connect ideas. Transitions can also signal a final point, indicating the close, or conclusion of the argument.

Transitions that Continue an Argument		Transitions that Signal a Final Point
In addition	Also	Finally
Additionally	Because	Lastly
Another reason	Similarly	

PRACTICE/APPLY

Write the following sentences on the board. In their Writer's Notebooks, have students rewrite the sentences, adding transitions to connect the ideas and make the argument "stick together." Model adding a transition to help students get started: *It helps the environment because fewer trees have to be cut down.* Point out that you connected two ideas by adding the transition *because*.

> Everyone should recycle paper. It helps the environment. Fewer trees have to be cut down. There is less trash. It makes you feel good that you are not wasteful.

Conferencing Routine

Dynamic Feedback System

Step 1 Read and appreciate the writing.

Step 2 Notice how the student uses the targeted skill (for example, strengthening an argument: Ask: *How did the writer make his or her argument more convincing?*).

Step 3 Write comments that show how the writing has an impact on you. Direct your comments to those places in the piece where the student has used the targeted skill.

Step 4 Meet with the student and give him or her a revision assignment.

Write Effective Comments

Ideas At least one of your comments should highlight the way the student strengthens an argument in the writing. Here are some sample comments.

- This detail really proves your argument.

- This reason helps me understand why you feel that way.

- I am not convinced by this reason. What details can you add to make it stronger?

Revision Assignments

Ideas Here are some examples of effective revision assignments for strengthening an argument.

Revise
- **Reread your entry.** *Choose one reason that you feel strongly about. Now add two sentences that give me more specific details about the reason you chose.*

Revise
- **[Underline a section.]** Mark a specific section of a student's writing and then ask the student to revise it in a specific way.

Revise
- **[Underline a section.]** *Read the part that I underlined. Rewrite it, adding reasons that will convince your audience to agree with you.*

Teacher-to-Teacher

Over-the-Shoulder Conferences

Use these quick, focused opportunities to comment while students are writing.

- **Step 1** Quietly move close enough to a student that you can read the journal entry he or she is writing.

- **Step 2** Read part of what you see. You don't need to start from the beginning or read the entire piece.

- **Step 3** Show the student a spot in the writing where he or she is using a particular skill or describing something that piques your interest.

- **Step 4** Whisper a sentence or two about why you noticed that spot in the writing, and ask a question that will nudge the student to add a strong reason or detail.

- **Step 5** Move on to the next student. Select students strategically. You should see 12–15 students in a 15-minute period.

Research Proven Writing Approach

The Writers' Express
Immediate Impact. Lasting Transformation.   wex.org

Me and Uncle Romie **395B**

---

nonexamples, including antonyms for the word. (Example: *short* or *one-story building, low-rise*)

RELATED WORDS

- Help students generate words related to *collage.* The classification of words can help improve students' vocabularies.

- Students can create a word web of art-related words, with other forms of art listed in one oval, such as *painting, sketch, sculpture,* and *mural.*

- Another oval might name different materials that artists use, such as *canvas, paintbrushes,* and *easel.*

- Other ovals might list topics for artwork, such as *portrait* and *landscape,* or places to see artwork, such as *gallery, museum,* and *exhibit.*

- Have students use a dictionary to add additional words to their list.

Use the additional selection word *saxophone* as a springboard for students to learn other words.

- Write *saxophone.* Underline *saxo-* and explain that *saxophone* is the name of a musical instrument invented by a man named Adolphe Sax.

- Underline *-phone* and have students name other words they know that contain this word part, such as *telephone, megaphone,* and *speakerphone.* Explain that *phone* comes from the Greek root *phōnē,* meaning "voice" or "sound," and that all these words are related to sound.

- Have students list other words containing the related forms *phon-* or *phono-.* Add words not included, such as *phonics* and *phonograph.* Discuss how these words relate to sound.

information they learned from this week's readings.

- **ELL** Provide the Day 4 sentence stems for students needing extra support.

PERIODIC REVIEW

- Check students' mastery of all the words from Unit 3. Use the Day 1 prompts from each week. Continue to use these words during classroom discussions to reinforce their meanings and usage.

Me and Uncle Romie **395D**

5-Day Vocabulary

Connect Language Arts

WHOLE GROUP

✓ **VOCABULARY**
• Tested Words

SPELLING
• Compound Words

✓ **GRAMMAR**
• Irregular Verbs

SMALL GROUP
• Differentiated Instruction, pp. 395I–395HH

Build Robust Vocabulary

Day 1 — Teach/Practice

CONNECT TO WORDS

■ Practice this week's vocabulary words using the following prompts:

1. What makes *skyscrapers* different from other buildings?
2. What types of materials can be used to make a *collage*?
3. What is the difference between a *barbecue* and a picnic?
4. What would the weather be like on a *glorious* day?
5. What kinds of animals might be *strutting*?
6. Why are *swarms* of bees

Day 2 — Review

CONNECT TO WORDS

■ Review the definitions of this week's vocabulary words using **Student Book** pages 370–371. Then discuss each word using these prompts:

1. What kind of *skyscraper* would you build?
2. How would you make a *collage* about a hobby you have?
3. During what season would you be most likely to have a *barbecue*?
4. What has been the most *glorious* moment of your life so far?
5. What is the difference between

Connect
Spelling

5-Day Spelling

Compound Words

Go to pages T14–T15 for **Differentiated Spelling Lists**.

Spelling Words

fishbowl	grandparent	newborn
lookout	railroad	bedspread
backyard	snowstorm	yourself
desktop	loudspeaker	overdo
campfire	bookcase	clothesline
overhead	bedroom	undertake
waterproof	blindfold	

Review dresses, arrows, babies
Challenge eyesight, paperweight

Dictation Sentences

1. The cat peered into the <u>fishbowl</u>.
2. The airport has a <u>lookout</u> tower.
3. Sam camped out in his <u>backyard</u>.
4. Papers lay on the <u>desktop</u>.
5. We cooked over a <u>campfire</u>.
6. He heard thunder <u>overhead</u>.
7. Luckily, the tent was <u>waterproof</u>!
8. Anna's **grandparent** is visiting.
9. We boarded the <u>railroad</u> car.
10. School closed for the <u>snowstorm</u>.
11. The principal spoke over the **loudspeaker**.
12. Every shelf of the <u>bookcase</u> is full.
13. David has drums in his **bedroom**.
14. The <u>blindfold</u> covered my eyes.
15. The <u>newborn</u> mice were tiny.
16. We bought a new <u>bedspread</u>.
17. Did you build that by <u>yourself</u>?
18. Try not to <u>overdo</u> it.
19. I hung sheets on a <u>clothesline</u>.
20. Let's <u>undertake</u> the journey.

Review/Challenge Words

1. The little girls bought new <u>dresses</u>.
2. <u>Arrows</u> pointed to the exits.
3. We laughed and smiled at the <u>babies</u>.
4. Eagles have sharp <u>eyesight</u>.
5. I have a glass <u>paperweight</u>.

Words in **bold** are from this week's selections.

395E Unit 3 Week 5

Day 1 — Pretest

ASSESS PRIOR KNOWLEDGE

■ Model for students how to spell the word *sunglasses*. Segment the longer word into shorter words. Point out that *sunglasses* is a compound word made up of the words *sun* and *glasses*.

■ Use the Dictation Sentences. Say the underlined word, read the sentence, and repeat the word. Have students write the words.

■ Have students self-correct their tests. Point out that they should begin by identifying the shorter words that are in the compound word.

■ Have students cut apart the **Spelling Word Cards BLM** on **Teacher's Resource Book** page 58 and figure out a way to sort them. Have them save the cards for use throughout the week.

Day 2 — Word Sorts and Review

SPIRAL REVIEW

Review the plural word endings *-s, -es,* and *-ies.* Have students find plural words in this week's readings.

WORD SORTS

■ Have students take turns sorting the spelling words and explaining how they sorted them. When students have finished the sort, discuss any words that they may have found challenging to read or sort.

■ Review the spelling words, pointing out the short words that form the compound words. Use the cards on the Spelling Word Cards BLM. Write the words *roadway, walkway, underway, highway, undercover, underground,* and *driveway* on the board. Model how to sort the compound words by the shorter words within them.

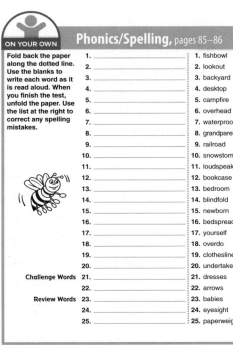

Day 3 | Word Meanings

CONTEXT CLUES

Write the following sentences. Ask students to copy the sentences into their Writer's Notebooks, filling in the blanks with spelling words.

1. When we camped out in our _____, my dad had to build a _____ to keep warm. (*backyard, campfire*)

2. As we trudged though the freezing _____, we were glad that our boots were warm and _____. (*snowstorm, waterproof*)

Challenge partners to work together to write three more sentences, each of which contains two spelling words. Ask students to draw pictures that represent each word.

Day 4 | Proofread

PROOFREAD AND WRITE

Write these sentences on the board. Have students circle and correct each misspelled word.

1. Carrie placed the fishebowl on the bookase. (*fishbowl, bookcase*)

2. The loudspeker in the railrode station was not working. (*loudspeaker, railroad*)

3. The blue bedspred matched the colors on the desktopp. (*bedspread, desktop*)

Error Correction Remind students that they can break apart each compound word and use the shorter words' spellings and meanings to help them determine the spelling and meaning of the compound word.

Day 5 | Assess and Reteach

POSTTEST

Use the Dictation Sentences on page 395E for the Posttest.

If students have difficulty with any words in the lesson, have them place the words on a list called *Spelling Words I Want to Remember* in their Writer's Notebooks. Look for students' use of these words in their writings.

HOMEWORK — Phonics/Spelling, page 88

backyard	clothesline	blindfold	overhead	snowstorm
bedspread	desktop	lookout	bookcase	undertake
bedroom	fishbowl	loudspeaker	railroad	waterproof
campfire	grandparent	overdo	newborn	yourself

A. What is the Meaning?

Find the word from the spelling list that matches each definition below.

1. flat surface to write on — **desktop**
2. covers a bed — **bedspread**
3. shelf unit for holding books — **bookcase**
4. room where you sleep — **bedroom**
5. cloth covering the eyes — **blindfold**
6. for outdoor warmth and cooking — **campfire**
7. to dry clothing outside — **clothesline**
8. behind a house — **backyard**

B. What's the Word?

Complete each sentence with a spelling word.

9. One of my chores is to clean out our fish Milo's **fishbowl**.
10. My **grandparents** moved to Florida where it never snows.
11. Stay on the **lookout** for our turn.
12. The principal announced on the **loudspeaker** that school would be closed because of the storm.
13. A **newborn** baby is really tiny.
14. Take a break when shoveling snow. You don't want to **overdo** it.
15. The clouds **overhead** were dark and heavy.
16. Will the **railroad** shut down because of the ice?

ON YOUR OWN — Phonics/Spelling, page 89

A. Proofreading

There are six spelling mistakes in the story below. Circle the misspelled words. Write the words correctly on the lines below.

With his ⟨desk top⟩ microscope, Jack could see the beauty of snowflakes. They were tiny but had intricate designs. Each one was different, and they were all spectacular.

But Jack was sad because he knew that most people could not see the beauty of snowflakes. They did not have a microscope. It was like they had a ⟨blind fold⟩ on. So, he decided to ⟨under take⟩ a new project to let them see for themselves. For a long time, he was on the ⟨look out⟩ for a camera that could photograph snowflakes, but there was none. He'd have to make it himself.

He read a ⟨book case⟩ full of books about cameras and started putting one together. It took many tries, but when he finished his camera, he could take pictures of snowflakes and say to anyone he met, "See for ⟨your self⟩ how beautiful snowflakes are."

1. **desktop** 3. **undertake** 5. **bookcase**
2. **blindfold** 4. **lookout** 6. **yourself**

B. Writing Activity

Jack's favorite thing about the snow is snowflakes. Write a letter to a friend describing your perfect day in the snow. Include four spelling words in your writing. Answers will vary.

HOMEWORK — Phonics/Spelling, page 90

Look at the words in each set below. One word in each set is spelled correctly. Use a pencil to fill in the circle next to the correct word. Before you begin, look at the sample set of words. Sample A has been done for you. Do Sample B by yourself. When you are sure you know what to do, you may go on with the rest of the page.

Sample A:
- Ⓐ birfday
- Ⓑ berthday
- Ⓒ ● birthday
- Ⓓ burthday

Sample B:
- Ⓔ noatbook
- Ⓕ notebook
- Ⓖ ● notebook
- Ⓗ notbook

1. Ⓐ bakyard / Ⓑ backyard / Ⓒ bakeyard / Ⓓ bacyard
6. Ⓔ deasktop / Ⓕ disktop / Ⓖ desktop / Ⓗ desktopp
11. Ⓐ loudspeaker / Ⓑ lowdspeaker / Ⓒ loudspeeker / Ⓓ lowdspeeker
16. Ⓔ nueborn / Ⓕ newborn / Ⓖ nooborn / Ⓗ neweborn

2. Ⓔ beadspred / Ⓕ bedspred / Ⓖ bedsprede / Ⓗ bedspread
7. Ⓔ fishboll / Ⓕ fishbowl / Ⓖ fichbowl / Ⓗ fishbole
12. Ⓔ overdo / Ⓕ overdoo / Ⓖ overdew / Ⓗ ovredo
17. Ⓐ snostorm / Ⓑ snoestorm / Ⓒ snowstoorm / Ⓓ snowstorm

3. Ⓐ bedroom / Ⓑ bedrome / Ⓒ beddroom / Ⓓ bedrom
8. Ⓔ grandparent / Ⓕ grandpairent / Ⓖ granparent / Ⓗ granparint
13. Ⓐ overhed / Ⓑ overhead / Ⓒ ovurhead / Ⓓ overhede
18. Ⓔ undertaik / Ⓕ undartaik / Ⓖ undertake / Ⓗ unndertake

4. Ⓔ kampfire / Ⓕ campfyre / Ⓖ kampfyre / Ⓗ campfire
9. Ⓐ blinedbold / Ⓑ blyndfold / Ⓒ blindfold / Ⓓ flindfould
14. Ⓔ boukcase / Ⓕ bookase / Ⓖ bookcase / Ⓗ bookcaise
19. Ⓐ watterproo / Ⓑ waterproof / Ⓒ waterprouf / Ⓓ watterprou

5. Ⓐ clothesline / Ⓑ closeline / Ⓒ clowsline / Ⓓ closelyne
10. Ⓔ lookout / Ⓕ lokout / Ⓖ loukout / Ⓗ lookowt
15. Ⓐ raleroad / Ⓑ railrode / Ⓒ ralerode / Ⓓ railroad
20. Ⓔ yurself / Ⓕ yourcelf / Ⓖ yorself / Ⓗ yourself

---

2. It ~~grow~~ colder after we went outside.

3. I ~~know~~ it was a good idea to wear my gloves, hat, and scarf.

4. The snow and ice leave the trees glistening and white.

5. The path ~~lead~~ us straight to the forest.

6. I ~~keep~~ my hands in my pockets.

7. We ~~choose~~ the first day of winter to take pictures of the forest.

8. The winds ~~blow~~ drifts of snow against the bare trees.

Ever since she was a little girl, Margaret had know she wanted to be a photographer. By the age of 15, she had winned three photography awards. Now 30 years old, she has write a guide for beginning photographers. She has maked photography her life's work.

B. Circle the letter before the correct irregular verb and helping verb that completes each sentence.

3. The weather _____ colder and windier since this morning.
   a. has become
   b. have become
   c. has became
   d. have became

4. Before she retired, the professor _____ a career out of studying snowflakes.
   a. has maded
   b. has make
   c. had make
   d. had made

Daily Language Activities

Write the sentences on the board.

DAY 1

Approaching

SMALL GROUP

	Daily Planner
DAY 1	• Prepare to Read • Academic Language • Vocabulary (Preteach)
DAY 2	• Comprehension • Leveled Reader Lesson 1
DAY 3	• Phonics/Decoding • Leveled Reader Lesson 2
DAY 4	• Phonics/Decoding • Vocabulary (Review) • Leveled Reader Lesson 3
DAY 5	• High-Frequency Words • Fluency • Self-Selected Reading

LOG ON **StudentWorks** Plus
Interactive Student Book

If you wish to preteach the main selection, use StudentWorks Plus for:

• Vocabulary Preteaching
• Word-by-Word Highlighting
• Think Aloud Prompts

Academic Language

Academic words include those harder Tier 2 words that appear in much of students' reading materials as well as the language of instruction. The words chosen for instruction were selected from the **Living Word Vocabulary** list and Avril Coxhead's list of **High-Incidence Academic Words**.

Approaching Level

Prepare to Read

Objective Preview *Me and Uncle Romie*
Materials • **StudentWorks Plus** • self-stick notes

PREVIEW TEXT

- Have students preview *Me and Uncle Romie* using **StudentWorks Plus**, the interactive eBook. This version of the selection contains oral summaries in multiple languages, story recording, word-by-word highlighting, Think Aloud prompts, and comprehension-monitoring questions.

- Remind students that listening carefully to and following along with the word-by-word reading will help them prepare for the reading of the selection with the class. Have students place self-stick notes on any challenging words or places that confuse them. Discuss these with students prior to the reading of the selection with the rest of the class.

- Ask students to write three or four sentences in their Writer's Notebooks telling what they learned about visiting a big city.

Academic Language

Objective Teach academic language
Materials • none

PRETEACH LANGUAGE OF INSTRUCTION

Tell students that there are many important lesson words you will be using this week. You want them to become familiar with these words *before* the lessons. These words also appear in the directions of the tests they will be taking this year.

Preteach the following academic words: *historical fiction, character, setting, plot, visualize, theme,* and *rate*.

- Define each word using student-friendly language. Tell students that *historical fiction* is a story that includes real people and events along with fictional characters and plots. For example, a story about George Washington as a young boy might include some fictional playmates.

- In addition, relate each word to known words. For example, connect *setting* to *where and when* or *time and place, visualize* to *vision,* and *rate* to *speed*.

- Highlight these words when used throughout the week, and reinforce their meanings.

Approaching Level

Phonics/Decoding

Objective   Decode compound words

Materials
- **Approaching Reproducible,** p. 127
- **Word-Building Cards**

PHONICS MAINTENANCE

Tier 2

- Display the **Word-Building Cards**. Ask: *What long word do we get if we put these two short words together?* Keep the card with the word *foot*. Replace the card *ball* with the card *step* and then with the card *print*. Have students say each word (*footstep* and *footprint*) and explain its meaning.

- Review that some long words can be divided into two shorter words. Write the words *sidewalk, weekend,* and *birthday* on the board. Model how to divide each compound word into two smaller words. Say each word, and ask students its meaning. Relate the meanings of the shorter words within each compound to the meaning of the whole word.

- Dictate the following compound words for students to spell: *baseball, ballgame, someone, rooftop, eyelash, homework, workshop, bedroom.* Write each word on the board, and have students self-correct their work.

RETEACH SKILL

Compound Words   Review how to divide each of the dictated compound words into two smaller words. Say each word, and ask students its meaning. Then display the Word-Building Cards and review the spelling of each word.

- Write the words below on the board. Model how to decode the first word in each row, and then guide students as they decode the remaining words. For the multisyllabic words, divide the words into syllables using the syllable-scoop technique to help students read one syllable at a time.

- When completed, point to the words in random order for students to chorally read. Repeat several times.

campfire	campground	underground	underwater
eyeball	eyelash	eyebrow	eyewitness
snowball	snowflake	snowdrift	snowmobile
baseball	softball	basketball	ballroom
bedroom	bathroom	bedside	footrest
grandson	grandmother	daybreak	breakfast

Approaching Reproducible, page 127

> When two smaller words are put together to make one larger word, the new word is called a **compound word**.
> The small words can help you figure out how to say the compound word and, sometimes, tell you what it means.
> ***backyard*** = ***back*** + ***yard*** = a yard in back of a house

A. Write the two smaller words that form each compound word. Then write the meaning of the compound word.

1. raindrop   rain   +   drop
Meaning: a drop of rain

2. snowflake   snow   +   flake
Meaning: a flake, or crystal, of snow

3. southeast   south   +   east
Meaning: the direction between south and east

B. Match a word from the box with the words below to create compound words. Then write a sentence using the new word.
Possible responses provided.

pour	storm	set

4. sun   set
The sunset was beautiful.

5. thunder   storm
The thunderstorm was over quickly.

Approaching Level

Vocabulary

Objective Preteach selection vocabulary

Materials
- **Visual Vocabulary Resources**
- **Approaching Reproducible,** p. 128
- **Vocabulary Cards**

PRETEACH KEY VOCABULARY

Tier 2

Introduce the Words Use the **Visual Vocabulary Resources** to preteach the key selection words *skyscrapers, collage, barbecue, glorious, strutting*, and *swarms*. Use the following routine that appears in detail on the cards.

- Define the word in English, and provide the example given.

- Define the word in Spanish, if appropriate, and indicate if the word is a cognate.

- Display the picture, and explain how it illustrates or demonstrates the word. Then engage students in structured partner-talk about the image, using the key word.

- Ask students to chorally say the word three times.

- Point out any known sound-spellings or focus on a key aspect of phonemic awareness related to the word.

- You may wish to also distribute copies of the Vocabulary Glossary in the **ELL Resource Book**.

REVIEW PREVIOUSLY TAUGHT VOCABULARY

Display the **Vocabulary Cards** from the previous four weeks. Say the meanings of each word, one by one, and have students identify them. Then point to words in random order for students to provide definitions and related words they know.

Context Clues Remind students that context clues are clues within the text that help a reader figure out what a word means. Examples and definitions are two types of context clues. Have students write a context sentence for each vocabulary word. For example, *My favorite part of our trip to the zoo was when we saw the peacocks* strutting *around.*

Corrective Feedback

Throughout the lessons, provide feedback based on students' responses. If the answer is correct, ask another question. If the answer is tentative, restate key information to assist the student. If the answer is wrong, provide corrective feedback such as hints or clues, refer to a visual such as a Vocabulary Card or story illustration, or probe with questions to help the student clarify any misunderstanding.

Approaching Reproducible, page 128

| strutting | swarms | barbecue |
| skyscrapers | glorious | collage |

A. Use a vocabulary word to complete each sentence.

1. I enjoy eating hotdogs and hamburgers at a ___barbecue___.
2. The sun was shining and the air was warm. It was a ___glorious___ summer day.
3. I made a ___collage___ using leaves, fabric, and string.
4. The ___skyscrapers___ downtown are the tallest buildings I have ever seen.
5. ___Swarms___ of bees buzzed around the new blossoms.
6. I watched the rooster ___strutting___ across the barnyard.

B. Choose two vocabulary words and use each one in a sentence. Possible responses provided.

7. We're working on a *collage* in art class.

8. The marching band was strutting across the field.

Approaching Level

Vocabulary

Objective Review vocabulary and high-frequency words

Materials • **Vocabulary Cards** • **High-Frequency Word Cards**

REVIEW VOCABULARY

Review the Words Display the **Vocabulary Cards** *skyscrapers, collage, barbecue, glorious, strutting*, and *swarms*. Point to each word, read it aloud, and have students chorally repeat.

Then provide the following word sets. Ask students to name the word in each set that is <u>not</u> related to the other words.

- skyscrapers, tall, city, farm
- collage, test, scraps, art
- barbecue, meat, pancakes, grill
- glorious, disappointing, wonderful, perfect
- strutting, proud, walking, shy
- swarms, few, moving, many

HIGH-FREQUENCY WORDS

Tier 2

Top 250 Words The ability to read accurately and effortlessly the most frequently used words in written English will help students develop reading fluency. Display **High-Frequency Word Cards** 81–120. Then do the following:

- Display one card at a time and ask students to chorally state each word.
- Have students spell each word aloud.
- Ask students to write each word in their Writer's Notebooks as they state aloud each letter. Then have them read the word again.
- When completed, quickly flip through the word card set as students chorally read the words.
- Provide opportunities for students to use the words in speaking and writing. For example, provide sentence starters, such as *When I had to _____, it made me feel _____,* for oral and written practice. Or point to a word card, and ask a question, such as *What word means the opposite of this word?* (when pointing to the *never* word card).
- Continue the routine throughout the week.

ELL

Practice Vocabulary Pair students of different proficiency. Orally model the vocabulary in sentences. For example: *I used photographs from old magazines to make a collage.* On the board, provide sentence frames for pairs to copy and complete using the vocabulary. For example: *The winner of the competition was _____ proudly.* (strutting)

Word Webs

Have students create word webs in their Writer's Notebooks for each vocabulary word. Write the related words provided, and ask students to add other words, phrases, and illustrations.

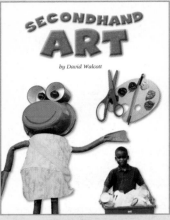

SECONDHAND ART
by David Walcott

Student Book

Approaching Level

Comprehension

Objective Reteach monitor comprehension and character, setting, plot

Materials • **Student Book:** "Secondhand Art"

RETEACH STRATEGY: VISUALIZE

Tier 2

- **Define** Review with students that when you visualize, you create pictures in your mind based on details an author provides. As an example, say the words *fluffy, soft, baby, meow*. Ask what students visualize.

  Relate the word *visualize* to the word *vision* and the root *vis*, which means "see." Suggest that vision is using your eyes to see and visualizing is using your mind to see.

- **Relate to Real Life** Ask students to imagine that it is a hot summer day and they are very thirsty. All the way home, they think about a big, cold glass of water with ice cubes floating in it. That is visualizing. You are creating a picture in your mind of how the water looks.

- **Set Purposes** Remind students that good readers visualize to help them understand what they are reading. They create mental images of the characters and events in the story.

RETEACH SKILL: CHARACTER, SETTING, PLOT

- **Define** Remind students that a character is a person or an animal in a story, that the setting tells when and where the story takes place, and that the plot is the series of events in a story.

- **Relate to Real Life** Instruct students to recall a recent fun activity. Ask: *What happened in this activity? When and where did it happen? Were you the only person participating in the activity, or were others involved? How did everybody get along?* Relate students' answers to the terms *plot, setting,* and *character,* respectively.

- **Set Purposes** Remind students that good readers look for story details that help them visualize or understand the characters, setting, and plot. Have them consider how these elements work together to make the story interesting. It can also help to explain the relationships between the characters and the changes the characters undergo.

- **Apply** Work with students to identify the characters, setting, and plot in "Secondhand Art." Have students visualize and monitor their comprehension as they read. Students will apply this strategy and skill to a simpler text as they read *Girl Arranging Her Hair.*

Corrective Feedback

Read each paragraph with students. Ask: *Which character is this paragraph mostly about? What is the character like? How can you tell?* Have students underline the details in the paragraph that give clues about the personality of one of the story characters.

Approaching Level

Leveled Reader Lesson 1

Objective Read to apply skills and strategies

Materials • **Leveled Reader:** *Girl Arranging Her Hair*

Leveled Reader

BEFORE READING

Preview and Predict Have students read the title and preview the first chapter. Ask students to make predictions about the characters, setting, and plot in this section. Students should note any questions they have before they read.

 Review the Vocabulary Words Have students read the vocabulary words on the inside front cover. Briefly define each and ask students to state related words they have learned.

Set a Purpose for Reading *Let's read to find out what the title of this story might mean.*

DURING READING

STRATEGY
VISUALIZE

Remind students that when you visualize, you use descriptive details in the text to picture the characters, settings, or events in your mind.

 SKILL
CHARACTER, SETTING, PLOT

Remind students to look for key details about the characters, setting, and plot in the story as they read. Read Chapter 1 with students. Help students begin a Story Flowchart.

As you read, help students decode unknown words. In addition, ask open-ended questions to facilitate rich discussion, such as *Where and when does this story take place? How would you feel if someone asked to paint your picture? Will the painting make Louise famous? Why or why not?* Build on students' responses to help them develop a deeper understanding of the text.

Stop after every two pages, and ask students to summarize what they have just read, focusing on the characters, setting, and plot. Help struggling students reread difficult pages or passages. Then model identifying details about them.

AFTER READING

Have students compare this story to real life. Say: *The painting shown on page 13 is real. How realistic does the story seem?* Have students identify character, setting, and plot details that support their answer.

Leveled Reader

Approaching Level
Leveled Reader Lesson 2

Objective Reread to apply skills and strategies and develop fluency
Materials
- **Leveled Reader:** *Girl Arranging Her Hair*
- **Approaching Reproducible,** p. 131

BEFORE READING

 Review the Strategy and Skill Review students' completed Story Flowcharts from the first read. Remind students that visualizing means creating a mental picture based on details from the text. Also remind students that a character is a person or an animal in a story, the setting is when and where the story takes place, and the plot is the series of events in a story.

Review the Vocabulary Words Have students search the book for each vocabulary word. Ask students to read aloud the sentence containing the word and state the word's definition or provide related words. Point out any context clues provided, such as surrounding words that offer examples, definitions, or descriptions.

Set a Purpose for Reading *Let's reread to check our understanding of the characters, setting, and plot in this story and to work on our reading fluency.*

DURING READING

Reread *Girl Arranging Her Hair* with students. Have them read silently, two pages at a time, or read aloud to a partner. Stop and have students summarize before they read the next two pages. Model oral summaries, as needed.

AFTER READING

Check Comprehension Have partners complete the Comprehension Check on page 16. Review students' answers. Help students find evidence for their answers in the text.

MODEL FLUENCY

Model reading the fluency passage on **Approaching Reproducible** page 131. Tell students to pay close attention to your rate as you read. Then read one sentence at a time, and have students echo-read the sentences, copying your rate.

During independent reading time, have students work with a partner using the fluency passage. One student reads aloud, while the other repeats each sentence back. If students need additional support, have them listen to the "practice speed" version of the passage on the **Fluency Solutions Audio CD.**

Approaching Reproducible, page 131

As I read, I will pay attention to my reading rate in order to match the action in the story.

	"Me?" asked Louise. "She asked for me?"
7	"Yes, Louise," said her mother, smiling. "Madame
14	Cassatt wants you to model for a painting. Will you do it?"
26	Louise could not have been more surprised. She didn't
35	think anyone would want to paint a picture of her. After
46	all, she was not at all like the beautiful women usually
57	found in paintings. She was just a fourteen-year-old girl.
66	"You know Madame Cassatt," said her mother. "She is
75	the American. She comes to the bakery almost every day."
85	"Oh," said Louise, nodding. "The tall lady?"
92	"Yes," said her mother. "What should we tell her? It is
103	all right with Papa and me. Madame Cassatt is honest.
113	She can be trusted. Of course it is your decision. She has
125	offered to pay." Her mother paused. "We could
133	pay for your lessons with the singing master." 141

Comprehension Check

1. How can you tell that Louise is not stuck up or vain? **Plot Development**
   She is surprised that Madame Cassatt wants to paint her. Louise thinks that she is not at all like the beautiful women she sees in paintings.
2. What opportunity has Louise been offered? **Plot Development**
   A painter, Madame Cassatt, has asked 14-year-old Louise to model for a painting.

	Words Read	–	Number of Errors	=	Words Correct Score
First Read		–		=	
Second Read		–		=	

Approaching Level

Leveled Reader Lesson 3

Objective Build fluency

Materials
- **Leveled Reader:** *Girl Arranging Her Hair*
- **Approaching Reproducible,** p. 131

FOCUS ON FLUENCY

Timed Reading Tell students that they will be doing a final timed reading of the fluency passage on **Approaching Reproducible** page 131 that they have been practicing. With each student, follow these directions:

- Place the passage facedown.

- When you say "Go," the student begins reading the passage aloud.

- When you say "Stop," the student stops reading the passage.

As they read, note words students mispronounce and their overall rate. Stop after one minute. Help students record and graph the number of words they read correctly.

REREAD PREVIOUSLY READ BOOKS

- Distribute copies of the past six **Leveled Readers**. Have students select two to reread. Tell students that rereading these books will help them develop their skills. The more times they read the same words, the quicker they will learn these words. This will make the reading of other books easier.

- Circulate and listen in as students read. Stop students periodically and ask them how they are figuring out difficult words and how they are monitoring their comprehension. Note students who need additional work with specific decoding or comprehension skills.

- Encourage students to read other previously read Leveled Readers during independent reading time or for homework.

Meet Grade-Level Expectations

As an alternative to this day's lesson, guide students through a reading of the On Level Leveled Reader. See page 395U. Since both books contain the same vocabulary, phonics, and comprehension skills, the scaffolding you provided will help most students gain access to this more challenging text.

Book Talk

Bringing Groups Together Students will work with peers of various language and reading abilities to discuss this week's Leveled Readers. Refer to page 158 in the **Teacher's Resource Book** for more about how to conduct a Book Talk.

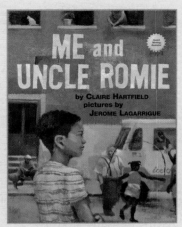

Student Book

Student Book

Approaching Level

Fluency

Objectives Reread selections to develop fluency; develop speaking skills

Materials • **Student Book:** *Me and Uncle Romie*, "Computers: The Future of Art"

REREAD FOR FLUENCY

- Have students reread a portion of *Me and Uncle Romie*. Suggest that they focus on two to four of their favorite pages from the selection. Work with students to read the pages with the appropriate rate.

- Provide time for students to read their sections of text to you. Comment on their rate, and provide corrective feedback by modeling proper fluency.

DEVELOP SPEAKING/LISTENING SKILLS

- Have students practice reading a half-page passage from the nonfiction article "Computers: The Future of Art."

- Work with students to read with an appropriate rate. Model reading a few lines at a time. Emphasize the flow of the instructions and the attention given to certain instructions through your rate. Have students repeat.

- Provide time for students to read aloud their passage to partners. Ask students to name ways in which their partner made the instructions clear with his or her voice.

- Challenge students to summarize the instructions from the article for the class, as if giving part of a research presentation or how-to lesson.

Decodable Text

Use decodable stories in the **Teacher's Resource Book** to help students build fluency with basic decoding patterns.

Approaching Level

Self-Selected Reading

Objective   Read independently to identify character, setting, and plot

Materials   • **Leveled Classroom Library** • other fiction books

APPLY SKILLS AND STRATEGIES TO INDEPENDENT READING

■ **Read Independently** Have students choose a fiction book, such as a **Leveled Classroom Library** book, for sustained silent reading. (See the **Theme Bibliography** on pages T8–T9 for book suggestions.) Remind them that visualizing means creating a mental picture to help make sure they understand what they have read so far. Review with students that a character is a person or an animal in a story, the setting tells when and where the story takes place, and the plot is the series of events in a story. Have students read their books and record details in a Story Flowchart.

■ **Show Evidence of Reading** While reading, students may generate a reading log or journal. After reading, ask students to use their Story Flowchart to write or orally state a summary of the book, maintaining meaning and logical order. Provide time for students to share their summaries and other comments through Book Talks. Ask: *Which character, setting detail, or event did you find most interesting? Why?*

Approaching

Leveled Classroom Library
See Leveled Classroom
Library lessons on pages T2–T7.

Daily Planner

DAY 1	• Vocabulary • Phonics
DAY 2	• Leveled Reader Lesson 1
DAY 3	• Leveled Reader Lesson 2
DAY 4	• Fluency
DAY 5	• Self-Selected Reading

ELL

Practice Vocabulary Pair ELL students with native speakers. On the board, provide sentence frames for pairs to copy and complete using the vocabulary and additional words when necessary. For example: *The city has lots of tall _____ and huge _____.* (skyscrapers; buildings)

On Level

Vocabulary

Objective Review vocabulary
Materials • **Vocabulary Cards**

REVIEW PREVIOUSLY TAUGHT WORDS

Review the Words Display the **Vocabulary Cards** for *skyscrapers, collage, barbecue, glorious, strutting,* and *swarms.* Point to each word, read it aloud, and have students chorally repeat.

Then ask students to describe the following:

- a place where they might see *skyscrapers*
- what they might include in a *collage* about their life so far
- a time when they ate *barbecue*
- a *glorious* day they can remember
- someone they have seen *strutting*
- a place where they might see *swarms* of people

Phonics/Word Study

Objective Decode multisyllabic compound words
Materials • **Word-Building Cards**

RETEACH SKILL

- **Compound Words** Show the **Word-Building Cards** for *side, walk, ways, step,* and *mother.* Review the spelling of each word part. Then review how to combine the short words into compound words such as *sidewalk, walkways, sidestep,* and *stepmother.* Write the compound words on the board, divide each one into its two smaller words, and verify the spelling.

- Write the words below on the board. If necessary, divide the words into syllables using the syllable-scoop technique to help students read one syllable at a time. When completed, point to the words in random order for students to chorally read.

footnote	footpath	bookmobile	bookkeeper
pathway	blueprint	candlestick	thunderstorm
blackberry	underpass	underhanded	straightaway

- **Spelling** Dictate the following words for students to spell: *rainfall, daylight, lighthouse, fingerprint, underground.* Guide students to use the Word-Building Cards and model how to segment words.

On Level

Fluency

Objective Reread selections to develop fluency and speaking skills

Materials • **Student Book:** *Me and Uncle Romie*, "Computers: The Future of Art"

REREAD FOR FLUENCY

- Have students reread *Me and Uncle Romie*. Work with students to read with the appropriate rate. Model as needed.

- Provide time for students to read a section of text to you. Comment on their rate and provide corrective feedback as needed.

DEVELOP SPEAKING/LISTENING SKILLS

- Have students practice reading a passage from the nonfiction article "Computers: The Future of Art."

- Work with students to read with an appropriate rate. Model reading a few lines at a time. If you model reading the instructions, emphasize the flow of the steps and the attention given to certain steps through your rate. Have students repeat.

- Provide time for students to read aloud their passage to partners. Ask students to name ways in which their partner made the instructions clear with his or her voice.

- Challenge students to summarize the instructions from the passage for the class, as if giving part of a research presentation or how-to lesson.

Self-Selected Reading

Objective Read independently to identify character, setting, and plot

Materials • **Leveled Classroom Library** • other fiction books

APPLY SKILLS AND STRATEGIES TO INDEPENDENT READING

- **Read Independently** Have students choose a fiction book for sustained silent reading. (See the **Theme Bibliography** on pages T8–T9 for book suggestions.) Have students read their books and record details in their Story Flowchart.

- **Show Evidence of Reading** While reading, students may generate a reading log or journal. After reading, ask students to use their Story Flowchart to write or orally state a summary of the book, maintaining meaning and logical order. Provide time for students to share their summaries and other comments through Book Talks. Ask: *Which character, setting detail, or event did you find most interesting? Why?*

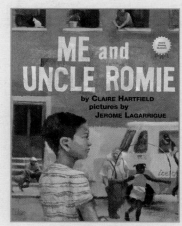

Student Book

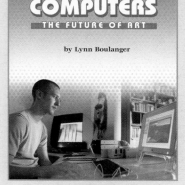

Student Book

On Level

Leveled Classroom Library
See Leveled Classroom Library lessons on pages T2–T7.

Leveled Reader

On Level

Leveled Reader Lesson 1

Objective Read to apply strategies and skills

Materials • **Leveled Reader:** *Beautiful or Not*

BEFORE READING

Preview and Predict Have students read the title and preview the book by reading the chapter titles and looking at the illustrations. Ask students to predict what they think this book is about and what its characters, setting, and plot might be like.

 Review the Vocabulary Words Have students read the vocabulary words on the inside front cover. Ask students to state related words they have learned. Review definitions, as needed.

Set a Purpose for Reading *Let's read to find out what the title means.*

DURING READING

 STRATEGY
VISUALIZE

Remind students that when you visualize, you create a mental image from details the author provides in the text.

SKILL
CHARACTER, SETTING, PLOT

Remind students that a character is a person or an animal in a story, the setting is when and where the story takes place, and the plot is the series of events in a story.

Read Chapter 1 with students. Ask open-ended questions to facilitate rich discussion, such as *How would you describe the relationship between Carly and her brother? How could the author have explained this more clearly?* Build on students' responses to help them develop a deeper understanding of the text. Have students fill in the details they have learned so far in their Story Flowchart. Then continue reading.

Context Clues Have students point out this week's new vocabulary words. Remind students to look for definitions, examples, or other context clues that help clarify each word's meaning.

AFTER READING

Have students compare this story to real life. Ask: *Would you use the term* realistic fiction *to describe this story? Why or why not?* Tell students to analyze and discuss the characters, setting, and plot in this story.

On Level

Leveled Reader Lesson 2

Objectives Reread to apply skills and strategies; develop fluency
Materials   • **Leveled Reader:** *Beautiful or Not*   • **Practice Book,** p. 131

BEFORE READING

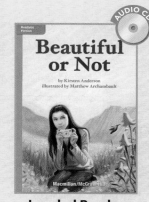

Leveled Reader

Review the Strategy and Skill Review students' completed Story Flowcharts from the first read. Remind students that visualizing means picturing the events in the story to make sure they understand what they have read so far.

Review that a character is a person or an animal in a story, the setting is when and where the story takes place, and the plot is the series of events in a story. If students' Story Flowcharts are incomplete, provide a model chart or use a student chart and revise it as a group. Have students copy the revised chart in their Writer's Notebooks.

Set a Purpose for Reading *Let's reread to check our understanding of the book's characters, setting, and plot, and to work on our reading fluency.*

DURING READING

Reread *Beautiful or Not* with students. Have them read silently, two pages at a time, or read aloud to a partner. Stop and have students summarize before reading the next two pages. Model making oral summaries, as needed.

AFTER READING

Check Comprehension Have partners complete the Comprehension Check on page 20. Review students' answers. Help students find evidence for their answers in the text.

MODEL FLUENCY

Model reading the fluency passage on **Practice Book** page 131. Tell students to pay close attention to your rate as you read. Then read one sentence at a time and have students echo-read the sentences, copying your rate.

During independent reading time, have students work with a partner using the fluency passage. One student reads aloud while the other repeats each sentence back. If students need additional support, have them listen to the "practice speed" version of the passage on the **Fluency Solutions Audio CD**.

Book Talk

Bringing Groups Together Students will work with peers of various language and reading abilities to discuss this week's **Leveled Readers**. Refer to page 158 in the **Teacher's Resource Book** for more about how to conduct a Book Talk.

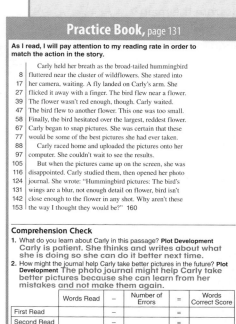

Practice Book, page 131

As I read, I will pay attention to my reading rate in order to match the action in the story.

Carly held her breath as the broad-tailed hummingbird
8 fluttered near the cluster of wildflowers. She stared into
17 her camera, waiting. A fly landed on Carly's arm. She
27 flicked it away with a finger. The bird flew near a flower.
39 The flower wasn't red enough, though. Carly waited.
47 The bird flew to another flower. This one was too small.
58 Finally, the bird hesitated over the largest, reddest flower.
67 Carly began to snap pictures. She was certain that these
77 would be some of the best pictures she had ever taken.
88   Carly raced home and uploaded the pictures onto her
97 computer. She couldn't wait to see the results.
105   But when the pictures came up on the screen, she was
116 disappointed. Carly studied them, then opened her photo
124 journal. She wrote: "Hummingbird pictures: The bird's
131 wings are a blur, not enough detail on flower, bird isn't
142 close enough to the flower in any shot. Why aren't these
153 the way I thought they would be?" 160

Comprehension Check

1. What do you learn about Carly in this passage? **Plot Development**
   Carly is patient. She thinks and writes about what she is doing so she can do it better next time.
2. How might the journal help Carly take better pictures in the future? **Plot Development** The photo journal might help Carly take better pictures because she can learn from her mistakes and not make them again.

	Words Read	–	Number of Errors	=	Words Correct Score
First Read		–		=	
Second Read		–		=	

Daily Planner	
DAY 1	• Leveled Reader Lesson 1
DAY 2	• Leveled Reader Lesson 2
DAY 3	• Phonics
DAY 4	• Vocabulary • Fluency
DAY 5	• Self-Selected Reading

ELL

Self-Monitor Vocabulary
Have student pairs of different proficiency identify and define unfamiliar words from the main selection using a dictionary. Challenge students to use the new words in sentences. Monitor students as they complete the activity.

Beyond Level

Phonics/Word Study

Objective   Decode multisyllabic compound words
Materials   • none

EXTEND/ACCELERATE

■ **Read Multisyllabic Compound Words**   Write the words below on the board. Challenge students to read the words, using known word parts. When completed, point to the words in random order for students to chorally read.

sunscreen	sunlight	sunglasses	sunflower
boardwalk	boardinghouse	lighthearted	fingerprinted
waterfront	watermelon	waterproofing	straightforward
undergrowth	overshadowing	overprotective	underestimated

■ **Define the Words**   Ask students to use their knowledge of word parts to figure out the meanings of the above words. Then have partners find the words in a dictionary and confirm or revise the meanings. Challenge students to use these words in this week's writing assignments.

■ **Spell Compound Words**   Dictate the following words for students to spell: *outbreak, eyewitness, thunderstorm, straightaway, throughout.* Write the words for students to self-correct.

Vocabulary

Objectives   Review setting and description; write a personal narrative
Materials   • none

ENRICH VOCABULARY

■ **Review Setting and Description**   Remind students that the author of *Me and Uncle Romie* used descriptions to help readers picture events in two different settings: New York City and a small town in North Carolina. Have students compare details about each setting. Discuss how the details make both places, though distinct, seem interesting. What words bring each setting to life?

■ **Write a Personal Narrative**   Have students think about a time when they spent a day at a crowded parade, street fair, carnival, or an amusement park. Challenge them to write a personal narrative about their day, using the vocabulary words from this week's selections. Have students use vivid descriptions in their writing.

Gifted & Talented

Beyond Level

Fluency

Objectives Reread selections to develop fluency; develop speaking skills
Materials • **Student Book:** *Me and Uncle Romie*, "Computers: The Future of Art"

RERED FOR FLUENCY

- Have students reread *Me and Uncle Romie*. Work with students to read the selection using an appropriate rate.

- Provide time for students to read a section of text to you. Comment on their rate and provide corrective feedback.

DEVELOP SPEAKING/LISTENING SKILLS

- Have students practice reading the nonfiction article "Computers: The Future of Art."

- Work with students to read with an appropriate rate. Model reading a few lines at a time. Emphasize the flow of the numbered steps and the attention given to certain steps through your rate. Have students repeat.

- Provide time for students to read aloud their passage to partners. Ask students to name ways in which the reader made the instructions clear with his or her voice.

Self-Selected Reading

Objective Read independently to identify the character, setting, and plot
Materials • **Leveled Classroom Library** • other fiction books

APPLY SKILLS AND STRATEGIES TO INDEPENDENT READING

- **Read Independently** Have students choose a fiction book for sustained silent reading. (See the **Theme Bibliography** on pages T8–T9 for book suggestions.) Have students read their books and record details in a Story Flowchart.

- **Show Evidence of Reading** While reading, students may generate a reading log or journal. After reading, ask students to use their Story Flowchart to write a summary of the book, maintaining meaning and logical order. Provide time for students to share their summaries and comments through Book Talks. Ask: *Which character, setting detail, or event did you find most interesting? Why?*

- **Evaluate** Have students pair up for a debate. One person from each group is for the use of technology in the arts and one is against. Each student should give reasons to support their position.

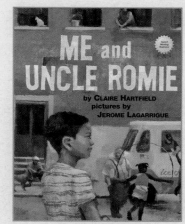

Student Book

Student Book

Beyond
Leveled Classroom Library
See Leveled Classroom
Library lessons on pages T2–T7.

Gifted Talented

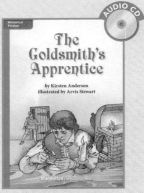

Beyond Level

Leveled Reader Lesson 1

Objective Read to apply strategies and skills

Materials • **Leveled Reader:** *The Goldsmith's Apprentice*

BEFORE READING

Preview and Predict Have students preview the book by reading the title and chapter titles and looking at the illustrations. Ask students to predict what this book is about as well as the types of characters, setting, and plot they might encounter.

 Review the Vocabulary Words Have students read the vocabulary words on the inside front cover. Ask students to state each definition and any related words they have learned.

Set a Purpose for Reading *Let's read to find details about the characters, setting, and plot of this story.*

DURING READING

 STRATEGY
VISUALIZE

Have students define the term *visualize.* Remind students that monitoring their comprehension means pausing to make sure they understand what they have read. Visualizing will help them do that.

SKILL
CHARACTER, SETTING, PLOT

Tell students to define the terms *character, setting,* and *plot.* If necessary, remind students that a character is a person or an animal in a story, that the setting is when and where the story takes place, and that the plot is the series of events in a story.

Read the book with students. Ask open-ended questions to facilitate rich discussion, such as *What type of character is the apprentice? How can you tell? What is his relationship with Benvenuto like? Explain.* Build on students' responses to help them develop a deeper understanding of the text. Have students fill in the Story Flowchart independently as they read.

AFTER READING

Relate to Real Life Have students relate this story to real life. Ask: *If you could become someone's apprentice, who would it be? Why?* Have students discuss their answers with a partner.

Analyze Ask students to create a Venn diagram to analyze how Uncle Romie and a character from this book are alike and different.

Beyond Level

Leveled Reader Library

Leveled Reader Lesson 2

Objective   Reread to apply skills and strategies and develop fluency

Materials
- **Leveled Reader:** *The Goldsmith's Apprentice*
- **Beyond Reproducible,** p. 131

BEFORE READING

Review the Strategy and Skill Review students' completed Story Flowcharts from the first read.

Remind students that a character is a person or an animal in a story, that the setting is when and where the story takes place, and that the plot is the series of events in a story. If students' Story Flowcharts are incomplete, provide a model chart or use a student chart and revise it as a group. Have students copy the revised chart in their Writer's Notebooks.

Set a Purpose for Reading *Let's reread to check our understanding of the book's characters, setting, and plot, and work on our fluency.*

DURING READING

Have students reread *The Goldsmith's Apprentice* silently or with a partner. If reading in pairs, prompt students to stop every two pages and summarize or ask their partner probing questions.

AFTER READING

Check Comprehension Have students independently complete the Comprehension Check on page 20. Review students' answers. Help students find evidence for their answers in the text.

Synthesize Have students write a list of questions they would ask Benvenuto Cellini about his work. Ask: *Would he like using the latest technology in his art? Why or why not? Discuss with a partner.*

Gifted Talented

MODEL FLUENCY

Model reading the fluency passage on **Beyond Reproducible** page 131. Tell students to pay close attention to your rate as you read. Then read one sentence at a time, and have students echo-read the sentences, copying your rate.

During independent reading time, have students work with a partner using the fluency passage. One student reads aloud, while the other repeats each sentence back. Students can check their fluency by reading along with the "expert speed" version of the passage on the **Fluency Solutions Audio CD**.

Historical Fiction

The Goldsmith's Apprentice

by Kirsten Anderson
illustrated by Arvis Stewart

Macmillan/McGraw-Hill

Leveled Reader

Book Talk

Bringing Groups Together
Students will work with peers of various language and reading abilities to discuss this week's Leveled Readers. Refer to page 158 in the **Teacher's Resource Book** for more about how to conduct a Book Talk.

Beyond Reproducible, page 131

As I read, I will pay attention to my reading rate in order to match the action in the story.

	"Over here, over here!"
4	I followed the voice and found Benvenuto lurking around the
14	corner of Signor Agnolo's shop.
19	"Hold on," he said. "I'll go with you on your errand."
30	"Aren't you supposed to be working?" I asked.
38	"Yes, but it's a **glorious** summer afternoon," Benvenuto said.
47	"I thought I'd rather come with you than sit in a dark workshop."
60	"Signor Agnolo will be angry," I said.
67	"No, he won't. I'll finish my work when I get back, and then
80	he won't have anything to complain about—if he even notices
91	I'm gone," he added, smiling mischievously.
97	I knew he was right. Benvenuto Cellini was by far the most
109	talented of the apprentices at Signor Agnolo's goldsmith shop.
118	He could finish any amount of work faster than anyone else. It would
131	be twice as good, too. Signor Agnolo knew that if he got rid of
145	Benvenuto, he would go to another shop. Then that goldsmith
155	would benefit from his talent.
160	My parents had sent me to Signor Agnolo's only three months ago,
172	right after my twelfth birthday. It was time for me to learn a trade. 186

Comprehension Check

1. What can you tell about Benvenuto's character? **Plot Development**
   Benvenuto is talented, mischievous, and persuasive.
2. What is Benvenuto trying to accomplish in his conversation? **Plot Development** He is trying to join his friend on an errand.

	Words Read	−	Number of Errors	=	Words Correct Score
First Read		−		=	
Second Read		−		=	

ELL — ENGLISH LANGUAGE LEARNERS

Daily Planner

DAY 1	• Build Background Knowledge • Vocabulary
DAY 2	• Vocabulary • Access to Core Content *Me and Uncle Romie*
DAY 3	• Vocabulary • Grammar • Access to Core Content *Me and Uncle Romie*
DAY 4	• Vocabulary • Writing/Spelling • Access to Core Content "Computers: The Future of Art" • Leveled Reader *Everyday Beauty*
DAY 5	• Vocabulary • Leveled Reader *Everyday Beauty* • Self-Selected Reading

LOG ON StudentWorks Plus
Interactive Student Book

Use StudentWorks Plus for:
- Vocabulary Preteaching
- Word-by-Word Highlighting
- Think Aloud Prompts

Cognates

Help students identify similarities and differences in pronunciation and spelling between English and Spanish cognates.

expression	*expresión*
mural	*mural*
barbecue	*barbacoa*
glorious	*glorioso*
visualize	*visualizar*
verb	*verbo*
definition	*definición*
example	*ejemplo*

Prepare to Read

Content Objective Describe visiting family away from home
Language Objective Use key words to describe how art can remind us of our past
Materials • **StudentWorks Plus**

BUILD BACKGROUND KNOWLEDGE

All Language Levels

- Have students preview *Me and Uncle Romie* using **StudentWorks Plus**, which contains oral summaries in multiple languages, online multilingual glossaries, word-by-word highlighting, and questions that assess and build comprehension.

- Students can build their word-reading fluency by reading along as the text is read or by listening during the first reading and, at the end of each paragraph, returning to the beginning of the paragraph and reading along.

- Students can build their comprehension by reviewing the definitions of key words in the online glossary and by answering the comprehension questions. When appropriate, the text required to answer the question is highlighted to provide students with additional support and scaffolding.

- After reading, students can respond in writing to a question that links the story to their own experiences, such as *Have you ever spent time with your relatives? Who did you visit? What did you do?*

Academic Language

Language Objective Use academic language in classroom conversations

All Language Levels

- This week's academic words are **boldfaced** throughout the lesson. Define the word in context, and provide a clear example from the selection. Then ask students to generate an example or a word with a similar meaning.

Academic Language Used in Whole Group Instruction

Theme Words	Key Selection Words	Strategy and Skill Words
expression **memorial** **mural**	**skyscrapers** **collage** **barbecue** **glorious** **strutting** **swarms**	**visualize** **character, setting, plot** **irregular verbs** **definitions** **examples**

Vocabulary

Language Objective Demonstrate understanding and use of key words by describing a visit to the city

Materials • **Visual Vocabulary Resources**
• **ELL Resource Book**

PRETEACH KEY VOCABULARY

Use the **Visual Vocabulary Resources** to preteach the key selection words *skyscrapers, collage, barbecue, glorious, strutting,* and *swarms*. Focus on two words per day. Use the following routine, which appears in detail on the cards.

Beginning/Intermediate

■ Point out any known sound-spellings, or focus on a key aspect of phonemic awareness related to the word.

All Language Levels

■ Define the word in English, and provide the example given.

■ Define the word in Spanish, if appropriate, and indicate if the word is a cognate.

■ Display the picture, and explain how it illustrates the word. Engage students in a structured activity using the key word.

■ Ask students to chorally say the word three times.

■ Distribute copies of the Vocabulary Glossary on **ELL Resource Book**, page 170.

PRETEACH FUNCTION WORDS AND PHRASES

All Language Levels

Use the Visual Vocabulary Resources to preteach the function words and phrases *window shop, blast past, curl up,* and *stretch up to the sky*. Focus on one word or phrase per day. Use the detailed routine on the cards.

■ Define the word in English and, if appropriate, in Spanish. Point out if the word is a cognate.

■ Refer to the picture and engage students in talk about the word. For example, students will partner-talk using sentence frames.

■ Ask students to chorally repeat the word three times.

TEACH BASIC WORDS

Beginning/Intermediate

Use the Visual Vocabulary Resources to teach the basic words *apartment, studio, stoop, ferry, rooftop,* and *subway*. Teach these "city" words using the routine provided on the card.

Visual Vocabulary Resources

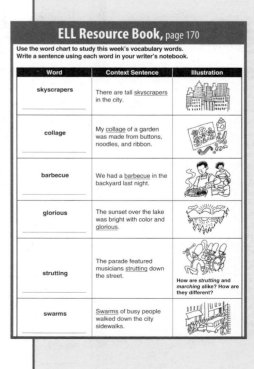

ELL Resource Book, page 170

Use the word chart to study this week's vocabulary words.
Write a sentence using each word in your writer's notebook.

Word	Context Sentence	Illustration
skyscrapers	There are tall <u>skyscrapers</u> in the city.	
collage	My <u>collage</u> of a garden was made from buttons, noodles, and ribbon.	
barbecue	We had a <u>barbecue</u> in the backyard last night.	
glorious	The sunset over the lake was bright with color and <u>glorious</u>.	
strutting	The parade featured musicians <u>strutting</u> down the street.	How are *strutting* and *marching* alike? How are they different?
swarms	<u>Swarms</u> of busy people walked down the city sidewalks.	

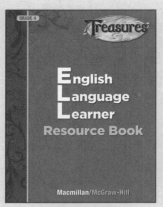

ELL Resource Book

ELL ENGLISH LANGUAGE LEARNERS

Access to Core Content

Content Objective Read grade-level text

Language Objective Discuss text, using key words and sentence frames

Materials • **ELL Resource Book,** pp. 158–169

✔ PRETEACH MAIN SELECTION (PAGES 372–389)

All Language Levels

Use the Interactive Question-Response Guide on **ELL Resource Book** pages 158–167 to introduce students to *Me and Uncle Romie*. Preteach half of the selection on **Day 2** and half on **Day 3**.

- Use the prompts provided in the guide to develop meaning and vocabulary. Use the partner-talk and whole-class responses to engage students and increase student talk.

- When completed, have partners reread the story.

PRETEACH PAIRED SELECTION (PAGES 392–393)

All Language Levels

Use the Interactive Question-Response Guide on ELL Resource Book pages 168–169 to preview the paired selection "Computers: The Future of Art." Preteach the selection on **Day 4**.

Beginning	Intermediate	Advanced
Identify Characters During the Interactive Reading, select several illustrations that show characters. Describe the characters in the illustrations and have students retell what you said.	**Describe** During the Interactive Reading, select a few lines of text that describe character, setting, or plot. After you have read and explained it, have students describe character, setting, or plot based on the text.	**Explain** During the Interactive Reading, select a passage of text. After you have read and explained it, have students describe the character, setting, and plot based on the text.

ELL ENGLISH LANGUAGE LEARNERS

Fluency

Content Objectives Reread selections to develop fluency; develop speaking skills
Language Objective Tell a partner what a selection is about
Materials • **Student Book:** *Me and Uncle Romie,* "Computers: The Future of Art"
• **Teacher's Resource Book**

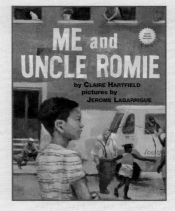

REREAD FOR FLUENCY

> **Beginning**

- Have students read the decodable passages in the **Teacher's Resource Book**, page 19.

> **Intermediate/Advanced**

- Have students reread two to four of their favorite pages of *Me and Uncle Romie,* based on their levels. Help students read the pages with appropriate pacing. For example, read each sentence of the first paragraph and have students echo. Then have students continue by chorally rereading additional paragraphs.

- Provide time for students to read their sections of text to you. Comment on their pacing, and provide corrective feedback by modeling proper fluency.

Student Book

DEVELOP SPEAKING/LISTENING SKILLS

> **All Language Levels**

- Have students practice reading "Computers: The Future of Art." Work with students to read with appropriate pacing.

- Provide time for students to read aloud a passage from article to a partner, then tell their partner about the instructions. Provide the sentence frame *These instructions are about* ___.

Self-Selected Reading

Content Objective Read independently
Language Objective Orally retell information learned
Materials • **Leveled Classroom Library** • other fiction books

APPLY SKILLS AND STRATEGIES TO INDEPENDENT READING

> **All Language Levels**

- Have students choose a fiction book for independent reading. (See the **Theme Bibliography** on pages T8–T9.)

- After reading, ask students to orally summarize and share their reactions to the book with classmates. Ask: *Would you recommend this book to a classmate? Why or why not?*

Leveled Classroom Library
See Leveled Classroom
Library lessons on pages T2–T7.

Transfer Skills

The Verbs *to Have* and *to Be* Students who speak Hmong and Khmer may have problems with irregular subject-verb agreement because verb forms do not change to indicate the number of the subjects in their primary language. Give students additional practice selecting the correct form of *have* and *be* in written sentences. See language transfers on pages T16–T31.

Corrective Feedback

During Whole Group grammar lessons, follow the routine on the **Grammar Transparencies** to provide students with extra support. This routine includes completing the items with English Language Learners while other students work independently, having students reread the sentences with partners to build fluency, and providing a generative task such as writing a new sentence using the skill.

Grammar

Content Objective Identify irregular verbs

Language Objective Speak in complete sentences, using sentence frames

IRREGULAR VERBS

Beginning/Intermediate

■ Review irregular verbs. Explain that the past-tense forms of irregular verbs do not end in *-ed*. Write on the board: *Sarah spent the summer at her uncle's house.* Underline the verb. Explain that *spent* is the past-tense form of the irregular verb *spend*. Repeat with the sentence: *He made the collage of the party.* Point out that *made* is the past-tense form of the irregular verb *make*.

All Language Levels

■ Review irregular verbs with students. Write the below sentences on the board. Have students choose the verb form that correctly completes each sentence. Have them say: ____ *is the past-tense form of* ____.

> They ____ on the grass and watched the trains. (sitted, sat)
>
> We ____ fun at the art show. (had, haved)
>
> He ____ the perfect collage for his room. (found, finded)
>
> We ____ our aunt and uncle every summer. (seed, saw)

PEER DISCUSSION STARTERS

All Language Levels

■ Write the following sentences on the board.

> *If I made a collage, I would* ____.   *I read about* ____.

■ Pair students and have them complete each sentence frame. Ask them to expand on their sentences by providing as many details as they can from this week's readings. Circulate, listen in, and take note of each student's language use and proficiency.

Beginning	Intermediate	Advanced
Identify Verbs Describe the illustrations in *Me and Uncle Romie* to students. Ask: *What do you see?* Help them point and name verbs. Help students identify the past-tense form and tell whether the verb is an irregular verb.	**Use Verbs** Ask students to describe the illustrations in *Me and Uncle Romie.* Have them use complete sentences. Ask students to use an irregular verb in a sentence.	**Use Verbs** Ask students to describe the illustrations in *Me and Uncle Romie.* Then have them identify irregular verbs that they used.

Writing/Spelling

Content Objective Spell words correctly

Language Objective Write in complete sentences, using sentence frames

All Language Levels

■ Write the key vocabulary words on the board: *skyscrapers, collage, barbecue, glorious, strutting, swarms*. Have students copy each word on their **WorkBoards**. Help them say each word and then write a sentence for it. Provide sentence starters, such as:

> *Looking at the skyscrapers, I felt ____.*
>
> *A collage of my life would include ____.*
>
> *At the barbecue, we ate ____.*
>
> *The day was glorious because ____.*
>
> *He was strutting through the hall because ____.*
>
> *Swarms of people gathered to ____.*

Beginning/Intermediate

■ Help students spell words using their growing knowledge of English sound-spelling relationships. Model how to segment the word students are trying to spell, and attach a spelling to each sound (or spellings to each syllable if a multisyllabic word). Use the **Sound-Spelling Cards** to reinforce the spellings for each English sound.

Advanced

■ Dictate the following words for students to spell: *snowball, bathroom, basketball, underwater, eyesight*. Use the Sound-Spelling Cards to guide students as they spell each word.

■ When completed, review the meanings of words that can be easily demonstrated or explained. Use actions, gestures, and available pictures.

Sound-Spelling WorkBoard

Phonics/Word Study

For English Language Learners who need more practice with this week's phonics/spelling skill, see the Approaching Level lesson on page 395J. Focus on minimal contrasts, articulation, and those sounds that do not transfer from the student's first language to English. See language transfers on pages T16–T31.

Leveled Reader

Vocabulary

Preteach Vocabulary Use the routine in the **Visual Vocabulary Resources**, pages 435–438, to preteach the ELL Vocabulary listed in the inside front cover of the **Leveled Reader**.

ELL ENGLISH LANGUAGE LEARNERS

Leveled Reader

Content Objective Read to apply skills and strategies

Language Objective Retell information, using complete sentences

Materials
- **Leveled Reader:** *Everyday Beauty*
- **ELL Resource Book,** p. 171
- **Visual Vocabulary Resources,** pp. 435–438

BEFORE READING

All Language Levels

- **Preview** Read the title *Everyday Beauty*. Ask: *What is the title? Say it again.* Repeat with the author's name. Then page through the book. Use simple language to tell about each page. Immediately follow up with questions, such as *How is Carly feeling? How can you tell? What animal is this? What is it doing?*

- **Review Skills** Use the inside front cover to review the comprehension skill and vocabulary words.

- **Set a Purpose** Say: *Let's read to find out what Carly learns about taking better photos.*

DURING READING

All Language Levels

- Have students read each page aloud using the differentiated suggestions. Provide corrective feedback, such as modeling how to blend a decodable word or clarifying meaning by using techniques from the Interactive Question-Response Guide.

- **Retell** After every two pages, ask students to state the main ideas they have learned so far. Help them to complete the Setting Flowchart. Restate students' comments when they have difficulty using story-specific words. Provide differentiated sentence frames to support students' responses and engage students in partner-talk where appropriate.

Beginning	Intermediate	Advanced
Echo-Read Have students echo-read after you.	**Choral-Read** Have students chorally read with you.	**Choral-Read** Have students chorally read.
Check Comprehension Point to pictures and ask questions, such as *Where is the hummingbird? Point to it.*	**Check Comprehension** Ask questions or provide prompts, such as *Have you seen skyscrapers? Describe them.*	**Check Comprehension** Ask: *What did Carly learn? Which sentences tell you important ideas about what she learned?*

ELL ENGLISH LANGUAGE LEARNERS

AFTER READING

Use the chart below and Think and Compare questions in the Leveled Reader to determine students' progress.

Think and Compare	Beginning	Intermediate	Advanced
1 Look at page 14. What does Carly do with Margaret Bourke-White's photographs? What does Carly learn about photography? *(Character, Setting, Plot)*	Possible responses: Nonverbal response. Make collage. Make things beautiful.	Possible responses: Carly made a collage with the photographs. She learned that photographs can make things look beautiful.	Possible responses: Carly made a collage on the wall using the photographs. She learned that she doesn't have to photograph just beautiful things. Ordinary things can also look beautiful in photographs.
2 Carly takes photographs of Fort Peck Lake. If you were taking pictures of Fort Peck Lake, what would you photograph? Why? *(Apply)*	Possible responses: Nonverbal response. Animals. Ducks. Like animals.	Possible responses: I want to take pictures of animals at the lake. They are interesting.	Possible responses: I would want to photograph animals and plants at the lake because they are very different from each other. They would be interesting.
3 Look at Margaret Bourke-White's photographs in chapter 3. How do you think photographs can make ordinary things look glorious? *(Evaluate)*	Possible responses: Nonverbal response. Make pretty.	Possible responses: Photographs can make things look beautiful.	Possible responses: Photographers can use light and size to make ordinary things look beautiful.

BOOK TALK

Develop Listening and Speaking Skills Distribute copies of **ELL Resource Book**, page 171, and form small groups. Help students determine the leader to discuss the Book Talk questions. Tell students to remember the following while engaged in the activity:

- Employ self-corrective techniques and monitor their own and other students' language production. Students should ask themselves: *What parts of this passage were confusing to me? Can my classmates help me clarify a word or sentence that I don't understand?*

- Express opinions, ideas, and feelings on a variety of social and academic topics. Ask: *What do you think about the characters in the story?*

ELL Resource Book

Book Talk

Bringing Groups Together Students will work with peers of varying language abilities to discuss the Book Talk questiions. Form groups so that students who read Beyond Level, On Level, Approaching Level, and ELL Leveled Readers are in the same group for the activity.

Progress Monitoring

Weekly Assessment

ASSESSED SKILLS

- Vocabulary: Vocabulary Words, Context Clues/Examples and Definitions
- Comprehension: Character, Setting, Plot
- Grammar: Irregular Verbs
- Phonics/Spelling: Compound Words

Selection Test for **Me and Uncle Romie** *Also Available*

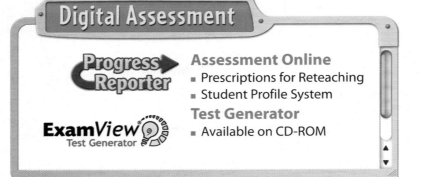

Digital Assessment

Progress Reporter

Assessment Online
- Prescriptions for Reteaching
- Student Profile System

ExamView Test Generator

Test Generator
- Available on CD-ROM

Fluency Assessment

Assess fluency for one group of students per week. Use the Oral Fluency Record Sheet to track the number of words read correctly. Fluency goal for all students: **102–122 words correct per minute (WCPM)**.

Approaching Level	Weeks 1, 3, 5
On Level	Weeks 2, 4
Beyond Level	Week 6

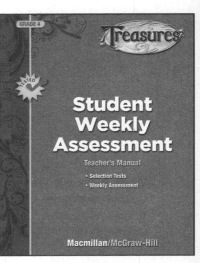

**Weekly Assessment
Unit 3 Week 5**

Fluency Assessment

Diagnose		Prescribe
Review the assessment answers with students. Have them correct their errors. Then provide additional instruction as needed.		
	IF...	**THEN...**
VOCABULARY WORDS **VOCABULARY STRATEGY** Context Clues/Examples and Definitions	0–2 items correct . . .	See **Vocabulary Intervention Teacher's Edition.** **LOG ON** Online Practice: Go to **www.macmillanmh.com.** **CD-ROM** Vocabulary PuzzleMaker
COMPREHENSION Skill: Character, Setting, Plot	0–3 items correct . . .	See **Comprehension Intervention Teacher's Edition.** **SPIRAL REVIEW** See Character, Setting, Plot lesson in Unit 4 Week 1, page 429B.
GRAMMAR Irregular Verbs	0–1 items correct . . .	See **Writing and Grammar Intervention Teacher's Edition.**
PHONICS AND SPELLING Compound Words	0–1 items correct . . .	**LOG ON** Online Practice: Go to **www.macmillanmh.com.** See **Phonics Intervention Teacher's Edition.**
FLUENCY	98–101 WCPM	**AUDIO CD** Fluency Solutions Audio CD
	0–97 WCPM	See **Fluency Intervention Teacher's Edition.**

Response to Intervention

To place students in Tier 2 or Tier 3 Intervention use the *Diagnostic Assessment*.

Tier 2

Tier 3

- Phonics
- Vocabulary
- Comprehension
- Fluency
- Writing and Grammar

Week 6 ★ At a Glance

Review and Assess

Writing Project
- **Persuasive Essay**
- **Writer's Resources:** Use the Internet

Show What You Know
- **Test Practice**
- **Literacy Activities:** Comprehension, Word Study, Drama, Genre Study

Theme Project
- **Famous Speeches**
- **Research Strategy:** Record Information
- **Listening/Speaking**

Computer Literacy
- **Digital Media**

Media Literacy
- **Advertising Techniques**

Assessment
- **Unit Assessment**

Key

 **Tested in program**

Digital Learning

Digital solutions to help plan and implement instructions

☑ **Teacher Resources**

LOG ON ▷

ONLINE www.macmillanmh.com

▶ **Teacher's Edition**
- Lesson Planner and Resources also on CD-ROM

TeacherWorks Plus

▶ **Formative Assessment**
- ExamView® on CD-ROM also available

Progress Reporter

▶ **Instructional Resources**
- Unit Videos
- Classroom Presentation Toolkit

VIDEO

▶ **Professional Development**
- Video Library

Professional Development

☑ **Student Resources**

LOG ON ▷

ONLINE www.macmillanmh.com

▶ **Interactive Student Book**

StudentWorks Plus

▶ **Leveled Reader Database**

▶ **Activities**
- Research Toolkit
- Oral Language Activities
- Vocabulary/Spelling Activities

AUDIO CD **Listening Library**
- Recordings of Student Books and Leveled Readers

AUDIO CD **Fluency Solutions**
- Fluency Modeling and Practice

Show What You Know

Spiral Review

Show What You Know provides a spiral review of reading comprehension and vocabulary skills and strategies previously taught. After reading fiction and nonfiction selections, students will answer questions that assess reading comprehension and vocabulary.

Have students turn to page 397 in the **Student Book** and read "Diary of a Scarecrow's Helper" independently. Distribute pages 9–10 from **Show What You Know**. Have students complete the questions.

Share Your Thinking

After students have completed the questions, model your own thinking on how to arrive at correct answers.

Question 1 Draw Conclusions
What happens before March 15?

Tell students that they must **connec**t the details in the story to find the **unstated** answer. The entry tells that there was a winter storm, and that Jack's pole snapped in two. (D) AUTHOR AND ME

Question 2 Prefixes *In the March 22 entry, what does the word <u>redo</u> mean?*

Students must **connect** the clues in the word with the **unstated** answer. The prefix *re-* means "again," so *redo* means "to do again." (H) AUTHOR AND ME

Show What You Know

Review

- Make Inferences
- Draw Conclusions
- Fact and Opinion
- Prefixes
- Line Graph

Diary of a Scarecrow's Helper

March 15

Oh no! They're getting rid of Jack Patches! Mom and I planned a visit to the community garden today to help clean up for spring. When we arrived, something felt peculiar. At first I couldn't figure it out. Then, as I was putting some old planting ties on the garbage pile, I saw a familiar old hat. Our wonderful scarecrow was lying in pieces in the trash.

I talked to Mr. Collins, the garden supervisor. He told me that there was a terrible storm this winter. The metal pole that Jack used to hang on snapped in two because it was rusty and old. Mr. Collins thinks it would be dangerous to try to put Jack back up, so he's getting rid of him.

I'm really unhappy and I'm going to miss him.

March 16

I keep thinking about Jack Patches lying in the garbage pile. I've got to do something. I can't let him stay there! But what can I do? I called Mr. Collins. He keeps saying that it is

396

Genre

Fiction

Fiction is a story that comes from imagination and not from fact.

Setting: The time and place where the story takes place

Characters: The people or animals in the story

Plot: The structure of the story; how the events are arranged in a story

Theme: The central lesson or message of the story

not safe to put Jack back up because the metal post is sharp and rusty. Besides, Jack's shirt is a mess. It practically rotted away. And his face is ruined, too. His button eyes fell off and his nose is coming loose.

March 17

I had a dream about Jack Patches. He was holding his nose in his hands and asked me to help him. What can I do?

March 18

I called Mr. Collins again. He agreed to keep Jack for at least a week. Then I talked to my uncle, who is really good with tools and wood. He says it won't be hard to fabricate a new support for Jack.

March 22

Uncle Jorge and I went back to the garden with a brand new post. Mr. Collins agreed that the new post looked very safe and sturdy. Uncle Jorge taught me how to plant a post safely. We placed the post into the concrete and held it there until it hardened, or set, enough that we could remove our hands. Tomorrow the concrete will be set, and we can put Jack back together. I brought his face home with me so I can redo it.

March 23

Jack Patches is back! He looks better than ever. Uncle Jorge donated a new shirt to replace the old one that was threadbare and faded. I finished sewing his face together this morning. His shiny new blue button eyes look terrific. He's so happy to be back that he's smiling. Well, he sort of has to, because I sewed him that way. But I'm sure everyone who visits the garden and sees him will smile, too!

397

GRADE 4

Treasures

Show What You Know

Spiral Review

Macmillan/McGraw-Hill

pages 9–10

Question 3 Make Inferences *Mr. Collins did not put Jack Patches back up because he —*

Remind students to **connect** the clues in the story to find the **unstated** answer. Mr. Collins says it would be dangerous to rehang Jack Patches, meaning he does not want the scarecrow to hurt anyone. (A) AUTHOR AND ME

Question 4 Make Inferences *The reader can tell that the writer of this diary plans to —*

Students should **connect** the clues in the story with one of the answer choices. The writer visits the garden often and cares a lot about it, so he probably plans to grow vegetables. (G) AUTHOR AND ME

Question 5 Draw Conclusions *How is Jack Patches improved by March 23? Explain your answer and support it with evidence from the diary.* AUTHOR AND ME

Possible response: He has a new shirt and is supported by a new post. His face has been sewn back together, and he has new button eyes.

Use the Short-Answer Reading Rubric on page 170 in the Teacher's Resource Book to score students' written responses.

Have students turn to page 398 in the **Student Book** and read "Silent Spring No Longer: Rachel Carson" independently. Distribute pages 11–12 from **Show What You Know**. Have students complete the questions.

Share Your Thinking

After students have completed the questions, model your own thinking on how to arrive at correct answers.

Question 1 Fact and Opinion *Look at the chart below. Which of the following belongs in the empty rectangle?*

Explain that this is a fact and opinion chart and that students are asked to fill in an opinion. Students must **connect** the clues in the story with the answer. Choice D says the birds that you hear each spring are wonderful, which is the author's opinion. (D) AUTHOR AND ME

Question 2 Line Graph *Look at the line graph on page 399. In which year was the population of bald eagles smallest?*

Remind students to look at the graph on page 399. Students must **combine** the information in the graph to find the **stated** answer. The bald eagle population was the lowest in 1963. (F)

THINK AND SEARCH

Silent Spring No Longer:
RACHEL CARSON

RACHEL CARSON WAS BORN on a farm in Springdale, Pennsylvania, in 1907. It was here, through the gentle encouragement of her mother, that she learned to love nature. When Carson went to college, she took her love of nature with her. She majored in marine biology, the study of life in the sea.

After college Carson taught for five years before joining the U.S. Bureau of Fisheries. She wrote for a radio show that explored life in the seas. It was called "Romance Under the Waters." Carson's writing was wonderful and made the sea come alive. She also wrote three books about the sea: *Under the Sea Wind*, *The Sea Around Us*, and *The Edge of the Sea*.

398

Genre

Biography

In a biography, the author tells about the life of another person.

5 Ws and an H: The author tells who the person is; what the person does or has accomplished; how, when, and where the person lives; and why he or she is important.

Elements of Fiction: Biographies may also include elements of fiction such as character, plot, setting, conflict, and theme.

Text Features: Biographies often include pictures or other graphics, such as time lines, that provide additional information about a person's life achievements and family.

These books all became bestsellers and won many awards. Carson soon left her job so she could become a full-time writer.

In the late 1940s and 1950s, people used chemicals called pesticides to kill unwanted insects. One of these pesticides was DDT. Scientists began to learn that DDT did kill harmful insects, but it also killed birds. Birds took the chemical into their bodies when they ate insects infected with it. The chemicals made the birds' eggs very frail. The delicate eggs broke easily, and many baby birds did not hatch. Birds such as peregrine falcons and bald eagles began to die out.

Rachel Carson became concerned about this problem. She spent a lot of time gathering facts. Then she wrote a book called *Silent Spring*. In the book she wrote about how birds were dying because of DDT.

Companies that made the chemicals tried to say that Carson was mistaken. President John F. Kennedy called for testing of chemicals used as pesticides. Tests showed that Carson was right. Pesticides were harming the environment and causing birds to die out.

Rachel Carson published *Silent Spring* in 1962. Carson did not get to see her work change history because she died in 1964. The use of DDT in the United States was banned in 1972. Since then birds that were in danger of dying out were saved and have come back. Now each spring you can hear these wonderful birds singing in the trees. Thanks to Rachel Carson, spring is not silent.

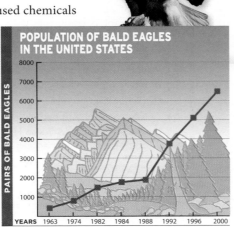

POPULATION OF BALD EAGLES IN THE UNITED STATES

This line graph shows how the population of bald eagle pairs increased after DDT was banned in the United States.

399

pages 11–12

Question 3 Line Graph *Look at the line graph on page 399. What happened between 1988 and 1992?*

Students must **connect** details from the graph to find the **unstated** answer. Between 1988 and 1992, the bald eagle population grew quickly from about 2000 pairs to about 4000 pairs. (C) AUTHOR AND ME

Question 4 Prefixes *In the third paragraph, the word* unwanted *means —*

Students must **connect** the word clues to find the **unstated** answer. The prefix un- means "not," so unwanted means "not wanted." (G) AUTHOR AND ME

Question 5 Fact and Opinion *What is one fact that Rachel Carson wrote about in* Silent Spring? *Explain your answer and support it with evidence from the article.* AUTHOR AND ME

Possible response: She wrote about how birds were dying because of DDT. The article says, *Pesticides were harming the environment and causing birds to die out.*

Use the Short-Answer Reading Rubric on page 170 in the Teacher's Resource Book to score students' written responses.

Show What You Know

Spiral Review

Show What You Know Unit Review provides a spiral review of the core skill taught in this unit. Students will review by answering questions and completing short, targeted activities.

Have students turn to pages 400 and 401 of the **Student Book**. Have students note their responses on a separate sheet of paper.

Share Your Thinking

Read the questions for each activity in the Student Book with students. If additional review is needed, go back to the lessons in the Teacher's Edition if necessary.

Comprehension: Point of View
Review with students the difference between first- and third-person narration in a story. Have them offer examples of stories they have read on their own that use one of these points of view. Read the activity on page 400 of the Student Book. Have students work individually to write a paragraph about the difference between first- and third-person points of view.

Comprehension

Point of View

- Point of view refers to the way a narrator tells a story. A first-person narrator tells the story in his or her own words. A third-person narrator tells the story from one character's point of view.

- Which stories in this unit are written from a first-person point of view? Which stories are written from a third-person point of view?

- Choose a story and explain the difference between first- and third-person point of view. How would the story be different if the point of view changed?

Genre

Elements of a Play

- A play is a story that is intended to be performed. It has features such as a prologue or epilogue, stage directions, scene descriptions, and dialogue.

- With a partner look at the play *Ranita, The Frog Princess* on page 342. Identify the setting, characters, stage directions, and dialogue.

- Think of a story that both of you know such as "The Three Little Pigs." Pick a scene from the story and make it into a scene from a play by adding: setting, characters, stage directions, and dialogue.

400

Listening/Speaking

Discuss the impact that media presentations can make. For example, ask how the experience of seeing a play performed on television is different from the experience of reading the play.

Remind students that they need to distinguish between information in media texts, such as live news coverage, and in fictional material, such as dramatic productions. Students should carefully consider the purpose of the presentation. Is the main goal to entertain, to inform, or to persuade? How can they tell?

Discuss criteria that students can use to evaluate different types of media presentations and create rubrics summarizing those criteria. Then have students view various media presentations and present reviews to the class based on the criteria you established together.

Word Study

Analogies Using Synonyms and Antonyms

- An analogy shows how two pairs of words are related. For an analogy to make sense, the words in each pair must be related in the same way. If the words in one pair are synonyms then the words in the second pair must be synonyms.

- The following analogies use either synonyms or antonyms.

  slender is to thin as big is to _____
  quiet is to loud as whisper is to _____

- Write these analogies on a separate sheet of paper, identify if they are synonyms or antonyms, and choose the word that best completes each analogy.

Context Clues

- Context clues, such as definitions, can help you figure out the meaning of an unfamiliar word. For example: *That car runs on solar energy which is energy that comes from the sun.*

- Sometimes there is an example in a sentence that will help you figure out the meaning of an unfamiliar word. For example: *A popular national monument, such as the Liberty Bell, has thousands of visitors each year.*

- Write the following three words in sentences: *island, shellfish, predator.* Include context clues that provide either a definition or an example to help make the meaning of each word clear. Then trade papers with a partner.

StudentWorks *Plus* **Interactive Student Book**
Media Literacy Activities www.macmillanmh.com

401

Genre: Elements of a Play Ask students to offer some examples of structural elements of a play. Help them make a list on the board. Read the activity on page 400 of the Student Book. After students have completed the activity with their partners, have them perform their scenes for the class. **To review, see page 360 of the Teacher's Edition.**

Word Study: Analogies Using Synonyms and Antonyms Explain to students that analogies can help you understand the relationships between words. Read the activity on page 401 of the Student Book. Have students complete the activity. Then have students work with a partner to write their own analogies using synonyms and antonyms. Partners can switch analogies with other pairs. **To review, see page 340 of the Teacher's Edition.**

Word Study: Context Clues Have students discuss ways of learning word meanings. They may mention dictionaries, thesauruses, and context clues. Read the activity on page 401 of the Student Book. Allow students to work individually to complete the activity. Then have them trade their work with a partner. **To review, see page 370 of the Teacher's Edition.**

StudentWorks *Plus*
Interactive Student Book
Media Literacy Activities
See Teacher's Edition p. 401J.

- Identify effective features of a persuasive essay
- Plan and organize ideas by using a graphic organizer to prewrite
- Draft and revise a persuasive essay
- Proofread, publish, and present a persuasive essay

Materials

- Writing Transparencies 47–52
- Teacher's Resource Book, pp. 171, 211

Features of a Persuasive Essay

- It is a **nonfiction** work
- It establishes the **writer's opinion** or **position**
- It tries to convince or **persuade** others to agree with the writer's thinking or take a certain action
- It **supports** the position with convincing reasons
- It organizes reasons in a **logical order**, includes helpful transition words, and concludes strongly
- It includes **persuasive language** such as *should*, *best*, and *must*

ELL

Build Persuasive Language Have students try to persuade partners to feel the same way they do about an issue. Help them list examples of persuasive language, such as *you should*, *it's important to*, and *it's better to*.

Persuasive Essay

Read Like a Writer

Read the following excerpt from the "I Have a Dream" speech by Dr. Martin Luther King, Jr. Explain to students that this excerpt is an example of persuasive writing. Ask students to listen for

- Dr. King's **opinion**, or what he thinks or believes;
- what Dr. King wants the **audience** to think or do;
- the reasons, details, facts, and persuasive language Dr. King uses to **support** his opinion or position;
- the **logical order** of the reasons.

I Have a Dream

Five score years ago, a great American, in whose symbolic shadow we stand today, signed the Emancipation Proclamation.

But one hundred years later, the Negro still is not free....

And as we walk, we must make the pledge that we shall always march ahead. We cannot turn back. . . .We can never be satisfied as long as our children are stripped of their selfhood and robbed of their dignity by signs stating "For Whites Only." We cannot be satisfied as long as a Negro in Mississippi cannot vote and a Negro in New York believes he has nothing for which to vote. No, no, we are not satisfied and will not be satisfied until justice rolls down like waters and righteousness like a mighty stream.

Discuss the Features

After reading, discuss the following questions with students.

- **What does Dr. King want the audience to do?** (He wants people to continue to work for equal rights. He wants the nation to ensure equal rights for all.)
- **How does Dr. King use language to persuade his audience?** (He uses words that call readers to action, such as *must*. He uses strong words , such as *never* and *always*. He also repeats words and phrases for emphasis.)

Prewrite

Set a Purpose Remind students that the purpose of a persuasive essay is to convince an audience to think, feel, or behave in a certain way, or to take or avoid a certain action.

Know the Audience Emphasize that understanding the audience is one key to effective persuasive writing. The writer must know what the audience thinks is important and choose reasons, facts, and examples that will appeal to their concerns.

Choose a Topic Ask students to think of stories they have read that have made them examine issues they care about. Tell students to choose an issue for which they can give strong reasons, facts, and examples. Ask questions to guide the class to plan the writing: *What is your opinion about the issue you chose? What do you want your audience to think or do about this? What reasons will persuade your audience?*

Minilesson **Organization**

Display **Writing Transparency 47**. Explain that together you will follow Kayla's progress as she develops her persuasive essay. Kayla arrived at her topic after reading *Dear Mrs. LaRue*. In the story, Mrs. LaRue narrowly escaped two traffic accidents. This made Kayla think about the importance of traffic safety, including wearing a helmet while riding a bike. Point out these details in Kayla's web:

- She states her opinion about wearing bike helmets.

- She supports her opinion with three convincing reasons.

- She uses opinion words such as *should*.

Organize Ideas Tell students they will make an Organizing Web to plan their persuasive essays. Tell them to write their opinion in the center oval and the reasons and details in the outer ovals.

Peer Review

Think, Pair, Share Have students explain their opinions to a partner, and have partners propose reasons for these opinions. Tell students to add additional details to their webs, supporting these reasons, before drafting their essays.

Flexible Pairing Option Pair students who have different issues or who hold different opinions on the same issue.

Writing Prompt
Write a composition about an important issue in your school or community. Explain your opinion by using descriptive language that will communicate your ideas and feelings. Remember to include facts, reasons, and details to support your opinion.

Transparency 47

Organizing Web

- could save lives and reduce head injuries
- could stop kids from being embarrassed about wearing a helmet
- Students should wear bike helmets if they ride bikes to school.
- could help kids get in the habit of wearing helmets whenever they ride

Writing Transparency

Draft

Minilesson Strong Reasons

Display **Writing Transparency 48** and read it with students. As you discuss Kayla's draft, point out the following features:

- Kayla's opening paragraph starts out with a question and ends with her **opinion**.

- Kayla's reasons are designed to **persuade the audience**. She gives supporting details that are important to them—safety, discouraging teasing, and teaching good habits.

- She organizes her reasons in a **logical order** and concludes with a strong statement.

- She uses **opinion words**, such as *should* and *best*.

Review Your Web Have students review their webs. As they write, tell them to refer to their webs regularly as they organize reasons, facts, and examples that support their opinions.

Write the Draft Remind students that the purpose of a draft is to get their ideas on paper. Tell students: *The most important thing to remember when writing a draft is to try to think of as many strong reasons as you can and write them down. You will have a chance to revise and proofread in later stages.* Share the following tips:

- Start by clearly stating your opinion in your introduction. You may want to open with a question that you answer.

- Present convincing reasons in the body of the essay.

- Organize reasons in a logical way, such as from weakest to strongest, to build the strength of your argument. Conclude with a convincing statement that restates your opinion.

- Include strong opinion words, such as *should*, *must*, and *best*.

Writer's Resources

Use the Internet Tell students that the Internet can be a valuable resource for locating statistics and other facts to use as support in their essays. Point out that not all Internet information is current or reliable. Government agencies, libraries, museums, and educational institutions usually provide the most reliable information. Before allowing students access to the Internet, review Internet safety rules and school policy.

ELL

Build Language Ask students to point out the supporting details in Kayla's draft. Discuss how the details support each reason. Then ask students to look at each of their reasons and review their supporting details. Put students in pairs, and have them state each reason and give their details. Encourage students to help each other create stronger reasons by suggesting more details.

Transparency 48

Bike Helmets
by Kayla S.

Do you want all students who ride bikes to be safe? for many years Ashford School has had a bike policy bike riders must register their bikes, park at the bike racks, and lock their bikes. Its a good policy but it's not enough. It would be best if the school made students wear bike helmets.

Bike helmets can reduce the risk of head injurys by as much as 85 percent. Hundreds of children die each year from bike accidents. A change to the school bike policy could save lives and prevent injurys!

The school should change its policy is to put an end to a student's worries over how he or she look. If everybody has to wear one, kids will stop teasing each other. Lots of kids are afraid that others will make fun of them for wearing a helmet.

Changing the school policy will also get students in the habit of wearing helmets. Pretty soon strapping on a bike helmet will be just as natural as putting on a coat or tying your shoes.

Changing the policy improves safety, ends concerns about looking different, and builds an important safety habit. Let's require helmets now.

Writing Transparency

Revise

Display **Writing Transparency 49** and point out ways that Kayla revises a good persuasive essay to make it excellent.

- She adds the phrase, "It's Time to Require" to the opening title and "Let's use our heads!" to the conclusion to clarify her opinion and to strengthen her opening and closing. (Voice)

- She revises a sentence in the first paragraph to include the opinion word *should*. She adds the descriptive words *stiff* and *strong* in the second paragraph to appeal to her readers' senses. (Development of Ideas/Word Choice)

- She adds a detail about head injuries to support her reason. (Organization)

- In the third paragraph, she adds the transition words *another reason* to help introduce a new point and rearranges two sentences to clarify meaning. (Conventions/Sentence Fluency)

Point out that Kayla still needs to proofread her essay to make final corrections. Then guide students to think about these elements as they evaluate and revise their persuasive essays:

Organization and Focus Do you clearly state your opinion and include only details that support it? Do you present the reasons in a logical order? Do you end with a concluding statement?

Development of Ideas/Word Choice Do you consider your audience and write to persuade them? Do you use strong reasons and supporting details? Do you use persuasive language such as *should* and *must*?

Conventions/Sentence Fluency Did you use different types of sentences, such as questions, commands, or exclamations? Did you use transitions to connect ideas?

Peer Review

Think, Pair, Share Ask students to read their revised drafts aloud to partners. Ask partners to tell which reasons are most convincing and why. If listeners find that a reason is weak, ask what reasons they could add that would convince them to feel differently.

Flexible Pairing Option Consider pairing students of similar abilities.

ELL

Read Silently Before students listen to a partner read aloud, allow time for them to read the draft silently. Provide each partner with a copy of the draft so one can read along as the other reads aloud.

Transparency 49

It's Time to Require **Bike Helmets**
by Kayla S.

Do you want all students who ride bikes to be safe? for many years Ashford School has had a bike policy bike riders must register their bikes, park at the bike racks, and lock their bikes. Its a good policy but it's not enough. It would be best if the school made students wear bike helmets.
should require that

Bike helmets can reduce the risk of head injurys by as much as 85 percent. Hundreds of children die each year from bike accidents. A change to the school bike policy could save lives and prevent injurys!
, which are stiff and strong.
Thousands more end up in the hospital with head injuries.

Another reason
The school should change its policy is to put an end to a student's worries over how he or she look. If everybody has to wear one, kids will stop teasing each other. Lots of kids are afraid that others will make fun of them for wearing a helmet.

Changing the school policy will also get students in the habit of wearing helmets. Pretty soon strapping on a bike helmet will be just as natural as putting on a coat or tying your shoes.

Changing the policy improves safety, ends concerns about looking different, and builds an important safety habit. Let's require helmets now.
Let's use our heads!

Writing Transparency

Speaking and Listening

Have students read their persuasive essays aloud and present their visuals. Share these strategies.

SPEAKING STRATEGIES

- Speak loudly and clearly, and read at an appropriate rate.
- Use gestures and facial expressions to enhance your presentation.
- Make eye contact with your listeners.

LISTENING STRATEGIES

- Give each speaker your full attention.
- Listen for enjoyment.
- Listen quietly and wait until the reader is done to make comments.
- Ask thoughtful questions.

Transparency 50

It's Time to Require **Bike Helmets**
by Kayla S.

Do you want all students who ride bikes to be safe? for many years Ashford School has had a bike policy bike riders must register their bikes, park at the bike racks, and lock their bikes. It's a good policy but it's not enough. It would be best if the school made students wear bike helmets.

should require that

Bike helmets can reduce the risk of head injurys by as much as 85 percent. Hundreds of children die each year from bike accidents. A change to the school bike policy could save lives and prevent injurys!

, which are stiff and strong,

injuries

Thousands more end up in the hospital with head injuries.

injuries

Another reason

The school should change its policy is to put an end to a student's worries over how he or she look. If everybody has to wear one, kids will stop teasing each other. Lots of kids are afraid that others will make fun of them for wearing a helmet.

Changing the school policy will also get students in the habit of wearing helmets. Pretty soon strapping on a bike helmet will be just as natural as putting on a coat or tying your shoes.

Changing the policy improves safety, ends concerns about looking different, and builds an important safety habit. Let's require helmets now.

Let's use our heads!

Writing Transparency

✔ Proofread/Edit

Minilesson Conventions

Display **Writing Transparency 50** to point out examples of Kayla's proofreading corrections.

- She capitalized the *f* in *for* in the second sentence and added a period at the end of the sentence.
- She added an apostrophe to the contraction *It's* and corrected the plural noun *injuries*.
- She changed *look* to *looks* to agree with its subject.

Have students read and reread their writing to correct mistakes in punctuation, spelling, sentence and paragraph structure, capitalization, and grammar. Suggest that they proofread for one kind of error, such as subject-verb agreement. Review the proofreading marks on page 171 of the **Teacher's Resource Book**. Have students apply them as they proofread.

Peer Review

Think, Pair, Share Have partners exchange papers and read aloud their partner's edited draft to look for errors. Encourage them to look and listen for errors in capitalization and ending punctuation.

TEACHER CONFERENCE

Use the rubric on page 401G to evaluate student writing and help you formulate questions to foster self-assessment.

- *Did you clearly state your opinion on the issue?*
- *Are your reasons supported by strong facts and examples?*
- *Will the audience be persuaded by your reasons?*

Publish and Share

Ask students to write fluidly and legibly in cursive or joined italic or type a final copy of their persuasive essays. Remind them to correctly form letters and use appropriate spacing between words, sentences, and paragraphs. Encourage students to submit their essays to the school newspaper, if appropriate.

PRESENTATION Invite students to give speeches based on their persuasive essays. Have them use visual supports, such as charts.

Using Rubrics

READ AND SCORE

Display **Writing Transparency 51**. Tell students to follow along as a volunteer reads the persuasive essay aloud. Then have students use the student rubric on page 211 of the **Teacher's Resource Book** to assess the writing sample. Guide students to understand that this persuasive essay is only a fair writing sample, which would score a 2, and that they will work together in groups to improve it.

RAISE THE SCORE

Point out the following shortfalls in the writing sample:

Focus and Coherence The writer does not provide a clear statement of opinion in the first paragraph. The reasons are not as well-developed as they could be.

Organization The essay contains two sentences about separating dogs from people when one is sufficient.

Development of Ideas/Word Choice The writer does not use strong opinion words to show that this issue matters to him, and so is less persuasive to the audience.

Have students work in small groups to revise the persuasive essay. Remind them to refer to the student rubric.

SHARE AND COMPARE

Ask groups to share their revised version with the class and explain how they improved the writing. Display **Writing Transparency 52** to show the same essay written at an exceptional level. Have each group compare its revised version with the transparency. Remind students that although two papers vary, they may both be excellent. Have students review their own persuasive essays.

Objective

- Revise a persuasive essay to raise the writing score from a 2 to a 4

CREATE A RUBRIC

Teacher-Developed Rubric
You may want to copy, enlarge, and then distribute the blank rubric form on page 216 in the Teacher's Resource Book. Remind students that the rubric should assess whether or not the persuasive essay focuses on the topic, is logically organized, includes ample development of supporting ideas, and demonstrates a strong command of language and conventions.

Transparency 52

Good Dogs
by Trent L.

Are you thinking of getting a new cuddly puppy? Do you already have a dog? If the answer to either of these questions is yes, then I have a message for you. Take your pet to dog school!

Each year millions of pet owners give up on their wild, barking, disobedient dogs, but they don't need to. Puppy preschool classes and obedience classes can teach a dog how to behave.

A trained dog is happy. It won't misbehave as much and have to be separated from people. Dog training is also good for dog owners. It teaches you about patience and about setting limits for your pet. In addition training classes stress the importance of rewarding good behavior.

Obedience classes are worth your time. Many animal shelters have free classes, or classes at other places may charge a small fee. Yet the rewards are many. You and your dog will have happier lives!

Writing Transparency

4-Point Persuasive Writing Rubric

Use this four-point rubric to assess student writing.

4-POINT SCORING RUBRIC

4 Excellent	3 Good	2 Fair	1 Unsatisfactory
Focus and Coherence Sustained focus shows how ideas are related. Introduction and conclusion add depth and sense of completeness.	**Focus and Coherence** Focus generally shows clear relationship between ideas. Introduction and conclusion add some depth and sense of completeness.	**Focus and Coherence** Somewhat focused paragraphs may shift quickly among related ideas. Introduction and conclusion may be superficial, but composition has some sense of completeness.	**Focus and Coherence** Weak connection to prompt and abrupt shift among ideas show lack of focus. Composition lacks completeness, with minimal, if any, introduction and conclusion.
Organization Logical and controlled progression of thought, with meaningful transitions. Organizational strategy enhances presentation of ideas.	**Organization** Generally logical and controlled progression of thought, with mostly meaningful transitions. Generally effective organizational strategy is not affected by minor wordiness or repetition.	**Organization** Progression of thought may not be logical and needs more meaningful transitions. Organizational strategy is not effective, with some wordiness or repetition.	**Organization** Progression of thought is not logical, and transitions are minimal or lacking. No evidence of organizational strategy, with random, wordy, or repetitive ideas.
Development of Ideas/ Word Choice Thorough, insightful development of ideas creates depth of thought. Shows interesting connections between ideas and willingness to take compositional risks. Precise word choice enhances quality of content.	**Development of Ideas/ Word Choice** Development of ideas reflects some depth of thought. Presentation of some ideas may be thoughtful but shows little evidence of willingness to take compositional risks. Word choice suits purpose.	**Development of Ideas/ Word Choice** Superficial development of ideas, using lists or brief explanations, is general, inconsistent, or contrived and shows little evidence of depth of thinking. Word choice does not suit purpose.	**Development of Ideas/ Word Choice** General or vague development of ideas. Omits words or uses chosen words incorrec
Voice Authentic and original writing expresses unique perspective and sustains connection with reader.	**Voice** Mostly authentic and original writing generally expresses unique perspective and generally sustains connection with reader.	**Voice** Somewhat authentic or original but shows little unique perspective and fails to sustain connection with reader.	**Voice** Shows little or no sense of individual voice and no connection with reader.
Conventions/Sentence Fluency Demonstrates consistent command of spelling, capitalization, punctuation, grammar, usage, and sentence structure. Words, phrases, and sentence structure enhance overall effectiveness of communication.	**Conventions/Sentence Fluency** Demonstrates good command of spelling, capitalization, punctuation, grammar, usage, and sentence structure. Generally appropriate words, phrases, and sentence structure contribute to overall effectiveness of communication.	**Conventions/Sentence Fluency** Demonstrates limited command of spelling, capitalization, punctuation, grammar, usage, and sentence structure. Simple or inaccurate words or phrases and some awkward sentences limit overall effectiveness of communication.	**Conventions/Sentence Fluency** Demonstrates little or no command of spelling, capitalization, punctuation, grammar, usage, and sentence structure. May be difficult to read. Misused omitted, or awkward words, phrases, or sentences interfere with communication.
Presentation Handwriting or typing is neat, consistent, and error free.	**Presentation** Margins are mostly even. Font is appropriate or handwriting is neat and mostly consistent.	**Presentation** Margins are inconsistent. Font is inappropriate or handwriting is difficult to read.	**Presentation** Spacing is uneven. Format is confusing or absent or handwriting is illegible in parts.

Anchor Papers

Use these Anchor Papers in the **Teacher's Resource Book** to evaluate students' writing.

Teacher's Resource Book, page 227

Teacher's Resource Book, page 228

Teacher's Resource Book, page 229

Teacher's Resource Book, page 230

Anchor Papers

Persuasive Essay Score: 4 Points

It's Time to Require Bike Helmets
by Kayla S.

Do you want all students who ride bikes to be safe? For many years Ashford School has had a bike policy. Bike riders must register their bikes, park at the bike racks, and lock their bikes. It's a good policy, but it's not enough. The school should require that students wear bike helmets when they ride their bikes to school.

Bike helmets, which are stiff and strong, can reduce the risk of head injuries by as much as 85 percent. Hundreds of children die each year from bike accidents. Thousands more end up in the hospital with head injuries. A change to the school bike policy could save lives and prevent injuries!

Another reason the school should change its policy is to put an end to a student's worries over how he or she looks. Lots of kids are afraid that others will make fun of them for wearing a helmet. If everybody has to wear one, kids will stop teasing each other.

Changing the school policy will also get students in the habit of wearing helmets. Pretty soon strapping on a bike helmet will be just as natural as putting on a coat or tying your shoes before you ride.

To sum up, changing the bike policy improves safety, ends concerns about looking different, and builds an important safety habit. Let's use our heads! Let's require bike helmets in our community.

Focus and Coherence The essay is focused and complete. The writer presents a clear opinion supported by solid reasons. The strong introduction and conclusion add clarity and depth.

Organization The writer presents her reasons in a logical order and uses meaningful transitions.

Development of Ideas/Word Choice The writer's ideas are well-developed. Reasons are supported by facts, details, and examples.

Strong word choice adds to the effectiveness of each argument.

Voice The writer's tone is serious, as is appropriate to her topic. She demonstrates her strong feelings about the issue and engages the reader directly.

Conventions/Sentence Fluency The writer is skilled in most writing conventions. Varied sentence structure contributes to the flow of her writing.

Short-Answer Response Rubric

Use the Short-Answer Reading Rubric to score students' short-answer responses to the weekly Comprehension Check questions and the short-answer questions on weekly and unit assessments.

SHORT-ANSWER READING RUBRIC			
3 Excellent	**2** Good	**1** Fair	**0** Unsatisfactory
An **exemplary** response must • be thoughtful and insightful; • be strongly supported with accurate/relevant textual evidence; • show depth of understanding and ability to effectively connect textual evidence to the idea, analysis, or evaluation.	A **sufficient** response must • be reasonable; • be supported with accurate/relevant textual evidence; • be clear and specific.	A **partially sufficient** response may • be reasonable; • be supported by general, incomplete, partially accurate/relevant textual evidence, if any; • weakly connect textual evidence to the idea, analysis, or evaluation; • be somewhat unclear or vague.	An **insufficient** response may • be too general or vague to determine whether it is reasonable or unreasonable; • not address the question or answer a different question than the one asked; • not be based on the selection; • incorrectly analyze or evaluate the text; • offer only incomplete or irrelevant textual evidence, if any; • lack clarity.

Evidence may consist of a direct quotation, a paraphrase, or a specific synopsis.

Unit 3 Computer Literacy

Objective

- Discuss the differences in various written conventions used for digital media

Materials

- www.macmillanmh.com
- Web site article; e-mail

Vocabulary

blog a Web site where entries that are written in a narrative, personal style are posted.

hyperlink text on a Web page that can be clicked on with a mouse and that takes you to another part of the site or a different Web page

cite to quote and credit an original information source

LOG ON ▶ LEARN IT

Computer Literacy
Focus on Keyboard and Internet Skills and Media Literacy
www.macmillanmh.com

Safety Alert

Remind students to think about the sources of Web pages they find. How do they know that the Web page is a reliable source, containing correct information? Students should verify information by checking at least one other source.

Digital Media
Written Conventions

ACCESS PRIOR KNOWLEDGE

Discuss with students:

- How is writing an e-mail different from writing a business letter? (E-mails are casual and do not use formal language. Business letters have an opener, a closer, and use formal language.)

- How is reading a science article about snakes on a Web site different from reading a **blog** entry about snakes? Which one is more likely to include photos, captions, and **hyperlinks**? (The science article uses formal language and will cite sources. The article is more likely to contain graphics and hyperlinks.)

EXPLAIN

Introduce the lesson vocabulary by writing each word on the board and asking for a definition.

- Tell students that it is important to understand the written conventions that are used in different types of digital media. This will help them evaluate the credibility of a Web page as a source of information.

MODEL

- Show students an article on a reputable Web site. Point out that the information is organized and clearly presented.

- Then show students a sample e-mail or online journal entry about the same subject. Ask students to point out the differences in language. Explain that although the two pieces of writing may contain similar information, the science article is a more credible source of information for a report or research project.

Technology Makes a Difference

Using Citations

- ▶ When you **cite** a source, you give credit to the person whose work you are using

- ▶ Different types of sources get different types of citations. For a book, include the author, title, place of publication, publisher, and year of publication. For a Web site, include the author, the site's name, the date you accessed the information, and the exact Web address.

Media Literacy
Advertising Techniques

ACCESS PRIOR KNOWLEDGE

Discuss with students:

- *Why do you think companies would want to have their logo in as many public places as possible?*

- *Do you think people buy the products they see advertised every day on billboards or television commercials? Why or why not?*

- In a 10-minute exercise, identify as many logos as possible within your classroom. Make a chart of the most popular logos and discuss with students why these logos are so popular.

EXPLAIN

Introduce the lesson vocabulary by writing each word on the board and asking for its definition.

- **Logos** are special designs that identify a company or organization and appear on all of its products, in all of its advertisements, etc.

- Logos are an example of an advertising **strategy**. They are powerful tools that can have both positive and negative impacts on consumer behavior. If people like a certain brand, they are more likely to buy the product with the brand logo. The reverse is also true. If they see the logo of a brand they dislike, they will not buy the product.

- The most successful logos are very simple. They can include words and/or **symbols**.

MODEL

- Ask students to create a **logo** that represents their personality. The logo might include their initials, a symbol of their favorite sport or hobby, their favorite colors, or anything else that is specific to them. Students should be able to discuss how they made the decision of which elements to include in their logo.

- Either individually or in small groups, give students an imaginary budget to develop a multimillion-dollar product and advertising campaign. Provide students with guidelines that describe their product and the product's target audience.

- Instruct students to come up with a logo and an advertising **slogan** for their product. Students should use art materials to produce their logo and present their finished logo and slogan to their classmates.

Objectives

- Explore how different advertisement techniques impact consumer behavior
- Identify how design techniques used in media can influence the message

Materials

- Examples of popular logos and advertising slogans

LOG ON

StudentWorks *Plus*

Interactive Student Book

Media Literacy Activities
Lessons that help students explore the effects of advertisement techniques and media influence.

Theme Project Wrap-Up
Research/Organizing and Presenting Ideas

After students complete Step 1, Step 2, Step 3, and Step 4 of their projects, have them work on the following:

 Create the Presentation Have students read all or part of the speech or written message they researched to the class. As an introduction, they should explain who wrote or spoke the message and what ideas he or she was trying to communicate. Afterward, they should present a conclusion about why the message is important. Have students use note cards as memory aids and use visuals to clarify and add interest.

 Review and Evaluate Use these checklists to help you and your students evaluate their research and presentation.

Teacher's Checklist

Assess the Research Process

Planning the Project
- ✔ Brainstormed possible speeches or writings.
- ✔ Identified credible sources.
- ✔ Successfully located information.

Doing the Project
- ✔ Paraphrased information and took notes.
- ✔ Organized information.
- ✔ Cited valid and creditable sources.

Assess the Presentation

Speaking
- ✔ Used correct grammar to communicate ideas.
- ✔ Recited speech/writing clearly, accurately, and with feeling.
- ✔ Spoke loudly and clearly.

Representing
- ✔ Spoke at an even pace.
- ✔ Made eye contact with the audience.
- ✔ Expressed an opinion and supported it.

Assess the Listener

- ✔ Listened quietly and politely.
- ✔ Held questions and comments until end of presentation.
- ✔ Asked relevant questions or made relevant comments.
- ✔ Connected own ideas to those of speaker.

Student's Checklist

Research Process
- ✔ Did you take notes?
- ✔ Did you record your sources?
- ✔ Did you organize the information?

Presenting

Speaking
- ✔ Did you rehearse enough?
- ✔ Did you speak loudly and clearly?
- ✔ Did you make eye contact with the audience?

Representing
- ✔ Did you present your information in an interesting way?
- ✔ Did you use gestures appropriately?
- ✔ Did your visuals help your presentation?

SCORING RUBRIC FOR THEME PROJECT

4 Excellent	**3** Good	**2** Fair	**1** Unsatisfactory
The student • presents the information in a clear and interesting way; • uses visuals that effectively present important information; • includes an effective introduction and conclusion.	The student • presents the information in a fairly clear way; • uses visuals that present relevant information; • includes an introduction and conclusion.	The student • struggles to present the information clearly; • may use few, adequate visuals; • includes either an introduction or conclusion.	The student • may not grasp the task; • may present sketchy information in a disorganized way; • does not have an introduction or conclusion.

Home-School Connection

Invite family members and students from other classes to the presentation of the projects.

■ Have students present a brief introduction about the theme, their presentations, and what they have learned about the power of words.

■ As part of your character-building feature on respect, have students point out statements/opinions/arguments of fellow students that they found interesting.

Big Question Wrap-Up

Review the Big Question with students. Have them use their organizers and what they learned to help them respond to the following questions: *What is the meaning of the saying "The pen is mightier than the sword"? Is writing or speaking a stronger form of communication? Why? What message would you like to communicate to your family?*

Administer the Test

UNIT 3 TEST

TESTED SKILLS AND STRATEGIES

COMPREHENSION STRATEGIES AND SKILLS

- Strategies: Generate questions; monitor comprehension; visualize
- Skills: Make inferences; draw conclusions; fact and opinion; theme; character, setting, plot

VOCABULARY STRATEGIES

- Base words
- Context clues
- Prefixes
- Latin prefixes
- Analogies: Synonyms and antonyms

TEXT FEATURES AND STUDY SKILLS

- Tool bars
- Line graph
- Using a computer
- Multiple-step instructions

GRAMMAR, MECHANICS, USAGE

- Action verbs
- Verb tenses
- Main and helping verbs
- Linking verbs
- Irregular verbs
- Subject-verb agreement
- Punctuation for dialogue
- Punctuation in contractions

WRITING

- Persuasive

Use Multiple Assessments for Instructional Planning

To create instructional profiles for your students, look for patterns in the results from any of the following assessments.

Fluency Assessment

Plan appropriate fluency-building activities and practice to help all students achieve the following goal: **102–122 WCPM**.

Running Records

Use the instructional reading level determined by the Running Record calculations for regrouping decisions.

Benchmark Assessment

Administer tests four times a year as an additional measure of both student progress and the effectiveness of the instructional program.

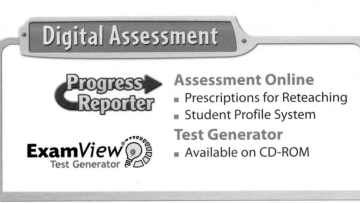

Digital Assessment

Progress Reporter

Assessment Online
- Prescriptions for Reteaching
- Student Profile System

Test Generator

ExamView Test Generator
- Available on CD-ROM

Analyze the Data

Use information from a variety of informal and formal assessments, as well as your own judgment, to assist in your instructional planning. Students who consistently score at the lowest end of each range should be evaluated for Intervention. Use the **Diagnostic Assessment** for guidelines for decision making.

Diagnose		Prescribe
ASSESSMENTS	**IF...**	**THEN...**
UNIT TEST	0–21 questions correct	Reteach tested skills using the **Intervention Teacher's Editions**.
FLUENCY ASSESSMENT		
Oral Reading Fluency	98–101 WCPM	 Fluency Solutions Reteach using the **Fluency Intervention Teacher's Edition**.
	0–97 WCPM	
RUNNING RECORDS	Level 28 or below	Reteach Comprehension skills using the **Comprehension Intervention Teacher's Edition**. Provide additional Fluency activities.

Response to Intervention

To place students in Tier 2 or Tier 3 Intervention use the *Diagnostic Assessment*.

Tier 2

- Phonics
- Vocabulary
- Comprehension
- Fluency
- Writing and Grammar

Tier 3

Glossary

Introduce students to the Glossary by reading through the introduction and looking over the pages with them. Ask the class to talk about what they see.

Words in a glossary, like words in a dictionary, are listed in **alphabetical order**. Point out the **guide words** at the top of each page that tell the first and last words appearing on that page.

ENTRIES

Point out examples of **main entries**, or entry words, and entries. Read through a sample entry with the class, identifying each part. Have students note the order in which information is given: entry word(s), syllable division, pronunciation respelling, part of speech, definition(s), example sentence(s).

Note if more than one definition is given for a word, the definitions are numbered. Note the format used for a word that is more than one part of speech.

Review the **parts of speech** by identifying each in a sentence:

Inter.	*article*	*n.*	*conj.*	*adj.*	*n.*
Wow!	A	dictionary	and	useful	glossary

v.	*adv.*	*pron.*	*prep.*	*n.*
tell	almost	everything	about	words!

HOMOGRAPHS/HOMOPHONES/HOMONYMS

Point out that some entries are for multiple-meaning words called **homographs**. Homographs have the same spellings but have different origins and meanings, and, in some cases, different pronunciations.

Explain that students should not confuse homographs with **homophones** or **homonyms**. Homophones are words that have the same pronunciation but have different spellings and meanings. Homonyms are words that have the same pronunciation and spelling but have different meanings. Provide students with examples.

PRONUNCIATION KEY

Explain the use of the pronunciation key (either the short key, at the bottom of every other page, or the long key, at the beginning of the Glossary). Demonstrate the difference between primary stress and secondary stress by pronouncing a word with both. Pronounce the words both correctly and incorrectly to give students a clearer understanding of the proper pronunciations.

WORD HISTORY

The Word History feature explains the **etymology** of select words. Explain that etymology is the history of a word from its origin to its present form. A word's etymology explains which language it comes from and what changes have occurred in its spelling and/or meaning. Many English words are derivatives of words from other languages, such as Latin or Greek. Derivatives are formed from base or root words.

Glossary

What Is a Glossary?

A glossary can help you find the **meanings** of words in this book that you may not know. The words in the glossary are listed in **alphabetical order**. **Guide words** at the top of each page tell you the first and last words on the page.

Each word is divided into syllables. The way to pronounce the word is given next. You can understand the pronunciation respelling by using the **pronunciation key**. A shorter key appears at the bottom of every other page. When a word has more than one syllable, a dark accent mark (´) shows which syllable is stressed. In some words, a light accent mark (ˈ) shows which syllable has a less heavy stress. Sometimes an entry includes a second meaning for the word.

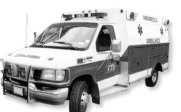

prehistoric

reptiles

808

Guide Words

First word on the page → **script/splendid** ← Last word on the page

Sample Entry

Pronunciation | Part of speech

Main entry & Syllable division → **sketch•es** (skech´əz) *plural noun.*
Simple drawings that are done → Definition
quickly. *I made several **sketches***
Example sentence → *before finally painting the tree.*

Pronunciation Key

Phonetic Spelling	Examples	Phonetic Spelling	Examples
a	at, bad, plaid, laugh	d	dear, soda, bad
ā	ape, pain, day, break	f	five, defend, leaf, off, cough, elephant
ä	father, calm		
âr	care, pair, bear, their, where	g	game, ago, fog, egg
e	end, pet, said, heaven, friend	h	hat, ahead
ē	equal, me, feet, team, piece, key	hw	white, whether, which
i	it, big, give, hymn	j	joke, enjoy, gem, page, edge
ī	ice, fine, lie, my	k	kite, bakery, seek, tack, cat
îr	ear, deer, here, pierce	l	lid, sailor, feel, ball, allow
o	odd, hot, watch	m	man, family, dream
ō	old, oat, toe, low	n	not, final, pan, knife, gnaw
ô	coffee, all, taught, law, fought	ng	long, singer
ôr	order, fork, horse, story, pour	p	pail, repair, soap, happy
oi	oil, toy	r	ride, parent, wear, more, marry
ou	out, now, bough	s	sit, aside, pets, cent, pass
u	up, mud, love, double	sh	shoe, washer, fish, mission, nation
ū	use, mule, cue, feud, few	t	tag, pretend, fat, dressed
ü	rule, true, food, fruit	th	thin, panther, both
ù	put, wood, should, look	th	these, mother, smooth
ûr	burn, hurry, term, bird, word, courage	v	very, favor, wave
ə	about, taken, pencil, lemon, circus	w	wet, weather, reward
b	bat, above, job	y	yes, onion
ch	chin, such, match	z	zoo, lazy, jazz, rose, dogs, houses
		zh	vision, treasure, seizure

809

Aa

ab•sorbed (ab zôrbd´) *verb.* Soaked up something such as a liquid or the sun's rays. *It was a hot day, so the plant **absorbed** the water immediately.*

a•chieved (ə chēvd´) *verb.* To have done or carried out successfully. *She studied hard and **achieved** the grade she wanted.*

ac•quaint•ance (ə kwān´təns) *noun.* A person one knows, but who is not a close friend. *Carole is an **acquaintance** from camp.*

ac•tive (ak´tiv) *adjective.* Lively, busy. *Carlos is always **active**; he hardly ever sits still.*

ad•vanced (ad vanst´) *adjective.* Beyond the beginning level; not elementary. *As a singer, Sheila was really **advanced** for her age.*

ag•ile (aj´əl) *adjective.* Able to move and react quickly and easily. *Bonita is an **agile** softball player.*

al•loy (al´oi) *noun.* A metal formed by fusing two or more metals. *Brass is an **alloy** of copper and zinc.*

a•maze•ment (ə māz´mənt) *noun.* Great surprise or wonder. *To the **amazement** of the audience, the children played some difficult music perfectly.*

am•bu•lance (am´byə ləns) *noun.* A special vehicle that is used to carry sick or injured people to a hospital. *My neighbor once had to call an **ambulance** to take him to the hospital.*

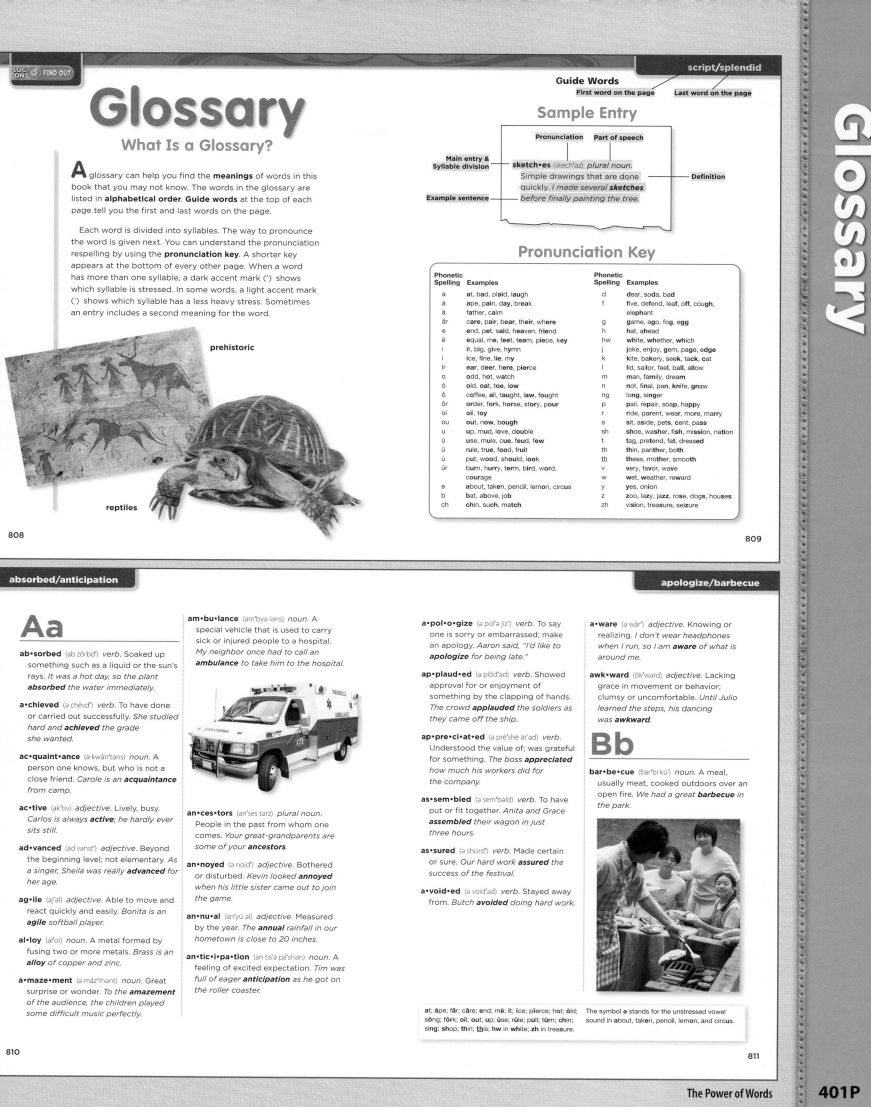

an•ces•tors (an´ses tərz) *plural noun.* People in the past from whom one comes. *Your great-grandparents are some of your **ancestors**.*

an•noyed (ə noid´) *adjective.* Bothered or disturbed. *Kevin looked **annoyed** when his little sister came out to join the game.*

an•nu•al (an´yü əl) *adjective.* Measured by the year. *The **annual** rainfall in our hometown is close to 20 inches.*

an•tic•i•pa•tion (an tis´ə pā´shən) *noun.* A feeling of excited expectation. *Tim was full of eager **anticipation** as he got on the roller coaster.*

---

a•pol•o•gize (ə pol´ə jīz´) *verb.* To say one is sorry or embarrassed; make an apology. *Aaron said, "I'd like to **apologize** for being late."*

ap•plaud•ed (ə plôd´əd) *verb.* Showed approval for or enjoyment of something by the clapping of hands. *The crowd **applauded** the soldiers as they came off the ship.*

ap•pre•ci•at•ed (ə prē´shē āt´əd) *verb.* Understood the value of; was grateful for something. *The boss **appreciated** how much his workers did for the company.*

as•sem•bled (ə sem´bəld) *verb.* To have put or fit together. *Anita and Grace **assembled** their wagon in just three hours.*

as•sured (ə shùrd´) *verb.* Made certain or sure. *Our hard work **assured** the success of the festival.*

a•void•ed (ə void´əd) *verb.* Stayed away from. *Butch **avoided** doing hard work.*

a•ware (ə wâr´) *adjective.* Knowing or realizing. *I don't wear headphones when I run, so I am **aware** of what is around me.*

awk•ward (ôk´wərd) *adjective.* Lacking grace in movement or behavior; clumsy or uncomfortable. *Until Julio learned the steps, his dancing was **awkward**.*

Bb

bar•be•cue (bär´bi kū´) *noun.* A meal, usually meat, cooked outdoors over an open fire. *We had a great **barbecue** in the park.*

---

at; āpe; fär; câre; end; mē; it; īce; pîerce; hot; ōld; sông; fôrk; oil; out; up; ūse; rūle; pùll; tûrn; chin; sing; shop; thin; this; hw in white; zh in treasure.

The symbol ə stands for the unstressed vowel sound in about, taken, pencil, lemon, and circus.

810

811

bar•gained (bär′gīnd) *verb.* To have talked over the terms of an agreement or sale. *My dad **bargained** with the salesperson to get a deal on our new car.*

bid•ding (bid′ing) *noun.* A period in which bids, offers of payments, are made or received. *The auction house started the **bidding** for the antiques.*

bor•der (bôr′dər) *noun.* A line between one country, state, county, or town and another. *A river runs along the **border** between the two states.*

boy•cotts (boi′kots) *plural noun.* Protests in which people refuse to buy from or work for a person, nation, or business. *The **boycotts** against the unfair company were very successful.*

Word History

Boycotts comes from Charles Boycott, who was shunned by Irish farmers for his harsh actions against them.

brit•tle (brit′əl) *adjective.* Likely to break or snap. *Susan's fingernails became **brittle** and started to break.*

Cc

cam•ou•flage (kam′ə fläzh′) *verb.* To hide or conceal by using shapes or colors that blend with the surroundings. *The chameleon is able to **camouflage** itself by changing the color of its skin.*

car•at (kar′ət) *noun.* A unit of weight equal to 1/5 of a gram, usually used to measure gems. *The ring had a three **carat** diamond in the center.*

chal•leng•es (chal′ənj ez) *plural noun.* Those things that call for work, effort, and the use of one's talents. *Ted's greatest **challenges** are in Art and Spanish.*

char•i•ty (char′i tē) *noun.* The giving of help to the poor or needy. *After the flood, some of the families refused to accept any **charity**.*

cir•cu•lar (sûr′kyə lər) *adjective.* Having or making the shape of a circle. *The referee's arm made a **circular** motion as he blew the whistle.*

cit•i•zen (sit′ə zən) *noun.* A person who was born in a country or who chooses to live in and become a member of that country. *Carmine is an Italian **citizen** but often visits the United States.*

civ•il•i•za•tions (siv′əl ə zā′shənz) *plural noun.* Human societies in which agriculture, trade, government, art, and science are highly developed. *Charles studies the ancient **civilizations** of Asia.*

cli•mate (klī′mit) *noun.* The average weather conditions of a place or region through the year. *Most deserts have a hot, dry **climate**.*

clus•tered (klus′tərd) *verb.* To have grown, or grouped together, things of the same kind. *The grapes were **clustered** in a bunch.*

col•lage (kə läzh′) *noun.* A picture made by pasting paper, cloth, metal, and other things in an arrangement on a surface. *Once I made a **collage** of my day's activities by using clippings from magazines.*

Word History

Collage comes from the French word *collage*, from *colle*, meaning "glue" or "paste."

col•o•ny (kol′ə nē) *noun.* A group of animals or plants of the same kind that live together. *I found a **colony** of ants in my yard.*

at; āpe; fär; câre; end; mē; it; īce; pîerce; hot; ōld; sōng; fôrk; oil; out; up; ūse; rūle; pùll; tûrn; chin; sing; shop; thin; this; hw in white; zh in treasure. The symbol ə stands for the unstressed vowel sound in about, taken, pencil, lemon, and circus.

---

con•duc•ted (kən dukt′tid) *verb.* To have directed, led, guided, or transmitted. *When Susie lost her sneaker, she **conducted** a search of the entire locker room.*

con•sist•ed (kən sis′təd) *verb.* Contained; was made up. *The batter **consisted** of a cup of flour, one egg, and a cup of milk.*

con•vinced (kən vinst′) *verb.* To have caused a person to do or believe something. *Raj finally **convinced** his father he was old enough to go on the trip.*

crank•y (krang′kē) *adjective.* To be cross or in a bad temper; grouchy. *Roni is always **cranky** before she's had breakfast.*

cur•i•ous (kyùr′ē əs) *adjective.* Eager to learn new, strange, or interesting things. *We were all **curious** to know who our new teacher might be.*

cur•rent (kûr′ənt) *noun.* A portion of a body of water or of air flowing continuously in a definite direction. *The **current** took the raft far out to sea.*

Dd

dec•ades (dek′ādz) *plural noun.* Periods of ten years. *Our family has lived in the same city for nearly six **decades**.*

Word History

Decades comes from the Greek *deka*, meaning "ten."

de•cayed (dē kād′) *adjective.* Having undergone the process of decomposition; rotted. *We walked in the woods past **decayed** stumps of trees.*

de•fend (di fend′) *verb.* Guard against attack or harm. *The rabbit could not **defend** itself against the snake, so it ran away.*

def•i•ni•tion (def′ə nish′ən) *noun.* An explanation of what a word or phrase means. *Our teacher Mr. Mitchell asked us what the **definition** of "like" is.*

de•mon•stra•ted (de′mən strā′təd) *verb.* Showed by actions or experiment. *The performer **demonstrated** great skill with both the piano and the drums.*

de•scen•dants (di send′ants) *plural noun.* People who come from a particular ancestor. *My neighbors are **descendants** of a French explorer.*

de•signed (di zīnd′) *verb.* To have made a plan, drawing, or outline of something. *Penelope's sister **designed** the perfect sundress for her.*

des•per•ate (des′pər it) *adjective.* Very bad or hopeless. *I needed money, but the situation was not **desperate**.*

di•ges•ted (di jes′tid) *verb.* To have broken down food in the mouth, stomach, and intestines. *After my dog had **digested** his dinner he was hungry again.*

dis•ap•point•ment (dis′ə point′mənt) *noun.* A feeling of being disappointed or let down. *Losing the match was a **disappointment**, but I still like tennis.*

dis•miss (dis mis′) *verb.* To discard or reject. *John was able to **dismiss** the story he heard as a rumor.*

dis•play (di splā′) *noun.* A show or exhibit. *The children's artwork is the main **display** on the family refrigerator.*

dis•rupt (dis rupt′) *verb.* To throw into disorder or confusion. *An argument might **disrupt** the meeting.*

diz•zy (diz′ē) *adjective.* Having the feeling of spinning and being about to fall. *I was **dizzy** when I got off the Ferris wheel.*

dove (dōv) *verb.* Plunged head first into water. *We watched as the woman **dove** perfectly off the board and into the deep pool.*

dove (duv) *noun.* A medium-size bird of the pigeon family. *The **dove** cooed quietly on the window ledge.*

draw•backs (drô′bāks) *plural noun.* Things that make something more difficult or unpleasant. *One of the **drawbacks** of his job is the long hours.*

drought (drout) *noun.* A period of time in which there is little or no rainfall. *The terrible August **drought** affected the wheat crop.*

at; āpe; fär; câre; end; mē; it; īce; pîerce; hot; ōld; sōng; fôrk; oil; out; up; ūse; rūle; pùll; tûrn; chin; sing; shop; thin; this; hw in white; zh in treasure. The symbol ə stands for the unstressed vowel sound in about, taken, pencil, lemon, and circus.

Glossary

Dust Bowl (dust bŏl) *noun*. The region in the central United States that suffered from the great dust storms of the 1930s. *Oklahoma was part of the* ***Dust Bowl***.

Ee

eaves·drop·ping (ēvz'drŏp'ĭng) *noun*. Listening to other people talking without letting them know you are listening. *He was* ***eavesdropping*** *on her neighbors.*

ech·o·lo·ca·tion (ĕk'ō lō kā'shən) *noun*. A way to find out where objects are by making sounds and interpreting the echo that returns. *Bats rely on* ***echolocation*** *when they hunt for insects.*

ee·rie (îr'ē) *adjective*. Strange in a scary way. *We heard an owl's* ***eerie*** *hooting as we walked home in the dark.*

e·lec·tri·cal (ĭ lĕk'trĭ kəl) *adjective*. Relating to the form of energy carried in wires for use to drive motors or as light or heat. *Dad carefully connected the* ***electrical*** *cables to the new DVD player in the den.*

e·merge (ĭ mûrj') *verb*. To come into view or become known. *After months in hibernation, the bears* ***emerge***.

en·coun·ter (ĕn koun'tər) *verb*. To meet or face, usually unexpectedly. *Katie listens to the traffic report so she does not* ***encounter*** *any delays.*

en·cour·aged (ĕn kûr'ĭjd) *verb*. To have inspired with courage, hope, or confidence. *The bright sunlight* ***encouraged*** *us to continue our hike.*

end·less (ĕnd'lĭs) *adjective*. Having no limit or end. *The line of people for the show seemed* ***endless***.

en·dured (ĕn dŭrd' or ĕn dyŭrd') *verb*. Survived or put up with. *The workers* ***endured*** *the hot sun all day.*

e·nor·mous (ĭ nôr'məs) *adjective*. Much greater than the usual size, amount, or degree; extremely large. *The* ***enormous*** *pumpkin weighed over 300 pounds.*

en·ter·pris·ing (ĕn'tər prī'zĭng) *adjective*. Showing energy and initiative; willing or inclined to take risks. *Brian, an* ***enterprising*** *young man, ran for class president and won.*

e·sta·blished (ĭ stăb'lĭshd) *verb*. To have begun, created, or set up. *We* ***established*** *a scholarship in memory of my mother.*

e·va·po·rate (ĭ văp'ə rāt') *verb*. To change from a liquid or solid into a gas. *Heat makes water* ***evaporate***.

Word History
Evaporate comes from the Latin *evaporatus*, "dispersed in vapor," from *ex*, "out," and *vapor*, "exhalation."

e·ven·tu·al·ly (ĭ vĕn'chū ə lē) *adverb*. In the end; finally. *We* ***eventually*** *got a DVD player because the good movies were not being shown on television.*

ex·as·per·at·ed (ĕg zăs'pər ăt'əd) *verb*. Annoyed greatly; made angry. *Helping me with my math so* ***exasperated*** *my dad that my mom took over.*

ex·po·sure (ĕk spō'zhər) *noun*. The condition of being presented to view. *After each* ***exposure*** *to the new toy, the dog began to recognize it and would pick it up without being asked.*

Ff

fam·ished (făm'ĭsht) *adjective*. Very hungry; starving. *After a long day of running and swimming, the children were* ***famished*** *and wanted to eat as soon as possible.*

flinched (flĭncht) *verb*. Drew back or away, as from something painful or unpleasant; winced. *When the door suddenly slammed, Myra* ***flinched***.

fool·ish·ness (fū'lĭsh nəs) *noun*. The act of not showing good sense. *I wanted to race across the street, but my mom will not allow that* ***foolishness***.

frag·ile (frăj'əl) *adjective*. Easily broken; delicate. *My toothpick ship is too* ***fragile*** *to take to show-and-tell.*

freeze-dried (frēz'drī'd) *verb*. To dry while frozen under high vacuum for preservation. *On the camping trip, John mixed a cup of boiling water with a teaspoon of* ***freeze-dried*** *coffee.*

fre·quent·ly (frē'kwənt lē) *adverb*. Happening often. *I* ***frequently*** *eat cereal for breakfast.*

fron·tier (frŭn tîr') *noun*. The far edge of a country, where people are just beginning to settle. *Many Americans moved to the* ***frontier*** *in covered wagons.*

fu·els (fū'əlz) *plural noun*. Substances burned as a source of heat and power, such as coal, wood, or oil. *When the world runs out of fossil* ***fuels***, *we will be forced to use alternate energy sources.*

at; āpe; fär; câre; end; mē; it; īce; pîerce; hot; ōld; sông; fôrk; oil; out; up; ūse; rūle; pull; tûrn; chin; sing; shop; thin; this; hw in white; zh in treasure.

The symbol ə stands for the unstressed vowel sound in about, taken, pencil, lemon, and circus.

Gg

gaped (gāpt) *verb*. Stared with the mouth open, as in wonder or surprise. *The audience* ***gaped*** *at the acrobats.*

gen·u·ine (jĕn'ū ĭn) *adjective*. Sincere; honest. *My friends and I made a* ***genuine*** *effort to help all the kids that were new to the school.*

glanced (glănsd) *verb*. To take a brief or hurried look. *He* ***glanced*** *at the magazines on the table.*

glist·ened (glĭs'ənd) *verb*. To shine with reflected light. *The snow on the fir trees* ***glistened*** *in the sun.*

globe (glōb) *noun*. Earth (as a shape). *Our* ***globe*** *is the home of billions of people.*

glo·ri·ous (glôr'ē əs) *adjective*. Having or deserving praise or honor; magnificent. *The colors of the maple leaves in autumn are* ***glorious***.

Great De·pres·sion (grāt'dē prĕsh'ən) *noun*. A worldwide economic downturn that began in 1928. *My grandparents tell stories about how difficult it was to find a job during the* ***Great Depression***.

guard·i·an (gär'dē ən) *noun*. A person or thing that guards or watches over. *My older brother sometimes acts like he is my* ***guardian***.

Hh

hab·i·tat (hăb'ĭ tăt') *noun*. The place where an animal or plant naturally lives and grows. *A swamp is a common* ***habitat*** *for many creatures.*

han·dy (hăn'dē) *adjective*. Within reach, nearby; easy to use. To **come in handy** is to be useful. *It's amazing how many times a dictionary can* ***come in handy***.

harm·less (härm'lĭs) *adjective*. Not able to do damage or hurt. *My dog looks mean, but really she is* ***harmless***.

head·lines (hĕd'līnz) *plural noun*. Words printed at the top of a newspaper or magazine article. *The most important news has the biggest* ***headlines***.

hi·ber·nate (hī'bər nāt') *verb*. To sleep or stay inactive during the winter. *Bears eat a lot to get ready to* ***hibernate***.

hi·lar·i·ous (hi lâr'ē əs) *adjective*. Very funny. *Keisha tells* ***hilarious*** *jokes that make everyone laugh.*

hoist·ing (hoist'ĭng) *verb*. Lifting or pulling up. ***Hoisting*** *logs out of the water, the men soon grew tired.*

Ii

i·den·ti·fied (ī dĕn'tə fīd') *verb*. Proved that someone or something is a particular person or thing. *The fingerprints on the gold watch* ***identified*** *the butler as the thief.*

im·pres·sive (ĭm prĕs'ĭv) *adjective*. Deserving admiration; making a strong impression. *The track team won five races, which was its most* ***impressive*** *result all year.*

in·ci·dent (ĭn'sĭ dənt) *noun*. An event or act. *After the pep rally, there was a funny* ***incident*** *involving bales of hay and the school mascot.*

in·de·pen·dence (ĭn'dĭ pĕn'dəns) *noun*. Freedom from the control of another or others. *America gained its* ***independence*** *from Great Britain.*

in·jus·tice (ĭn jŭs'tĭs) *noun*. Lack of justice; unfairness. *The workers felt it was an* ***injustice*** *that they could not vote on the issue.*

in·sec·ti·cides (ĭn sĕk'tĭ sīdz') *plural noun*. Chemicals for killing insects. *Our family room was sprayed with* ***insecticides***.

at; āpe; fär; câre; end; mē; it; īce; pîerce; hot; ōld; sông; fôrk; oil; out; up; ūse; rūle; pull; tûrn; chin; sing; shop; thin; this; hw in white; zh in treasure.

The symbol ə stands for the unstressed vowel sound in about, taken, pencil, lemon, and circus.

The Power of Words

Glossary

Glossary

in•spire (in spīr′) *verb*. To stir the mind, feelings, or imagination. *Nature can **inspire** some people to write poetry.*

in•sult (in′sult) *noun*. A remark or action that hurts someone's feelings or pride. *It would be an **insult** not to invite Marta to the party.*

in•tel•li•gent (in tel′i jənt) *adjective*. Able to understand and to think especially well. *An **intelligent** person was needed to solve the difficult puzzle.*

in•ter•act (in′tər akt′) *verb*. To act together, toward, or with others. *My teacher and our class **interact** on a daily basis.*

in•ter•fere (in′tər fîr′) *verb*. To take part in the affairs of others when not asked; to meddle. *My mom hates to **interfere** with my business, but she often gives me good advice.*

in•ter•vals (in′tər vəlz) *plural noun*. The spaces or time between two things. *There are **intervals** of 50 miles between each rest stop on the highway.*

in•ves•ti•gates (in ves′ti gāts′) *verb*. Looks at something carefully in order to gather information. *Every morning, our dog Lulu **investigates** our yard for cats.*

Word History
Investigates comes from the Latin *investigare*, meaning "to track."

is•sues (ish′üz) *plural noun*. 1. Subject matters under discussion. 2. Individual copies of a magazine. *1. My brother and I disagree on certain **issues**. 2. All the **issues** of my favorite comic book were stacked on the shelf.*

i•tems (ī′təmz) *noun*. Things in a group or list. *Christine always makes a list of the **items** she needs from the grocery store.*

Jj

jour•ney (jûr′nē) *noun*. A trip, especially one over a considerable distance or taking considerable time. *Ping made a **journey** to China to meet his grandparents and uncles.*

jum•ble (jum′bəl) *noun*. A confused mixture or condition; mess. *My messy room is a **jumble** of toys and books.*

Ll

la•bor (lā′bər) *noun*. 1. Hard work. 2. People who work at jobs that require physical strength. *1. We all needed naps after a day of **labor** in the yard. 2. The **labor** unions asked for better pay.*

leg•a•cy (leg′ə sē) *noun*. Something handed down from the past; heritage. *The medical research foundation she founded will be her **legacy**.*

leg•en•dary (lej′ən der′ē) *adjective*. Relating to a legend, or a story that has been handed down for many years and has some basis in fact. *Johnny Appleseed's efforts to spread the apple tree have become **legendary**.*

log•i•cal (loj′i kəl) *adjective*. Sensible; being the action or result one expects. *When it rains, I do the **logical** thing and put my bicycle in the garage.*

loos•ened (lü′sənd) *verb*. Made looser; set free or released. *Brad **loosened** his necktie when the ceremony was over.*

lum•ber•ing (lum′bər ing) *adjective*. Moving in a slow, clumsy way. *Put a **lumbering** hippo in the water, and it becomes a graceful swimmer.*

lurk (lûrk) *verb*. To lie hidden. *Many animals **lurk** in their dens so they can surprise their prey when it walks by.*

Mm

mag•ni•fy (mag′nə fī′) *verb*. To make something look bigger than it really is. *Devices such as microscopes help to **magnify** small things.*

mas•sive (mas′iv) *adjective*. Of great size or extent; large and solid. *The sumo wrestler had a **massive** chest.*

at; āpe; fär; câre; end; mē; it; īce; pîerce; hot; ōld; sōng; fôrk; oil; out; up; ūse; rüle; púll; tûrn; chin; sing; shop; thin; <u>th</u>is; hw in white; zh in treasure.

The symbol ə stands for the unstressed vowel sound in about, taken, pencil, lemon, and circus.

820   821

midst (midst) *noun*. A position in the middle of a group of people or things. *"There is a poet in our **midst**," said the principal, "and we need to clap for her."*

mi•grant work•ers (mī′grənt wûr′kərz) *plural noun*. Persons who move from place to place for work. *The **migrant workers** traveled from farm to farm.*

mis•chief (mis′chif) *noun*. Conduct that may seem playful but causes harm or trouble. *The kittens were always getting into **mischief** when we weren't home.*

mis•un•der•stood (mis′un dər stúd′) *verb*. Understood someone incorrectly; got the wrong idea. *I **misunderstood** the directions my teacher gave and did the wrong page for homework.*

mo•ti•vate (mō′tə vāt′) *verb*. To provide with a move to action. *The thought of a college scholarship will always **motivate** me to study hard.*

mut•tered (mut′ərd) *verb*. Spoke in a low, unclear way with the mouth closed. *I could tell he was mad by the way he **muttered** to himself.*

mys•te•ri•ous (mi stîr′ē əs) *adjective*. Very hard or impossible to understand; full of mystery. *The fact that the cookies were missing was **mysterious**.*

Nn

nat•u•ral (nach′ər əl) *adjective*. 1. Unchanged by people. 2. Expected or normal. *1. We hiked through **natural** surroundings of woods, streams, and meadows. 2. The **natural** home of the dolphin is the open ocean.*

ne•glec•ted (ni glekt′əd) *verb*. Failed to give proper attention or care to; failed to do. *I **neglected** to finish my science project and could not present it at the fair.*

now•a•days (nou′ə dāz′) *adverb*. In the present time. *People hardly ever write with typewriters **nowadays**.*

nu•mer•ous (nü′mər əs or nū′mər əs) *adjective*. Forming a large number; many. *The mountain climbers faced **numerous** problems, but they still had fun.*

nu•tri•ents (nü′trē ənts or nū′trē ənts) *plural noun*. Substances needed by the bodies of people, animals, or plants to live and grow. *Sometimes we get ill because we are not getting the proper **nutrients**.*

Oo

o•be•di•ence (ō bē′dē əns) *noun*. The willingness to obey, or to carry out orders, wishes, or instructions. *It is important to show **obedience** to safety rules.*

Word History
Obedience comes from the Latin word *obedire*, meaning "to hearken, yield, or serve."

o•pin•ions (ə pin′yənz) *plural noun*. Beliefs or conclusions based on a person's judgment rather than on what is proven or known to be true. *I want to find out what my classmates' **opinions** are about recycling.*

op•por•tu•ni•ties (op′ər tü′ni tēz) *plural noun*. Good chances or favorable times. *School offers students many **opportunities** to join clubs and organizations.*

or•a•to•ry (ôr′ə tôr′ē) *noun*. Eloquence and skill in public speaking. *The President was a master of campaign **oratory**.*

out•stretched (out′strechtd′) *adjective*. Stretched out; extended. *His **outstretched** palm held the quarter I had dropped.*

o•ver•flow•ing (ō′vər flō′ing) *verb*. To be so full that the contents flow over. *The trunk was **overflowing** with old toys.*

at; āpe; fär; câre; end; mē; it; īce; pîerce; hot; ōld; sōng; fôrk; oil; out; up; ūse; rüle; púll; tûrn; chin; sing; shop; thin; <u>th</u>is; hw in white; zh in treasure.

The symbol ə stands for the unstressed vowel sound in about, taken, pencil, lemon, and circus.

822   823

Pp

par•a•lyzed (par'ə līzd') *adjective.*
1. Having lost movement or sensation in a part of the body. 2. Powerless or helpless. *Sue was **paralyzed** by stage fright.*

part•ner•ship (pärt'nər ship) *noun.* A kind of business in which two or more people share the work and profits. *Janell, Pat, and Erik formed a gardening **partnership**.*

pe•cul•iar (pi kūl'yər) *adjective.* Strange; not usual. *I had the **peculiar** feeling that I was being watched.*

per•sis•tence (pər sis'təns) *noun.* The ability to keep trying in spite of difficulties or obstacles. *In order to run a business, a person must have a lot of **persistence**.*

phras•es (frāz'iz) *plural noun.* Groups of words expressing a single thought but not containing both a subject and predicate. *When I proofread my report, I made **phrases** into complete sentences.*

pol•i•cy (pol'i sē) *noun.* A guiding plan that people use to help make decisions. *The school has a strict "no t-shirt" **policy**.*

pos•i•tive (poz'i tiv) *adjective.* Certain; sure. *I am **positive** I left my backpack right here on the counter.*

pre•his•tor•ic (prē'his tôr'ik) *adjective.* Belonging to a time before people started recording history. *Explorers found **prehistoric** drawings along the cave walls.*

pro•claimed (prə klāmd' or prō klāmd') *verb.* Announced publicly. *The principal **proclaimed** May 20 as the day for our class trips.*

prop•er•ties (prop'ər tēz) *plural noun.* Characteristics of matter that can be observed. *Scientists measured the **properties** of gold in their lab.*

pro•test•ed (prō test'əd) *verb.* Complained against something. *When the workers lost their jobs in the factory, they **protested**.*

pur•chased (pûr'chəsd) *verb.* Got by paying money; got by sacrifice or hardship. *Sally **purchased** the chess board using what she saved from her monthly allowance.*

Rr

ranged (rānjd) *verb.* To go between certain limits. *The prices for a music player **ranged** from fifty to two hundred dollars.*

re•al•is•tic (rē'əlis'tik) *adjective.* Seeing things as they are; practical. *I dream of being a famous rock star, but I should also be **realistic** and stay in school.*

reef (rēf) *noun.* A ridge of sand, rock, or coral at or near the surface of the ocean. *Boaters have to be careful not to scrape against the **reef** below.*

ref•er•ence (ref'ər əns or ref'rəns) *noun.* A statement that calls or directs attention to something. *The speech makes a **reference** to a play written by William Shakespeare.*

re•form (ri fôrm') *noun.* A change for the better. *She worked for a **reform** of the political system.*

reg•is•ter (rej'i stər) *noun.* 1. A formal record or list. 2. The range of a voice or instrument. *verb.* To enroll. *Every college student must **register** before attending class.*

re•lays (rē'lāz) *plural noun.* Fresh sets, teams, or supplies that replace or relieve another. *Post office workers work in **relays** in order to get your letters from one place to another quickly.*

at; āpe; fär; câre; end; mē; it; īce; pîerce; hot; ōld; sông; fôrk; oil; out; up; ūse; rūle; pùll; tûrn; chin; sing; shop; thin; this; hw in white; zh in treasure. | The symbol ə stands for the unstressed vowel sound in about, taken, pencil, lemon, and circus.

---

re•leased (ri lēsd') *verb.* To have set free or loose. *The girl opened the gate to the pen and **released** the pigs.*

re•lo•cat•ed (rē lō'kā tid) *verb.* To have moved to a different location. *The store **relocated** down the block from the park.*

rep•tiles (rep'tīlz) *plural noun.* Cold-blooded vertebrates of the group Reptilia, which includes lizards, snakes, alligators, crocodiles, and turtles. *Most **reptiles** lay eggs, although some give birth to live young.*

res•i•dent (rez'i dənt) *noun.* A person who lives in a particular place. *The new **resident** shocked neighbors by planting the entire front yard with sunflowers.*

re•spon•si•bil•i•ty (ri spon'sə bil'i tē) *noun.* The quality or condition of having a job, duty, or concern. *Taking care of the dog was my **responsibility**.*

roamed (rōmd) *verb.* Moved around in a large area. *The grizzly bear **roamed** over the valley and the nearby mountains.*

route (rūt or rout) *noun.* A road or course used for traveling. *Trucks must follow a special **route**.*

rum•bling (rum'bling) *noun.* A heavy, deep, rolling sound. *The **rumbling** of thunder woke me up.*

Ss

sanc•tu•ar•y (sangk'chū er'ē) *noun.* A protected place for wildlife where predators are controlled and hunting is not allowed. *My friend runs a **sanctuary** for injured hawks and owls.*

scorn•ful•ly (skôrn'fəl ē) *adverb.* In a way that shows that something or someone is looked down upon and considered bad or worthless. *The critic was unhappy with the new artist's paintings so he spoke **scornfully** about them.*

seg•re•ga•tion (seg'ri gā'shən) *noun.* The practice of setting one racial group apart from another. *The Civil Rights movement fought against **segregation**.*

se•lec•ting (si lek'ting) *verb.* Picking out among many; choosing. *I spent a long time **selecting** the right gift.*

self•ish (sel'fish) *adjective.* Thinking only of oneself; putting one's own interests and desires before those of others. *A second piece of cake sounded good, but I didn't want to be **selfish**.*

sen•si•ble (sen'sə bəl) *adjective.* Having or showing sound judgment; wise. *If you make a mistake, the **sensible** thing to do is apologize.*

sev•er•al (sev'ə rəl or sev'rəl) *adjective.* More than two, but not many. *Louisa slept for **several** hours.*

shim•mer (shim'ər) *verb.* To shine with a faint, wavering light; glimmer. *The lake began to **shimmer** in the rays of the setting sun.*

silk•en (sil'kən) *adjective.* 1. Made of silk. 2. Like silk in appearance. *1. The queen's **silken** robe was exquisite. 2. Antonio wrote a poem about the girl's long **silken** hair.*

Silk Road (silk rōd) *noun.* A trade route that connected China with the Roman Empire. *The **Silk Road** was about 4,000 miles long.*

sim•i•lar (sim'əl ər) *adjective.* Having many but not all qualities alike. *Zack and Nick have **similar** haircuts.*

sky•scrap•ers (skī'skrā'pərz) *plural noun.* Very tall buildings. *The city has many **skyscrapers**, and some of them are 50 stories tall!*

slen•der (slen'dər) *adjective.* Thin, especially in an attractive or graceful way. *The swan stretched its long **slender** neck and flapped its wings.*

slith•ered (slith'ərd) *verb.* Slid or glided like a snake. *When the snakes **slithered** across the ground, they moved quickly and hardly made a sound.*

snick•er•ing (snik'ər ing) *verb.* Laughing in a mean or disrespectful manner. *The children stopped **snickering** when their mother told them to be kinder.*

at; āpe; fär; câre; end; mē; it; īce; pîerce; hot; ōld; sông; fôrk; oil; out; up; ūse; rūle; pùll; tûrn; chin; sing; shop; thin; this; hw in white; zh in treasure. | The symbol ə stands for the unstressed vowel sound in about, taken, pencil, lemon, and circus.

soft•ware (sôft′wâr′) *noun.* Written or printed programs of information that are used on a computer. *The artist used a new design **software** to help plan her latest sculpture.*

sol•i•tar•y (sol′i ter′ē) *adjective.* Living, being, or going alone. *After everyone else quit, Jim was the **solitary** player left in the game.*

Word History

Solitary comes from the Latin *solitarius,* meaning "alone, lonely."

sores (sôrz) *plural noun.* Places where the skin has been broken and hurts. *My hands had **sores** after raking leaves all morning with no gloves on.*

spe•cial•ized (spesh′ə līzd′) *verb.* To have concentrated on a particular product, activity, branch of a profession, or field of study. *When she went to cooking school, she **specialized** in bread baking.*

spe•cial•ty (spesh′əl tē) *noun.* A special thing that a person knows a great deal about or can make very well. *Making quilts is my aunt Lisa's **specialty**.*

spin•off (spin′ôf′) *noun.* A product derived from another field. *This new plastic used in eyeglass frames is a **spinoff** from the aerospace industry.*

strikes (strīks) *plural noun.* 1. The stopping of work to protest something. 2. Pitched balls in the strike zone or that a batter swings at and misses. *1. The workers threatened **strikes** if conditions did not improve. 2. One rule of baseball is three **strikes** and you're out.*

strut•ting (strut′ing) *verb.* Walking in a self-important way. *When Marilyn returned from her trip to Europe, she came **strutting** in showing off her new Italian boots.*

stur•dy (stûr′dē) *adjective.* Having strength; hardy. *The bookshelf we built was **sturdy** enough to hold our entire collection of books.*

sub•urbs (sub′ûrbz) *plural noun.* The areas around a city where people live. *Many people commute from the **suburbs** to the city using public transportation.*

Word History

Suburbs comes from the Latin *suburbium*—from *sub-* "under" and *urbs,* meaning "city."

sul•tan (sul′tən) *noun.* The king or ruler in certain Muslim countries. *Modern-day Turkey was ruled by a **sultan** at one time.*

swarms (swôrmz) *plural noun.* Large groups of insects flying or moving together. *When the hive fell, **swarms** of angry bees flew out.*

Tt

tan•gles (tang′gəlz) *plural noun.* Knotted, twisted, confused masses. *The garden hose had not been rolled back up and was full of **tangles**.*

tech•nique (tek nēk′) *noun.* A method or way of bringing about a desired result in a science, an art, a sport, or a profession. *Part of Orli's **technique**, when she is running, is to breathe in and out through her mouth.*

Word History

Technique comes from the Greek word *teknikos,* meaning "relating to an art or a craft."

tech•nol•o•gy (tek nol′ə jē) *noun.* Electronic products and systems that have various uses. ***Technology** has changed the ways that artists create their work.*

tel•e•graph (tel′i graf′) *noun.* A system or equipment used to send messages by wire over a long distance. *Before the telephone, a **telegraph** may have been used to relay a message.*

tem•po•rar•y (tem′pə rer′ē) *adjective.* Lasting or used for a short time only. *We recorded a **temporary** message for the answering machine.*

at; āpe; fär; câre; end; mē; it; īce; pîerce; hot; ōld; sông; fôrk; oil; out; up; ūse; rūle; pull; tûrn; chin; sing; shop; thin; this; hw in white; zh in treasure. The symbol ə stands for the unstressed vowel sound in about, taken, pencil, lemon, and circus.

ter•ri•to•ry (ter′i tôr′ē) *noun.* Any large area of land; region. *My brother's **territory** for selling medical office supplies is North Carolina.*

threat•ened (thret′ənd) *adjective.* Having a sense of harm or danger. ***Threatened** by the hawk circling above, the mouse escaped under a log.*

trans•form (trans fôrm′) *verb.* To change in form, appearance, or structure. *To **transform** a barn into a modern home, you need to invest a lot of time and expense.*

Word History

Transform comes from the Latin *transformare,* meaning "to change in shape."

trans•la•tion (trans lā′shən) *noun.* A changing of a speech or piece of writing into another language. *Maria's grandmother spoke only Spanish, so Maria needed a **translation** of the letter from her.*

Uu

un•fair (un fâr′) *adjective.* Not fair or just. *Punishing all of us for the actions of my little sister seemed **unfair**.*

un•ions (ūn′yənz) *plural noun.* Groups of workers joined together to protect their jobs and improve working conditions. *Some labor **unions** stage strikes to get workers the safety equipment they need.*

u•nique (ū nēk′) *adjective.* Having no equal; the only one of its kind. *The Everglades is **unique** in that there is no other place on Earth like it.*

un•sta•ble (un stā′bəl) *adjective.* Not settled or steady; easily moved or put off balance. *Although the raft looked **unstable**, it floated very well.*

Vv

var•ied (vâr′ēd) *adjective.* Consisting of many different kinds. *The organisms in this coral reef are **varied**.*

ven•ture (ven′chər) *noun.* A business or some other undertaking that involves risk. *Rea's new **venture** was a carpet-cleaning service.*

vi•o•lat•ed (vī′ə lā′tid) *verb.* To have failed to obey; to have broken. *Mel was yelled at because she **violated** the "no talking during a test" rule.*

vis•i•bly (viz′ə blē) *adverb.* Plainly seen. *The firemen were **visibly** fatigued.*

vol•un•teer (vol′ən tîr′) *noun.* A person who offers to help or does something by choice and usually without pay. *I am a **volunteer** at the nursing home.*

W

week•days (wēk′dāz′) *plural noun.* The days of the week except Saturday and Sunday. *We go to school only on **weekdays**.*

at; āpe; fär; câre; end; mē; it; īce; pîerce; hot; ōld; sông; fôrk; oil; out; up; ūse; rūle; pull; tûrn; chin; sing; shop; thin; this; hw in white; zh in treasure. The symbol ə stands for the unstressed vowel sound in about, taken, pencil, lemon, and circus.

Glossary

Additional Resources

Contents

Instructional Routines

Professional Development

- Read the routine prior to using *Treasures*. Use the Routine QuickNotes as a reminder of key routine steps throughout Unit 3, or as needed.

- View the online classroom video clip through **TeacherWorks Plus**. Watch master teachers use these routines.

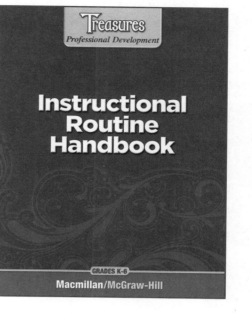

1. **Phonological Awareness/ Phonemic Awareness**
   Rhyme
   Oddity Tasks
   Sound Categorization
   Oral Blending
   Oral Segmentation
   Manipulation

2. **Phonics**
   Blending
   Introducing Sound-Spelling Cards
   Letter Recognition
   Building Words
   Building Fluency
   Reading Decodables
   Multisyllabic Words Routine

3. **Fluency**
   Strategies

4. **Vocabulary**
   Define/Example/Ask Routine
   Strategies

5. **High-Frequency Words**
   Read/Spell/Write Routine
   Reading Pre-decodables

6. **Spelling**
   Dictation

7. **Comprehension**
   Strategies
   Skills
   Reading Big Books
   Reading Student Book

8. **Writing**
   Conferences
   Revision Assignments
   Writing Process
   Using Rubrics
   Using Anchor Papers
   Writers' Express Sequence

9. **Research Process**
   Big Question Board

10. **Classroom Management**
    Workstation Flip Charts
    Contracts
    Centers
    Small Groups

11. **Listening/Speaking/Viewing**

12. **Assessment**

Objectives

- **Generate questions**
- **Distinguish fact and opinion**
- **Make inferences about people and events**

Genre Literary Nonfiction/Biography

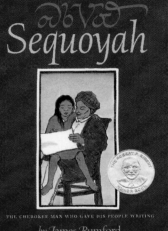

Approaching Level

Summary

Written in poetic prose, this book is the story of how a brilliant Cherokee Indian named Sequoyah created a writing system for the Cherokee language. The Cherokee were then able to read and write in their own language.

FYI for your information

Creating a system of writing based on an existing language is a feat few individuals have accomplished. The Cherokee system is not based on individual letters, as is the English language. Rather, it is based on a syllabary of 84 signs, one for each syllable in the Cherokee language.

Sequoyah
by James Rumford

Before Reading

BUILD BACKGROUND

Brainstorm lists of inventions and inventors with students. Write their responses on the board. Ask students:

- *How do inventors think of things to invent?*
- *What would you invent to make your life easier or better?*
- *What would have been a difficult thing to invent? Why?*

PREVIEW AND SET PURPOSES

Tell students to look at the cover illustration, read the title, and page through the book. Point out that the writing is in two languages: English and Cherokee. Have students set a purpose for reading, such as to learn what inventing has to do with this other language in the book.

During Reading

APPLY COMPREHENSION SKILLS AND STRATEGIES

The following are suggestions for dividing the reading into manageable sections. For each section, Think Alouds and discussion questions are provided. Use these to review comprehension strategies and skills taught in this unit.

Pages 1–10

STRATEGY
GENERATE QUESTIONS

Teacher Think Aloud I know that generating questions as I read can help me to clarify meaning, understand the author's purpose for writing, or locate a specific answer in the text. It can also help me identify any techniques of persuasion the author might use. Here's a question I can ask as I begin to read: If Sequoyah was not a brave fighter or a good leader, what did he do to become famous? I will read on to see if my question is answered.

Fact and Opinion Authors may state their opinion about a topic at the beginning of a book. They often use persuasive techniques to convince us their opinion is right. What statement does this author make about Sequoyah? (Through the words of others, he states that Sequoyah was famous for fighting bravely, leading well, and being tall and strong, but not in a way that we would normally think.)

STRATEGY
GENERATE QUESTIONS

Teacher Think Aloud As I read, I pause to ask myself questions. This helps me understand key ideas, events, and details in a text. As I read these pages, I ask myself, *Why did people burn down Sequoyah's cabin? What did Sequoyah learn from this disaster?*

Make Inferences *What clues help you infer that Sequoyah was a man of confidence and determination?* (Although he was disabled, he worked as a metalworker. He loved the Cherokee people and was proud of his culture. He did not want the Cherokee to disappear into the white man's world.)

STRATEGY
GENERATE QUESTIONS

Teacher Think Aloud Asking questions can help me understand the author's purpose for writing something. The author has included a chart at the end of the book. It shows the symbols that were used in Sequoyah's writing system. Why would the author include this? I think the author included this so the reader could use Sequoyah's invention by translating some of the Cherokee words.

Fact and Opinion *What two facts about Sequoyah can you list from these pages? How could you verify these facts?* (Possible responses: Sequoyah created a writing system for the Cherokee. A statue of Sequoyah stands in the U.S. Capitol. These facts can be verified using a reference book or reliable web site.)

After Reading

LITERATURE CIRCLES

Use page 253 in the **Teacher's Resource Book** to review Listening and Speaking guidelines for a discussion. Use these questions to guide a discussion of the book in small groups:

- *What is the most memorable part of the book? Explain.*

- *What questions do you still have about Sequoyah or the Cherokee? How could you find answers to these questions?*

- *Why was Ayoka important in letting people know about the writing system?*

Write About It

Have students take the part of either Sequoyah or one of the people who were uncertain about his writing system. Then have students write a letter to a friend or relative expressing that point of view. Tell students to be persuasive and try to convince the person to believe the way he or she does.

Social Studies
Connect to Content

NATIVE AMERICAN LANGUAGES

Sequoyah invented a written language in order to preserve his native Cherokee language. Have students research a language of a Native American nation from your state. Have them look for definitions and pronunciations of some words and phrases, and organize the information into a chart that resembles a dictionary page. Tell students to present their findings to the class.

Classroom Library

Objectives

- **Monitor comprehension**
- **Analyze character, setting, plot**
- **Generate questions**
- **Draw conclusions about characters**
- **Select, respond to, and view texts recognized for quality and literary merit**

Genre | Literary Text/Fiction

On Level

Summary

In Los Angeles during the 1920s, Jeannie Sloan tells of how she and her sister Marguerite meet their new neighbors, the Hanisians. In particular, the girls befriend Francie Hanisian, whose cerebral palsy isolates her from everyone else. Marguerite risks her own social standing to teach Francie to read and write, an act that ultimately unites the entire neighborhood during a very special holiday party.

FYI for your information

Cerebral palsy describes several disorders of the brain. The word *cerebral* means "of the brain," and *palsy* is a condition in which parts of the body move uncontrollably. Cerebral palsy results from brain damage either before birth or shortly afterward.

Circle of Giving

by Ellen Howard

Before Reading

BUILD BACKGROUND

Explain to students that *Circle of Giving* tells the story of characters who have recently moved into a neighborhood during the 1920s. During that time, over 80 years ago, many physical disabilities remained a mystery. Create a chart that allows students to suggest differences between then and now. Ask students:

- *How would you learn about your new neighborhood if your family moved from one place to another today? How is that different from the 1920s?*

PREVIEW AND SET PURPOSES

Tell students to look at the contents page and predict some of the main events of the novel. Have them set a purpose for reading, such as discovering why the book's title is also the title of the final chapter.

During Reading

APPLY COMPREHENSION SKILLS AND STRATEGIES

Follow these suggestions to divide the reading into manageable sections. Think Alouds and discussion questions accompany each section. These will help students understand and review the comprehension strategies and skills.

Chapters 1–5

STRATEGY
MONITOR COMPREHENSION

Teacher Think Aloud Good readers monitor their comprehension, especially at the beginning of a new book. I will read slowly to make sure that I understand who the main characters are and where the story takes place. I will pay extra attention to the problem these characters face.

Character, Setting, Plot Who are the main characters in this book? How are they related? (Jeannie and Marguerite are the main characters. They are sisters.)

Chapters 6–9

STRATEGY
GENERATE QUESTIONS

Teacher Think Aloud Generating questions can help me clarify the characters and plot of the story. Jeanne and Marguerite visit their neighbor Francine, who has cerebral palsy. I ask myself *Will they be able to teach Francine to read?* As I read, I will think about this question and look for clues.

Character, Setting, Plot What character traits best describe Marguerite? Why? (Marguerite is a strong, determined person. She makes a decision to teach Francie how to read and write and sticks to it. She even risks her own social standing.)

Chapters 10–14

STRATEGY
MONITOR COMPREHENSION

Teacher Think Aloud As I read this section of the book, I might come across words and terms I don't know. I can stop and reread any sections of text that have unfamiliar words and look for clues in the surrounding sentences that may help me understand what they might mean.

Draw Conclusions *What conclusion can you draw about Jeanne's character after she first hears Francie pronounce words?* (Although the jacks game was important to Jeanne, it was not as important as hearing Francie speak and knowing that Francie and Marguerite care about her.)

Chapters 15–18

STRATEGY
GENERATE QUESTIONS

Teacher Think Aloud As I read, I pause to ask myself questions. This helps me to be sure I understand key ideas, events, and details in the story. As I read, I'll look for the answer to this question: *What will be Francie give to her mother as a Christmas gift? How does Marguerite help?*

Character, Setting, Plot How have the neighbors' impressions of Francie changed after the party? How does this affect their behavior toward her? (They realize that Francie can express herself by speaking, reading, and writing and that her strong will to overcome her disabilities deserves their support.)

After Reading

LITERATURE CIRCLES
Use page 253 in the **Teacher's Resource Book** to review Listening and Speaking guidelines for a discussion. Use these questions to guide a discussion of the book in small groups:

- *What does the author mean by a "circle of giving"?*
- *How do you think life will change in the Sloans' neighborhood after the holiday party?*

Write About It
Tell students to put themselves at the scene of the holiday party. Have them select a character from the story and write about what gift they might have given him or her. They should use vivid words to set the scene and describe what they see, smell, hear, and feel. Remind them to make sure that their sentences have proper subject-verb agreement.

Social Studies
Connect to Content

SIGNS OF THE TIMES

Circle of Giving takes place in Los Angeles during the 1920s. Have students use almanacs, history books, or the Internet to research events and popular trends (games, songs, fashion, etc.) associated with that place and time. Then have students compare and contrast their findings to the present-day equivalents.

Classroom Library

Objectives

- Monitor comprehension
- Draw conclusions
- Generate questions
- Distinguish fact and opinion

Genre Informational Text/Expository

Beyond Level

Summary

Harriet Hemenway and Minna Hall are outraged when they see women sporting dead birds on their fancy hats. They write letters to the women of Boston inviting them to the first informal meeting of what became the Audubon Society. Hemenway and Hall are also successful in getting men to lobby legislatures to pass laws to save birds.

FYI for your information

The Audubon Society is named for John James Audubon (1785–1851). He traveled to paint and describe the birds of America. His prints are considered major works of art. Today, the Audubon Society works to protect birds and their habitats all over the world.

She's Wearing a Dead Bird on Her Head

by Kathryn Lasky

Before Reading

BUILD BACKGROUND

Have students think about a time when they saw something they did not think was right, such as the mistreatment of an animal, or a person doing something dangerous. Ask:

- *How might you persuade someone to stop doing something you think is wrong?*

- *Is it usually easy or difficult to persuade someone to change his or her behavior? Why?*

PREVIEW AND SET PURPOSES

As students look at the illustrations, talk about the mood set by the art. Will this be a serious or a humorous book? Then tell students to set a purpose for reading, such as to find out about the bird hats.

During Reading

APPLY COMPREHENSION SKILLS AND STRATEGIES

Students may want to read the book in one sitting. Use the following Think Alouds and discussion questions to review comprehension strategies and skills taught in this unit.

Pages 1–14

STRATEGY
MONITOR COMPREHENSION

Teacher Think Aloud At the beginning of the book, I read more slowly to make sure I understand who the characters are and what the problem in the book might be. I can always reread if I find I don't understand what is going on. So far, the two main characters are Harriet Hemenway and her cousin Minna. The problem is that birds are being killed to be used in fashion. Harriet and Minna want to stop this practice.

Draw Conclusions From the information given in this section, what conclusion can you draw about how Harriet and Minna feel about birds? What clues lead you to this conclusion? (Harriet and Minna love birds and are sad that they are not protected. Harriet becomes upset after seeing a woman wearing a bird in her hat. On her way to see Harriet, Minna looks for birds in the trees because they make her heart swell.)

STRATEGY
GENERATE QUESTIONS

Teacher Think Aloud I know that Harriet, Minna, and other women of their day didn't have the same rights as women today. Still, why would they need men who could go into state legislatures and Congress? I can generate a question to help me understand. How could the U.S. Congress help Harriet and Minna with their cause? Perhaps laws could be passed to stop hatmakers from using bird feathers.

Fact and Opinion Harriet and Minna convinced women that "killing birds was wrong" and that "birds as hat decorations made women look silly." Are these statements facts or opinions? (The statements cannot be proven, so they must be opinions.)

STRATEGY
GENERATE QUESTIONS

Teacher Think Aloud As I continue reading, another question comes to mind. If Harriet and Minna cannot vote, how do they have the power to change laws? I read on to find my answer. Harriet and Minna teach and organize people and write letters about bird conservation to lawmakers. Eventually, laws are passed to protect the birds.

Draw Conclusions What do Harriet and Minna do that leads to the enforcement of laws protecting birds? (They go to New York, purchase hats with birds on them, and get information from the hatmakers about the suppliers of the illegal feathers. They give this information to the authorities, who arrest the suppliers.)

After Reading

LITERATURE CIRCLES

Use page 253 in the **Teacher's Resource Book** to review Listening and Speaking guidelines for a discussion. Use these questions to guide a discussion of the book in small groups:

- *What two problems did Hall and Hemenway have to solve? How did they solve these problems?*

- *What cause might the ladies work on if they were alive today?*

Write About It

Have students think about something they feel passionate about. Possible topics might be pollution, the benefits of exercise, or saving endangered animals. Tell students to write a short essay persuading readers to believe as they do. They should use persuasive language and supporting details.

Connect to Content

THE AUDUBON SOCIETY

Have students research the Audubon Society using books, reference materials, and the Internet. Tell students to note what issues of bird conservation the Society is working on. Tell students to find out how the conservation of habitats affects the survival of birds. When the class reconvenes, have spokespeople share what they learned about this organization.

Classroom Library

Theme Bibliography

Additional Readings

30 MINUTES DAILY

By the Authors and Illustrators

For additional information on authors, illustrators, and selection content, go to www.macmillanmh.com.

Scacco, Linda. *Always My Grandpa: A Story for Children About Alzheimer's Disease.* **Illustrated by Nicole Wong. American Psychological Association, 2005.** Through vivid pictures and text, join one child's journey to accept his grandfather's illness.

`APPROACHING`

Teague, Mark. *Detective LaRue: Letters from the Investigation.* **Scholastic, 2004.** When two cats disappear, Ike becomes the leading suspect and decides to solve the case himself.

`APPROACHING`

Related to the Theme
(spans 3+ grade levels)

Use these and other classroom or library resources to ensure students are reading at least 30 minutes a day outside of class. Enlist the help of your school librarian to teach students how to use library resources, such as card catalogs and electronic search engines, to find other books related to the unit theme.

Friedman, Lise. *Break a Leg! The Kid's Guide to Acting and Stagecraft.* **Workman Publishing, 2002.** Theater games, improvisation, backstage life, and miming are addressed in this book about stagecraft.

`APPROACHING`

Goble, Paul. *Iktomi and the Buzzard: A Plains Indian Story.* **Orchard Books, 1994.** In this traditional Lakota trickster tale, Iktomi tries to fool a buzzard into carrying him across a river.

`APPROACHING`

Ashabranner, Brent K. *On the Mall in Washington D.C.: A Visit to America's Front Yard.* **Twenty-First Century Books, 2002.** A guide to the National Mall in Washington, D.C.

`ON LEVEL`

Davies, Jacqueline. *The Boy Who Drew Birds: A Story of John James Audubon.* **Houghton, 2004.** Watercolor paintings and collages depict the childhood of the famous painter and naturalist.

`ON LEVEL`

Bloom, Harold. *Thornton Wilder.* **Chelsea House, 2002.** Wilder was able to dramatize the extraordinary things about ordinary life. Two of his plays, *Our Town* and *The Skin of Our Teeth*, are examined.

`BEYOND`

Creech, Sharon. *The Wanderer.* **HarperCollins, 2000.** Sophie and her cousin record their transatlantic crossing aboard a ship on its way to England.

`BEYOND`

Library Resources

Genre Study

Have students select a theme-related book in the library. Remind students that fiction and nonfiction books are found in different places in the library. Point out that fiction books are arranged alphabetically by the author's last name and nonfiction books are found by the subject.

Once students have read a book, they should write a response to it that shows their understanding. Have them compare and contrast the book with other books of this genre, explaining why they did or did not like this particular book and how they feel about the genre as a whole.

Deedy, Carmen Agra. *The Yellow Star.* **Peachtree, 2000.** The story of a Danish king's courage in wearing a yellow armband during World War II as an act of solidarity with his Jewish subjects.
ON LEVEL

Teague, Mark. *Flying Dragon Room.* **Blue Sky Press, 1996.** With the help of Mrs. Jenkins's special tools, Patrick builds a fabulous place of his very own. Come experience his colorful adventure.
APPROACHING

Lagarrigue, Jerome. *Freedom Summer.* **Atheneum, 2001.** The friendship between two boys, one of whom is black and the other white, is powerfully rendered in the text and beautiful illustrations.
APPROACHING

Halvorsen, Lisa. *Letters Home from Yellowstone.* **Blackbirch, 2000.** Here is a first-person account of a trip to Yellowstone that describes its wildlife, boiling mud pools, and its geyser, "Old Faithful."
APPROACHING

Orr, Wendy. *Nim's Island.* **Knopf, 2001.** When her father disappears, a young girl is left with only a sea lion, an iguana, and a mysterious new e-mail friend.
APPROACHING

Schanzer, Rosalyn. *How We Crossed the West: The Adventures of Lewis and Clark.* **National Geographic, 1997.** The explorers' journals provide a good introduction to the expedition.
APPROACHING

Peterson, Lenka. *Kids Take the Stage.* **Back Stage Books, 1997.** A "how-to" book for children about stagecraft and putting on a play.
ON LEVEL

Roop, Peter. *Good-bye for Today: The Diary of a Young Girl at Sea.* **Atheneum, 2000.** Nine-year-old Laura writes in her journal about her voyage from Japan to the Arctic Sea aboard a whaling ship.
ON LEVEL

Thompson, Lauren. *One Riddle, One Answer.* **Scholastic, 2001.** A sultan's daughter, who loves numbers and riddles, devises a plan to find a man who will become her husband.
ON LEVEL

Partridge, Elizabeth. *Kogi's Mysterious Journey.* **Dutton, 2003.** Kogi is a painter unable to capture the beauty that inspires him until he steps out of his body and experiences life as a fish.
BEYOND

Rosen, Michael. *Shakespeare: His Work and His World.* **Candlewick Press, 2001.** An inspiring introduction to one of the greatest writers of all time, with a focus on some of his plays.
BEYOND

Szabo, Corinne. *Sky Pioneer: A Photobiography of Amelia Earhart.* **National Geographic, 1997.** An upbeat biography of this pioneer, with photographs and quotations from Earhart herself.
BEYOND

Selection Honors, Prizes, and Awards

Dear Mrs. LaRue

Unit 3, p. 296
by *Mark Teague*
Booklist Editor's Choice (2002), *New York Times* Best Illustrated Book, *Publishers Weekly* Best Books of the Year

Author/Illustrator: *Mark Teague,* winner of Nevada's Young Readers' Award (1998) and Washington Children's Choice Picture Book Award (1999) for *The Secret Shortcut;* Christopher Medal (2000) and ABC Children's Booksellers Choices Award (2001) for *How Do Dinosaurs Say Goodnight?*

Ranita, the Frog Princess

Unit 3, p. 342
by *Carmen Agra Deedy*
Illustrated by *Renato Alarcão*

Author: *Carmen Agra Deedy,* winner of the North Dakota Flicker Tale Children's Book Award (1997) for *The Library Dragon;* the Jane Addams Peace Association Honor Book Award (2001), the Christopher Award (2001), Bologna Ragazzi Award (2001), and Parents' Choice Gold Award (2000) for *The Yellow Star: The Legend of King Christian X of Denmark*

Me and Uncle Romie

Unit 3, p. 372
by *Claire Hartfield*
Illustrated by *Jerome Lagarrigue*
Smithsonian Notable Book (2002), Junior Library Guild Choice

Illustrator: *Jerome Lagarrigue,* winner of the Coretta Scott King Award for a New Artist (2002)

Resources

Audio Bookshelf
44 Ocean View Drive
Middletown, RI 02842
800-234-1713
www.audiobookshelf.com

Discovery Education
One Discovery Place
Silver Spring, MD 20910
800-323-9084
http://discoveryeducation.com

Dorling Kindersley
375 Hudson Street
New York, NY 10014
Tel: 800-631-8571
Fax: 201-256-0000
http://us.dk.com

GPN Educational Media
1407 Fleet Street
Baltimore, MD 21231
800-228-4630
http://shopgpn.com

Innovative Educators
P.O. Box 520
Montezuma, GA 31063
888-252-KIDS (5437)
Fax: 888-536-8553
www.innovative-educators.com

Library Video Co.
P.O. Box 580
Wynnewood, PA 19096
800-843-3620
www.libraryvideo.com

Listening Library
400 Hahn Road
Westminster, MD 21157
800-733-3000
http://randomhouse.biz/educators/

Live Oak Media
P.O. Box 652
Pine Plains, NY 12567
800-788-1121
www.liveoakmedia.com

Macmillan/McGraw-Hill
220 East Danieldale Road
DeSoto, TX 75115-9960
Tel: 800-442-9685
Fax: 972-228-1982
www.macmillanmh.com

Microsoft Corp.
One Microsoft Way
Redmond, WA 98052
800-642-7676
www.microsoft.com

National Geographic Society
1145 17th Street N.W.
Washington, DC 20036
800-647-5463
www.nationalgeographic.com

Recorded Books
270 Skipjack Road
Prince Frederick, MD 20678
800-638-1304
www.recordedbooks.com

Sunburst Communications
Sunburst Technology
1550 Executive Drive
Elgin, IL 60123
888-321-7511 ext.3337
www.sunburst.com

Tom Snyder Productions
100 Talcott Avenue
Watertown, MA 02472
800-342-0236
www.tomsnyder.com

Weston Woods
143 Main Street
Norwalk, CT 06851
800-243-5020
www.teacher.scholastic.com/products/
westonwoods/

Web Sites

Go to **www.macmillanmh.com**.
Use the zip code finder to locate other resources in your area.

The Academy of Natural Sciences
http://www.ansp.org/

Acadia National Park
http://www.nps.gov/acad

Agriculture in the Classroom
http://www.agclassroom.org/

Arches National Park
http://www.nps.gov/arch

Asian American History Resources Online - CET
http://www.cetel.org/res.html

Association of Zoos and Aquariums
http://www.aza.org/

Bronx Zoo
http://www.bronxzoo.com/

Cincinnati Zoo
http://www.cincinnatizoo.org/

Colonial Williamsburg
http://www.history.org/

Denali National Park and Preserve
http://www.nps.gov/dena

Ellis Island
http://www.ellisisland.org/

Glacier National Park
http://www.nps.gov/glac

Grand Canyon National Park
http://www.nps.gov/grca

Grand Teton National Park
http://www.nps.gov/grte

High Museum of Art, Atlanta
http://www.high.org/

International Civil Rights Center and Museum
http://www.sitinmovement.org/

Japanese American National Museum
http://www.janm.org/

K12Station – Library of K–12 Education Links
http://www.k12station.com/k12link_library.html

Kids.gov
http://www.kids.gov/

KidsHealth in the Classroom
http://classroom.kidshealth.org/

Meteorology
http://www.wxdude.com/

The Metropolitan Museum of Art, New York
http://www.metmuseum.org/

Minneapolis Institute of Arts
http://www.artsmia.org/

Minnesota Zoo
http://www.mnzoo.com/

MoMA | The Museum of Modern Art
http://www.moma.org/

Monterey Bay Aquarium
www.montereybayaquarium.org

Mount Rushmore National Memorial
http://www.nps.gov/moru

Museum of Fine Arts, Boston
http://www.mfa.org/

Museum of Science, Boston
http://www.mos.org/

Museum of Science and Industry, Chicago
http://www.msichicago.org/

NASA
http://www.nasa.gov/

NASA Kids' Club
http://www.nasa.gov/audience/forkids/kidsclub/flash/index.html

National Air and Space Museum
http://www.nasm.si.edu/

National Civil Rights Museum
http://www.civilrightsmuseum.org/home.htm

National Museum of African American History and Culture
http://nmaahc.si.edu/

National Museum of American History
http://americanhistory.si.edu/

National Museum of the American Indian
http://www.nmai.si.edu/

National Museum of Women in the Arts
http://www.nmwa.org/

National Music Museum
http://www.usd.edu/smm/

National Park Service
http://www.nps.gov/

National Weather Service Education Resources
http://www.nws.noaa.gov/om/edures.shtml

National Women's History Museum
http://www.nwhm.org/

National Zoo
http://nationalzoo.si.edu/

Native American Facts for Kids: Resources on American Indians for Children and Teachers
http://www.native-languages.org/kids.htm

New England Aquarium
http://www.neaq.org/index.php

New York Aquarium
http://www.nyaquarium.com/

Newseum
http://www.newseum.org/

Omaha's Henry Doorly Zoo
http://www.omahazoo.com/

Philadelphia Museum of Art
http://www.philamuseum.org/

Philadelphia Zoo
http://www2.philadelphiazoo.org/

Plimoth Plantation
http://www.plimoth.org/

Redwood National and State Parks
http://www.nps.gov/redw

Rocky Mountain National Park
http://www.nps.gov/romo

Saint Louis Art Museum
http://www.slam.org/

San Diego Zoo
http://www.sandiegozoo.com/

San Francisco Museum of Modern Art
http://www.sfmoma.org/

Shedd Aquarium
http://www.sheddaquarium.org/

Smithsonian Education
http://www.smithsonianeducation.org/

Smithsonian: Science and Technology
http://www.si.edu/Encyclopedia_SI/science_and_technology/

Space Center Houston
http://www.spacecenter.org/

Tennessee Aquarium
http://www.tennis.org/

United States Holocaust Memorial Museum
http://www.ushmm.org/

University of California Museum of Paleontology
http://www.ucmp.berkeley.edu/

The White House Historical Association
http://www.whitehousehistory.org/

Yellowstone National Park
http://www.nps.gov/yell

Yosemite National Park
http://www.nps.gov/yose

Zion National Park
http://www.nps.gov/zion

Unit 3

Week		Vocabulary	Differentiated Spelling
1	When I Went to the Library	weekdays slithered genuine apologize harmless ambulance	**APPROACHING** dirty, purse, birth, curl, nurse, purr, person, shirt, worse, hurl, twirl, third, herb, turkey, turns, surf, perfect, serve, learn, pearl **ON LEVEL** dirty, purse, birth, curl, curve, curb, **person**, shirt, worse, hurl, twirl, swirl, herb, turkey, turnip, purpose, blurred, sternly, serpent, pearl **BEYOND** squirming, purse, birthmark, superbly, curved, curbed, further, whirlwind, permit, hurl, dangerous, swirl, herbs, turkey, turnip, purpose, blurred, sternly, serpent, pearl
2	Dear Mrs. LaRue	neglected appreciated misunderstood desperate endured obedience	**APPROACHING** hour, lambs, knew, wrist, knee, thumbs, honest, answer, knot, plumber, honor, known, combs, wrap, knives, climb, knob, crumb, heir, write **ON LEVEL** hour, lambs, knew, wrench, kneel, thumbs, honest, answer, **honesty**, plumber, honor, **known**, combs, wrapper, knives, doubt, knead, wriggle, heir, wrinkle **BEYOND** autumn, lambs, knowledge, wrench, kneel, thumbs, honesty, wreckage, resign, plumber, honorable, knapsack, combs, wrapper, knives, doubt, knead, wriggle, heiress, wrinkle
3	Words Add Up to Success	dismiss interact motivate conceived definition	**APPROACHING** center, once, dance, germs, nice, bridge, change, chance, cement, cage, strange, police, urge, orange, ounce, ginger, pages, arrange, sponge, gyms **ON LEVEL** center, once, **scene**, germs, spice, bridge, badge, circus, cement, glance, strange, police, certain, orange, ounce, ginger, wedge, arrange, sponge, village **BEYOND** officers, general, difference, passage, decision, exchange, badge, circus, cement, audience, manager, introduce, certain, orange, ounce, gingerly, scene, arranged, languages, villagers

Key Spelling words in bold appear in the selection.

 LOG ON For additional spelling activities, go to www.macmillanmh.com.

Unit 3 (continued)

Week		Vocabulary	Differentiated Spelling
4	**Ranita, The Frog Princess**	selfish cranky commotion exasperated specialty famished	**APPROACHING** clams, mints, props, friends, dresses, parents, caves, glasses, hobbies, tigers, couches, arrows, holidays, babies, ranches, flowers, mistakes, berries, mosses, armies **ON LEVEL** clams, mints, props, arches, dresses, parents, caves, glasses, hobbies, engines, couches, arrows, enemies, babies, ranches, patches, mistakes, **supplies**, mosses, armies **BEYOND** tipis, mints, belongings, arches, dresses, parents, batteries, trophies, hobbies, engines, couches, arrows, enemies, babies, ranches, patches, mistakes, supplies, mosses, armies
5	**Me and Uncle Romie**	skyscrapers collage barbecue glorious strutting swarms	**APPROACHING** fishbowl, lookout, backyard, desktop, campfire, overhead, waterproof, grandparent, railroad, snowstorm, classroom, airport, bedroom, anyway, newborn, footstep, yourself, overdo, driveway, undertake **ON LEVEL** fishbowl, lookout, backyard, desktop, campfire, overhead, waterproof, **grandparent**, railroad, snowstorm, **loudspeaker**, bookcase, **bedroom**, blindfold, newborn, bedspread, yourself, overdo, clothesline, undertake **BEYOND** fishbowl, courtroom, backyard, heartbroken, campfire, overhead, waterproof, grandparent, teammate, snowstorm, loudspeaker, bookcase, skateboard, blindfold, eyesight, bedspread, undergrowth, gentleman, clothesline, undertake

---

Key Spelling words in bold appear in the selection.

 LOG ON For additional spelling activities, go to **www.macmillanmh.com**.

Word List **T15**

Language Transfers:

The Interaction Between English and Students' Primary Languages

Dr. Jana Echevarria
California State University, Long Beach

Dr. Donald Bear
University of Nevada, Reno

It is important for teachers to understand why English Language Learners (ELLs) use alternative pronunciations for some English words. Many English sounds do not exist or transfer to other languages, so English Learners may lack the auditory acuity to "hear" these English sounds and have difficulty pronouncing them. These students are not accustomed to positioning their mouth in a way the sound requires. The charts that appear on the following pages show that there is variation among languages, with some languages having more sounds in common and thus greater transfer to English than others.

For example, an English speaker may be able to pronounce the /r/ in the Spanish word *pero* ("but"), but not the /rr/ trill in *perro* ("dog"). The English speaker may also lack the auditory acuity to detect and the ability to replicate the tonal sounds of some Chinese words. Similarly, a Vietnamese speaker may have difficulty pronouncing /th/ in words such as *thin* or *thanks*.

Further, English Language Learners make grammatical errors due to interference from their native languages. In Spanish, the adjective follows the noun, so often English Language Learners say "the girl pretty" instead of "the pretty girl." While English changes the verb form with a change of subject (*I walk. She walks.*), some Asian languages keep the verb form constant across subjects. Adding /s/ to the third person may be difficult for some English Language Learners. Students may know the grammatical rule, but applying it consistently may be difficult, especially in spoken English.

When working with English Language Learners, you should also be aware of sociocultural factors that affect pronunciation. Students may retain an accent because it marks their social identity. Speakers of other languages may feel at a social distance from members of the dominant English-speaking culture.

English Language Learners improve their pronunciation in a non-threatening atmosphere in which participation is encouraged. Opportunities to interact with native English speakers provide easy access to language models and give English Language Learners practice using English. However, students should not be forced to participate. Pressure to perform—or to perform in a certain way—can inhibit participation. In any classroom, teacher sensitivity to pronunciation differences contributes to a more productive learning environment.

Phonics, word recognition, and spelling are influenced by what students know about the sounds, word structure, and spelling in their primary languages. For example, beginning readers who speak Spanish and are familiar with its spelling will often spell short *o* with an *a*, a letter that in Spanish makes the short *o* sound. Similarly, English Language Learners who are unaccustomed to English consonant digraphs and blends (e.g., /ch/ and *s*-blends) spell /ch/ as *sh* because /sh/ is the sound they know that is closest to /ch/. Students learn about the way pronunciation influences their reading and spelling, beginning with large contrasts among sounds, then they study the finer discriminations. As vocabulary advances, the meaning of words leads students to the sound contrasts. For example, *shoe* and *chew* may sound alike initially, but meaning indicates otherwise. Students' reading and discussions of what they read advances their word knowledge as well as their knowledge in all language and literacy systems, including phonics, pronunciation, grammar, and vocabulary.

Phonics Transfers:

Sound Transfers

This chart indicates areas where a positive transfer of sounds and symbols occurs for English Language Learners from their native languages into English. This symbol (✔) identifies a positive transfer. "Approximate" indicates that the sound is similar.

Sound Transfers	Spanish	Cantonese	Vietnamese	Hmong	Korean	Khmer
Consonants						
/b/ as in bat	✔	approximate	approximate	approximate	approximate	✔
/k/ as in cake, kitten, peck	✔	✔	✔	✔	✔	✔
/d/ as in dog	✔	approximate	approximate	✔	approximate	✔
/f/ as in farm	✔	✔	✔	✔		
/g/ as in girl	✔	approximate	✔	approximate	approximate	
/h/ as in ham	✔	✔	✔	✔	✔	approximate
/j/ as in jet, page, ledge		approximate	approximate		approximate	
/l/ as in lion	✔	✔	✔	✔	✔	
/m/ as in mat	✔	✔	✔	✔	✔	✔
/n/ as in night	✔	✔	✔	✔	✔	✔
/p/ as in pen	✔	✔	✔	approximate	✔	✔
/kw/ as in queen	✔	approximate	✔		✔	✔
/r/ as in rope	approximate					✔
/s/ as in sink, city	✔	✔	✔	✔	✔	approximate
/t/ as in ton	✔	✔	approximate	approximate	✔	✔
/v/ as in vine	✔		✔	✔		
/w/ as in wind	✔	✔			✔	✔
/ks/ as in six	✔				✔	✔
/y/ as in yak	✔	✔		✔	✔	✔
/z/ as in zebra			✔			
Digraphs						
/ch/ as in cheek, patch	✔	approximate		✔	✔	✔
/sh/ as in shadow			✔	✔	✔	
/hw/ as in whistle					✔	✔
/th/ as in path	approximate		approximate			
/TH/ as in that	approximate					
/ng/ as in sting	✔	✔	✔	✔	✔	approximate

Sound Transfers	Spanish	Cantonese	Vietnamese	Hmong	Korean	Khmer
Short Vowels						
/a/ as in cat	approximate		approximate	✔	✔	
/e/ as in net	✔	approximate	approximate		✔	
/i/ as in kid	approximate	approximate			✔	
/o/ as in spot	approximate	approximate	approximate	approximate	approximate	✔
/u/ as in cup	approximate	approximate	✔		✔	✔
Long Vowels						
/ā/ as in lake, nail, bay	✔	approximate	approximate	approximate	✔	✔
/ē/ as in bee, meat, cranky	✔	approximate	✔	✔	✔	✔
/ī/ as in kite, tie, light, dry	✔	approximate	✔	✔	✔	✔
/ō/ as in home, road, row	✔	approximate	approximate		✔	
/ū/ as in dune, fruit, blue	✔	approximate	✔	✔	✔	✔
/yü/ as in mule, cue	✔	approximate			✔	
r-Controlled Vowels						
/är/ as in far	approximate	approximate				
/ôr/ as in corn	approximate	approximate				
/ûr/ as in stern, bird, suburb	approximate	approximate				
/âr/ as in air, bear						
/îr/ as in deer, ear						
Variant Vowels						
/oi/ as in boil, toy	✔	approximate	approximate		✔	✔
/ou/ as in loud, down	✔	approximate	✔	approximate	✔	✔
/ô/ as in law	approximate	✔	✔	approximate	approximate	✔
/ô/ as in laundry	approximate	approximate	✔	approximate	approximate	✔
/ôl/ as in salt, call	approximate	approximate			approximate	✔
/ü/ as in moon, drew	✔	approximate	approximate	✔	✔	✔
/u̇/ as in look		approximate	approximate		approximate	✔
/ə/ as in askew			approximate		✔	

Phonics Transfers:
Sound-Symbol Match

Sound-Symbol Match	Spanish	Cantonese	Vietnamese	Hmong	Korean	Khmer
Consonants						
/b/ as in bat	✔		✔			
/k/ as in cake	✔		✔			
/k/ as in kitten	✔		✔	✔		
/k/ as in peck						
/d/ as in dog	✔		✔	✔		
/f/ as in farm	✔			✔		
/g/ as in girl	✔		✔			
/h/ as in ham			✔	✔		
/j/ as in jet, page, ledge						
/l/ as in lion	✔		✔	✔		
/m/ as in mat	✔		✔	✔		
/n/ as in night	✔		✔	✔		
/p/ as in pen	✔		✔	✔		
/kw/ as in queen			✔			
/r/ as in rope	approximate					
/s/ as in sink, city	✔		✔			
/t/ as in ton	✔		✔	✔		
/v/ as in vine	✔		✔	✔		
/w/ as in wind	✔					
/ks/ as in six	✔					
/y/ as in yak	✔			✔		
/z/ as in zebra						
Digraphs						
/ch/ as in cheek, patch	✔					
/sh/ as in shadow						
/hw/ as in whistle						
/th/ as in path			✔			
/TH/ as in that						
/ng/ as in sting	✔		✔			
Short Vowels						
/a/ as in cat			✔	✔		
/e/ as in net	✔		✔			
/i/ as in kid						
/o/ as in spot			✔	✔		
/u/ as in cup						

Sound-Symbol Match	Spanish	Cantonese	Vietnamese	Hmong	Korean	Khmer
Long Vowels						
/ā/ as in lake						
/ā/ as in nail						
/ā/ as in bay						
/ē/ as in bee						
/ē/ as in meat						
/ē/ as in cranky						
/ī/ as in kite, tie, light, dry						
/ō/ as in home, road, row						
/ū/ as in dune			✔	✔		
/ū/ as in fruit, blue						
/yü/ as in mule, cue						
r-Controlled Vowels						
/är/ as in far	✔					
/ôr/ as in corn	✔					
/ûr/ as in stern	✔					
/ûr/ as in bird, suburb						
/âr/ as in air, bear						
/îr/ as in deer, ear						
Variant Vowels						
/oi/ as in boil	✔		✔			
/oi/ as in toy	✔					
/ou/ as in loud						
/ou/ as in down						
/ô/ as in law						
/ô/ as in laundry						
/ôl/ as in salt	✔					
/ôl/ as in call						
/ü/ as in moon, drew						
/ù/ as in look						
/ə/ as in askew						

How to Use the Phonics Transfer Charts

To read and speak fluently in English, English Language Learners need to master a wide range of phonemic awareness, phonics, and word study skills. The Phonics Transfer Charts are designed to help you anticipate and understand possible student errors in pronouncing or perceiving English sounds.

1. Highlight Transferrable Skills If the phonics skill transfers from the student's primary language to English, state that during the lesson. In most lessons an English Language Learner feature will indicate which sounds do and do not transfer in specific languages.

2. Preteach Non-Transferrable Skills Prior to teaching a phonics lesson, check the chart to determine if the sound and/or spelling transfers from the student's primary language into English. If it does not, preteach the sound and spelling during Small Group time. Focus on articulation, using the backs of the small **Sound-Spelling Cards**, and the minimal contrast activities provided.

3. Provide Additional Practice and Time If the skill does NOT transfer from the student's primary language into English, the student will require more time and practice mastering the sound and spellings. Continue to review the phonics skill during Small Group time in upcoming weeks until the student has mastered it. Use the additional resources, such as the extra decodable stories in the **Teacher's Resource Book**, to provide oral and silent reading practice.

Teaching Supports for Students Transitioning from Spanish to English

The **Sound-Spelling Cards** have been created to assist you in working with English Language Learners. For example:

1. The dotted border on many of the cards indicates that the sound transfers from Spanish to English. On these cards, the same image is used in both English and Spanish (e.g., *camel/camello*). Therefore, students learning the sound in Spanish can easily transfer that knowledge to English.

2. Students whose primary language is not English will need additional articulation support to pronounce and perceive non-transferrable English sounds. Use the articulation photos on the backs of the Sound-Spelling Cards and the student-friendly descriptions of how to form these sounds during phonics lessons.

Sound-Spelling Cards

Transfer Skill Support

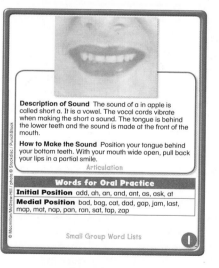

Articulation Support

Grammar Transfers:
Grammatical Form

This chart can be used to address common mistakes that some English Language Learners make when they transfer grammatical forms from their native languages into English.

Grammatical Form	Transfer Mistakes in English	Native Language	Cause of Difficulty
Nouns			
Plural Marker -s	**Forgets plural marker -s** *I have 3 sister.*	Cantonese, Haitian Creole, Hmong, Korean, Vietnamese, Khmer	Native language does not use a plural marker.
Countable and Uncountable Nouns	**Confuses countable and uncountable nouns** *the homeworks* or *the informations*	Haitian Creole, Spanish	Countable and uncountable nouns are different in English and native language.
Possessives	**Uses prepositions to describe possessives** *the book of my brother* as opposed to *my brother's book*	Haitian Creole, Hmong, Spanish, Vietnamese	Possession is often described using a prepositional phrase.
	Avoids using 's *dog my father* as opposed to *my father's dog*	Haitian Creole, Vietnamese, Khmer	A noun follows the object in the native language.
Articles			
	Consistently omits articles *He has book. They want dog not cat.*	Cantonese, Haitian Creole, Hmong, Korean, Vietnamese, Khmer	There is no article in the native language or no difference between *the* and *a*.
	Overuses articles *The English is difficult. The soccer is popular in the Europe.*	Haitian Creole, Hmong, Spanish	Some languages use articles that are omitted in English.
a/an	**Mistakes one for a/an** *She is one nurse.*	Haitian Creole, Hmong, Vietnamese	The native language either does not use articles or uses articles differently.
Pronouns			
Gender-Specific Pronouns	**Uses pronouns with the inappropriate gender** *He is my sister.*	Cantonese, Haitian Creole, Hmong, Korean, Spanish, Khmer	The third person pronoun in the native language is gender free, or the personal pronoun is omitted.
	Uses inappropriate gender, particularly with neutral nouns *The day is sunny. She is beautiful.*	Spanish	Nouns have feminine or masculine gender in the native language, and the gender may be carried over into English.

Grammatical Form	Transfer Mistakes in English	Native Language	Cause of Difficulty
Pronouns			
Object Pronouns	**Confuses subject and object pronouns** *Her talks to me.*	Cantonese, Hmong, Khmer	The same pronoun form is used for subject and object in the native language.
	Omits object pronouns *That girl is very rude, so nobody likes.*	Korean, Vietnamese	The native language does not use direct objects.
Pronoun and Number Agreement	**Uses the wrong number for pronouns** *I saw many red birds. It was pretty.*	Cantonese, Korean	The native language does not require number agreement.
Subject Pronouns	**Omits subject pronouns** *Mom isn't home. Is at work.*	Korean, Spanish	Subject pronouns may be dropped because in the native language the verb ending gives information about the number and/or gender.
Pronouns in Clauses	**Omits pronouns in clauses** *If don't do homework, they will not learn.*	Cantonese, Vietnamese	The native language does not need a subject in the subordinate clause.
Pronouns and Nouns	**Overuses pronouns with nouns** *This school, it very good.*	Hmong, Vietnamese	This is popular in speech in some languages. The speaker mentions a topic, then makes a comment about it.
	Avoids pronouns and repeats nouns *Carla visits her sister every Sunday, and Carla makes a meal.*	Korean, Vietnamese	In the native language, the speaker repeats nouns and does not use pronouns.
Pronoun *one*	**Omits the pronoun *one*** *I saw two dogs, and I like the small.*	Spanish	Adjectives can stand alone in the native language, but English requires a noun or *one*.
Possessive Forms	**Confuses possessive forms** *The book is my.*	Cantonese, Hmong, Vietnamese	Cantonese and Hmong speakers tend to omit the final *n* sound, which may create confusion between *my* and *mine*.

Grammar Transfers:
Grammatical Form

Grammatical Form	Transfer Mistakes in English	Native Language	Cause of Difficulty
Verbs			
Present Tense	**Omits -s in present tense, third person agreement** *He like pizza.*	Cantonese, Haitian Creole, Hmong, Korean, Vietnamese, Khmer	Subject-verb agreement is not used in the native language.
Irregular Verbs	**Has problems with irregular subject-verb agreement** *Tom and Sue has a new car.*	Cantonese, Hmong, Korean, Khmer	Verbs' forms do not change to show the number of the subject in the native language.
Inflectional Endings	**Omits tense markers** *I study English yesterday.*	Cantonese, Haitian Creole, Hmong, Korean, Vietnamese, Khmer	The native language does not use inflectional endings to change verb tense.
Present and Future Tenses	**Incorrectly uses the present tense for the future tense** *I go next week.*	Cantonese, Korean	The native language may use the present tense to imply the future tense.
Negative Statements	**Omits helping verbs in negative statements** *Sue no coming to school.*	Cantonese, Korean, Spanish	The native language does not use helping verbs in negative statements.
Present-Perfect Tense	**Avoids the present-perfect tense** *Marcos live here for three months.*	Haitian Creole, Vietnamese	The native language does not use the present-perfect verb form.
Past-Continuous Tense	**Uses the past-continuous tense for recurring action in the past** *When I was young, I was talking a lot.*	Korean, Spanish	In the native language, the past-continuous tense is used but in English the expression *used to* or the simple past tense is used.
Main Verb	**Omits the main verb** *Talk in class not good.*	Cantonese	Cantonese does not require an infinitive marker when using a verb as a noun. Speakers may confuse the infinitive for the main verb.
Main Verbs in Clauses	**Uses two or more main verbs in one clause without any connectors** *I took a book went studied at the library.*	Hmong	In Hmong, verbs can be used consecutively without conjunctions or punctuation.
Linking Verbs	**Omits the linking verb** *He hungry.*	Cantonese, Haitian Creole, Hmong, Vietnamese, Khmer	In some languages, *be* is implied in the adjective form. In other languages, the concept is expressed with a verb.
Helping Verb in Passive Voice	**Omits the helping verb in the passive voice** *The homework done.*	Cantonese, Vietnamese	In Cantonese and Vietnamese, the passive voice does not require a helping verb.

Grammatical Form	Transfer Mistakes in English	Native Language	Cause of Difficulty
Verbs			
Passive Voice	**Avoids the passive voice** *They speak English here.* *One speaks English here.* *English is spoken here.*	Haitian Creole	The passive voice does not exist in the native language.
Transitive Verbs	**Confuses transitive and intransitive verbs** *The child broke.* *The child broke <u>the plate</u>.*	Cantonese, Korean, Spanish	Verbs that require a direct object differ between English and the native language.
Phrasal Verbs	**Confuses related phrasal verbs** *I ate at the apple.* *I ate up the apple.*	Korean, Spanish	Phrasal verbs are not used in the native language, and there is often confusion over their meaning.
Have* and *be	**Uses *have* instead of *be*** *I have thirst.* *He has right.*	Spanish	Spanish and English have different uses for *have* and *be*.
Adjectives			
Word Order	**Places adjectives after nouns** *I saw a car red.*	Haitian Creole, Hmong, Spanish, Vietnamese, Khmer	Nouns often precede adjectives in the native language.
	Consistently places adjectives after nouns *This is a lesson new.*	Cantonese, Korean	Adjectives always follow nouns in the native language.
***-er* and *-est* Endings**	**Avoids *-er* and *-est* endings** *I am more old than you.*	Hmong, Korean, Spanish, Khmer	The native language shows comparative and superlative forms with separate words.
***-ing* and *-ed* Endings**	**Confuses *-ing* and *-ed* forms** *Math is bored.*	Cantonese, Korean, Spanish, Khmer	Adjectives in the native language do not have active and passive meanings.
Adverbs			
Adjectives and Adverbs	**Uses an adjective where an adverb is needed** *Talk quiet.*	Haitian Creole, Hmong, Khmer	Adjectives and adverb forms are interchangeable in the native language.
Word Order	**Places adverbs before verbs** *He quickly ran.* *He ran quickly.*	Cantonese, Korean	Adverbs usually come before verbs in the native language, and this tendency is carried over into English.
Prepositions			
	Omits prepositions *I like come school.*	Cantonese	Cantonese does not use prepositions the way that English does.

How to Use the Grammar Transfer Charts

The grammar of many languages differs widely from English. For example, a student's primary language may use a different word order than English, may not use parts of speech in the same way, or may use different verb tenses. The Grammar Transfer Charts are designed to help you anticipate and understand possible student errors in speaking and writing standard English. With all grammar exercises, the emphasis is on oral communication, both as a speaker and listener.

1. **Highlight Transferrable Skills** If the grammar skill transfers from the student's primary language to English, state that during the lesson. In many lessons an English Language Learner feature will indicate which skills do and do not transfer.

2. **Preteach Non-Transferrable Skills** Prior to teaching a grammar lesson, check the chart to determine if the skill transfers from the student's primary language into English. If it does not, preteach the skill during Small Group time. Provide sentence frames and ample structured opportunities to use the skill in spoken English. Students need to talk, talk, and talk some more to master these skills.

3. **Provide Additional Practice and Time** If the skill does NOT transfer from the student's primary language into English, the student will require more time and practice mastering it. Continue to review the skill during Small Group time. Use the additional resources, such as the grammar lessons in the **Intervention Kit** (K–3) or review lessons, in upcoming weeks.

4. **Use Contrastive Analysis** Tell students when a skill does not transfer and include contrastive analysis work to make the student aware of how to correct their speaking and writing for standard English. For example, when a student uses an incorrect grammatical form, write the student sentence on a **WorkBoard**. Then write the correct English form underneath. Explain the difference between the student's primary language and English. Have the student correct several other sentences using this skill, such as sentences in their Writer's Notebooks.

5. **Increase Writing and Speaking Opportunities** Increase the amount of structured writing and speaking opportunities for students needing work on specific grammatical forms. Sentence starters and paragraph frames, such as those found in the lessons, are ideal for both written and oral exercises.

6. **Focus on Meaning** Always focus on the meanings of sentences in all exercises. As they improve and fine-tune their English speaking and writing skills, work with students on basic comprehension of spoken and written English.

To help students move to the next level of language acquisition and master English grammatical forms, recast their responses during classroom discussions or provide additional language for them to use as they respond further. Provide leveled-language sentence frames orally or in writing for students to use as they respond to questions and prompts. Below are samples.

English Language Learner Response Chart

Beginning (will respond by pointing or saying one word answers)	**Sample Frames** (simple, short sentences) *I see a _____.* *This is a _____.* *I like the _____.*
Early Intermediate (will respond with phrases or simple sentences)	**Sample Frames** (simple sentences with adjectives and adverbs added, and compound subjects or predicates) *I see a _____ _____.* *The _____ animal is _____.* *There are _____ and _____.*
Intermediate (will respond with simple sentences and limited academic language)	**Sample Frames** (harder sentences with simple phrases in consistent patterns; some academic language included) *The animal's prey is _____ because _____.* *The main idea is _____ because _____.* *He roamed the park so that _____.*
Early Advanced (will begin to use more sophisticated sentences and some academic language)	**Sample Frames** (complex sentences with increased academic language, beginning phrases and clauses, and multiple-meaning words) *When the violent storm hit, _____.* *As a result of the revolution, the army_____.* *Since most endangered animals are _____, they _____.*
Advanced (will have mastered some more complex sentence structures and is increasing the amount of academic language used)	Use the questions and prompts provided in the lessons for the whole group. Provide additional support learning and using academic language. These words are boldfaced throughout the lessons and sentence starters are often provided.

Cognates

Cognates are words in two languages that look alike and have the same or similar meaning (e.g., *school/escuela, telephone/teléfono*) and can be helpful resources for English Language Learners. This list identifies some Spanish cognates for the academic language used during the lessons.

Students must also be aware of false cognates—words that look similar in two languages, but have different meanings, such as *soap* in English and *sopa* (meaning *soup*) in Spanish.

accent	*acento*	**context**	*contexto*
action	*acción*	**contrast**	*contrastar*
action verb	*verbo de acción*	**definition**	*definición*
adjective	*adjetivo*	**demonstrative**	*demostrativo*
adverb	*adverbio*	**denotation**	*denotación*
alphabetical order	*orden alfabético*	**description**	*descripción*
analogy	*analogía*	**dialogue**	*diálogo*
analyze	*analizar*	**dictionary**	*diccionario*
antecedent	*antecedente*	**direct**	*directo*
antonym	*antónimo*	**effect**	*efecto*
apostrophe	*apóstrofe*	**evaluate**	*evaluar*
article	*artículo*	**event**	*evento*
author	*autor*	**example**	*ejemplo*
cause	*causa*	**exclamation**	*exclamación*
classify	*clasificar*	**family**	*familia*
combine	*combinar*	**fantasy**	*fantasía*
compare	*comparar*	**figurative**	*figurativo*
complex	*complejo*	**fragment**	*fragmento*
comprehension	*comprensión*	**future**	*futuro*
conclusion	*conclusión*	**generalization**	*generalización*
confirm	*confirmar*	**generalize**	*generalizar*
conjunction	*conjunción*	**glossary**	*glosario*
connotation	*connotación*	**Greek**	*Griego*
consonant	*consonante*	**homophone**	*homófono*

idea	*idea*	**prefix**	*prefijo*
identify	*identificar*	**preposition**	*preposición*
illustration	*ilustración*	**prepositional**	*preposicional*
indirect	*indirecto*	**present**	*presente*
introduction	*introducción*	**problem**	*problema*
irregular	*irregular*	**pronunciation**	*pronunciación*
language	*lenguaje*	**punctuation**	*puntuación*
Latin	*Latín*	**reality**	*realidad*
myth	*mito*	**relationship**	*relación*
negative	*negativo*	**sequence**	*secuencia*
object	*objeto*	**singular**	*singular*
opinion	*opinión*	**solution**	*solución*
order	*orden*	**structure**	*estructura*
origin	*orígen*	**subject**	*sujeto*
paragraph	*párrafo*	**suffix**	*sufijo*
part	*parte*	**syllable**	*sílaba*
perspective	*perspectiva*	**synonym**	*sinónimo*
persuasion	*persuación*	**technique**	*técnica*
phrase	*frase*	**text**	*texto*
plural	*plural*	**theme**	*tema*
possessive adjective	*adjetivo posesivo*	**verb**	*verbo*
predicate	*predicado*	**visualize**	*visualizar*
prediction	*predicción*	**vowel**	*vocal*

ELL ENGLISH LANGUAGE LEARNERS

The **English Language Learners** in your classroom have a variety of backgrounds. An increasing proportion of English Language Learners are born in the United States. Some of these students are just starting school in the primary grades; others are long-term English Language Learners, with underdeveloped academic skills. Some students come from their native countries with a strong educational foundation. The academic skills of these newly arrived students are well developed and parallel the skills of their native English-speaking peers. Other English Learners immigrate to the United States with little academic experience.

These English Learners are not "blank slates." Their oral language proficiency and literacy in their first languages can be used to facilitate literacy development in English. Systematic, explicit, and appropriately scaffolded instruction and sufficient time help English Learners attain English proficiency and meet high standards in core academic subjects.

Beginning

This level of language proficiency is often referred to as the "silent" stage, in which students' receptive skills are engaged. It is important that teachers and peers respect a language learner's initial silence or allow the student to respond in his or her native language. It is often difficult for teachers to identify the level of cognitive development at this stage, due to the limited proficiency in the second language. It is important to realize that these beginning students have a wide range of abilities in their first language. They are able to transfer knowledge and skills from their first language as they develop English and learn grade-level content. Beginning students include those with limited formal schooling: young students just starting school, as well as older students. Other beginning students have had schooling in their native language and are academically parallel to nativeEnglish-speaking peers.

The Beginning Student...

- recognizes English phonemes that correspond to phonemes produced in primary language;
- is able to apply transferable grammar concepts and skills from the primary language;
- initially demonstrates more receptive than productive English skills;
- produces English vocabulary to communicate basic needs in social and academic settings;
- responds by pointing to, nodding, gesturing, acting out, and manipulating objects/pictures;
- speaks in one-or two-word responses as language develops;
- draws pictures and writes letters and sounds being learned.

Early Intermediate

At this level, students are considered more advanced beginning English Learners. They are developing early production skills, but their receptive skills are much more advanced than their speaking ability. At this stage it is critical that the students continue to listen to model speakers.

The Early Intermediate Student...

- recognizes English phonemes that correspond to phonemes produced in primary language;
- is able to apply transferable grammar concepts and skills from the primary language;
- understands more spoken English than the beginning student;
- speaks in one- or two-word utterances;
- may respond with phrases or sentences;
- produces English vocabulary words and phrases to communicate basic needs in social and academic settings;
- begins to ask questions, role-play, and retell;
- begins to use routine expressions;
- demonstrates an internalization of English grammar and usage by recognizing and correcting some errors when speaking and reading aloud;
- increases correct usage of written and oral language conventions.

Intermediate

Students at this level begin to tailor their English language skills to meet communication and learning demands with increasing accuracy. They possess vocabulary and knowledge of grammatical structures that allow them to more fully participate in classroom activities and discussions. They are generally more comfortable producing both spoken and written language.

The Intermediate Student...

- pronounces most English phonemes correctly while reading aloud;
- can identify more details of information that has been presented orally or in writing;
- uses more complex vocabulary and sentences to communicate needs and express ideas;
- uses specific vocabulary learned, including academic language;
- participates more fully in discussions with peers and adults;
- reads and comprehends a wider range of reading materials;
- writes brief narratives and expository texts;
- demonstrates an internalization of English grammar and usage by recognizing and correcting errors when speaking and reading aloud.

Early Advanced

Students at this language proficiency level possess vocabulary and grammar structures that approach those of an English-proficient speaker. These students demonstrate consistent general comprehension of grade-level content that is presented.

The Early Advanced Student...

- applies knowledge of common English morphemes in oral and silent reading;
- understands increasingly more nonliteral social and academic language;
- responds using extensive vocabulary;
- participates in and initiates more extended social conversations with peers and adults;
- communicates orally and in writing with fewer grammatical errors;
- reads with good comprehension a wide range of narrative and expository texts;
- writes using more standard forms of English on various content-area topics;
- becomes more creative and analytical when writing.

Advanced

The student at this language proficiency level communicates effectively with peers and adults in both social and academic situations. Students can understand grade-level text but still need some English language development support, such as preteaching concepts and skills. While the English language proficiency of these students is advanced, some linguistic support for accessing content is still necessary.

The Advanced Student...

- understands increasingly more nonliteral social and academic language;
- responds using extensive vocabulary;
- communicates orally and in writing with infrequent errors;
- creates more complex narratives and expository writing in all content areas.

English Language Learner Profiles
Facilitating Language Growth

Beginning

Student's Behaviors	Teacher's Behaviors	Questioning Techniques
■ Points to or provides other nonverbal responses ■ Actively listens ■ Responds to commands ■ Understands more than he or she can produce	■ Gestures ■ Focuses on conveying meanings and vocabulary development ■ Does not force students to speak ■ Shows visuals and real objects ■ Writes words for students to see ■ Pairs students with more proficient learners ■ Provides speaking and writing frames and models	■ Point to the _____. ■ Find the _____. ■ Put the _____ next to the _____. ■ Do you have the _____? ■ Is this the _____? ■ Who wants the _____?

Early Intermediate

Student's Behaviors	Teacher's Behaviors	Questioning Techniques
■ Speaks in one- or two-word utterances ■ Uses short phrases and simple sentences ■ Listens with greater understanding	■ Asks questions that can be answered by yes/no ■ Asks either/or questions ■ Asks higher-order questions with one-word answers ■ Models correct responses ■ Ensures supportive, low-anxiety environment ■ Does not overtly call attention to grammar errors ■ Asks short "wh" questions	■ Yes/no (Did you like the story?) ■ Either/or (Is this a pencil or a crayon?) ■ One-word responses (Why did the dog hide?) ■ General questions that encourage lists of words (What did you see in the book bag?) ■ Two-word responses (Where did I put the pen?)

Intermediate

Student's Behaviors	Teacher's Behaviors	Questioning Techniques
■ Demonstrates comprehension in a variety of ways ■ Speaks in short phrases or sentences ■ Begins to use language more freely	■ Provides frequent comprehension checks ■ Asks open-ended questions that stimulate language production	■ Why? ■ How? ■ How is this like that? ■ Tell me about _____. ■ Talk about _____. ■ Describe _____. ■ What is in your book bag?

Early Advanced

Student's Behaviors	Teacher's Behaviors	Questioning Techniques
■ Participates in reading and writing activities to acquire information ■ Demonstrates increased levels of accuracy and correctness and is able to express thoughts and feelings ■ Produces language with varied grammatical structures and academic language ■ May experience difficulties in abstract, cognitively demanding subjects	■ Fosters conceptual development and expanded literacy through content ■ Continues to make lessons comprehensible and interactive ■ Teaches thinking and study skills ■ Continues to be alert to individual differences in language and culture	■ What would you recommend/why? ■ How do you think this story will end? ■ What is this story about? ■ What is your favorite part of the story? ■ Describe/compare _____. How are these similar/different? ■ What would happen if _____? ■ Why do you think that? Yes, tell me more about _____.

Fostering Classroom Discussions

Strategies for English Language Learners

One of the most effective ways in which to increase the oral language proficiency of your English Language Learners is to give students many opportunities to do a lot of talking in the classroom. Providing the opportunities and welcoming all levels of participation will motivate students to take part in the class discussions. You can employ a few basic teaching strategies that will encourage the participation of all language proficiency levels of English Language Learners in whole class and small group discussions.

☑ WAIT/DIFFERENT RESPONSES

- Be sure to give students enough time to answer the question.
- Let students know that they can respond in different ways depending on their levels of proficiency. Students can
  - answer in their native language;
  - ask a more proficient ELL speaker to repeat the answer in English;
  - answer with nonverbal cues (pointing to related objects, drawing, or acting out).

> **Teacher:** Where is Charlotte?
>
> **ELL Response:** (Student points to the web in the corner of the barn.)
>
> **Teacher:** Yes. Charlotte is sitting in her web. Let's all point to Charlotte.

☑ REPEAT

- Give positive confirmation to the answers that each English Language Learner offers. If the response is correct, repeat what the student has said in a clear, loud voice and at a slower pace. This validation will motivate other ELLs to participate.

> **Teacher:** How would you describe the faces of the bobcats?
>
> **ELL Response:** They look scared.
>
> **Teacher:** That's right, Silvia. They are scared. Everyone show me your scared face.

☑ REVISE FOR FORM

- Repeating an answer allows you to model the proper form for a response. You can model how to answer in full sentences and use academic language.
- When you repeat the answer, correct any grammar or pronunciation errors.

> **Teacher:** Who are the main characters in the story *Zathura*?
>
> **ELL Response:** Danny and Walter is.
>
> **Teacher:** Yes. Danny and Walter <u>are</u> the main characters. Remember to use the verb <u>are</u> when you are telling about more than one person. Let's repeat the sentence.
>
> **All:** Danny and Walter <u>are</u> the main characters.

☑ REVISE FOR MEANING

- Repeating an answer offers an opportunity to clarify the meaning of a response.

> **Teacher:** Where did the golden feather come from?
>
> **ELL Response:** The bird.
>
> **Teacher:** That's right. The golden feather came from the Firebird.

☑ ELABORATE

- If students give a one-word answer or a nonverbal cue, elaborate on the answer to model fluent speaking and grammatical patterns.
- Provide more examples or repeat the answer using proper academic language.

> **Teacher:** Why is the girls' mother standing with her hands on her hips?
>
> **ELL Response:** She is mad.
>
> **Teacher:** Can you tell me more? Why is she mad?
>
> **ELL Response:** Because the girls are late.
>
> **Teacher:** Ok. What do you think the girls will do?
>
> **ELL Response:** They will promise not to be late again.
>
> **Teacher:** Anyone else have an idea?

☑ ELICIT

- Prompt students to give a more comprehensive response by asking additional questions or guiding them to get to an answer.

> **Teacher:** Listen as I read the caption under the photograph. What information does the caption tell us?
>
> **ELL Response:** It tells about the butterfly.
>
> **Teacher:** What did you find out about the butterfly?
>
> **ELL Response:** It drinks nectar.
>
> **Teacher:** Yes. The butterfly drinks nectar from the flower.

Making the Most of Classroom Conversations

Use all the speaking and listening opportunities in your classroom to observe students' oral language proficiency.

- Response to oral presentations
- Responding to text aloud
- Following directions
- Group projects
- Small Group work
- Informal, social peer discussions
- One-on-one conferences

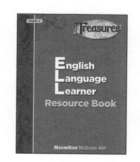

The **English Language Learner Resource Book** provides Speaking and Listening Checklists to help you monitor students' oral language proficiency growth.

Treasures

Support for Students with Dyslexia

Characteristics of Dyslexia

A student with dyslexia is a student who continually struggles with reading and spelling but displays an ability to learn when there are no print materials involved. Even though the student receives the same classroom instruction as most other students, he continues to have difficulties with reading and spelling.

Students identified with dyslexia often have difficulties in the following areas

- reading words in isolation
- decoding nonsense words accurately
- oral reading (slow and inaccurate)
- learning to spell

The difficulties in these areas are usually the result of student's struggles with:

- phonological awareness: segmenting, blending, and manipulating words
- naming letters and pronouncing their sounds.
- phonological memory
- rapid naming of the letters of the alphabet or familiar objects

Effective Instruction

To address the needs of a student with dyslexia, instruction should be delivered in small groups. The instruction should be explicit, intensive, employ multisensory methods, as needed, and be individualized. It should include instruction on:

- phonemic awareness that has students detect, segment, blend and manipulate sounds
- phonics, emphasizing the sound/symbol relationships for decoding and encoding words
- morphology, semantics and syntax
- fluency with patterns of language
- strategies for decoding, encoding, word recognition, fluency and comprehension

Resources:
The International Dyslexia Association Website: www.interdys.org
The Dyslexia Handbook: Procedures Concerning Dyslexia and Related Disorders (Revised 2007) Texas Education Agency, Austin, TX, Publication Number: GE8721001

Treasures Reading and Language Arts Program

Treasures is a scientifically-based core program that offers sequential, explicit, and effective instruction in phonological awareness, phonics, morphology, fluency, vocabulary, and reading comprehension. Students are given many opportunities to practice and review these skills to help prevent reading difficulties before they begin.

Tier 2 INTERVENTION

Weekly Small Group Lessons
Intervention Teacher's Editions

Tier 2 Instruction is provided in weekly small group lessons in the *Treasures* **Teacher's Editions**. These lessons provide targeted instruction in priority skills taught in the week. *Tier 2 Intervention* **Teacher's Editions** provide additional instruction for struggling students in the areas of phonemic awareness, phonics, vocabulary, fluency, and comprehension, grammar and writing.

Tier 3 INTERVENTION

Reading Triumphs
Intervention Program

Reading Triumphs provides intensive instruction. Explicit, sequential lessons delivered through clear instructional routines for all the key components of reading are embedded in the program. The "no assumption instruction" allows for both teacher and student success.

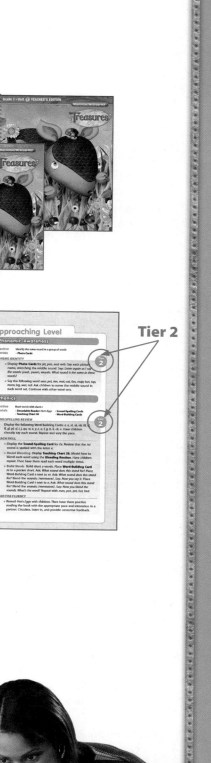

A

B

C

Key 3 = Unit 3

Key 3 = Unit 3

G

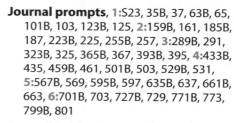

M

U

Index

Key 3 = Unit 3

The publisher gratefully acknowledges permission to reprint the following copyrighted material.

"I Have a Dream," excerpt from speech by Dr. Martin Luther King, Jr. Copyright © 1963 by Writers House. Used by permission of Writers House.

Photography

All photos by Ken Karp or Ken Cavanagh for MacMillan/McGraw-Hill except the following:

iv: (tl, tcl, tcr, ccl, bl, br) Macmillan/McGraw-Hill; (tr) Deborah Attoinese Photography; (ccr, cr) Anthony Colella/Richter-Colella Studios; (cl) Photography by Monet. v: (br) Macmillan/McGraw-Hill; (tl) Doug Martin; (tr) Ferguson & Katzman Photography. xii: (br) Thomas Kitchin & Victoria Hurst/Getty Images. xiii: (br) Macmillan/McGraw-Hill. 267A–B: Photodisc/Fotosearch. 267C: (bl) Michael & Patricia Fogden/Minden; (cl) John Cancalosi/DRK; (l) Daryl Balfour/Getty Images; (tc) Bruce Coleman, Inc/Alamy; (tr) Michael Fogden/Animals Animals. 267I: Courtesy Scholastic. 291B: (b) Gabe Palmer/Corbis. 292A–B: Radius Images/Alamy. 292C: (bl) Royalty-Free/Corbis; (cl) Ulrike Schanz/Animals Animals; (tl) Mary Grace Long/Asia Images/Getty Images; (r) Okapia/Hund/Kramer/Photo Researchers. 292I: Courtesy Scholastic. 326A–B: Digital Vision/Fotosearch. 326I: Courtesy Scholastic. 338A–B: Digital Vision/PunchStock. 338I: Courtesy Scholastic. 367B: (b) Jim Cummings/Corbis. 368A–B: John Anderson/Alamy. 368B: (l) Chris Steele-Perkins/Magnum. 368C: (tl) Getty Images; (cl) Comstock Images/Getty Images; (cr) Photodisc/Getty Images; (r) Frank Chmura/Alamy. 368I: Courtesy Scholastic. 396A–B: Brad Perks Lightscapes/Alamy. 401B–F: Macmillan/McGraw-Hill. 401H: (br) Royalty Free/Corbis. 401L: (br) Dennis MacDonald/age fotostock. Teacher's Notes: (marker) Royalty Free/Corbis; (sharpeners) Pixtal/PunchStock.

Acknowledgments

The publisher gratefully acknowledges permission to reprint the following copyrighted material:

"Adelina's Whales" text and photographs by Richard Sobol. Text and photographs copyright © 2003 by Richard Sobol. Reprinted by permission of Dutton Children's Books, a division of Penguin Books USA Inc.

"The Adventures of Ali Baba Bernstein" by Johanna Hurwitz. Copyright © 1985 by Johanna Hurwitz. Reprinted by permission of William Morrow and Company.

"The Ant and the Grasshopper" retold and illustrated by Amy Lowry Poole. Copyright © 2000 by Amy Lowry Poole. Reprinted by permission of Holiday House.

"The Astronaut and the Onion" by Ann Cameron from GLORIA RISING. Text copyright © 2002 by Ann Cameron. Reprinted by permission of Frances Foster Books, an imprint of Farrar, Straus and Giroux.

"At Home in the Coral Reef" by Katy Muzik, illustrated by Katherine Brown-Wing. Text and illustrations copyright © 1992 by Charlesbridge Publishing. Reprinted by permission.

"Because of Winn-Dixie" by Kate DiCamillo from BECAUSE OF WINN-DIXIE. Copyright © 2000 by Kate DiCamillo. Reprinted by permission of Candlewick Press.

"Brave New Heights" by Monica Kulling from MORE SPICE THAN SUGAR: POEMS ABOUT FEISTY FEMALES compiled by Lillian Morrison. Compilation copyright © 2001 by Lillian Morrison. Reprinted by permission of Marian Reiner from the author.

"The Cricket in Times Square" by George Selden, illustrated by Garth Williams from THE CRICKET IN TIMES SQUARE. Copyright © 1960 by George Selden Thompson and Garth Williams. Reprinted by permission of Farrar, Straus and Giroux. [McGraw-Hill acknowledges the use of a trademark due to illustrator restrictions.]

"Dear Mrs. LaRue" written and illustrated by Mark Teague. Copyright © 2002 by Mark Teague. Reprinted by permission of Scholastic Press, a division of Scholastic, Inc.

"How Ben Franklin Stole the Lightning" by Rosalyn Schanzer. Copyright © 2003 by Rosalyn Schanzer. Reprinted by permission of HarperCollins Publishers.

"I Love the Look of Words" by Maya Angelou from SOUL LOOKS BACK IN WONDER. Copyright © 1993 by Tom Feelings. Reprinted by permission of Dial Books, a division of Penguin Books USA Inc.

"Ima and The Great Texas Ostrich Race" by Margaret Olivia McManis, illustrated by Bruce Dupree. Text copyright © 2002 by Margaret McManis. Illustrations copyright © 2002 by Bruce Dupree. Reprinted by permission of Eakin Press/A Division of Sunbelt Media, Inc.

"Leah's Pony" by Elizabeth Friedrich, illustrated by Michael Garland. Text copyright © 1996 by Elizabeth Friedrich. Illustrations © 1996 by Michael Garland. Reprinted by permission of Boyds Mills Press.

"The Life and Times of the Ant" by Charles Micucci from THE LIFE AND TIMES OF THE ANT. Copyright © 2003 by Charles Micucci. Reprinted by permission of Houghton Mifflin Company.

"Light Bulb" and "Lightning Bolt" by Joan Bransfield Graham from FLICKER FLASH. Text copyright © 1999 by Joan Bransfield Graham. Reprinted by permission of Houghton Mifflin Company.

"Me and Uncle Romie" by Claire Hartfield, paintings by Jerome Lagarrigue. Text copyright © 2002 by Claire Hartfield, paintings copyright © 2002 by Jerome Lagarrigue. Reprinted by permission of Dial Books, a division of Penguin Books USA Inc.

"Mighty Jackie: The Strike-Out Queen" by Marissa Moss, illustrated by C. F. Payne. Text copyright © 2004 by Marissa Moss, illustrations copyright © 2004 by C. F. Payne. Reprinted by permission of Simon & Schuster Books for Young Readers.

"Mountains and plains" and "No sky at all" from AN INTRODUCTION TO HAIKU: AN ANTHOLOGY OF POEMS AND POETS FROM BASHŌ TO SHIKI. Copyright © 1958 by Harold G. Henderson. Reprinted by permission of Doubleday Anchor Books, a Division of Doubleday & Company, Inc.

"My Brother Martin: A Sister Remembers, Growing Up with the Rev. Dr. Martin Luther King, Jr." by Christine King Farris, illustrated by Chris Soentpiet. Text copyright © 2003 by Christine King Farris, illustrations copyright © 2003 by Chris Soentpiet. Reprinted by permission of Simon & Schuster Books for Young Readers.

"My Brothers' Flying Machine" by Jane Yolen, paintings by Jim Burke. Text copyright © 2003 by Jane Yolen, illustrations copyright © 2003 by Jim Burke. Reprinted by permission of Little, Brown and Company.

"My Diary from Here to There" story by Amada Irma Pérez, illustrations by Maya Christina Gonzalez from MY DIARY FROM HERE TO THERE. Story copyright © 2002 by Amada Irma Pérez, illustrations copyright © 2002 by Maya Christina Gonzalez. Reprinted by permission of Children's Book Press.

"Mystic Horse" by Paul Goble. Copyright © 2003 by Paul Goble. Reprinted by permission of HarperCollins Publishers.

"The New Kid" from AT THE CRACK OF THE BAT: Baseball Poems compiled by Lillian Morrison, illustrated by Steve Cieslawski. Text copyright © 1992 by Lillian Morrison. Illustrations copyright © 1992 by Steve Cieslawski. Reprinted by permission of Hyperion Books for Children.

"Roadrunner's Dance" by Rudolfo Anaya, pictures by David Diaz. Text copyright © 2000 by Rudolfo Anaya, illustrations copyright © 2000 by David Diaz. Reprinted by permission of Hyperion Books for Children.

"Snowflake Bentley" by Jacqueline Briggs Martin, illustrated by Mary Azarian. Text copyright © 1998 by Jacqueline Briggs Martin, illustrations copyright © 1998 by Mary Azarian. Reprinted by permission of Houghton Mifflin Company.

"The snow is melting" and " Winter solitude" from THE ESSENTIAL HAIKU: VERSIONS OF BASHŌ, BUSON, AND ISSA. Introduction and selection copyright © 1994 by Robert Hass. Unless otherwise noted, all translations copyright © 1994 by Robert Hass. Reprinted by permission of The Ecco Press.

Excerpt from "So Long, It's Been Good to Know Yuh." Words and music by Woody Guthrie. www.woodyguthrie.org Copyright © 1940 (Renewed), 1950 (Renewed), 1951 (Renewed) by TRO-Folk. Reprinted by permission of The Richmond Organization (TRO).

"A Walk in the Desert" by Rebecca L. Johnson with illustrations by Phyllis V. Saroff from A WALK IN THE DESERT. Text copyright © 2001 by Rebecca L. Johnson, illustrations copyright © 2001 by Phyllis V. Saroff. Reprinted by permission of Carolrhoda Books, Inc.

"When I Went to the Library" by Ken Roberts from WHEN I WENT TO THE LIBRARY edited by Debora Pearson. Copyright © 2001 by Ken Roberts. Reprinted by permission of Groundwood Books/Douglas & McIntyre.

"Wild Horses: Black Hills Sanctuary" by Cris Peterson, photographs by Alvis Upitis. Text copyright © 2003 by Cris Peterson, photographs copyright © 2003 by Alvis Upitis. Reprinted by permission of Boyds Mills Press, Inc.

ILLUSTRATIONS

Cover Illustration: Gloria Domingo Manuel.

10–31: Maya Christina Gonzalez. 40–41: Ginger Nielson. 42–59: Brian Biggs. 60–63: Olwyn Whelan. 65: Ken Bowser. 80: Kim Johnson. 82–97: Anna Rich. 120–121: Robert Casilla. 125: Viviana Diaz. 140–155: Chris Soentpiet. 166–183: C.F. Payne. 184–185: Steve Cieslawski. 220–223: Ande Cook. 230–251: Paul Goble. 258–259: Darryl Ligasan. 270: Ann Boyajian. 272–285: Nicole Wong. 296–319: Mark Teague. 330: Dean Macadam. 340–341: David LaFleur. 342–361: Renato Alarcão. 362: Wendy Born Hollander. 363: (tr)(m) Renato Alarcão; (bl)(cr) Wendy Born Hollander. 364: (t) Renato Alarcão; (tr)(bl) Wendy Born Hollander. 365: (bkgd) Renato Alarcão; (insets) Wendy Born Hollander. 372–391: Jerome Lagarrigue. 396–397: Susan Swan. 408–409: Loretta Krupinski. 410–429: Garth Williams. 433: Argosy. 440–455: Charles Micucci. 456–459: Amy Lowry Poole. 465: Bridget Starr Taylor. 476–477: James Bentley. 478–497: Bruce Dupree. 508–525: Jim Burke. 527: Jim Burke. 528–529: Bandelin-Dacey Studios. 532–533: Bill Cigliano. 534–535: Argosy. 548: Laura Westlund. 550–559: Phyllis V. Saroff. 574–595: David Diaz. 614–631: Katherine Brown-Wing. 632–635: David Groff. 658: Richard Sobol. 660–661: Jesse Reisch. 664–665: Fabricio Vandenbroeck. 666–667: Marion Eldrige. 676–677: Stacey Schuett. 678–697: Michael Garland. 706–707: Greg Shed. 708–723: Ying-Hwa Hu & Cornelius Van

832

Wright. 746–769: Mary Azarian. 770–771: Tina Fong. 778–797: Rosalyn Schanzer. 802–803: Stacey Schuett. 804: Paul Mirocha.

PHOTOGRAPHY

iv: Purestock/SuperStock. v: (t) Jeff Greenberg/PhotoEdit; (b) © 2005 Twentieth Century Fox. All rights reserved. vi: Kayte M. Deioma/PhotoEdit. vii: (t) Brian Bahr/Getty Images. viii: Masterfile. ix: Masterfile. x: Bob Daemmrich/PhotoEdit. xi: Bill Heinsohn/Alamy. xii: (tl) Lon Lauber/OSF/Animal Animals/Earth Scenes. (cl) Martin J. Miller/Visuals Unlimited; (cl-bkgd) Tom Bean. xiii: William Smithey Jr/Getty Images. xiv: Comstock/SuperStock. xv: AP Images/Neil Eliot. 2-3: Purestock/SuperStock. 4: Veronique Krieger/Getty Images. 4-5: Ryan McVay/Getty Images. 5: Bettmann/Corbis. 6-7: Jose Luis Pelaez/Corbis. 8: Rusty Hill/FoodPix/Jupiter Images. 9: David Hiser/Getty Images. 30: (tl, c) Children's Book Press. 32: (bl) Ted Streshinsky/Corbis. 33: (c) Morton Beebe/Corbis; (br) Najlah Feanny/Corbis. 34: (bl) Arthur Schatz/Time Life Pictures/Getty Images; (tr) PunchStock. 35: Walter P. Reuther Library/Wayne State University. 37: Myrleen Ferguson Cate/PhotoEdit. 38-39: Tom & Dee Ann McCarthy/Corbis. 58: (bl) Brian Biggs; (tr) Ben Hurwitz. 65: Photodisc/Getty Images. 66–67: Jeff Greenberg/PhotoEdit. 68: (t) Getty Images; (cr) Russel Illig/Photodisc/PunchStock; (br) C Squared Studios/Getty. 70-71: (all) Mi Won Kim /Time For Kids. 72: (t) Esta Shapiro/Time For Kids; (bl) Courtesy David Hsu. 73: Courtesy David Hsu. 74: Lewis Wickes Hines/Corbis. 77: (tcr) Brand X Pictures/PunchStock; (cr) PhotoLink/Getty Images. 78-79: Mitch Tobias/Masterfile. 81: Stock Trek/Getty. 96: (tl) Das Anuda/Courtesy Farrar, Straus and Giroux; (cr) Courtesy Anna Rich. 98: NASA Johnson Space Center Collection. 98-99: (bkgd) NASA/CORBIS. 99: (br) PatitucciPhoto/Aurora Photos; (t) NASA Johnson Space Center Collection. 100: (tr) GustoImages/Artemi Kyriacou/Jupiter Images. 100-101: (bkgd) BigStockPhoto. 101: (tr) NASA/Roger Ressmeyer/Corbis; (br) NASA/Corbis. 103: Dan Bigelow/Getty Images. 104-105: Don Mason/Blend Images/Jupiter Images. 106:Steven Weinrebe/Index Stock Imagery. 107: Don Smetzer/Stone/Getty Images. 108-114: © 2005 Twentieth Century Fox. All rights reserved. 116-117: (bkgd) Wetzel & Company. 117: © 2005 Twentieth Century Fox. All rights reserved. 120: (tr) Courtesy Candlewick Press; (bl) © 2005 Twentieth Century Fox. All rights reserved. 121: © 2005 Twentieth Century Fox. All rights reserved. 124: © 2005 Twentieth Century Fox. All rights reserved. 125: Ryan McVay/Getty Images. 126: Brand X Pictures/PunchStock. 128: Michael Okoniewski/AP-Wide World Photos. 129: (br) Michael Okoniewski/AP-Wide World Photos; (bl) Hemera Technologies/Alamy. 131: (cr) Nic Hamilton/Alamy; (tr) Ryan McVay/Getty Images; (br) Pixtal/PunchStock. 132-133: Kayte M. Deioma/PhotoEdit. 134: Digital Vision Photography/Veer. 134-135: Ingram Publishing/AGEfotostock. 135: Owen Franken/Corbis. 136-137: Corbis. 138: Bettmann/Corbis. 139: (cl,cr) Bettmann/Corbis. 154: (c) Courtesy Chris Soentpiet/www.soentpiet.com. 156: Bettmann/Corbis. 156-159: Macmillan/McGraw-Hill. 157: AP Photo. 158: Jack Balletti/Bettmann/Corbis. 161: Michael Newman/PhotoEdit. 162-163: Lori Adamski Peek/Getty Images. 164: Bettmann/Corbis. 165: Bernard Hoffman/Getty. 182: (cr) Courtesy C.F. Payne. 187: Royalty-Free/Corbis. 188-189: Brian Bahr/Getty Images. 190: (t) Brian Nicholson/AP Photo; (b) Bryn Lennon/Getty Images. 191: (tr) Al Grillo/AP Photo; (bl) Phil Cole/Getty Images. 192: Brian Bahr/Getty Images. 193: (tr) Todd Warshaw/Pool/Getty Images; (bl) Petros Giannakouris/AP Photos. 194: Nadia Borowski Scott/Zuma Press/Newscom. 195: (tr) STR/AFP/Getty Images; (b) Petros Giannakouris/AP Photo. 196:Tamara Reynolds. 199: (bl) Photodisc/PunchStock; (bc) Ana de Sousa/Shutterstock; (r) Stockdisc/PunchStock. 200-201: Steve Bloom Images/Alamy. 202: Scott Neville/AP Photos. 204-217: (all) Alvis Upitis. 218: (tl) Boydsmills Press; (cr) Alvis Upitis. 218-219: Alvis Upitis. 225: Kevin Peterson/Stone/Getty Images. 226-227: Carson Ganci/Design Pics Inc./Alamy. 228: TiConUno s.r.l./Alamy. 228-229: (bkgd) Photographers Choice RF/SuperStock. 229: Macmillan/McGraw-Hill. 250: Courtesy Paul Goble. 252: (bl) Getty Images; (bkgd) Wetzel & Company. 253: Getty Images. 253-255: (bkgd) Wetzel & Company. 257: Robert Llewellyn/Alamy. 260: (br) Michael St. Maur Sheil/Corbis; (t) Jerry Driendl/Getty Images. 260-261: Jerry Driendl/Getty Images. 261: (tr) Stockbyte/PunchStock; (cr) Royalty-Free/Corbis; (bl) McVay/Getty Images. 264-265: Masterfile. 266: Dennis MacDonald/AGEfotostock America. 266-267: Gary He/Macmillan/McGraw-Hill. 267: Charles Krupa/AP Images. 268-269: Whit Preston/Stone/Getty Images. 271: (tl) Daryl Balfour/Getty Images; (cr) Stephen Cooper/Getty Images. 284: (t) Courtesy Groundwood Books; (cr) Courtesy Nicole Wong. 286: John Cancalosi/DRK. 287: Michael & Patricia Fogden/Animal Animals; (bl) Bruce Coleman, Inc/Alamy. 288: (t) Michael Fogden/Animal Animals; (bl) Bruce Coleman, Inc/Alamy. 291: Tipp Howell/Getty Images. 292-293: Masterfile Royalty-Free. 294: (bl) Ulrike Schanz/Animal Animals; (b) Royalty-Free/Corbis. 295: Mary Grace Long/Asia Images/Getty Images. 318: Courtesy Scholastic. 320: Okapia/Hund/Kramer/Photo Researchers.

321-323: Manuela Hartling/Reuters/Corbis. 325: Royalty-Free/Corbis. 326-327: Masterfile. 328: Time & Life Pictures/Getty Images. 329: (tl) Time & Life Pictures/Getty Images; (tr) Corbis. 331: Marc Longwood. 332: Eric L. Stewart/Lyon College. 333: Warner Brothers/Everett Collection. 337: (tcr, br) Brand X Pictures/PunchStock; (cr) Siede Preis/Getty Images; (bl) PhotoLink/Getty Images; (bc) Ana de Sousa/Shutterstock; (b) Michael Scott/Macmillan/McGraw-Hill. 338: Group 4/Image Source Black/Alamy. 360: (tl) Courtesy Peachtree Publishers; (br) Courtesy Renato Alarcāo. 367: Amos Morgan/Getty Images. 368-369: Jeff Greenberg/Alamy. 370: (bl) Chris Steele-Perkins/Magnum; (bc) Getty Images; (br) Comstock Images/Getty Images. 371: Photodisc/Getty Images. 390: (cl) Courtesy of Penguin Group; (tr) Photo by Jessica Tampas. Courtesy Claire Hartfield. 392: Frank Chmura/Alamy. 395: Alan Levenson/AGEfotostock America. 398: Time & Life Pictures/Getty Images. 399: Danita Delimonte/Alamy. 401: (bl) Pixtal/PunchStock; (cr) Stockdisc/PunchStock. 402-403: Bob Daemmrich/Photo Edit. 404: Marta Lavandier/AP Images. 404-405: (bkgd wooden blocks) Dynamic Graphics/Jupiter Images; (bkgd wood texture) Dynamic Graphics/PunchStock; (bkgd close-up of wood grain) Ryan McVay/Getty Images. 405: The Granger Collection, New York. 406-407: Gabe Palmer/Corbis. 428: (tl) Marcia Johnston. Courtesy Farrar, Straus & Giroux; (cr) Courtesy Estate of Garth Williams c/o Frost National Bank. 430: (tr) B. G. Thomson/Photo Researchers; (cr) Karen Marks/Bat Conservation International/Photo Researchers. 430-431: Steve Kaufman/Corbis. 431: Pat Little/AP Images. 432: Jeff Lepore/Photo Researchers. 432-433: Tim Flach/Stone/Getty Images. 435: Dan Bigelow/Getty Images. 436-437: Michael & Patricia Fogden/Corbis. 438: Masterfile. 439: Steve Hopkin/Ardea. 454: Anita Lambrinos/Courtesy Charles Micucci. 461: Amos Morgan/Getty Images. 462-463: Bill Heinsohn/Alamy. 464: Bob Stefko/Getty Images. 465: (tr) Bettmann/Corbis; (tl) Christopher and Sally Gable/Getty Images. 466: Stephen Pingry/AP Photo. 467: AGEfotostock/SuperStock. 468: Doug Mazell/Jupiter Images. 469: Mary Altaffer/AP Photo. 470: OJPhotos/Alamy. 473: (cr) Ryan McVay/Getty Images; (bl) PhotoLink/Getty Images; (bc) Ana de Sousa/Shutterstock; (br) Photodisc/PunchStock. 474-475: Troy Wayrynen. 496: (tl) Justin A. Woods; (br) Donna Freeman courtesy of Pelican Publishing Company. 498: Richard Hutchings. 499: North Wind Picture Archives/Alamy. 500: (tl) The Ima Hogg Papers/The Center for American History/The University of Texas at Austin; (b) Travelwide/Alamy. 501: Thais Llorca/epa/Corbis. 503: Rubberball Productions/Getty Images. 504-505: Library of Congress/Getty Images. 506-507: Bettmann/Corbis. 507: Science Museum, London/Topham-HIP/Image Works. 526: (tr) Jason Stemple/Curtis Brown Limited; (bcl) Courtesy Jim Burke. 531: Frank Siteman/AGEfotostock America, Inc. 537: (l) Brand X Pictures/PunchStock; (cr) Ken Cavanagh/Macmillan/McGraw-Hill; (br) Stockbyte/PunchStock. 538-539: Lon Lauber/OSF/Animal Animals/Earth Scenes. 540: George H. H. Huey/Corbis. 540-541: Brand X Pictures/PunchStock. 541: Jeff Foott/Getty Images. 542-543: Stephen Krasemann/NHPA. 544: Jack Barrie/Bruce Coleman. 545: Dave Tipling/Alamy. 546-547: Bruce Clendenning/Visuals Unlimited. 547: Martin J Miller/Visuals Unlimited. 549: (tr) Steve Warble; (b) Brian Vikander. 550: Barbara Gerlach/Visuals Unlimited. 551: (t) Richard Day/Daybreak Imagery; (b) Tom Bean. 552: (tr) Bayard A. Brattstrom/Visuals Unlimited; (b) Rob Simpson/Visuals Unlimited. 553: John Cunningham/Visuals Unlimited. 554: (t) LINK/Visuals Unlimited; (b) John and Barbara Gerlach/Visuals Unlimited. 555: Hal Beral/Visuals Unlimited. 556: Malowski/Visuals Unlimited. 557: John Gerlach/Visuals Unlimited. 558: (tr) Barbara Gerlach/Visuals Unlimited; (b) Joe McDonald/Visuals Unlimited. 559: Tom J. Ulrich/Visuals Unlimited. 560-561: Bruce Clendenning/Visuals Unlimited. 562: (tr) Courtesy Lerner Publishing Group; (b) Martin J Miller/Visuals Unlimited. 562-563: Bruce Clendenning/Visuals Unlimited. 563: (bl) Barbara Gerlach/Visuals Unlimited; (bc) Rob Simpson/Visuals Unlimited; (br) Steve Warble. 564: Mitsuaki Iwago/Minden Pictures. 565: (tl) Steve Kazlowski/Danita Delimont.com; (br) Robert W. Ginn/Alamy. 566: (tl) Inside OutPix/PunchStock; (cl) Renee Morris/Alamy; (bc) blickwinkel/Alamy; (br) Andrew Harrington/Alamy. 567: Royalty-Free/Corbis. 569: Jim Jordan/Getty Images. 570-571: Joel Sartore/National Geographic Image Collection. 572-573: John Cancalosi/Ardea. 573: ZSSD/SuperStock. 590: (tl) Photo by Mimi. Courtesy Rudolfo Anaya; (cr) Courtesy of David Diaz. 597: BananaStock/Alamy. 598-599: William Smithey Jr/Getty Images. 600: Frank Staub/Index Stock Imagery. 601: Corey Rich/Aurora Photos. 602-603: Ken Wilson/Wildfaces. 605: William Campbell/Corbis Sygma. 606: Galen Rowell/Corbis. 609: (cr) PhotoLink/Getty Images; (bc) Ana de Sousa/Shutterstock; (br) Stockbyte/PunchStock. 610-611: Jupiter Images/Comstock/Alamy. 612: (t) Boden/Ledingham/Masterfile; (bl) Brandon Cole Marine Photography/Alamy. 612-613: Boden/Ledingham/Masterfile. 613: Brandon Cole/Visuals Unlimited. 616-629: (bkgd) Wetzel & Company/Janice McDonald. 630: Yuusuke Itagaki, Courtesy Charlesbridge Publishers. 630-631: (bkgd) Wetzel & Company/

Acknowledgments

Janice McDonald. 637: BananaStock/AGEfotostock. 638-639: (bkgd) James Watt/Animal Animals/Earth Scenes. 640: (tr) Amos Nachoum/Corbis; (br) Roger Tidman/Corbis. 640-641: (bkgd) Stephen Frink Collection/Alamy. 642-657: Richard Sobol. 658: (author) Courtesy Robert Sobol. 658-659: Richard Sobol. 663: (cr) Rubberball Productions/Getty Images. 669: (cr) Stockdisc/PunchStock; (br) Tracy Montana/PhotoLink/Getty Images. 670-671: Comstock/SuperStock. 672: Comstock/SuperStock. 673: Underwood & Underwood/Corbis. 672-673: Digital Vision/Getty Images. 674-675: Corbis. 696: Alice Garland. 698-699: Corbis. 699: Dorothea Lange/Stringer/2005 Getty Images. 700: (t) John Springer Collection/Corbis; (c) Bettmann/Corbis. 703: Comstock Images/Alamy. 704-705: The Granger Collection, New York. 722: (tr) Rob Layman; (cl) Courtesy Cornelius Van Wright and Ying-Hwa Hu. 724: James L. Amos/Corbis. 724-725: Joe Ginsberg/Getty Images. 725: (t) Pat Roque/Associated Press; (b) Joe Ginsberg/Getty Images. 726: (t) Victoria & Albert Museum, London/Art Resource, NY. 726-727: Joe Ginsberg/Getty Images. 727: ImageDJ/Jupiter Images. 729: Tipp Howell/Getty Images. 730-731: Damian Dovarganes/AP Photo. 732: Brian Harkin/Getty Images. 733: (all) Taro Yamasaki. 734: Ric Francis/AP Photo. 735 (all) Arthur Schatz/Time Life Pictures/Getty Images. 736-

737: Aurelia Ventura/La Opinion Photos/Newscom. 738: Staples, Inc. 741: (br) Royalty-Free/Corbis; (bc) Ana de Sousa/Shutterstock. 742-743: Randy Olson/National Geographic/Getty Images. 744: Gary Buss/Getty Images. 745: Richard Hutchings/Corbis. 768: (tl) Sharron L. McElmeel/McBookwords LLC; (cr) Courtesy Mary Azarian. 773: ImageState/Alamy. 774-775: Justin Sullivan/Getty Images. 776: (tr) Schenectady Museum; Hall of Electrical History Foundation/Corbis; (bl) W. Dickson/Corbis. 777: Bettmann/Corbis. 796: Courtesy Roz Schanzer. 801: Michael Newman/PhotoEdit. 804-805: Chris Howes/Wild Places Photography/Alamy. 807: (tr) Stockdisc/PunchStock; (br) Photodisc/PunchStock. 808: (l) Digital Vision Ltd./Getty Images; (r) Ingram Publishing/Alamy. 810: Comstock/Alamy. 811: Photodisc Collection/Getty Images. 814: Creatas/SuperStock. 815: Adam Jones/Visuals Unlimited. 818: Jeremy Woodhouse/Getty Images. 819: Charles George/Visuals Unlimited. 821: Mel Curtis/Getty Images. 822: Jeff Foott/Discovery Images/Getty Images. 825: Digital Vision Ltd./Getty Images. 826: (r) S. Solum/PhotoLink/Getty Images; (l) Ingram Publishing/Alamy. 829: Digital Vision Ltd. 830: Peter Yates/Corbis. 831: Robert Harding World Imagery/Getty Images.